Metadata and Semantics

T0191652

Metadata and Semantics

Edited by

Miguel-Angel Sicilia
University of Alcalá
Madrid, Spain

Miltiadis D. Lytras
University of Patras
Patras, Greece

 Springer

Editors:
Miguel-Angel Sicilia
Universidad de Alcalá de Henares
Depto. Ciencias de la Computación
Ctra. Barcelona Km 33.6
Campus E. Politecnica
28871 Alcalá De Henares Madrid
Spain
msicilia@uah.es

Miltiadis D. Lytras
University of Patras
Research Academic Computer Tech. Inst.
Computer Engineering & Informatics Dept.
Patras, Greece
lytras@ceid.upatras.gr

ISBN-13: 978-1-4419-4600-3   e-ISBN-13: 978-0-387-77745-0

Food and Agriculture Organization of the United Nations retains the copyright of the following chapters included in this book:

    Comparing Different Metadata Application Profiles for Agricultural Learning Repositories
    Metadata Application Profile for Agricultural Learning Resources
    A Distributed Architecture for Harvesting Metadata Describing Organizations in the
    Agriculture Sector

The views expressed in this publication are those of the author(s) and do not necessarily reflect the views of the Food and Agriculture Organization of the United Nations.

Printed on acid-free paper

springer.com

Preface

Metadata can be defined as structured data about an object that supports some function(s) related to that object described, achieving a degree of uniformity in description by means of schemas. Metadata schemas are structured representations of information for a given use or domain, following some rules of well-formedness and quality and in most cases being open specifications. Schemas are often produced by communities of practice, and in some cases, they reach the status of formal standard. There is not a single language to express metadata in digital form, but XML and RDF are nowadays the more common choices. Formal ontology has emerged recently as a knowledge representation infrastructure for the provision of shared semantics to metadata, which essentially forms the basis of the vision of the Semantic Web. In consequence, ontologies and annotations that use ontologies can be considered a very specific kind of metadata, especially targeted to machine-understandability by means of using formal logics. Ontology annotations complement existing metadata schemas with richer semantics that can be used for automated reasoning. Metadata is a product that once created and properly managed becomes an *asset* for some functions that in turn produce some kind of *value*. It has been proposed elsewhere that there are at least three levels of increasing metadata functionality:

(1) support data discovery;
(2) facilitate acquisition, comprehension and utilization of data by humans; and
(3) enable automated data discovery, ingestion, processing and analysis

Thus, metadata is used for different purposes and with different objectives. Also, metadata does not come without a cost, but it is expensive to create if some quality is required. As a consequence of the above "metadata research" can be seen as a multi-disciplinary field, obviously encompassing Information Technology but also inputs from other disciplines as management or knowledge organization.

These topics of metadata, semantics and ontologies were the core areas of the 2nd International Conference on Metadata and Semantics Research (MTSR'07). There are a few conferences related to metadata either directly or indirectly, and several devoted to Semantic Web issues. However, MTSR is unique in gathering together researchers from different disciplines and with diverse backgrounds. This fosters an atmosphere of cross-fertilization which is the main objective of the conference.

MTSR'07 took place at the Corfu Island in Greece, from 1st to12th of October 2007, thanks to the support of the Ionian University. The Ionian University opened to students in 1985, and it is nowadays a modern and dynamic institution, with six academic departments and nine postgraduate programmes. There were two interesting special sections, one on Agricultural Metadata & Semantics and a second one on Metadata and Semantics for Pervasive Computing. Invited speakers were Grigoris Antoniou (University of Crete and FORTH), Jorge Cardoso (University of Madeira, Portugal) and Gauri Salokhe (FAO).

MTSR'07 received around 120 submissions, of which 60 were selected for the conference, and most of them are collected in this book in revised form. The peer review process had in consequence two rounds. The first one was for the selection of the papers to be presented at the conference. Then, after the conference, programme committee members had the chance to have an additional review, especially in cases in which the presentation of the paper at the conference had raised relevant comments, criticisms or suggestions. This book is the result of that post-conference process of review.

The book can be considered a view of the changing landscape of metadata and semantics research. There are some topics that are currently under intense activity, notably metadata in agriculture and metadata in the management of cultural assets. This reflects some bursts of activity fostered by strong institutions in the area, however, metadata and semantics spans every domain in which locating, relating or exploiting digital assets represents a need.

We hope the compilation of chapters in this book serve the purpose of providing a good overview of the state of the art in metadata and semantics.

Miguel-Angel Sicilia
Miltiadis Lytras

Table of Content

Metadata integration and applications

Semantic Web applications

Ontology engineering and related techniques

Metadata and semantics for pervasive computing

A Hybrid Ontology and Visual-based Retrieval Model for Cultural Heritage Multimedia Collections

Stefanos Vrochidis, Charalambos Doulaverakis, Anastasios Gounaris,
Evangelia Nidelkou, Lambros Makris, Ioannis Kompatsiaris

Abstract The contribution of this paper is the introduction of a hybrid multimedia retrieval model accompanied by the presentation of a search engine that is capable of retrieving visual content from cultural heritage multimedia libraries as in three modes: (i) based on their semantic annotation with the help of an ontology; (ii) based on the visual features with a view to finding similar content; and (iii) based on the combination of these two strategies in order to produce recommendations. The main novelty is the way in which these two co-operate transparently during the evaluation of a single query in a hybrid fashion, making recommendations to the user and retrieving content that is both visually and semantically similar.

1 Introduction

Multimedia content management plays a key role in modern information systems. To provide advanced functionalities for the manipulation and knowledge retrieval from such visual content as those provided for text processing, a key aspect is the development of more efficient search engines for imagefiles.

To date, two main approaches to image search engine techniques have been proposed, namely annotation-based and content-based. The former is based on image metadata or keywords that annotate the visual content or they refer to the properties of the image file. Several variants of annotation-based multimedia search engines have been proposed. Some of them assume manual annotation (e.g., [2]), while others provide support for automatic annotation. This search approach has benefitted significantly from the advances in ontologies [3] and the Semantic Web (e.g., [5]), so that annotations can have well-defined semantics.

Stefanos Vrochidis, Charalambos Doulaverakis, Anastasios Gounaris,
Evangelia Nidelkou, Lambros Makris, Ioannis Kompatsiaris
Informatics and Telematics Institute, Thessaloniki, Greece e-mail: {stefanos, doulaver, gounaris, nidelkou, lmak, ikom}@iti.gr

However, annotation and semantic-based search are often insufficient when dealing with visual content. When searching through cultural heritage material for example, it is very common to look for images that are visually similar but may be annotated in a different way (thus a strict annotation search cannot retrieve all relevant images). In addition, in many cases, manual annotation is not available or is incomplete. To tackle this problem, a second complementary approach has been devised: content-based search. The core idea is to apply image processing and feature extraction algorithms to the visual content and extract low-level visual features, such as color layout and edge histogram [6].

This paper focuses on a hybrid retrieval model by combining in an novel way the content and annotation based approaches. A search engine has been developed implementing this model using images from the culture domain. The remainder of the paper is structured as follows. Section 2 introduces the retrieval model. The implementation and evaluation procedures are presented in Section 3, while results of the hybrid engine and insights into the performance of the different approaches appear in Section 4. Eventually, section 5 concludes the paper.

2 Hybrid Retrieval of Visual Content

As mentioned previously, the search engine described hereby supports three modes of queries and retrieval of images, namely:

1. content-based retrieval,
2. ontology-based retrieval, and
3. hybrid retrieval, which builds upon the combination of the two aforementioned methods.

2.1 Combining Visual and Semantic Information

The main objective behind this retrieval model is to allow a user to complement a query primarily addressed using one of the visual or semantic mode with the other. Starting with one mode, information arising from the complementary mode is used to enhance the results and provide recommendations.

The mathematical model of the hybrid retrieval system is described below for both cases. Lets assume that the function $Sem(data_{rdf}, q_{sem})$ is producing the desired output given the data and the query based on the semantic data formed in RDF[1] language by retrieving the results from the Knowledge Base:

$$Res_{sem} = Sem(data_{rdf}, q_{sem}) \tag{1}$$

---

[1] http://www.w3.org/RDF/

where $data_{rdf}$ are the metadata stored in RDF in the Knowledge Base and q_{sem} is the query string in RDFQL or SeRQL.

In a similar way, the function: $Vis(data_{desc}, q_{vis})$ outputs the results from content-based search using as data the extracted descriptors of the multimedia content and the proper input from the user.

$$Res_{vis} = Vis(data_{desc}, q_{vis}) \qquad (2)$$

where $data_{desc}$ represent the extracted descriptors of the multimedia content and q_{vis} represents the desirable input (i.e one or a set of images) for which visually matching content expected to be retrieved and displayed. The function $Vis(data_{desc}, q_{vis})$ outputs Res_{vis} in a specific ranking based on the similarity coefficient which derives from the calculation of the distances of the extracted descriptors for the objects included in the query.

Subsequently, two cases of hybrid search are defined: (i) the visual search, where the system produces visually similar results with the initial object accompanied by a set of recommendations deriving from the transparent semantic query that the visual results produce; and (ii) the semantic search, where a user can submit a query by browsing the ontology fields and acquire the results that illustrate the content which satisfies the constraints of the query complemented by recommendations based on visual similarity of the initial results.

In visual search the output consists of two sets of results: the initial results produced by Res_{vis} and the set of recommendations Rec_{sem} based on semantic search and given by:

$$Rec_{sem} = Sem(data_{rdf}, ResToQ_{sem}(Res_{vis})) \iff \qquad (3)$$

$$Rec_{sem} = Sem(data_{rdf}, ResToQ_{sem}(Vis(data_{desc}, q_{vis}))) \qquad (4)$$

where the function $ResToQ_{sem}$ creates a new query based on the first set of the results in order to retrieve the semantically related content. This function could be based on a combination of several algorithms in order to output a query which contains the information from the visual results. The algorithm adopted for the tests and the evaluation with the search engine for cultural content was based on the semantic concept which appeared more frequently between the results.

The final set of results Res is the set of results from visual similarity Res_{vis} enhanced by the recommendation results Rec_{sem}:

$$Res = Res_{vis} \cup Rec_{sem}. \qquad (5)$$

On the other hand, when a Semantic search occurs the results that are produced consist of: the first set provided by Res_{sem} and the second set Rec_{vis} illustrating the recommendations:

$$Rec_{vis} = Vis(data_{desc}, ResToQ_{vis}(Res_{sem})) \iff \qquad (6)$$

$$Rec_{vis} = Vis(data_{desc}, ResToQ_{vis}(Sem(data_{rdf}, q_{sem}))) \qquad (7)$$

where the function $ResToQ_{vis}$ constructs a query taking into account the visual features of the initial results. The algorithm used for this function produces descriptors of an average hypothetical object by averaging the descriptors of the results.

The final set of results is:

$$Res = Res_{sem} \cup Rec_{vis}. \tag{8}$$

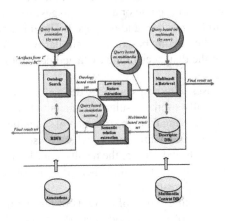

Fig. 1 Hybrid retrieval model architecture.

The architecture of the Hybrid retrieval model is illustrated in Figure 1.

2.2 Content-based Retrieval

In this retrieval mode, described by (2), users are able to perform a visual-based search by taking advantage of low-level multimedia content features.

In this mode, the user provides, as the input query, an example of the multimedia content she or he is interested in, and the system performs a visual similarity-based search and the relevant results are retrieved. The analysis of 2D images is performed using the approach described in [4] and involves the extraction of MPEG-7 features.

2.3 Ontology-based Retrieval

This search mode, described by (1), is more appropriate for the cases in which the user knows to an adequate degree of confidence the semantic annotation of the material he or she is searching for and for the cases. To submit a query, the user provides constraints on the concepts of the five ontologies of Section 3.2. During search time, the system retrieves the semantically connected content according to user's selections.

Figure 2 illustrates the application of this technique by presenting a proper interface for ontology based search.

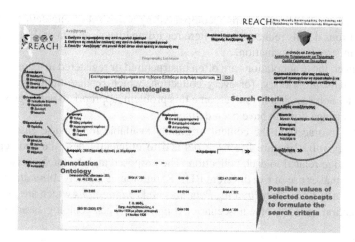

Fig. 2 Search engine interface

3 Search Engine and Evaluation Corpus

The evaluation procedure took place with the employment of a search engine based on the aforementioned retrieval model and it is capable of retrieving cultural visual content.

3.1 Visual Content

The main content provider is the Center for Greek and Roman Antiquity (KERA)[2], which offers a large collection of inscriptions and coins while a rich collection of

---

[2] http://www.eie.gr/nhrf/institutes/igra/index-en.html

Greek paintings is provided by the Greek museum: Teloglion Foundation of Art[3].
Finally, Alinari[4]Photographic Archives offered a large collection of black and white
photographs.

3.2 Ontology

Cultural heritage collections are accompanied by a rich set of annotations that describe various details related to each item regarding historical data or details regarding administrative information.

However, these annotations are often unstructured or registered in a non-standard
form, usually proprietary, for every collection, which renders them unusable for
inter-collection searching. To overcome this problem, appropriate ontologies for the
cultural heritage domain have been defined.

Taking into account the content originally available for our use case scenario
an ontology infrastructure has been defined to efficiently describe and represent
all knowledge related to each collection. The proposed architecture consists of two
layers and makes use of five different RDF(S) ontologies, namely *Annotation*, which
is generic, and *Coins*, *Inscriptions*, *Paintings* and *Photographs* which are specific to
the collection itemsets of our scenario. (Figure 3). These ontologies are detailed
below.

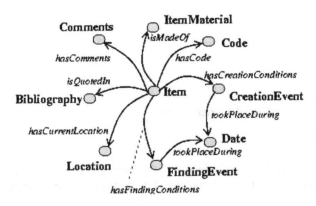

Fig. 3 A graphical representation of the concepts in the ontology and their relations.

A large set of information fields inside the image annotation set is common for
each item, regardless of the collection that is part of. As such, it was decided to

---

[3] http://web.auth.gr/teloglion/
[4] http://www.alinari.com/

use a separate, higher-level ontology specifically intended for representing this kind of concepts and relations, which cover information like date and place of creation, current location, construction material, dimensions, etc.

The properties that are specific to a collection item category are captured by complementary ontologies; more specifically there is a separate ontology for each category, as the particular details that correspond to the collection items can vary greatly for each class. As a further step, to support interoperability of the system with other semantic-enabled cultural heritage systems, the aforementioned ontologies were mapped to the CIDOC-CRM [1] core ontology.

3.3 Ground Truth Definition

The ground truth used in order to evaluate the results of the experiments were different for each retrieval mode. Regarding the content-based experiments as ground truth was considered the (subjective) visual similarity of the objects. The results from ontology-based queries could be easily evaluated due to the existing annotations. The recommendations, which are results of the hybrid mode, are considered to be results semantically or visually related to the initial set of the results.

4 Results

In this section the advanced functionalities of the hybrid search engine are demonstrated through use cases and insights into the performance of the two search flavors are provided.

4.1 Hybrid Search: Use Cases

The hybrid search engine is capable of detecting implicit semantic relationships between visually dissimilar images, and extract the relevant artefacts. To demonstrate this capability, two use cases are presented in this section, which are summarized in Figures 4 and 5.

In the first use case (Figure 4), the input query is the painting "Holly monastery of Saint Paul" (1933), which is created by Reggos Polykleitos. During the content-based search visually similar inscriptions are extracted (Figure 4a). To fire an ontology-based search, the system retrieves the most common semantic feature, which happens to be the name of the painter. The first set of results shows visually similar images by illustrating mostly paintings with monasteries and buildings while the recommendations include paintings of the same painter who has created paintings of similar themes (monastery, churches, etc.) and in addition a portrait which cannot be retrieved by visual similarity (Figure 4).

Fig. 4 The first use case: (a) initial set of results derived from visual similarity search, (b) set of recommendations based on a complementary semantic query

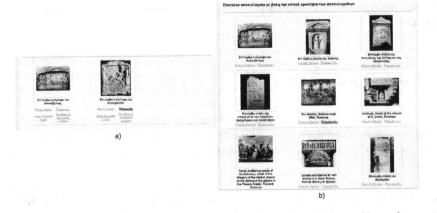

Fig. 5 The second use case: (a) initial set of results based on a semantic query, (b) set of recommendations includes visually similar images

The second use case follows the opposite approach where the initial query is based on ontology fields while the set of recommendations derives from visual similarity (Figure 5). In this scenario, the user searches for inscriptions characterized as anaglyphs. The first set of results includes the two inscriptions which are named as anaglyphs (Figure 5a) while the recommendations provide results visually similar with the two inscriptions.

4.2 Performance Insights

The experiments were conducted on a PC, with a P5 3.0GHz Intel CPU and 1GB RAM. The knowledge base containing the ontological metadata is Sesame 1.2 running a MySQL DBMS at the back-end. MySQL is also used to store the actual non-multimedia content and the links to the multimedia files. The dataset is consisted of roughly 4000 images including inscriptions, coins, paintings and photographs along with a complete set of semantic annotations. The visual descriptors are stored in a collocated MPEG-7 XM server.

Figure 6 shows the Precision-Recall diagram for the content-based retrieval. The curves correspond to the mean precision value that was measured after several retrieval tasks. For the ontology-based search since it is based on selecting available concepts describing the content, the estimation of Precision-Recall diagram is not relevant.

The average response time for the ontology-based search is 0.163 sec, while for the content-based search is 0.773 sec.

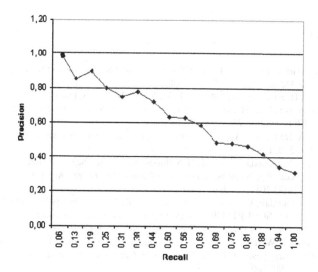

Fig. 6 Precision-Recall diagram for the content-based method.

5 Conclusions

In this paper, a novel retrieval model for handling visual and multimedia digital libraries is presented in an efficient and effective manner. The retrieval model proposed model adopts three methods for retrieval: two autonomous and one combinational. The ontology-based method makes use of the formal, logic-based representation of semantic mark-up metadata accompanying each collection, while an illustrative user interface is used for graphical query formulation. This method is appropriate when the user is interested in semantically similar results. The content-based method makes use of the low-level visual characteristics of the multimedia material, in order to retrieve items with similar appearance. The hybrid method, which is the main contribution of this work, makes a combined use of the previous two methods.

6 Acknowledgments

This work was supported by the project REACH "New forms of distributed organization and access to cultural heritage material" funded by the General Secretariat of Research and Technology of Hellas-Greece and by the project CHORUS "Coordinated approacH to the EurOpean effoRt on aUdiovisual Search engines" funded by the European Commission.

References

1. M. Doerr. The CIDOC-CRM An Ontological Approach to Semantic Interoperability of Metadata. *AI Magazine*, 24(3):75–92, Fall 2003.
2. M. Flickner, H. Sawhney, W. Niblack, J. Ashley, Q. Huang, B. Dom, M. Gorkani, J. Hafner, D. Lee, D. Petkovic, D. Steele, and P. Yanker. Query by image and video content: The QBIC system. *IEEE Computer*, 28(9):23–32, 1995.
3. T. Gruber. A Translation Approach to Portable Ontology Specifications. *Knowledge Acquisition*, 5:199–220, 1993.
4. V. Mezaris, I. Kompatsiaris, and M. G. Strintzis. Still Image Segmentation Tools for Object-based Multimedia Applications. *International Journal of Pattern Recognition and Artificial Intelligence*, 18(4):701–725, June 2004.
5. P. Sinclair, S. Goodall, P. Lewis, K. Martinez, and M. Addis. Concept browsing for multimedia retrieval in the SCULPTEUR project. In *Multimedia and the Semantic Web, held as part of the 2nd European Semantic Web Conference, Heraklion, Crete, Greece*, May 2005.
6. A. Smeulders, M. Worring, S. Santini, A. Gupta, and R. Jain. Content-based image retrieval at the end of the early years. *IEEE Transactions on Pattern Analysis and Machine Intelligence*, 22(12):1349–1380, 2000.

Towards a Definition of Digital Information Preservation Object

Hugo Quisbert, Margarita Korenkova, Ann Hägerfors

Abstract In this paper, we discuss long-term digital preservation from an information perspective, rather than the predominant approaches; the Archival and the Technocratic Approach. Information lives longer than people, tools (software) and organizations live. The Information Continuum Model provides support for this standpoint. However, we find that there exists no concept to support practical action in preservation from the information perspective. Existing concepts as information object, digital object, preservation object, electronic record, information package and significant properties are context dependent and focus on the object to be preserved, rather than preservation of information. Consequently, they are not suitable for realizing the information perspective in long-term digital preservation. The concept of Digital Information Preservation Object is therefore introduced and a tentative definition of the concept is presented.

1 Introduction

During the last years, development of digital technologies has been very fast and for the most unpredictable. Consequently, the amount of information created in electronic form is growing exponentially. [18] According to Runardotter et al., [25] digital information has to be available for the future society by legal, historical and democratic reasons.

The solutions that are today for preservations and foremost to make digital material accessible for long time are insufficient. Archival inquiry "Archives for Everyone – Now and in the Future", called attention to these great shortcomings and argued that models, methods and platform-independent software for preservation of the digital material are omitted largely. [19] On one hand, the "problem" with digital preservation is the lack of proven methods to ensure that the digital information will continue to exist [26]. On the other hand, the software currently available does not include good tools for saving digital recorded information in the face of rapid hardware and software obsolescence [12]. One of the challenges to be addressed is how to preserve information through technology

Hugo Quisbert, Luleå University of Technology, Division of Systems Sciences
University Area, 971 87 Luleå, Sweden, Hugo.Quisbert@ ltu.se
Margarita Korenkova, Luleå University of Technology, Division of Systems Sciences
University Area, 971 87 Luleå, Sweden, Margarita.Korenkova@ltu.se
Ann Hägerfors, Luleå University of Technology, Division of Systems Sciences
University Area, 971 87 Luleå, Sweden, Ann.Hagerfors@ltu.se

changes. [12] Within the practice of preservation, archives are still using methods developed since 1970-1980. These methods cause losing functionalities of records when archiving. Archival Science has not developed as rapid as information technology. Digital material is needed to be migrated and/or emulated to be preserved. [25]

Information Systems Sciences have no methods that in the same degree as Archival Science deal with long-term, "forever" perspectives. The transition between paper-based media to digital media was not preceded by a strategy for long-term digital preservation. This phenomenon explained in terms of lack of knowledge and experience when handling digital material. [25]

Society and information curators have to face the challenge of finding some sustainable solutions to ensure that digital recorded information of today become accessible and understandable in the future. Otherwise, digital material and likewise one part of society's future cultural heritage and history are in danger of disappearing forever. Consequently, legal and democratic demands cannot be fulfilled. [19] According to Gladney [12] technology has influence in almost every aspect of long-term digital preservation and it is not widely believed these solutions can be achieved solely through technological means. To find solutions to the problem much research was limited to technical aspects of preservation but our research has taken another view on long-term digital preservation, which puts information in focus. This paper therefore discusses the concept of information as central for long-term digital preservation.

2 Facing Long-term Digital Preservation

The authors of this paper are connected to the Long-term Digital Preservation Centre (LDP Centre) in Sweden. The major activities of the LDP Centre concern research and systems development within the field of long-term digital preservation. The LDP Centre has adopted, at this stage, migration as method for preservation and developed a model for structure for Information Package in accordance with [4]. This structure was (and is) intended to be used by archive creating organizations, in order to later deliver digitally recorded information to archives. The base-structure consists of different sets of metadata according to well-established international metadata standards such as METS, EAC, EAD, PREMIS, etc.

We found out that the existing models for structuring information about the object to be preserved, produces problems in implementation. As we can realize, these structures are used as "wrappers" carrying metadata sometimes overlapping one another. Consequently, dealing with all these structures causes both intellectual complications and technical implementation difficulties. We, at the LDP Centre, have experienced that all these structures have some kind of inherent philosophy, which focuses on special features, or attributes of digital material. Here we did three significant observations: 1) the used structures do not focus specifically on information, 2) using several structures sometimes causes an intellectual "mess" due to their inherent philosophies (such as ontological confusion), and 3) the used structures are inherited from the archival world and they support legislative (or authority) records more than digitally recorded information in general. We also found out that putting many efforts on these structures, made us loss focus on that we believe is important to preserve, information. It is obvious that technical or other aspects of digital material to be preserved are indeed important to deal with, but those are just means of preserving information while the digital "technology is a live".

Another issue concerns the fact that it was archival institutions that early experienced the need of digital preservation. Consequently, (archival) metadata standards were developed in order to support digital preservation. The archival inheritance spokes for the principle of provenience as one of the stone corners in long-term digital preservation, because this principle supports authenticity and trustworthiness of any kind of digitally recorded information. Consequently, today's "solutions", based on the Archival and/or the Technocratic Approach supports preservation only in a (relatively) short-term.

To approach a solution concerning how to preserve information through technology changes and surpassing the archival inheritance, the LDP Centre's research activities have taken a new view, which puts information in focus. This includes the development of a detached *Digital Information Preservation Object* that is independent of technology and deals with the question of provenience in a rather new way. Such preservation object might be transferred between different technologies. This is viewed as the main key to a viable solution for long-term digital preservation. Such view demands a higher-level perspective of information and its continuing value without neglecting the constant changing technical aspects of digital preservation.

3 Developing the Information Approach

This paper is a result of two research activities, literature review and interaction in the developing R&D team at the LDP Centre. The literature review was carried out with the purpose of developing a definition of Digital Information Preservation Object and the interaction helped to gather data about the developed structure through seminars, (informal) "interviews" and systems development meetings.

There is a large quantity of literature about the concept of information. Nevertheless, in comparison, the quantity of literature in the field of long-term digital preservation is relatively small. The process of critical selection of relevant literature was based on guidelines such as "well known writers", "established perspectives and/or schools", in order to address the key sources, key theories and definitions of the topic [13]. Since our intention was to provide a broad view on the subject, the initial literature review made it clear that several research projects have shown its own approaches to what we call Digital Information Preservation Object. In our work, we tackle questions like: What are the elements of the

Information Approach? What properties/characteristics constitute a definition of the notion Digital Information Preservation Object?

Since the LDP Centre intends to develop a general preservation model in which Digital Information Preservation Object is the mediator for preservation, this paper will have influence for further research as well as for what methods, models and techniques that will be developed and used. Furthermore, our result will influence the development of the information systems intended to serve long-term digital preservation.

3.1 On Information

The term information is used with different meanings by different groups and in different contexts [17] and there is no well-defined definition of the terms "data" and "information" [6]. A common and short definition is that information is interpreted data [3]. Hence, data is signs used to represent information [17], or signs which carries with them, the possibility to compose and/or decompose the text, photo, music etc. from which it is derived. Thus, retrieving the source provides access to information and we can start reading/viewing/listening but also interpreting and analysing the information existing in the source. This results in the creation of knowledge, that is, we learn from information.

The central idea is that data become information by a process of interpretation [17]. Langefors [ibid.] states, "One of the central insights from infology is that data or texts do not "contain" information (knowledge) but will only, at best, represent the information to those who have the required "pre-knowledge"". Dealing with information systems require a broad view of information, since using a computer implicitly involves information services of some kind, that is, we get service by being informed by data. According to Langefors [17] it is necessary to define information as knowledge, since "information is knowledge and not physical signs". He regards information as knowledge structured in such a way that it is communicated. Because of this, it can also be stored, which leads to information being stored knowledge. [17]

Checkland & Holwell [6] provides the view that information is a service that supports decision making within organizations. Data are facts and a starting point for mental processes. They introduce the concept of "capta", which is the result of selection of certain data (we pay attention to, create some new category or get surprised by the data). In other words, data that catches our interest transforms to capta, the consciousness of something. This signifies that turning data into information is done through a mental process and during that process the data changes shape, and will ultimately lead to knowledge. Once we have selected, paid attention to or created some data, or turned it into capta, we relate it to other things or put it in a context, we attribute meaning to it, and we once again convert it, this time to information. This can be done individually or collectively and this process, selection and conversion of data into meaningful information can lead to larger structures of interconnected information, or what we call knowledge. The interpretation process [17] emphasizes is implicit in this reasoning. We agree with Langefors with his notion that in order to understand information people has to have pre-knowledge. This we see as knowledge that consists of the ability to assimilate the information, but also to have an understanding of the information content, or the subject in focus. If these abilities are found, new knowledge is created the moment someone (individually or in a group) thinks of an issue. When people's ideas, or knowledge, are being shaped and transferred to a medium they are made available for others to share. Hence, the knowledge has now once again become information and exists physically (or digitally), available for people who need it in order to learn and increase their knowledge of something, for example within an organization.

3.2 Information Continuum Perspective

Runardotter et al., [25] put information in a long-term digital preservation context that is a new circular view of the information life cycle. The authors manifested that information is a living concept and is in progress during constant ongoing process. The statement is based on that information is constantly shaped and reshaped, evolving through time, picking up further information or losing some parts and in that way information is all the time under reconstruction. To keep information alive demands a set of ongoing activities, both organizational and technical. The idea of living spiral is also supported by the Records Continuum Model and Information Continuum Model [32] [33]. According these models information and records continues to evolve in space/time and therefore are no end products. [25] The named models are founded on Giddens' structuration theory. This theory of time/space distanciation has been translated into a "rhythm" for information processing derived from the processes of creating information, capturing it as recorded information, organising it and bringing it together within the plural domains of competition. Each item of information once created, may or may not be recorded, stored and managed in ways that can benefit individuals, groups, communities, and can push that information out into the plural domains of the further reaches of space/time. The continua (the dimensions of the model) in the Information Continuum Model are collectively meant to focus analytical attention on the nature of recorded information as an allocative resource, something to be shared and to be used within our activities. The continua in the Records Continuum Model collectively are meant to focus analytical attention on the nature of recorded information as an authoritative resource, something to be relied on not because of its content but because of the way, it has been created and maintained with some continuing contact to the original specificities of its occurrence. [33]

According to Upward [31], information (and its reconstituted products) outwardly spiral from the original act of creation of a document. In the Information Continuum Model, information is derived from a principle source (for example, an information object such as an interview), and becomes transformed through the agency of people and technologies for different purposes. Information Objects are both embedded in the "context of the action in which they are part, and are recursively involved". [28]

We could use Giddens own "words" and transform these to our vocabulary of Information Continuum. Giddens "structure" equals to rules and resources organized as properties of systems. Systems equal to reproduced relations between actors or collectivities organized as social practices. Finally, structuration equals to the continuity or transformation of structures, and therefore the reproduction of systems [16] [11]. The dynamic of structuration is crucial in our view. "Social practices evolve over time and space and has to replicate even to stay the same" [24] (the essence of long-term digital preservation). The term of continuity, (i.e. continuum) promotes the reproduction of systems (i.e. memory traces, organized social practices) by means of digitally recorded information and its continuing value. Information is seen as an (allocative) resource, something to be shared and to be used within our activities [33] [25]. In the long-term gaining access to digitally recorded information (through long-term digital preservation activities) will tell us what sorts of things were out there in the world. We could summarize our view in simple words, as digital preservation will ensure, through the continuing value of information, that social systems will be reproduced as memory tracks of human activities.

4 Predominant Approaches in Long-term Digital Preservation

In our research, we could observe two predominant approaches trying to define the object of preservation, Archival (including Records Management) and a technical (or merely a technocratic) perspective.

4.1 The Object of Preservation in the Archival Approach

One definition of Preservation Object is given by Dollar [8] as "Preservation Objects are those to be archived. These objects are physically compounded by set of files in maybe different formats. The objects logically are compounded by data – the content for instance birth date of a person, and metadata – that should describe the context when the birth date of a particular person was used".

Preservation makes the record a vital component in the memory of organizations, individuals and in some cases of society [29]. A record is more than just information, it is supposed to be trustworthy i.e. being able to serve as evidence, and support accountability. The time for preservation could vary from days or months up to hundreds of years. [10][29] The International Standards Organization definition of records is: "Information created, received, and maintained as evidence and information by organizations or person, in pursuance of legal obligations or in transaction of business." [15] In the Guide for Managing Electronic Records of the International Council on Archives, from an archival perspective, a similar definition of record is given as "recorded information produced or received in the initiation, conduct or completion of an institutional or individual activity and that comprises content, context and structure sufficient to provide evidence of the activity." Records can occur in different forms and representations. They are usually represented as logically delimited information objects, for example, as distinct documents. [14] However, increasingly we find records in the form of distributed objects, such as relational databases and compound documents.

According to Thomassen [29] a record has four characteristics, which make the record unique in relation to other types of information: 1) Records serve as evidence over actions and transactions, 2) Records support accountability, 3) Records are related to processes, i.e. information that is generated by, and linked to some work processes, and 4) Records are going to be preserved, some even for eternity.

Cox [7] have stated that the evidential value of a record can only exist if the content, structure and context are preserved. The context is the link between different records that belongs together and to the process where the record was created. According to Dollar [8], the electronic record is more of a logical entity, where integral parts can be managed at different places within an information system, or even in different information systems.

The question "What is a record" has been one of the fundamental issues in debates and discussions in archiving and digital preservation over the past twenty years. Attempts to arrive at general definition of an *electronic record* were made in the last decade by several research projects and have by now being replaced by more constructive approaches that define the properties and functionalities of electronic records, which need to be preserved in a given context. An electronic record can be understood as a package or a set of technical properties and possibilities, and of administrative context where some of these technical possibilities were put to use. [26]

In contrast, one approach in Digital Libraries that might have a significant difference is proposed by Nichols [21]. In this approach, the concept of "artefact" is central and defined as "a physical object produced at sometime in the past, and attesting to a given set of practices, thinking, and ways of viewing the world, but whose importance will be defined by present and foreseeable future needs and use. The value of the artefact is strongly influenced, but not completely determined by, the document/object's features that are unique". [21] An artefact is then an object with a set of values such as Evidential, aesthetic, Associational, Market and Exhibition value. An artefact is of value to the extent that it testifies to the information being original, faithful, fixed, or stable. Although, this approach does not mention the term record but "artefact", we interpret this approach to be similar to the Archival Approach.

The definitions of records are to some extent usable in our perspective. We perceive the evidentiallity of records as the major focus of Archiving and Records Management and less focus is given to records as informational source.

Thomassen [29] gives emphasis on the need of preservation of records in order to be reused as memory traces. This encompasses our Continuum perspective, which is beyond of just records. The "big difference" is that our perspective is turning the precedence of information in relation to Archiving. Another difference is that our perspective deal with any kind of digitally recorded information as evidence of human activities not just with records as legal evidence.

4.2 The Object of Preservation in the Technocratic Approach

A definition of Digital Object is given by Blanchi & Petrone [2] as "a unique identified data abstraction that encapsulates content and access policies while providing a high-level, self-describing, type definition. Digital Objects are described through the use of an abstract typing mechanism that we refer to as content type". The concept of Information Package of the OAIS Reference Model [4] states that data is interpreted using its Representation Information (described in metadata), which produces information, necessary to interpret that content. In order to preserve successfully such a generic Information Object, it is critical for an Open Archival Information System (OAIS) to identify clearly and understand the Data Object and its associated Representation Information, which together forms what, is called an Information Package. Objects, according to PREMIS [23], can be bitstreams, files or representations. Further, the notion Preservation Object can be compared to the approach of Persistent Object articulated by the US National Archives (NARA) and the San Diego Supercomputing Centre (SDSC). This method presumes that all records can be represented as objects with their specific characteristics and behaviour [26].

The concept of Significant Properties, proposed by the National Library of Australia (NLA) [20], are functions or characteristics of an object that are essential to the meaning of it. Preservation of digital objects, in this approach, are going to necessitate changes in look, feel, functionality or content if the object is to remain usable at all. In the Cedars project [5], Significant Properties were associated with the Underlying Abstract Form (UAF) of an object. Therefore, objects with the same UAF have the same significant properties. The PREMIS [23] working group, following on the work of OAIS, Cedars and NLA, defined Significant Properties as "characteristics of a particular object subjectively determined to be important to maintain through preservation actions", noting that "Significant properties may be objective technical characteristics subjectively considered to be particularly important, or subjectively determined characteristics". Further, the FEDORA architecture [22] conceptualize a Digital Object as having: 1) a structural kernel, which encapsulates content as opaque byte stream packages and, 2) an interface, or behaviour, layer that gives contextual meaning to the data in the Digital Object. One useful metaphor for a Digital Object is that of a cell.

A similar approach is given by Saidis et al. [27] as Digital Object Prototypes (DOPs) that has constituent components as files, metadata, behaviours and relationships. A DOP is a digital object type definition that provides a detailed specification of its constituent parts and behaviours. Digital objects are conceived as instances of their respective prototypes. The approach to Digital Libraries proposed by Arms et al. [1] described the "digital object" in a slightly different manner. The main building blocks in this approach are: "digital objects", which are used to manage digital material in a networked environment. From a computing view, the digital library is built up from simple components, notably digital objects. A digital object is a way of structuring information in digital form. [1]

Very common are the terms: "data abstraction", "data""bitstreams", "files", "instantiation", "characteristics and behaviour", "functions", "functionality", "objective technical characteristics", "structural kernel", "encapsulates opaque byte stream packages", "interface", "metadata", "behaviours and relationships", "manage digital material in a networked environment", "stored". The ontology of this approach shows that the terms utilized come from computer science in general and at some extent from Object Oriented terminology. This spokes for data management through information systems making data central. The term object is also important, being conceptualization of data (such as files, bitstreams, etc.) having some behaviour (its functionality or implemented functions in as information system). No emphasis is made on information neither on its contents as traces of human activities.

5 Towards a Definition of Digital Information Preservation Object

Every other approach to define the object of preservation has focused from different perspectives of preservation and from different characteristics of the digital object using its own ontology. Furthermore, we found that 1) there is no existing or established definition of Digital Information Preservation Object, 2) existing concepts are context dependent and focuses specifically on object to be preserved. After our study we came to conclusions that research carried out so far do not handle Digital Information Preservation Object from Information Continuum perspective and do not contribute with any definition of the notion Digital Information Preservation Object. However, the studied research results merely focus on the structure and physical nature of the digital object. Their described abstractions are conceptualizations of the underlying physical level. Nevertheless, although these approaches support our activities to some extent, the definitions provided by these approaches are not suitable for our view, hence; we experienced the emergence of an own definition of Digital Information Preservation Object that specifically focuses on information. However, this study gave us insights to take another perspective. To define the notion of Digital

Information Preservation Object it is needed to take a standpoint. We cannot begin the definition from structure of the object; nonetheless, we will begin definition from a global view. If we start from the structure, we are viewing an object as a delimited entity at structural level, since our focus is on information, not the object itself. We want to distinguish the conventional view to the object that is a construction, a container or a carrier to hold together the elements (depending on level of conceptualization) from the view that is to see an object from continuum perspective. An object there is a piece or pieces of information that reflects human action in a social context in the continuum.

Our intention (or level of abstraction) lay merely in the general level or, so to say, we try to define DIPO at an "ethereal" level; we want to define the "thing" DIPO. We take stand in the philosophy of Dooyeweerd who stated that Meaning rather than Existence is the primary property in created reality [9]. In our perspective, this view encompasses the Information Continuum Model perspective in which put the continuing value of information (i.e. its reconstruction of human social actions) as the meaning (*raison d'être*) of the DIPO.

The DIPO is a recorded result of action of humans in the form of information pieces. This information is categorized in an information type from social context. These information pieces can have relationships to other information pieces either within its own physical carrier or toward other objects. The vital characteristic of the information object from continuum perspective is that new object can be created through the combination of information pieces that can be a piece of other objects. In that way, the information will be reused in another context and reproducing human social actions. It means that information can be related to processes (that is generated by, and linked to work processes). Furthermore, the information in the object has to serve as evidence over actions and transactions as well.

References

1. Arms W., Blanchi C., Overly E.: An Architecture for Information in Digital Libraries. D-Lib Magazine (1997)
2. Blanchi, C., Petrone, J.: An Architecture for Digital Object Typing. Corporation for National Research Initiatives. Reston, Virginia (2001)
3. Bratteteig, T and Verne, G.: Feminist, or merely critical? In search of Gender Perspectives in Informatics. In Mörtberg, C, ed. Where do we go from here? Feminist Challenges of Information Technology. Division gender and Technology. Luleå University of Technology, Luleå. pp. 39-56 (2000)
4. CCSDS: Reference Model for an Open Archival Information System (OAIS) – Blue book. National Aeronautics and Space Administration (2002)
5. Cedars Project Team and UKOLN: Metadata for Digital Preservation: the Cedars Project outline specification: draft for public consultation, unpublished, www.leeds.ac.uk/cedars.pdf (2000)
6. Checkland, P and Holwell, S.: Information, Systems and Information Systems – making sense of the field. Wiley & Sons Ltd, Chichester, England (1998)

7. Cox, R. J.: Managing Records as Evidence and Information. Quorum Books.(2001)
8. Dollar, C M.: Authentic Electronic Records: Strategies for long-term access. Cohasset Associates Inc. (2000)
9. Dooyeweerd H.: A New Critique of Theoretical Thought . Vol. 1. The Edwin Mellen Press (1997)
10. Duranti, L.: Concepts, Principles, and Methods for the Management of Electronic Records. The Information Society (2001) 17, 271-279
11. Giddens A.: The Constitution of Society. Polity Press. (1984)
12. Gladney, H. M.: Preserving Digital Information. Springer (2007)
13. Hart, C.: Doing a Literature Review. Sage Publications Ltd (1998)
14. ICA Committee on Current Records in an Electronic Environment: Electronic Records: A Workbook for Archivists. Draft (2005)
15. International Standards Organization. Iso 15489-1.: Information and Documentation and Records Management part 1: General. International Standards Organization (2001)
16. Jones M., Orlikowski W., Munir K.: Structuration Theory and Information Systems: A Critical Reappraisal. In Mingers J. & Willcocks L. (Eds.): Social Theory and Philosophy for Information Systems. Wiley (2004)
17. Langefors B.: Essays on Infology. Dept. of Information Systems. Göteborg University, Göteborg (1993)
18. Lim Siew Lin, Chennupati K. Ramaiah Pitt Kuan Wal: Problems in the preservation of electronic records. Library Review, (2003) Vol. 52, nr. 3, pp. 117-125
19. Marklund, K.: Archives for Everyone – Now and in the Future. Government Offices of Sweden. SOU 2002:78 (in Swedish) (2002)
20. National Libraries of Australia. Digital Preservation Policy (2002)
21. Nichols, S.: Artifacts in Digital Collections. 67th IFLA Council and General Conference. August 16-25 (2001)
22. Payette, S. and Lagoze, C.: Flexible and Extensible Digital Object and Repository Architecture (FEDORA). Department of Computer Science Cornell University. Springer-Verlag (1998)
23. PREMIS Working Group. Data Dictionary for Preservation Metadata: final report of the Premis Working Group. Dublin, OCLC Online Computer Library Center and Mountain View, RLG, www.oclc.org/research/projects/pmwg/premis-final.pdf (2005)
24. Rose J.: Structuration Theory and Information system Development – Frameworks for Practice. Proceedings of The 9th European Conference on Information Systems. (2001)
25. Runardotter, M., Quisbert, H., Nilsson J., Hägerfors, A., Miriamdotter, A.: The Information Life Cycle – Issues in Long-term Digital Preservation. Proceedings IRIS 28 – Information system research seminar in Scandinavia (2005)
26. Ruusalepp, R.: Digital preservation in archives: An overview of Current Research and Practices. Swedish National Archives, Sweden (2005)
27. Saidis, K., Pyrounakis, G., Nikolaidou, M., and Delis, A.: Digital Object Prototypes: An Effective Realization of Digital Object Types. Department of Informatics and Telecommunications, Libraries Computer Center, University of Athens. Springer-Verlag (2006)
28. Stillman L. J. H. Understandings of Technology in community-Based Organizations: A Structurational Analysis. Dr. Thesis. Faculty of Information Technology, Monash University (2006)
29. Thomassen, T.: A first introduction to archival science. Archival Science, (2001) Vol. 1, pp 373-385
30. Upward, F.: Structuring the Records Continuum - Part One: Postcustodial principles and properties. First published: Archives and Manuscripts, (1996) 24 (2)

31. Upward, F.: Structuring the Records Continuum, Part Two: Structuration Theory and Recordkeeping. First published: Archives and Manuscripts, (1997) 25 (1)
32. Upward, F.: Modeling the Continuum as Paradigm Shift in Recordkeeping and Archiving Process and Beyond – a Personal Reflection. Records Management Journal. (2000) Vol. 10, nr 3. pp 115-139
33. Upward, F.: Community Informatics and the Information Processing Continuum. Proceedings of the Constructing and sharing memory: community informatics, identity and empowerment conference. Centre for Community Networking Research (CCRN) (2006)

Semantic Application Profiles: A Means to Enhance Knowledge Discovery in Domain Metadata Models

Dimitrios A. Koutsomitropoulos, George E. Paloukis and Theodore S. Papatheodorou

Abstract. Ontologies on the Semantic Web form a basis for representing human-conceivable knowledge in a machine-understandable manner. Ontology development for a specific knowledge domain is however a difficult task, because the produced representation has to be adequately detailed and broad enough at the same time. The CIDOC-CRM is such an ontology, pertaining to cultural heritage, which we align to the Semantic Web environment: first transforming it to OWL and then profiling it not in the usual flat metadata sense, but by refining and extending its conceptual structures, taking advantage of OWL semantics. This kind of profiling maintains applicability of the model, while enabling more expressive reasoning tasks. To this end, we construct a mechanism for acquiring implied and web-distributed information that is used to conduct and present a series of experimental inferences on the CRM profiled form.

1 Introduction

The CIDOC Conceptual Reference Model [1] is an ontology that attempts to model the knowledge domain of cultural heritage. As every human conceivable domain, cultural heritage is very hard to be accurately modeled. In addition and due to its nature, cultural heritage information use to be hidden in libraries and museum archives, and when available on-line are poorly or not at all structured. Moreover, the CIDOC-CRM has been recently appointed an ISO standard status (ISO-21127), a fact that further stresses its importance as a common conceptual basis between cultural heritage applications.

High Performance Information Systems Laboratory,
School of Engineering, University of Patras,
Buidling B, 26500 Patras-Rio, Greece
{kotsomit, gpalouk, tsp}@hpclab.ceid.upatras.gr

Using the CIDOC-CRM standard as our conceptual basis, we first create its machine meaningful counterpart by expressing it in the Web Ontology Language (OWL), a W3C standard. This process does not merely amount to a simple syntax transformation. Rather, taking advantage of OWL most expressive (but, simultaneously, decidable) structures we also enrich and upgrade the model, thus further narrowing the conceptual approximation [4].

To avoid making the model too specific, we incorporate the OWL statements in different documents that involve concrete instances of the CRM's concepts and roles. This approach not only demonstrates the distributed knowledge discovery capabilities inherent in web ontologies; at the same time it suggests a *semantically enhanced application profiling* paradigm: this kind of profiling takes the usual metadata-specific sense, where it is seen as an aggregation of disparate metadata elements [5], a step further: It does not so much deal with a horizontal extension of the ontology, but rather extends it in a semantic manner, as may dictated by a particular application.

The next step is to take advantage of this new ontology mostly by being able to reap the benefits of our semantic extensions. Thus we employ a methodology [6] and implement a prototype web application, the Knowledge Discovery Interface (KDI) to be able to pose reasoning-based intelligent queries to the CRM profiled form.

The rest of this paper is mainly organized as follows: First we give an overview of the metadata application profiling idea and approaches. Then we present our process of transforming and profiling the CIDOC-CRM, pointing out our extensions and discussing semantic profiling; following there are the inferences conducted on the CRM using the KDI and their results. Finally, we summarize potential future work and the conclusions drawn from our approach.

2 Metadata Application Profiling

The need for efficient resource description in electronic archives quickly identified the lack of uniform ways for representing and maintaining information about resources. These pieces of information, known as *metadata* would therefore be organized in concrete schemata produced and managed by content authorities, institutions and domain experts. The XML language eased this process by providing an official syntax for expressing both schemata and actual metadata information in machine readable format.

However, as these schemata tended to proliferate day by day, focusing on a particular domain of interest or function, there was often the case where particular developer's needs were not satisfied by any existing schema or some elements he may find suitable where scattered over various standard implementations. Metadata application profiling came then as a natural means to overcome these obstacles while respecting the standards *raison d'être*: As defined in [3] application profiling is the assemblage of metadata elements selected from one or more metadata schemas and their combination in a compound schema. Let's briefly examine an application profiling example [9]:

```
<?xml version="1.0"?>
<record
xmlns="http://example.org/learningapp/"
xmlns:xsi="http://www.w3.org/2001/XMLSchema-
instance"
xsi:schemaLocation="http://example.org/learningapp/
schema.xsd"
xmlns:dc="http://purl.org/dc/elements/1.1/"
xmlns:ims="http://www.imsglobal.org/xsd/imsmd_v1p2">
   <dc:title>
     Frog maths
   </dc:title>
   <dc:description>
     Simple maths games for 5-7 year olds.
   </dc:description>
   <ims:typicallearningtime>
     <ims:datetime>
       0000-00-00T00:15
     </ims:datetime>
   </ims:typicallearningtime>
</record>
```

This is an instantiation of mixing Dublin Core elements with IMS learning metadata. It is noticeable that the most important means for actually implementing an application profile are *namespaces*. In the example above dc represents elements from the Dublin Core set, while ims denotes IMS-originating metadata. Namespaces play a crucial role not only in identifying provenance of distinct schemata, but also as a means to separate and then merge different elements and vocabularies.

It is clear that metadata schemata attempt to capture and convey human conceivable knowledge in the most basic unambiguous machine-compatible form: A horizontal aggregation of definitions (possibly with sub-elements) with specified value restrictions and formats that is expressed (most often) in XML. Metadata standards are perfectly successful in this manner; at the same time their representation of knowledge is considered quite poor and distanced from machine-understandability.

On the other hand, the Semantic Web and its ontologies give the chance of more accurate modeling of domain knowledge: ontologies are essentially metadata schemata with precisely defined meaning and richer relations between elements and concepts of a conceptual model. With this new toolbox at hand a series of possibilities is now opened that may further ease the development of enhanced metadata profiles. These include a novel method for creating a metadata application profile, not just by combining, refining or restricting elements, but by the semantic extension of the model, and that is exactly what we are trying to do in the following section.

3 Transforming the CIDOC-CRM

CIDOC-CRM includes about 84 concepts and 139 roles, not counting their inverses (that is, a total of 278 roles) (Figure 1). In terms of expressivity, the CRM employs structures enabled by RDF(S), which may be summarized as follows:

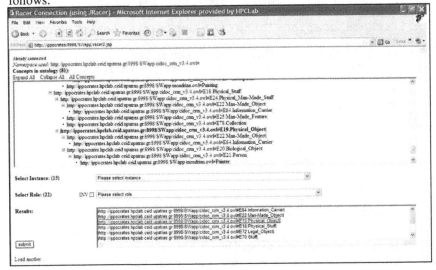

Fig. 1. CIDOC-CRM taxonomy as shown by the KDI.

- Concepts as well as roles are organized in hierarchies.

- For every role, concepts are defined that form its domain and its range.

- For every role, its inverse is also defined, as a separate role, because RDF(S) cannot implicitly express inversion relation between two roles.

- There is no distinction between object and datatype properties (roles) as in OWL; Rather, roles that are equivalent to datatype properties have rdf:Literal as their range.

As of Jan. 2005 there exists an OWL transcription of the CRM's RDF document. However this version adds only role specific constructs (inversion, transitivity etc) which, semantically, do not exceed OWL Lite.

To create a CIDOC-CRM semantic application profile, we follow a twofold approach: First we transcode it in an appropriate and expressive format (namely OWL); Next, we commence with its actual profiling, first by strengthening its intension, i.e. the general knowledge about the domain [8] and then by refining the model for the needs of a particular application.

Although the CRM syntactic processing is not straightforward, in the following we are focusing on the semantic transformation of the model, the details of the transcoding being presented in [7].

3.1 Semantic Intension and Refinement

This phase of CRM upgrading includes its semantic augmentation with OWL-specific structures up to the OWL DL level, so as to enable a satisfactory level of reasoning, as well as its completion with some concrete instances.

This has been conducted in two steps: first, we added expressions that pertain to the model itself, so as to better capture intended meaning of properties and classes by taking advantage of OWL vocabulary. Second, added further subclasses and *semantic constraints* on them that actually profile the model for the specific case of paintings and painters in general. As an application scenario we have chosen to model facts from the life and work of the Dutch painter Piet Mondrian. Let's examine these steps in detail:

Core Intension Strengthening

In this step, we do not add any new classes or entities that extend the CRM. Instead, we try to better approximate the core model's conceptualization by using OWL statements that allow for its more precise implementation. In particular:

- We modelled minimum and maximum cardinality restrictions by using unqualified number restrictions (owl:minCardinality, owl:maxCardinality).
- We modelled inverse roles, using the owl:inverseOf operand.
- We included a symmetric role example, using the rdf:type= "&owl;Symmetric" statement.

Note that RDF(S) being CRM's favoured implementation, there is no way to express such constraints. For the purpose of our work, we have not exhaustively quantified the CRM properties, but applied constraints to some ones, used and instantiated in our Mondrian example (see Section 4).

Clearly, the additions above actually refine the core model in a way that achieves to expand the *intensional knowledge* of the schema using constructs and means provided only in a Semantic Web infrastructure.

Application Refinement

During this step, we create some specific CRM concept and role instances pertaining to our particular application. We also include axiom and fact declarations that only OWL allows to be expressed, as well as new roles and concepts making use of this expressiveness.

- We added the classes: "Painting" as subclass of CRM's "Visual_Item", "Painting_Event", a subclass of "Creation_Event" and "Painter" a subclass of "Person".
- We added a data type property "hasURL" as a sub-property of "has_current_location".
- We semantically characterized above concepts based on existential and universal quantification, by using the owl:hasValue, owl:someValuesFrom and owl:allValuesFrom expressions, which ultimately enable more complex inferences.

This is another direction of semantic profiling: We added new elements bearing their own namespace, but then we semantically entangled them with each other and with the model's own definitions, thus imposing *semantic refinements* for our own specific case.

3.2   A Semantic Profiling Technique

The above discussion introduces the process of creating semantic application profiles and suggests a universal paradigm for Semantic Web metadata applications. Although we applied this technique specifically on CIDOC-CRM, it can be easily seen that it fits any other domain of interest. Independently of the domain chosen, one has first to consider a suitable machine readable implementation for the model, which, for the time being, is offered by the OWL specifications.

Given a proper syntax, it is worth examining the possibilities of better capturing the intensional knowledge of the model, taking advantage of any particular vocabulary the representation language may offer. In this way the conceptualization of the model is strengthened and its potential ensured.

At some point the initial model may be found inadequate for the specific application needs. As is the case with traditional metadata profiling, other ontological and metadata schemata may have to be considered and mixed with the original, thus revisiting the initial step. In addition, one can devise appropriate constructs in order to narrow the semantics of the intended application.

One of the main concerns when developing an application profile is to ensure the source schema is not affected and its general applicability maintained. To achieve this, in addition to namespaces, OWL provides an explicit inclusion mechanism through the `<owl:imports>` statement. In our case, we chose to include our semantic ornaments in three new OWL documents, namely: crm_core_profile.owl for the core intension, crm_paint_profile.owl for the application refinement and mondrian.owl as the instantiation of the above[2]. In this

---

[2]All documents are available under
http://ippocrates.hpclab.ceid.upatras.gr:8998/SWapp/

way we preserve the original model and we also show Semantic Web capabilities for ontology integration and distributed knowledge discovery.

4 Results

In the following we present the results from some experimental inference actions conducted on the CRM augmented OWL form using our KDI. The KDI is a web application, providing intelligent query submission services on Web ontology documents and is detailed in [6].

Inferences performed can be divided in two categories: *Positive* inferences where, based on the concept and role axioms as well as the ontology facts we conclude new, not explicitly expressed facts and *negative* inferences where, based on the ontology axioms and facts we detect unsatisfiability conditions on concepts and instances.

4.1 Positive Inferences

The following code is a fragment from mondrian.owl stating that a "Painting_Event" is in fact a "Creation_Event" that "has_created" "Painting" objects only:

```
<owl:Class rdf:ID="Painting_Event">
  <rdfs:subClassOf
  rdf:resource="&crm;E65.Creation_Event"/>
  <rdfs:subClassOf>
    <owl:Restriction>
      <owl:onProperty
      rdf:resource="&crm;P94F.has_created"/>
      <owl:allValuesFrom rdf:resource="#Painting"/>
    </owl:Restriction>
  </rdfs:subClassOf>
</owl:Class>
<Painting_Event rdf:ID="Creation of Mondrian's
composition">
```

Top Concept: **T**

P94F.has_created: **R**

Painting_Event: **C**

Painting: **D**

Creation of Mondrian's
Composition: **i₁**

Mondrian's Composition: **i₂**

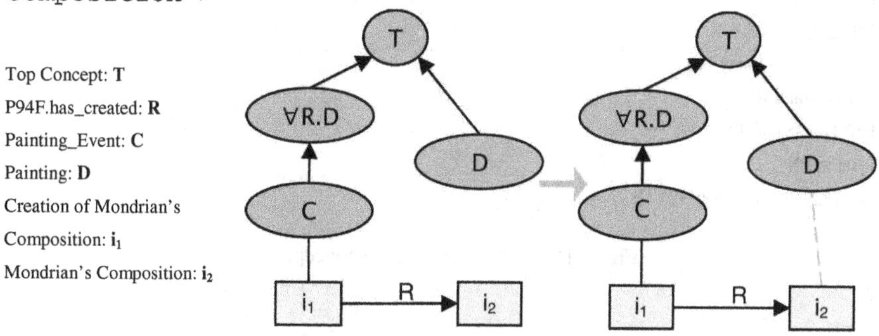

Fig. 2. Inference example using value restriction.

```
<crm:P94F.has_created rdf:resource="#Mondrian's
    composition"/>
</Painting_Event>
```

The above fragment is graphically depicted in the left part of Figure 2. Creation of Mondrian's Composition" (i_1) is an explicitly stated "Painting_Event" that "has_created" (R) "Mondrian's composition" (i_2). Now, asking the KDI to infer "what is a painting?" it infers that i_2 is indeed a painting (right part of Figure 2), correctly interpreting the value restriction on role R.

4.2 Negative Inferences

In CRM, temporal events may have a time-span. Naturally, a "Person" cannot have a time-span, unless it is also a "Temporal Entity". In the following we state that "Persons" and "Temporal Entities" are disjoint concepts and we attempt to define the class of "Painters with time-span".

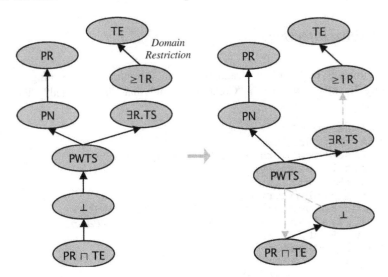

Bottom Concept: ⊥

P4F.has_time-span: **R**

E2. Temporal_Entity: **TE**

E21.Person: **PR**

E52.Time-Span: **TS**

Painter: **PN**

Painter_with_time-span: **PWTS**

Fig. 3. Detecting unsatisfiable concepts.

```
<owl:ObjectProperty rdf:ID="P4F.has_time-span">
  <rdfs:domain rdf:resource="#E2.Temporal_Entity"/>
</owl:ObjectProperty>
<owl:Class rdf:about="&crm;E2.Temporal_Entity">
  <owl:disjointWith rdf:resource="&crm;E21.Person"/>
</owl:Class>
<owl:Class rdf:about="#Painter">
  <rdfs:subClassOf rdf:resource="&crm;E21.Person"/>
</owl:Class>
<owl:Class rdf:ID="Painter_with_time-span">
  <rdfs:subClassOf rdf:resource="#Painter"/>
  <rdfs:subClassOf>
    <owl:Restriction>
      <owl:onProperty rdf:resource="&crm;P4F.has_time-
        span"/>
      <owl:someValuesFrom rdf:resource="&crm;E52.Time-
        Span"/>
    </owl:Restriction>
  </rdfs:subClassOf>
</owl:Class>
```

The above fragment is graphically depicted in Figure 3. A "Painter with time-span" is defined as a "Painter" (known subclass of "Person") that "has time-span" some "Time-Span" instances. However, individuals that "have time-span" are required to belong to the "Temporal Entity" class, as dictated by the corresponding domain restriction. Therefore, apart from being a "Person", a "Painter with time-span" must also be a "Temporal Entity". On the other hand "Persons" and "Temporal Entities" are disjoint, so their intersection represents the bottom (always empty) concept. Thus, a "Painter with Time-Span" can never exist, as its class is inferred to be equivalent to the bottom concept. The KDI correctly detects the unsatisfiability of this class by pointing it out with red colour in the taxonomy.

5 Conclusions and Future Work

In this paper we attempted to deploy a working platform upon which we experimented with the application of Semantic Web techniques and ideas on the cultural heritage domain. Concurrently, we suggested a practice that can easily be followed in any other domain of interest.

First we have shown the Semantic Web capabilities for knowledge discovery with web ontologies. We conducted and presented a series of successful experimental results possible only after aligning our ontological model to the Semantic Web standards. A side product of this process is the strengthening of the argument that OWL and its most expressive decidable subset, OWL DL, may be recommended for modeling domain metadata and be fruitful in that way.

Doing so, we elaborated a novel technique for creating metadata application profiles, by taking advantage of the Semantic Web toolbox. This technique, involves semantic enrichment of the metadata model and then deepening of its structures and definitions in accordance to specific needs. Having the CIDOC-CRM as a starting point, our approach can be likewise applied in any other knowledge domain.

A possible combination of semantic profiling with traditional metadata profiling practices like namespace inclusion and merging may be worth to examine as future work. The combination for example of a CRM profile with a flat metadata schema (e.g. Dublin Core) should allow for the interchangeable use of both their element sets, provided this is done in a semantically consistent and productive manner, i.e. simple metadata elements are not treated naively as annotations.

To this end, of particular interest is looking into the upcoming OWL 1.1 [2] specification and especially its concept of *punning* as a meta-modeling principle, based on which a name definition may have variable semantic interpretation depending on the ontological context.

Acknowledgments. Dimitrios Koutsomitropoulos is partially supported by a grant from the "Alexander S. Onassis" Public Benefit Foundation.

References

1. Crofts N, Doerr M, Gill T (2003) The CIDOC Conceptual Reference Model: A standard for communicating cultural contents. Cultivate Interactive, 9. http://www.cultivate-int.org/issue9/chios/
2. Cuenca Grau B, Horrocks I, Parsia B et al (2006) Next Steps for OWL. In Proc. of the OWL Experiences and Directions Workshop (OWLED'06)
3. Duval E, Hodgins W, Sutton S et al (2002) Metadata Principles and Practicalities. D-Lib Magazine, 8. http://www.dlib.org/ dlib/april02/weibel/04weibel.html
4. Guarino N (1998) Formal Ontology and Information Systems. In N. Guarino (ed.): Formal Ontology in Information Systems. Proc. of FOIS'98. IOS Press
5. Heery R, Patel M (2000) Mixing and Matching Metadata Schemas. Ariadne, 25. http://www.ariadne.ac.uk/issue25/app-profiles/intro.html
6. Koutsomitropoulos DA, Fragakis MF, Papatheodorou TS (2006) Discovering Knowledge in Web Ontologies: A Methodology and Prototype Implementation. In Proc. of SEMANTICS 2006. OCG 151-164
7. Koutsomitropoulos DA, Papatheodorou TS (2007) Expressive Reasoning about Cultural Heritage Knowledge Using Web Ontologies. In Proc. of 3d International Conference on Web Information Systems and Technologies (WEBIST 2007). WIA track, pp.276-281

8. Nardi D, Brachman RJ (2007) An Introduction to Description Logics. In Baader F, Calvanese D, McGuiness DL et al (eds) The Description Logic Handbook, 2nd edn. Cambridge
9. Powell A, Johnston P (2003) Guidelines for implementing Dublin Core in XML. DCMI Recommendation. http://dublincore.org/documents/dc-xml-guidelines/

Ontology for Preservation of Interactive Multimedia Performances

Kia Ng [1], Tran Vu Pham[1], Bee Ong[1], Alexander Mikroyannidis[1],
and David Giaretta[2]

Abstract. Preservation of interactive multimedia performances is becoming important as they are getting more and more popular in the performing arts communities. Preservation does not only require keeping all the necessary components for the production of a performance but also the knowledge about these components so that the original production process is repeated at any given time. Ontologies provide the means for semantic processing, cataloguing and querying on preserved digital objects. In this paper, a domain ontology is introduced for describing the complex relationships amongst different components of a performance to support its preservation.

1   Introduction

Interactive multimedia technologies are popularly used in contemporary performing arts, including musical compositions, installation arts, dance, etc. Typically, an Interactive Multimedia Performance (IMP) involves one or more performers who interact with a computer based multimedia system making use of multimedia contents that may be prepared as well as generated in real-time including music, manipulated sound, animation, video, graphics, etc. The interactions between the performer(s) and the multimedia system can be done in a wide range of different approaches, such as body motions [14], movements of traditional musical instruments, sounds generated by these instruments [18], tension of body muscle using bio-feedback [12], heart beats, sensors systems, and many others[3]. These "signals" from performers are captured and processed by the

---

[1] Interdisciplinary Centre for Scientific Research in Music (ICSRiM), School of Computing & School of Music, University of Leeds, Leeds LS2 9JT, UK

[2] STFC, Rutherford Appleton Laboratory, Oxfordshire OX11 0QX, UK
caspar@icsrim.org.uk – www.icsrim.org.uk/caspar

multimedia systems. Depending on specific performances, the "signals" will be mapped to multimedia contents for generation using a mapping strategy. Depicted in Fig. 1 is a typical IMP process based on the MvM (Music via Motion) interactive performance system, in which performer's motion is captured in 3D and translated into multimedia contents [14].

IMPs are usually *ad hoc*. In order to keep a performance alive through time, not only its output, but also the whole production process to create the output needs to be preserved. In addition to the output multimedia contents, related digital contents such as mapping strategies, processing software and intermediate data created during the production process (e.g. data translated from "signals" captured) have to be preserved, together with all the configuration, setting of the software, changes (and time), etc. The most challenging problem is to preserve the knowledge about the logical and temporal relationships amongst individual components so that they can be properly assembled into a performance during the reconstruction process.

The preservation of IMPs produced by the MvM system comprises part of the Contemporary Arts testbed dealing with preservation of artistic contents, which is one of the three testbeds of the EU project CASPAR (Cultural, Artistic and Scientific knowledge for Preservation, Access and Retrieval - www.casparpreserves.eu). The other two are Scientific and Cultural testbeds, which regard scientific data of high volume and complexity, as well as virtual cultural digital content respectively.

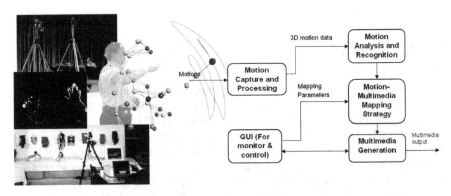

Fig. 1. An example of IMP production process using the MvM (Music via Motion) system [14]

This paper introduces an ontology approach to describing an IMP and its internal relationships to support the preservation process. The proposed ontology is an extension of the CIDOC Conceptual Reference Model (CIDOC-CRM), which is an ISO standard for describing cultural heritage [4, 5, 9]. The next section of the paper discusses various metadata approaches in digital preservation.

---

[3] See New Interfaces for Musical Expression (NIME) conference series - http://www.nime.org

The applicability and limitations of CIDOC-CRM for modelling IMPs to support their preservation are analysed in Section 3. In Section 4, the proposed extensions for CIDOC-CRM are presented. Finally, the paper is concluded and some plans for future work are provided.

2 Metadata and Ontologies for Digital Preservation

Metadata and ontologies have been proven an important factor in digital preservation. Currently, the most popular metadata model used in digital archives is Dublin Core [3]. It was developed as a basic metadata set for discovery of digital records on the Internet. It is now widely used in digital library community for interoperability. However, it is descriptive and too simple for use in a digital preservation process due to the lack of mechanism for describing the relationship amongst digital objects. This is one of the key requirements for digital preservation, such as in the case of preserving IMPs as described in this paper.

Metadata element sets designed specifically for preservation purposes include those developed by RLG Working Group on Preservation Issues of Metadata (RLG) [1], CURL Exemplars in Digital Archives (CEDARS) project (www.leeds.ac.uk/cedars) [2], the metadata of the National Library of Australia (NLA) [13] and the Networked European Deposit Library (NEDLIB) [11]. The RLG elements are for describing structure and management of digital image files in preservation archives. The scope of applicability of RLG elements is therefore limited. It also lacks the capability to describe the relationships amongst related digital objects. CEDARS, NLA and NEDLIB element sets are more comprehensive and also compliant to OAIS Reference Model. A consensus effort has been carried out by the OCLC/RLG Working Group on Preservation Metadata to develop a common Metadata Framework to Support the Preservation of Digital Objects, which was based largely on CEDARS, NEDLIB and NLA element sets [15]. The Preservation Metadata Implementation Strategies (PREMIS) Working Group later built on this framework a PREMIS data model and a data dictionary for preservation metadata [16].

Relationships and dependencies can be better described in an object oriented way using ontologies. In the Fedora project, a small simple set of relationship ontologies was used together with Dublin Core [7]. An ontology has been developed based on MPEG-7 standard [10] for describing structure and conceptual related aspects of audio-visual contents [17]. The CIDOC Conceptual Reference Model (CRM) is being proposed as a standard ontology for enabling interoperability amongst digital libraries [4, 5, 9]. CIDOC-CRM defines a core set concepts for physical as well as temporal entities. This is very important for describing temporal dependencies amongst different objects in a preservation archive. A combination of core concepts defined in CIDOC-CRM and multimedia content specific concepts of MPEG-7 for describing multimedia objects in museums has also been introduced. A harmonisation effort has also been carried out to align the Functional Requirements for Bibliographic Records (FRBR) [8] to

CIDOC-CRM for describing artistic contents. The result is an object oriented version of FRBR, named FRBRoo [6].

3   CIDOC-CRM for Digital Preservation

CIDOC-CRM was originally designed for describing cultural heritage collections in museum archives. In museums, CIDOC-CRM is used to describe things and events from the past. Similarly, in preservation domain, today's things and events are documented for the future. Due to this similarity and its wide coverage, CIDOC-CRM has attracted attention from preservation communities as core ontology for enabling semantic interoperability amongst digital archives.

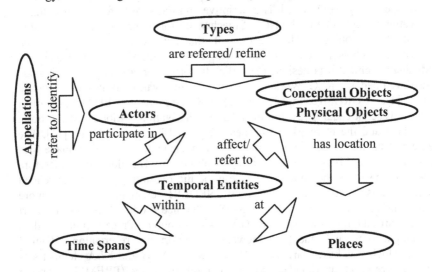

Fig. 2. The meta-schema of CIDOC-CRM [4]

The meta-schema of CIDOC-CRM is illustrated in Fig. 2. CIDOC-CRM's conceptualisation of the past is centred on Temporal Entities (e.g. events). People (Actors) and objects (Conceptual Objects and Physical Objects) involved, time (Time-Spans) and Places are documented via their relationships with the Temporal Entities. Appellations and Types are generally used for identification and classification. For example, an MvM performance can be described as an event. Participants of the performance are Actors, tools and instruments used in the performances are Physical Objects, etc. The mapping of a performance to the meta-schema of CIDOC-CRM is shown in Fig. 3. Appellation and Types are omitted in this diagram.

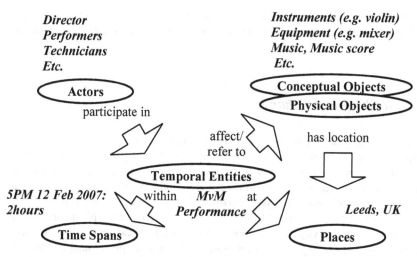

Fig. 3. Mapping an MvM performance details to CIDOC-CRM meta-schema

The CIDOC-CRM vocabulary can be used to describe a performance at a high level. However, more specialised vocabularies are necessary for the interactive performing art domain to precisely describe the relationship amongst the elements of a performance. For example, it is necessary to model how equipments are connected together in the performance. Some concepts representing digital objects have been very recently introduced in CIDOC-CRM for digital preservation purposes. Nevertheless, there is a need for documenting the relationships amongst software applications, data, and operating systems, as well as the operations performed on them. In addition, CIDOC-CRM is designed primarily for the documentation of what has happened, whereas in digital preservation, it is also required to document the reconstruction of a past event from preserved components.

4 Extending CIDOC-CRM for Preservation of IMPs

The CIDOC-CRM ontology is being extended for describing IMP in digital preservation context. The extended ontology is domain specific. It does not alter any concepts defined in CIDOC-CRM. Instead, the extended ontology is a specialisation of CIDOC-CRM concepts for IMP and digital preservation domain. Specifically, the extension is developed for the following objectives:

- To provide a domain specific vocabulary for describing an IMP. The description includes details on how the archived performance was carried out and how possibly it can be recreated.

- To provide a vocabulary for describing the interrelationships between digital objects and the operations performed on them in the digital preservation context.

4.1 Describing Performances

The scope of description is the information about the performance, its various activities, actors, equipment, instruments and digital objects involved in the performance. Configuration – how different elements are associated with each other – is also of particular importance. The centre of the description is the "IMP1.Performance" object[4]. "IMP1.Performance" is a specialisation of CIDOC-CRM "E7.Activity" and also of "E63.Beginning of Existence". This means that a performance is an activity and it brings something into existence. Entities and properties for describing the relationships between a performance and its components are shown in Fig. 4.

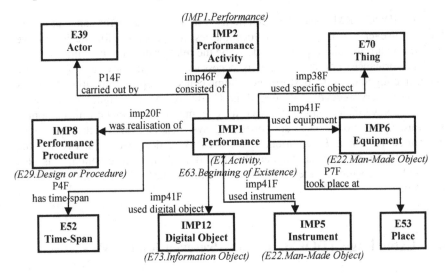

Fig. 4. "IMP1.Performance" entity and its components: new concepts are attached with the names (in brackets) of their direct parent from CIDOC-CRM.

More specifically, the following concepts have been introduced:

---

[4] The extended concepts are prefixed by IMP and an identification number. The original CIDOC-CRM entity and property names are prefixed by E and P respectively.

- "**IMP2.Performance Activity**": for describing activities of a performance. For example, in an MvM performance, "capturing of 3D motion data" can be modelled as an activity. "IMP2.Performance Activity" is designed as a specialisation (subclass) of "IMP1.Performance" as any activity within a performance can be seen as a performance itself. The temporal order in which performance activities were carried can be modelled using properties inherited from "E7.Activity".

- "**IMP5.Instrument**": a specialisation of CIDOC-CRM "E22.Man-Made Object" for modelling musical instruments (e.g. cellos, violins, drums, etc.) used in a performance.

- "**IMP6.Equipment**": a specialisation of CIDOC-CRM "E22.Man-Made Object" for modelling equipment used in a performance. Equipment can be a microphone, a sound mixer or a computer, etc. Computer related equipment is further classified into "IMP7.Computer_Hardware" in the extended model to better describe their relationships with computer software.

- "**IMP8.Performance Procedure**": a specialisation of CIDOC-CRM "E29.Design or Procedure", which is a subclass of "E73.Information Object" for describing the procedure in which a performance should be carried out. A performance procedure may consist of other performance procedures. Similar to performance activities, the procedures need to be executed in a particular temporal order in order to achieve the desired performance. However, as CIDOC-CRM is aimed at describing what has happened, whereas performance procedures usually tell what is supposed to happen, CIDOC-CRM does not have precise vocabulary for describing temporal order of execution of performance procedures. New properties have been introduced for "IMP8.Performance Procedure" to deal with this requirement.

- "**IMP12.Digital Object**": a specialisation of "E73.Information Object". "IMP12.Digital Object" and its specialisations are discussed in detail in Section 5.2.

Configuration of a performance, e.g. assignment of actors to roles, connections of tools, or association between data and processing applications, can be described using "IMP29.Performance Attribute Association" and its subclasses: "IMP3.Data Application Association", "IMP4.Actor Role Association" and "IMP30.Equipment Pairing". "IMP29.Performance Attribute Association" is a specialisation of "E7.Activity".

4.2 Describing Digital Objects

Digital objects are not well covered by CIDOC-CRM. In essence, a digital object is a stream of bits. This bits once interpreted carry some kind of information, e.g. a text document, a picture or a set of instruction. Strictly under CIDOC-CRM definition, the stream of bits is an information object ("E73.Information Object"). However, by itself, it does not have much meaning to a human being. Only the information it carries, once interpreted by a computer, is understandable. From this point of view, a digital object is an information carrier, which is a characteristic of physical objects under CIDOC-CRM definition. In this extension, digital objects are classified under "IMP12.Digital Object", which is a subclass of "E73.Information Object". Information carrying characteristic of digital objects are modelled using properties of "IMP12.Digital Object" and its specialisations. Hierarchical structure of "IMP12.Digital Object" and its subclasses is shown in Fig. 5.

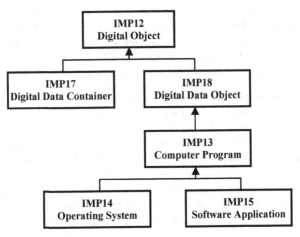

Fig. 5. Classification of digital objects

"IMP12.Digital Object" has two direct subclasses: "IMP17.Digital Data Container" and "IMP18.Digital Data Object". A digital data container ("IMP17.Digital Data Container") is a container of one or more digital data objects ("IMP18.Digital Data Object"). An example of digital data container is a file. The bit stream contained within the file is considered as a digital data object. This separation is necessary to model a bit stream in memory or in cases where multiple bit streams carrying different information carried by a single digital data container. A special type of digital data object is a computer program (IMP13.Computer Program). In this case, the bit stream is a set of instructions to be executed by a computer. There are two specialisations of computer programs: "IMP14.Operating System" and "IMP15.Software Application".

Relationships between digital objects are modelled through their types. An example of such a relationship is between software applications and operating systems. Each class under "IMP12.Digital Object" has a type, which is specified under CIDOC-CRM "E55.Type", associated with it. With the above example, suppose that there is an operating system type "Windows" and a software application type "Microsoft Office", and it is described that software application type "Microsoft Office" "can run on" operating system type "Windows" then it can be inferred that any application having type "Microsoft Office" can run on operating system having type "Windows". Modelling the relationships between digital objects using type will reduce the complexity when handling individual instances.

Operations on digital objects can be described using "IMP26.Digital Object Operation", which is a specialisation of CIDOC-CRM "E5.Event". A number of subclasses of "IMP26.Digital Object Operation" have also been defined to deal with common operations such as creation, duplication, transformation, modification, access and deletion. This is necessary in preservation context, where history of a digital object (provenance information) needs to be documented.

5 Conclusion

This paper introduces characteristics of IMPs and their requirements for digital preservation. It notes that metadata and ontologies play a very important role in digital preservation process, in particular for describing representation information, provenance and other information related to a digital object as defined by the OAIS Reference Model. An ontology approach has been considered, by extending the current concepts defined in CIDOC-CRM, for preservation of IMPs. A number of concepts for performing art domain as well as for digital objects have been proposed. This extension is designed specifically for describing an IMP and its internal relationships. It can also be used together with FRBRoo if there is the need for describing the conception process of the performance (the process of translating the initial idea of the composer into a performance plan). The new concepts are currently being evaluated using MvM performance data available at ICSRiM and further in the contemporary arts testbed of the CAPSAR project. Finally, the newly proposed concepts will be examined and verified by relevant communities for acceptance to ensure successful implementations in the future.

Acknowledgements. Work partially supported by European Community under the Information Society Technologies (IST) programme of the 6th FP for RTD - project CASPAR. The authors are solely responsible for the content of this paper. It does not represent the opinion of the European Community, and the European Community is not responsible for any use that might be made of data appearing therein.

References

[1]   Berger, B., Coleman, J., Cromwell-Kessler, W., Dale, R., DeCandido, B., Montori, C., and Ross, S. RLG Working Group on Preservation Issues of Metadata - Final Report. RLG and Preservation 1998.

[2]   Day, M. Metadata for Preservation - CEDARS Project Document AIW01. UKOLN 1998.

[3]   DC Dublin Core Metadata Initiative. http://dublincore.org/.

[4]   Doerr, M. *The CIDOC CRM - an Ontological Approach to Semantic Interoperability of Metadata.* AI Magazine, 2003. **24**(3).

[5]   Doerr, M., "Increasing the Power of Semantic Interoperability for the European Library", in *ERCIM News*, vol. 66, 2006.

[6]   Doerr,   M.   and   LeBoeuf,   P.   FRBRoo   Introduction. http://cidoc.ics.forth.gr/frbr_inro.html, 2006.

[7]   Fedora Overview: The Fedora Digital Object Model. 2006.

[8]   FRBR Functional Requirements for Bibliographic Records - Final Report. International Federation of Library Associations and Institutions (IFLA), Frankfurt am Main, Germany 1997.

[9]   Gill, T. *Building semantic bridges between museums, libraries and archives: The CIDOC Conceptual Reference Model.* First Monday, 2004. **9**(5).

[10]   ISO Information Technology – Multimedia Content Description Interface (MPEG-7). Standard   No.   ISO/IEC   15938:2001.   International   Organization   for Standardization(ISO) 2001.

[11]   Lupovici, C. and Masanes, J. Metadata for long term-preservation. NEDLIB 2000.

[12]   Nagashima, Y. *Bio-Sensing Systems and Bio-Feedback Systems for Interactive Media Arts.* In *Proceedings of the 2003 Conference on New Interfaces for Musical Expression (NIME-03).* 2003. Montreal, Canada.

[13]   National Library of Australia Preservation Metadata for Digital Collections. http://www.nla.gov.au/preserve/pmeta.html, 1999.

[14]   Ng, K. C. *Music via Motion: Transdomain Mapping of Motion and Sound for Interactive Performances.* Proceedings of the IEEE, 2004. **92**(4).

[15]   OCLC/RLG Working Group on Preservation Metadata Preservation Metadata and the OAIS Information Model - A metadata framework to support the Preservation of digital objects. 2002.

[16]   PREMIS Data Dictionary for Preservation Metadata - Final Report of the PREMIS Working Group. OCLC and RLG 2005.

[17]   Troncy, R. *Integrating Structure and Semantics into Audio-Visual Documents.* In *Proceedings of the the 2nd International Semantic Web Conference.* 2003. Florida, USA.

[18]   Young, D., Nunn, P., and Vassiliev, A. *Composing for Hyperbow: A Collaboration Between MIT and the Royal Academy of Music.* In *Proceedings of the International Conference on New Interfaces for Musical Expression.* 2006. Paris, France.

NCD Recommendation for the National Standard for Describing Digitized Heritage in Serbia

Zoran Ognjanović, Tamara Butigan-Vučaj, Bojan Marinković[1]

Abstract In this paper we present a proposal for the national standard for describing digitized assets of movable heritage in Serbia. The proposal was made by the National center for digitization and supported by the Committee for digitization of the UNESCO commission of Serbia. The main objective of the proposal is to guarantee interoperability among resources available by different providers and compatibility with the most popular existing international standards.

1 Introduction

The document [12] "Recommendations for coordination of digitization of cultural heritage in South-Eastern Europe" accepted at the South-Eastern Europe regional meeting on digitization of cultural heritage (Ohrid, Macedonia, 17-20 March 2005) says that the current digitization practice in SEE is still not matching the priorities communicated on the EU-level and that the rich cultural content of the region is still underrepresented in the electronic space. One of the main principles accepted by the participants of the Meeting says that "It is recognized that knowledge of the cultural and scientific heritage is essential for taking decisions concerning its digitization and for interpreting the digitized resources. For this reason, inventorying and cataloging should precede or accompany the digitization of cultural and scientific assets."

Zoran Ognjanović
Mathematical Institute, Serbian Academy of Sciences and Arts, Kneza Mihaila 35, Belgrade, Serbia, e-mail: zorano@mi.sanu.ac.yu

Tamara Butigan-Vučaj
Digital Library Department, National Library of Serbia, Skerlićeva 1, Belgrade, Serbia e-mail: tamara@nbs.bg.ac.yu

Bojan Marinković
Mathematical Institute, Serbian Academy of Sciences and Arts, Kneza Mihaila 35, Belgrade, Serbia, e-mail: bojanm@mi.sanu.ac.yu

Concerning the Meeting conclusions Serbian National Center for Digitization (NCD) recognized the metadata problem as the most sophisticated one in the cataloging phase of digitization. There are a lot of metadata schemes for describing digitized assets of heritage, but not the universal one. Serbian national heritage is described after different standards, according to the nature of assets, but once being digitized, national heritage needs one metadata standard before including in the national database of digital objects. The standard should guarantee interoperability among resources available by different providers and compatibility with the most popular existing international standards. Thus, the proposal contains two parts:

- description of metadata related to individual assets of movable heritage[1] and
- mappings from/to some internationally recognized and/or widely used standards.

This proposal is carried out by the Mathematical Institute of the Serbian Academy of Sciences and Arts and the National Library of Serbia, but also supported by the National Museum (Belgrade), and the Historical Archive of Belgrade. These institutions together with Faculty of Mathematics (Belgrade), Archaeological Institute Belgrade, Archive of Republic Serbia, Serbian Institute for Monument Protection and Yugoslav Film Archive are founding members of the NCD [8]. Main goals of the NCD are to establish coordination of activities of local research and cultural institutions in the digitization field and to promote a national strategy for the cultural and scientific heritage digitization.

The proposal is also accepted by the Committee for digitization of the UNESCO commission of Serbia.

2 Why national standard?

Why national standard? To answer this question, we give a short overview of the current state-of-the-art in Serbia and the related international standards.

2.1 State-of-the-art in Serbia

At the moment, there is no wide spread metadata standard for describing digitized heritage in Serbia. Actually, although the digitization process is entering most of the institution caring about national heritage, there is no metadata standard formally accepted at the state level, and we face this *metadata problem*, let us call it in that way. Different providers of heritage resources (libraries, museums, archives, some research institutions) use international standards appropriate for their specific fields,

---

[1] The term *movable heritage* covers: library, archive and museum objects, furniture, scientific papers, machinery, religious object, photos, natural items, etc.

or ad-hock methods, or old procedures for describing cultural assets in classical format (formulated in 1980s or early 1990s). In fact, some providers wait for some solution of the metadata problem and do not do anything related to digital cataloging. It means that our digital catalogs, if exist at all, cannot help in communication between different kinds of providers and users.

2.2 International standards

There are plenty of metadata standards for describing heritage resources, for example:

- Dublin Core [4],
- EAD [5],
- MARC [7],
- TEL AP [11],
- FRBR [2, 6] etc.

Dublin Core is developed and maintained by the Dublin Core Metadata Initiative (DCMI). The goal of DCMI is to promote interoperable metadata standards and develop specialized metadata vocabularies for describing resources. Although this standard can be applied to every kind of resources ensuring interoperability, as it is noted in [3], the problem is that the DC Element Set (Simple DC) is rather restricted and different information must be grouped into one element. More recently, DCMI has allowed some refinements of Simple DC - so called Qualified DC, so that it is possible to develop DC Application Profiles for specific applications and domains. It is important to emphasize that it is possible to lose some information in the process of reducing Qualified DC to Simple DC values. It might be noted that we could use Qualified DC to describe our approach. From our point of view, in this moment more important issue is to define *what* data should be included in the metadata standard, which is the subject of this paper, than to chose *how* to express them in one or the other format. However, one of the first steps we plan to carry out will be to develop the corresponding Qualified DC description.

The other above mentioned standards are mainly related to some special subdomains of heritage. Encoded Archival Description (EAD) is focused on the archival resources with the goal to allow describing them and to make them accessible to users.

Similarly, the MARC standards are used mostly for the representation and communication of bibliographic and related information in machine-readable form. Another librarian-supported standard is The European Library Application Profile (TEL AP). TEL AP for objects is based on the proposal of Dublin Core Metadata Initiative - Libraries Working Group for the Library Application Profile from 2002. TEL Metadata Working Group is responsible for additions and changes made on the basic document for TEL purposes, the functionality of the Portal at the first place. National Library of Serbia became the full partner of The European Library in 2005 and getting known with the TEL AP concept was a kind of inspiration for the NCD metadata model. The TEL Metadata Registry of terms is currently in development, as well as TEL AP for objects, TEL AP for collections and future TEL AP for services. Functional requirements for bibliographic records (FRBR) is a conceptual, object-oriented model for metadata records, born also in the library world. The model is based on three groups of entities. The first one presents the products of intellectual or artistic endeavor being described, by four entities: work, expression, manifestation and item. Two entities: person and corporate body are in the second group, connected to the responsibility for the intellectual or artistic content, the production and distribution, or the custodianship of these products. The third group is covering subject area for intellectual or artistic endeavor with four entities: concept, object, event and place. FRBR is extendable to archives, museums and publishing area.

Up to our knowledge, in the field of museums, there is no widely accepted metadata standards. We are aware of a set of recommendations called Spectrum, the UK Museum Documentation Standard [10]. Thus, from our point of view, although these standards are very important and useful in the corresponding subdomains of digitized heritage, they are partially incompatible, and cannot be directly used to cover the whole domain of heritage.

Having all that in mind, the NCD decided, according to its coordinating role in the digitization field in Serbia, to take care and obligatory to try to solve this metadata problem and define a unique metadata core to assure the interoperability between various digital resources of national cultural and scientific heritage.

3 Methodology

At the beginning of the project some requirements were determined to accommodate more-or-less divergent descriptive practices and to articulate needs of different specific heritage contexts. More precisely, the requirements were:

- the definition should be rich enough so that it could be used to describe assets from libraries, museums, and archives, as well as from the other providers (research institutions, for example),
- the definition should be flexible enough to allow translation to and from international standards,
- the definition should allow: multilingual description of cultural and scientific assets and use of some pre-defined dictionaries for the particular elements as much as possible.

The underlying idea, as it is mentioned in Introduction, is that the description of cultural assets based on this metadata set should be used to make decisions about future digitization. For this reason, the proposal contains more structured and detailed elements than it is usually the case.

Fig. 1 The intended architecture of the metadata description system

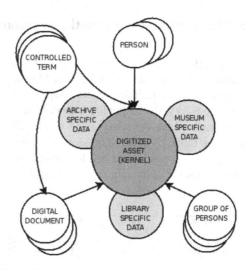

4 Description of the standard

According to the previous requirements, the following five basic objects were distinguished:

- *Person*, and *Group-of-persons* for entities that have intellectual or some other important contribution to the creation of assets, that are subjects of and/or owners of cultural heritage assets,
- *Digital-document*, for an individual file containing digital representation of the corresponding asset,
- *Digitized-asset*, for the digitized asset of heritage, and
- *Controlled-term*, for elements of a pre-defined dictionary.

Figure 1 contains a structure based on the above mentioned set of meta-data objects, where the nodes represent the objects, and the arcs represent relationships between them. This structure forms a unique core representing an intersection of descriptions of assets from libraries, museums, and archives. However, our proposal allows some extensions related to the particular fields of interests.

The object Controlled-term corresponds to standardized data values that can be used to improve access to information about heritage. Those values should be organized in a structured controlled vocabulary which offers preferred terms and synonyms, as for example in [1].

The sets of meta-data that corresponds to each of these objects were defined. They contain a descriptive and an administrative part. The administrative part identifies authors and/or owners of descriptions, assets of heritage and their digital representations. Note that, if appropriate, a description of access rights is also available to limit access to (parts of) resources. The following provides an abbreviated version of the descriptions of the mentioned objects (the full description in Serbian is available [9]).

5 Translations to international standards

As a particular part, the proposal defines mappings to and from some international standards for meta-data (Dublin Core Metadata Element Set, The European Library Application Profile, Table of Core Metadata Elements for Library of Congress Digital Repository Development, Encoded Archival Description). An example of the translation of the elements of the objects Digital-document and Digitized-asset is given in Table 1. As it can be seen, some different elements of our objects must be grouped into one element and for some elements there are no corresponding translations in some of the mentioned standards.

NCD	DC	ISAD	EAD	TEL AP	Library of Congress
Description	description	3.3.1	scopecontent	description	description summary
Type	type	3.1.5	genreform	type	original content type
Material	medium	3.1.5	physdesc	format.medium	
Rights	rights	3.4.2	userestrict	rigths	access rights
Access rights	accessRights	3.4.1	accessrestrict	rights	access category
Note		3.6.1	note, odd		
Capture device(s)			daodesc		capture device ID
MIME format(s)	Format		daodesc	format	internet media type

Table 1 Mappings to/from international standards

6 Conclusion

In this paper we present a proposal for a metadata description of individual assets of movable heritage. The main objective of the proposal is to guarantee:

- interoperability among resources available by different providers, and
- compatibility with the most popular existing international standards.

The proposal is made and will be maintained and further developed by the most of the leading Serbian institutions in the field of digitization gathered in the Serbian National Center for Digitization. It will be submitted to the Serbian Ministry of culture to officially accept it as the metadata format for the future central national catalog of individual assets of (digitized) movable heritage. The expected official support will be especially important concerning the issue of creating an appropriate thesaurus.

An object-oriented approach is used in defining the proposed metadata description. As technical benefits of such an approach, we would like to mention:

- *modularity*, which makes it much easier to change individual components of the description
- *reusability* of objects, which makes it possible that the same object can be used many times in the system (for example, a person could be in the same time an author of more than one asset, a member of some group of authors, owner of some files, etc.)

The proposed metadata model is FRBR-ized in the domain of the second FRBR group of entities with person and group of persons with all the basic FRBR attributes for these entities. The future creation of a database of Serbian digitized heritage based on the NCD metadata standard will be the opportunity to implement some more aspects of the FRBR-model, like providing the easier access to users for particular segments of digital collections.

Since the proposed set of metadata is related to individual objects of movable heritage, the plan of the NCD is to define similar sets of metadata related to:

- non movable heritage and
- heritage collections.

Finally, we believe that developing the national metadata standard has a broader mission than the description itself. It is the potential influence on the subjects dealing with all kinds of national heritage preservation to think further in the direction of building the future heritage digital replica overcoming the differences and rivalry at national and international level, with the long-term goal to improve presence of Serbian heritage on the Internet.

Appendix

Example 1. In this example we illustrate how to describe a book of a well-known Serbian comediograph Branislav Nušić. The book, Autobiography, belongs to the collection of the Serbian Children's digital library [13]. The illustrator of the edition, published by Kreativni centar, is Dobrosav Živković, and the editors are Simeon Marinković and Slavica Marković. Digitization of the book was performed by Nikola Pavlović from National library of Serbia. The author of the metadata records is Tamara Butigan.

Table 2 contains a record which corresponds to the author. Table 3 contains a record which corresponds to the digital version of the book. Table 4 contains a record which corresponds to the "hardcopy" version of the book.

Descriptive	
Name	
* First_name	Branislav
* Family_name	Nušić
Name_version	
* First_name	Ben
* Family_name	Akiba
Date_of_birth	1864
Date_of_death	1938
Sex	male
Biography	
* Biography_in_Serbian	http://sr.wikipedia.org/wiki/ Бранислав_Нушић
* Biography_in_other_languages	http://en.wikipedia.org/wiki/Branislav_Nusic
Administrative	
Record_Creation_Date	30/3/2007
Record_Creator	T. Butigan
Record_Owner	NBS

Table 2 PERSON – author

Descriptive	
Title	
* Title in Serbian	Digitalizovana dečja knjiga Autobiografija, Branislava Nušića
* Title in English	Digitized children's book: Autobiography written by Branislav Nusic
Creator	
* Identifier	ID (Nikola Pavlović)
* Role	programmer
Location of digital document	http://www.digital.nbs.bg.ac.yu/decije/jpg/nusauto/
Administrative	
Archive date	2004
Digital document format	jpg
Size	17.9MB
Digital document MIME format	image
Capture device	Epson GT 15000
Rights	NBS gained rights from the publishing house
Access rights	Unlimited
Digital object owner	NBS
Record creation date	30/3/2007
Record creator	T. Butigan
Record owner	NBS

Table 3 Digital_document

Descriptive	
Title	
* Original name	Аутобиографија
* Name in Serbian	Autobiografija
* Name in English	Autobiography
Creator	
* Identifier	ID (Branislav Nušić)
* Role	writer
Contributor	
* Identifier	ID (Dobrosav Živković)
* Role	illustrator
Contributor	
* Identifier	ID (Simeon Marinković)
* Role	editor
Contributor	
* Identifier	ID (Slavica Marković)
* Role	editor
Classification	
* Classification_scheme	UDK
* Classification_identifier	821.163.41-93
Description	
* Description_in_Serbian	Autobiografija poznatog srpskog pisca Branislava Nušića ispričana u formi šaljivog romana. Sadrži i kraća objašnjenja manje poznatih reči
* Description_in_English	Autobiography of famous Serbian writer Branisav Nusic but written as a funny story. Vocabulary sections included.
Date_and_provenance	
* Date of origin	2001
* Provenance of origin	Belgrade
* Version of the cultural monument	First issue
Dimension	
* Dimension name	Number of pages
* Dimension value	283
Dimension	
* Dimension name	Book back height
* Dimension value	24 cm
Type	text
Acquisition	
* Type of acquisition	Legal deposit
* Date of acquisition	06/2001

Owner	NBS
Source object ID	II449580
Administrative	
Rights	Publishing house Kreativni centar
Access rights	Unlimited
Record creation date	30/01/2007
Record creator	T. Butigan
Record owner	NBS
Extensions for standard edition	
Publisher	Kreativni centar
Language	scc
Edition	Collection Pustolovine
Identifier	ISBN 86-7781-042-0

Table 4: Digitalized asset

References

1. The Art & Architecture Thesaurus, AAT,
   http://www.getty.edu/research/conducting_research/vocabularies/aat/.
2. A weblog about FRBR: Functional Requirements for Bibliographic Records, www.frbr.org,
   2007.
3. I. Buonazia, M. E. Masci, D. Merlitti, *The Project of the Italian Culture Portal and its Development. A Case Study: Designing a Dublin Core Application Profile for Interoperability
   and Open Distribution of Cultural Contents*, ELPUB2007. Openness in Digital Publishing:
   Awareness, Discovery and Access - Proceedings of the 11th International Conference on
   Electronic Publishing held in Vienna, Austria 13-15 June 2007, Edited by: Leslie Chan and
   Bob Martens. 393–494, 2007.
4. The Dublin Core Metadata Initiative, http://dublincore.org/.
5. Encoded Archival Description, http://www.loc.gov/ead/.
6. IFLA Study Group, Functional Requirements for Bibliographic Records,
   www.ifla.org/VII/s13/frbr/frbr.pdf, 1998.
7. MARC Standards, http://www.loc.gov/marc/.
8. National Center for Digitization, http://www.ncd.matf.bg.ac.yu.
9. Recommendation for the National Standard for Describing Digitized Heritage in Serbia,
   2007. http://www.ncd.matf.bg.ac.yu/?page=news&lang=sr&file=predlogStandardaMetadata.
   htm
10. SPECTRUM, the UK Museum Documentation Standard,
    http://www.mda.org.uk/spectrum.htm.
11. The European Library, http://www.theeuropeanlibrary.org/
12. Recommendations for coordination of digitization of cultural heritage in South-Eastern Eu-
    rope, Conclusions of the Regional Meeting on Digitization of Cultural Heritage, Ohrid,
    Macedonia, 17-20 March 2005, Review of the National Center for Digitization, 2 -7, 2005.
    (http://elib.mi.sanu.ac.yu/files/journals/ncd/7/ncd07002.pdf)
13. Serbian Children's digital library, http://digital.nbs.bg.ac.yu/decije/

The Human Art of Encoding: Markup as Documentary Practice

Paul Scifleet[1], Susan P. Williams[1] and Creagh Cole[2]

Abstract. This paper describes the Markup Analysis Project, a research initiative of the Information Policy and Practice Research Group at the University of Sydney to investigate frameworks for understanding the complex interactions evident in digital document development. Although markup languages are now widely deployed to identify and define the structural and contextual characteristics of electronic documents, to date, very little work has been undertaken to evaluate how the encoded elements of a markup language are being used by human authors and systems developers in practice. Our study addresses this by reviewing the literature of the field in search for common threads that will support a framework for a practice oriented view. We conclude that a clear understanding of digital representation as a documentary practice is absent from mainstream considerations digital document development and make recommendations for its inclusion.

1. Introduction

In *What is history?* E.H. Carr invited us to entertain the idea that an historic fact is one that is repeated so often that it is accepted as true [1]. For many working within the scholarly domain of our cultural institutions: Universities, Museums, Libraries, Archives, the irony behind Carr's essay will not be lost. When you are surrounded by the records of time, with evidence of so many past events comprising the identity, heritage and culture of society, chance can seem to play a disproportionate role in determining which stories are told, how they are told, and even which stories will never be told. To accept the idea that an historic fact

---

[1] Business Information Systems, Faculty of Economics & Business,
The University of Sydney, Sydney NSW 2006, Australia.
(p.scifleet, s.williams)@econ.usyd.edu.au

[2] School of Philosophical and Historical Enquiry,
The University of Sydney. Sydney NSW 2006, Australia.
creagh.cole@arts.usyd.edu.au

occurs by chance would of course undermine the importance of what Carr is saying: facts which are repeated most often are really repeated because there is a high level of trust in the process of historiography that supports the assertion.

Methodologies for establishing the reliability of evidence are central to the custodial role information professionals have in managing the records of society. The raison d'être of custodial institutions is premised on principles of information management that have been developed to ensure evidence is preserved, stored, retrieved, accessed and presented correctly. While the underlying motivation is to share information, the requirements of the task have always extended beyond simple, unmediated maintenance of artefacts, to authenticating, witnessing and verifying the integrity, authority and context of the evidence they contain. Many of the qualities reflected in this custodial warrant are clearly not immutable. Information management deals with complex phenomena in complex environments [2]. The claims made about an artefact through its documentation are as situated and bound by context as the source material itself. Judgments, even argument are inherent in our empirical observations and description precisely because the objects we are interested in stand in direct relation to the observer. The professional community has not shied away from the subjective agency implicit in their roles and ongoing debate about the extent of passive and active involvement of practitioners in documentation is as prevalent now in electronic scholarly communication as it was at the time of Carr's observations.

> "If you find it in the documents it is so. But what, when we get down to it, do these documents –the decrees, the treaties, the rent-rolls, the blue books, the official correspondence, the private letters and diaries - tell us?" [1:16]

The body of literature concerning documentary practice is now so large that it's hard to agree with the occasional claim that this field is inadequately represented or under-theorized. Yet there is an increasingly apparent gap between digital document management as it is presented within the theoretical space of research literature and the everyday work of developers. In this paper we bring this disjoint to the foreground by returning to some of the key questions asked by the leading theorists and practitioners of documentation over the past 50 years.

While most commentators seem willing to concede that current technologies are adequate for document creation, storage and retrieval, there is an ongoing concern about the accuracy and correctness of the representation of information contained in documents themselves and their suitability in meeting the descriptions needs of users. There is a growing number of case studies published by practitioners that give voice to the challenges of content development, yet these projects are advancing in a rapidly changing information management environment that allows little opportunity to gain an understanding of the experience practitioners share at an aggregate level.

There is now a noteworthy echo among researchers that error prone, idiosyncratic practice may turnout to be the hallmark of markup language innovation. Alongside these concerns is an acknowledgement that the functionality achieved through markup languages has been less than was expected and diffusion slower than anticipated [8]. The outcomes of this 'first wave' of descriptive encoding should not be surprising. Digital content developers are faced on a daily basis, some times text by text with profound questions about the nature of a document and its digital identity. There is an ontological complexity here that has occupied a theoretical space in the research literature, but that is rarely addressed in application. In practice we might assume that the documents themselves will somehow reveal their own best description or, that somehow common sense will prevail, but this seems contrary to all that we know about the task of assigning meaning to artefacts.

It is hard to comment on these issues with any certainty. A major challenge is that to date empirical studies of encoding practice remain thin on the ground. In this paper we begin to address this challenge by presenting a framework for investigating the emergent processes of document encoding. We argue for a practice oriented view of encoding that accounts for the situated, contextual nature of practice itself or, as E.H. Carr would have referred to it, there is a need to understand the *processing process* [1].

Our study begins by reviewing the literature of this field in a search for the common threads that will support a framework for such a practice oriented view. Moreover we conclude that a clear understanding of digital representation as documentary practice has been absent from mainstream considerations of markup and digital document development and make recommendations for its inclusion.

2. The practice of documentation

Best practice in documentation is the overriding concern of information management. It is the arrangement and description of information resources that makes all the other aspects of custodianship possible, yet its perfection has been allusive. In 1951, Suzanne Briet, the French documentalist and author of *Qu'est ce que la documentation?*[3] described the growing endeavor of documentation as a 'new cultural technique' involving processes for selection, synthesis and interpretation of information [3,4]. Centres for documentation, she said, were places that presented a point of view in accordance with their own specialization and through this specialization they were charged with the role of analytical and sometimes critical resumes. The agency presented by Briet is carefully considered. Documentalists are seen as subject specialists who understand the techniques and forms of documentation well enough to comment on sources materials, while at the same time balancing, respecting and maintaining the intellectual integrity of the material. Yet ultimately this "respect pour le fond", when juxtaposed with the

---

[3] Suzanne Briet's book entitled "Q'uest ce que la documentation?" was originally published in 1951 in French. The page numbers cited in all references to the 1951 work in this paper are those of the English translation edited by Day, Martinet and Anghelescu published by Scarecrow Press in 2006.

role of commentary, presents a dilemma of interference with evidence that has influenced methodologies across all branches of information management. Documentation is a highly contextualized activity that is intimately tied to the practitioner [3]. At the time of her writing, Briet's position contrasted sharply with the traditional ambitions of librarianship where a more objective bibliographic control of information resources (by author-title-subject) was promoted as the best way of managing artefacts for location, retrieval and delivery to the reader. Yet even the simplest dimensions of bibliographic control have never been straightforward. Selecting, acquiring and presenting the materials required by their users has always presented libraries with complex questions of what constitutes the item being cataloged: is it the organic (abstract) work created by an author or is it the dimensions of the concrete entity that embodies an author's work that should be described? [5:15]. In more recent times, the situated, contemporary nature of cataloging and the potential biases inherent in the designation of subject headings has been highlighted [6] yet, interference as a positive force continues to cross many branches of information management. This is perhaps most evident in archival science where early discussions about the passive, moral and physical defence of records inherited organically from previous administrations is now counterbalanced by modern practice where archivists are actively involved in determining (selecting, appraising and disposing of) the records of corporate and social accountability. While records are kept as reliable memories of the past, it must also be acknowledged, as Suzanne Briet does, that documentation can "… in certain cases, end in a genuine creation through the juxtaposition, selection and comparison of documents and the production of auxiliary documents." [4:16]

What concerns us here is not the rights or wrongs of different approaches but the level of complexity inherent in all approaches to documentation and the tensions this presents to the practitioner. *It might be historical information, but is it real now? Is it falsified history? Is it current information? Or is it falsified current information?* [7]. For the documentalist, what is the objective truth to be described? How is it best described? Documents are not self evident, self revealing entities [8].

In this environment the working tools of standards, guidelines and principles of best practice have provided some basis for acceptable levels of neutrality and reliability in the description and management of discrete information artefacts; but descriptive practice has also been an emergent practice that is localized and dependent on context and circumstance. Even when underlying methodologies of information management have been shared by practitioners from the top down, their implementation has varied widely from one custodial institution to the next.

The themes of fifty years ago are remarkably similar to the themes of today. Even so, until recently, the work of the documentalist has been clearly bounded by the separation of the artefact from its description:

"The proper job of documentation agencies is to produce secondary documents, derived from those initial documents that these agencies do not ordinarily create, but which they sometimes preserve." [3:25]

From the advent of filing card systems to the implementation of networked computer systems, the developing methodologies of documentary practice are inseparable from the technologies available to them. Yet as the number of documents in existence grows and the technologies designed to manage them improves there is an increasingly apparent gap between document management as it is presented within the theoretical space of research literature and the everyday work of developers. Within the literature there has been significant variation and tension between views of digital documents as objects requiring structured management and as information to be classified, represented and communicated. This tension is readily observed in the application of markup languages for document definition. Descriptive markup languages have the peculiar role of structuring the form of a content object *and* providing a reference to its meaning. While the benefits of defining complex document structures in this way are now widely acknowledged, practice within the custodial institutions and by individual practitioners remains largely unexplored.

3. Markup Languages in practice

We contend that technological innovations resulting from the adoption of descriptive markup languages have presented organizations with forms of documentation that are often difficult to reconcile with existing information management processes. Generalized markup languages allow us to consider texts as databases rather than as artefacts whose sole purpose is to be presented in an appropriate form. This view of text as database, that is open to multiple outputs and subject to continual alteration seems fundamentally different to the discrete artefact of the documentary tradition. It is a representation of text as data where inline markup languages have the peculiar role of being both the carrier of content and a reference to its meaning. Encoding text provides us not only with the key elements for structuring an electronic document it also serves as the method for transmitting our understanding of those elements, and as such, it is as much a commentary as it is a technical mechanism [9]. It is the role of markup as a commentary on the source that we contend requires more consideration.

While the benefits of representing complex document structures through descriptive markup languages are now widely acknowledged, the implications of this new approach to our understanding of documents is profound. Descriptive encoding is a process of categorizing data streams, representations or specific occurrences of content within a document, as either belonging or not belonging to a named element [10]. It is this practice of codifying and categorizing content into a generic type of document (e.g. a TEI document, an XBRL, a LegalML document, a Web document) that provides markup with its distinct advantage in the management of electronic documents. By bringing together data with the descriptive elements of a markup language digital content is being made more comprehensible and accessible than has previously been possible. It allows computerized systems to move away from the complex intertwined streams of data, programmed scripts and rules, that have been the common mode of electronic data management, towards systems where the elements of content in electronic texts are easily recognized and immediately available for processing in any environment. It is this simple architecture that is the foundation of Tim Berners-Lee's, Semantic Web, where properly designed digital content objects with *well defined meaning*, will allow software agents to interact with discrete units of information to *deliver sophisticated services* that are familiar representations of real world phenomena [11].

It is important to note that within the new research agenda for digital content development we are being presented with an ideal of intelligent semantic systems that step well beyond the benefits that typified the markup language 'advantage table' of the 1990s. Then the improved efficiencies of document engineering were multiple outputs and new composite products; improved validation and accuracy; better information storage and retrieval; long term archival management; and greater interoperability and exchange; now the implicit identification of meaning that is inherent in any descriptive task has been acknowledged and moved to the Internet; and its taking centre stage.

We can't but help think back to Seymour Lubetzky:

The essence of the modern concept of cataloging, which might more appropriately be called "bibliographic cataloging," has gradually emerged from a growing realization of the fact that the <u>book</u> (i.e. the material recorded) and the <u>work</u> (i.e. the intellectual product embodied in it) are not coterminous; that in cataloging, the <u>medium</u> is not to be taken as synonymous with the <u>message</u>; that the book is actually only one representation of a certain work which may be found in a given library or system of libraries in different media (as books, manuscripts, films, phonerecords, punched and magnetic tapes, Braille), different forms (as editions, translations, versions), and even under different titles [5:5].

In principle markup languages are not concerned with the physical form of texts but with the meaning that can be provided by describing the logical content they embody. It is this process of categorizing and codifying content objects as either belonging or not belonging to a class of things that seems to share much in common with traditional aspects of librarianship. Yet there are now a large and growing number of cases studies giving voice to the challenges of content development, and these studies seem to indicate that recording the cognitive space of content for digital systems is a far more difficult task than it has been with the physical systems that preceded them. Some of the most important questions raised in Information Systems design seem to be the familiar questions of documentation: *What is the information we are sharing? What do the elements of encoded data represent? What is the appropriate unit of information? How do we achieve acceptable degrees of accuracy, authenticity, consistency and reliability?* Yet the environment for digital documentation is still not clearly understood.

Although encoding guidelines exist for most markup languages, it is increasingly apparent that providing organizations with the apparatus to construct digital objects does not resolve issues of assigning 'meaning' to the content elements of text. That a document type definition is much more than the formal expression of its rules is slowly being acknowledged, yet there is still little discussion of other protocols that may, or should be, in place [12]. Problems in encoding seem to be resolved by reference to published 'tag libraries' that license some options as a valid expression of a document while discounting others as incorrect. While the structured hierarchy of descriptive markup is adequate for the purpose of storage and access to digital texts, there are problems arising from generalised definitions and encoding rules not appropriate to organizational contexts or specific instances of an object. The heterogeneous nature of information means that people often disagree with the content models presented in guidelines. There are concerns about the accuracy of the encoded text and concerns that idiosyncratic practice may well be the legacy of the first years of markup language practice [8]. Guidance when sought is often provided by the consortia managing a particular markup language yet it is questionable that this should be the role of standards developers. It is the nature of these dimensions of digital document development that must be better understood if processes for information design and management are to be improved.

The rapidly changing information management environment in which new documentary practices are emerging has placed the experience gained from project to project well ahead of the development of shared methodologies for understanding, adopting and implementing markup language vocabularies. In this environment, the research question of *'how are markup languages being used?'* is least clearly understood; an answer to this question is our primary research objective. Until then any unified view of practice over the last decade is hard to provide and largely unexplored, thus leading to our second research objective: *understanding the process of documentation evident in digital content development.*

4.   Taking a practice view

To date very little work has been undertaken to evaluate how systems developers and the (human) encoders of digital documents are resolving the tensions of documentation and implementing markup languages. There is a large and growing amount of research in Computer Science and Information Technology that focuses on the construction and automation of 'ontologies' however, these projects rarely acknowledge difficulties inherent in applying the elements of representation. Typical research into semantic systems involves the development of a classification schema to describe resources for a specific application and a demonstration of network software interacting with these resources [13].While the knowledge gained through this activity aims to be stable over time and available for solving problems across multiple applications, more often then not what is being presented are singular, novel applications that have been 'tweaked' to ensure project goals are achieved within the limited time frame set for them [13].

The quality of developmental work is not at issue here, what needs to be noted is that the experience of lead projects is not being translated into methodologies for improved implementation.

One community particularly sensitive to the implications of the changing documentary practice described here is the Text Encoding Initiative (TEI). The TEI is an international endeavor to develop guidelines for the preparation and interchange of electronic texts for scholarly research. The TEI provides a tag set (a vocabulary expressed as XML) of over 400 named elements along with guidelines for their use in the preparation of electronic texts. While the intent of TEI is to provide a means of encoding source texts of all descriptions, it is weighted towards the scholarly editing of works in the humanities [14]. It is supported by a vital user community that continues to develop the markup language as a vocabulary adequate for academic, library and archival description of source documents. While the tag set does not satisfy all aspects of textual description, it succeeds in defining a general purpose vocabulary that has the potential to meet the majority of scholarly requirements in text studies. The relative maturity and stability of the tag set, which commenced as a Standard Generalized Markup Language (SGML) document type in 1987, has ensured it a position of familiarity that is attractive to a very large number of projects. It has been widely adopted as the standard for the production of electronic versions of scholarly texts. Importantly the TEI is observed by a much larger community of content developers and has been the model of other markup languages, including for example Extensible Business Reporting Language (XBRL) [15]. Over the last 20 years there have been sporadic debates within the TEI community on the value of markup languages and the role of humanities computing that have had far wider implications than might be expected. As with all markup languages, the TEI assumes there are general textual features that are structural rather than presentational, and their identification reveals a deeper reality than can be achieved at the level of presentation. Modeling the text is a process of material definition where meaning is assigned to artefacts. Yet, what is that reality? There is an ontological question at the heart of the debates of, 'what is text, really?' that must impact on our understanding of what it is we are documenting [16]. Are we to take a strictly realist view in this matter or consider our textual descriptions, in a more constructivist way? Irrespective of position, the debates are not superfluous to practice. Within the TEI community there has been an intense consideration of the philosophical issues underlying practice because the implementation of *ontology* presents some immediate concerns.

Many of the difficulties that arise in markup practice occur because normalizing the constituent parts of digital content (a document or record) into a single classification scheme is highly problematic. Documents are not static or limited constructs that can be described once and maintained for all time. All classification is variable and likely to change over time as documents take on different roles in different contexts. Considering the potential life cycle of even a simple corporate record such as a payroll register demonstrates the point: our payroll register was first used by a large industrial manufacturer to ensure the correct distribution of weekly wages; thirty years later it has joined legal proceedings in a workers compensation hearing because a number of former employees who have contracted Mesophelioma (resulting from exposure to asbestos) are seeking compensation. Using current markup languages, at least two, and potentially more, different vocabularies could be used to describe the record over time. Firstly, a vocabulary describing the payroll register for organizational purposes would be required. Later the legal record will be managed by the records administration unit of the Courts and will require additional description for the administration of legal evidence. Finally, as a record of social and historic significance, additional descriptive metadata will be required for the long term preservation of the record.

In a previous paper we argued that the text ontology debates of the TEI community need to be informed by a better appreciation of real world practices in text encoding. Implementing the TEI guidelines is not simply a case of picking up a manual and applying the TEI tag set. The TEI is variously a standard, a series of committees to manage its development, a consortium of contributing institutions, the requirements of individual institutions and a practising community of encoders [8]. The work of text encoding is itself undertaken by individuals (sometimes teams of encoders) from diverse backgrounds, who are contending with different organizational and social contexts that will ultimately reveal themselves in the decisions they make about encoding. All markup language implementation projects are faced with this same complex of situated social activity when constructing digital documents.

Making sense of practice then requires, not only an understanding of the artefact to be described but an understanding of where that object is situated in relation to the documentalist at different stages in a process of description. It presupposes a range of questions that must be addressed *in situ*: *What does the data represent? What is the information we are sharing? What is the appropriate unit of information? What is enough information? What constitutes meaningful content in the documents we encode?*

Answering the questions of documentation then involves much more than getting the static representation of page structures right in valid, well formed XML. Indeed we would argue that, for the documentalist, commenting on the meaningful dimensions of a text is a form of knowledge transfer with experts bringing their expertise to the representation of each work (i.e. from the knower to the artefacts they know about). Here then, the relational idiom seems paramount: What holds this differentiated practice together may well be the relationship between documentalist and the document [17].

5. Is there a process emergent in practice?

In addressing these questions, documentalists are faced with a difficult problem but it is not insoluble. Reconciling the difficulties of heterogeneous data management has always been a major focus of information research, particularly in the field of data description and management. It can be demonstrated that typically, when agreement is reached at a conceptual level improvement in the development and management of information systems follows. The widespread adoption and use of the *systems development life cycle* (SDLC) as a conceptual framework for sense making is perhaps the most widely known example of this [18]. The system development life cycle describes a sequence of common activities in all systems development projects. Its enunciation has allowed particular objectives and methods to be associated with each stage of the cycle, allowing developers to understand and evaluate similar objectives in widely divergent projects and develop appropriate design solutions from the insight the model provides. Across time the sequence of objectives and methods associated with the model have been refined and improved. The SDLC did not precede systems development but rather emerged through practice as more and more organizations engaged in the development of in-house systems across the 1960s and 1970s. It typifies a common pattern in information management; as technology is applied to new areas, new processes result; "...new kinds of systems and new development methods are also created" [19:181]. Following on from the SDLC different information systems design models and methodologies have emerged for different systems (for example, transaction processing systems, enterprise resource planning systems, decision support systems, all present different conceptual design frameworks), but all share the common objective of improving practitioner confidence in decision making by identifying and incorporating structures that are common to different types of systems into the design process. Part of the objective of systems design modeling has been to "...reduce developer uncertainty by restricting the range of allowable system features and development activities to a more manageable set" [19:181]. Yet not all processes are highly structured. Nor is it desirable to make all processes highly structured. It can have the effect of restraining creativity to a rigid set of allowable design principles. Human sense making requires understanding to evolve in a recursive, participatory manner, with processes emerging through trial and error, and the experience gained from problem solving [19].

Our research proposes a similar approach to the human encoding experience by asking, what patterns are emerging in practice? By exploring methods for documentary analysis and document definition in encoding we aim to investigate the viability of a conceptual framework for sense making that will allow us to witness the processes that are emergent digital documentation. By investigating *'how markup languages are being used in practice'* and accounting for this complexity through the provision of a framework, it should be possible to identify common themes across implementation projects. Ultimately this should present the encoders of digital documents with a design process to support their work.

There are obvious situational differences between the communities of interest who define the markup languages that are used to encode documents, the organizations that adopt them, the systems developers that apply them and the users that employ them for encoding. These differences give rise to and accentuate problems in decision making that need to be managed through improved information policy, and accounted for in the development of processes for document production and management. Our approach proposes a theoretical and analytical framework for examining the relationship that the encoders of digital documents have with markup languages; from the *community* level (where markup languages are developed) to the *organizational* level (where markup languages are selected for implementation) and at the *implementation* level (where particular choices are made about the way markup languages are applied).

6. The Markup Analysis Project

With this notion of practice as a dynamic and emergent relationship between the encoder and the digital document in mind the Markup Analysis Project (MAP) commenced in December 2006 with a survey of the Text Encoding Initiative's community of practitioners. 130 institutions located around the world were invited to participate in the study; the response to the study and its objectives has been extremely favorable with a total of 32 participants.

In essence our study is a *markup usage* study. Understanding documentary practice requires a view of practice that allows us to investigate the artefacts that are in a process of being materially defined, the digital text itself. To achieve this objective several data collection techniques have been employed; the study comprises three interrelated activities: a questionnaire based survey of practitioners involved in the process of document markup; an in-depth analysis of the marked up texts themselves and follow up interviews with practitioners to extend and deepen the survey and text analysis findings. The three approaches also provide a means to triangulate and confirm the findings as they arise.

Questionnaire based survey. MAP participants completed a questionnaire based survey comprising over 66 items. The aim of the survey is to explore community, organizational and implementation level contexts of electronic text production across the participating community. The questionnaire addresses factors influencing text encoding: governance, funding, organizational objectives and responsibilities, along with the disposition and structure of the materials themselves. Many of these factors will inevitably be realized through the digital text object itself.

Encoded text analysis. By examining the encoding used to structure the text it is possible for us to analyse the documents produced across multiple projects at once, to identify, compare and analyze the patterns of encoding. Survey participants submitted between 5 and 10 TEI encoded text files that they considered representative of their work, along with any associated files (e.g. Document Type Definitions (DTD), other schema files, character and entity files) for analysis. The analysis of encoded documents is undertaken with analytical software (developed in-house) that reports on tag usage (i.e. the occurrence of elements and attributes used) in batches of encoded documents. By interpreting and reporting on the markup applied within documents we are able to extend our analysis beyond participant responses to the application of the markup choices they have made.

Participant Interviews. The survey was designed to bring sense to the scale and type of interactions that are taking place across many projects at once and, with that objective in mind, participant interviews were included to allow us to return to, verify and expand on findings from the first two components of the study. Our objective here has been to support findings with practitioner accounts of encoding that will support a clearer understanding of how practices are evolving.

Data analysis. The method of analysis chosen here is essentially one of content analysis "...a research technique for the objective, systematic and quantitative description of the manifest content of media." [20]. However there are some important differences between traditional content analysis and the analysis we have undertaken. Whereas content analysts typically define categories for encoding text in order to make valid inferences between the data they collect and the subject of their enquiry, our study needs to remain agnostic on the encoding of the texts. Our approach is essentially epistemic: we are not interested in individual texts, individual practice, assessing productivity or isolating examples of good and bad practice. Our focus has been only on the shared experience of practice the study might reveal. This approach to analysis means we have also to stay independent of any single markup language and establish procedures that might be used to investigate document encoding in any domain.

While the availability of software capable of parsing and interpreting encoded documents provides the opportunity to process a large amount of quantitative data quickly, so far, other studies (of HTML encoding) taking this approach have had only limited success in explaining the phenomena they witness [see 21,22]. The challenge for *markup analysis* is to move beyond 'counting tags' to an understanding of the phenomena of changing human communication that is presented in the widespread categorisation of digital documents that is now underway across many different types of organizations. Our study then, is premised on understanding the relationship of encoders to documents and addresses this problem by triangulating patterns of markup usage in its context.

7.   Conclusion

Between January and September 2007 over thirty institutional and individual TEI practitioners, representing thirteen different countries will have participated in the Markup Analysis Project. A corpus of over 150 digital texts (comprising more than 220mbs of electronic files) has been submitted for analysis. The texts contributed are a remarkable testament to the diversity of organizations, geography, history, languages and culture represented in digital form and a valuable insight into the significance of the Text Encoding Initiative in making these works accessible.

By addressing the question: *How are markup languages being used in practice?* This study contributes to our understanding of documentary practice as it extends to digital documentation.   Through the development of analytical software, the research is making inroads into the development of new applications for content analysis in the field of scholarly communication and electronic publishing. It is envisioned that over time, the development of analytical methods for markup analysis will contribute to:

- managing changing standards (e.g. identifying redundant and changing elements within documents);
- comparing, synchronizing and merging different information sets;
- supporting confidence in the decision making required in the implementation of markup languages
- educating and training users involved in the design and development of markup based systems; and
- supporting research activities specific to organizational content or academic enquiry.

References

1. Carr, E.H.: What is history? 2nd edition. Penguin Books, London UK. (1961)
2. Buckland, M: What is a "document"? J. Am Soc Inf Sci 48(9), 804--809 (1997)
3. Briet, S.: Qu'est-ce que la documentation? EDIT, Paris (1951)
4. Day R.E., Martinet, L. and Anghelescu, H.G.B. What is Documentation? English Translation of the Classic French Text. Scarecrow Press, Lanham MD, (2006)
5. Lubetsky, S.: Bibliographic Dimensions in Information Control. Institute of Library research, University of California, Los Angeles. California, USA (1968)
6. Bowker, G.C. and Starr, S.L.: Sorting Things Out: Classification and Its Consequences. The MIT Press, Cambridge MA (1999)
7. Kent, W.: Data and Reality. 2nd edition. 1st Books Library, Bloomington, IN (2000)
8. Cole, C. and Scifleet, P.: In the Philosophy Room: Australian Realism and Digital Content Development. Literary and Linguistic Computing. 21(2), 15—167 (2006)
9. Smith, B. : Textual deference. Amercian Philosophical Quarterly, 28, 1—13 (1991)
10. Sperberg-McQueen, C. M.: Classification and its Structures. In Schreibman, S., Siemens, R., and Unsworth, J. (eds). A Companion to Digital Humanities. Blackwells, Malden, MA (2004)
11. Berners-Lee, T., Hendler, J., and Lassila, O.: The Semantic Web. Scientific American 17 May 2001 http://www.scientificamerican.com (2001)
12 Dubin, D., Huitfield, C., Renear, A. and Sperberg-McQueen C. M. XML Semantics and Digital Libraries. Joint Conference on Digital Libraries. ACM, Houston, Texas. pp.303—305 (2003)
13. Morse, Emile L.: Evaluation Methodologies for Information Management Systems. D-Lib Magazine. 8 ,9 http://www.dlib.org/dlib/september02/morse/09morse.html (2002).
14. Sperberg-MacQueen. C.M. and Burnard, L.: Guidelines for Electronic text Encoding and Interchange. The TEI Consortium http://www.tei-c.org/P4X/index.html (2004)
15. Debreceny, R. and Gray G.L.: The production and use of semantically rich accounting reports on the Internet: XML and XBRL. International Journal of Accounting Information Systems. 2, 47-74, (2001)

16. Renear, A.: Out of Praxis: three (Meta) theories of textuality. In Sutherland, K. (ed), Electronic Text: Investigations in Method and Theory. Oxford University Press, Oxford 107—126 (1997)
17. Knorr-Cetina, K.: Objectual practice. In Schatski, T. R., Schatski, Knorr-Cetina, K. & von Savigny, E. (eds), The Practice Turn in Contemporary Theory. Routledge. London, UK: (2001)
18. Royce, W.W.: Managing the development of large software systems Proceeding of IEEE, WESCON, August, 1-9, (1970)
19. Markus, L M., Majchak A., Grasser, L.: A design theory for systems that support emergent knowledge processes. MIS Quarterly, 26(3), 179—212, (2002)
20. Weber, R.P.: Basic Content Analysis. 2nd edition. Sage Publications, Newbury Park CA. (1990)
21. Woodruff, A., Aoki, P.M. Brewer, E., Gauthier, P. and Rowe, L.A.: An Investigation of Documents from the World Wide Web. Computer Science Division – EECS University of Berkeley. http://bmrc.berkeley.edu/research/publications/1996/113/index.html (1995)
22. Zhang, J., and Jastram, I:. A study of metadata element co-occurrence. Online Information Review 30(4) ,428—453 (2006)

Metadata for describing learning scenarios under the European Higher Education Area paradigm

Ana-Elena Guerrero[1], Julià Minguillón[1], Lourdes Guàrdia[2], and Albert Sangrà[2]

Abstract I

n this paper we identify the requirements for creating formal descriptions of learning scenarios designed under the European Higher Education Area paradigm, using competences and learning activities as the basic pieces of the learning process, instead of contents and learning resources, pursuing personalization. Classical arrangements of content based courses are no longer enough to describe all the richness of this new learning process, where user profiles, competences and complex hierarchical itineraries need to be properly combined. We study the intersection with the current IMS Learning Design specification and the additional metadata required for describing such learning scenarios. This new approach involves the use of case based learning and collaborative learning in order to acquire and develop competences, following adaptive learning paths in two structured levels.

1 Introduction

The adoption of the European Higher Education Area (EHEA) model, also known as the Bologna process, has changed completely the way institutions need to face educating people, which are now considered to be lifelong learners since the very first moment they start higher education, shifting from content-based courses to competence development. The design of a competence-based curriculum demands to rethink and redesign programs and courses and stimulates the application of social-constructivist pedagogical approaches that

---

[1]Estudis d'Informàtica, Multimèdia i Telecomunicacions
[2]Psychology and Educational Science Studies
Universitat Oberta de Catalunya
Rb. Poble nou 156, 08018 Barcelona
e-mail: {aguerreror,jminguillona,lguardia,asangra}@uoc.edu

are learner and community-centered. Personalization becomes a useful tool for providing learners with adaptive learning paths according to their specific needs and particularities.

With the creation of the new European Higher Education Area, distance and open education is changing the followed approaches until now. E-learning should be encouraged and trained to acquire and further develop their e-competences. E-learning courses should guarantee high quality standards, achieving an equal acceptance of skills as those acquired via classical learning, in order to be attractive for professionals. Learners become the center of any educational action and, in the case of blended or virtual learning environments, it is very important to provide them with the appropriate guidance (tutoring, counseling, personalized feedback, etc.) avoiding the classical isolation that learners in distance education suffer from. Furthermore, the new EHEA pushes learners towards a lifelong learning scenario, where education is needed through all of life. Competences are not just "chunks" of information that can be assimilated easily, but must be continuously acquired, developed and updated by means of well designed learning paths, during long periods of time. Personalization is therefore a key factor to help learners to define their starting point in any educational experience, and the paths they need to follow to achieve the desired competence level. Learning paths must be defined taking into account the user profile, but also the hierarchical structure of degrees, courses, subjects, etc., and personalization has a different meaning according to the context where is employed. Nevertheless, learning environments are not prepared yet for describing the learning process based on competences including personalization issues. Furthermore, most of the current e-learning standards and recommendations focus on content description and packaging, and there is only one specification available for describing the learning process (IMS Learning Design, [1]), but it is very limited for providing complete and flexible descriptions for all the elements interacting in a virtual learning scenario taking into account the new requirements of the EHEA paradigm, where activities, resources and learner profiles have to be strongly related with ICT competences.

This paper is organized as follows: Section 2 briefly describes the Universitat Oberta de Catalunya (UOC) experience and the virtual e-learning environment used for supporting lifelong learning and the official masters and degrees. We also describe a pilot educational experience that has been designed following the new requirements imposed by the EHEA paradigm. Section 3 describes the learning scenarios created in this educational experience and the relationship with the current e-learning standards and specifications for describing them. Finally, the discussion of the work presented in this paper, the open issues and the current and future research lines are summarized in Section 4.

2 Developing competences in a virtual learning scenario

The Universitat Oberta de Catalunya[1] (in English Open University of Catalonia) is an institution which has emerged from the knowledge society. The mission is to provide people with training throughout their lives. To this end, it offers intensive use of information and communications technologies (ICT), thereby enabling us to overcome the barriers imposed by time and space for offering an educational model based on personalized attention for each individual student.

Among many other possibilities, the university offers several official degrees and several masters which have been partially or totally adapted to the directives given by the EHEA. One of them is the International Master on Education and ICTs. The International Master in Education and ICTs was one of the first courses adapted to the Bologna process, and all the requirements for describing competences, creating adaptive learning paths, personalization issues, using different learning strategies and methodologies and so have arisen from its adaptation.

2.1 From learning contents to learning activities

Master degrees are designed as a sequence of subjects which allow learners to create their own learning paths. Learners acquire and develop competences with the aim of achieving the appropriate level for facing real problems in the professional field. The main point is that within each subject learning scenarios are created for facilitating the learning process through the use of a virtual learning environment. Learning resources, activities and a teaching plan (which defines all the details of the learning process) are designed for acquiring the main and specific competences according to the Bologna process for each professional profile. The teaching plan becomes a first step towards a formal description of all the elements involved in the learning process: leaner profiles, competences, activities and learning resources. Subjects are arranged in semesters and they must be taken according to a higher level plan, taking into account that several competences can be developed in parallel and/or in consecutive subjects.

In this sense, learners create their own learning paths, developing competences (both transversal and specific) with the aim of achieving the appropriate level for facing real problems in the professional field or as the first step towards the consecution of a Ph.D. degree, according to their learning goals. Some of these competences are developed across several subjects (transversal competences and a few specific ones), while others (the rest of the specific ones) are developed in a single specialization subject. The same

---

[1] http://www.uoc.edu

competence can be developed at different levels and in different contexts. It is important to ensure that the learning path followed by the learner covers all the required competences and the learning goals. This flexibility can be seen as a first step towards a personalized learning process through adaptive formative itineraries, both inter-subject and intra-subject, following a hierarchical structure of two levels. At the bottom level, each subject is thought as a small learning scenario where several learning situations are presented to learners. Learners must demonstrate the already acquired competences, by using and developing them, and then incorporating new ones. At the top level, subjects are arranged according to the educational system structure (academic semesters), which is not always coherent with the concept of continuous competence development, as there is not a direct relationship between competences and subjects.

2.2 Personalization issues

Personalization is a key aspect for improving user experience and increasing satisfaction, involving him or her into the activity being performed, pursuing fidelity [2]. In the particular case of virtual learning environments, personalization has different goals, although not very different from those defined previously: increasing fidelity is a synonym for reducing dropout, the main problem of distance education. Following [3], a meaningful learning is produced when learners are able to connect their knowledge with the previous one they have. That means students can put into practice their competences in each case of study and learn new ones that complement and reinforce their professional skills. Developing transversal competences usually involves collaborating with other learners in the same learning scenario, so an interpersonal development is converted in an intrapersonal development by means of social interaction along learning process. Competence development implies designing learning activities which promote using, acquiring and putting into practice other competences, which overlap and are semantically related to each other. Competences are usually defined by long textual sentences (i.e. "Developing educational designs related to virtual teaching and learning environments") which makes impossible obtaining formal descriptions unless they are decomposed in smaller pieces, namely learning activities. Personalization is no longer just adapting the contents and/or the syllabus for each student; personalization must be designed using competences as the main element of the learning process. Personalization in virtual learning scenarios can be described according to two dimensions (which are not completely orthogonal): the elements which are taken into account for designing and executing learning paths, namely maps of competences, subjects arranged in learning paths, and learning activities within a subject; and the analysis level used for describing the possible actions [4], namely lifelong learning (long term), academic semester (med term) and user sessions (short term). Table 1 summarizes the intended uses and implications of the combination of both dimensions.

Table 1 Intended uses of personalization in virtual learning environments.

	Creating the map	Creating the path	Supervising the path
Short Term	—	—	Improving interaction
Med Term	Subject planning	Adaptive paths	Learning activities
Long Term	Curricula planning	Progressive degrees	Fighting dropout

Designing any long term educational action composed by several subjects must be combined in order to acquire and develop competences taking into account personalization issues creates new requirements for its formal description that are not available through the use of the current e-learning standards and specifications. It is necessary to evolve from content oriented standards (LOM) to activity based ones (IMS LD) and then towards higher level specifications that allow the description of hierarchical structures such as those required for personalization issues using competences, see [5] for a compilation of educational uses of learning objects and learning designs, including pedagogical issues.

2.3 Adapting the Bologna process

The International Master on Education and ICTs is structured in two academic years (four academic semesters) with 45 ECTS credits. Each semester, students enroll in one or more subjects with the aim of acquiring competences oriented to a professional area related with education and ICT, according to their profiles and preferences. All the learning process is supported by the virtual learning environment, which provides students with the teaching plan and all the learning resources, following the new EHEA paradigm but using the classical semester-subject structure. It includes four types of subjects, with different educational focus depending on the professional skills to be developed: Initial, Basic, Specialization and Application subjects. While initial and basic subjects focus on basic e-learning subjects for the development of a quality professional level of practice, specialization and application subjects focus on acquiring applied knowledge and consolidating the professional skills that have been developed throughout the master. The variety of user profiles and interests creates several possible paths, although most students follow the recommendations given by the teachers and tutors. This creates a complex map of competences and learning paths which needs to be formally described in order to provide learners with recommendations for choosing according to their profile.

3 Metadata for describing learning situations and learning scenarios

Each subject in the official master is designed as one or more learning situations trying to reproduce real professional situations where experts in one field need to apply practical knowledge for solving a problem, in a virtual learning environment. This methodology, which tries to ensure a high quality of the learning process, takes into account all the elements in the field of actuation and it reproduces them in terms of learning activities; these activities are designed with all the learning goals in mind, in a hierarchical structure, as follows:

```
Educational offers
    → Semesters (top level)
        → Subjects (bottom level)        ← "Imposed" structure
            → Learning situations
                → Competences      ← "Desired" structure
                    → Learning goals
                        → Activities
                            → Resources
```

This structure is currently partially supported by the teaching plan, a document with the description of the subject, which is human-readable, but non machine-readable. Each teaching plan has been designed in basis of three premises: (1) a sound formulation of competences and learning goals; (2) the design of learning activities which are diversified and coherent with the competences to be developed; and (3) the design of evaluation activities which prioritize the gathering of evidences that the proposed competences have been properly acquired.

Among other methodological tools, and for the purpose of our research, we define case-based learning (CBL) as an instructional strategy that uses case study as a resource and the case method as the learning scenario description where learners and instructor interact [6]. Most professors using case study describe it as a descriptive document, delivered as a narrative that is based on a real situation or event. The case tries to facilitate a balanced relationship between the multidimensional representation of the context, its participants and the reality of the situation. The concept of case in itself has an internal structure which is independent of the final activities and resources used in its implementation, and this fact can be used to generate different case studies from a subset of case patterns and a collection of learning resources, following an instructional design approach [6, 7]. At the bottom level, we need formal representations for case-based learning scenarios, which involve all the elements in the learning process (learners, activities, competences, resources, etc.), and all the relationships between these elements. Our goal is to provide a mechanism for learning path design according to learner preferences and already acquired competences, learning goals and directions given by instructional designers and teachers. In the particular case of the IMS LD specification, it is necessary to adapt the particular needs of the virtual learning scenario to the specifications available following the directions given in [6], where competences are used to describe goals, prerequisites and outcomes of the learning activities. In this sense, there is a lack of standards for describing competences at a rich semantic level, because IMS RDCEO, which is mentioned by IMS LD as a possible competency standard for describing objectives, is not enough to represent the hierarchical structure and all the relationships identified previously.

3.1 Current specifications and standards

In fact, new standards and specifications such as IMS LD are more oriented towards describing learning scenarios than just contents. The IMS LD specification tries to describe all the aspects and the elements more related to the learning process in itself, such as sequencing or role playing, that is, the second level of description as aforementioned. It seems clear that all this information cannot be stored in the learning objects, but in a higher semantic level. Although the IMS LD specification may seem too complex for practical applications, its flexibility and multilevel description capabilities allow the specification of any learning process ranking from simple educational itineraries to complex learning processes including personalization and collaborative working capabilities. Nevertheless, both content description standards (such as LOM [8], for example) and learning process description specifications (such as IMS LD) lack from a formal description for the concept of competence. In [9] a proposal for formal description of required and acquired competences following the most well known taxonomies [10, 11, 12] is presented, and the use of ontologies for standard integration and extension is discussed, following the approach described in [7]. Other works about competence design and taxonomies in the same direction have been also considered [13, 14].

In IMS LD, "Learning-objectives" within an "Activity" is precisely the place to describe competences, but using a more textual approach. Each learning objective is described using, at least, two basic fields, a text based description and a type, which can be one (and only one) of the following: skill, knowledge, insight, attitude, competency and other. Therefore, any extension to include a more comprehensive description of competences should be included here, using the proposal presented in this paper. IMS LD will probably become a standard for defining complex learning processes, including personalization issues. Therefore, it would be interesting to study how to include our proposal in the IMS LD specification taking also into account not only competences but also activities and roles in a personalized learning process. Nevertheless, personalization capabilities of the current IMS LD specification are clearly insufficient for describing the complex requirements of Table 1. Although IMS LD can be used for describing the learning scenarios needed by each subject, the description of the elements of any e-learning process and all the interactions between such elements is not yet a simple question. Two basic levels of description can be identified: the first level, pointed towards content management through the use of learning objects, describes the aspects directly related to the educational content. The second level describes the interactions between such learning objects and the users within the framework defined by the learning process. This separation is needed to ensure reutilization of learning resources in different contexts.

For the first level, the LOM standard [8] defines a structure for interoperable descriptions of learning objects. In this case, a learning object is defined as any entity, digital or non-digital, that may be used for learning, education or training. Notice that we do not use the classical definition of learning object from Wiley [15] because it does not include non-digital resources, which are still heavily used at the UOC virtual campus. Nevertheless, although there are several other definitions for learning objects, all of them coincide in a single desired behaviour: reusability. For the second level, we need additional standards and specifications for describing the learning profiles, the competence maps, and the learning process itself beyond IMS LD. As stated in [16], both IEEE Personal and Private Information (PAPI) [17] and IMS Learner Information Package (LIP) [18] overlap in describing user profiles. On the one hand, the main interest of IEEE PAPI is to supply the minimum set with information that can allow follow-up of the student performance during its study. On the other hand, IMS LIP offers richer structures and it takes into the main characteristics of the user, like goals and interests (not covered to IEEE PAPI), and it also describes the characteristics of the student with views to the personalization contents. It is extensible, provides best practice guides and that makes it easier to use and of reading. In any case, it is possible to pass a user profile to IEEE PAPI from IMS LIP.

Following [19], it is necessary to establish the models used to describe the learning scenario, namely Domain, User, Context, Instruction and Adaptation. Each model defines one or more elements of the learning process, which are related each other but current standards do not reflect these relationships. Table 2 shows the current standards and specifications that might be used to describe the proposed virtual learning environment with personalization and competence based instructional design capabilities. "P" means that the current standard or specification has a relationship with the concept we want to represent, but only partially. On the other hand, "C" means that the current standard or specification is enough to fully describe the proposed element.

Table 2 Current standards and specifications for system requirements (P=partial, C=Complete).

	LOM	IMS LD	RDCEO	PAPI/LIP	OKI
Competence map			C		
Competence profile		P	P	P	
Competence itineraries	P	P			
Teaching plans	P	P	P	P	P
Learning situations	P	P			P
Learning activities	P	C			P
Learning resources	C				P

Taking into account the limitations and gaps between this set of standards and specifications is also necessary to create an ontology (or several) for ensuring that all elements involved in a competence based design process are covered. As described in [7], it is possible to use an ontology for describing not only standards, but also the relationships that occur between the elements that take part of such standards, which cannot be part of the learning object instances, thus providing coherence to metadata instances and referring to the appropriate domains. As shown in Table 2, there are main gaps in the competence related concepts which need to be solved for creating learning paths attending personalization issues in a learning scenario based on competences. Ontologies will allow us to add extensions and new rules for covering the disadvantages of the current standards, such as formal definitions for competences or competence maps.

4 Discussion

Virtual learning environments are becoming true learning scenarios for both blended and pure virtual distance education. Classical learning content management systems will become obsolete if they just provide learners with contents and syllabus. The new EHEA paradigm, which bases the design of any educational offer in terms of competence acquisition and development, promotes personalization as a way to ensure a proper development for each learner, taking into account his or her particularities, preferences, the already acquired competences and the desired learning goals. Activities for developing competences, and not contents, are the basic pieces for designing educational experiences. This means that classical e-learning standards and specifications need to be rethought in order to incorporate this new vision. Furthermore, personalization means different things depending on the elements taken into account and the level of application, and the complexity of all the possibilities is beyond the capacity of the current standards. The IMS LD specification is the first step towards a complete description of the elements in the learning process, although it is still far from providing complete descriptions with the required level of detail, including adaptive learning paths for competence development. It needs to be used in combination with other e-learning standards and specifications, and semantic interoperability is not always ensured and, in fact, very limited.

The UOC virtual campus is undergoing a major revision (both in technological and methodological aspects) with the inclusion of new web 2.0 tools for teaching and learning, personalization issues and adopting a web services based architecture using OKI. The International Master on Education and ICTs will be used as a pilot experience for providing learners with adaptive learning paths and a complete curriculum based on competence evaluation, acquisition and development. The concept of teaching plan is also under development as it is clear that it cannot be only a sequence of learning activities involving the use of learning resources, but it has to reflect the higher level competence maps and personalization issues through the use of user profiles.

Current and future research lines in this subject include the creation of pilot subjects including both case based learning and workgroups, using IMS LD as the starting point for the formal definitions. As several IMS LD based courses will be available, a higher level definition taking into account the competence map will be needed to provide the adaptive learning paths according to user profile. The use of ontologies for creating relationships between the elements described by different e-learning standards and recommendations is also an interesting issue which needs to be deeply developed yet.

Acknowledgements

This paper has been partially supported by a Spanish government grant under the project PERSONAL (TIN2006-15107-C02-01).

References

1. IMS: WG12: Learning Design. Available at http://www.imsglobal.org/learningdesign (2003)
2. Kasanoff, B.: Making it Personal: how to profit from personalization without invading privacy. Perseus Publishing (2001)
3. Ausubel, D.P., Noval, J.D., Hanessian, H.: Educational Psychology. A cognitive view. Holt, Rinehart and Winston, New York (1978)
4. Mor, E., Minguillón, J., Garreta-Domingo, M., Lewis, S.: A three-level approach for analyzing user behavior in ongoing relationships. In: Proceedings of the 12th International Conference on Human-Computer Interaction, Beijing, China (2007) 971–980
5. Minguillón, J.: Education and pedagogy with learning objects and learning designs. Computers in Human Behavior **23** (2007) 2581–2584

6. Guardia, L., Sangrá, A., Maina, M.: Case method in vtle: An effective tool for improving learning design. In: Proceedings of the 4th EDEN Research Workshop, Barcelona, Spain (2006)
7. Sicilia, M.A.: Ontology-based competency management: Infrastructures for the knowledge-intensive learning organization. In: Intelligent learning infrastructures in knowledge intensive organizations: A semantic web perspective, Idea Group (2005) 302–324
8. IEEE: WG12: Learning Object Metadata. Available at http://ltsc.ieee.org/wg12/index.html (2002)
9. Guerrero, A.E., Minguillón, J.: Metadata for describing educational competencies: The uoc case. In: Proceedings of the Second International Conference on Web Information Systems and Technologies. (2006) 275–280
10. Biggs, J.B.: Evaluating the Quality of Learning- the SOLO Taxonomy. Academic Press, New York (1982)
11. Bloom, B.: Taxonomy of Educational Objectives, Handbook I: The Cognitive Domain. David McKay Co Inc, New York (1956)
12. González, J., Wagenaar, R.: Tuning educational structures in Europe. Technical report (2003) Available at http://www.relint.deusto.es/TuningProject/index.htm.
13. Ng, A., Hatala, M., Gasevic, D. In: Ontology-based Approach to Learning Objective Formalization. IGP (2007)
14. Woelk, D.: E-learning semantic web services and competency ontologies. In: Proceedings of World conference on educational multimedia, hypermedia and telecommunications. (2002) 2077–2078
15. Wiley, D.A.: The Instructional Use of Learning Objects. Agency for Instructional Technology (2002)
16. Chatti, M.A., Klamma, R., Quix, C., Kensche, D.: Lm-dtm: An environment for xml-based, lip/papi-compliant deployment, transformation and matching of learner models. In: ICALT, IEEE Computer Society (2005) 567–569
17. IEEE: WG12: Personal and Private Information. (Available at http://edutool.com/papi/)
18. IMS: WG12: Learner Information Package. (Available at http://www.imsglobal.org/profiles/index.html)
19. Aroyo, L., Dolog, P., Houben, G., Kravcik, M., Naeve, A., Nilsson, M., Wild, F.: Interoperability in personalized adaptive learning. Educational Technology & Society 9 (2006) 4–18

Metadata Encoding for the Levels of Scientific Research

Nikoletta Peponi[1], Marios Poulos[2] and Theodoros Pappas[3]

Abstract   A description of the designing of a special DTD (Document Type Definition) for the scientific method is reported and an analysis of the creation of a DTD according to the separation that T.Pappas gives in his book Methodology of scientific research in the humanism[4] is presented. According to this separation the researching process consists of five levels: the subject selection, the strategy designation for the development of study, the collection and indexing of bibliographical material, the evaluation and classification of bibliographic material and the process and writing of study. Each level is part in sublevels in proportion with the separation that is already given in the book. In the second chapter of the paper we describe the methodology followed in order to create the DTD. We conclude by proposing future plans which will enrich, organize and develop further the already existing DTD.

1. Introduction

A definition given in the concept of scientific research is: *The systematic, controlled, empirical and critical investigation of hypothetical propositions about the presumed relations among natural phenomena*[5]. Scientific research aims at the audit examination and presentation of a scientific sector. Its main objective is the re-examination of existing knowledge and description of a concrete subject

---

[1] nikpeponi@gmail.com
[2] Dept. Of Archives and Library Sciences, Palea Anaktora 49100, Corfu, Greece, mpoulos@ionio.gr
[3] Dept. Of Archives and Library Sciences, Palea Anaktora 49100, Corfu, Greece, thpappas@ionio.gr

[4] *Η μεθοδολογία της επιστημονικής έρευνας στις ανθρωπιστικές επιστήμες*, εκδ. Μ. Καρδαμίτσα, Αθήνα 2002, 190 σελ.

[5] Kerlinger, Fred N. (1964), *Foundations of Behavioral Research*, New York: Holt Rinehart.

along with the formulation of a new innovating theory. The researcher, at the beginning of his study should find through programmed and systematic collection, analysis and interpretation of data, the proofs in order to support his positions. Research must follow a concrete methodology, based on logical and predefined activities. The scientific method attempts to minimize the influence of bias or prejudice in the experimenter when testing a hypothesis or a theory, and it is never based on propaedeutic conclusions.

According to T.Pappas, scientific research can distribute in many sectors by specific measures. Some examples are given below: the opportunity of developing the researching results in terms of their application (technology, theory), the expedient goal (descriptive/declaratory), the usable method (experimental, historical, clinical, ethnographic, multicultural etch), the form and the proving ground (quantitative or qualitative, laboratorial, bibliographic), the time of elaboration (synchronic, diachronic), the number of the researchers (teamwork or personal work), and finally the number of the examinant (sampling, gallop poll or personal research).

In all circumstances scientific research has some basic feature; some of them are mention further down. First of all scientific research, concerns the discovery, accumulation and analysis of new knowledge. Therefore some of the most important issues are the thorough examination of the related bibliography so as for the researcher to be informed on the already existing studies in order to be aware of his/her own offer to the existing knowledge. Furthermore, researchers should manage to reach a well-formed and systematic gathering of all information and data processing. Another feature of scientific research according to T. Pappas is the sincere devotion towards the process of research which should be based on firm and logic analysis of information. Finally, regarding the style of a scientific study, researchers should use an impersonal – documentary language in order to achieve objectivity and validation of scientific results.

2. A DTD for Scientific Research

In order to promote and organize further the procedure of scientific research in a practical way, we decided to create a special DTD which will offer to the researchers a handy tool for the better organization of their studies. As we mention earlier, the right organization and methodology are necessary measures for the fulfilment of scientific research. On this account the existence of a DTD will accommodate the inquiry not only for the writer of the study, but also for every interested in the specific information.

2.1 Levels of Researching Process

Scientific research elaborates for a specific purpose which may be to bear up an aspect, or to compare and contrast two theories, or even to present and explain a specific study. In all cases the main purpose is to boost and add up to research and science by aiming at the creation of something prototypical and new. Scientific method is a body of techniques for investigating phenomena and acquiring new knowledge, as well as for correcting and integrating previous knowledge. It is based on gathering observable, empirical, measurable evidence, subject to specific principles of reasoning. As T.Pappas mentions in his book *'Methodology of scientific research in the humanism'* (Παππάς, 2002:71) researching process consists of five levels:

- subject selection (subject selection)

- strategy designation for the development of study (strategy)

- collection and indexing of bibliographical material (collection and indexing of b)

- evaluation and classification of bibliographic material (classification of bibliography)

- process and writing of study (writing of study)

2.2 Mark up for Scientific Method

Until now no special DTD for scientific method has been developed. In order to facilitate and organize the researching process there is a need of developing a special DTD which will create a mark up language that will cover the description of scientific method and metadata for researching process.

3. Methodology

The elaboration and designing of a special DTD for the researching process requires a specific and correctly structured methodology. As far as the designing of the special DTD concerns, it will be parted in 5 main areas. These areas correspond to the five levels of researching process.

3.1 The First Area

Further down we appose the code text and also the graphical display of the XML Schema:

```
<xs:schema xmlns:xs="http://www.w3.org/2001/XMLSchema"
elementFormDefault="qualified"
attributeFormDefault="unqualified">
        <xs:element name="scientific_research">
                <xs:annotation>
                        <xs:documentation>the procces of
scientific research</xs:documentation>
                </xs:annotation>
                <xs:complexType>

        <xs:sequence>
```

Fig. 1. The graphical display represents the beginning of the XML Schema.

The *first area* concerns the subject selection, a procedure that determines the value and the possibility of the research's realization.

The process of subject selection underlies of the scientific research. The subject of the study can be specified by the supervisor professor or can be suggested by the researcher. There are many places where someone can derive ideas for a researching study such as papers, articles, proceedings, books or from a personal thought etc. A scientific research could be an article that is a summary study which publishing in a scientific journal, a monograph that is a specialized study in a prototypical subject, an essay or thesis. Before the researcher selects the eligible subject, he/she must search if the sources of the material are available and approachable. We have enriched the *source of material* element by adding one more subclass of elements. These elements are: ISBN, ISSN, URL, DOE, and ISBD. The ISBN element contains two more sub elements, the *book* and the *conference*. In the *book* element we have added a Boolean attribute, so as to clarify if the material (book) has a publisher or not. In the same way, we added in the *conference* element a Boolean attribute so as for the researcher to be able to check if the source of the material (conference) is an academic institute or not. With these extensions we tried to encode information on the valence (positive/negative) of citations. Furthermore availability of data and access of material, time, skill and knowledge are fundamental elements. In addition time is a major element for the right process of the scientific research. Time and expected results are bound together. Ultimately, the element skill and knowledge deals with the capability of the researcher and the contribution of his/her study to the scientific sector. In terms of the relevance of material to bibliometry and general studies of sociology of science we also added in the *subject selection* element a parameter of *relevance* which has taken a normalized String attribute so that the researcher has the possibility to check the relevance of the material in a range of four steps: non related, shortly related, related and very related.

There are many areas that add up to the scientific research such as economy, history, philology, mathematics, physics, chemistry etch as well as philosophy, arts, literature, political science, culture, spiritual issues etc.

3.2 The Second Area

The strategy to follow for the development of study is analyzed at the *second area*.
Below is the diagram of the strategy element:

```
<xs:element name="strategy">
  <xs:complexType>
    <xs:sequence>
      <xs:element name="goals"
type="xs:string"/>
      <xs:element name="suggestions"
type="xs:string"/>
      <xs:element name="activities"
type="xs:string"/>
      <xs:element
name="definition_of_priorities" type="xs:string"/>
```

```
            <xs:element name="time_at_disposition"
type="xs:string"/>
            </xs:sequence>
            </xs:complexType>
            </xs:element>
```

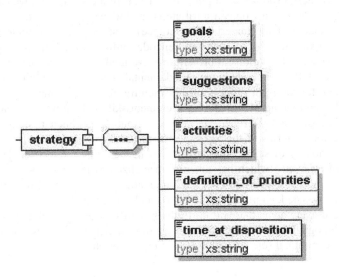

Fig. 2. The graphical display represents the second level of scientific research.

3.3 The Third Area

Goals and suggestions made by the researcher, activities to follow in order to achieve these goals, the definition of priorities and time at disposition are measures that describe the development of study.

Bibliography comprises the main component for the study. The material collection derives from various sources that diversify according to the nature of the source (books, articles, papers, journal, data base etc). These considerations concern the *third area*, the collection and indexing of bibliography material.

3.4 The Fourth Area

The evaluation and classification of bibliography – the *fourth area* – refers firstly to the formulation and the organization of the material collected and secondly to the value and production of new knowledge (scientific, social etc).

```
                    <xs:element
name="classification_of_bibliography">
                    <xs:complexType>
                    <xs:sequence>
                    <xs:element name="formulation"
type="xs:string"/>
                    <xs:element name="organization"
type="xs:string"/>
                    <xs:element
name="value_of_new_knowledge" type="xs:string"/>
                    <xs:element
name="production_of_new_knowledge" type="xs:string"/>
                    </xs:sequence>
                    </xs:complexType>
                    </xs:element>
```

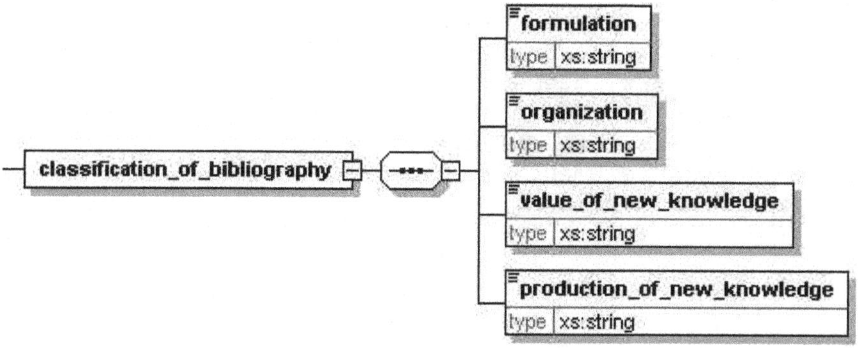

Fig. 3. The graphical display represents the fourth level of scientific research.

3.5 The Fifth Area

The fifth and last area concerns the process and writing of study and deals with the composition of the text, the structure of the study, the proper use of language and style, footnotes and the proper way to expose and retrieve the information offered in the study (references).

```
<xs:element name="writing_of_study">
     <xs:complexType>
     <xs:sequence>
     <xs:element
name="the_composition_of_the_text" type="xs:string"/>
     <xs:element
name="the_structure_of_the_study" type="xs:string"/>
     <xs:element
name="the_proper_use_of_language_and_style"
type="xs:string"/>
          <xs:element name="footnotes"
type="xs:string"/>
     <xs:element
name="the_proper_way_to_expose_information"
type="xs:string"/>
          </xs:sequence>
          </xs:complexType>
          </xs:element>
        </xs:sequence>
        </xs:complexType>
       </xs:element>
      </xs:schema>
```

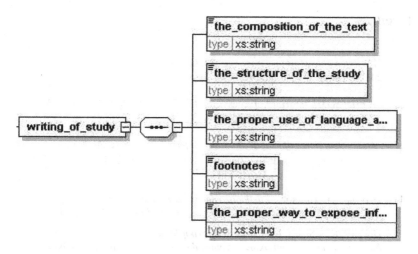

Fig. 4. The graphical display represents the fifth level of scientific research.

4. Future Plans

Considerations on scientific method, elaboration and designing of a special DTD could be enriched further. More specialize DTD can be created focusing on different types of scientific research. For example the creation of a DTD that will describe exclusively articles, or monographs, or thesis etc. In this way scientific research will be more organized and the work of researchers will be facilitated.

To sum up, the developing of a unified model/ontology of existing format by using a tool as Protégé, comprise a challenge and a future goal, so as to develop further our study.

References

1. *[1] "Extensible Markup Language (XML) 1.0 (Fourth Edition)"*, [access at 24/3/07] <http://www.w3.org/TR/REC-xml/>

2. *"A brief SGML tutorial"*, [access at 24/3/07] <http://www.w3.org/TR/WD-html40-970708/intro/sgmltut.html#h-2.3.3.2>

3. *"DTD_Overview.pdf (application/pdf Object)"*, [access at 24/3/07] <http://www.idevelopment.info/data/Programming/java/xml/DTD_Overview.pdf>

4. Θεόδωρος Γ. Παππάς, *Η μεθοδολογία της επιστημονικής έρευνας στις ανθρωπιστικές επιστήμες*, εκδ. Μ. Καρδαμίτσα, Αθήνα 2002, 190 σελ.

5. Howard, K. – Sharp, J.A., *Η Επιστημονική Μελέτη. Οδηγός σχεδιασμού και διαχείρισης πανεπιστημιακών ερευνητικών εργασιών*, μτφρ. Β.Νταλάκου, Αθήνα, εκδ. Gudenberg, 1996.

6. Τσιμπούκης, Κ. *Τρόπος συγγραφής μιας επιστημονικής εργασίας*, Αθήνα, 1986

7. Eco, U., *Πως γίνεται μια διπλωματική εργασία*, μτφρ. Μ. Κονδύλη, Αθήνα, εκδ. Νήσος, 1994.

8. *APPENDIX E: Introduction to the Scientific Method*
   http://teacher.nsrl.rochester.edu/phy_labs/AppendixE/AppendixE.html

Metadata Encoding for the Documents based on the Rules of Diplomatics Science

Sylvia Poulimenou[1], Spyros Asonitis[2] and Marios Poulos[3]

Abstract This paper addresses the issue of metadata in Diplomatics science. Due to the fact that there is no metadata schema in order to describe in detail the information held in Diplomatics documents and to face the problem of factitiousness, the creation of an appropriate schema is explained and further explored in this paper. This schema is meant to be used for a strict category of documents of Diplomatics which are called *Privilegia* and the reason for that restriction is due to the intense controversy of the structure of Diplomatics documents during various time periods and production mechanisms that make each category or subcategory to vary.

1 Introduction

1.1 Diplomatics

Diplomatics is the science concerned with the authenticity of documents [1]. Documents are critically studied via typical rules that apply to written acts in affinity with their production mechanisms [5, 1]. Diplomatics was born in 1659 and was named after the term *diploma* that rises in history several centuries ago,

---

[1] web222spider@yahoo.gr

[2] Dept. of Archives and Library Sciences Ionian University, Palea Anaktora 49100, Corfu, Greece, asonitis@ionio.gr

[3] Dept. of Archives and Library Sciences Ionian University, Palea Anaktora 49100, Corfu, Greece, mpoulos@ionio.gr

typically from the Romans Time. At that period it specified the written permission for using the means (*cursus publicus*) of the Empires Post [3]. The most recent definition of diploma is a document that was folded in order to assure its secrecy or authenticity. Diplomatics is separated in periods due to the diversity of documents, which is caused by the also diverse mechanisms that produced them through out the ages. Diplomas are separated in categories that apply to a certain period of time and in that period to sub categories that apply to different types of diplomas, where there are also several types of other categorization [5, 3, 1]. In this paper not all categories are to be included, but a specific sub category called *Byzantine Imperial Diplomas* that donated a privilege (*Privilegia/* Chrysobulls/ Golden Bulls) [1]. In this sub category there are three types of diplomas Chrysobull logos, Chrysobull Sigillia (*sigillium*), Chrysobull precept (*praeceptum*). That category is to be studied from the view of critical analysis by a diplomatist, commonly known as *critical edition* of a text.

Keywords for this paper: Diplomatics, metadata, critical edition, Privilegia, diplomas, Chrysobull logos, Chrysobull Sigillia, sigillium, Chrysobull precept, praeceptum, transcription.

1.2 Structure of a Diploma

It is important to emphasize that most kinds of diplomas that apply at the same period share a common structure, at a very general level though. Lots of differences rise through one sub period to another and through different types of diplomas. In order to understand the layout of the schema it is necessary to describe the structure of the Byzantine Imperial Diplomas where the Chrysobulls belong. Furthermore raises the necessity of describing the special features of Chrysobulls. In addition since the subject of this article contain the encoding not only of Chrysobulls but moreover of the critical edition of that type of text, one must consider of the rules that apply to the critical edition.

At this part of the article two parameters are going to be basically presented and are going to be analyzed during presentation of the schema that will be able to encode the critical edition of a Chrysobull. A common Byzantine Imperial Diploma is divided in two parts, the actual text and the parts of the diploma that provide an introduction and a closure. The actual text is named *text* and the introduction and closure as a part are defined as *protocol*. Moreover the introduction is defined as protocol and closure as eschatocol.

The process that is followed to accomplish a critical edition lies in four steps:

- Presenting the actual diploma that contains general information about its category and providing a description of the diploma.
- The process of the critical edition that mainly applies to the transcription of the text according to some basic rules of Diplomatics.

- Comments on the diploma, such us pointing out general observations concerning its subject and annotation of specific names.
- Finally the critical edition is accomplished via supplements such as alphabetical tables and facsimiles of the actual diploma.

The essence of Diplomatics lays in the possibility of a document being factitious [4]. That can be examined from several parameters and mainly if it doesn't match to its time structure. A factitious diploma is a verisimilitude document to an original document and was created as an attempt to give the impression of being authentic [4, 1]. Moreover, there is the essence of personal gain that led the person creating a factitious document [3]. Diplomas can be categorized using factitiousness as criteria into original diplomas, copies from the Imperial Secretariat and copies that had a certain receiver. Moreover another way that diplomas can be delivered is as copies that can be found inside another diploma, imitations and factitious diplomas.

There are ten main criteria [3, 1] of authenticity that apply to all diplomas. In Diplomatics, to understand whether a diploma is factitious or not, it needs to be tested with the main criteria and then with the criteria that come as a result of it's time diversity.

Prior work in the metadata science comes from *Tomaž Erjaveci, Matija Ogrin* [6] that have begun an important attempt of digitizing critical editions of older Slovenian texts, via *Text Encoding Initiative (TEI)*, also applying the P4 version and in the end creating a strict schema in order to specialize the use of TEI, having as a result the *Web library of critical editions of Slovene literature*. Another important attempt coming from the Bancroft Library and Charles Faulhaber [8] that undertook the sponsorship of a TEI SCHEMA that would serve the transcription of medieval and renaissance manuscripts, the ds3.schema, which has been processed further from many workshops of Berkley since and comes as a transcription software package. Also *J.W.J. Burgers* and *F.G. Hoekstra* [7] from the Institute for Netherlands History (ING) in order to make accessible a large amount of documents that apply to the Dutch historiography of the 1314-1345 which haven't been studied sufficiently due to the fact that they cannot be found in a modern edition, has begun a project. Another attempt coming from *Michael Gervers and Michael Margolin* [7] that created an application in XML, of metadata that could be attached to Latin Medieval Charters that also included possible encoding of diplomatic text. For the last two attempts there are no other information mainly because thy where presented in the Digital Diplomatics Conference held in Munich from the 28-2-07 to 2-3-07.

2 Methodology

2.1 Mark up for Diplomas

In order to categorize diplomas so that they are retrievable and of a clear structure semantically for Diplomatics scientists and for all the scientific community there is the need for developing a special SCHEMA [9, 10, 11] which will create a mark up language that will cover their structure and the necessary metadata for Diplomatics. Moreover the criteria [1] that express their possible factitiousness need to be enfolded at the schema.

In order to create a schema that gave the possibility of encoding Chrysobulls several parameters were taken into consideration as mentioned above. The root element <diploma> of the diploma.schema consists of three complex elements <presentation>, <transcription>, <dobs>. The alphabetical tables and facsimiles are not going to be included in this survey and are to be included in future adjustments of this article as added databases.

As can be understood that applies to the four steps of accomplishing the critical edition that where mentioned above. All four are enfolded in more detail as it supposed to according to specific Diplomatics guidelines [3].

2.1.1 The element <presentation>

The element <presentation> is divided in two complex elements <genchar>, that provides more sub elements that describe in a general way the diploma and <desc> that with several sub elements gives a more detailed description of the diploma (and its possible copies).

The complex element <genchar> consists of three sub elements. The first sub element <category> states the category of the diploma and can be either Chrysobull logos, Chrysobull Sigillia, Chrysobull precept. It can be repeated if more than one category is mentioned at the diploma. <Category> consists of two sub elements <line> and <cattype>. The element <line> indicates the actual line where the definition is found in the diploma and provides two attributes, "pagetype" and "pagenote". At the element <cattype> the category of the diploma can be declared. The second sub element is <chron> that states the date of the diploma and contains the attribute "actualdate", to declare the date in a proper and standardized form. The third sub element is <abstract> that applies to a couple of lines which summarise the diplomas content.

The complex element <desc> consists of the sub element <descitem>, due to the fact that at the beginning of the critical edition the diplomatist is providing the description of possible several versions that exist of the actual diploma. The element <descitem> can be repeated as many times as it is needed.

In the element <descitem> can be found 12 sub elements that give a full description of the diploma (each version). It consists of <state>, <material>, <materialobs>, <dimension>, <ink>, <writing>, <lingobs>, <sealdesc>, <diplobs>, <mendocs>, <ppindex>, <pans>.

Each sub element of <descitem> consists of more appropriate sub elements which is not necessary to be mentioned. A brief analysis of the twelve sub elements of <descitem> follows:

- The element <state> describes the diplomas condition. Via "grade" attribute it is possible to describe the extent of the diplomas condition.
- The element <material> indicates the material on which the diploma was written. It can be stated through the attribute "mtype" that stands for material type. Possible values are "parchment", "paper", and "papyrus" and as default value is used "paper".
- The element <materialobs> contains observations relative to the material of the diploma. It consists of several sub elements that most of them contain the attribute "exists".
- <dimension> consists of many sub elements in order to state the total dimension of the diploma and of its separate parts and contains the attribute "measurement".
- The element <ink> states the inks colour and it can be used once or unbounded times and contains the attribute "col" to determine the ink colour.
- The element <writing> can be used to describe the texts writing.
- The element <lingobs> can be used to state observations about the language and the spelling of the diploma.
- The element <sealdesc> can contain observation about the seal and can consist of several sub elements <sobs>, which stands for seal observations. <sobs> contains the attribute "type" that indicates the part of the seal that the observation is addressed to.
- The element <diplobs>, contains the sub element <diobs> that can contain observations from Diplomatics point if view and also contains an attribute "type".
- The element <mendocs> gives the opportunity to declare in detail mentioned documents at the current diploma in the form of a sub element <item>.
- The element <ppindex> stands for previous published index and it can be used as a way of reference to different critical editions of the same diploma.
- Finally the element <pans> where can be mentioned editions with facsimiles.

2.1.2 The element <transcription>

The element <transcription> consists of the actual text.

The element <protokollo> consists of three main sub elements, <invocatio>, <intitulatio> and <inscriptio> that are named after the three areas in which the protocol of a Byzantine Imperial diploma is divided. Invocation is the part of protocol that the invocation of Devine is actualized by the writer. Intitulatio was the part of the protocol that declared the Emperors titles. Finally inscriptio (or *pertinentia*) was the part of protocol that especially at the Chrysobull Logos consists of a standard phrase [1] *"Pasin οις to paron ημων eusebéς epideiknutai sigillion"*.

All these three main sub elements, <invocatio>, <intitulatio> and <inscriptio>, share a list of ten sub elements, that give the opportunity to the Diplomatics scientist to describe some difficulties that come across while transcripting the text. In Diplomatics some punctuation marks are used in order to describe those difficulties. To each marking of the chosen punctuation marks have been assigned special meanings, that in this article where translated to elements. Moreover the elements <invocatio>, <intitulatio> and <inscriptio> are the ones that embody the protocol of the diploma therefore they are mixed elements. They consist of ten sub elements and #PCDATA:

1. The element <nametype> is used to represent any type of name in the text. To be more descriptive there is the attribute "is" with possible values "person", "place" and "organization". Furthermore the attribute "id" that is an ID type and can be used to assign a unique identifier.
2. The element <linenumber> can enfold the whole line that the Diplomatics scientist transcripts. In Diplomatics, texts have their lines numbered.
3. The element <fromremains> contains added letters from the Diplomatics scientist, as transcription of letters that were not clear and the text provided some remains.
4. The element <abbranalysis> contains the analysis of an abbreviation.
5. The element <destrwords> contains words that the Diplomatics scientist added in place of destroyed words.
6. The element <missingwords> in an empty element that can be used in case that destroyed words cannot be added. The Diplomatics scientist can use the attribute "wordcount" to declare the actual number of the destroyed words.
7. The element <ommitedtext> declares that the original writer of the diploma has omitted a part out of negligence.
8. The element declares that the original writer of the diploma out of negligence has written the same word twice.
9. The element </notunderstandeblepart> declares a part of the text that the Diplomatics scientist cannot understand. This can be done since someone can actually copy-paste that part of the text to another document and use a special punctuation to declare the fact. In this schema though, the use of an empty element, </notunderstandeblepart>, declares the fact, but does not provide the possibility to see the actual text. Therefore it is omitted and is part of future plan in this research.

10. The element <differ> contains a part of the text that for some reasons may differ from the previous part. In order to determine the reason of difference the attribute "how" can be used.

The element <keimeno> consists of five main sub elements that also apply to five areas that the Diplomatics scientists divide the diplomas text. That five sub elements are named after these areas that are arrenga, narratio, dispositio, sanctio, corroboratio. Arrenga is the part of diploma that applies to a typical introduction to what the text is about. At narratio the actual subject of the diploma is unfolded. Dispositio contains the Emperors decision. Sanctio contains sanctions in case that anyone does not apply with the diplomas content that declares the Emperors will. Finally corroboratio was the part that provided ratification of the diploma via a typical phrase that was written at the end of text. These five sub elements <arrenga>, <narratio>, <dispositio>, <sanctio> and <corroboratio> share the same 10 sub elements as <invocatio>, <intitulatio> and <inscriptio>.

Finally the element <esxatokollo> that consists of six sub elements, <datum>, <standardphrase>, <legimus>, <subscriptio>, <rednote> and <rapnotes>. The element <datum> contains chronology, which can be found in lots of forms therefore there is the attribute "type" in order to declare the type of chronology. The element <standardphrase> contains the standard phrase "εν ω και το ημέτερον υπεσημήνατο κράτος" which is usually found at this part of a diploma usually from the 13th century and contains the attribute "exists", in case that the standard phrase is omitted. The element <legimus> declares that the word *legimus* exists at eschatocol, which is very important because it is a part of the ratification of the diploma and it contains the attribute "exists" and the attribute "ink", for the specification of the color of the ink that legimus was written. The element <subscriptio> is the actual ratification of the diploma due to the fact that it consists of words or phrases that the Emperor him self has written, or his signature. For that reason the element <subscriptio> consists of the sub elements <word>, <phrase>, <signature> that each contain specific domain of the sucscriptio. The element <word> contains words written by the hand of the Emperor, the element <phrase> likewise. The element <signature> consists of a description of the Emperors signature. Due to the fact that the Emperors signature is very important, there is the necessity of creating an image database that would provide a collection of signatures from various Emperors of the Byzantine Era. This database could be used to link each signature to the <signature> element. In this article the actual signature is omitted but a creation of the image database is in future plans. The element <rednote> is an element that contains specific type of notes that are usually found at eschatocol and are called release notes (simiwseis apolisews). Finally the element <rapnotes> contains specific notes that are usually found at eschatocol and are called reporter notes (simeiwseis eishghtwn). These notes are written by the person who reported the diploma to the Emperor.

The elements <datum>, <standardphrase>, <legimus>, <word>, <phrase>, <signature>, <rednote> and <rapnotes> contains the ten basic sub elements that help to the difficulties that the Diplomatics scientist can come across during the transcription process.

2.1.3 The element <dobs>

The element <dobs> is the main element that gives the opportunity to the Diplomatics scientist to point out special observations concerned in Diplomatics. It consists of three main sub elements <gendobs>, <notes> and <criteria>.

The element <gendobs> can contain information about the semantic of the diploma. In order to categorise its semantic the attribute "seman" is used and the values to be chosen are "hist" for historic, "admin" for administrative, "soc" for social, "finan" for financial and "leg" for legal.

The element <notes> consists of the sub element <ref> that can appear in the xml from zero to unbounded times. Via <ref> the diplomatist can reference to names and terms and describe them further by giving more details and information. For that reason it contains two attributes, "reftype" that indicates whether the reference is about an actual name or a term and "refpoint" that is IDREF type and can connect the actual name or term of the text with the note of the Diplomatics scientist.

Finally the element <criteria>, that contains 10 actual Diplomatics criteria that are mainly filled by using the logic "true or false". That is why the most of them contain an attribute "false" with values "yes" or "no". Generally the attribute "false" means factitious in this schema.

The element <hand> via "false" attribute answers the question whether the writing type doesn't correspond to the writing of that chronological period.

The element <langslip> contains possible language errors that are divided to 3 sub elements <orthslip> for orthographic errors, <syntslip> for syntactic errors, <style> for the style of language at that period of time.

The element <otslip> stands for other possible language slips and contains two sub elements that represent them, <anachr> and <geoslip>. The element <anachr> answers whether the anachronism phenomenon was found and the element <geoslip> is referring to geographical errors.

The element <matord> stands for material ordinary and contains information about any material anomalies compared with the chronological time habit. The material observations are divided to three sub elements, <shapeordin> that declares whether the shape of the material applies to its time period and is condidered normal, <cut> that has to do with the way that the material was cut and <sealcon> that has to do with the way that the seal is connected to the diploma.

The element <decoratives> has to do with decoration observations.

The element <skips> has to do with omissions and contains observations about inserted words (parenthetes lekseis), whether some of them where omitted or none written. The attribute "extent" is used with values "word" or "total".

The element <empsign> contains observations about the Emperors signature.

The element <blackdate> describes whether the whole date is written in black ink. It is important because some parts of the date where written in red ink

The element <discords> answers the question whether the indictio, which is a type of chronology, matches the annus mundi. It uses three attributes, "exists" that answers whether there is a difference between the two dates, the attribute "from" and "to" that declare the types of the two dates.

Finally the element <cratos> that answers the question whether the word «Κράτος» exists as the first word of the last line of the diploma. It uses the attribute "false", "firstword" and "lastline".

2.2 Implementation of the dtd

In order to develop a special SCHEMA for diplomas a certain methodology was followed. Firstly there was the need of studying an exact category of diploma [3, 1] its sub categories and their structure. Secondly understanding the process that is followed in Diplomatics at the examination of a diploma [2]. Finally the attempt to develop a SCHEMA [9, 10, 11] that would be able to mark up such documents in a way that would serve Diplomatics.

2.3 Resume general plan of implementation

Having the knowledge that all diplomas of the same period share a very general though common structure; the schema described at this paper has used them as basic fields for its development. Continuing these fields have been enriched with all other elements and attributes that can mark up effectively from the Diplomatics point of view diplomas. Moreover were included description details that a Diplomatics scientist includes at the examination of a document in order to create a critical edition [2].

The SCHEMA was parted in 3 main sections that apply to the basic guidelines that define some basic steps in order to create a critical edition. The first section has been devoted in presenting the document and its possible copies. The second section has been devoted for marking up the actual document. The third section has been devoted in Diplomatics observations most relative to subjects as possible fictitiousness of the document, how the fictitious document was created, the reasons and time period of fictitiousness. At this part the factitiousness criteria have been enfolded.

3 Future plans

The future plans of this paper are firstly to complete the SCHEMA. That means that there are some serious adds that need to be done. These adds are referring to the creation of data bases. In order to be complete this schema needs to be accompanied with a database of names and places, another with rare names (alphabetical tables), another with images of the Emperors signatures. Moreover other databases that are needed are for images of destroyed parts of the text and another for images of facsimiles.

After the completion of the SCHEMA future plans are to enrich it for being able to describe not only a sub category (special type in a time period) of diploma, but to describe all types of diplomas that belong to a certain time period. Moreover to develop ontology that in association with the SCHEMA, will be able to determine whether a diploma is fictitious or not.

Nevertheless, it should be pointed out that the necessity of an expert cannot be replaced by a directed via rules machine and this possibility remains to be seen scientifically.

References

1. Ασωνίτης Σπύρος Ν, *Σημειώσεις παραδόσεων Βυζαντινής Διπλωματικής*, Ιόνιο Πανεπιστήμιο, Τμήμα Αρχειονομίας και Βιβλιοθηκονομίας, Κέρκυρα 2005.
2. Βρανούση Έ, *Έγγραφα Πάτμου*. Ι. Αυτοκρατορικά. ΚΒΕ/ΕΙΕ, Αθήνα 1980.
3. Καραγιαννόπουλος Ι.Ε., *Βυζαντινή Διπλωματική*. (Β' ελληνική έκδοσις του έργου των F. Dolger-J. Karayannopoulos, Byzantinische Urkundenlehre. I. Die Kaiserurkunden, Munchen 1968), Θεσσαλονίκη 1972.
4. Πιτσάκης Κ.Γ, Έγκλημα χωρίς τιμωρία; Τα πλαστά στη βυζαντινή ιστορία, στο *Έγκλημα και τιμωρία στο Βυζάντιο*, (επιμέλεια Σ. Τρωιάνος), Αθήνα 1997.
5. Tessier G, Διπλωματική. Στο έργο Ιστορία και μέθοδοι της (Encyclopedie de la Pleiade), τ. Β΄, τεύχος 2, Αθήνα 1981, 219-276.
6. Tomaž Erjaveci, Matija Ogrin. *Digitisation of Literary Heritage Using Open Standards in Proceedings of eChallenges e-2005*. Ljubljana: Jožef Stefan Institute, 2005. [Access in 31-3-07], <http://nl.ijs.si/et/Bib/eChallenges05-ZRC.pdf>
7. "Conference Digital Diplomatics", Munich:International Center for Science and the Humanities,   2007.   [Access   in   31-3-07]   <http://www.cei.uni-muenchen.de/DigDipl07/programm.php?lang=en>
8. "Transcription SCHEMA TEI Extension – Digital Scriptorium", [Access in 31-3-07] <http://sunsite3.berkeley.edu/scriptorium/technical/transcription_tei.html>
9. "Extensible Markup Language (XML) 1.0 (Fourth Edition)", [access at 24/3/07] <http://www.w3.org/TR/REC-xml/>
10. "A brief SGML tutorial", [access at 24/3/07] <http://www.w3.org/TR/WD-html40-970708/intro/sgmltut.html#h-2.3.3.2>
11.   "SCHEMA_Overview.pdf   (application/pdf   Object)", [access   at   24/3/07] <http://www.idevelopment.info/data/Programming/java/xml/SCHEMA_Overview.pdf>

Formalizing Dublin Core Application Profiles – Description Set Profiles and Graph Constraints

Mikael Nilsson, Alistair J. Miles, Pete Johnston, Fredrik Enoksson[1]

Abstract. This paper describes a proposed formalization of the notion of Applications Profiles as used in the Dublin Core community. The formalization, called Description Set Profiles, defines syntactical constraints on metadata records conforming to the DCMI Abstract Model using an XML syntax. The mapping of this formalism to syntax-specific constraint languages such as XML Schema is discussed.

Introduction

The term *profile* has been widely used to refer to a document that describes how standards or specifications are deployed to support the requirements of a particular application, function, community or context, and the term *application profile* has recently been applied to describe this tailoring of metadata standards by their implementers (Heery & Patel, 2000).

Since then, the Dublin Core Metadata initiative (DCMI) has published a formalization of the Dublin Core metadata model called the DCMI Abstract Model (Powell et al, 2007), which provides the necessary foundation for a formalization of application profiles that lends itself to machine processing.

This paper describes a proposed formalization of the notion of Applications Profiles as used in the Dublin Core community, called "Description Set Profiles", or *DSPs*. This formalization is simplified by focusing on the core aspect of application profiles: the need for syntactically constraining the metadata instances.

---

[1]   mikael@nilsson.name, A.J.Miles@rl.ac.uk, Pete.Johnston@eduserv.org.uk, fen@csc.kth.se

Dublin Core Application Profiles

As described in the "Singapore Framework for Dublin Core Application Profiles" (Singapore Framework, 2008), a DSP is part of a documentation package for Dublin Core Application Profiles (DCAPs) containing

- Functional requirements, describing the functions that the application profile is designed to support, as well as functions that are out of scope

- Domain model, defining the basic entities and their relationships using an formal or informal modeling framework.

- Description Set Profile, as described in this paper

- Usage guidelines, describing how to apply the application profile, how the used properties are intended to be used in the application context etc.

- Encoding syntax guidelines, defining application profile-specific syntaxes, if any.

The DSP thus represents the machine-processable parts of a Dublin Core Application Profile.

There are existing attempts at defining a formal model for Dublin Core Application Profiles. Two important attempts have been documented in CEN CWA 14855, defining an overarching model for documenting application profiles, and CEN CWA 15248 that defined a machine-processable model for DCAPs.

These models depend on single-resource model for application profiles, where the DCAP describes a single resource and its properties. In the light of emerging multi-entity application profiles such as the Eprints Application Profile (Allinson et al 2007), where a five-entity model is used, a one-entity DCAP model is clearly insufficient. Also, earlier attempts at defining DCAPs have not had the benefit of a formal model for Dublin Core metadata, the DCMI Abstract Model, (Powell et al, 2007).

The Singapore Framework described above is intended to support DCAPs at the level of complexity represented by the ePrints DCAP.

Description Set Profiles

The DSP model relies on the metadata model defined in the DCMI Abstract Model and constrains the set of "valid" metadata records. Thus, a DSP defines a set of metadata records that are valid instances of an application profile. The Description Set Profile model is being developed within the Dublin Core

Architecture Forum and is in progress of being put forward as a DCMI Working Draft.

The first part of the paper describes the design of the DSP specification in the context of Dublin Core Application Profiles, uses it is intended to support, and some examples of applying it to relevant problems. Later in the paper, we discuss how the approach could be generalized to graph-based metadata such as RDF, and the potential benefits of such an approach.

The Role of Application Profiles

The process of "profiling" a standard introduces the prospect of a tension between meeting the demands for efficiency, specificity and localization within the context of a community or service on the one hand, and maintaining interoperability between communities and services on the other. Furthermore, different metadata standards may provide different levels of flexibility: some standards may be quite prescriptive and leave relatively few options for customization; others may present a broad range of optional features which demand a considerable degree of selection and tailoring for implementation.

It is desirable to be able to use community- or domain-specific metadata standards – or component parts of those standards – in combination. The implementers of metadata standards should be able to assemble the components that they require for some particular set of functions. If that means drawing on components that are specified within different metadata standards, that should be possible. They should also be safe in the knowledge that the assembled whole can be interpreted correctly by independently designed applications. Duval et al (2002) employ the metaphor of the Lego set to describe this process: an application designer should be able to "snap together" selected "building blocks" drawn from the "kits" provided by different metadata standards to build the construction that meets their requirements, even if the kits that provide those blocks were created quite independently.

In a Dublin Core Application Profile, the terms referenced are, as one would expect, terms of the type described by the DCMI Abstract Model, i.e. a DCAP describes, for some class of metadata descriptions, which *properties* are referenced in statements and how the use of those properties may be constrained by, for example, specifying the use of *vocabulary encoding schemes* and *syntax encoding schemes*. The DC notion of the application profile imposes no limitations on whether those properties or encoding schemes are defined and managed by DCMI or by some agency: the key requirement is that the properties referred to in a DCAP are compatible with the RDF notion of property.

It is a condition of that abstract model that all references to terms in a DC metadata description are made in the form of URIs. Terms can thus be drawn from any source, and references to those terms can be made without ambiguity. This set of terms can be regarded as the "vocabulary" of the application or community that the application profile is designed to support. The terms within that vocabulary may also be deployed within the vocabularies of many other DCAPs.

It is important to realize that the semantics of those terms is carried by their definition, independent of any application profile. Thus, semantic interoperability is addressed outside of the realm of application profiles, and therefore works between application profiles. Instead, application profiles focus on the *set of metadata records* that follow the same guidelines. Therefore, application profiles are more about high-level syntactic or structural interoperability than about semantics.

The Design of Description Set Profiles

The Dublin Core Description Set Profile model is designed to offer a simple constraint language for Dublin Core metadata, based on the DCMI Abstract Model and in line with the requirements for Dublin Core Application Profiles as set forth by the Singapore Framework. It constrains the resources that may be described by descriptions in the description set, the properties that may be used, and the ways a value may be referenced.

A DSP does, however, *not* address the following:

- Human-readable documentation.

- Definition of vocabularies.

- Version control.

A DSP contains the formal syntactic constraints only, and will need to be combined with human-readable information, usage guidelines, version management, etc. in order to be used as an application profile. However, the design of the DSP information model is intended to facilitate the merging of DSP information and external information of the above kinds, for example by tools generating human-readable documentation for a DCAP.

A DSP describes the structure of a Description Set by using the notions of "templates" and "constraints".

A *template* describes the possible metadata structures in a conforming record. There are two levels of templates in a Description Set Profile:

- **Description templates**, that contains the statement templates that apply to a single kind of description as well as constraints on the described resource.

- **Statement templates**, that contains all the constraints on the property, value strings, vocabulary encoding schemes, etc. that apply to a single kind of statement.

While templates are used to express structures, *constraints* are used to limit those structures. Figure 1 depicts the basic elements of the structure.

Thus, the DSP definition contains constructs for restricting

- what properties may be used in a statement and the multiplicity of such statements

- what languages and syntax encoding schemes may be used for literals and value strings, and if they may be used or not

- what vocabulary encoding schemes and value URIs that may be used, and if they may be used or not.

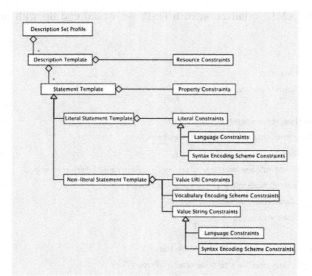

Figure 1: Templates and constraints in a DSP

The DSP specification also contains a pseudo-algorithm that defines the semantics of the above constraints, i.e. how an application is supposed to process a DSP. The algorithm takes as input a description set and a DSP, and gives the answer "matching" or "non-matching".

The Book DSP example

To show some of the features of the DSP model, consider the example of an application profile that wants to describe a book and its author. We would like to describe the following:

- A book

  ○ The title (dcterms:title) of the book (a literal string with language tag)

  ○ The creator (dcterms:creator) of the book, described separately

    ■ A single value string for the creator is allowed

    ■ No value URI for the creator is allowed

    ■ No vocabulary encoding scheme for the creator is allowed

- The Creator of the book

  ○ The name (foaf:name) of the creator (a literal string)

Using the XML serialization of a DSP, we would end up with the following XML:

```
<DescriptionSetTemplate>
  <DescriptionTemplate maxOccur="1" minOccur="1">

    <StatementTemplate maxOccur="1" type="literal">
      <Property>http://purl.org/dc/terms/title</Property>
      <LiteralConstraint>
        <SyntaxEncodingSchemeOccurrence>disallowed</SyntaxEncodingSchemeOccurrence>
        <LanguageOccurrence>optional</LanguageOccurrence>
      </LiteralConstraint>
    </StatementTemplate>

    <StatementTemplate maxOccur="1" type="nonliteral">
      <Property>http://purl.org/dc/terms/creator</Property>
      <NonliteralConstraint descriptionTemplateID="creator">
        <ValueURIOccurrence>disallowed</ValueURIOccurrence>
        <VocabularyEncodingSchemeOccurrence>disallowed</VocabularyEncodingSchemeOccurrence>
        <ValueStringConstraint maxOccur="1">
          <SyntaxEncodingSchemeOccurrence>disallowed</SyntaxEncodingSchemeOccurrence>
          <LanguageOccurrence>disallowed</LanguageOccurrence>
        </ValueStringConstraint>
      </NonliteralConstraint>
```

```
    </StatementTemplate>
  </DescriptionTemplate>
  <DescriptionTemplate maxOccur="1" minOccur="1">
    <StatementTemplate maxOccur="1" type="literal">
      <Property>http://xmlns.com/foaf/0.1/name</Property>
      <LiteralConstraint>
        <SyntaxEncodingSchemeOccurrence>disallowed</SyntaxEncodingSchemeOccurrence>
        <LanguageOccurrence>disallowed</LanguageOccurrence>
      </LiteralConstraint>
    </StatementTemplate>
  </DescriptionTemplate>
</DescriptionSetTemplate>
```

The above XML documents the Book DSP in a machine-processable way. The DSP describes a class of description sets matching the given constraints on the book and creator descriptions.

We will now see how such a format can be used.

Using DSPs

A Description Set Profile can be used for many different purposes, such as:

- as a formal representation of the constraints of a Dublin Core Application Profile
- as a syntax validation tool
- as configuration for databases
- as configuration for metadata editing tools

The DSP specification tries to be abstract enough to support such diverse requirements.

Formal documentation: The Wiki DSP generator

An example of where DSPs fills the purpose of formal documentation is the Wiki

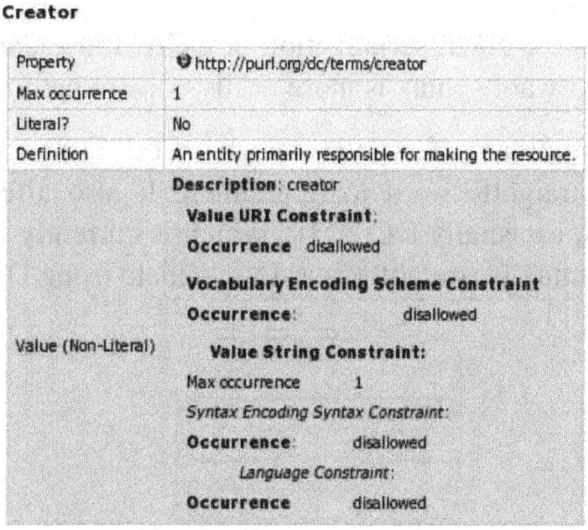

Creator

Property	http://purl.org/dc/terms/creator
Max occurrence	1
Literal?	No
Definition	An entity primarily responsible for making the resource.
Value (Non-Literal)	**Description**: creator **Value URI Constraint**: **Occurrence** disallowed **Vocabulary Encoding Scheme Constraint** **Occurrence**: disallowed **Value String Constraint:** Max occurrence 1 *Syntax Encoding Syntax Constraint*: **Occurrence**: disallowed *Language Constraint*: **Occurrence** disallowed

Figure 2: An HTML rendering of the DSP Wiki syntax

DSP generator used by the Dublin Core project and developed by one of the authors, Fredrik Enoksson. The software adds markup definitions to a wiki system (currently a MoinMoin installation) that generates a HTML-formatted display of the DSP, intermingled with human-readable text. Upon request, the software can generate an XML file.

The Wiki can then be used to host both the human-readable application profile guidelines and the XML version, maintained in a single place. See Figure 2 for the HTML output for the Book DSP example.

The wiki syntax is defined in Enoksson (2007).

Syntax validation

Validating metadata using a DSP can be done directly by an implementation of the DSP model in a custom validation tool. A more promising approach, however, is to leverage the widespread tool support for validating existing concrete syntaxes and, in particular, for XML validation.

Given a concrete XML syntax for DCAM-based metadata, such as DC-XML (currently being defined by the DCMI), a DSP can be converted to a syntax-specific validating schema. In the XML case, there are multiple options, such as XML Schema, RelaxNG and SchemaTron, each supporting different complexity in constraints. The authors are currently experimenting with translations from a DSP to these schema languages.

Interesting to note is that the complexity of such a translation is dependent on multiple factors:

- The flexibility of the schema language. XML Schema has well-documented difficulties in expressing certain forms of constraints, that are simple to express in RelaxNG, etc.

- The options available in a DSP. If the model allows for too complex constraints, translating them into a schema language will prove difficult.

- The design of the XML serialization of DCAM metadata. A more regular and straightforward syntax is more easily constrained.

The above considerations affects the design of the DSP specification – it is desirable that it be straightforward to implement. It also affects the design of Dublin Core syntaxes, especially DC-XML, which is currently under revision – it is desirable that the syntax is straightforward to validate using DSPs.

Metadata editors

DSPs have successfully been used to configure metadata editors. The SHAME metadata editing framework (Palmér et al 2007) is a RDF-based solution for generating form-based RDF metadata editors. The DSP XML format is translated to the form specification format of SHAME, and then used to create an editor. See Figure 3 for an example editor generated from a definition of a "Simple Dublin Core Application Profile".

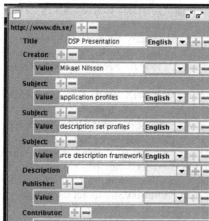

Figure 3: The SHAME editor configured by a DSP

Conclusions

The definition of a formal model for Description Set Profiles marks an important milestone in the evolution of the Dublin Core Metadata Initiative, and is a validation of the DCMI Abstract Model as a foundation for defining application profiles. Still, the model has yet to be validated by wide deployment and implementation, and many important issues remain to be studied. A few initial proofs of the concepts have been realized – using DSP for formal documentation, using DSPs to configure metadata editors, and using DSPs to generate XML Schemas for validation.

We expect that the next few years will show if DSPs solved the perceived problem or not. As part of the DC Singapore Framework for applications profiles, we hope that DSPs will serve the community's need for application profile definitions in support of quality control.

References

Allinson, J., Johnston, P., Powell, A. (2007), A Dublin Core Application Profile for Scholarly Works, *Ariadne Issue 50*, January 2007. Retrieved Sep 1, 2007, from http://www.ariadne.ac.uk/issue50/allinson-et-al/

Baker, T. (2003), DCMI Usage Board Review of Application Profiles. Retrieved Sep 1, 2007, from http://dublincore.org/usage/documents/profiles/

Baker, T. (2005), Diverse Vocabularies in a Common Model: DCMI at ten years, Keynote speech, DC-2005, Madrid, Spain. Retrieved Sep 1, 2007, from http://dc2005.uc3m.es/program/presentations/2005-09-12.plenary.baker-keynote.ppt

Bearman, D., Miller, E., Rust, G., Trant, J. & Weibel, S. (1999), A Common Model to Support Interoperable Metadata, *D-Lib Magazine*, January 1999. Retrieved Sep 1, 2007, from http://www.dlib.org/dlib/january99/bearman/01bearman.html

Brickley, D. & Guha, R. V. (2004), RDF Vocabulary Description Language 1.0: RDF Schema, *W3C Recommendation 10 February 2004*. Retrieved Sep 1, 2007, from http://www.w3.org/TR/rdf-schema/

Carroll, J.J., Stickler, P. (2004), TriX: RDF Triples in XML, Technical Report HPL-2004-56, HP Labs. Retrieved Sep 1, 2007, from http://www.hpl.hp.com/techreports/2004/HPL-2004-56.pdf

Dublin Core Application Profile Guidelines (2003), CEN Workshop Agreement CWA 14855. Retrieved Sep 1, 2007, from ftp://ftp.cenorm.be/PUBLIC/CWAs/e-Europe/MMI-DC/cwa14855-00-2003-Nov.pdf

The Dublin Core Singapore Framework, DCMI. Retrieved Sep 1, 2007, from http://dublincore.org/architecturewiki/SingaporeFramework

Duval, E., Hodgins, W., Sutton, S. & Weibel, S. L. (2002), Metadata Principles and Practicalities, *D-Lib Magazine*, April 2002. Retrieved Sep 1, 2007, from http://www.dlib.org/dlib/april02/weibel/04weibel.html

Enoksson, F., ed. (2007), Wiki format for Description Set Profiles. Retrieved Sep 1, 2007, from http://dublincore.org/architecturewiki/DSPWikiSyntax

Friesen, N., Mason, J. & Ward, N. (2002), Building Educational Metadata Application Profiles, *Dublin Core - 2002 Proceedings: Metadata for e-Communities: Supporting Diversity and Convergence*. Retrieved Sep 1, 2007, from http://www.bncf.net/dc2002/program/ft/paper7.pdf

Godby, C. J., Smith, D. & Childress, E. (2003), Two Paths to Interoperable Metadata, *Proceedings of DC-2003: Supporting Communities of Discourse and Practice – Metadata Research & Applications*, Seattle, Washington (USA). Retrieved Sep 1, 2007, from http://www.siderean.com/dc2003/103_paper-22.pdf

Guidelines for machine-processable representation of Dublin Core Application Profiles (2005), CEN Workshop Agreement CWA 15248. Retrieved Sep 1, 2007, from ftp://ftp.cenorm.be/PUBLIC/CWAs/e-Europe/MMI-DC/cwa15248-00-2005-Apr.pdf

Heery, R. & Patel, M. (2000), Application Profiles: mixing and matching metadata schemas, *Ariadne Issue 25*, September 2000. Retrieved Sep 1, 2007, from http://www.ariadne.ac.uk/issue25/app-profiles/

Heflin, J. (2004), OWL Web Ontology Language – Use Cases and Requirements, *W3C Recommendation 10 February 2004*. Retrieved Sep 1, 2007, from http://www.w3.org/TR/webont-req/

Johnston, P., (2005a), XML, RDF, and DCAPs. Retrieved Sep 1, 2007, from http://www.ukoln.ac.uk/metadata/dcmi/dc-elem-prop/

Johnston, P., (2005b), Element Refinement in Dublin Core Metadata. Retrieved Sep 1, 2007, from http://dublincore.org/documents/dc-elem-refine/

Klyne, G. & Carroll, J. J. (2004), Resource Description Framework (RDF): Concepts and Abstract Syntax, *W3C Recommendation 10 February 2004*. Retrieved Sep 1, 2007, from http://www.w3.org/TR/rdf-concepts/

Lagoze, C. (1996), The Warwick Framework – A Container Architecture for Diverse Sets of Metadata, D-Lib Magazine, July/August 1996. Retrieved Sep 1, 2007, from http://www.dlib.org/dlib/july96/lagoze/07lagoze.html

Lagoze, C., Sompel, H. Van de (2007), Compound Information Objects: The OAI-ORE Perspective. Retrieved Sep 1, 2007, from http://www.openarchives.org/ore/documents/CompoundObjects-200705.html

Manola, F. & Miller, E. (2004), RDF Primer, W3C Recommendation 10 February 2004. Retrieved Sep 1, 2007, from http://www.w3.org/TR/rdf-primer/

Nilsson, M., ed. (2007), DCMI Description Set Profile Specification. Retrieved Sep 1, 2007, from http://dublincore.org/architecturewiki/DescriptionSetProfile

Nilsson, M., Johnston, P., Naeve, A., Powell, A. (2007), The Future of Learning Object Metadata Interoperability, in Harman, K., Koohang A. (eds.) *Learning Objects: Standards, Metadata, Repositories, and LCMS* (pp 255-313), Informing Science press, ISBN 8392233751.

Palmér, M., Enoksson, F., Nilsson, M., Naeve, A. (2007), Annotation profiles: Configuring forms to edit RDF. *Proceedings of the international conference on Dublin Core and metadata applications 2007: Application Profiles: Theory and Practice*, Singapore, Aug 27 - 31 2007. Retrieved Sep 15, 2007, from http://www.dcmipubs.org/ojs/index.php/pubs/article/viewFile/27/2

Powell, A., Nilsson, M., Naeve, A., Johnston, P. (2007), DCMI Abstract Model, *DCMI Recommendation*. Retrieved Sep 1, 2007, from http://dublincore.org/documents/abstract-model/

Uschold, M. & Gruninger, M. (2002), Creating Semantically Integrated Communities on the World Wide Web, Invited Talk, Semantic Web Workshop, Co-located with WWW 2002, Honolulu, HI, May 7 2002. Retrieved Sep 1, 2007, from http://semanticweb2002.aifb.uni-karlsruhe.de/USCHOLD-Hawaii-InvitedTalk2002.pdf

Capturing MPEG-7 Semantics

S.Dasiopoulou and V.Tzouvaras and I.Kompatsiaris and M.G.Strintzis

Abstract The ambiguities due to the purely syntactical nature of MPEG-7 have hindered its widespread application as they lead to serious interoperability issues in sharing and managing multimedia metadata. Acknowledging these limitations, a number of initiatives have been reported towards attaching formal semantics to the MPEG-7 specifications. In this paper we examine the rationale on which the relevant approaches build, and building on the experiences gained we present the approach followed in the BOEMIE project.

1 Introduction

Multimedia content is omnipresent on the Web, rendering the availability of interoperable semantic content descriptions a key factor towards realising applications of practical interest. The recent literature includes a number of efforts towards extracting well-defined descriptions, utilising the formal and exchangeable semantics provided by ontologies and the Semantic Web. However, descriptions of multimedia content come intertwined with media related aspects, for which a unified representation is also required to ensure truly interoperable multimedia metadata.

The MPEG-7 standard [5] constitutes the greatest effort towards a common framework to multimedia description. However, despite providing a wide coverage

S.Dasiopoulou, M.G.Strintzis
Information Processing Laboratory, Aristotle University of Thessaloniki, Greece, e-mail: dasiop@iti.gr

V.Tzouvaras
Image, Video and Multimedia Systems Laboratory, National Technical University of Athens, Greece, e-mail: tzouvaras@image.ntua.gr

I.Kompatsiaris
Informatics and Telematics Institute, Centre for Research and Technology Hellas, Thessaloniki, Greece, e-mail: ikom@iti.gr

of the aspects of interest, MPEG-7 leads to a number of ambiguities that hinder the interoperability and sharing of the resulting descriptions, due to its XML Schema implementation lack of explicit semantics and the allowed flexibility in using the provided description tools.

To overcome the resulting ambiguities and align with the Semantic Web initial for machine understandable metadata, a number of efforts towards adding formal semantics to MPEG-7 through its ontological representation have been reported. Different approaches have been followed, ranging from those targeting direct translations pertaining to the MPEG-7 specifications, to those focusing more on the need for unambiguous, well-defined semantics of the corresponding descriptions. In the following we examine the existing approaches and discuss on the respective design rationales and issues raised. Based on such study, we present the Multimedia Content Ontology (MCO) developed within the BOEMIE project[1] for the purpose of capturing content structure and decomposition semantics in a rigid way.

The remainder of the paper is organised as follows. Section 2, briefly overviews on MPEG-7 and highlights the inherent interoperability issues, while Section 3 goes through the existing MPEG-7 ontologies, focusing on the different engineering principles followed. Section 4, presents the proposed MCO ontology, examining the objectives, engineering methodology and attained value. Finally, Section 5, concludes the paper and discusses future perspectives.

2 MPEG-7 Interoperability Issues

The MPEG-7 standard, known as ISO/ICE 15938, constitutes the greatest effort towards a common framework to multimedia description. Formally named "Multimedia Content Description Interface", it was developed by the Moving Pictured Expert Group, a working group of ISO/IEC. It aims to provide a rich set of standardised tools for the description of multimedia content and additionally support some degree of interpretation of the information's meaning, enabling thus smooth sharing and communication of multimedia metadata across applications and their efficient management, e.g. in terms of search and retrieval.

MPEG-7 consists of four main parts: the Description Definition Language (DDL), i.e. the XML-based language building blocks for the MPEG-7 metadata Schema, the Visual and Audio parts that include the description tools for visual and audio content respectively, and the Multimedia Description Schemes (MDSs), the comprise the set of Description Tools (Descriptors and Description Schemes) dealing with generic as well as multimedia entities. Generic entities are features, which are used in audio and visual descriptions and therefore "generic" to all media (e.g. vector, time, etc.). Apart from these, more complex Description Tools have been defined that can be grouped into five categories according to their functionality: i) content description, which address the representation of perceivable information, ii) content

---

[1] http://www.boemie.org/

management, which includes information about media features, creation and usage of audiovisual content, iii) content organisation, iv) navigation and access, which refers to summaries specifications and variations of content, and v) user interaction that addresses user preferences and usage history pertaining to the consumption of multimedia content. Consequently, using MPEG-7 one can construct descriptions referring to the media itself, the content conveyed, management and organisation aspects.

MPEG-7 is implemented in the form of XML Schemas that define how well-formed and valid content descriptions can be constructed. However, the intended semantics of the provided description tools are available only in the form of natural language documentation accompanying the standard's specifications, thereby leaving proper use of the description tools in the responsibility of each application/system. For example, the conceptual difference between *StillRegion* and *VideoSegment* is not, and cannot be, reflected in the corresponding XML schemas. Further ambiguities result from the flexibility adopted in the MPEG-7 specifications: the provided tools and descriptions are not associated with unique semantics. For example, the MovingRegion DS can be used to describe an arbitrary set of pixels from an arbitrary sequence of video frames, one pixel of a video frame, a video frame or even the full video sequence. This is contrary to the human cognition that perceives each of the aforementioned as conceptually different notions. Obviously such flexibility leads to many problems in terms of interoperability of the produced descriptions, and particularly with respect to the preservation of intended semantics.

In addition, MPEG-7 aiming to provide a generic framework for multimedia content description rather than committing to specific application aspects provides significant flexibility in the usage of the provided description tools. For example, describing an image of Zidane scoring can be done using among others keywords or free text, and can be done either at image or image region level, with all possible combinations conveying exactly the same meaning. However, in this paper we focus on media rather than content aspects of multimedia metadata; consequently issues related to the utilisation, alignment and coupling of domain ontologies with multimedia ones are out of scope.

As direct result of the aforementioned, different applications may produce perfectly valid MPEG-7 metadata that are however non-interoperable to each other as they implicitly conform to different conceptualisations. This practically means, that in order to access and retrieve such metadata in a uniform and integrated way, appropriate mappings and customised queries translations (e.g., expansions) need to be pre-defined.

3 State of the Art MPEG-7 Ontologies

Motivated by the advances in content annotation brought by, within the Semantic Web content, research in multimedia analysis and annotations shifted towards the exploration of Semantic Web technologies, especially for expressing the extracted content descriptions. However, as multimedia come in two layers, soon the need to formalise semantics at media level as well became apparent. As described in the following, a number of approaches have been reported targeting (partial) translations of MPEG-7 into an ontology. However, the standard's normative semantics force each author to decide individually how to interpret the semantics from the syntax and description provided, inevitably leading to different methodologies for mapping the provided XML Schema to RDFS/OWL models.

Chronologically, the first initiative to make MPEG-7 semantics explicit was taken by Hunter [3]. The RDF Schema language was proposed to formalize the Multimedia Description Scheme and the Descriptors included in the corresponding Visual and Audio parts, while later the proposed ontology was ported to OWL [4]. The translation follows the standards specifications and preserves the intended flexibility of usage, while making explicit the semantics related to the implied hierarchy by formalizing the "is-a" relations through subclass relations. As a result, the different segment types are treated as both segments (due to the subclass relation with respect to the Segment class) and multimedia content items (due to the subclass relation with respect to the MultimediaContent class). Such an approach, simplifies on one hand addresses issues with respect to part-whole semantics, e.g. a query for an image depicting Zidane would return images containing a still region depicting Zidane, but retains the issues related to semantic ambiguities, e.g. it is still not possible to differentiate conceptually a moving region from a frame or a video segment.

Two RDFS MPEG-7 based multimedia ontologies have been developed within the aceMedia project [1] in order to address the representation of the multimedia content structure and of visual description tools. The use of RDFS restricts the semantics captured to subclass and domain/range relations, however, the defined content and segment concepts are kept distinct, contrary to the approach of [4]. Furthermore, additional concepts that represent notions common to humans, such as the Frame concept, have been introduced to represent content decomposition aspects (and semantics) not present in MPEG-7.

Another effort towards an MPEG-7 based multimedia ontology has been reported within the context of the SMART Web project [6]. The developed ontology focuses on the Content Description and Content Management DSs. Two disjoint top level concepts, namely the MultimediaContent and the Segment, subsume the different content and segment types. A set of properties representing the decomposition tools specified in MPEG-7 enables the implementation of the intrinsic recursive nature of multimedia content decomposition. Although in this approach, axioms have been used to make explicit parts of the MPEG-7 intended semantics, ambiguities are present due to the fact that in many cases the defined concepts and properties semantics lie in linguistic terms used.

Contrary to the aforementioned efforts that target partial translations of MPEG-7 in a manual fashion, an initiative towards a more systematic approach to translate the complete MPEG-7 to OWL has been reported in [2]. The proposed approach is based on a generic XML Schema to OWL mapping designed to ensure that the intended semantics are preserved. The resulting MPEG-7 ontology has been validated in different ways, one of which involved its comparison against [4], which showed their semantic equivalence. However, as the resulting ontology is an OWL Full ontology, issues emerge with respect to the complexity and decidability of the applicable inferences. Another related activity refers to the work conducted in the context of the DS-MIRF framework [8], where a methodology has been presented for translating the complete MPEG-7 MDS (including content metadata, filtering metadata etc.) into OWL. The main characteristic of this approach is that the resulting MPEG-7 ontology is used as a core ontology in order to integrate domain specific annotations.

Similar to the efforts of porting MPEG-7 to an ontology, Troncy et. al. proposed to represent both the Schema and the semantics of DAVP using Semantic Web technologies [7]. An ontology has been developed to capture the DAVP Schema semantics while additional rules have been defined to capture additional constraints. Although contributing towards less ambiguous descriptions semantics and usage, the proposed approach .

4 The BOEMIE approach

From the aforementioned, it is clear that two core issues with respect to formalising MPEG-7 semantics include: modelling unambiguously conceptually distinct entities, and capturing the logical relations semantics of the considered entities. Building on the experiences gained from the existing literature, two ontologies have been implemented to address structural and audiovisual descriptors within the BOEMIE project. In the following we exemplify the proposed approach for the so called Multimedia Content Ontology (MCO), the ontology that addresses the semantics of content structure and decomposition.

Taking into account the intertwined in multimedia content media and content layers, multimedia ontologies are involved in analysis, annotation and retrieval. As such, an ontology addressing multimedia content structural aspects needs to provide the means to represent the following types of knowledge:

- The different types of media content considered, e.g. images, captioned images, web pages, video, etc.
- The semantics of decomposition of the corresponding media types into their constituent parts according to the level of the produced annotations, and
- Logical relations among the different media types, e.g. a web page may consist of a text extract, two images, and an audio sample.

Based on the identified MPEG-7 interoperability issues and the solutions proposed in the existing literature, three main challenges have been identified with respect to reaching a well-defined conceptualisation, providing cleaner semantics:

- MPEG-7 allows different Segment DS types to be used for representing the same multimedia entity. For example, to represent an image one can use both the Still-Region DS and the VideoSegment DS.

- The provided Segment Description Tools do not have unique semantics in themselves either. For example, the MovingRegion DS can be used to describe an arbitrary set of pixels from an arbitrary sequence of video frames, one pixel of one video frame, a full video frame or even the full video sequence.
- The above ambiguities extend to the decomposition relations among the different multimedia content items and types of multimedia segments. For example, a video can be temporally decomposed into segments of both the VideoSegment type and of the StillRegion type, while StillRegion type segments may result as well from a spatial decomposition

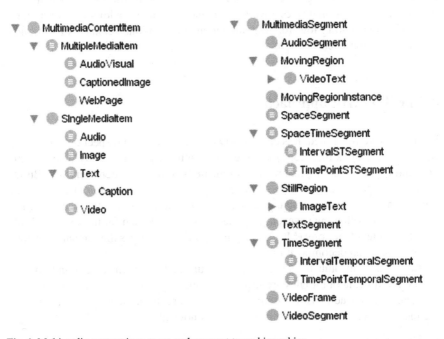

Fig. 1 Multimedia content item types and segment types hierarchies.

4.1 Multimedia Content Ontology Engineering

The MCO engineering starts with the identification of the different types of multimedia content addressed and the introduction of respective concepts. The concepts of SingleMediaItem and MultipleMediaItem have been introduced to discriminate between multimedia content items consisting of a single media item and composite ones that contain multiple different media content items (e.g., a captioned image is be defined as a type of composite content that includes an image and an associated text). Figure 1 illustrates the respective content item hierarchy. Axioms have been included to formally capture the definitions of the composite items based on the different types of content they may include, while for the single media content items respective axioms have been introduced only this time based on their decomposition properties.

The class MultimediaSegment has been introduced to represent the different types of constituent segments into which the different single media content items can be decomposed. The different types of multimedia segments have been further grouped with respect to the decomposition dimension, namely spatial, where only position information is required to identify the desired segment, temporal, where information with respect to the time point or interval is required to define the corresponding segment, and spatiotemporal, where both position and time related information is required, thus leading to the following hierarchy. As result the classes: *SpaceSegment*, *TimeSegment* and *SpaceTimeSegment* have been defined, while appropriate axioms have been introduced to define the kind of decompositions applicable to each of the three multimedia segment types, as shown in Table 1. The applicable decompositions are a direct result (semantically) of the aforementioned definitions of what constitutes a spatial, temporal and spatiotemporal segment respectively.

Table 1 Illustrative segment types definitions referring localisation attributes.

$$SpaceSegment \equiv \exists\ hasSegmentLocator.SpaceLocator$$
$$SpaceSegment \equiv \forall\ hasSegmentLocator.SpaceLocator$$
$$SpaceSegment \sqsubseteq \forall\ hasSegmentDecomposition.SpaceSegment$$
$$TimeSegment \equiv \exists\ hasSegmentLocator.TimeLocator$$
$$TimeSegment \equiv \forall\ hasSegmentLocator.TimeLocator$$
$$TimeSegment \sqsubseteq \forall\ hasSegmentDecomposition.(TimeSegment \sqcup SpaceTimeSegment)$$
$$SpaceTimeSegment \equiv \exists\ hasSegmentLocator.SpaceLocator$$
$$SpaceTimeSegment \equiv \exists\ hasSegmentLocator.TimeeLocator$$
$$SpaceTimeSegment \sqsubseteq \forall\ hasSegmentDecomposition.SpaceTimeDecomposition$$

Given the types of single media items addressed, corresponding classes of the different decomposition segments have been included, basing the definitions on restrictions with respect to the corresponding segment locator and decomposition properties. In Figure 1, the corresponding segment type hierarchy is depicted, while in Table 2, indicative segment type definitions are provided.

The concept SegmentLocator has been introduced to represent the different types of locators one can use to identify a particular segment (spatial, such as a visual mask, and temporal, such as a time interval).

A number of additional properties, not directly related to the structure of multimedia content but necessary within the BOEMIE analysis and interpretation, have been defined. These include the association of a content item with the URL providing the physical location of the file, the association of a segment/content item

Table 2 Illustrative segment types definitions referring decomposition attributes.

StillRegion ⊑ ∀ hasSegmentSpaceDecomposition StillRegion
StillRegion ⊑ ∃ hasSegmentSpaceDecomposition StillRegion
StillRegion ⊑ ∀ hasSegmentLocator.SpaceLocator
StillRegion ⊑ ∃ hasSegmentLocator.SpaceLocator
MovingRegion ⊑ ∀ hasSegmentSpaceTimeDecomposition MovingRegion
MovingRegion ⊑ ∃ hasSegmentTimeDecomposition MovingRegion
MovingRegion ⊑ ∀ hasSegmentLocator.SpaceLocator
MovingRegion ⊑ ∃ hasSegmentLocator.TimeLocator

to the domain concepts it depicts and its respective ABox (as a URL including the respective domain-specific instances).

The aforementioned definitions, in combination with the disjointness axiom defined between the MultimediaContentItem and MultimediaSegment classes, enforce distinct semantics to the different segment and decomposition types, overcoming the respective ambiguities present in relevant MPEG-7 specifications part and in parts of the existing MPEG-7 ontologies. Thus, cleaner semantics are achieved, while, and most importantly, well-defined inference services can be applied to ensure the semantic coherency of the produced annotations. The corresponding ontology files can be accessed at *http://www.boemie.org/*.

4.2 Instantiation Example

In this subsection, we provide an annotation example based on the developed Multimedia Content Ontology. Assuming a captioned image depicting Feovana Svetlanova's pole vault trial, the assertions utilising the proposed MCO are shown in Table 3, where the *N3* notation has been used for readability purposes, and *aeo* corresponds to the athletics domain ontology that provides the domain specific vocabulary. Contrary to the use of pure XML Schema, the underlying MPEG-7 based ontology assists in meaning disambiguation. For example, assuming the mco:Image assertion was omitted, i.e. that the type of individual *Image1* is not explicitly specified, there would be no ambiguity to whether it represents a content item or a segment. The ontology axioms explicitly entail that only members of the mco:Image class can be decomposed into still regions, while at the same time participating in decompositions of content items encompassing more than one modality. Were it pure XML, this would not have been possible, unless the decomposition tools, specific to the referred segment type had been used. Furthermore, ambiguities related to equivocal semantics are alleviated; for example, the mco:Image assertion specifically represents an instance of a still image, neither a partition of it (a still region), nor a frame of a video sequence. The aforementioned example, despite being a very simple one, already showed some advantages from deploying formal semantics. As the complexity of content descriptions increases, such benefits manifest themselves further.

Table 3 Example annotation utilising the MCO of an image depicting a high jump attempt of an athlete.

$$mco : Image(Image1)$$
$$mco : Caption(Caption1)$$
$$mco : CaptionedImage(CaptionedImage1)$$
$$mco : contains(CaptionedImage1, Image1)$$
$$mco : contains(CaptionedImage1, Caption1)$$
$$mco : hasURL(CaptionedImage1, ``http : //..pole_vault1.jpg")$$
$$mco : StillRegion(StillRegion1)$$
$$mco : hasMediaDecomposition(Image1, StillRegion1)$$
$$mco : Mask(Mask1)$$
$$mco : hasSegmentLocator(StillRegion1, Mask1)$$
$$hasURL(Mask1, ``http : //..mask - url.."$$
$$mco : hasMediaDecomposition(Image1, StillRegion2)$$
$$mco : StillRegion(StillRegion2)$$
$$mco : hasSegmentLocator(StillRegion2, Contour2)$$
$$mco : Contour(Contour2)$$
$$hasURL(Contour2, ``http : //..contour - url..")$$
$$mco : depicts(StillRegion1, PersonFace1)$$
$$aeo : PersonFace(PersonFace1)$$
$$mco : depicts(StillRegion2, HorizontalBar1)$$
$$aeo : HorizontalBar(HorizontalBar1)$$
$$mco : TextSegment(TextSegment1)$$
$$mco : hasMediaDecomposition(Caption1, TextSegment1)$$
$$mco : TokenLocator(TokenLocator1)$$
$$mco : hasSegmentLocator(TextSegment1, TokenLocator1)$$
$$mco : StartCharacter(StartCharacter1)$$
$$mco : EndCharacter(EndCharacter1)$$
$$mco : hasOffsetValue(StartCharacter1, ``0")$$
$$mco : hasOffsetValue(EndCharacter1, ``17")$$
$$mco : depicts(TextSegment1, PersonName1)$$
$$aeo : PersonName(PersonName1)$$
$$aeo : hasPersonNameValue(PersonName1, ``FeovanaSvetlanova")$$

5 Conclusions and Perspectives

MPEG-7 constitutes the greatest effort towards standardised multimedia content descriptions, comprising a rich set of broad coverage tools. Aiming to serve as a common framework, it builds on a generic schema, allowing for great flexibility in its usage, a feature partially accountable for the confronted interoperability issues, the other main reason being the lack of formal semantics that would render such descriptions unambiguous. On the other hand, the Semantic Web provides the languages and means to express, exchange and process the semantics of information.

The aforementioned study reveals two core issues with respect to formalizing MPEG-7 intended semantics: modelling unambiguously conceptually distinct entities, and capturing the logical relations semantics of the considered entities. The former is a prerequisite to ensure interoperability among the different existing MPEG-7 ontologies, and to allow the definition of respective mappings. The latter forms a key enabling factor for truly utilizing the expressivity and inference services provided by ontologies. The significance of providing interoperable formal semantics is further emphasized by initiatives such as the Multimedia Semantics (MMSEM) Incubator Group[2], a standardization activity of the World Wide Web Consortium (W3C) that aims at providing a common framework for achieving semantic interoperability and the Common Multimedia Ontology Framework[3].

The presented Multimedia Content Ontology although not providing an immediate solution towards interoperable multimedia metadata, constitutes a valuable contribution towards a cleaner conceptualisation of media related aspects that allows the utilisation of ontology reasoners in order to assess the semantic consistency of the produced annotations. Ensuring precise media semantics is of significant importance for the realisation of a multimedia enabled Web, as it strongly relates to the feasibility of applications involving semantic handling of multimedia content, as for example multimedia presentation generation applications, hypermedia ontology-frameworks, and of course all services involving semantic-based annotation and retrieval of multimedia content.

Acknowledgements This work was partially supported by European Commission under contract FP6-027538 BOEMIE. Also supported by the research project PENED 2003 Ontomedia (03EΔ475), cofinanced 75% of public expenditure through EC-European Social Fund, 25% of public expenditure through Greek Ministry of Development-General Secretariat of Research and Technology and through private sector, under measure 8.3 of OPERATIONAL PROGRAMME "COMPETITIVENESS"in the 3rd Community Support Programme.

References

1. Bloehdorn, S. et. al. : Semantic Annotation of Images and Videos for Multimedia Analysis. Proc. ESWC, Heraklion, Crete, Greece, May 29 - June, 592–607 (2005)
2. Garcia, R., and Celma, O.: Semantic Integration and Retrieval of Multimedia Metadata. Proc. ISWC, Galway, Ireland, Nov. 6-10 (2005)
3. Hunter, J.: Adding Multimedia to the Semantic Web: Building an MPEG-7 Ontology. Proc. 1st Semantic Web Working Symposium, Stanford University, California, USA, July 30 - August 1, 261–283 (2001)
4. Hunter, J., Drennan, J., Little, S.: Realizing the Hydrogen Economy through Semantic Web Technologies. IEEE Intelligent Systems, (1):January, 40–47 (2004)
5. Martinez, J.M. (editor). : Overview of the MPEG-7 Standard (v4.0) ISO/MPEG N3752.
6. Oberle, D. et.al. : DOLCE ergo SUMO: On Foundational and Domain Models in SWIntO (SmartWeb Integrated Ontology). Tech. Report, AIFB, University of Karlsruhe. July (2006)
7. Troncy, R. et. al.: Enabling Multimedia Metadata Interoperability by Defining Formal Semantics of MPEG-7 Profiles. Proc. SAMT, Athens, Greece, December 6-8, 41–55 (2006)
8. Tsinaraki, C. et. al.: Ontology-Based Semantic Indexing for MPEG-7 and TV-Anytime Audiovisual Content. Multimedia Tools Appli. 26(3), 299–325 (2005)

---

[2] $http://www.w3.org/2005/Incubator/mmsem/$

[3] $http://www.acemedia.org/aceMedia/reference/multimedia\_ontology/$

On the requirements of Learning Object Metadata for adults' educators of special groups

Maria Pavlis Korres[1]

Abstract In the development of educational material for adults' educators of special groups within an e-learning environment it is important to follow the IEEE Learning Object Metadata (LOM) specifications in order to enhance the retrieval, interoperability, and reusability. One of the factors affecting directly the educational procedure is the compatibility between educator and learners. In order to provide the proper educational material to each educator, its important properties have to be linked with the existing IEEE LOM elements and a number of additional LOM elements have to be defined and proposed as extensions, vocabularies and ontologies. In this case the adults' educator of special groups is defined under "intended user role", the "educational objectives" are customized and the notion of the new term "compatibility" is accommodated under a new purpose in the classification category "special attributes". In this way, the proper Learning Object (LO) according to each educator's needs can be retrieved by using the Learning Object's Metadata.

1. Introduction

E-learning material and applications help educators to overcome problems of conventional learning, such as place, time and cost, enhancing also personalized learning [1, 5, 14, 26, 28, 31, 32]

In the context of e-learning technology, standards are generally developed to be used in systems design and implementation for the purposes of ensuring retrieval, interoperability and reusability. These attributes should apply to the systems themselves, as well as the content and the metadata they manage [10]. The development of technical standards and specifications in e-learning can be seen as part of the maturation of this recently emerging field or industry [10].

Maria Pavlis Korres
Computer Science Dept., University of Alcalá, Spain, email:eumarcor@otenet.gr

According to the widely accepted IEEE Learning Object Metadata (LOM) specifications [15], the characteristics of a Learning Object (LO) are grouped under certain categories: general, life-cycle, meta-metadata, technical, educational, rights, relation, annotation, classification. However, the LOM standard is a general-purpose specification and in many cases it does not capture the specificities of certain domains. The notion of profiles serves as a means for devising specializations of the LOM schema for concrete purposes. *The specific purpose considered here is that of the training of adults' educators of special groups.*

2. Adults' educators of special groups

With the term *special group* we define the social group whose characteristics (social, cultural, ethnic, linguistic, physical etc.) cause to its members social exclusion, marginalization and stigmatization (i.e. immigrants, Gypsies, repatriated-refugees, prisoners/ex-cons, ex-addicts, persons with special needs etc).

For the effective training of adults' educators of special groups one of the key elements is the specialization on adults' education focusing on *the characteristics of adults as learners, the effective ways through which adults are learning* and *the role of the educator* [17, 18, 25].

Additionally, educators of special groups need extra training, on *the characteristics of the special group they have to deal with* and they also need *to be aware of their own attitudes towards the group, to reflect critically on these attitudes and to seek transformation and improvement* [9, 11, 12, 13, 24, 29].

A further analysis of the above elements is important in order to provide the necessary background information on adults' educators of special groups.

2.1 Special characteristics of adults as learners and the requirements for effective adult learning

Adults as learners have specific characteristics that set them apart from children. As one might expect, these characteristics are varied, however there seems to be a general consensus in the literature [3, 7, 17, 19, 25] on some common characteristics that have an impact on learning efficacy and the overall classroom experience:

a. Adults participate in the learning process with specific intents, goals and expectations
b. Adults already have certain knowledge and experience as well as fixed perspectives
c. Adults have already developed personal styles of learning
d. Adults are bound to self-directed activities throughout their lives
e. Adults have to deal with certain obstacles on their learning process

The main requirements for effective adult learning are defined by taking into consideration the above mentioned characteristics and looking into bibliography [6, 7, 16, 23, 25]. These requirements are:

a. Education is centered on the learner
b. The active participation of the learners is both encouraged and intended
c. The creation of a learning environment based on communication, cooperation and mutual respect.

2.2 Requirements for the effective training of special groups

Further to the specific characteristics and requirements of adults as learners, the educator of special groups has to deal with issues such as prejudices, stereotypes, discrimination, stigma and social exclusion.

The recognition, knowledge, appreciation and respect of the diversity of the special group by the educators through critical reflection [4] as well as the transformation of the educators themselves [12, 22] is necessary for a multicultural educational environment, which values diversity and appreciates differences [27]. In any situation in which the participants' experiences are ignored or devalued, adults will perceive this as rejecting not only their experience, but rejecting themselves as persons [20].

The acquisition of the essential knowledge about adults and special groups and, more importantly, the development of the desired skills, as well as the development and transformation of the required attitudes are indispensable to all adults' educators of special groups, regardless of the topic each educator is teaching.

3. Compatibility between educator and learner in adults' education of special groups

With the term *compatibility* we refer to the level of knowledge and positive attitude of the educator, as well as his/her acceptance of the special group.

The type of compatibility between adults' educators of special groups and the respective learners varies in relation with the parameters that define the specific special group itself. These parameters can be *social, cultural, ethnic, linguistic or physical.*

The higher the level of compatibility between educator and learner, the more efficient will be their approach to the special group, regardless of the subject the educator is teaching. When we have to deal with a special group, the knowledge, the positive attitude and the respect of the characteristics of the group not only facilitate the communication between educator and learners which is essential for the educational procedure [9], but also satisfies the safety, the love and belonging as well as the self-esteem needs of the learners for their social acceptance, and ensures that their identity is not threatened. The above needs have to be satisfied in order for the learners to be able to satisfy the cognitive needs (the desire to know and to understand) according to Maslow's hierarchy of needs [21].

If the compatibility between educator and special group is not taken into account there is a risk to either provide to an educator boring and oversimplifying material or a complex and difficult one. This, in other words, means that one might fail matching the educational material with the needs and the interests of each educator and affect negatively the educational outcome.

4. Learning Objects and their Metadata

The training material for the adults' educators of special groups is LOs. In order for these LOs to be described properly, their important properties have to be linked with the existing IEEE LOM elements and a number of additional LOM elements must be defined and proposed as extensions.

Metadata systems allow for extensions so that particular needs of a given application can be accommodated [8]. Such extensions may take the form of new terms for existing vocabularies, new vocabularies for existing elements or new elements.

As [30] quotes Online education is still too much in its infancy to presume to create all necessary and adequate meta-data fields and vocabularies. Therefore, it is also possible to include concepts that are not included in the standard LOM. This is one of the intended purposes of Classification.

In the present application which is the development of educational material for the training of adults' educators of special groups within an e-learning environment, we have to form new terms and taxonomies/ontologies which further specify existing vocabularies (5.5. intended end user role) and create extensions in the form of taxonomies/ontologies which indicate the educational objectives, and the new element of compatibility between educator and learner (9.1.classification.purpose). These taxonomies/ontologies will provide the proper information pertaining to the particular domain of the training of adults' educators of special groups under the broad term purpose.

As the notion of compatibility could not be presented in any of the existing purposes in classification category, a new purpose under the name "special attributes" is created in order to accommodate compatibility between educator and learner, as well as provide space where any learning object with specific attributes can be accommodated under classification purpose.

More precisely:

a.   The following diagram is indicative of this proposal and presents a hierarchical taxonomy beginning with the broad term "intended end user role" and refining its vocabulary term "teacher":

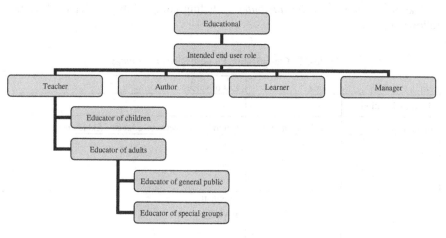

Fig 4.1.: *A new taxonomy refining the term "teacher"*

b.   In category 9.1.Classification.Purpose existing taxonomies serving the description of the educational material are used and new taxonomies/ontologies are created in order to provide the proper information pertaining to the particular domain of the training of adults' educators of special groups.

The information about the educational domain in which a Learning Object belongs contained in standard classification schemes {i.e.LCC (Library of Congess Classification)} is either too general (i.e. LB 1705-2286: Education and training of teachers and administrators, LC212-212.863: The discrimination in education,) or too specific (i.e. LC2667-2698: Latin Americans.Hispanic Americans, LC3503-3520: Romanies. Gypsies). Therefore, we can not properly and accurately classify our significant information (compatibility between educator and learner) in any of the existing categories.

In the following example existing taxonomies have been used under existing purposes, *discipline* and *educational objectives*, and a new purpose, *special attributes,* has been added with a new taxonomy under the broad term "compatibility between educator and learner".

9.1.Classification.Purpose.*Dicsipline* / taxonpath: LCC / taxon id: L / entry:education / taxon id: LC1390-5160.3 / entry: Education of special classes of persons / taxon id: LB1705-2286 / entry: Education and training of teachers and administrators.

9.1.Classification.Purpose.*Educational objectives* / taxonpath: "Bloom's learning taxonomy" [2] / "http://www.nwlink.com/~donclark/hrd/bloom.html / Cognitive objectives, Affective objectives.

The new purpose *special attributes* including compatibility is depicted in the following table:

Table 4.1.: Classification.Purpose.*Special attributes*

No	Name	List of values
9.1.Classification	-	-
purpose	Special attributes	Compatibility between educator and learner
-	-	Cultural
		Ethnic
		Social
		Linguistic
		Physical

In reference with the element compatibility, we must define the vocabulary to be used:

- *Social compatibility*: It defines the level of knowledge, of positive attitude and acceptance of the social status of the special group by the educator.

- *Cultural compatibility*: It describes the level of knowledge, of positive attitude and acceptance of the culture of the special group by the educator
- *Ethnic compatibility*: It describes the level of knowledge, of positive attitude and acceptance of the ethnic identity of the special group by the educator
- *Linguistic compatibility*: It describes the level of knowledge, positive attitude and acceptance of the linguistic identity and specialties of the special group by the educator
- *Physical compatibility*: It describes the level of knowledge, positive attitude and acceptance of the disabilities/impairments of the special group by the educator
- *Values* for all the above types of compatibility are: very low, low, medium, high, very high

It is obvious that without the new taxonomies for the extension of existing vocabularies and the new extensions created for the classification of the compatibility between educator and learner, a learning object dealing with these issues will be lacking the necessary metadata which would ensure its interoperability, retrieval and reusability.

5.   Example

In order to specify the LOM profile for a LO concerning adults' educators of special groups in a more concrete manner, an example is provided, based on a LO for the training of educators for the special group of Gypsies (Roma) in Greece. The educators who address to special groups are not a homogenous group. That means that they have different levels of compatibility with the special group. It is fundamental for the educational procedure to assess and improve the level of the educators' compatibility with the group with which they are dealing. It is also important for the educational material to match with their needs and interests.

The example LO consists of oral instructions in romanes (gypsy language) to fill a simple form in greek. The instructions contain only some greek words like certification, deadline and prohibited.

The educators implementing this activity have the opportunity to realize and empathize the linguistic difficulties which Gypsies are facing when they have to deal with the authorities and fill up forms in greek. After that, the educators are asked to fill a questionnaire in greek language concerning the difficulties they faced.

This LO is addressed to educators with very low linguistic and cultural compatibility. Assuming that one of our educators is a Gypsy, one has worked with Gypsies in the past and another has never been in contact with Gypsies, it is obvious that the above LO has different value for each one of them, because of the different compatibility of each educator in the linguistic and cultural sector.

The only way to avoid giving the same educational material to both the gypsy (for whom it has no meaning) and a person with no previous contact with gypsies(for whom it is very important) is the proper description of the LO through its metadata.

The main metadata of this LO according to IEEE LOM [15] specifications will be:

1.General / 1.2.Title: Linguistic difficulties of Gypsies(Roma) learners / 1.3.Language: "el" "rom" / 1.4.Description: An activity which focuses on the linguistic difficulties which the Gypsies (Roma) learners face in daily life and in the learning procedures / 1.5.Keywords: oral language, bilingualism, linguistic difficulties.

4.Technical / 4.1.Format: Audio WAV, Text.

5.Educational / 5.1.Interactivity type: Mixed / 5.2.Learning resource type: Narrative, Text, Questionnaire / 5.3.Interactivity level: Low / *5.5.Intented end user role: Adults' Educator of special groups* /, 5.6.Context: Training: Continuous professional development / 5.8.Difficulty: Easy.

9.1.Classification.Purpose.Discipline: LC1390-5160.3 / Education of special classes of persons / LB1705-2286 / Education and training of teachers and administrators.

9.1. Classification.Purpose.Educational objectives: Specialization on Gypsies issues, Realization and awareness of stereotypes, prejudices and attitudes concerning Gypsies.

A new purpose *special attributes* is created to accommodate the notion of compatibility, as shown in the following table.

Table 5.1.: Classification.Purpose.Special attributes (example)

Element	Sub-element	Datatype	Values
9.Classificati on	9.1.Purpose.Speci al attributes	Compatibility between educator and learner	
-	-	Linguistic Cultural	Very low Very low

By including the new taxonomy in the metadata of the specific LO it becomes apparent that this LO is addressed only to educators with very low linguistic and cultural compatibility.

6. Conclusion

In order to enhance retrieval, interoperability, portability and reusability of Learning Objects for the training of adults' educators of special groups their metadata have to be described and classified under IEEE LOM specifications with the appropriate extensions, vocabularies and taxonomies/ ontologies. Moreover, the additional purpose "special attributes" in classification catergory allows the proper description of any LO containing properties that could not be classified under IEEE LOM specification.

References

1. Beatty, K.: Describing and Enhancing Collaboration at the Computer. Canadian Journal of Learning and Technology, Volume 28(2) Spring / printemps (2002)
2. Bloom, B.S., Krathwohl D.R.: Taxonomy of Educational Objectives. New York, David McKay, (1964)
3. Brookfield, S.: Understanding and Facilitating Adult Learning. Open University Press (1986)
4. Brookfield, S. Becoming a Critically Reflective Teacher. Jossey-Bass Publishers, San Francisco (1995)
5. Conceicao, S.: Faculty lived experiences in the online environment. Adult Education Quarterly, Vol. 57, No. 1, pp. 26-45 (2006)
6. Courau, S.: Les outils d'excellence du formateur. 2th edition, ESF editeur, Paris (1994)
7. Cross, K.P. : Adults as Learners. Jossey-Bass, San Francisco (1981)
8. Duval, E., Hodgins W., Sutton S., Weibel S. L.: Metadata, principles and practicalities. D-LibMagazine,8(4) (2002) Retrieved in March 2007 from http://www.dlib.org/dlib/april02/weibel/04weibel.html,
9. Freire, P.: The pedagogy of the oppressed. New York: Herder and Herded (1970)
10. Friesen, N.: Interoperability and Learning Objects: An Overview of E-Learning Standardization. Interdisciplinary Journal of Knowledge and Learning Objects 1 (2005)
11. Goffman, E.:, Stigma: Notes on the Management of Spoiled Identity. Prentice-Hall (1963)
12. Gorski, P.: Transforming Myself to Transform My School (2001) retrieved in March 2007 from www.edchange.org/multicultural/papers/edchange_10thinls.html

13.G.S.A.E. (General Secretariat of Adults' Education, Greek Ministry of Education) : Educational curriculum for the training of Gypsy Mediators. European Initiative:Employment/Integra 1998-2000. Athens (1999)

14.Hew, K. F, Cheung, W. S.: An exploratory study on the use of asynchronous online discussion. In hypermedia design, Nanyang Technological University Singapore, retrieved in May 2007 in www.usq.edu.au/electpub/e-jist/docs/Vol6_No1/an_exploratory_study_on_the_use_.htm

15.IEEE LOM - http://ltsc.ieee.org/wg12/files/LOM_1484_12_1_v1_Final_Draft.pdf

16.Jaques, D. : Learning in groups. Kogan Page (2000)

17.Jarvis, P.:, Adult and continuing education. Theory and practice. London and New York, Routledge (1995)

18.Knowles, M. S : Andragogy in Action. Applying modern principles of adult education. San Francisco: Jossey Bass (1984)

19.Knowles, M. S.; The adult learner: A neglected species. Gulf Publishing, Houston (1990)

20.Knowles M.S.: The Adult Learner. Gulf Publishing Company, Houston, Texas (1998)

21.Maslow, A.: Motivation and Personality. 2nd. ed., New York, Harper & Row (1970)

22.Mezirow J.: Transformative dimensions of adult learning. San Francisco, Jossey-Bass (1991)

23.Noye, D., Piveteau, J. : Guide pratique du formateur. INSEP Editions (1997)

24.Quicke, J., Beasley, K. Morrison, C.; Challenging Prejudice through Education. The Falmer Press, U.K. London, (1990)

25.Rogers, A.: Teaching Adults. Open University Press (1996)

26.Sadler-Smith E., Smith P.: Strategies for accommodating individuals' styles and preferences in flexible learning programmes . British Journal of Educational Technology, Vol 35 No 4 , pp. 395-412 (2004)

27.Shaw -Cooper, C.: Critical issue: educating teachers for diversity. Retrieved in March 2007 from www.ncrel.org/sdrs/areas/issues/educatrs/presrvce/pe300.htm

28.Smith R.: Working with difference in online collaborative groups. Adult Education Quarterly, Vol. 55, No. 3, pp. 182-199 (2005)

29.Tomlinson, S.: A Sociology of Special Education. London :Routledge and Kegan Paul (1982)

30.Wason, T.: Dr. Tom's Taxonomy Guide: Description, Use and Selections, (2006) http://www.twason.com/drtomtaxonomiesguide.html

31.Ziegahn, L.: Talk' about culture online: The potential for transformation. Distance Education, 22:1, pp. 144 - 150 (2001)

32.Ziegahn, L.: Critical Reflection on cultural difference in the Computer Conference. Adult Education Quarterly, 11 2005; vol. 56: pp. 39 – 64 (2005)

Abbreviations

IEEE: Institute of Electrical and Electronics Engineers
LCC: Library of Congess Classification
LOM: Learning Object Metadata
LO(s): Learning Object(s).

Quality Metrics in Learning Objects

Juan F. Cervera, María G. López-López, Cristina Fernández, Salvador Sánchez-Alonso

Abstract. In today's rapidly evolving society, the range and depth of information available to us is quickly growing which affects educational institutions, who find it difficult to keep their programmes up to date, whilst students struggle to find the right information. The paradigm of learning objects is an emerging technology aimed towards facilitating the managements of the massive amount of (educational) resources available. Enabling users relying on this paradigm to use concise and high quality pieces of knowledge within different contexts represents a key challenge. Therefore, when designing learning objects, reusability must be a key consideration. Bearing this in mind, the current lack of metrics to help measure quality and reusability represents a major issue. Specific metrics for learning objects will eventually appear, probably based on extended and improved metadata. In the meantime, there remains the need to measure the potential reusability of the existing base of learning objects. This paper attempts to bridge this gap by analysing and developing adapted metrics for learning objects, based on existing metrics used in other disciplines such as software engineering.

1 Introduction

This paper extends the theoretical framework proposed by Cuadrado in his paper about learning object reusability metrics [1], which explores the possibility of using existing metrics, such as Chidamber and Kemerer Object Oriented metrics [2], and adapting them to the domain of learning objects (LO).

Juan F. Cervera
Information Engineering Research Unit, University of Alcalá, Alcalá de Henares, SPAIN, jfcervera@gmail.com
María G. López-López
Centro de Investigación en Sistemas de Información (CISI), Escuela de Computación, Facultad de Ciencias, Universidad Central de Venezuela, Caracas, Venezuela, lopezgertrudis@gmail.com
Cristina Fernández
Information Engineering Research Unit, University of Alcalá, Alcalá de Henares, SPAIN
Salvador Sánchez-Alonso
Information Engineering Research Unit, University of Alcalá, Alcalá de Henares, SPAIN, salvador.sanchez@uah.es

135

The objective of this paper is to show how we adapted, applied and tested statistically some of the metrics proposed in [1] to LOs. The purpose of this exercise was to see if these adapted metrics could provide useful results about reusability and quality of LOs, by means of correlations between the metrics and metadata. The metrics we adapted and tested were as follows: Weighted Methods per Class (WCM), Depth of Inheritance Tree (DIT), Response for a Class (RFC), Coupling Between Objects (CBO) and Lack of Cohesion on Methods (LCOM).

In order to check whether the metrics performed consistently across different knowledge areas, they were applied to two random samples of LOs selected from the Merlot repository 1; one for Computer Science LOs and another one for Biology LOs. The metadata fields used were size in bytes, granularity, number of links, peer review average (Merlot-exclusive), and member comments average (Merlot-exclusive).

2 Adapted Object-Oriented metrics

Object Oriented Software engineering techniques have been a source of influence on the design of LOs [3] [4]. In this sense, LOs can be considered particular software pieces oriented towards human interaction. Some metrics developed in the context of Software Engineering, which work with concepts such as dependency and complexity, may have a clear correlation with LO technology [1]. The original Chidamber and Kemerer Object oriented (OO) metrics to measure reusability [2] needed to be adapted before they could be used with LOs. This section explains the adaptation of each metric that we used.

2.1 Weighted Methods per Class (WMC)

The definition of this metric, according to [2], is as follows: "WMC relates directly to Bunge's definition of complexity of a thing, since methods are properties of object classes and complexity is determined by the cardinality of its set of properties. The number of methods is, therefore, a measure of class definition as well as being attributes of a class, since attributes correspond to properties". The approach taken in [1] to adapting this metric for LOs is as follows: "The resulting metric for learning objects would be consistent with the current consideration that only learning objects of "fine granularity" may offer a high degree of reusability".

One of the IEEE LOM metadata fields is the *aggregation level* of the LO, which is based on the granularity of the LO and measured on a scale from 1 to 4, 1 being the smallest level of aggregation and 4 the largest level of granularity. We have used this value for the adapted WCM metric.

---

1 http://www.merlot.org

2.2 Depth of the Inheritance Tree (DIT) / Response for Class (RFC)

According to [2], DIT is defined as follows: "Depth of inheritance of the class is the DIT metric for the class. In cases involving multiple inheritance, the DIT will be the maximum length from the node to the root of the tree." The definition for RFC is "The response set of a class is a set of methods that can potentially be executed in response to a message received by an object of that class".

As explained in [1], "Inheritance depth as a driver for increased complexity applies in a similar way to LOs, since subtyping entails the requirement of more detailed metadata elements".

As subtyping applied to LO is still in the early stages, the right kind of information for calculating a DIT metric is, unfortunately, not available in the metadata. Therefore, most existing learning objects will never contain this information.

The approach we have used consists of checking the depth of the links of a LO, as this information is available in the current metadata. This approach keeps the original idea of Depth and, as it is applied to links and it also resembles concepts from the RFC metric.

2.3 Coupling Between Objects (CBO)

The definition given for this metric, according to [2] is "CBO for a class is a count of the number of other classes to which it is coupled". In [1], Cuadrado argues that this metric can be directly applied to a LO's relationship with other LOs and can be defined with current metadata.

Therefore, we have adapted this metric by checking the coupling of a LO with other LOs. Had LOM metadata been available, this information could have been extracted from the relation metadata field. As it was not, it has been calculated manually. Every link to a different LO was counted towards the value of the metric; LOs with no links to other LOs were given a value of 0 for this metric.

2.4 Lack of Cohesion on Methods (LCOM)

The definition of this metric according to [2] is "The LCOM is a count of the number of method pairs whose similarity is 0 (i.e. σ() is a null set) minus the count of method pairs whose similarity is not zero. The larger the number of similar methods, the more cohesive the class ...". In [1], Cuadrado reasons that "... it can be stated that learning objectives [..] can be regarded metaphorically as attributes of the class. In consequence, disparateness of objectives [..] are indicators for ill-defined objectives, which hampers reuse".

Consequently, this metric was adapted by checking whether the objectives/subjects of a LO were concrete enough, or whether it was possible to split the LO into several, more concrete LOs. The metric was measured by the number of different objectives that could be extracted into smaller LOs, being 0 when a single educational objective was covered.

3 Analysis and results

To analyse the aplicability of existing OO metrics to the LOs domain, we run correlations between the adapted metrics and empirical metadata. As previously said, part of this data has been obtained from the Merlot repository, while the remainder was calculated by hand.We have selected two groups of 25 LOs from two different knowledge areas: Computer Science and Biology. The LOs have been randomly selected from theMerlot repository. The metadata obtained and calculated for each LO was as follows:

- Title: The title of the LO
- URL: The URL of the LO
- WCM: The results of the adapted WCM metric
- DIT/RFC: The results of the adapted DIT/RFC metric
- CBO: The results of the adapted CBO metric
- LCOM: The results of the adapted LCOM metric
- Size: Size of the LO in bytes
- NL: Number of links
- PR: Peer reviews average from the Merlot repository
- MC: Member comments average from the Merlot repository

In this section we present the correlations obtained between the metrics and the metadata using three different correlation coefficients: Pearson's correlation coefficient (P), Kendall's tau-b coefficient (K) and Spearman's rho coefficient (S). Table 1 shows the correlation coefficients obtained in the Computer Science group, where we found significant correlations between the CBO metric and the Number of Links at the 0.01 level for all types of correlation. We also found a significant correlation level of 0.05 between the LCOM metric and the Number of Links, but only for the Pearson correlation.

---

[1] http://www.merlot.org

Table 1. Pearson, Kendall and Spearman Correlation results obtained in LOs of Computer Science.

	Size	NL	PR	MC
WMC	P=-0,179	P=0,209	P=0,096	P=0,209
	K=-0,165	K=0,237	K=-0,005	K=0,237
	S=-0,190	S=0,279	S=-0,002	S=0,279
DIT/RFC	P=-0,056	P=0,074	P=0,293	P=0,011
	K=0,043	K=0,168	K=0,177	K=-0,091
	S=0,042	S=0,218	S=0,205	S=-0,123
CBO	P=0,160	P=0,963**	P=0,158	P=-0,199
	K=0,261	K=0,879**	K=0,281	K=-0,123
	S=0,334	S=0,961**	S=0,359	S=-0,163
LCOM	P=0,102	P=0,635*	P=-0,153	P=0,058
	K=0,110	K=0,297	K=-0,032	K=0,049
	S=0,159	S=0,354	S=-0,039	S=0,049

- P: Pearson's correlation coefficient
- K: Kendall's Tau-b correlation coefficient
- S: Spearman's rho coefficient

** Correlation is significant at the 0.01 level (2-tailed)
* Correlation is significant at the 0.05 level (2-tailed)

Table 2 shows the correlation coefficients obtained for the Biology group, where we obtained significant correlations between the WCM metric and the Number of Links at the significance level of 0.01 for the Kendall and Spearman correlations and at the significance level of 0.05 for the Pearson correlation. We obtained correlations between the CBO metric and the Number of Links at the 0.01 level in all correlation types. We also obtained significant correlations between the CBO metric and the Peer Reviews Average at the 0.01 level for the Kendall and Spearman correlations and at the 0.05 level for the Pearson correlation.

Table 2. Pearson, Kendall and Spearman Correlation results obtained in LOs of Biology.

	Size	NL	PR	MC
WCM	P=0,278	P=0,497*	P=0,215	P=0,303
	K=0,280	K=0,524**	K=0,117	K=0,278
	S=0,342	S=0,634**	S=0,143	S=0,317
DIT/RFC	P=0,017	P=0,189	P=0,204	P=0,104
	K=0,010	K=0,272	K=0,265	K=0,060
	S=0,031	S=0,371	S=0,343	S=0,084
CBO	P=0,075	P=0,633**	P=0,448*	P=0,186
	K=0,211	K=0,633**	K=0,449**	K=0,109
	S=0,224	S=0,784**	S=0,549**	S=0,138
LCOM	P=0,026	P=0,297	P=0,281	P=0,021
	K=0,104	K=0,270	K=0,179	K=-0,005
	S=0,151	S=0,343	S=0,208	S=-0,007

- P: Pearson's correlation coefficient
- K: Kendall's Tau-b correlation coefficient
- S: Spearman's rho coefficient

** Correlation is significant at the 0.01 level (2-tailed)
* Correlation is significant at the 0.05 level (2-tailed)

4 Conclusions and future work

The correlation data calculated shows that the CBO metric has a strong correlation with the metadata Number of Links. As the adapted CBO metric is based on the number of links to other LOs, this result was expected.

The CBO metric has a less strong but, nevertheless, noticeable correlation with the Peer Reviews Average metadata for the Biology group only. The LCOM metric displays a noticeable correlation with the metadata Number of Links for the Pearson's coefficient in the Computer Science group only. If we consider that LOs covering several objectives are more likely to have additional links to access every objective, we would have expected a stronger correlation with this metric.

The WMC metric displays a strong correlation with the metadata Number of Links for the Biology group only. The DIT/RCF metric does not display any particular correlation with any metadata.

With the exception of the CBO metric in the Biology group, there are no strong correlations between any of the other metrics and the Peer Reviews Average metadata, nor between the metrics and the Member Comments Average metadata. Taking into account that these fields provide a measure of the quality of the LO based on evaluation by experts and end users, ideally we would look for stronger correlations between the metrics and these two metadata. This result suggests that the Peer Reviews Average and Member Comments Average metadata in the Merlot repository do not consider the reusability of LOs.

Taking into account the lack of strong correlations based on this analysis alone, we feel that further work along these lines could yield more conclusive results. However, it is important to stress that there are no theoretical requirements to have strong correlations between metrics and LO metadata. Therefore, the lack of strong correlations should not necessarily be taken as an indicator of metric validity.

In summary, we feel that we need to broaden the study scope to encompass a greater number of metrics, a larger number of LOs and an additional number of statistical and empirical tests, which should be applied to a greater number of knowledge areas, in order to prove whether using metrics borrowed from other areas of software engineering can be applied to LOs.

---

[1] http://www.merlot.org

References

1. Cuadrado JJ, Sicilia MA (2005). Learning Object Reusability Metrics: Some Ideas from Software Engineering, International Conference on Internet Technologies and Applications ITA 2005
2. Chidamber S, Kemerer C (1994). A metric suit for object oriented design, IEEE Transactions on Software Engineering, 20(6)
3. Sosteric M, Hesemeier S (2002). When a Learning Object is not an Object: A first step towards a theory of learning objects. International Review of Research in Open and Distance Learning Journal, 3(2)
4. Sicilia MA, Sachez-Alonso S (2003). On the Concept of 'Learning Objeject Design by Contract', WSEAS Transactions. on systems, Oct. 2003, vol. 2, issue 3

A New Proposal for Heterogeneous Data Integration to XML format. Application to the Environment of Libraries

Ana Mª Fermoso[1*], Roberto Berjón [1], Encarnación Beato[1], Montserrat Mateos[1], Miguel Angel Sánchez[1], Maribel Manzano García[1], María José Gil[2]

Abstract   Organizations have to work with large volumes of information at different formats. In this context they are necessary tools and formats like XML, to integrate these data and solve the heterogeneity problem. In this paper we proposed a new software tool called XDS. XDS (eXtensible Data Sources) is a new system to integrate data from relational databases, native XML databases and XML documents. On the other hand, the environment of libraries has also their bibliographical catalogues at different sources and formats. Therefore, we show the use and validity of the XDS system in this environment obtaining the results in a bibliographical format like MODS (Metadata Object Description Schema). Hereby the resources of different bibliographical catalogues can be consulted obtaining the results in a common format as MODS.

1 Introduction

Nowadays organizations have to work with a large variety of data from heterogeneous sources. In this context it could be necessary to use tools as mediators to integrate these different data to a common format like XML. XML has reached the facto standard to present and exchange information between organizations.

[1] Universidad Pontificia, Escuela Universitaria de Informática, Salamanca, España
{rberjonga, afermosoga, ebeatogu, mateossa, msanchezvi, mmanzanoga}@upsa.es
[2] Universidad de Deusto, E.S.I,D.E., Bilbao, España marijose@eside.deusto.es

* This research has been financed by Junta Castilla y León government inside the project *"Estudio sobre integración y acceso único a recursos documentales informatizados"* (PON06B06)

In this paper we describe the XDS tool. XDS is a system to integrate information to XML from some of the most common type of data sources: relational databases, native XML databases, and XML documents.

On the other hand, the environment of libraries is also suffering important changes mainly in two aspects, their content digitalization and their migration to the web environment from where libraries have also to offer their services. Hereby, it would be very useful a unique access to the libraries catalogues and resources with independency of their storage sources and format data.

In the libraries world have appeared new bibliographical formats XML based like MODS (Metadata Object Description Schema) [11]. The advantage of this format is not only it is based on XML, but it derives from the MARC format, the most extended bibliographical format.

Bearing these premises in mind, the XDS tool has been used to access bibliographical catalogues of different sources and libraries, obtaining the results in the bibliographical MODS format.

In the next sections first we are going to describe the XDS tool. Second we are going to make a comparative study of the more important formats of bibliographical cataloguing based on XML. Finally, it appears the use of the XDS tool in a real environment to access a bibliographical database obtaining the queried results in the MODS format.

2 XDS

After different studies about the integration of data from heterogeneous sources, mainly relational and XML sources, since it appears in [1], [2] y [5], there can be deduced the desirable and necessary requirements to integrate information of different sources using XML:

- The information could come simultaneously from different sources.
- The types of the acceded data sources are relational databases, native XML databases and XML documents
- Every source could be queried using its own syntax to take advantage of its maximum functionality.
- The query language of the user requests should be XML
- The user should be able to define the structure of the XML output result

From all this requirements it has been develop the XDS tool. First we are going to describe their architecture and then its components and its query language.

2.1 XDS Architecture

The tool has two main modules called *XDSConnections* and *XDSQuery*. The *XDSConnections* module takes charge of making the queries over the information data sources and to return the results of these queries in XML format, although the original sources did not have this format. The second module, *XDSQuery*, looks after processing the client requests and the results of the queries obtained from the different data sources.

The *XDSConnections* has a configuration XML document which describes each of the data sources that can be accessed and the possible queries to each of them. This queries are made in the own query language of each source. Every time client wishes to obtain information from an information source, he will have to identify the source, the native query to obtain this information, as well as the possible parameters of this selected query.

Once it has been analyzed the configuration document, it is created an object for each source. Each of these objects will contain others objects, one for each specified query for this source. For each of these query objects exist a module to allow to fix the query parameters defined in the query, making the nested operation if this operation has been specified in the configuration document and making the information translation from relational to XML format.

The *XDSQuery* module takes of to process the user request and calls the *XDSConnections* module each time it is necessary to obtain information from a specific source. A user request is a query written in a language also called XDSQuery. This language has a large similarity with the XQuery language, as we will see in a next section.

In the following sections we are going to described in more detail the features of these two modules.

2.2 XDS Connections

The *XDSConnections* defines the different data sources and the native queries that will be able to be made over them. This definition is made using a XML document that will follow the XMLSchema represented in the Figure 1.

This XML document includes a `<connection>` tag for each information source. In this element are defined the necessary parameters to establish the database connection (`<parameter>` tags) and the queries over this data sources (`<query>` tags). The `<connection>` tag has two attributes: `name` and `type`. The `name` attribute identify the data source, since in the same XML document it is possible to define several sources. The `type` attribute define the type of the source. There are three possible types or values of this attribute: `file`, for XML documents; `SQL` for relational or XML-Enabled databases; and `Tamino` for the native XML databases, since this is the only XML native database supported by the moment by the XDS tool.

The <query> tag has also the name and type attributes. The name attribute gives a name to the query to identify it. The type attribute defines the language used for the queries, since in some sources like Tamino is possible to use more than one, XQuery or X-Query.

The <query> tag includes the following tags: <statement>, <parameters>, <nesting> y <rowSchema>.

The <statement> tag describes the native query. The <parameters> contains the parameters defined in the query. The <nesting> and <rowSchema> tags describe respectively, the nested operation over the relational data, and the transformation structure or schema to translate the relational information from the relational to XML format.

We are going to study in detail this two *nesting* and *schema* elements.

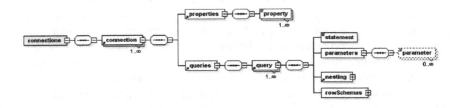

Fig. 1. Format of the XDSConnections

2.2.1 Nesting

The nested relational NF^2 model described in [4], [6], [7] y [8] is useful to represent objects with hierarchical structure. This relational model removes the first formal form (1FN) from the basic relational model, since it allows to define relations where multi-value and/or composed attributes appear.

It would be very useful if the SQL queries could obtain NF^2 views. That is, to next the result of a queried by one or more queried fields. The schema of this operation is showed in the Figure 2.

Each <query> tag has a <nesting> tag to attain the NEST operation. Inside a <nesting> tag it is possible to define various nesting levels using <nested> tags. It must be defined, for each <nested> tag, the field or fields by the ones it will be made the nested process. That is, the field which has the same value in the query results. Moreover, each <nested> tag has a name attribute to define the name of the new tag in the XML output. This XML output tag will have like nested fields, the rest of the fields that are not included in the elements or tags of type <field>.

Fig. 2. Format of the `<nesting>` tag

2.2.2 XDSSchema

In XDS all the information obtained from the data sources must be of XML type. In this sense, id the sources are of SQL type will be necessary to realize a transformation from the relational data obtained from the queries, to XML.

XDS can do this transformation in two different ways: using a specific output format defined by the user *(XDSSchema)* or using a canonical transformation model if the user does not define any rules. This canonical transformation will be the default transformation if the user not specified any other. It is very similar to the default XML output obtaining in Oracle after the transformation of the results obtained by a SQL statement, to the XML format.

XDSSchema is the tool provided to the user by XDS to specify the XML output format, that is, the XML structure of each of the records returned by a query. If the user wants to use a *XDSSSchema* he must add a `<rowSchema>` tag to the `<rowSchemas>` tag of the query. The `<rowSchema>` tag is shown in the Figure 3.

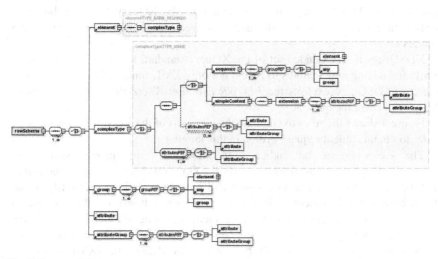

Fig. 3. Format of the `<rowSchema>` tag.

The XDSSchema uses an extended set of the elements of the W3C XMLSchema standard. These XML tags or elements are: `<element>`, `<complexType>`, `<sequence>`, `<group>`, `<attribute>`, `<attributeGroup>`, `<simpleContent>`, `<extension>` and `<any>`.

XDSSchema adds some additional attributes to the standard attributes of these XMLSchema elements. These new attributes allow to identify the origin of the information in the database records. These attributes are: `field`, `newF2` and `occursField`.

The `field` attribute defined in `<element>`, `<attribute>` and `<any>` tags (`<any>` is used when the information obtained from the database is XML) refers to the field of the database record that has the information associated to these XML tags.

A `<rowSchemas>` tag can have so many `<rowSchema>` tags as different transformations the user want to make. When the user executes an XDSQuery sentence will have to indicate what transformation he wants to apply to the results of the SQL query (each `<rowSchema>` tag has a `name` attribute to identify it) and the *root element* of the applied XDSSchema.

2.3 XDSQuery

XDSQuery is the name of the component that processes the client requests and their results, but it is also the name of the language used by the clients to query the data sources. This language is very similar to the XQuery language but it is written in XML. In this way the user can create and modify more easily the queries.

XDSQuery is an extended set of the XQuery standard language, but writing in XML and adding new features to access not only XML sources, but also relational sources. XDSQuery exploits the *FLOWR (For-Let-Where-Return)* expression of XQuery to make the queries.

Figure 4 shows the rules to combine the elements of the XDSQuery language in order to obtain a client request written in this language.

The `<datasource>` tag indicates in XDSQuery the queried source. Its `connection` and `query` attributes identify the connection name to the data source and the native query to execute, which will have been defined previously in the XDSConnections document. If it is a *sql* data source, it will be also possible to specify the XDSSchema and the root element, using the `schema` and `root` attributes, to apply to the output result. If these attributes are not specified in the request to a *sql* source, it will be applied by default the XML canonical transformation model.

Moreover, in a request to a *sql* source, the `<datasource>` tag can also have parameters for the query.

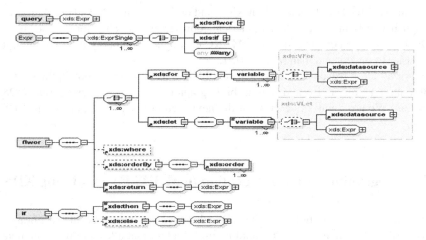

Fig. 4. Format of the XDSQuery tags

3 Languages Based on XML in the Bibliographical Environment

Nowadays libraries should provide different services using Internet. To provide all these services it is necessary to work with different products of different vendors. Therefore it is indispensable to use standards.

In this research we are going to centre in the most important standard languages based on XML and used to catalogue the bibliographical resources.

First we are going to make a classification of the most important of these languages and then we will justify why we have selected one of them.

MARC [9] is the most extended format to catalogue bibliographical information, but it is not based on XML based and in addition it uses numerical fields to codify the information. To solve this complexity they are appearing new cataloguing languages based in the use of tags like XML.

Dublin Core, MARCXML and MODS are three languages based on XML to codify representations summarized of the bibliographical resources in the catalogues of the libraries.

MARCXML [10] is XML based and derived from MARC, but it continues using numerical representations in its XML tags, therefore its comprehension is complicated yet.

Dublin Core [3] is XML based and does not use numerical representation in their XML tags, but it is not compatible with the MARC representation. Therefore is easier to understand but less compatible with the traditional catalogues in MARC format.

Finally, MODS [11] is based on XML and derived from MARC, besides it uses English words in its tags, not numerical representations. Therefore, opposite to Dublin Core the compatibility with MARC catalogues is supported. In addition, it is easier to understand than MARCXML.

For all these reasons, we have selected MODS as language to obtain the results of data integration from different bibliographical catalogues, using our XDS system. We are going to describe in the next section this application of the XDS tool.

4 Bibliographical Data Integration to MODS Format Using XDS

In order to check the utility of the XDS, this tool has been used in the libraries context. In this environment it would be useful a tool that allows to integrate data of different bibliographical catalogues, where each of one can be stored in different sources and with different formats. MODS is one of the most extended bibliographical format, XML based and proceeding of MARC format.

In this section it will be described the use of XDS tool to access bibliographical catalogues, obtaining the results in a bibliographical format XML based like MODS.

In this case study it will be queried a bibliographical catalogue stored in a relational database, to obtain the description of the library resources in MODS format. To obtain it, it has been created a connection to the database (*connections.xml* file) that includes various SQL queries that will be combined at the end in a XDSQuery to obtain the final result. Due to the fact that the information comes from a relational database which stores the bibliographical catalogue, it has been necessary indicate how to make the transformation from the relational data to XML in order to obtain the results in MODS format. To obtain them, for every SQL query an XDSSchema has been defined by the rules that have to follow.

Next code shows a part of the configuration file *connections.xml*. This file contains the connection to the database which stores the library catalogue, the partial SQL query and the associated XSDSchema to transform the query results to MODS language.

```
<?xml version = '1.0' encoding = 'ISO-8859-1'?>
<connections xsi:noNamespaceSchemaLocation="file:///C:/schemas/connection.xsd"
xmlns:xsi="http://www.w3.org/2001/XMLSchema-instance">
  <connection name="Oracle" type="sql">
    <properties>
      <property name="url">jdbc:oracle:thin:@localhost:1521:orcl</property>
      <property name="driver">oracle.jdbc.OracleDriver</property>
      <property name="user">MODS</property>
      <property name="password">MODS</property>
    </properties>
    <queries>
      <query name="ResourceByRecordIdentifier">
        <statement>SELECT R.RECORD_IDENTIFIER, R.RECORD_CONTENT_SOURCE, R.TITULO, T.NOMBRE
        TYPE_OF_RESOURCE,
```

```
FROM RESOURCES R, TYPES_OF_RESOURCES T
WHERE T.CODIGO = R.TYPEOFRESOURCE
    AND R.RECORD_IDENTIFIER = ?
</statement>
<parameters>
  <parameter name="$RECORD_ID" index="1" typeName="VARCHAR" sqlTypeName="VARCHAR2"/>
</parameters>
<nesting/>
<rowSchemas>
  <rowSchema name="schema0">
    <element name="resource">
      <complexType>
        <sequence>
          <element name="titleInfo" type="titleInfo_TYPE"/>
          <element name="typeOfResource" field="TYPE_OF_RESOURCE"/>
          <element name="recordInfo" type="recordInfo_TYPE"/>
        </sequence>
      </complexType>
    </element>
    <complexType name="titleInfo_TYPE">
      <sequence>
        <element name="title" field="TITULO"/>
      </sequence>
    </complexType>
    <complexType name="recordInfo_TYPE">
      <sequence>
        <element name="recordIdentifier" field="RECORD_IDENTIFIER"/>
        <element name="recordContentSource" minOccurs="0" nillable="false"
                 occursField="RECORD_CONTENT_SOURCE" field="RECORD_CONTENT_SOURCE"/>
      </sequence>
    </complexType>
  </rowSchema>
</rowSchemas>
</query>
```

Finally, in Table 1 appears the XDSQuery query sent by the user and the final obtained result.

Table 1. XDSQuery query and MODS results

XDSQuery Query	MODS Result

`<?xml version = '1.0' encoding = 'ISO-8859-1'?>`
`<xds:query xsi:schemaLocation="file:///C:/XDS4/xdsquery.xsd"`
`   mlns:xsi="http://www.w3.org/2001/XMLSchema-instance"`
`   xmlns:xds="http://rberjon.eui.upsa.es/XDSQuery">`
`<mods version="3.0"`
`   xsi:schemaLocation="http://www.loc.gov/mods/v3`
`   http://www.loc.gov/standards/mods/v3/mods-3-0.xsd">`
`<xds:flwor>`
`<xds:for>`
`  <xds:variable name="$src" select="/resource">`
`  <xds:datasource connection="Oracle"`
`         query="ResourceByRecordIdentifier"`
`         schema="schema0" root="resource">`
`  <xds:parameter name="$RECORD_ID">001</xds:parameter>`
`  </xds:datasource>`
`  </xds:variable>`
`</xds:for>`
`<xds:let>`
`<xds:return>`
`  {$src/titleInfo}`
`  {$src/typeOfResource}`
`</xds:return>`
`</xds:flwor>`
`</mods>`
`</xds:query>`
	`<?xml version = '1.0' encoding = 'ISO-8859-1'?>`
	`<mods version="3.0"`
	`   xsi:schemaLocation="http://www.loc.gov/mods/v3`
	`   http://www.loc.gov/standards/mods/v3/mods-3-0.xsd">`
	`<titleInfo>`
	`  <title>J2EE Applications and BEA Weblogic Server</title>`
	`</titleInfo>`
	`<typeOfResource>text</typeOfResource>`
	`</mods>`

5 Conclusions

The XDS software tool allows to query XML and relational data or a combination of this type of data sources, integrating the results in a XML format. In addition, it allows to access these sources using their native language in order to take advantage of their maximum functionality.

The tool also offers a great flexibility to transform the relational data to a XML representation, since the user can specify different schemes of transformation for the XML results.

About XDSQuery, the extensible language used to make the client requests, it is a XML language. Hereby it will be possible to create and/or modify queries in an easy way.

In addition to all these advantages, the XDS tool has been tested in real environments obtaining very satisfactory results. XDS has been used in the environment of libraries to obtain the information about the resources from their catalogues stored in different sources, in a common bibliographical format as MODS.

We can conclude the XDS tool is a good solution to obtain XML data from different types of XML and relational sources. That is, it is a tool that contributes to the heterogeneous data integration in an exchange of information based on XML. The problem of the heterogeneous data also appears in the bibliographical catalogues, where XDS can be used to obtain the results of the catalogues queries in the bibliographical MODS format.

Acknowledgments   We thank the collaboration of Junta Castilla y León to finance this work.

References

1. Berjón R, Fermoso A, Gil MJ (2005) Obtención de XML a partir de información residente en bases de datos. XDS, una nueva propuesta. In:Proceedings of Conferencia Ibero-Americana WWW/Internet 2005. IADIS, Lisboa
2. Berjón R, Fermoso A, Gil MJ (2005) Obtaining database information in XML. In: Proceedings of International Conference e-Society. INSTICC Press, Lisboa: 656-660.
3. DCMI (2007) Dublin Core Metadata Initiative. http://es.dublincore.org/. Accessed 3 September 2007
4. Elmasri R, Navathe S (2002) Fundamentals of database systems. Addison Wesley
5. Fermoso A, Berjón R (2007) Business information integration from XML and relational databases sources. In: Adaptive Technologies and Business integration: Social, Managerial and Organizational Dimensions. Idea group reference, Hersey
6. Fischer PC, Van Gucht D (1984) Weak multivalued dependencies. In: Proceedings of the 3rd ACM SIGACT-SIGMOD symposium on Principles of database systems
7. Roth MA, Korth, HF, Silberschatz A (1988) Extended algebra and calculus for nested relational databases. ACM Trans. Database Systems 13(4):389-417
8. Silberschatz A, Korth, H, Sudarshanm Database System Concepts. McGraw-Hill

9. The library of Congress: MARC Standards (2007).. http://www.loc.gov/marc/marc.html. Accessed 3 September 2007
10. The library of Congress: MARCXML. MARC 21 XML Schema (2007). http://www.loc.gov/standards/marcxml/. Accessed 3 September 2007
11. The library of Congress: MODS. Metadata Object Description Schema (2007). http://www.loc.gov/standards/mods. Accessed 3 September 2007

Identifying Inference Rules for Automatic Metadata Generation from Pre-existing Metadata of Related Resources

Merkourios Margaritopoulos, Isabella Kotini, Athanasios Manitsaris and Ioannis Mavridis[1]

Abstract Manual indexing of learning resources according to metadata standards is a laborious task. The introduction of automatic metadata generation methods is a developing research field with diverse approaches, which appears as an option having the advantage of the economy of work for not having to manually create metadata. In this paper, a methodology for automatic generation of metadata which exploits relations between resources to be described is introduced and examples and empirical data on the application of the methodology to the LOM (Learning Object Metadata) standard are presented. The methodology comprises the execution of consecutive steps of actions aiming at identifying inference rules for automatic generation of a resource's metadata based on pre-existing metadata of its related resources.

1 Introduction

Metadata is structured data which describes the characteristics of a resource and is usually defined as "data about data" ([7], [15]). IEEE in [16] filters this definition as "information about an object". Metadata share many similar characteristics to the cataloguing that takes place in libraries, museums and archives. Moreover, metadata have the advantage to remain independent from the objects they describe and store information not present in the described object (such as usage rights, or third party annotations). In the educational domain these objects are called learning objects ([9], [15], [16]). As the population of learning objects is increasing exponentially, while particular learning needs are developing equally rapidly, possible lack of information or metadata about the objects is restricting the ability to locate, use and manage them. The adoption of standard structures for

[1] Department of Applied Informatics, University of Macedonia, 156 Egnatia Street 54006, Thessaloniki, Greece, {mermar, ikotin, manits, mavridis}@uom.gr

the interoperable description of learning objects has been a major step towards the definition of a common indexing background. LOM standard ([16]), ambitiously, defines almost 80 elements for the description and management of learning objects. Yet, not only the number, but, also, the diversity of the elements in this metadata specification has created implementation difficulties. Such a dense metadata set becomes by itself a source of trouble to potential indexers, since the use of the metadata set, in its entirety, is a complex and resource demanding task. In [17] this problem is called "metadata bottleneck". Several studies on the use of LOM metadata have been carried out by researchers, providing interesting conclusions on the way they are used by indexers ([11], [20], [21]).

A solution to the problem of manual indexing is the involvement of automatic metadata generation techniques ([12], [13]). Automatic metadata generation is based on exploiting several sources from which metadata values can emerge. These sources of information are known as document content analysis, document context analysis and composite documents structure ([3]). Among these three sources of information for automatic metadata generation, composite documents structure is a highly interesting approach with an efficient application to collections of objects. Objects, related to each other with some kind of relation, create together a whole and therefore, it is possible that several of their metadata elements are influenced by each other. As [8] notes, metadata generation through "related content" is a method of metadata propagation parallel to basic object-oriented modelling concepts like inheritance; hence the authors strongly encourage the research community to tackle this issue.

This paper is organised as follows: Section 2 presents the motivation for the proposed methodology based on related work on the issue of automatic metadata generation by exploiting relations between resources. The focus is on educational resources. In Section 3, a solid methodology for the identification of inference rules that automatically generate metadata values of a resource based on pre-existing metadata of its related resources is introduced. Section 4 provides some examples and empirical data for the practical application of the proposed methodology to the LOM metadata schema. Finally, in Section 5, a conclusion is drawn and plans for future work are presented.

2   Motivation from Related Work

Several research efforts dealing with the issue of automatic metadata generation through related resources with considerable interesting results have been undertaken ([1], [2], [6], [10], [14], [19]). The study of these efforts, which take advantage of already described related resources to produce new metadata descriptions of a resource, reveals that the set of inference rules used in these approaches is a core element, since it is the means for determining the metadata values. Each one of the above referenced research efforts incorporates a set of logic rules the application of which (usually by means of using a rule or inference engine) produces implicit propositions for the values of metadata of related resources.

Defining logic rules is an intellectual task, which has to take into account the semantics of the relations and the metadata. Inference rules proposed by the researchers, usually, coincide (there is a relative uniformity in defining the kinds of rules – inheritance, aggregation, etc.). However, sometimes, they diverge due to differences in the perceived semantics of the relations and the metadata elements. In this regard, the majority of the rules used by the researchers are considered to be heuristic rules, since they are not mathematical propositions applied globally, but solid results of experience. For example, in [20] the educational context of an object is considered to be the same with that of an object being part of the first one, while in [2] such an inference is not adopted.

As a result of the above discussion, becomes apparent the need for a generic, common framework methodology to define a guided process for the identification of the complete set of inference rules suggesting the metadata of a resource based on the metadata of its related resources. The research work presented in this paper stems from the observation that the process of defining such rules must follow a well-formed theoretical construction based on the semantics of the relations connecting the resources. For this reason, a generic methodology for identifying inference rules, based on existing relations between resources is introduced. The methodology aims at enriching the existing relations by identifying new (implicit) ones, and, using existing metadata to compute the influenced metadata of related resources. The application of this methodology can be accomplished regardless of the metadata schema and the semantics of the relations used.

3 Generic Methodology for Identifying Inference Rules

Since the following presentation of the generic methodology focuses on indexing learning objects using LOM, LOM relations are put into consideration. The relations defined by LOM are directly adopted from Dublin Core metadata set ([4], [5]). The semantics of the relations of Dublin Core suggest a certain semantical perspective for the relations between general resources and documents, which mainly serves the administrative needs of librarians ([10], [22]). In addition, the way Dublin Core relations are defined cannot properly serve the needs of an educational environment where learning objects described with the LOM standard will be used. Thus, a slight modification to the semantics of these relations is a first necessary step before applying the proposed methodology. The approach presented in this article has been greatly influenced by the definition of the semantics for the six pairs of LOM relations proposed by [10].

The identification of inference rules to generate metadata values of a resource by exploiting a net of existing relations between the resources, is a process that comprises four consecutive steps each of which is elaborated in the following subsections.

3.1 Step 1: Locating Connection Features

In most cases, the semantics of a relation connecting two resources is defined in free text describing the concept of relating two resources with this relation, or is implied from the meaning of the verb or the noun used to specify the relation with no further explanations. Thus, the adoption of logic inferences regarding interconnected properties of the resources is a demanding intellectual task. In order to come up with such inferences, one has to locate the interrelated properties of the resources connected with a relation that specify this connection on the basis of similarities or differences. In the rest of this paper these properties are called *"connection features"*. Connection features may be stated explicitly in the definition of the semantics of a relation. However, in other cases, connection features may be implied. For example, the definition of the semantics of the relation "IsVersionOf" of Dublin Core ([4], [5]) clearly highlights the connection features "Format" and "Creator" (the related resources have the same format and the same creator), whereas, one can presume the connection feature "Topic area" (different versions of a resource belong to the same topic area).

Apart from relations referring to semantic characteristics of the resources they connect, structural relations (part – whole relations) connecting the related resources are also included in the definition of connection features ("part" or "subset, "whole" or "superset" connection features). For the optical representation of a set of relations and the connection features of each, in order to extract logic inferences, the use of a 2-dimensional table for assisting the identification of the inference rules is proposed in [18]. The rows of the table consist of the set of relations under consideration, while its columns contain their connection features. The connection features depicted in the table are defined as common properties of the two related resources, as well as properties influenced by each other in a specific way. Thus, the interrelation of the connection features of a relation does not, necessarily, take the form of equality. It is possible that a relation defines a certain type of differentiation. For the relation "IsLessSpecificThan" in [10], the connection feature "Level of details" is defined, since the values of this property of the two connected resources with this relation are influenced by each other in a specific way (one lower than the other).

3.2 Step 2: Creating Inference Rules for New Implicit Relations

It is possible that the relations the members of a set of resources are connected to each other with, can be enriched by applying certain inference rules to generate new implicit relations from the already existing ones. Such a process involves two substeps:

- Firstly, a number of rules for the generation of new relations are created by exploiting the *mathematical properties* of the relations. Since the relations in question are all binary relations (having two arguments), they are equipped, as the case may be, with common properties of binary relations (concepts of set theory in Mathematics), such as inverse, symmetric relations, transitivity, etc. For example, transitivity in the relation "IsPartOf" of LOM leads us to the rule: «If resource a "IsPartOf" resource b and resource b "IsPartOf" resource c, then resource a "IsPartOf" resource c».

- Secondly, one takes advantage of the connection features defined in the previous step to create rules for getting new relations by means of *"relation transfer"*. Relation transfer states that if resource a is connected to resource b with relation σ, then it is also connected with the same relation to all other resources connected to b through a certain connection feature (the relation is transferred to them). For example (using LOM relations), the relation "IsReferencedBy" connecting resource a to resource b can be transferred to all resources sharing the same "Intellectual content" with b (such as all resources related to each other with the relation "IsFormatOf"). The resulting rule is: «If a "IsReferencedBy" b and b "IsFormatOf" c then a "IsReferencedBy" c». This sort of propositions can be depicted by adding the symbol "v" in the table produced in the previous step ([18]). Symbol "v" depicts the proposition «resource a is connected to resource b with relation σ, as well as any other resource connected to b through the connection feature appearing in the respective column of the table» and facilitates the formulation of the respective inference rule of relation transfer.

3.3 Step 3: Mapping Connection Features to Metadata Elements

The connection features, thought as properties of resources, can be mapped to certain metadata elements of the schema used for describing the resources. The interrelation of the connection features of two resources (through the relation they are connected with) is translated into the interrelation of their respective metadata elements. Thus, considering the LOM metadata schema ([16]), the connection feature "Intellectual content" is mapped to metadata elements which are affected by the content of the resources (such as "1.4 General.Description" and "1.5 General.Keyword"). Consequently, resources connected to each other with a relation that uses this connection feature (such as "IsFormatOf" which prescribes that the connected resources have the same intellectual content), will have their respective metadata elements interrelated the same way as their connection features (i.e. equal). Furthermore, the connection feature "Whole" can be mapped to LOM elements expressing properties of learning objects which can influence the same properties of an object that contains them, like "1.3 General.Language", "1.5 General.Keyword", "5.9 Educational.Typical learning time", "6. Rights.Cost", etc. In this regard, the connection feature "Understanding" can be mapped to LOM metadata elements that can be influenced by the notion of understanding the learning objects by their users, which are "5.6 Educational.Context", "5.7 Educational.Typical age range" and "5.11 Educational.Language".

3.4 Step 4: Specifying the Influence Type of the Metadata Elements' Values

An inference rule generating the value of a metadata element exploits the relations that use the connection features corresponding to the element, as its conditions part. For each and every one of these relations a single rule is created. For example, for the metadata element "1.3 General.Language" two rules are created having as their conditions part the relations "HasPart" and "IsPartOf" (as the connection features "Whole" and "Part" were mapped to this metadata element – since it is not hard to conclude that the value of "1.3 General.Language" of a learning object can influence the value of this element of a learning object that either contains or is part of the first one).

The actions part of every rule deals with specifying the exact type of influence for the metadata elements values. The value of a metadata element may be influenced in one of the following three types:

- *Inclusion of metadata values* from related resources, according to which a resource's metadata element values (with cardinality greater than 1) are added (included) to the values of the same metadata element of a related resource. A resource can include metadata values from its parts as a result of a whole relation (the inclusion relations of the resources are transferred to their metadata elements).
- *Computation of metadata value* from metadata values of related resources. The metadata element value of a resource is the result of a mathematical or logic expression (which has to be specified) of metadata element values of related resources.
- *Restriction of the range of values* of a metadata element, according to which the range of values of a metadata element of a resource is not the complete value space defined by the specification of the standard, but a proper subset of it computed from the values of the same metadata element of related resources (the exact expression has to be specified).

The first two types of influence automatically generate metadata values, while the third one facilitates the task of manual indexing. Thus, the rules are formatted as: «If resource *a* is related to resource *b* with relation σ, then the value of the metadata element *m* of *a* is determined by the value of metadata element *m* of *b* according to one of (the above) three defined types of influence».

Considering the above stated examples, in order to get the actions part of the rules, one has to specify the exact type of influence for the metadata element values. Thus, if learning object *a* contains ("HasPart") learning object *b*, the value of the metadata element "1.3 General.Language" of *b* will be included ("inclusion of metadata values" type of influence) to the values of the same metadata element of *a*. Following the same logic, if a learning object "IsPartOf" two or more learning objects, then the range of values of its language will be restricted ("restriction of the range of values" type of influence) to the intersection of the values of the languages of its two supersets.

4   Application Example

Applying the proposed methodology to LOM, more than 80 inference rules were created. A brief description of the reasoning followed to obtain a small sample of such rules, which affect the values of certain LOM metadata fields, follows:

- Metadata field "1.5 General.Keyword": The connection feature "Intellectual content" of the relation "IsFormatOf" can be mapped to this element (keywords are determined by the content of an object). The value of this metadata element of a learning object is directly connected to the value of this element of a related object which they share the same intellectual content with. The influence type of the element's value is "computation of metadata value" (equality). In free text, the rule takes the form "learning objects that differ only in their format (they have the same content), will have the same keywords".
- Metadata field "1.8 General.Aggregation Level": It maps to the connection feature "Whole" ("Superset") of the relation "HasPart", in the sense that the value of this metadata element of a learning object is affected by the value of the same element of objects that are parts of the object to be indexed. Ignoring any formal notation, the rule may be expressed as "the aggregation level of the superset will be greater by 1 than the maximum aggregation level of its parts" (since a collection of learning objects of some aggregation level constitutes a learning object with aggregation level increased by 1). The influence of the element's value is done through "computation of metadata value".
- Metadata field "4.1 Technical.Format": This element maps to the connection feature "Format" of the relation "IsVersionOf". "Computation of metadata value" (equality) is the influence type of the element's value. Equality of these metadata elements of the related objects is obvious, since "different versions of a learning object maintain the same technical format".
- Metadata field "5.4 Educational.Semantic Density": It maps to the connection feature "Intellectual content" of the relation "IsFormatOf" (the semantic density of a learning object is a property of its content). The influence of the element's value is done through "computation of metadata value" (equality). Thus, the rule, in free text, is formulated as "learning objects that differ only in their format (they have the same content) will have the same semantic density".

- Metadata field "5.7 Educational.Typical Age Range": It maps to the connection feature "Understanding" of the relation "Requires", in the sense that the value of this metadata element of the object to be indexed can be affected by the value of the same element of the objects required in order for the first one to be understood. The influence of the element's value is of type "restriction of the range of values". The rule, in simple words, is expressed as "if a learning object requires others, then the typical age range of its intended user will be greater than the maximum typical age range of the objects it requires".

- Metadata element "5.11 Educational.Language": It maps to the connection feature "Understanding" of the relation "IsRequiredBy", in the sense that the value of this metadata element of the object to be indexed can be affected by the value of the same element of the object that requires it in order to be understood. "Computation of metadata value" (equality) is the type of influence of the element's value. Simply put, the rule takes the form "if a learning object is required by another one, then the human language used by the typical intended user of this object will be the same with the corresponding language of the object that requires it".

- Metadata element "6.1 Rights.Cost": This element maps to the connection feature "Part" ("Subset") of the relation "IsPartOf", in the sense that the value of this metadata element of a learning object which is part of others can be affected by the value of this element of the objects containing it. The element's value is influenced through "computation of metadata value" (equality on condition). Without any formal notation, the rule can be expressed as "if a learning object is part of other ones, then there is no cost in it, if at least one of the objects containing it has no cost".

In order to demonstrate the effectiveness of the created rules in the automatic generation of metadata of related learning objects, and, thus, prove the practical application of the proposed approach, an application scenario is introduced involving four learning objects (a, b, c and d) the LOM descriptions of the three of which (a, b and c) are already stored in a database, while the fourth one (d) is intended to be indexed. More specifically, learning objects are defined as: a is a Microsoft Word file containing a differential calculus exercise; b is a postscript file which contains the entire manual of the calculus theory; c is a web page containing a part of calculus theory regarding differential calculus; d is a web page containing the calculus theory taken from the contents of learning object b. The relations connecting objects a, b and c (as they are already registered in the database) are: "a IsReferencedBy b", "a IsReferencedBy c", "b References a", "c References a".

In order to take advantage of the created inference rules, so as to automatically index learning object d, one has to provide the relations connecting d to the already indexed learning objects. Thus, he/she manually fills out the relations "d IsFormatOf b" and "d HasPart c". Considering inverse relations and relation transfer, implicit relations automatically produced are: "b HasFormat d", "c IsPartOf d", "a IsReferencedBy d" (as a result of relation transfer – "a

IsReferencedBy *b*" and "*b* HasPart *d*"), "*d* References *a*". As a result of relation "*d* IsFormatOf *b*", applying specific rules of computation of metadata value (in this case, equality), metadata fields of *d* inherited from *b* are: "1.2 General.Title", "1.4 General.Description", "1.5 General.Keyword", "1.6 General.Coverage", "5.2 Educational.Learning Resource Type", "5.5 Educational.Intended End User Role", "5.6 Educational.Context" and all fields of category "9 Classification" (providing the purpose of classification is related to the content of the learning objects). As a result of relation "*d* HasPart *c*", applying either specific rules of inclusion of metadata values, or specific rules of computation of metadata value, metadata fields of *d*, the values of which are partly influenced by the same metadata values of *c*, are: "1.3 General.Language", "1.8 General.Aggregation.Level", "2.2 Lifecycle.Status", "2.3 Lifecycle.Contribute", "4.1 Technical.Format", "4.4 Technical.Requirement", "5.1 Educational.Learning Resource Type", "5.8 Educational.Difficulty", "5.9 Educational.Typical Learning Time", "5.11 Language", "6.1 Rights.Cost", "6.2 Rights.Copyright and Other Restrictions", "8 Annotation".

The outcome of this process is that a considerable number of initially empty fields of a learning object, which has not been indexed, is automatically populated with values computed from the values of respective metadata fields of already indexed related learning objects.

5 Conclusion – Future work

In this paper, a step-by-step methodology to guide the process of identifying a set of inference rules for generating metadata of a resource, based on the metadata of its related resources was introduced. The presentation of the methodology is accompanied with examples for its practical application to LOM metadata schema demonstrating the effectiveness of the proposed approach in the automatic generation of metadata. The process is integrated in a theoretical construction, the foundation of which is the semantics of the relations connecting the resources to be indexed.

At present, there is an on-going work to apply the entire set of the rules created, by means of using a software module which carries out the automatic generation of metadata and stores them in a LOM native XML database. The whole project is being developed as an Integrated Metadata Management System (IMMS) that incorporates the abilities for editing, storing, retrieving and automatically generating new metadata.

References

1. Bourda Y, Doan B-L, Kekhia W (2002) A semi-automatic tool for the indexation of learning objects. In Proceedings of World Conference on Educational Multimedia, Hypermedia and Telecommunications 2002 (pp. 190-191). Chesapeake, VA: AACE.
2. Brase J, Painter M, Nejdl W (2003) Completion axioms for learning object metadata - Towards a formal description of LOM. In 3rd international conference on advanced learning technologies (ICALT). Athens, Greece.
3. Cardinaels K, Meire M, Duval E (2005) Automating metadata generation: the simple indexing interface. In Proceedings of the 14th international conference on World Wide Web, Chiba, Japan.
4. Dublin   Core   Metadata   Initiative   (2002)   DCMI   Metadata   Terms http://dublincore.org/documents/dcmi-terms/. Accessed 15 March 2007.
5. Dublin Core Metadata Initiative (2005) Using Dublin Core – The Elements http://dublincore.org/documents/usageguide/elements.shtml. Accessed 15 March 2007.
6. Doan B-L, Bourda Y (2005) Defining several ontologies to enhance the expressive power of queries. In volume 143 of CEUR, workshop Proceedings, on Interoperability of web-based Educational Systems, held in conjunction with WWW'05 conference, Chiba, Japan, Technical University of Aachen (RWTH).
7. Duval E (2001) Metadata Standards: What, Who & Why? Journal of Universal Computer Science, Vol. 7, no 7, 2001, pp. 591-601.
8. Duval E, Hodgins W (2004) Making metadata go away - hiding everything but the benefits. In DC-2004: Proceedings of the International Conference on Dublin Core and Metadata Applications, pp. 29–35.
9. E-Learning Consortium (2003) Making sense of learning specifications and standards: A decision's maker's guide to their adoption (2e). The Masie Centre. http://www.masie.com/standards/s3-2nd-edition.pdf. Accessed 15 March 2007.
10. Engelhardt M et al (2006) Reasoning about eLearning Multimedia Objects. In J. Van Ossenbruggen, G. Stamou, R. Troncy, V. Tzouvaras (Ed.) Proc. of WWW 2006, Intern. Workshop on Semantic Web Annotations for Multimedia (SWAMM).
11. Friesen N (2004) International LOM Survey: Report (Draft). http://dlist.sir.arizona.edu/403/01/LOM_Survey_Report2.doc. Accessed 15 March 2007.
12. Greenberg J, Spurgin K, Crystal A (2005) AMeGA (Automatic Metadata Generation Applications) Project, University of North Carolina.
13. Greenberg J, Spurgin, K, Crystal A (2006) Functionalities for Automatic-Metadata Generation Applications: A Survey of Metadata Experts' Opinions. International Journal of Metadata, Semantics and Ontologies. Vol. 1, No. 1, 2006.
14. Hatala M, Richards G (2003) Value-added metatagging: Ontology and rule based methods for smarter metadata. In RuleML, pp. 65–80.
15. Horton W, Horton K (2003) E-learning Tools and Technologies. Indianapolis: Wiley Publishing.
16. IEEE. 1484.12.1 (2002) Draft Standard for Learning Object Metadata. Learning Technology Standards   Committee   of   the   IEEE.   http://ltsc.ieee.org/wg12/files/LOM_1484_12_1_v1_Final_Draft.pdf. Accessed 15 March 2007.
17. Liddy E D et al (2002) Automatic metadata generation & evaluation. In Proceedings of the 25th Annual International ACM SIGIR Conference on Research.
18. Margaritopoulos M, Manitsaris A, Mavridis I (2007) On the Identification of Inference Rules for Automatic Metadata Generation. In Proceedings of the 2nd International Conference on Metadata and Semantics Research (CD-ROM), Ionian Academy, Corfu, Greece.
19. Motelet O (2005) Relation-based heuristic diffusion framework for LOM generation. In Proceedings of 12th International Conference on Artificial Intelligence in Education AIED 2005 - Young Researcher Track, Amsterdam, Holland.

20. Najjar J, Ternier S, Duval E (2003) The Actual Use of Metadata in ARIADNE: an Empirical Analysis. In Proceedings of ARIADNE Conference 2003.
21. Sicilia M A et al (2005) Complete metadata records in learning object repositories: some evidence and requirements. International Journal of Learning Technology, 1(4), pp. 411-424.
22. Steinmetz R, Seeberg C (2003) Meta-Information for Multimedia eLearning. Computer science in perspective, Springer-Verlag New York, Inc.

Semi – automated tool for characterizing news video files, using metadata schemas

Stefanos Asonitis, Dimitris Boundas, Georgios Bokos, and Marios Poulos[1]

Abstract. The size increment of online TV's video repositories, rises the necessity of an effective automated video content-based retrieval service. Our project will give a partial answer to that problem by developing a semi-automated tool for characterizing broadcast news video files. Our tool will be constituted of two sections. In the first section, the repositories' video files will be separated from their audio content. Then the audio content will be characterized by a classification system in two predefined categories,: news and sports. In the second section the audio files will be described using proper description languages such as NewsML and SportsML, thus characterizing the initial video file they came from. The effectiveness of our semi-automated tool will be tested in a local repository of news video files, created by a customizable, focuses on video files, data mining web crawler.

1 Introduction

The size increment of online TV's video repositories, rises the necessity of an effective video, content-based, retrieval service [4]. An effective video retrieval service should based on metadata, describing the repositories' resources. Metadata's approach in video retrieval gives the advantage to an XML application

---

[1] Stefanos Asonitis
Dept. Of Archives and Library Sciences, Ionian University, Palea Anaktora, 49100 Corfu, Greece, email: asostef@gmail.com

Dimitris Boundas,
Dept. Of Archives and Library Sciences, Ionian University, Palea Anaktora, 49100 Corfu, Greece, email: boundas7@yahoo.gr

Georgios Bokos,
Dept. Of Archives and Library Sciences, Ionian University, Palea Anaktora, 49100 Corfu, Greece, email: gbokos@ionio.gr

Marios Poulos
Dept. Of Archives and Library Sciences, Ionian University, Palea Anaktora, 49100 Corfu, Greece, email: mpoulos@ionio.gr

to examine the metadata associative to a source (video file) and if and only if the metadata correspond to the user's criteria, only then the user could go on to a download procedure of the main content of the source. Thus the user avoids a useless downloading procedure, not corresponding to his criteria, gaining time and bandwidth usage.

A global metadata implementation, suitable for any video files repository is complex, due to many different metadata standards [6]. In this paper we present the methodology of a semi-automated tool, designed for creating videos repositories containing news and sports video files. The creation of the repository based on a hand crafted data mining web crawler and a classification system, characterizing video files in two predefined categories: news and sports. Then each video category, news and sports, can effectively described using proper markup languages, such as NewsML and SportsML correspondence. A manual, NewsML and SportsML metadata approach will be implemented only in a limited number of video resources of our repository

2 Methodology

2.1 Web Crawler Creation

Our workbench includes the creation of a customizable data mining web crawler[3] focuses on video files, which means that our crawler will not only be capable of searching across the internet and index links including .mov, .avi or other video formats files, but also it will be capable of downloading the video files in a local repository. Due to the size of the video files our crawler will act in two steps.[13]

First Step: In the first step the crawler creates the video files location index. At the beginning of the first step the user feeds the crawler with a set of URLs, thus creating a predefined URL list, from which the crawler will start searching the web. Additionally the user feeds the crawler with a set of file extensions (such as .avi, .mov) possibly containing video content.

Fig. 1 illustrates the crawler operation during the first step of its action.

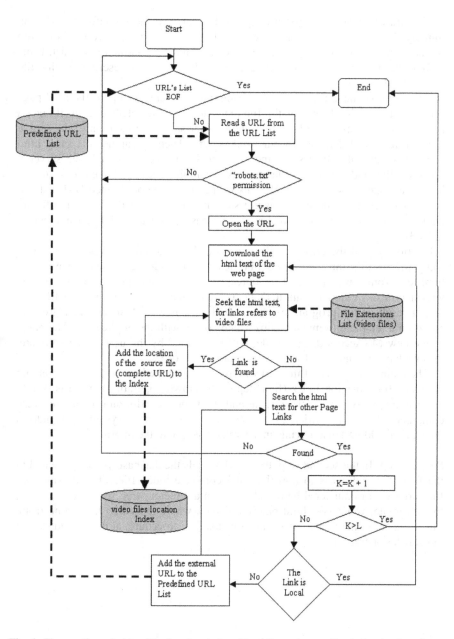

Fig. 1. The creation of video files location index. The (*discontinuous lines*) plot the data flow to/from the repository. The (*letter K*) represents the counter for the number of visited links and the (*letter L*) represents the maximum number of visited links. If K>L then the crawler stops searching the web.

The crawler reads the first html page that finds in the predefined URL list. Initially the crawler looks for a file named "robots.txt" in the root of the web server containing the html page, already read from the predefined URL List. If the "robots.txt" file exists, the crawler reads the robot policy as described in that file and adapted to it [14].

Assuming we have the necessary permissions, the crawler opens the html page and searches the html text for the file extensions we are interesting in. If such a file extension exists in the html text, the crawler stores the location of the source file to a relational database in our local system. Then it searches the same html page for other links. In case it finds a local link to the examined web server it opens the link and downloads the html text, searching again for video files. In case it finds an external link, it adds the link to the end of the predefined URL list and so on. The retrieving procedure won't stop until the user of the crawler software clicks a cancel button or until the crawler has visited a predefined number of links[3].

The first step of the crawler will be hand-coded in Microsoft Visual Basic 6.0, using Microsoft's internet access libraries for opening URLs and downloading html text from a web page. The source code will be interpreted to an .exe file, named vlf.exe (Video Location Finder). Each time we run the vlf.exe file, the output result of the program execution will be a new MSAccess database file, based on a template (template.mdb) which comes with the application. The name of the new MSAccess database file, will be entitled by the user of the software, thus we have an .mdb file for each execution of vlf.exe.

The main advantages of the software packet, described previously, for creating the video files location Index (first step of the crawler operation) are: it is simply consists of just two files: the vlf.exe and the template.mdb. and it runs in every computer uses a Microsoft Windows operating system (Windows 98/ME/NT/2000/X) also having an active connection to the internet.

Second Step: In the second step, the crawler reads the database we have created in the first step and starts to download the complete video files. The downloaded files are saved to our local hard disk drive, in a directory tree structure according to the remote web server html pages structure, where the video files came from. Fig. 2 illustrates the workflow or the downloading procedure, at the second step of the crawler operation.

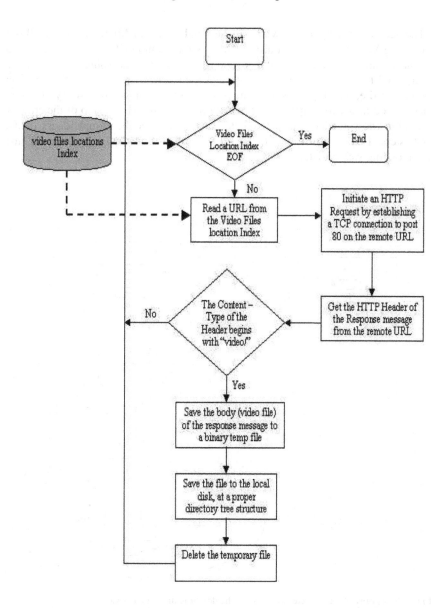

Fig. 2. The workflow of downloading procedure, during the second step of the crawler operation. The (*discontinuous lines*) plot the data flow to/from the repository.

The second step of the crawler will be hand-coded in Microsoft Visual Basic 6.0, using Microsoft's internet access libraries for opening URLs and downloading a binary data file from a remote location via HTTP. The source code will be interpreted to an .exe file, named vd.exe (Video Downloader). Each time we run the vd.exe file, the output result of the program execution is a repository of video files, stored in our local hard disk drive. Notice that the second step of the crawler operation (downloader) can be executed any time after the completeness of the first step. Fig. 3 illustrates the workfow of a complete operation of the downloading web crawler.

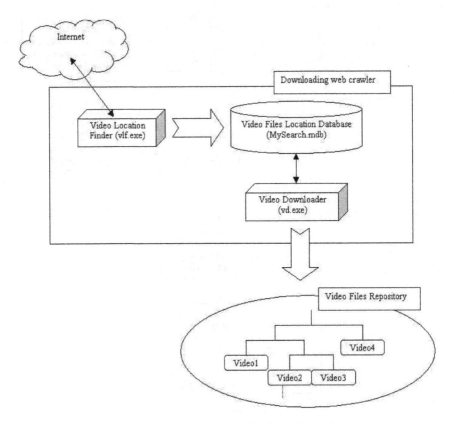

Fig. 3. Workflow of a complete operation of the downloading web crawler

2.2 Video Classification

The repositories' video files will be separated from their audio content. At this stage the audio signal is classified, using computer algorithms, into two predefined categories namely news and sports. Classification is based on quantitative low-level features of the original signal. This is actually a two step procedure, at first a set of features is extracted from the original signal and then these features are fed to a classifier. There is a great number of proposed classifiers such as neural networks, support vector machines and genetic algorithms.[1,5,8,9]

2.3 Describing the audio files

The most important markup languages for data news interchange, are NewsML(News Markup Language) and SportsML(Sports Markup Language).

NewsML

The main target of NewsML [10] language is to ascribe successfully the news' information, in an interchange procedure, regardless of the source type of the context (text, picture, or even video). NewsML is based on XML and other coherent models. NewsML is a compatible, extensible and flexible frame for describing news information. It has the capability of handling huge digitalized collections of news' information, contemporaneously taking care of their metadata and the relationship among the collections. News' interchange is a transmission's procedure focused not only on the content of data news, but also on data describing the news' content in a brief and concise way. Information for broadcasting and the direction of the broadcast are also important in a procedure of interchanging news information. NewsML language allows multiple presentations of the same information and handles arbitraries mixtures of types, languages and coding.

News data can be transferred as individual modules or as a part of relatives modules comprising a news packet. Proper metadata must exist in a news data transformation procedure, to ensure effective production, reproduction, transformation and use of the news context, including classification and searching. News packets may contain various types of content, such as text, images, video, sound. The news packet may also exist in various formats such as interpretations of the news text in multiple languages, or presentation of the news images in alternative image formats.

The main use of NewsML is the news interchange, but it is also used for creation, handling and publishing a collection of a news repository in a network environment, or in an isolated file system environment. News events evolves gradually, so there exists the necessity for updates, extensions and replacements with recently data. Finally a very important factor in news environment is the authentication of the metadata and the news content itself. The value of a news information arises from its reliability. NewsML administrates efficiently that factor.

The structure of NewsML

NewsML structure consists of four levels [2]. Each level is represented of a "news object". The assessment of the term "news object" is indicated in NewsML specifications and represents one of the basic components of NewsML documents. The news objects are: NewsEnvelope, NewsItem, NewsComponent and ContentItem. Each of the four levels in NewsML structure provides additional functions which are named from inner to outer core, as follows:

1. **Exchange** level → represented of **NewsEnvelope** object
2. **Management** level → represented of **NewsItem**
3. **Structure** level → represented of **NewsComponent**
4. **Content** level → represented of **ContentItem**.

The ContentItem level

The core of NewsML focuses on the news content itself. Basically the ContentItem constitutes the section comprises of the data and metadata, extracted of a news event. ContentItem has the capability of representing any kind of information file, such as text, image, flash animation, video, of any other kind of multimedia. The ContentItem comprises of an integument/packet which makes the content itself and the metadata which describe the technical data of other physical characteristics of the content, tangible to a NewsML processor.

The answer to the question "why metadata are included in the ContentItem object", is that the metadata provision gives the advantage to a NewsML application, to examine the metadata associative to a NewsML source and then, if and only if the metadata corresponded to our criteria, to go on with the downloading procedure of the main content of the source, thus gaining time and bandwidth of a useless downloading procedure, not corresponded to our searching criteria.

NewsML anticipates several types of metadata, in its Content level: media type, format type, mime type, notation and a set of other characteristics.

ContentItems can by classified in several ways. Media type is allocated in sub element MediaType using FormalName. The values assigned to FormalName are limited and come from a controlled glossary defined from the NewsML language itself. Examples of media types are: XML, JPEG, Audio and MPEG. In that way, the recipient of the NewsML document, knows the type of the source and therefore the proper working–out way. MimeType has a similar role in the NewsML architecture. MimeType takes, for example, the following values: "text/xml", "image/jpeg", "audio/x-wav". "video/mpeg". The characteristics in the examined categories, meaning the audio and visual schema, arise as follows:

1. Audio: the audio objects assigned of the following characteristics: Audio Coder, Audio Coder Version, Total Duration, Average Bit Rate, Sample Size, Sample Rate and Audio Channels.
2. Video: the video objects assigned of the following characteristics: Video Coder, Video Coder Version, Vbr, Width, Height, Total Duration, Frames Total, Key Frames, Pixel Depth, Frame Rate, Average Bit Rate, Sampling and Redirector.

SportsML

The procedure which takes place in managing sports events using SportsML is respectively similar to the usage of NewsML in news events. SportsML [11] gives someone the benefit to describe a sport event, by answering questions like "how, what, when, where and why". A SportsML document can be very simple or very complicated, in proportion to the described source and the requirements of the managers and the users of the shortage information. Team names, player names, results, standings, statistics and other important information are handled in a formal way reducing the time needed to prepare sports events for publication. Information for each championship can also be stored in SportsML, in an effective way, making easier the processing of standings, playoff matches, and the results.

SportsML language endorses the identification, the description and the creation of a huge number of sports metadata. The most important are:

1. Results: The winner and score balances. The final score in a match and the players who score in a football or american football match, or the player who accomplishes the most points in a basketball match.
2. Programs: Who faces whom and fixtures.
3. Results: Who are the champions, who takes part in European championship, in Copa Libertadores, etc. and those who are near to bumping in lower standing.
4. Statistics: Who are the most valuable players
5. News: How do we combine the publication coverage of an athletic event and the data streaming according to the event.? How are the metadata "packed" in a group with the sports events?

The SportsML model consists of a core DTD including a property frame. SportsML describes a huge era of sports events. The sports events coverage is implemented through the DTD's core. Further, SportsML consist of several "embedded" DTDs for a specific field event. The fact, that there are only seven field events (football, basketball, volleyball, tennis, baseball, hockey and american football) covered from the first edition of SportsML, doesn't mean that SportsML bounds in those fields. DTD's core provides a remarkable start point for the development of other embedded DTD cores in the body of SportsML.

We should mention that the sports markup language cooperates with MPEG-7, the standard for multimedia metadata [12]. That cooperative schema, between

SportsML and MPEG-7, gives the ability to extract information, data and metadata broadcasted during a sport event, or a sport TV airing.

The extracted information, is filtered via the MPEG-7 standard and then is modified from the seven SportsML's DTDs and distributed, in a unique form, to all the sports news agencies. So is accomplished a powerful environment for semantic annotation and personalized access to any sporting service

Conclusion and future work

We described a semi-automated tool characterizing broadcast news video files, using NewsML and SportsML schemas. Our tool consists of a downloading web crawler focuses on video files, a signal separator insulating audio signal from downloaded video files and a neural network classifying the audio signal into two predefined categories named news and sports. Finally we create metadata files, describing our resources, using NewsML and SportsML, only in a limited number of news and sports broadcast video files [7], gathered in the previous steps of the methodology. Fig. 4 illustrates a global aspect of the semi-automated tool architecture.

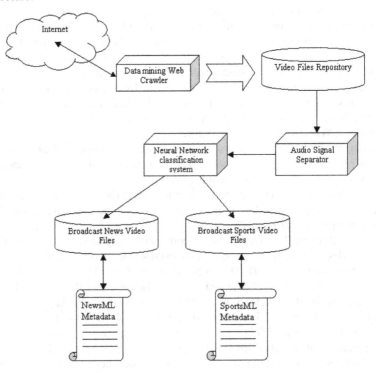

Fig. 4. A global aspect of the semi-automated tool architecture

A total humanly metadata approach on the last step is unrealistic due to the number of resources requiring metadata. As future work, an automated metadata implementation, via application development [6], is necessary to complement the described in this paper methodology, cutting out the manual creation of metadata files.

This semi-automated tool can be used for video files harvesting, broadcasting videos classification and in its final form (including automated metadata implementation) for video retrieval services.

References

1. Adami, N., Bugatti, A., Leonardi, R., Migliorati, P.: Low Level Processing of Audio and Video Information for Extracting the Semantics of Content. IEEE Fourth Workshop on Multimedia Signal Processing (2001)
2. Allday, T.: "NewsML: enabling a standards-led revolution in news publishing?". Reuters Media Group, EBU Technical Review (2001).
3. Barrat, K., Miller, R.: SPHINX: A Framework for Creating Personal, Site-Specific Web Crawlers. Printed in Computer Network and ISDN Systems v.30. Brisbane, Australia, pp. 119-130 (1998)
4. Brown, M., Foote, J., Jones, K., Young, S.: Automatic Content-Based Retrieval of Broadcast News: Proceedings of the third ACM international conference on Multimedia, pp. 35-43 (1995)
5. Fogarty, T. C.: Classifier systems for control. IEEE Colloquim on Genetic Algorithms for Control Systems Engineering (1993)
6. Greenberg, J., Spugrin, K. & Crystal, A. : Functionalities for automatic metadata generation applications: a survey of metadata experts' opinions, International Journal of Metadata, Semantics and Ontologies vol. 1 no. 1 pp. 3-20 (2006)
7. Kokaram, A., Rea, N., Dahyot, R., Tekalp, M., Bouthemy, P. , Gros, P. , Sezan, I. : Browsing sports video: trends in sports-related indexing and retrieval work. IEEE Signal Processing Magazine, Volume 23, Issue 2, pp. 47 – 58 (2006)
8. Michel, P., Kaliouby, R.: Real time facial expresion recognition in video using support vector machines. In Proceedings of ICMI'03.
9. Nitanda, N., Haseyama, M., Kitajima, H.: Accurate Audio-Segment Classification Using Feature Extraction Matrix. IEEE International Conference on Acoustics, Speech, and Signal Processing (2005)
10. The NewsML, www.newsml.org .
11. The SportsML, www.sportsml.org .
12. Tsekeridou, S., MPEG-7 MDS based application specific metadata model for personalized multi-service access in a DTV broadcast environment.
13. Wales, C., Kim, S., Leuenberger, D., Watts, W., O Weinrothl, O.: IPTV – The Revolution is Here. cs.berkeley.edu (2005.)

14. Welz, M., Hutchison, A. : Modulating Access Control at the Application for Closely Coupled Intrusion Detection, 1st Computer Science Mini Conference, Cape Town, South Africa (2002)

Exploring aspects of scientific publishing in astrophysics and cosmology: the views of scientists

Panayiota Polydoratou and Martin Moyle[1]

Abstract Scientists in astrophysics and cosmology make much use of the arXiv repository. Concerns raised by scientists in those fields about publication costs and delays, and the transparency and validity of the peer review process, raised questions about levels of satisfaction with existing publishing models. This paper discusses the results from a community survey in the fields of astrophysics and cosmology, conducted as part of an investigation into the feasibility of an "overlay journal" model in these disciplines. Six hundred and eighty three (683) researchers provided information about their academic/research background, their research practices, and their attitudes, both as producers and consumers of information, to the traditional journal publishing system, and gave their reaction to the overlay publication model. The survey results indicate that scientists in these disciplines are, in general, favourably disposed towards new publishing models, although some important caveats and concerns, particularly regarding quality, were highlighted.

Introduction

The Repository Interface for Overlaid Journal Archives (RIOJA) project (http://www.ucl.ac.uk/ls/rioja) is an international partnership of academic staff, librarians and technologists from UCL (University College London), the University of Cambridge, the University of Glasgow, Imperial College London and Cornell University. It aims to address the issues around the development and implementation of a new publishing model, the overlay journal - defined, for the purposes of the project, as a quality-assured journal whose content is deposited to and resides in one or more open access repositories. The project is funded by the Joint Information Systems Committee (JISC, http://www.jisc.ac.uk/), UK, and runs from April 2007 to June 2008.

---

[1] University College London

The impetus for the RIOJA project came directly from academic users of the arXiv (http://arxiv.org) subject repository. For this reason, arXiv and its community is the testbed for RIOJA. arXiv was founded in 1991 to facilitate the exchange of pre-prints between physicists. It now holds over 460,000 scientific papers, and in recent years its coverage has extended to mathematics, nonlinear sciences, quantitative biology and computer science in addition to physics. arXiv is firmly embedded in the research workflows of these communities.

This paper discusses the results from a study which, as part of the RIOJA project, surveyed the views of scientists in the fields of astrophysics and cosmology regarding an overlay journal model. To gather background to their views on publishing, the respondents were asked to provide information about their research, publishing and reading patterns. The use of arXiv in this community and their response to a potential overlay publishing model were also in addressed in the survey. Respondents were asked to provide feedback about the suggested model; to indicate the factors that would influence them in deciding whether to publish in a journal overlaid onto a public repository; and to give their views on the relative importance of different features and functions of a journal in terms of funding priorities.

Literature Review

The overlay concept, and the term "overlay journal" itself, appear to be attributed to P. Ginsparg (1996). J W T Smith (1999) made a significant contribution to the concept of overlay journals by discussing and comparing functions of the existing publishing model with what he referred to as the "deconstructed journal". Although aspects of overlay have been introduced to journals in some subject domains, such as mathematics, overlay journals have not yet been widely deployed.

Halliday and Oppenheim (1999), in their report regarding the economics of Digital Libraries, recommended further research, in the field of electronic publishing in particular. Specifically, they suggested that the costs of electronic journal services should be further investigated, and commented that the degree of functionality that users require from electronic journals may have an impact on their costs.

Self-archiving and open access journals have been recommended by the Budapest Open Access Initiative (http://www.soros.org/openaccess/read.shtml) as the means to achieve access to publicly-funded research. The overlay model has the potential to combine both these "Green" (self-archiving) and "Gold" (open access journal) roads to open access. Hagemmann (2006) notes that *overlay journals complement the original BOAI dual strategy for achieving Open Access..."* and suggests that the overlay model could be the next step to open access. Factors such as the expansion of digital repositories, the introduction of open source journal management software, an increasing awareness within the scholarly community at large of the issues around open access, and an increasing readiness within the publishing community to experiment with new models, suggest that the circumstances may now be right for an overlay model to succeed. The RIOJA survey was designed to test the reaction of one research community, selected for its close integration with a central subject repository, to this prospective new model.

Aims and objectives

The aims of the survey were to explore the feasibility of a new journal publishing model in the field of astrophysics and cosmology, and to gather structured community input towards the refinement of a demonstrator journal. In particular, the objectives were:

• To gain a snapshot of research practice in this discipline, with particular reference to information-seeking, repository use and publication.
• To explore the ideal functional requirements of a community-led journal in astrophysics and cosmology, in order to inform further investigation into the costs associated with a sustainable implementation of the RIOJA model.
• To identify factors critical to the successful academic take-up of a journal founded on the principle of overlaid quality certification.

Methodology

The RIOJA project is currently being carried out in six overlapping packages, addressing technical developments in support of the overlay model, as well as its sustainability. . This paper discusses the results from an online questionnaire survey, aiming to explore the views of scientists in the fields of astrophysics and cosmology on the feasibility of an overlay journal model. The Times Higher Education Supplement World Rankings was used to identify scientists in the top 100 academic and 15 non-academic institutions in the fields of astrophysics and cosmology, so as to receive feedback from the research community at an international level. Additionally, the invitation to participate in the survey was posted to a domain-specific discussion list, "CosmoCoffee" (http://www.cosmocoffee.info).
The survey was launched on June 8th 2007, and closed on July 15th. The questionnaire comprised 5 sections. The first section aimed to gather demographic and other background information about the respondents. Sections 2 and 3 were designed to gather information about the research norms and practices of the scientists, from their perspectives as both creators and readers of research. Section 4 aimed to identify issues around the researchers' use of arXiv; and the final section sought their views regarding the viability of the overlay journal model.

The target group was restricted to scientists who have completed their doctoral studies, and who therefore could be assumed to have produced some publication of their research or to be in the process of publishing their research outcomes.

Definition and scope

For the purpose of this paper an overlay journal is defined as a quality-assured journal whose content is deposited to and resides in one or more open access repositories

The chosen sample placed some limitations on the survey. Identifying and collecting contact details for the scientists proved to be a difficult and lengthy process, for various reasons. For instance, astrophysics research groups in academic institutions often conduct interdisciplinary research, and can be spread across more than one department such as physics, mathematics and astronomy. In most cases, contact details for scientists, academic and research staff were not disclosed on institutional Web sites, and visits to various additional Web pages were required. Additionally, academic institutions are dynamic organisations, and academic and research staff can hold positions in more than one institution. Some overlap of contacts was therefore inevitable, although duplication was avoided wherever possible. These limitations should be borne in mind when the survey results are considered.

Results

The following sections present the results from the online questionnaire survey. 4012 scientists were contacted, and six hundred and eighty three (683), or 17%, responded.

Some identity characteristics

The first section of the questionnaire aimed to gather information that would allow the RIOJA team to draw an indicative profile of the scientists who participated in the questionnaire survey. In particular, almost a quarter of the responses came from scientists with professorial status (163 people, 24% of base=683). This was followed by Research Fellows (135 people, 20%), Lecturers (79 people, 12%), Senior Research Fellows (81 people, 12%) and Research Associates (81 people, 12%). The remainder of the response was divided between Readers, Senior Lecturers, and other categories. Almost half of the scientists (46%) reported having over 10 years of post-doctoral research experience. The vast majority

(90%) indicated that their primary responsibility was research. Teaching (38%) and heading a research group/unit (21%) also featured highly as indicative responsibilities of the scientists. The English language was reported as the mother tongue of almost half (51%) of respondents.

Publishing research outputs and reading patterns in astrophysics and cosmology

The second section of the questionnaire was designed to gather information about the information-seeking and publishing patterns of scientists in the fields of astrophysics and cosmology. The following issues were explored in particular:

- Whether scientists in those fields still require journals to publish their research.
- What factors affect their decisions on where to publish

The first choice of research output for the vast majority of the researchers (663 people) was papers for submission to peer-reviewed journals. The scientists reported that, on average, they each produced 13 papers over a two year period. The second most popular research output was papers for conference proceedings. Both of those findings confirm the importance that peer-reviewed journals and peers in general, play in the validation and dissemination of research in this discipline.

The journals in which the respondents had mostly published their research were: "The Astrophysical Journal" (476 people), "Monthly Notices of the Royal Astronomical Society" (382) and "Astronomy and Astrophysics" (331). These 3 journals are among the top 10 journals in terms of ISI impact factor. Irrespective of ongoing discussions in the literature about the validity of citation analysis, these findings indicate that it does currently have a bearing on scientists' decisions on where to publish.

The researchers were also asked to rank the importance of several factors which might influence their decision on where to publish. The majority of the researchers (494 people) reported that the quality of the journal as perceived by the scientific community was very important to them. Other important factors were the impact factor of the journal (330), and being kept up-to-date during the refereeing process (346). Factors that were deemed to range from neither important nor unimportant, to unimportant, were whether the journal is published by their professional society (473), and whether the journal is published in print (463). These results are presented in the following table.

Table 1. Factors affecting the decision of where to publish

Statement	Rating	% agree		
Perceived quality of the journal by the scientific community		97.3	±	1.2
High journal impact factor		88.9	±	2.4
Being kept up-to-date during the refereeing process		81.6	±	3
Other factors (please specify)		75.3	±	9.4
Inclusion in indexing/abstracting services (e.g. ISI Science Citation Index)		67.9	±	3.6
Reputation of the editor/editorial board		66.2	±	3.6
Journals that do not charge authors for publication		64.5	±	3.6
Open Access Journals (journals whose content is openly and freely available)		52.8	±	3.8
Low or no subscription costs		33.9	±	3.6
Journals which publish a print version		29.8	±	3.5
Journals published by my professional society		26.9	±	3.4
Journals which have a high rate of rejection of papers		21.1	±	3.1

Key: Very unimportant | Fairly unimportant | Neither | Fairly important | Very important

Other factors that were specifed as important by respondents emphasised the process of peer review - in particular, the speed, quality and reliability of the process. Some comments on the *speed of peer review* concerned the role of the editorial team and other support services (e.g. publishers' role). Comments show that an easily accessible editorial team that keeps scientists informed at each stage of the review process while responding promptly and reliably to questions is desirable. Also welcomed, perhaps as an alternative, would be access to an online system that allows authors to keep track of the peer review process, supplemented by a clear statement how the review is conducted and the assessment criteria in place Comments about the *quality of peer review* raised issues around the transparency of the process, the selection of the referees and a proven record of past refereeing alongside what a respondent called *"respected peer review".* Furthermore, comments also referred to the competence, care, efficiency and responsibility of editors and editorial boards. The subject coverage of the journal, the efficiency and ease of use of the submission system, handling of images and various file formats (eg LaTex), and the time that it takes for a paper to reach publication were also noted as influential factors.

Use of the arXiv and other services

The scientists were asked to indicate the means they employ for keeping up to date with advances in their fields. The majority of the respondents (549 people, 80.4% of base=683) visit the arXiv and in particular the "new/recent" section to keep up to date with new research. This finding confirms the role of the arXiv in these fields as an active and vital point for publicising research. In addition to arXiv's "new/recent" service, 396 people (58%) noted that they visit the ADS website to look for new papers. This shows that indexing services still have a place in this community Those who noted "other" in their response mentioned their reliance on information from and discussions with colleagues, journal alerting services (such as RSS and table of contents), attendance at conferences and workshops, and visiting SPIRES.

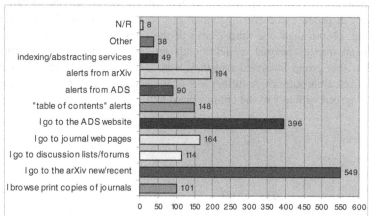

Fig. 1. Sources used for keeping up to date with research advances

The scientists were also asked to indicate the locations they turn to retrieve the full text of potentially interesting papers. E-print repositories (such as the arXiv) were denoted as the primary source of information for accessing the full text of a paper by 610 people (89% of base=683, Fig. 2.). The second most-preferred option (443 scientists, 65%) is to visit the journal's website.. Those who indicated "other" sources (111 people, 16.3%) referred mainly to the ADS services and to SPIRES.

Sources for obtaining the full text of papers

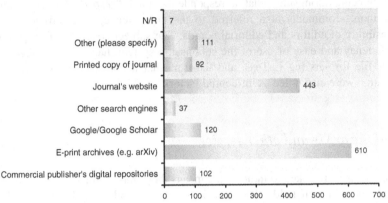

Fig. 2. Sources used for accessing the full text of papers

Overlay journal model

More than half of the respondents to the questionnaire survey (53%) were favourably disposed to the overlay journal as a potential future model for scientific publishing. More than one third (35%) of the respondent, however, noted that although an overlay journal model sounds interesting they did not consider it important: this group indicated that they were fairly satisfied with their current access to research outputs. A further 7% of the scientists either did not reply, or said they agreed with any of the options provided.

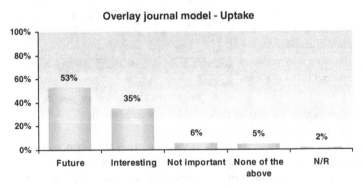

Fig. 3. Overlay journal model – Uptake

Many interesting comments were made in response to this question. Scientists who did not welcome the overlay journal model highlighted their currently unclear perception and understanding of the overlay journal model, and their concerns about new publishing models. Comments from all groups noted that forming an opinion about the possible role of overlay journal models in the future of publishing scientific journals would depend upon:

- "...how the journal was explicitly set-up in practice"
- "...I am concerned about long-term archiving, which assumes much greater importance when you are dealing with completed, peer-reviewed works as opposed to electronic preprints or open-access copies of material that is archived elsewhere"
- "...on how widely used by readers the system becomes. If no-one reads it, there's no point submitting to it"
- "An overlay of "accepted" papers is O.K. if the acceptance standards are objective"
- "if this is to replace all other journals, as it should, particular care has to be taken with the review process to allow authors to challenge the peer review or editor; parallel alternate structures need to be in place".

Additionally, concerns relating to the use of arXiv as the repository to be overlaid (policies about file sizes, submission, acceptance and citation of unrefereed papers, multiple versions of papers, etc.) were also raised by some of the respondents. For example:

- "...arXiv papers that are submitted before refereeing and then resubmitted 1-2 times are both annoying and scientifically irresponsible. If there was really a new category of arXiv that only had accepted papers, that is a plus, but even better would be to make it clearer to insist that papers should not even be posted on arXiv unless they have been reviewed..."
- "arXiv allows for replacements. Journal would need to specify which version was peer reviewed and should be considered as "published". This may lead to confusion".
- "A point I have with this new idea is: will the "accepted" papers be in the same repository of the "normal" arXiv (so that it will not be that easy to find them) or will there be a devoted repository which keep them separated from the others?"

Respondents to the questionnaire survey were asked to provide their views about what fraction of money, within a given budget, should be spent on different functions of a journal. We used a ranking scale of five points, ranging from "none", to little (1) and very little (2), moderate amount (3), and considerable (4) and most of the amount (5), with the additional option of "not sure". It was hoped that this would provide some indication of which journal functions the scientists considered important; the question was not designed to be the basis of a costing exercise for a potential new journal. Most of the responses indicated that the scientists place importance on the role of scientific and copy editors and ensuring the maintenance of the journal software. However, the majority of the respondents in every group emphasised the importance of the journal website, with the online archive of the journal's back issues also given some priority.

Table 2. Suggested expenditure/priorities by journal functions

Suggested expenditure/priority	None	1	2	3	4	5	Not sure
Paying scientific editors	23	23	60	240	141	15	21
Paying copy editors	8	28	73	256	134	6	15
Maintenance of journal software	4	20	73	238	147	9	30
Journal website	5	28	79	225	149	20	15
Online archive of journal's own back issues	9	27	52	202	189	18	19
Production of paper version	138	101	125	107	29	4	14
Extra features such as storage of associated data	30	63	105	182	100	6	26
Publisher profits	142	122	138	91	9	0	19
Paying referees	249	70	70	85	22	8	18
Other	3	1	1	1	3	2	3

Finally, the respondents were asked to indicate the factors that would encourage them to publish in an overlay journal (as defined by the RIOJA project), and whether they would be willing to participate in an overlay journal in some capacity. The most important factors which would encourage publication were the quality of other submitted papers (526), the transparency of the peer review process (410) and the reputation of the editorial board (386). They also provided a range of other factors that they considered important, among them the reputation of the journal; its competitiveness across other journals under the RAE (the UK's Research Assessment Exercise); the quality both of the journal's referees and of its accepted papers; a commitment to using free software; a commitment to the long-term archiving and preservation of published papers; relevant readership; acceptance and reputation of the journal in the scientific community; and its impact factor, which should only take into account citations to papers after final acceptance and not while residing on arXiv prior to "publication".

The questionnaire participants were asked to indicate their willingness, in principle, to participate in an arXiv-overlay journal. The vast majority of the scientists (549 people, 80% of base=683) stated that they would act as referees (**Fig. 4.**). Given the emphasis that the researchers placed on the process of peer review, noted throughout this report, this result suggests that there is genuine interest in contributing to the improvement of what they consider an important process. A willingness to referee for an overlay journal was expressed by over three quarters of respondents in each group, with Readers the only exception at 68%.

Willingness to participate

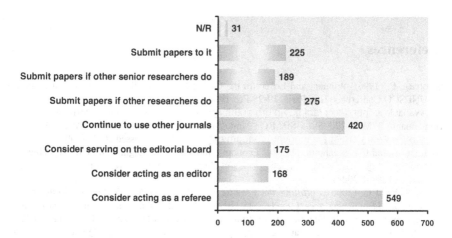

Conclusions and future work

The roles, responsibilities and experience of the respondents primarily involve research. The preferred output from their research is peer-reviewed journal article, which confirms the importance in this discipline of certification by quality-assured journals. The scientists indicated that the quality of any journal publishing model is very important to them, and they choose to publish in journals that demonstrate to them the endorsement of the scientific community, whether through readership levels, impact factor, or perceived quality of the editorial board and journal content.

In general the scientists were disposed favourably towards the overlay journal model. However, they raised several implementation issues that they would consider important, primarily relating to the quality of the editorial board and of the published papers, and to the long-term archiving of the accepted research material. The traditional publishing functions of copy editing and scientific copy editing remain important to researchers in these disciplines. The traditional printed volume is of little interest, but the scientists highlighted the long-term electronic archiving of the journal content as important.

The initial results from this survey suggest that scientists in the fields of astrophysics and cosmology are, in the main, positioned positively towards a new publishing model that, in a respondent's own words, "...*is more open, flexible, quicker (and cheaper?), and as "safe" or safer (i.e. ensuring science quality) as would be needed"*. A full examination of these results, together with the other findings from the RIOJA project, is expected to enrich our understanding of the many issues around the acceptance and sustainability of the overlay journal as a potential publishing model.

References

Ginsparg, P. (1996). Winners and Losers in the Global Research Village. Invited contribution, UNESCO Conference HQ, Paris, 19-23 Feb 1996.
    Available at: http://xxx.lanl.gov/blurb/pg96unesco.html (Last accessed 20/01/2008)
Haggemann, M. (2006). SPARC Innovator: December 2006. Available at: http://www.arl.org/sparc/innovator/hagemann.html (Last accessed 20/0/1/2008)
Halliday, L and C Oppenheim. (1999). Economic models of the Digital Library. Available at: http://www.ukoln.ac.uk/services/elib/papers/ukoln/emod-diglib/final-report.pdf (Last accessed 20/01/2008)
Prosser, David C. (2005) *Fulfilling the promise of scholarly communication - a comparison between old and new access models*, in Nielsen, Erland Kolding and Saur, Klaus G. and Ceynowa, Klaus, Eds. Die innovative Bibliothek : Elmar Mittler zum 65.Geburtstag, pp. 95-106. K G Saur. (Also available at http://eprints.rclis.org/archive/00003918) (Last accessed 20/01/2008)
Smith, J W T. (1999). The deconstructed journal: a new model for academic publishing. Learned Publishing, Vol. 12 (2), pp. 79-91
The Times Higher Education Supplement. (2006). World's top 100 in science. Available at: http://www.thes.co.uk/statistics/international_comparisons/2006/top_100_science.aspx (Last accessed 31/08/2007)
The Times Higher Education Supplement. (2006). World's top non university institutions in science.   Available   at: http://www.thes.co.uk/statistics/international_comparisons/2006/top_non_unis_science.aspx (Last   accessed   31/08/2007)

An RDF modification protocol, based on the needs of editing Tools

Fredrik Enoksson[1], Matthias Palmér[1], Ambjörn Naeve[1]

Abstract. The use of RDF on the web is increasing, unfortunately the amount of editing tools suitable for end users without knowledge of technicalities of the language are not so common. We believe that a vital ingredient for the editing tools to flourish is a working remote modification protocol. This will allow editing tools to be developed separately from triple-stores and make them more flexible and reusable. Several initiatives for remote modification exist already but have not gained wide-spread adoption. In this paper we will show that most of them fall short when it comes to edit arbitrary RDF constructs, especially in combination with typical requirements of editing tools. We will first list these requirements, then propose a solution that fulfills them and finally outline an implementation. With this implementation we will also demonstrate how Annotation Profiles, a configuration mechanism for RDF metadata editors, has the additional feature of making modification requests very precise.

1 Introduction

RDF is increasingly used for expressing metadata on the web, and consequently appropriate end-user editing tools are in demand. To become more user-friendly such editing tools need to hide the complex RDF-structure from the user. This is typically achieved by displaying the metadata in forms and focusing on a single or a few central resources at a time. Beyond the user-interface layer such editing tools need to access a triple-store where the RDF is stored. A common solution is to use the triple-stores own API. Unfortunately this approach makes it harder to separate editing tools from the underlying triple-store which has a negative impact on the variety of triple-stores and makes it harder to create well-designed editing tools. Hence, a common protocol for remote modification of RDF is desirable. Earlier initiatives, such as (Seaborne 2002) and (Nejdl 2002), have not gained

---

[1] Royal Institute of Technology(KTH/CSC), Lindstedtsv. 5, 100 44 Stockholm, Sweden
{fen,matthias,amb}@csc.kth.se

wide acceptance, probably due to the lack of a common query language, which more or less is a prerequisite. Now, when SPARQL and the closely related SPARQL-protocol for RDF (endorsed by W3C) has matured, the possibility of a wide acceptance of a remote modification protocol has increased. A recent initiative, SPARUL (Seaborne and Manjunath 2007), builds on top of SPARQL and looks promising, especially since much of the work done for supporting SPARQL in a triple-store can be reused. However, when taking a closer look, limitations from the perspective of an editing tool became visible. In this paper we will first consider the requirements on a protocol that supports remote modification from the perspective of an editing tool, then list possible approaches for a remote modification protocol, and finally discuss the reason why SPARUL will not be sufficient and also outline a simple solution in accordance with the introduced requirements for editing tools.

2 Remote Modification Protocol

The following list of requirements is not complete. Rather, it represents requirements from the perspective of editing tools. Even though these requirements might seem quite natural and simple, they are not so easy to fulfill, especially when taking into account the common usage of blank nodes in RDF .

Resource centric – all kinds of subgraphs reachable (possible via intermediate blank nodes) from a named node (resource identified through a URI) should be modifiable.

Concise modifications – The modification requests should be concise, not inefficient by transferring too much or too little data at a time.

Without side effects – parts of the graph that are not to be modified should be left intact. More specifically, you should not be required to have knowledge of all parts of the graph to be able to modify it successfully.

Application independent – There should not be any built-in knowledge in the protocol of specific properties or resources.

2.1 Different approaches to build a Remote Modification Protocol

The two naive approaches to support remote modification, i.e. transferring updates with one statement at a time or the entire RDF graph, are both flawed. Updating one statement at a time would yield a "chatty protocol" where a single update operation could require hundreds of requests. On the other hand, updating the entire RDF graph could result in the transfer of large amounts of data where large parts are sent unmodified back and forth. It would also be problematic to support simultaneous updates with this approach as the entire graph would have to be locked.

A better approach would be to transfer only deltas (differences) between RDF graphs as described in (Berners-Lee and Connolly 2006). The described strong delta is especially interesting as they can be applied to subsets of the whole RDF graph. Unfortunately, the outlined algorithm breaks down whenever there are blank nodes in the graph, unless there are unique ways to identify them. (Breaking or leaving orphaned blank nodes in the graph is of course not acceptable, see the requirement 'without side effects'.) The general problem of identifying blank nodes requires finding the largest common subgraph is a graph isomorphism problem which has been proven to be NP-complete (see discussion in (Berners-Lee and Connolly 2006)). Hence, another approach has been taken. The corresponding algorithm relies on knowledge of how the graph was constructed, i.e. according to which OWL ontology. Hence, if there are inbound functional or outbound inversely functional properties from a blank node to another identifiable node in the graph, the blank node can be identified. Unfortunately, there are a lot of real world situations when the data does not follow an OWL ontology, or even if there is an OWL ontology it may not be known by the tool, or there may not be enough functional or inversely functional properties to uniquely identify the blank nodes. Hence, this approach seem to be too brittle to base a remote modification protocol on it.

Another approach is transferring an easily identified subgraph that encompasses the modification. To avoid the problem of preserving identity of blank nodes, the subgraph should be defined in such a way that it shares no blank nodes with the rest of the graph. In the general case, this requirement could mean that the subgraph will be large, or even identical to the whole graph, for example if the graph consists solely of blank nodes. However, in nearly all real editing scenarios that we care about from the perspective of the requirement 'resource centric' listed above, there is a mixture of named nodes and blank nodes. Furthermore, the blank nodes are typically arranged into tree like data-structures that are reachable from the named nodes and not interconnected in a larger graph except via the named nodes. This is not something we postulate here, but rather a consequence of an established best practice where you name the resources that you express metadata on with URIs. From this observation we realize that a useful method of calculating a subgraph is the *anonymous closure* (or the closely related *concise bounded descriptions*), i.e. starting from a named resource and then recursively including all statements until other named resources are encountered.

It is important that the calculation of the subgraph is done deterministically, since with anonymous closure, it has to be done twice, first to be accessed for remote modification and second to be removed from the bigger graph before the modified subgraph is inserted. The alternatives, to calculating the subgraph twice, are either removing the subgraph directly or keeping a copy of the subgraph on the server side for later removal. The first alternative will yield a graph where data is missing from time to time, which should clearly be avoided. The second alternative requires a state -sensitive protocol and sessions to keep track of who initiated a modification on a specific subgraph. This should also be avoided both to avoid complexity and to be compatible with the principles of REST[2] (sometimes referred to as the architecture of the web). Hence, the preferred alternative is calculating the subgraph twice.

Even though the anonymous closure subgraph approach is simple and solves the problem with graphs that have blank nodes in them, it has to be complemented to allow 'concise modifications' of larger subgraphs including several named nodes. (See above for the 'concise modification' requirement.) If you know the names of all the named nodes you can simply take the anonymous closure of each of them. However, this is not always the case since you typically only know the name of one of the named nodes and how the other nodes are connected to it. In this case you have to express the relationship from the known named node to the other nodes in a query language and then require the anonymous closure of all the matches. With SPARQL this can be almost completely achieved with graph patterns and the DESCRIBE option. Unfortunately, DESCRIBE is formally undefined and left to the triple-store to implement However, for general purpose triple-stores the anonymous closure algorithm or it's close counterparts seems to be frequently used.

2.2 Why the SPARUL approach will not be sufficient

The main idea with SPARUL is to specify which statements to DELETE and which to INSERT into a specific model. In its simplest form, the statements are simply listed, and the approach has the limitations of sending deltas without the elaborate scheme to identify blank nodes as discussed above. Hence, in this simple case, statements with blank nodes can be inserted but never removed or modified. In the more advanced case, the delete and insert blocks contain templates which generate the statements to DELETE and INSERT via matching of a WHERE clause. Modifying subgraphs containing blank nodes is in this case possible but awkward since: First, it requires the WHERE clause to uniquely identify the right subgraph and capture the blank nodes in appropriate variables. Second the templates in DELETE and INSERT have to be carefully constructed to express the modification to be done. For simple and well-known metadata and specific applications this is perhaps feasible. But in general, the required algorithm would be complex and be executed in every compliant client that want to use the protocol. We argue that a better approach is to allow the DELETE to be combined with DESCRIBE based on the variables matched in WHERE. In this case it will be possible to delete a series of anonymous closures according to the principle described above and then list the modified subgraph to be inserted in INSERT.

---

2   http://www.ics.uci.edu/~fielding/pubs/dissertation/rest_arch_style.htm

3 Approach: Replacing subgraphs

We suggest a modification mechanism, along the lines of what was discussed in the last part of section 2.1, where an subgraph is calculated, retrieved, modified locally, and finally pushed back to the remote storage to replace the original subgraph. This approach has the benefit of not requiring knowledge in advance, such as SPARUL, of how the graph looks like. Instead, it is sufficient to know a starting point and in some cases a rough outline of what to modify. The subgraph calculated from this knowledge can be treated like any RDF graph, modified locally at leisure and then, pushed back to the remote storage where the modification is incorporated into the bigger graph. Hence, a related benefit compared to update languages such as SPARUL, editing tools need not make use of a specific update language since they can make the modifications directly in the RDF graph (The alternative, generating SPARUL updates from changes in the subgraph are nontrivial and will fail to do correct modifications in many situations involving blank nodes).

In the following section we go through how to use SPARQL and a new kind of SPARQL-based service at the remote storage fore realizing this approach.

3.1 Retrieving a proper subgraph to edit

In order to find the proper subgraph a resource is needed as a starting point. This is the central resource from which to start the search of what related resources that are to be edited. Since not all the resources connected to the starting point is known, a pattern has to be provided. This way arbitrarily deep constructs can be retrieved by using the DESCRIBE query in SPARQL. As stated above, DESCRIBE is not formally defined and can therefore return different answers for different implementations. For the purpose of retrieving a proper subgraph, all the direct properties of the resource, the Concise Bounded Description for the resource, and all properties for the resources matched in the pattern need to be returned. In the following, an example will be given where we want to edit the dc:title, dc:creator and dc:subject for a given resource. The RDF graph in the remote storage is depicted in figure 1.

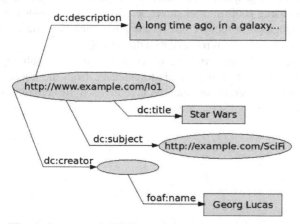

Fig. 1: An example RDF graph in the remote storage.

In order to retrieve the subgraph with a DESCRIBE-query, the following question provides enough information:

```
DESCRIBE <http://www.example.com/lo1> ?creator
?subject

WHERE
{ OPTIONAL {
    <http://www.example.com/lo1>
        <http://purl.org/dc/terms/creator>  ?creator .
}
    OPTIONAL {
        <http://www.example.com/lo1>
            <http://purl.org/dc/terms/subject> ?subject .
}
}
```

From the pattern in this example, a model with all properties and values for the resource http://www.example.com/lo1 will be returned, as well as all properties and values for potential resources matching the variables *?creator* and *?subject*. The reason that we do not include a title property in the query is because this is a direct property. The reason why we include subject and creator is that they might point to non-anonymous resources. The use of OPTIONAL for every property also assures that if one property will not match, a graph will anyway be returned (with all the properties) if such a resource exists.

3.2 Updating the remote storage

When the retrieved model has been modified by the application, the subgraph on the remote storage should be updated with these modification. An update-request to the remote storage consists of two parts: First, an indication of which subgraph to remove, and second, a subgraph to be inserted as a replacement. This subgraph has to be sent by serialising RDF into whatever serialisation is supported by the remote storage. The subgraph to remove can on the other hand be indicated by a query (that is, the same query used to retrieve it in the first place).

After the remote server has received the query to calculate the subgraph to remove and the model to insert, it first needs to calculate from the query what subgraph to remove from the server and then remove it. Then the subgraph to be inserted can be put into the model at the server.

4. Implementation

An implementation of the described approach in section 3 has been made by the authors of this paper. The remote storage used is version 3.1 of the *Joseki*[3] server and the editor application was implemented with the SHAME[4] code library. This is a code library used to built editors that can be configured with RDF metadata Annotation Profiles, as described in (Palmér et al. 2007) and (Palmér, Enoksson and Nilsson et al 2007).

An RDF metadata Annotation Profile consists of a *Form Template* and a *Graph Pattern*, where the latter can be used to fairly easily create a query used to retrieve the subgraph to edit from the remote storage. A Graph Pattern is expressed in an RDF query language like SPARQL. It defines the structure of the metadata to be edited and also acts as a template when new metadata structures are to be created. The Graph Pattern is a tree-structure where the root-node variable matches the resource to be edited, and intermediate resources are variable nodes that match nodes in the RDF-model. A query to send to the remote storage can be constructed from the Graph Pattern by removing the leaves from the Graph Pattern and then send it as a DESCRIBE query.

As the Annotation Profile is constructed from the perspective of usability for the end users, one can expect that it encompasses a suitable subgraph to update in one operation. Moreover, as the DESCRIBE query is constructed from the graph pattern, it will correspond to a *concise modification* (one of our requirements).

In our implementation this is sent to the Joseki server over HTTP, and the server returns the calculated subgraph, or an empty graph if no subgraph can be calculated.

Once the model has been retrieved, it is edited by applying the method that is described in (Palmér et al. 2007) and (Palmér, Enoksson and Nilsson et al 2007). The editing process, described shortly here, will match the Graph Pattern against the retrieved subgraph, and create bindings to the matching variables. These bindings are then combined with the Form Template that makes it possible to create a Graphical User Interface that hides the underlying complexity from the end-user. This GUI makes it possible for the end-user to modify the subgraph in a rather simple form-based manner.

When the changes to the subgraph are finished, an if the end user decides to save the modifications, the modified subgraph is serialised into RDF/XML and the query to calculate the original subgraph is expressed as a DESCRIBE query in SPARQL. As stated above, this is the same query as the one used to retrieve the subgraph. For the Joseki-server to perform the update, we have to implement and add a service called Update, which is called with these two arguments. On the Joseki server, the operation of removing the calculated subgraph is performed

---

3   http://www.joseki.org
4   http://kmr.nada.kth.se/shame

first, followed by inserting the modified subgraph. Joseki is using Jena to handle RDF, and the two operations are implemented using the methods *add* and *remove* defined in the interface Model of the Jena API.

5. Conclusion

In this paper we have described several initiatives/approaches to remotely edit RDF graphs, according to the requirements of being *Resource centric*, allowing *Concise modifications*, being *Without side effects*, and being *Application independent*. Specifically, we have discussed a recent initiative, SPARUL, which seems to be promising. However, we believe that it does not provide sufficient flexibility since it requires too much knowledge of the remote graph in advance. Moreover, we have argued that the only approach that could meet all the requirements for the needs of an editing tool is the one described in section 3. This approach relies on the facts that most graphs consist of a mixture of blank and non-blank nodes, and that replacing whole subgraphs calculated from one or a few starting points corresponds well to the extent of a typical update. The update is performed by retrieving a subgraph, modifying it and then submitting the modified subgraph back to replace the original.

In addition to the modification mechanism, this paper has shortly outlined how to use Annotation Profiles, a configuration mechanism for editing tools, in order to retrieve the subgraph needed for editing. Consequently, if such an approach is used, the modification protocol will work automatically, avoiding manual construction of queries.

A rather important issue that is out of the scope of this paper is how to handle concurrent changes of the same subgraph. Presently, the subgraph is not locked after the first retrieval of it, and changes could be done inside the same subgraph by another user. Additional to the risk of updates being overwritten falsely, this might lead to inconsistencies in the RDF, since differences in the queries used to extract the subgraph may lead to orphaned constructs. Some kind of additional restrictions on the queries may be needed for a consistent locking mechanism to be feasible.

Acknowledgement

This work has been carried out with financial support from the EU-FP6 project LUISA (http://www.luisa-project.eu), which the authors gratefully acknowledge.

References

Berners-Lee T, Connolly D (2006) Delta: an ontology for the distribution of differences between RDF graphs. http://www.w3.org/DesignIssues/Diff. Accesses 19 January 2008

Nejdl W, Siberski W, Simon B, Tane J (2002) Towards a Modification Exchange Language for Distributed RDF Repositories. In: Proceedings of the First International Semantic Web Conference on The Semantic Web. Springer, UK

Palmér M, Enoksson F, Naeve A (2007) LUISA deliverable 3.2: Annotation Profile Specification. http://luisa.atosorigin.es/www/images/comission_deliverables/WP3_D3.2_AnnotationProfileSpecification_Final.pdf. Accessed 19 January 2008

Palmér M, Enoksson F, Nilsson M, Naeve A (2007) Annotation Profiles: Configuring forms to edit RDF. In: Proceedings of the Dublin Core Metadata Conference. DCMI Conference Papers, United States

Seaborne A (2002) An RDF NetAPI. In: Proceedings of the First International Semantic Web Conference on The Semantic Web. Springer, UK

Seaborne A, Manjunath G (2007) SPARQL/Update A language for updating RDF graphs. Version 2. http://jena.hpl.hp.com/~afs/SPARQL-Update.html Accessed 19 January 2008

Pragmatic support for taxonomy-based annotation of structured digital documents

Lara Whitelaw[1] and Trevor Collins[2]

Abstract   The aim of the work presented here was to explore how taxonomy-based annotation could facilitate the use of digital library resources within a virtual learning environment for distance learning students. The approach taken is to provide support for the fine-grained annotation of course study materials so that relevant digital library resources can be retrieved and presented alongside the appropriate sections of a student's course materials. This paper introduces the course delivery model and discusses the process involved in developing a pragmatic tool to support annotation.

1.   The Open University digital library

The Open University, UK (OU) is a distance learning university with more than 180,000 students. The university uses blended learning techniques to teach students at a distance. In the past, OU courses have been very self-contained with students being provided with a course materials pack that contains all the resources they need to complete their course. More recently, OU courses have been making increasing use of activities that encourage the students to study beyond their course materials and explore their subject in a more independent manner (thereby, further developing their information literacy and transferable skills).

The wide-spread public take-up of internet access and the increasing availability of electronic journals and online databases have enabled the university to cre-

---

[1] Lara Whitelaw

The Open University Library, The Open University, Milton Keynes, UK., e-mail:
l.whitelaw@open.ac.uk

[2] Trevor Collins

Knowledge Media Institute, The Open University, Milton Keynes, UK., e-mail:
t.d.collins@open.ac.uk

ate an extensive online library of digital resources for our students. This currently provides access to 270 electronic databases containing approximately 15,000 journal titles. The subscription costs for e-resources are very high and there is pressure to raise awareness and increase uptake of the resources. Combined with the fact that Open University students are particularly time poor and on the basis of student feedback, the organisation is keen to identify and access relevant library resources at appropriate points within the course timelines, whilst ensuring that students are neither swamped by information overload, nor too overwhelmed and intimidated to interact with the resources.

Current practice in the OU is to create a metadata record for every course learning resource which goes through the university's print production system. These records are catalogued using the IEEE Learning Object Metadata standard, and the complexity and detail of the record varies based on the size and breadth of the resource. For example, a four-page assessment resource will have a less detailed record than a main text that may be several hundred pages long. The Resources for Learning by Exploration (ReFLEx) Project was developed to look at ways of improving access to course resources and exposing relevant library resources through the application of semantic web technologies to semi-automated metadata annotation. The project aimed to build on Spotlight Browsing technology developed in the CIPHER project [10].

2.   Research Context

The current state of metadata annotation technologies and automation developments for educational resources has been analysed in great detail recently in two major reports [11] [4]. The JISC State of the Art Review [11] recommended the need to investigate semi-automatic solutions to indexing and classification and highlighted that: "many argue for a combination of intellectual work and automatic assistance". The Automated Metadata Review of existing and potential metadata within Jorum and an overview of other automation systems [4] recommended: "a process of metadata generation followed by a process of cataloguing and then review should remain in place [within the Jorum system], and cataloguers should at least concept check selected entries which the system makes."

The Library of Congress funded Final Report for the AMeGA (Automated Metadata Generation Applications) Project [6], found that the two metadata functionalities strongly favoured by their metadata expert survey were: "Running automatic algorithm(s) initially to acquire metadata that a human can evaluate and edit [and] integrating content standards (e.g., subject thesauri, name authority files) into metadata generation applications" [6].

As has been found in a number of studies, providing access to online resources is not sufficient to ensure they are used effectively in a learning context [9] [12] [5]. In order to encourage the uptake of digital library services, the use of these resources should be embedded in the students' study activities. This can be facilitated by encouraging a close working relationship between the academicss involved in producing the course materials and the library staff delivering the supporting information services [3]. The following section introduces a delivery model that tries to foster such a relationship through the shared use of a set of annotation, recommendation and presentation support interfaces.

3. Course delivery model

In order to contribute to the student's achievement of the learning objectives for the course, the use of library resources must be pertinent to the section of the course, accurate in terms of the content they present, of a suitable level of detail, and appropriate for the study time available. To ensure these criteria are met, a tiered delivery model has been proposed consisting of the: annotation, selection and presentation of library resources within a virtual learning environment. The intention is to supplement metadata currently created by the library for the electronic course materials; the aim being to disaggregate resources into smaller component parts and provide child records for each of the disaggregated objects linked to the main catalogue record for the overall resource.

The delivery model is comprised of annotation, selection and presentation tiers. Annotation involves the creation of metadata for each section of the course materials. The selection tier incorporates the use of the course material metadata to find relevant resources, and the selection and recommendation of those resources to students. Finally, the presentation tier combines the structured course material content and the recommended resources in the students' interface to the learning environment.

The following section explains the form of annotation used in this context and discusses the iterative development of the annotation support tool.

4. Annotation support

The annotation used in this application involved the creation of domain specific metadata for each section of the course materials. This can then be used to help identify relevant resources either by search or information alerting services. Subject librarians and course teams worked together to identify domain taxonomies, which were used to create the document metadata. The subject based taxonomies have the benefits of a fixed vocabulary and hierarchical structure. Although taxonomies are not as expressive as ontologies, due to their simpler structure they are easier to apply. Pragmatically, using domain thesauri and taxonomies was seen as the option which could be developed and applied most consistently across the breadth and depth of subjects taught at the university. Although domain ontologies are increasing in number, it couldn't be guaranteed that there would be suitable ontologies for all the university's subject domains. We also felt that domain taxonomies would provide us with a sufficient level of richness for the task of identifying relevant articles and online resources. Therefore, the goal in this application was to support the human cataloguer in their selection of domain taxonomy terms for creating document section metadata.

Taxonomies follow a standard representation that identifies the preferred terms or 'go terms' (G), and non-preferred terms or 'stop terms' (S). For each of the go terms the taxonomy definition lists the broader (BT) and narrower (NT) go terms, and any related terms (RT). If a go term is used in preference to a stop term, the stop term is listed in the taxonomy under the go term as a 'use for' term (UF), conversely under each stop term the go term used in preference is listed as a 'use' term (USE).

Rather than fully automating the process, the system was designed to suggest terms for the cataloguer to validate and where necessary correct. The design of the taxonomy matching algorithm went through four iterations with the library cataloguer before finding an effective solution. This involved the library cataloguers evaluating the quality of the automated metadata produced by the algorithms and feeding this back to the developers in an iterative manner in order to improve the accuracy of the results. The library cataloguers involved in the evaluation are the same cataloguers that currently create the metadata records for the course materials. Their involvement in the project was invaluable, as their detailed knowledge of the resources selected for the pilot meant that the library was able to give highly detailed and structured feedback to the developers regarding the effectiveness of the tools.

The first version involved the use of a database's 'full text' search function, in which the taxonomy terms were matched against the text in each document section. In the second version this was extended by stemming both the taxonomy terms and the section text. In the third iteration an additional weighting was added to the matching of taxonomy terms and section headings. Finally, sentence frequency counts were used to replace the full text search approach; this involved counting the number of sentences in the stemmed document section containing the stemmed words in each go term or any associated 'use for' terms.

The fourth version was best suited to the cataloguer's approach to the task. The interface to the system shows the course document and the set of suggested taxonomy terms for each section (see Fig 1). When the cataloguer clicks on a taxonomy term, the taxonomy definition for that term is displayed and the occurrences of that term and any associated use for terms are highlighted in the displayed document section. A checkbox is listed to the side of each term for the cataloguer to indicate whether or not the term should be used as section metadata.

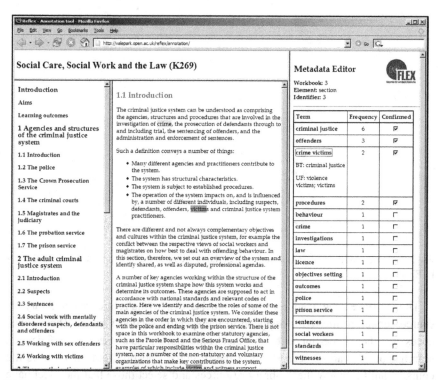

Fig 1. The course material annotation interface, as used by the library cataloguing staff. An interactive table of contents for the course document is shown on the left, a selected document section is shown in the middle of the screen, and a table of applicable taxonomy terms for the selected section is displayed on the right.

The initial trials looking at the use of this interface by library cataloguers has been very encouraging. The tool identifies the majority of relevant terms, and where inappropriate terms are suggested or appropriate terms are missed the interface supports the checking and correction of the section annotations.

Course staff and students are then presented with a web page that provides a browsable version of the course materials. The web presentation is produced from the XML schema that has been developed by the university, for use within a structured authoring environment and the OpenLearn project [2].

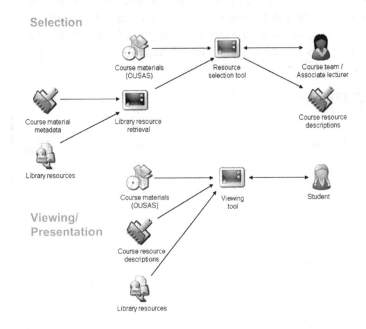

Fig 2. Selection of and viewing of library materials by course teams and students using the Re-FLEX tools

The interface developed to include a sidebar displaying references to library resources linked to the terms assigned to the specific section viewed. These references are then hyperlinked to the electronic library databases via a federated search tool. As can be seen in Fig 2 the resource selection tool then allows the course team to review these library resources and select those that they feel have most relevance for the students. The viewing tool then gives the students access to the course materials and the selected library resources. The interface also highlights terms and references that are contained in course indexes and glossaries or course readers and displays the resulting definitions and resources.

5. Cost benefit analysis results

As part of the pilot project the library carried out a cost benefit analysis, this took place at an early stage of the tool development. Of necessity, the current analysis is based largely on qualitative data. Further development of the tools will enable more quantitative data to be collated, interpreted and presented. The methodology has been to conduct a narrow cost benefit analysis focusing on the annotation support and the perceived benefits of the 2nd and 3rd tiers of the delivery model.

The quantitative data presented in the report was based on tools in the early stages of development. The average time spent using the annotation tool equated to one minute per page of the course materials, compared to 30-40 seconds when cataloguing using the university's traditional methods. The ReFLEx annotation tool allows the segmentation of materials to a much finer degree as can be seen in the example in Table 1 where the course material has been given 23 sibling records and 235 confirmed subject terms, with an average of 2.6 terms per page. Although the additional time taken can be seen as significant, achieving the same results from manual processes would not be feasible. It is anticipated that future iterations of the annotation tool would reduce process times during the human mediation phase of the annotation process.

Table 1. A Comparison of the number of terms created and the time taken to annotate an example OU course block under the existing document annotation process and the proposed section annotation process. The example text contains 23 sections in 90 pages (an average of 3.91 pages per section).

System	Number of terms	Time (mins)
Course material repository	34	40-60
ReFLEx	235	90

The cost benefit analysis report concluded that data gathered indicates the need for:

- Further research to explore solutions for factors expected to impact on the scalability and viable deployment of the annotation tool within Library workflows.
- Investigation of factors expected to impact on further development of the search, selection and viewing tools.

Fig 3 illustrates the potential benefits to be gained by users viewing course materials within a ReFLEx environment with persistent linking. The benefits of an optimised ReFLEx 3 tier delivery model are envisaged to be:

- Time savings achieved through a single interface displaying course materials and connecting end users, at the point of need, with Library resources relevant to the topic areas being covered by the unit of study.
- An opportunity to realise significant gains in designing innovative Library services aligned with end users' expectations.

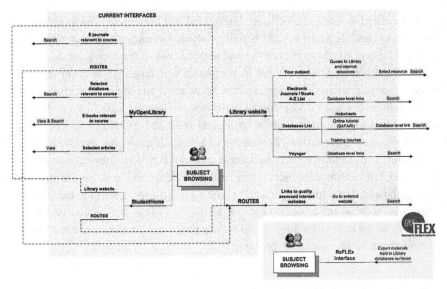

Fig 3. The Open University Library's current interfaces for subject browsing compared to ReFLEx.

6. Findings and future work

The initial findings of the project are that the tools developed by the ReFLEx Project enable:

- Richer concept mapping with semi-automated annotations of course material at a more granular level, than traditional cataloguing techniques.
- A context-sensitive interface for course teams, associate lecturers and students (end users), which supports the surfacing of expert materials held in library managed subscription databases alongside course materials.

Current and planned work for the project involves the importing of taxonomies represented using the Simple Knowledge Organisation System (SKOS) [1]. The Open University would like to see how use of SKOS might bridge the gap between library base thesauri and classification schemes, and semantic ontologies. Researchers at the University of Oregon have been applying SKOS to Library of Congress Subject Headings [7], [8]. Using the results of this work with the tools developed within the ReFLEx project would allow us to evaluate the approach at a more generic cross-domain level. Further evaluation of the delivery model, the online use of course materials with integrated library services and user testing with course teams and students are currently underway.

7. Conclusion

This paper has introduced a practical application of metadata in an educational context. The delivery model explains the context that determined the form of annotation support required. Various automation techniques were used during project testing. The techniques initially applied were relatively sophisticated but it was found that the transparency of term generation was important to engendering trust in the librarians and the course staff. It was found that the librarians and cataloguers had to understand how and why the terms were generated in order to feel confident that the appropriate terms were being used. This actually led to the use of less sophisticated methods of generating keyword terms than was initially envisaged.

This application supports the cataloguer's task of creating fine-grained taxonomy-based metadata. The semi-automated approach helps with the selection, validation and (where needed) correction of metadata terms. The resulting metadata is accessible to all users and the highlighting facility can be used to help illustrate the justification of the selected terms.

8. References

[1] "Simple Knowledge Organisation Systems home page." Available from http://www.w3.org/2004/02/skos/, (last accessed March 2007).

[2] "The Open University Open Learn project." Available from http://openlearn.open.ac.uk/ (last accessed March 2007)

[3] A. Adams and A. Blanford, "Digital libraries' support for the user's 'information journey'," presented at *Joint Conference on Digital Libraries (JCDL'05)*, Denver, Colorado, USA, 2005.

[4] K. Baird, "Automated Metadata: A review of existing and potential metadata automation within Jorum and an overview of other automation systems," *Edina*, Glasgow, July 2006

[5] G. Calverley and K. Shephard, "Assisting the uptake of on-line resources: Why good learning resources are not enough," *Computers & Education*, vol. 41 (2003), pp. 205-224.

[6] J. Greenberg, K. Spurgin, and A. Crystal, "Final Report for the AMeGA (Automatic Metadata Generation Applications) Project," Library of Congress, USA, February 2005.

[7] C. A. Harper, "Encoding Library of Congress Subject Headings in SKOS: Authority Control for the Semantic Web," *DC-2006: Proceedings of the International Conference on Dublin Core and Metadata Applications*, Manzanillo: Universidad de Colima, (2006), pp. 55-64

[8] C. A. Harper, Harper, B. B. Tillett, "Library of Congress controlled vocabularies and their application to the Semantic Web," *Cataloging & Classification Quarterly*, vol. 43, no. 3/4.(2007), pp 47-68

[9] A. Kirkwood, "Going outside the box: Skills development, cultural change and the use of on-line resources," *Computers & Education*, vol. 47 (2006), pp. 316-331.

[10]   Mulholand, P., Collins T. and Zdrahal, Z. "Spotlight browsing of resource archives," *ACM Conference on Hypertext and Hypermedia (HT '05)*, Salzburg, Austria (2005). Available from the ACM Digital Library.

[11]   D. Tudhope, T. Koch, and R. Heery, "Terminology Services and Technology: JISC State of the Art Review," Joint Information Systems Committee (JISC) of the Higher and Further Education Councils, UK, September 2006.

[12]   C. Urquhart, R. Lonsdale, R. Thomas, S. Spink, A. Yeoman, C. Armstrong, and R. Fenton, "Uptake and use of electronic information services: Trends in UK higher education from the JUSTEIS project," *Program: Electronic Library and Information Systems*, vol. 37 no. 3 (2003), pp. 167-180.

Encoding changing country codes for the Semantic Web with ISO 3166 and SKOS

Jakob Voss

Abstract This paper shows how authority files can be encoded for the Semantic Web with the Simple Knowledge Organisation System (SKOS). In particular the application of SKOS for encoding the structure, management, and utilization of country codes as defined in ISO 3166 is demonstrated. The proposed encoding gives a use case for SKOS that includes features that have only been discussed little so far, such as multiple notations, nested concept schemes, changes by versioning.

1 Introduction

1.1 Semantic Web

The Semantic Web is a vision to extend the World Wide Web to a universal, decentralised information space. To join in, information has to be expressed with the Resources Description Framework (RDF) in form of statements about resources. All resources are identified by Uniform Resource Identifiers (URIs) as defined in RFC 3986 [5]. URIs can identify documents, but also real-world objects and abstract concepts. In library and information science controlled vocabularies are used to uniformly identify objects — also across different databases. An example of such controlled vocabulary is ISO 3166 [8] that defines codes and names to identify countries and their subdivisions. To use ISO 3166 in Semantic Web applications for referring to countries, an encoding in RDF is needed. The encoding should include explicit relations between codes in ISO 3166 and define a way how to deal with changes. It is shown how the Simple Knowledge Organisation Systems (SKOS) can be

Verbundzentrale des GBV (VZG), Platz der Göttinger Sieben 1,
37073 Göttingen, Germany. e-mail: `jakob.voss@gbv.de`

used to encode ISO 3166, and which parts of it need to be redefined to do
so. Examples of RDF in this paper are given in Notation 3 (N3) [4].

1.2 ISO 3166 and other systems of country codes

Country codes are short codes that represent countries and dependent areas.
The most common code for general applications is ISO 3166, but there are
many other country codes for special uses. Country codes are managed by
an agency that defines a set of countries, with code, name and partly ad-
ditional information. Examples of relevant systems of country codes beside
ISO 3166 include codes that are used by the US government as defined by the
Federal Information Processing Standard (FIPS), codes of the International
Olympic Committee (IOC), codes of the World Meteorological Organization
(WMO), and numerical country calling codes assigned by the International
Telecommunications Union (ITU). Some country codes occur as part of more
general coding systems, for instance in the geographical table of Dewey Decimal Classification (DDC) that is used as a universal library classification.
Other systems also identify groups of countries such as the group identifiers
of International Standard Book Numbers (ISBN). More country code systems
are listed in the English Wikipedia [20]. The best public resource on country
codes on the Web is Statoids [10] that includes references and a history of
updated codes for many country subdivisions. GeoNames [19] is an open,
free-content geographical database that also contains countries and subdivisions. In contrast to ISO 3166 (which GeoNames partly refers to) GeoNames
already uses URIs and SKOS to publish its content, but changes are rather
uncontrolled because the database can be edited by anyone. Examples of
agencies that not define codes but names of countries and subdivisions are
the Board on Geographic Names (BGN) in the United States and the Permanent Committee on Geographical Names (StAGN) in Germany.

1.3 ISO 3166

ISO 3166 is an international standard for coding the names of countries and
its subdivisions. It consists of three parts. ISO 3166-1 (first published in 1974)
defines two letter codes, three letter codes and three digit numeric codes for
countries and dependent areas together with their names in English and
French. The standard is widely refered to by other standards. For instance
ISO 3166-2 is used for most of the country code top-level domains as defined
by Internet Assigned Numbers Authority (IANA) and the ICANN Country
Code Names Supporting Organisation (ccNSO). ISO 3166-2 (first published
1998) builds on ISO 3166-1 and defines codes for country subdivisions. Fig-

ure 1 shows the relations between ISO 3166, ISO 3166-1, and ISO 3166-2. ISO 3166-3 defines four letter codes for countries that merged, split up or changed the main part of their name and their two letter ISO 3166-1 codes since 1974. ISO 3166 is continuously updated via newsletters that are published by the ISO 3166 Maintenance Agency.[1] In November 2006 a second edition of ISO 3166-1 was published [8]. It contains a consolidation all changes to the lists of ISO 3166-1:1997, published in the ISO 3166 Newsletter up to V-12. Meanwhile this edition has been corrected by a technical corrigendum that was published in July 2007 [9].

1.4 SKOS

SKOS was first developed in the SWAD-Europe project (2002-2004). It is a RDF-based standard for representing and sharing thesauri, classifications, taxonomies, subject-heading systems, glossaries, and other controlled vocabularies that are used for subject indexing in traditional Information Retrieval. Examples of such systems are the AGROVOC Thesaurus, the Dewey Decimal Classification, and the dynamic category system of Wikipedia [17]. Encoding controlled vocabularies with SKOS allows them to be passed between computer applications in an interoperable way and to be used in the Semantic Web. Because SKOS does not carry the strict and complex semantics of the Web Ontology Language (OWL), it is also refered to as "Semantic Web light". At the same time SKOS is compatible with OWL and can be extended with computational semantics for more complex applications.[16] SKOS is currently being revised in the Semantic Web Deployment Working Group of W3C to become a W3C Recommendation in 2008.

2 Related Work

Use cases and application guidelines for SKOS can best be found at the SKOS homepage.[2] Guidelines for using SKOS to encode thesauri [2, 11] and classification schemes [18] been published, while the use to encode authority files and standards like ISO 3166 has not been analysed in detail so far. To a slightly lesser degree this also applies to revision and changes. Although changes are common in living Knowledge Organization Systems, research about this process is rare. The Fourth International Conference of the International Society for Knowledge Organization in 1996 [1] was about changes in general — but the change only dealed about getting existing systems digital, a task that is

---

[1] http://www.iso.org/iso/country_codes
[2] http://www.w3.org/2004/02/skos/

still not finished and will hopefully bring more interoperability with SKOS. In computer science Johann Eder has done some recent work about modelling and detecting changes in ontologies [6, 7]. He presented an approach to represent changes in ontologies by introducing information about the valid time of concepts. Following this, a changed concept must get a new URI which is compatible to the method presented in this paper. Bakillah et al. [3] propose a semantic similarity model for multidimensional databases with different geospatial and temporal data – however countries are more than simple, undisputed geographic objects. On the contrary is is unclear whether results from ontology evolution can be applied to knowledge organization systems. Noy and Klein[14] argue that ontology versioning is different from schema evolution in a database – the same applies to ontology versioning compared to changes in knowledge organization systems because the latter are mainly designed for subject indexing and retrieval without strict semantics and reasoning.

3 Encoding ISO 3166 in SKOS

3.1 Basic elements

The basic elements of SKOS are concepts (`skos:Concept`). A concept in SKOS is a resource (identified by an URI) that can be used for subject indexing. To state that a resource is indexed with a specific concept, SKOS provides the property `skos:subject`. The concepts of ISO 3166 are countries and their subdivisions. Hierarchical relations between concepts are encoded with `skos:broader` and `skos:narrower`. These relationships allow applications to retrieve resources that are index with a more specific concept when searching for a general term [12]. For representation and usage by humans, concepts are refered to by labels (names). SKOS provides the labelling properties `skos:prefLabel` and `skos:altLabel`. A concept should only have one `skos:prefLabel` at least per language – as shown below this causes problems due to the definition of 'language'. The following example encodes basic parts of ISO 3166 for two concepts: France and the subordinated region Bretagne are encoded together with their English names and their ISO codes `FR` ('France') and `FR-E` ('Bretagne'). Unless the ISO 3166 Maintenance Agency defines an official URI schema, unspecified namespace prefixes like `iso3166:` are used:

```
iso3166:FR a skos:Concept ;
  skos:prefLabel "France"@en ;
  skos:prefLabel "FR"@zxx ;
  skos:narrower iso3166:FR-E .

iso3166:FR-E a skos:Concept ;
```

```
skos:prefLabel "Bretagne"@en ;
skos:prefLabel "FR-E"@zxx ;
skos:broader iso3166:FR-E .
```

3.2 Notations

The main labels of ISO 3166 are not names but country codes. Such codes
are also known as notations in other knowledge organisation systems. The
final encoding method of notations in SKOS is still an open issue. The example above uses ISO 639-2 language code zxx for 'no linguistic content'
as proposed in [18]. This solution has some drawbacks: First the code was
introduced the IANA language subtag registry in 2006, so not every RDF
application may already be aware of it. Second the SKOS specification requires the skos:prefLabel property to be unique per concept and language,
so you can only specify one main notation per concept. The problem is caused
by the special treatment of languages in RDF which is a failure by design[3]
To bypass the limitation, notations could either be implemented by additional labeling properties or by private language tags. If you use additional
labeling properties for notations, SKOS must provide a way to state that a
given property defines a notation. This could be done with a new relation
skos:notationPropery:

```
iso3166: a skos:ConceptScheme ;
   skos:notationPropery iso3166:twoLetterCode ;
   skos:notationPropery iso3166:threeLetterCode ;
   skos:notationPropery iso3166:numericalCode .

iso3166:FR a skos:Concept ;
   skos:prefLabel "France"@en ;
   iso3166:twoLetterCode "FR" ;
   iso3166:threeLetterCode "FRA" ;
   iso3166:numericalCode "250" .
```

With RFC 4646 [15] you can now define private language tags in RDF. These
tags are seperated with the reserved single-character subtag 'x'. This way you
could define the new language tag x-notation for notations:

```
iso3166:FR a skos:Concept ;
   skos:prefLabel "France"@en ;
   skos:prefLabel "FR@x-notation-twoletter" ;
   skos:prefLabel "FRA@x-notation-threeletter" ;
   skos:prefLabel "250@x-notation-numerical" .
```

Another advantage of private language codes is that you can use them at
different levels, for instance de-x-notation for a German notation. No matter which solution will be used for encoding notations in SKOS, it has to be

---

[3] languages in RDF are not resources but absolute entities outside of RDF.

defined clearly in the SKOS standard or notations will not be usable among different applications.

3.3 Grouping

ISO 3166 is does not only consist of country codes but it also has an internal structure. First the three parts ISO 3166-1, ISO 3166-2, and ISO 3166-3 are concept schemes of their own but their concepts refer to each other. Second the country subdivisions as defined in ISO 3166-2 can be grouped and build upon another. For instance France is divided in 100 departments which are grouped into 22 metropolitan and four overseas regions, and Canada is disjointedly composed of 10 provinces and 3 territories. Figure 1 shows the structure of ISO 3166 with an extract of the definitions for France.

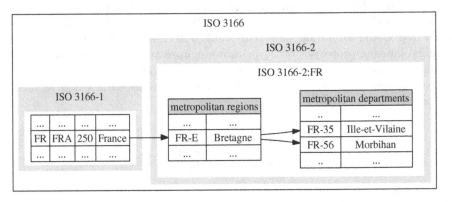

Fig. 1 Internal structure and grouping of ISO 3166

To encode groupings of concepts, SKOS provides the classes skos:Collection and skos:ConceptScheme and the properties skos:member and skos:inScheme. The current standard only allows skos:Collection to be nested. This is problematic for vocabularies like ISO 3166, that nested parts of which are also used independently. An easy solution is to make skos:ConceptScheme a subclass of skos:Collection. This way concept schemes can be nested via skos:member (figure 2).

3.4 Changes and versioning

SKOS provides concept mapping relations to merge and combine identfiers from different concept schemes. A first working draft of the SKOS map-

```
iso3166: a skos:ConceptScheme ;
  skos:member iso3166-1: ;
  skos:member iso3166-2: .

iso3166-1: a skos:ConceptScheme .
iso3166-2: a skos:ConceptScheme ;
  skos:member iso3166-2:FR .

iso3166-2:FR a skos:ConceptScheme ;
  skos:member iso3166-2:FR-regions ;
  skos:member iso3166-2:FR-departements .

iso3166-2:FR-regions a skos:Collection ;
  skos:member iso3166:FR-E .

iso3166-2:FR-departements a skos:Collection ;
  skos:member iso3166:FR-35 ;
  skos:member iso3166:FR-56 .
```

Fig. 2 Proposed encoding of figure 1 (without concepts)

ping vocabulary was published in 2004 [13]. It includes properties for concept equivalence (skos:exactMatch), specialization (skos:narrowMatch), and concept generalization (skos:broadMatch). In practise full one-to-one mappings between concept schemes are rare because of differences in definition, focus, politics, and update cycles. In the following it will be shown how mapping relations can be used to encode changes and versioning in ISO 3166. Mappings between different systems of country codes remains a topic to be analyzed in more detail. A promising candidate to start with for mapping to ISO 3166 would be the GeoNames database which already uses SKOS.[19]

Nationalists might have a different opinion, but countries are no stable entities: Contries come into existence, they can split and merge, change their names and area, or even disappear. To keep track of changes and the current situation, every modification in a schema of country codes needs to be documented for further lookup. The ISO 3166 Maintenance Agency uses newsletters and editions to publish updates. For Semantic Web applications these updates need to be explicitly specified in RDF. To develope a consistent encoding of changes, you must first consider all possible types of updates and paradigms of versioning. Types of changes are:

1. A new country arises
2. A country disappears
3. A country is split into two or more countries
4. Two or more countries unite (join)
5. A country remains but its identity changes

Type 1 and 2 are easy to model if there is no predecessor/successor but nowadays countries mostly arise from other countries (type 3 to 5). Easy examples of splits (type 3) are the division of Czechoslovakia (ISO code CS) into the Czech Republic (CZ) and Slovakia (SK) in 1993 and the division of Serbia and Montenegro (CS, until 2003 named Yugoslavia with code YU) into Serbia (RS) and Montenegro (ME) in 2006. An example of a simple join (type 4) is the German reunification in 1990. Other changes such as large reforms of country subdivisions and partly splits are more complex. They mostly imply that the identity of all involved entities change. To distinguish countries before and after a change, it is crucial to assigned a new URI for each version. The examples of Yugoslavia (which underwent several splits between 1991 and 2006) and the country code CS show that also controlled codes and names can be ambiguous if date is unknown and versioning is not respected.

You should keep in mind that changes in the basic structure of countries are political and can be highly controversial. This means that the existence and nature of a change depends on who and when you ask. Encoding schemes of country codes can only give you guidance how to consistently encode changes for reasoned retrieval but you first have to agree upon what happend with the involved entities.

The encoding of changes in ISO 3166 in SKOS will be shown with the example of Canada. Canada, the world second largest country in total area, is composed of 10 provinces and 3 territories. The provinces are independent states with own jurisdiction. In March 31, 1949 Newfoundland entered the Canadian confederation as the 10th province. The territories cover the parts of Canada that do not belong to provinces. They are created by the federal government and have less authority. The North-Western Territory was formerly much larger then today. It contained parts of current provinces and the area that now form the territories Yukon (since 1898) and Nunavut (1999). Between 1998 and 2002 the ISO 3166-2 entry of Canada has been changed three times. Figure 3 contains an overview of the changes:

- Newsletter I-1 (2000-06-21) Addition of 1 new territory: The new territory Nunavut split up from Northwest Territories.
- Newsletter I-2 (2002-05-21) Correction of name form of CA-NF: The name 'Newfoundland' changed to 'Newfoundland and Labrador'.
- Newsletter I-4 (2002-12-10) Change of code element of Newfoundland and Labrador: The country code CA-NF changed to CA-NL.

To model these changes, unique URIs must be defined for each version – at least when the definition of a country or country subdivision changed. For easy detection of the valid URI for a given date or newsletter, a directory structure of URLs with namespaces for each newsletter should be provided by the ISO 3166 Maintenance Agency. Changing country codes are then mapped to each other with the SKOS Mapping vocabulary. For codes that did not change with a newsletter, you could either provide new URIs and connect unmodified concepts with the owl:sameAs property from the OWL Web Ontology Language or just direct to the previous URI with a

Initial Version	Newsletter I-1	Newsletter I-2	Newsletter I-3	Newsletter I-4
CA-NF Newfoundland		CA-NF Newfoundland and Labrador		CA-NL Newfoundland and Labrador
CA-NT Northwest Territories	CA-NT Northwest Territories			
	CA-NU Nunavut			

Fig. 3 Changes of Canada in ISO 3166-2

HTTP 303 redirect. Support of any method in SKOS applications can be ensured by best practise rules in the final SKOS standards. Figure 4 contains an encoding of the changes of Canada in ISO 3166 as shown in figure 3. The change of Newfoundland to Newfoundland and Labrador in newsletter I-2 and I-4 is encoded by an exact mapping between sequent versions (`skos:exactMatch`) while the split of Northwest Territories in newsletter I-1 is encoded by an `skos:narrowMatch`. Unchanged country codes are connected with `owl:sameAs`.

```
@prefix iso3166-2-v0: <http://iso.org/iso3166/2/first/> .
@prefix iso3166-2-v1: <http://iso.org/iso3166/2/newsletter-1/> .
@prefix iso3166-2-v2: <http://iso.org/iso3166/2/newsletter-2/> .
@prefix iso3166-2-v3: <http://iso.org/iso3166/2/newsletter-3/> .
@prefix iso3166-2-v4: <http://iso.org/iso3166/2/newsletter-4/> .
@prefix iso3166-2-v4: <http://iso.org/iso3166/2/current/> .

iso3166-2-v0:CA-NF  owl:sameAs         iso3166-2-v1:CA-NF .
iso3166-2-v0:CA-NT  skos:narrowMatch   iso3166-2-v1:CA-NT .
iso3166-2-v0:CA-NT  skos:narrowMatch   iso3166-2-v1:CA-NU .

iso3166-2-v1:CA-NF  skos:exactMatch    iso3166-2-v2:CA-NF .
iso3166-2-v1:CA-NT  owl:sameAs         iso3166-2-v2:CA-NT .
iso3166-2-v1:CA-NU  owl:sameAs         iso3166-2-v2:CA-NU .

iso3166-2-v2:CA-NF  owl:sameAs         iso3166-2-v3:CA-NF .
iso3166-2-v2:CA-NT  owl:sameAs         iso3166-2-v3:CA-NT .
iso3166-2-v2:CA-NU  owl:sameAs         iso3166-2-v3:CA-NU .

iso3166-2-v3:CA-NF  skos:exactMatch    iso3166-2-v4:CA-NL .
iso3166-2-v3:CA-NT  owl:sameAs         iso3166-2-v4:CA-NT .
iso3166-2-v3:CA-NU  owl:sameAs         iso3166-2-v4:CA-NU .
```

Fig. 4 Encoding of changes of Canada in ISO 3166-2

4 Summary and Conclusions

With the Simple Knowledge Organisation System more and more thesauri, classifications, subject-heading systems, and other controlled vocabularies can be integrated into the Semantic Web. This will increase interoperability among Knowledge Organisation Systems which are already used and maintained for a long time and in many applications. One kind of Knowledge Organisation Systems are Country codes, a common type of authority files. This paper shows how in particular country codes from ISO 3166 can be encoded in RDF with SKOS. ISO 3166 and its parts are widely used and referred to by other applications and standards that could benefit from such a common encoding. ISO 3166 includes some particular features of controlled vocabularities that have not been discussed in detail so far in the context of SKOS. The hereby proposed encoding contains support of country names and codes (notations), internal structure and nested concept schemes (grouping), and versioning of changes. To explicitly support notations a notation property or a private language subtag (x-notation) has to be defined. Nested concept schemes can easily be supported by making skos:ConceptScheme a subclass of skos:Collection. Finally you can track changes by publishing new URIs for the concepts of each version of a concept scheme and interlink them with owl:sameAs and SKOS mapping relations.

To get a reliable RDF representation of ISO 3166, that other Semantic Web applications can build upon, the upcoming W3C Recommendation of SKOS must first be finalized with support of notations, grouping concept schemes and versioning. Second an URL scheme for country codes of ISO 3166 has to be defined by ISO, and third the ISO 3166 Maintenance Agency must regularly and freely publish versioned ISO 3166 data in SKOS. A public, official, RDF-representation of ISO 3166 will allow heterogeneous data on the web to be linked for homogeneous, semantic retrieval via aggregating resources. For instance statistics by the United Nations can be combined with encyclopaedic information by Wikipedia and visualised with geographical data by GeoNames. With controlled versioning and linking to specific versions you can also access historic information without having to update all involved datasets. Geographic data from GeoNames could be used to select a country or country subdivision by browsing on a map. Linked with ISO 3166 in SKOS then relevant past countries could be determined to extend searches in databases with other country codes. In this way ISO 3166 and other authority files will be the corner stones of connecting distributed data to a universal, decentralised information space.

References

1. Knowledge organization and change: Proceedings of the Fourth International ISKO

Conference . Indeks (1996)

2. van Assem, M., Malais, V., Miles, A., Schreiber, G.: A Method to Convert Thesauri to SKOS. The Semantic Web: Research and Applications pp. 95–109. DOI 10.1007/11762256_10

3. Bakillah, Mostafavi, Bédard: A Semantic Similarity Model for Mapping Between Evolving Geospatial Data Cubes. On the Move to Meaningful Internet Systems 2006: OTM 2006 Workshops (2006)

4. Berners-Lee, T.: Notation3 (N3) A readable RDF syntax

5. Berners-Lee, T., Fielding, R., Masinter, L.: Uniform Resource Identifier (URI): Generic Syntax. RFC 3986 (2005)

6. Eder, J., Koncilia, C.: Modelling Changes in Ontologies. Lecture Notes in Computer Science 3292 pp. 662–673 (2004)

7. Eder, J., Wiggisser, K.: Detecting Changes in Ontologies via DAG Comparison. Lecture Notes in Computer Science 4495 pp. 21–35 (2007)

8. International Organization for Standardization: Codes for the representation of names of countries and their subdivisions — Part 1: Country codes. ISO3166:1-2006 (2006)

9. International Organization for Standardization: ISO 3166-1 Technical Corrigendum 1. ISO3166:1-2006/Cor 1:2007 (2007)

10. Law, G.: Statoids. http://www.statoids.com (2007). [visited 2008-01-20]

11. Miles, A.: Quick Guide to Publishing a Thesaurus on the Semantic Web. http://www.w3.org/TR/swbp-thesaurus-pubguide (2005)

12. Miles, A.: Retrieval and the Semantic Web. http://isegserv.itd.rl.ac.uk/retrieval/ (2006)

13. Miles, A., Brickley, D.: SKOS Mapping Vocabulary Specification. http://www.w3.org/2004/02/skos/mapping/spec/ (2004)

14. Noy, N., Klein, M.: Ontology Evolution: Not the Same as Schema Evolution. Knowledge and Information Systems (2003)

15. Phillips, Davis: Tags for the Identification of Languages. RFC 4646 (2006)

16. Sanchez-Alonso, S., Garcia-Barriocanal, E.: Making use of upper ontologies to foster interoperability between SKOS concept schemes. Online Information Review **30**(3), 263–277 (2006). DOI 10.1108/14684520610675799

17. Voss, J.: Collaborative thesaurus tagging the Wikipedia way. http://arxiv.org/abs/cs/0604036v2 (2006)

18. Voss, J.: Quick Guide to Publishing a Classification Scheme on the Semantic Web. http://esw.w3.org/topic/SkosDev/ClassificationPubGuide (2006). [last changed 2006-09-11 13:08:41]

19. Wick, M.: Geonames. http://www.geonames.org (2007). [visited 2008-01-20]

20. Wikipedia: Country code. http://en.wikipedia.org/w/index.php?oldid=154259104 (2007)

Improving Accuracy of Tagging Systems Using Tag Qualifiers and Tagraph Vocabulary System

Syavash Nobarany[1] and Mona Haraty[2]

Abstract This short paper addresses the lack of accuracy in social tagging systems, as information retrieval systems, in comparison with traditional search-engines. The lack of accuracy is caused by the vocabulary problems and the nature of tagging systems which rely on lower number of index terms for each resource. Tagraph vocabulary system which is based on a weighted directed graph of tags, and Tag Qualifiers, are proposed to mitigate these problems and increase the precision and the recall of social tagging systems. Both solutions are based on community contributions, therefore specific procedures such as task routing should be used to increase the number of contributions and therefore to achieve a more accurate system.

1. Introduction

Collaborative tagging has become increasingly popular as a common way of organizing, sharing and discovering information. Properties and design of tagging systems are investigated in [1, 2, 3]. One of the important deficiencies of current tagging systems is the lack of accuracy about the way and the quantity with which a resource relates to a tag. Although in tagging systems keywords are detected with less error, the lack of accuracy in tagging leads to poor search results. In traditional search engines, relevance of a term to a resource is estimated using several methods such as calculating term frequency, which does not have any alternatives in tagging systems.

Another class of problems that are not limited to tagging systems and involve all information retrieval systems is the Vocabulary Problems, introduced by George Furnas et al [7]. An example of the Vocabulary Problems happens where different users use different tags to describe the same resources, which can lead to missed information or inefficient user interactions. We introduce a community-based approach to overcome the Vocabulary Problems without requiring either the rigidity

---

[1] Syavash Nobarany

School of ECE, University of Tehran, Tehran 14395-515, Iran, nobarany@gmail.com

[2] Mona Haraty

School of ECE, University of Tehran, Tehran 14395-515, Iran, haraty@gmail.com

and steep learning curve of controlled vocabularies, or the computational complexity of automatic approaches to term disambiguation.

2. Tag Qualifiers

Tags have several properties, which we call Tag Qualifiers. A basic qualifier, which can improve search results, is the Relevance Qualifier. Tags that are assigned to a resource are not equally relevant to the resource. Therefore, Relevance Qualifier can be defined to express their relevance. Relevance Qualifier is a key element for improving *precision* of tagging systems, which is defined as the number of relevant retrieved documents divided by the number of all retrieved documents. Assigning Relevance Qualifier is not easy for taggers and most users are not comfortable with using tag-qualifiers except when they are using them for special purposes such as using restriction qualifiers. Discussion on incentives in online social interaction can be found in [5] and [6]. A simple yet robust solution to this problem is using auto-assigned relevance qualifiers that can be calculated automatically using traditional information retrieval methods such as calculating term frequency usage and document frequency retrieval. This will reduce user obligation to assign Relevance qualifiers.

Another qualifier, which is already being used in tagging systems, is the Restriction Qualifier which may be implemented using a public-private property or, in a more precise manner, by mapping users to sets of permissions.

Beside general tag qualifiers, context-specific qualifiers can also be helpful in special purpose tagging systems. For example, in virtual learning environments, level of educational materials can be considered as a qualifier. Bookmarks, which are used to express user interest in a resource, also may have qualifiers. For example, Recommendation Qualifier can be used to express users' interest in a resource. This qualifier leads to a better ranking of results. Choosing the appropriate set of qualifiers can be considered as a part of the design of tagging systems.

3. Tagraph: Graph based vocabulary system

A common assumption in many information retrieval systems such as probabilistic systems is considering terms' occurrences independent from each other, which is incorrect in many situations. A famous counterexample for this assumption occurs when different users use different tags to describe the same resources. This is known as synonyms problem. However, this problem is not limited to synonyms. Consider a document tagged with the term 'EJB', and a query contains the term 'Java'. In this situation, EJB is not a synonym of Java, but their meanings are related. The document tagged with Java, however, may not necessarily be related to EJB. To deal with situations similar to the above example, Tagraph, a graph with tags as nodes and relationships between tags as arcs, is proposed. In Tagraph, arcs are directed since the relationships between tags are not necessarily two-way, as in the previous example. Tagraph is a weighted graph based on the strength of the relationship between a tag and its implementation. For example the relationship between JSF and MyFaces, an implementation of JSF, is stronger than the relationship between Java and JSF.

Relevance arcs can increase the *recall* of tagging systems, which is defined as the number of relevant retrieved documents divided by the number of relevant documents. Relevance arcs are transitive and their weights can be used to find out the relevance of two nodes that are not directly connected. Transitive relevance can be inferred using Equation 1. Source of the non-existent relevance arc is denoted as s, its destination is denoted as d and tags with direct relevance arc to source are denoted as i. This equation finds the strongest relationship between source and destination.

$$r_{sd} = MAX_i (r_{si} \times r_{id})$$ (1)

Homonyms problem is another important problem that influences tagging systems more than traditional search engines. This problem stems from the smaller number of index terms that are used to describe each document in tagging systems. Large number of index terms in traditional search engines can determine the context of a document, while in a tagging system many documents have less than three tags. Therefore, defining context of the tags deems necessary in tagging systems.

To overcome this problem, each node of the Tagraph has a set of context-definition terms. These terms are chosen from a predetermined hierarchy of terms. This solution can increase *precision* of tagging systems. A sample Tagraph is depicted in Figure 1.

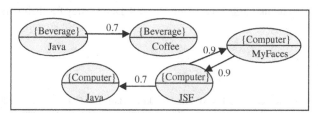

Fig. 1. Sample graphs in Tagraph system

Proposed system's performance is highly dependent on user interface design. Figure 2 shows a UI prototype, which allows context definition while tagging a resource. Similar procedure can be used in the query formulation UI.

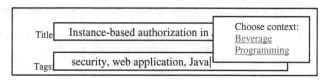

Fig. 2. AJAX based tagging UI with context selection

3.1 Discovering Tagraph edges and their weights

Finding and assigning relevance edges can be done automatically using WordNet. But still a community-based approach is needed to compensate for WordNet deficiencies such as inconsistencies. A system like SuggestBot introduced by Cosley et al. [4] which has increased the number of contributions in Wikipedia, can be used to take the most advantage of taggers. Task definition for Tagraph requires automatic document inspection to derive possible edges from co-occurrence of tags. Determining possible edges, assigning their weight can be suggested to taggers based on their history.

4. Conclusions

In this paper, we suggest using Tag Qualifiers to improve precision of tagging and search results through storing more information about each tag. Auto indexing also can be used to help taggers to assign relevance-qualifier to tags.

The Tagraph vocabulary system is proposed to overcome the Vocabulary Problems of tagging systems. These problems are mitigated using a community-based approach and the weighted directed graph of tags and their relevance. These solutions can improve precision and recall of tagging systems and a comprehensive evaluation is needed to verify the effectiveness of each solution.

Acknowledgments
We would like to thank Farid Vakil, Sam Vakil & Dan Cosley for their comments.

References

[1] Sen S, Lam S K, Cosley D, Rashid A M, Frankowski D, Harper F, Osterhouse J, Riedl J (2006) tagging, community, vocabulary, evolution. 20th anniversary conference on Computer supported cooperative work , pp. 181—190. ACM Press

[2] Marlow C, Naaman M, Boyd D, Davis M (2006) HT06, Tagging Paper, Taxonomy, Flickr, Academic Article, ToRead., seventeenth ACM conference on Hypertext and hypermedia , pp. 31—40. ACM Press

[3] Golber S, Huberman B A, The Structure of Collaborative Tagging System, Information Dynamics Lab: HP Labs, Palo Alto, USA, http://arxiv.org/abs/cs.DL/0508082

[4] Cosley D, Frankowski D, Terveen L, Riedl J (2007) SuggestBot: using intelligent task routing to help people find work in wikipedia. 12th international Conference on intelligent User interfaces, pp. 181—190. ACM Press

[5] Korfiatis N (2007) Social and Economic Incentives in Online Social Interactions: A Model and Typology. 30th Information Systems Research Seminar in Scandinavia IRIS.

[6] Ludford P, Cosley D, Frankowski D, Terveen L (2004). Think Different: Increasing Online Community Participation Using Uniqueness and Group Dissimilarity. CHI 2004, pp. 631--638. ACM Press

[7] Furnas G W, Landauer T K, Gomez L M, Dumais S T (1987) The vocabulary problem in human-system communication. Communications, 30 (11), 964 – 971. ACM Press.

Ensemble Learning of Economic Taxonomy Relations from Modern Greek Corpora

Katia Lida Kermanidis

Abstract. This paper proposes the use of ensemble learning for the identification of taxonomic relations between Modern Greek economic terms. Unlike previous approaches, apart from *is-a* and *part-of* relations, the present work deals also with relation types that are characteristic of the economic domain. Semantic and syntactic information governing the term pairs is encoded in a novel feature-vector representation. Ensemble learning helps overcome the problem of performance instability and leads to more accurate predictions.

1 Introduction

A domain ontology is the tool that enables information retrieval, data mining, intelligent search in a particular thematic domain. Ontologies consist of concepts that are important for communicating domain knowledge. These concepts are structured hierarchically through taxonomic relations. A taxonomy usually includes *hyperonymy-hyponymy* (is-a), and *meronymy* (part-of) relations.

Learning taxonomic relations between the concepts that describe a specific domain automatically from corpora is a key step towards ontology engineering. The advent of the semantic web has pushed the construction of concept taxonomies to the top of the list of interests of language processing experts.

A complete ontology, however, may also include further information regarding each concept. The economic domain, especially, is governed by more 'abstract' relations, that capture concept attributes (e.g. *rise* and *drop* are two attributes of

Katia Lida Kermanidis
Department of Informatics, Ionian University, Corfu, Greece, e-mail: kerman@ionio.gr

the concept *value*, a *stockholder* is an attribute of the concept *company*). Henceforth, this type of relation will be referred to as *attribute* relation. A term pair is governed by an attribute relation if it does not match the typical profile of an *is-a* or a *part-of* relation. All the aforementioned types of relations are henceforth called *taxonomic* in this paper.

The present work proposes a methodology for automatically detecting taxonomic relations between the terms that have been extracted from Modern Greek collections of economic texts. Unlike most previous approaches, that focus basically on hyponymy, in this work, meronymy as well as *attribute* relations are also detected. The work is part of an ongoing research effort to build an economic ontological thesaurus for Modern Greek.

A set of empirically selected features are proposed for taxonomy learning, that describe syntactic and semantic properties of the extracted term pairs. Each term pair, accompanied by its set of features, is classified into one of the taxonomy type classes, which indicates the type of taxonomic relation it belongs to. Therefore, each term pair is represented as a feature-value vector (instance).

One of the main ideas that this work has been based on, is the ability of the proposed methodology to be easily applied to other languages and other domains. For this reason, and unlike several previous approaches, the concept hierarchy is built from scratch, instead of trying to extend an already existing ontology. Furthermore, no use of external resources is made, e.g. semantic networks (like WordNet), grammars, or pre-existing ontologies.

This automatic nature of the process, and the use of minimal external resources does not allow individual stand-alone learning algorithms to predict new instance classes most accurately. Therefore, several ensemble learning setups are proposed in order to achieve optimal classification accuracy. Bagging, boosting and stacking schemes have been experimented with and comparative results are presented.

Another interesting aspect of the present work is the language itself. Modern Greek is a relatively free-word-order language, i.e. the ordering of the constituents of a sentence is not strictly fixed, like it is in English. The rich morphology, as well as other typical idiosyncrasies of the language (described in section 4) are taken into account throughout the present work.

2   Related Work

Previous approaches to taxonomy learning have varied from supervised to unsupervised clustering techniques, and from methodologies that make use of external taxonomic thesauri, to those that rely on no external resources.

Regarding previous approaches that employ clustering techniques, the work in [3] describes a conceptual clustering method that is based on the Formal Concept Analysis for automatic taxonomy construction from text and compares it to similarity-based clustering (agglomerative and Bi-Section-KMeans clustering). The automatically generated ontology is compared against a hand-crafted gold standard ontology for the tourism domain and report a maximum lexical recall of 44.6%.

Other clustering approaches are described in [6] and [19]. The former uses a syntactically parsed text (verb-subcategorization examples) and utilize iterative clustering to form new concept graphs. The latter also makes use of verb-object dependencies, and relative frequencies and relative entropy as similarity metrics for clustering.

In [18] the authors take advantage of a taxonomic thesaurus (a tourism-domain ontology) to improve the accuracy of classifying new words into its classes. Their classification algorithm is an extension of the kNN method, which takes into account the taxonomic similarity between nearest neighbors. They report a maximum overall accuracy of 43.2%.

[11] identifies taxonomic relations between two sections of a medical document using memory-based learning. Binary vectors represent overlap between the two sections, and the tests are run on parts of two Dutch medical encyclopedias. A best overall accuracy value of 88% is reported.

[24] proposes a methodology for extending lexical taxonomies by first identifying domain-specific concepts, then calculating semantic similarities between concepts, and finally using decision trees to insert new concepts to the right position in the taxonomy tree. The classifier is evaluated against two subtrees from GermaNet.

The authors in [15] interpret semantically the set of complex terms that they extract, based on simple string inclusion. They make use of a variety of external resources in order to generate a semantic graph of senses.

Another approach that makes use of external hierarchically structured textual resources is [13]. The authors map an already existing hierarchical structure of technical documents to the structure of a domain-specific technical ontology. Words are clustered into concepts, and concepts into topics. They evaluate their ontology against the structure of existing textbooks in the given domain.

[12] makes use of clustering, as well as pattern-based (regular expressions) approaches in order to extract taxonomies from domain-specific German texts.

The authors in [4] also make use of syntactic patterns to extract hierarchical relations, and measure the dissimilarity between the attributes of the terms using the Lance and Williams coefficient. They evaluate their methodology on a collection of forms provided by the state agencies and report a precision value of 73% and 85% for is-a and attributive relations respectively.

As can be seen, most previous approaches rely on the use of external resources, semantic networks, grammars, pre-existing ontologies, hierarchically structured corpora, and focus mainly on hyperonymy/hyponymy relations. In this work, merely an unstructured corpus is used and an attempt is made to learn a wider range of relation types.

3 Ensemble Learning

The standard supervised learning problem is described as a program that is given training examples as input in the form of $\{(x_1, y_1), \ldots, (x_n, y_n)\}$, where each x_i is a vector of feature-value pairs, and y_i is the value of the class label for the vector. The goal of the learning algorithm is to output a hypothesis h (classifier), which is an approximation of the real classification function $y=f(x)$. The learner then predicts the class value of new unseen (not present among the training examples) x vectors using the hypothesis.

An ensemble of classifiers is a set of individual (base) classifiers whose output is combined in order to classify new instances. The construction of good ensembles of classifiers is one of the most active areas of research in supervised learning, aiming mainly at discovering ensembles that are more accurate than the individual classifiers that make them up [5].

Various schemes have been proposed for combining the predictions of the base classifiers into a unique output. The most important are bagging, boosting and stacking. Bagging entails the random partitioning of the dataset in equally sized subsets (bags) using resampling [2]. Each subset trains the same base classifier and produces a classification model (hypothesis). The class of every new test instance is predicted by every model, and the class label with the majority vote is assigned to the test instance.

Unlike bagging, where the models are created separately, boosting works iteratively, i.e. each new model is influenced by the performance of those built previously ([7],[22]). In other words, new models are forced, by appropriate weighting, to focus on instances that have been handled incorrectly by older ones.

Finally, stacking usually combines the models created by different base classifiers, unlike bagging and stacking where all base models are constructed by the same classifier [5]. After constructing the different base models, a new instance is fed into them, and each model predicts a class label. These predictions form the input to another, higher-level classifier (the so-called meta-learner), that combines them into a final prediction.

4 Automatic Extraction of Economic Terms

The first step of the procedure proposed in this paper is the automatic extraction of economic terms, following the methodology described in [23]. A brief summary of the term extraction process is presented here.

4.1 Corpora

Corpora comparison was employed for the extraction of economic terms. Corpora comparison detects the difference in statistical behavior that a term presents in a balanced and in a domain-specific corpus.

The domain-specific corpus [10] is a collection of economic domain texts of approximately five million words of varying genre, which has been automatically annotated from the ground up to the level of phrase chunking. The balanced corpus ([8] [16]) is a collection of 300,000 words, manually annotated with morphological information.

4.2 Candidate terms

Noun and prepositional phrases of the two corpora are selected to constitute candidate terms, as only these phrase types are likely to contain terms.

Coordination schemes are detected within the phrases, and the latter are split into smaller phrases respectively. The occurrences of words and multi-word units (n-grams), pure as well as nested, are counted. Longer candidate terms are split into smaller units (tri-grams into bi-grams and uni-grams, bi-grams into uni-grams).

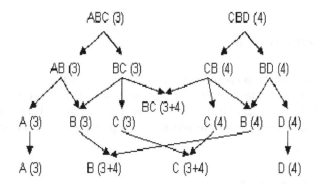

Fig. 1. Counting the occurrences of the nested candidate terms in the corpus.

Due to the relative freedom in the word ordering in Modern Greek sentences, bi-gram A B (A and B being the two lemmata forming the bi-gram) is considered to be identical to bi-gram B A, if the bi-gram is not a named entity. Their joint count in the corpora is calculated and taken into account. The resulting uni-grams and bi-grams are the candidate terms. The candidate term counts in the corpora are then used in the statistical filters.

Figure 1 shows the count calculation for the nested candidate terms. The two tri-grams, A B C and B C D occur in a corpus three and four times respectively. The accumulative counts of the nested terms are shown in parentheses.

4.3 Filtering

The domain-specific corpus available to us is quite large compared to the balanced corpus. As a result, several terms that appear in it, do not appear in the balanced corpus, making it impossible for them to be detected by corpora comparison. In order to overcome this problem, Lidstone's law [14] was applied to the candidate terms, i.e. each candidate term count was augmented by a value of $\lambda=0.5$ in both corpora.

Filtering was then performed in two stages: First the relative frequencies are calculated for each candidate term. Then, for those candidate terms that present a relative frequency value greater than 1, the Log Likelihood ratio (LLR) is calculated.

The LLR metric detects how surprising (or not) it is for a candidate term to appear in the domain-specific or in the balanced corpus (compared to its expected appearance count), and therefore constitute an economic domain term (or not). The term extraction methodology reaches a precision of 82% for the 200 N-best candidate terms.

5 Taxonomy Learning

The next phase of the proposed methodology constitutes the core of the current work and focuses on the syntactic and semantic information that has been taken into account for the identification of the taxonomic relations between the terms that were extracted in the previous phase. The proposed features are empirical.

5.1 Semantic context vectors

The sense of a term is strongly linked to the context the term appears in. To this end, for each extracted term semantic context vectors have been constructed, that are comprised by the ten most frequent words the term co occurs with in the domain-specific corpus.

A context window of two words preceding and two words following the term for every occurrence of the term in the corpus is formed. All non-content words (prepositions, articles, pronouns, particles, conjunctions) are disregarded, while acronyms, abbreviations, and certain symbols (e.g. %, €) are taken into account because of their importance for determining the semantic profile of the term in the given domain. Bi-grams (pairs of the term with each word within the con-text window) are generated and their frequency is recorded. The ten words that present the highest bi-gram frequency scores are chosen to form the context vector of the term.

5.2 Semantic similarity

For each pair of terms, their semantic similarity is calculated, based on their semantic context vectors. The smaller the distance between the context vectors, the more similar the terms' semantics. The value of semantic similarity is an integer with a value ranging from 0 to 10, which denotes the number of common words two context vectors share.

5.3 Semantic diversity

Another important semantic feature that is taken into account is how 'diverse' the semantic properties of a term are, i.e. the number of other terms that a term shares semantic properties with. This property is important when creating taxonomic hierarchies, because, the more 'shared' the semantic behavior of a term is, the more likely it is for the term to have a higher place in the hierarchy.

The notion of 'semantic diversity' is included in the feature set by calculating the percentage of the total number of terms whose semantic similarity with the focus term (one of the two terms whose taxonomic relation is to be determined) is at least 1.

5.4 Syntactic patterns

Syntactic information, regarding the linguistic patterns that govern the co occurrence of two terms, is significant for extracting taxonomic information. For languages with a relatively strict sentence structure, like English, such patterns are easier to detect [9], and their impact on taxonomy learning more straightforward.

As mentioned earlier, Modern Greek presents a larger degree of freedom in the ordering of the constituents of a sentence, due to its rich morphology and its complex declination system. This freedom makes it difficult to detect syntactic patterns, and, even if they are detected, their contribution to the present task is not that easily observable.

However, two Modern Greek syntactic schemata prove very useful for learning taxonomies. They are the attributive modification schema and the genitive modification schema. The first, known in many languages, is the pattern where (usually) an adjective modifies the following noun. The second is typical for Modern Greek, and it is formed by two nominal expressions, one of which (usually following the other) appears in the genitive case and modifies the preceding nominal, denoting possession, property, origin, quantity, quality. The following phrases show examples of the first (example 1) and the second (examples 2, 3 and 4) schemata respectively.

1. το   μετοχικό[ADJ]   κεφάλαιο[NOUN]
   the   stock   capital
2. η   κατάθεση[NOUN]   επιταγής[NOUN-GEN]
   the   deposit   check
   (the deposit of the check)
3. πρόεδρος[NOUN]   του   συμβουλίου[NOUN-GEN]
   head   the   council
   (head of the council)
4. αύξηση[NOUN]   του   κεφαλαίου[NOUN-GEN]
   increase   the   capital
   (capital increase)

Both these schemata enclose the notion of taxonomic relations: hyponymy relations (a check deposit is a type of deposit, a stock capital is a type of capital), as well as meronymy relations (the head is part of a council). The fourth example incorporates an attribute relation.

The distinction among the types of relations is not always clear. In the check deposit example, the deposit may also be considered an attribute of check, constituting thereby an attribute relation.

For each pair of terms, the number of times they occur in one of the two schemata in the domain-specific corpus is calculated. This information is basically the only language-dependent feature that is included in the methodology.

6 Classification Schemata and Results

After the process described in section 4, the 250 most highly ranked terms (according to the LLR metric) were selected, and each one was paired with the rest. The syntactic and semantic information described in the previous section has been encoded in a set of attributes that form a feature-value vector for each pair of terms (learning instance – as described in section 3). The term lemmata, their frequencies, and their part-of-speech tags were also included in the feature set.

The semantic relations of a total of 6000 term pairs were manually annotated by economy and finance experts with one of the four class label values: *is-a*, *part-of*, *attribute* relation and no relation (*null*). 9% of the term pairs belong to the *is-a* class, 17% belong to the *attribute* class and only 0,5% belong to the *part-of* class. The instances that belong to one of the first three classes are called *positive*, while those that belong to the *null* class are called *negative*.

Different classifiers lead to different results. Preliminary experiments have been run using various classification algorithms. *C4.5* is Quinlan's decision tree induction algorithm without pruning [21]. Decision trees were chosen because of their high representational power, which is very significant for understanding the impact of each feature on the classification accuracy, and because of the knowledge that can be extracted from the resulting tree itself. *IB1* is the implementation of the 1-Nearest neighbor instanced-based learning algorithm and is chosen to constitute a reference to a baseline classification performance. *SVM* is the Support Vector Machines classifier with a linear kernel. *SVM* cope well with the sparse data problem, and also with noise in the data (an inevitable phenomenon due to the automatic nature of the procedure described so far). A first degree polynomial kernel function was selected and the Sequential Minimal Optimization algorithm was chosen to train the Support Vector classifier [20]. *BN* is a Bayesian Network classifier, using a hill climbing search algorithm, and conditional probability tables are estimated directly from the data.

The performance metrics that are used to estimate classification accuracy are the *precision* and *recall* scores from the information retrieval domain. They are defined as

$$Precision = TP/(TP+FP) \tag{1}$$
$$Recall = TP/(TP+FN) \tag{2}$$

where *TP* (true positives) is the number of correctly classified positive instances, *FP* (false positives) is the number of negative instances that have been incorrectly classified as positive, and *FN* are the number of positive instances that have been incorrectly classified as negative. The two metrics can be combined in a single one, called *f-score*:

$$F\text{-}score = 2*Recall*Precision/(Recall+Precision) \tag{3}$$

Table 1 shows the f-score for each class achieved when trying to classify new term pairs using 10-fold cross validation. The dataset is divided into ten parts and ten experiments are run using one part for testing and the remaining nine for training. The results of the ten experiments are then averaged.

Table 1. Class f-score for various classifiers.

	C4.5	IB1	Naïve Bayes	SVM	BN
Is-a	0.808	0.694	0.419	0.728	0.762
Part-of	0.4	0	0	0	0
Attribute	0.769	0.765	0.77	0.788	0.775
Null	0.938	0.904	0.892	0.907	0.917

The poor results for the *part-of* relation are attributed mainly to its extremely rare occurrence in the data. The economic domain is more "abstract" and is governed to a large extent by other relation types.

To overcome this problem of performance instability among the various classifiers, the application of ensemble learning [17] is proposed. The combination of various disagreeing classifiers leads to a resulting classifier with better overall predictions [5]. Experiments have been conducted using the aforementioned classifiers in various combination schemes using bagging, boosting and stacking.

Table 2 shows the results using bagging. Experiments were run using several base classifiers and several bag sizes as a percentage of the dataset size. 50% bag size means that half of the dataset instances were randomly chosen to form the first training set, another random half is used to form the second training set etc. After repeating the process ten times (10 iterations), the datasets are used to train the same base learner. Majority voting determines the class label for the test instances. The best results are achieved with a decision tree base classifier, when using 50% of the instances to fill the bags.

Table 2. Results with bagging.

	C4.5		IB1		SVM	BN
Bag Size	50%	100%	50%	100%	50%	50%
Is-a	**0.856**	0.777	0.736	0.687	0.728	0.766
Part-of	**0**	0	0	0	0	0
Attribute	**0.809**	0.751	0.765	0.766	0.786	0.783
Null	**0.962**	0.935	0.912	0.904	0.908	0.909

Table 3 shows the results using boosting. Again, various experiments were conducted with different base learners. The best results are again obtained with a decision tree base learner. It is interesting to observe the detection of some part-of relations using boosting.

Table 4 shows the results with stacking. Different base classifiers were combined, and their predictions were given as input to the higher level meta-learner. The combined classifiers are the IB1 instance based-learner, the C4.5 decision tree learner, the Naïve Bayes learner, the Bayes Network classifier and the Support Vector Machine classifier. After running experiments with several combinations, it became obvious, that the greater the number and the diversity of the base classifiers, the better the achieved results. Using the same base learner combination, numerous experiments were run to compare meta-learners (shown in table 4). The best results are achieved using *SVM* as a meta-learner, but the results are very satisfactory with the other meta-learners as well. It is interesting to observe that even the simple lazy meta-learner, *IB1*, reaches an f-score higher than 81% for all three classes. This is attributed to the predictive power of the combination of base learners. In other words, the sophisticated base learners do all the hard work, deal with the difficult cases, and the remaining work for the meta-learner is simple.

Table 3. Results with boosting.

	C4.5	IB1	SVM	BN
Is-a	**0.772**	0.719	0.611	0.826
Part-of	**0.286**	0	0	0
Attribute	**0.762**	0.744	0.732	0.798
Null	**0.922**	0.903	0.92	0.944

Table 4. Results with stacking.

Meta-learner	C4.5	IB1	Naïve Bayes	SVM
Is-a	0.761	0.848	0.827	**0.853**
Part-of	0	0	0	**0**
Attribute	0.756	0.818	0.793	**0.835**
Null	0.94	0.952	0.947	**0.957**

7 Discussion

Comparing the results with ensemble learning (tables 2, 3 and 4) and simple learning (table 1), the positive impact of combining multiple classifiers into a single prediction scheme becomes apparent. Mistakes made by one single classifier are amended through the iterative process and the majority voting in bagging, through instance weighting, according to how difficult an instance is to predict, in boosting, and through combining the strengths of several distinct classifiers in stacking.

Among the several ensemble schemes, stacking achieves the highest results. As mentioned earlier, class prediction performance benefits significantly from combining different base learners, because, roughly speaking, the weaknesses of one classifier are 'overshadowed' by the strengths of another, leading to a significant improvement in overall prediction.

The part-of relation proves to be very problematic, even with meta-learning. This is not surprising, however, taking into account that only 0,5% of the data instances were labeled as *part-of* relations. This rare occurrence leads all learning algorithms to disregard these instances, except for the unpruned decision tree learner, either as a stand-alone classifier or as base classifier in a boosting scheme. When no pruning on the decision tree is performed, overlooking tree paths that might be important for classification is avoided, and, thereby, even very low frequency events may be taken into account.

The extracted relations are useful in many ways. They form a generic semantic thesaurus that can be further used in several applications. First, the knowledge is important for economy/finance experts for a better understanding and usage of domain concepts. Moreover, the thesaurus facilitates intelligent search. Looking for semantically related terms improves the quality of the search results. The same holds for information retrieval and data mining applications. Intelligent question/answering systems that take into account terms that are semantically related to the terms appearing in queries return information that is more relevant, more accurate and more complete.

The economic domain is governed by semantic relations that are characteristic of the domain (buy/sell, monetary/percentage, rise/drop relations etc.), and that have been included under the *attribute* relation label in this work. A more fine-grained distinction between these types of *attribute* relations is a challenging future research direction, providing information that is very useful for data mining applications in the particular domain.

8 Conclusion

This paper described the process of learning semantic relations between economic terms automatically from Modern Greek corpora. The presented methodology makes use of no external resources in order for it to be easily portable to other domains. The language-dependent features of the described approach are kept to a minimum, so that it can be easily adapted to other languages. Several ensemble learning schemes were experimented with in order to overcome the shortcomings of simple individual classifiers, leading to an overall f-score of 68,5%. Bearing in mind the use of minimal resources and the highly automated nature of the process, classification performance is very promising, compared to results reported in previous work.

References

1. Bay, S.: Combining Nearest Neighbor Classifiers Through Multiple Feature Subsets. In Proc. of the 15th International Conference on Machine Learning (1998) 37-45
2. Breiman, L.: Bagging predictors. Machine Learning 24 (1996):123-140
3. Cimiano, P., Hotho, A., Staab., S.: Comparing Conceptual, Divisive and Agglomerative Clustering fro Learning Taxonomies from Text. Proceedings of the European Conference on Artificial Intelligence (2004). Valencia, Spain

4. Degeratu, M., Hatzivassiloglou, V.: An Automatic Model for Constructing Domain-Specific Ontology Resources. Proceedings of the International Conference on Language Resources and Evaluation (2004): 2001-2004. Lisbon, Portugal
5. Dietterich, T.: Ensemble Learning. Tha Handbook of Brain Theory and Neural Networks. Second Edition. Cambridge MA: The MIT Press (2002)
6. Faure, D., Nedellec., C.: A Corpus-based Conceptual Clustering Method for Verb Frames and Ontology. Proceedings of the LREC Workshop on Adapting Lexical and Corpus Resources to Sublanguages and Applications (1998). Granada, Spain
7. Freund, Y., Schapire, R. E.: Experiments with a new boosting algorithm. Proceedings of the International Conference on Machine Learning (1996): 148-156. San Francisco
8. Hatzigeorgiu, N., Gavrilidou, M., Piperidis, S., Carayannis, G., Papakostopoulou, A., Spiliotopoulou, A., Vacalopoulou, A., Labropoulou, P., Mantzari, E., Papageorgiou, H., Demiros, I.: Design and Implementation of the online ILSP Greek Corpus. Proceedings of the 2nd International Conference on Language Resources and Evaluation (2000): 1737–1742. Athens, Greece
9. Hearst, M. A.: Automatic Acquisition of Hyponyms from Large Text Corpora. Proceedings of the International Conference on Computational Linguistics (1992): 539-545. Nantes, France
10. Kermanidis, K., Fakotakis, N., Kokkinakis, G.: DELOS: An Automatically Tagged Economic Corpus for Modern Greek. Proceedings of the Third International Conference on Language Resources and Evaluation (2002): 93-100. Las Palmas de Gran Canaria, Spain
11. Lendvai, P.: Conceptual Taxonomy Identification in Medical Documents. Proceedings of the Second International Workshop on Knowledge Discovery and Ontologies (2005): 31-38. Porto, Portugal
12. Maedche, A., Volz, R.: The Ontology Extraction and Maintenance Framework Text-To-Onto. Proceedings of the Workshop on Integrating Data Mining and Knowledge Mining (2001). San Jose, California
13. Makagonov, P., Figueroa, A. R., Sboychakov, K., Gelbukh, A.: Learning a Domain Ontology from Hierarchically Structured Texts. Proceedings of the 22nd International Conference on Machine Learning (2005). Bonn, Germany
14. Manning, C., Schuetze., H.: Foundations of Statistical Natural Language Processing. MIT Press (1999)
15. Navigli, R., Velardi, P.: Learning Domain Ontologies from Document Warehouses and Dedicated WebSites. Computational Linguistics, 50(2). MIT Press (2004)
16. Partners of ESPRIT-291/860,: Unification of the Word Classes of the ESPRIT Project 860. Internal Report BU-WKL-0376 (1986)
17. Opitz, D., Maclin, R.: Popular Ensemble Methods: An Empirical Study. Journal of Artificial Intelligence Research Vol. 11 (1999) 169-198
18. Pekar, V., Staab. S.: Taxonomy Learning –Factoring the Structure of a Taxonomy into a Semantic Classification Decision. Proceedings of the International Conference on Computational Linguistics (2002). Taipei, Taiwan
19. Pereira, F., Tishby, N., Lee, L.: Distributional Clustering of English Words. Proceedings of the 31st Annual Meeting of the Association for Computational Linguistics (1993)
20. Platt, J.: Fast Training of Support Vector Machines using Sequential Minimal Optimization. Advances in Kernel Methods - Support Vector Learning (1998), B. Schoelkopf, C. Burges, and A. Smola, eds. MIT Press.
21. Quinlan, R.: C4.5: Programs for Machine Learning, Morgan Kaufmann Publishers, San Mateo, CA (1993)

22. Schapire, R. E., Rochery, M., Rahim, M., Gupta, N.: Incorporating prior knowledge into boosting. Proceedings of the Nineteenth International Conference on Machine Learning (2002)
23. Thanopoulos, A., Kermanidis, K., Fakotakis, N.: Challenges in Extracting Terminology from Modern Greek Texts. Proceedings of the Workshop on Text-based Information Retrieval (2006). Riva del Garda, Italy
24. Witschel, H. F.: Using Decision Trees and Text Mining Techniques for Extending Taxonomies. Proceedings of the Workshop on Learning and Extending Lexical Ontologies by Using Machine Learning Methods (2005)

THE EXTENSION OF THE OMNIPAPER SYSTEM IN THE CONTEXT OF SCIENTIFIC PUBLICATIONS

Teresa Susana Mendes Pereira[1], Ana Alice Baptista[2]

Abstract Today the Internet is an important information source, which facilitates the search and access to information contents on the Web. In fact, the Internet has become an important tool used daily by scholars in the development of their work. However the contents published on the Web increase daily and consequently difficult the identification of new contents published in various information sources. In this context the RSS technology introduces a new dimension in the access and distribution mechanisms of new contents published by distributed information sources. In the scope of scientific contents the use of RSS technology helps the scholars to be up to date of new scientific resources provided by several and distributed information sources. An instance of the OmniPaper RDF prototype has been developed in order to instantiate the mechanisms of distributed information retrieval investigated in the context of the news published in newspapers and use them in the context of scientific contents. In addition a central metadatabase was developed through the RSS approach, in order to enable the scientific content syndication. This paper intends to describe the steps involved in the development of the instantiation system of the OmniPaper RDF prototype.

---

[1] Teresa Susana Mendes Pereira

Polytechnic Institute of Viana do Castelo, Superior School of Business Studies, Valença, Portugal, e-mail: tpereira@esce.ipvc.pt

[2] Ana Alice Baptista

University of Minho, School of Engineering, Information System Department, Guimarães, Portugal, e-mail: analice@dsi.uminho.pt

241

1 Introduction

Today the Web is an important and widely used information source. In fact the increased use of the Web associated to the constant evolution of technologies has promoted the development of sophisticated information systems to facilitate the access and dissemination of scientific contents produced by scientific communities. However, the Web provides several information sources and, consequently, the identification of new contents or updates demands time. In fact, users spend a lot of time tracking a set of information sources to check for new contents or updates and sometimes some of the resources are not even accessed.

RSS is an XML-based format to syndicate information, or metadata. The content syndication helps the user to be up to date of new contents published in different and distributed information sources and improves the visibility of the contents published, guaranteeing that the user becomes aware when new contents are published.

In the context of scientific contents the use of the RSS technology introduces important advantages in the distribution and dissemination process of the results produced by scientific communities. In spite of the RSS being primarily used in relaying the latest entries' headlines of the newspapers and weblogs, it has been adapted to a wide range of uses in the description of Web contents, to enhance the rapid dissemination of the contents. Some journals already use the RSS format in the description of the scientific articles published, such as D-Lib, Ariadne, Nature Publishing Group's (NPG), et cetera. In fact the syndication of metadata information of scientific contents has been contributing to the transformation of the current communication processes and information retrieval systems.

In the OmniPaper project were investigated and developed sophisticated mechanisms of distributed information retrieval in order to facilitate the access and distribution of the news contents published in the newspapers. These functionalities were supported by a semantic metadata layer. In order to take advantage of the search and browsing functionalities developed in the OmniPaper project, an instance of the OmniPaper RDF prototype was created in the context of scientific publication. In fact the whole RDF structure (described below) developed in the OmniPaper was used in the context of scientific contents in order to provide a mechanism to facilitate the distribution and dissemination of scientific research developments. The metadata layer followed an RSS approach in order to enable the syndication of the metadata information of the scientific contents.

This paper intends to describe the research work conducted in the implementation of the instantiated system of the OmniPaper RDF prototype and deepens each step shown below.

2 The RDF Prototype Developed in the OmniPaper Project

The OmniPaper (Smart Access to European Newspapers, IST-2001-32174) was a project from the European Commission IST (Information Society Technologies) program. The OmniPaper project aims to (1) find and test mechanisms for retrieving information from distributed sources in an efficient way; (2) Find and test ways for creating a uniform access point to several distributed information sources; (3) Make this access point as usable and user-friendly as possible; (4) Lift widely distributed digital collections to a higher level.

One of the principal aspects of the project is the whole metadata layer of the system that describes the metadata information of each local archive of digital news providers. This approach enables the user to search and navigate on the metadata information instead of performing integral text search, as it is usual in the most general information retrieval system. The OmniPaper architecture has two metadata layers: the Local Knowledge Layer and the Overall Knowledge Layer. The Local Knowledge Layer is composed of distributed metadatabases that contain standard semantic descriptions of all the existent articles provided by each digital news provider; this, enables a structured and uniform access to the available distributed archives. The Overall Knowledge Layer includes a conceptual layer which effort is to facilitate cross-archive browsing and navigation through the use of a web of concepts. Furthermore, this layer is enriched with multilingual and personalization functionalities for the interface with the user [15].

The steps followed in the development of the OmniPaper RDF prototype were [1]:
(1) Definition and development of the metadatabase. The definition of the metadata element set (the OmniPaper Application Profile) to be used in the descriptions of the articles was based on the Dublin Core Metadata Terms (DCMT) [3]. This choice stems from its rich semantic interoperability; it is an ISO standard (15836:2003) [8]; it is an ANSI/NISO standard (Z 39.85-2001) [9]; it has been a stable element set since 1996; it has been a Dublin Core Metadata Initiative (DCMI) recommendation since 1999 with its version 1.1; and finally due to the fact that is widely used metadata element set across boundaries of disciplines or application domains [1]. However the DCMT didn't contain all the necessary elements in the description of the news articles. Therefore a new namespace RDF Schema (called "omni") had to be defined in order to add the metadata elements established by the consortium partners [11].
(2) Definition and development of the conceptual layer (subject + lexical thesaurus). The goal of the conceptual layer was to have an ontology-based web of concepts linked to the articles [1]. The used solution was the International Press Telecommunications Council Subject Codes (IPTC SC). The IPTC SC is composed of a hierarchical three-level tree of subject codes, which describes the content of a set of concepts and has no associative relationship between its

concepts. To represent the IPTC SC, several ontology languages were analyzed and studied in order to select the one that best fits its hierarchical representation. However the IPTC SC in the semantically point of view is not that rich and, due to its simplicity, it was only necessary to define its hierarchical concepts. Therefore the RDF Schema language was chosen to complete the representation of the hierarchical tree represented in the IPTC SC [10].

The IPTC SC was then included in a metadatabase. The connection with the subject elements included in the hierarchical tree of the IPTC SC is made through the metadata element "dc:subject". Furthermore, in the OmniPaper application profile definition, the "rdfs:range" of the metadata element "dc:subject" are the IPTC Subject Codes. This means that the metadata element "dc:subject" only allows values originating from the IPTC SC [10].

In addition to the navigation and browsing functionalities through the concepts represented in the IPTC Subject Codes structure, another empowering information-organization tool was included and linked to the metadatabase: WordNet® [1]. The WordNet is "an on-line lexical reference system whose design is inspired by current psycholinguistic theories of human lexical memory. English nouns, verbs, adjectives and adverbs are organized into synonym sets, each representing one underlying lexical concept. Different relations link the synonym sets" [12].

An RDF-encoded version of the WordNet 1.6 was downloaded and stored in a local metadatabase. Its connection with the metadata elements of the articles stored in the metadatabase is performed through the metadata element "omni-keyList". This feature enables the user to perform query expansion and thus refine the search term introduced.

The system design of the OmniPaper RDF prototype is shown in figure 1.

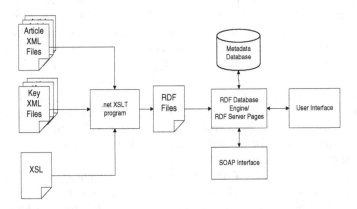

Fig. 1 OmniPaper RDF Prototype System Design

The combination of the subject thesaurus (IPTC SC) with a lexical thesaurus (WordNet), implemented in the OmniPaper RDF prototype to enhance both user queries and navigation is considered rare within RDF applications [1]. Moreover, the fact of these search and browsing functionalities, through the use of a subject thesaurus and a lexical thesaurus being supported by central RDF metadatabase, instead of the full text search, directly in the local archive, usually increase the response time and the results have low levels of precision and recall to the user.

In order to take advantage of the search and navigation functionalities and the whole RDF infrastructure developed in the OmniPaper RDF prototype, it was implemented a system which is an instance of the OmniPaper RDF prototype, in the context of scientific publication. The following sections present the work developed in the instantiation of the OmniPaper RDF prototype in the context of the scientific contents.

3 Instantiation of the OmniPaper RDF Prototype in the Context of Scientific Literature

The smart search mechanisms developed in the OmniPaper RDF prototype, previously presented, demonstrate that the OmniPaper RDF prototype goes far beyond the current full-text search methods. An instance of this prototype in the context of scientific literature aims to improve the daily work of scholars providing sophisticated mechanisms to access and search for new scientific contents.

The implemented system follows the concept of the OmniPaper RDF prototype. However the OmniPaper system was developed in the scope of the news published in newspapers, and its instantiation in the context of scientific publications required some changes at the level of the data and of some processes. In fact, the metadata element set was the principal change in the instantiation process of the OmniPaper RDF prototype, as a consequence of the specific features that characterizes the scientific contents. Another difference stands for the RSS approach followed in the definition of the metadata layer, while in the OmniPaper RDF prototype the metadata description followed the RDF/XML technology. However this can not be considered as a relevant difference because the RSS version 1.0 used, conforms the W3C's RDF specification and is extensible via XML-namespace and/or RDF based modularization [2]. The extensibility mechanisms built in to RSS 1.0 ensure the semantically rich metadata description of any resource which can be identified by a URI. For this reason, the RSS 1.0 was used for metadata encoding and also because it increases interoperability with other RDF/XML applications and enables the rich semantic description of Web resources. However, in the OmniPaper RDF prototype an RDF file holds one description about one article/resource that is stored in one of the local archives, while in the RSS approach is defined a RSS feed that contains a list of items containing titles, links, descriptions and other terms of a set of scientific articles. The differences between the two approaches are in metadata elements used in the description of the Web resources.

Finally, the last difference is related to the navigation functionality available in both systems. In the system developed in the scope of scientific literature it was considered more adequate to use the controlled vocabulary ACM CCS instead of the IPTC Subject Codes used in the OmniPaper RDF prototype. The use of the WordNet remained because it is a lexical thesaurus oriented to organize information, and therefore its use is not restricted to any specific kind of information resource.

4 Implementation of the Metadata Layer

As in the OmniPaper project, the principal aspect of the implemented system was the definition of the metadata layer. The purpose of the metadata layer is to support the search and navigation functionalities and facilitate the access to the contents presented within the feed repository. Another goal concerns the use of the central metadatabase to accomplish the syndication of contents, through the RSS approach. Providing the RSS feed to scholars, they can subscribe the feed and thus be aware of new scientific articles published in the distributed repositories, instead of accessing the different information sources to search for new contents that have been published.

The consumer of a scientific feed requires more information besides the regular metadata elements, usually used in the RSS documents as title, link and (optionally) description. In fact, the user requires more information about the article, in order to be able to cite, or produce a citation for a given article within a serial [5]. Consequently rich metadata was necessary in describing the article along with the article title, link and description. Thus, taking into account that the RSS 1.0 is based on RDF, makes the RSS 1.0 increasingly attractive to be used in the description of scientific publications and therefore ideally suited to the inclusion of supplementary metadata [6]. Several metadata standard vocabularies widely used in the domain of the scientific literature were analyzed in order to define a set of a metadata elements which best describe the features of the scientific contents. The vocabularies were analyzed in terms of the semantics of their elements, their usage in the community, and their interoperability across communities. This analysis resulted in the selection of the DCMT vocabulary in the definition of the metadata structure, since it provides a variety of metadata elements that conforms totality all the necessary descriptions requirements of the information resources used, it enables the metadata interoperability, and it is an ISO and an ANSI/NISO standard.

The selected elements were included in the application profile and the rules for metadata encoding were defined accordingly to the structure defined in the RSS template.

The encode of the metadata elements followed the recommendations made by Kokkelink and Schwänzl in the document "Expressing Qualified Dublin Core in RDF/XML" [7], although, it is still a DCMI candidate recommendation.

5 Implementation of the Conceptual Layer

The design of the system implemented in the context of scientific publications (shown in figure 2) is the same developed in the OmniPaper RDF prototype. The whole RDF model developed in the OmniPaper was instantiated in context of scientific literature. The changes performed were at the data level and in some processes.

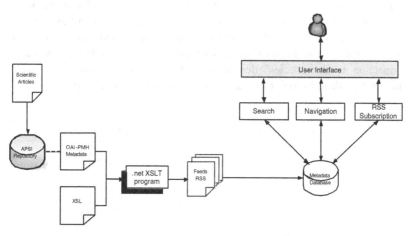

Fig. 2 System Design

The scientific contents used in the developed system are provided by the Associação Portuguesa de Sistemas de Informação (APSI) [13]. APSI has an institutional repository that stores, preserves, disseminates and enables access to the articles published in the Information Systems journal and articles published in the APSI' conference (CAPSI) proceedings.

APSI provided the metadata information of the articles in the XML OAI-PMH format. Then, in order to get these metadata information encoded accordingly to the RSS structure defined in the template, a stylesheet to perform the transformation was developed. This process resulted in the creation of the RSS feed organized by a list of items. Each item contains the metadata description of one article. RDF triples were extracted from the RSS feed and stored in the metadatabase, through the use of the RDF Gateway, a Microsoft Windows based native RDF database management system combined with a HTTP server. Some RDF Server Pages (RSPs) were defined in order to provide some functionally for the end user.

The metadatabase supports the navigation and browsing functionalities enabling the user to search through the metadata layer and not directly in the information source. In the development of the navigation mechanism it was used the available RDF-S version of the ACM CCS [14]. The scientific articles provided by APSI weren't classified neither using the ACM CCS nor any other controlled vocabulary, thus this work still had to be done manually. The connection between the ACM CCS subject tree to the metadatabase is performed through the "dc:subject" metadata element, as illustrated in figure 3. This fact allowed the user to subscribe the articles within a specific subject accordingly with the specific interest areas of each subscriber.

Besides this functionality, the use of the WordNet was also instantiated from the OmniPaper RDF prototype. The use of this lexical thesaurus improves the search procedure, since it allows the relationship of the input concept with others, enabling the user to perform query expansion and thus redefine his search. The connection to the articles' descriptions stored in the metadatabase was made through the "description" metadata element, as illustrated in figure 3.

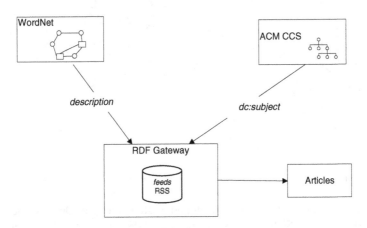

Fig. 3 Metadata semantic layer of the system

Furthermore, the metadatabase also enabled the syndication of scientific contents that are included in the RSS feed. In fact, the user doesn't need to check for new articles published in the APSI repository, because since the user subscribed the RSS feed he can be aware of new issues that have been published through an RSS Reader application with which the user is familiar with.

Figure 4 shows the interface of the implemented system.

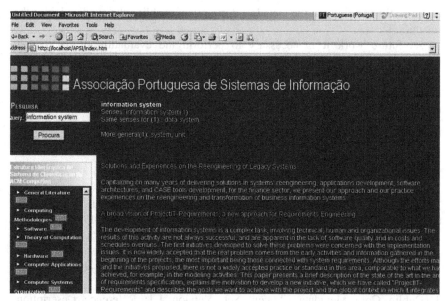

Fig. 4 Screenshot of the developed prototype

6 Conclusions and Future Work

The development of information and communication technologies, and the increase use of the Internet associated to the user needs have been contributing to a deep restructure of the traditionally means used in the publication of information. The RDF prototype implemented in the OmniPaper project has already proven to be an efficient system to search for news contents published in newspapers. Moreover the RDF application combines completely with subject ontology and a lexical thesaurus to enhance both user search and navigation. In this context, the instantiation of the OmniPaper RDF prototype in the scope of the scientific publication would improve the current mechanisms used to access and to distribute the scientific research developments. This article described the steps followed in the instantiation of the OmniPaper RDF prototype in the context of scientific publications. The main difference between the two systems was the use of the RSS technology in the metadata description, enabling the syndication of the scientific feeds.

As future work it is necessary to perform the evaluation of the system implemented, to determine the relevance of the results returned and its usability. It would also be interesting to harvest several repositories to the metadatabase implemented in this system, in order to provide a more complete service with more information.

References

1. Baptista, A. A.: Searching and browsing using RDF-Encoded Metadata: the case of OmniPaper. Canadian Journal of Communication. 29 (3), 317--328 (2004). Available from: https://repositorium.sdum.uminho.pt/handle/1822/5080.

2. RDF Site Summary (RSS) 1.0, http://web.resource.org/rss/1.0/spec#.

3. Dublin Core Metadata Element Set, Version 1.1: Reference Description, http://www.dublincore.org/documents/dces/.

4. Dublin Core Metadata Initiative Home Page, http://www.dublincore.org/.

5. Hammond, T.: Why Choose RSS 1.0? XML.com (2003). Available from: http://www.xml.com/pub/a/2003/07/23/rssone.html.

6. Hammond, T., Hannay, T. e Lund, B.: The Role of RSS in Science Publishing Syndication and Annotation on the Web. D-Lib Magazine, 10 (12) (2004). Available from: http://www.dlib.org/dlib/december04/hammond/12hammond.html.

7. Kokklink, S. e Schwänzl, R.: Expressing Qualified Dublin Core in RDF/XML [on-line]. Dublin Core Metadata Initiative (2002). Available from: http://www.dublincore.org/documents/2002/04/14/dcq-rdf-xml/.

8. National Information Standards Organization. The Dublin Core Metadata Element Set: An American National Standard/ developed by National Information Standards Organization (2001), http://www.niso.org/standards/resources/Z39-85.pdf

9. National Information Standards Organization. NISO Press Release - The Dublin Core Metadata Element Set Approved (2001), http://www.niso.org/news/releases/PRDubCr.html

10. Pereira, T. and Baptista, A. A.: Incorporating a Semantically Enriched Navigation Layer Onto an RDF Metadatabase. Engelen, J., Costa Sely., M. S., Moreira, Ana Cristina S., ed. In: Building digital bridges: linking cultures, commerce and science: Proceedings of the ICCC International Conference on Electronic Publishing, ELPUB, July 2004 Brasília, Brasil (2004). Available from: https://repositorium.sdum.uminho.pt/handle/1822/604.

11. Pereira, T., Yaginuma, T. and Baptista, A. A.: Perfil de Aplicação e Esquema RDF dos Elementos de Metadados do Projecto OmniPaper. In: CMLE'2003 – 3th Congresso Luso-Moçambicano de Engenharia. August 20, 2003. Maputo, Moçambique (2003). Available from: http://repositorium.sdum.uminho.pt/handle/1822/281

12. Princeton University Cognitive Science Laboratory. WordNet –A lexical database for the English language, http://www.cogsci.princeton.edu/~wn

13. Associação Portuguesa de Sistemas de Informação, http://www.apsi.pt/.

14. ACM Computing Classification System [1998 Version], http://dspace-dev.dsi.uminho.pt:8080/pt/addon_acmccs98.jsp

15. Paepen, B.: Blueprint: a universal standard model for efficient information retrieval. Technical Report of the OmniPaper Project, 28 February of 2005. Available from: http://www.omnipaper.org/

The Semantic Web: A mythical story or a solid reality?

Jorge Cardoso[1]

Abstract The Semantic Web vision has drove hundreds of practitioners to research and develop a new bread of applications that could take the full potential of the Web to the next level. While there is a fairly clear understanding of where Web 1.0 and Web 2.0 stand now a day, the current status and position of the Semantic Web, also known as Web 3.0, is not as clear and well defined. Therefore, in this paper we present a landscape that illustrates and captures the trends in the Semantic Web with the purpose of guiding future developments.

1. Introduction

The vision for a Semantic Web has been termed as *The Next Big Thing* for information system. The publication of the Scientific American Magazine article "The Semantic Web" in May, 2001, by Tim Berners-Lee, James Hendler and Ora Lassila has triggered a strong wave of research worldwide. Thousands of research papers have been written and hundreds of applications have been implemented. But what are the research trends. That is what we will address in this paper by presenting a summary of a survey (Cardoso, 2007) to gives an account of current Semantic Web practices. The findings reported in this article are based on 627 surveys that were filled in and conducted from 12 December 2006 to 26 January 2007.

2. Web.X – A story in 3 chapters

The Semantic Web has been coined Web 3.0. While previous Web technologies, such as Web 1.0 and Web 2.0, had a remarkable success, there is no consensus that Web 3.0 had, or will have in the future, the same levels of success. While

---

[1] SAP AG, Germany, jorge.cardoso@sap.com

some researchers believe that the Web 3.0 is still to come to delight users and take them to a new paradigm, others believe that it has been such as long time since the Semantic Web vision was introduced that it is becoming almost mythical.

The Web 1.0 classifies the very first applications for the Web which had the main objective to only provide information content to end users. Web 2.0 brought interactivity to users. Features such as tagging, social networks, online media, content aggregation and syndication (RSS), mashups and folksonomies became common on the Web.

Web 1.0 and Web 2.0 successes are undeniable. Success stories are available at the distance of a mouse click. Web 1.0 has deliver innovative solutions such as DoubleClick, mp3.com, Britannica Online, personal websites, screen scraping, and content management systems. Web 2.0 has engineered landmarks such as Google AdSense, Flickr, BitTorrent, Napster, Wikipedia, and del.icio.us.

But what about the Web 3.0? When will the Semantic Web arrive? The building blocks are already available: RDF, OWL, and microformats are a few of them. During the 2007 Semantic Technology Conference, several new and robust startups companies based on – Semantic Web technologies – have demonstrated their interest and commitment to this new concept for their business. But while it seems that we getting close to deliver the promised automated applications, we are still a few years away from unleashing the killer-app. Interesting companies that are actively trying to implement the Semantic Web include Twine, Garlik, and Hakia. Twine is a real application of the Semantic Web that gives users a superior way to share, organize, and find information with people they trust. It uses the Semantic Web, natural language processing, and machine learning to make your information and relationships more expressive. Garlik is using Semantic Web technologies to help users monitor their personal information online and protect themselves against identity theft. Hakia is a semantic search engines with a focus on natural language processing methods to try and deliver search results based on analyzing semantics and not keywords.

According to Google search engine, the number of queries for "Semantic Web" keywords has dropped since 2004. Figure 1 shows a trend in Semantic Web popularity. What does this empirical trend represented the semantic research field?

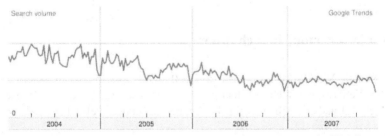

Fig 1. Volume of search queries for the keywords "Semantic Web"

On the one hand, this can be explained by the fact that the hype is fading away and that people are losing interested in Semantic Web solutions. On the other hand, it can be explained by the fact that the concept is already accepted and understood by many people and, therefore, it does not need to be searched for. To better understand the current research and industrial efforts to make the Semantic Web a reality, and not a mythical story, we have carried out a survey in 2006 and 2007. The results are summarized in the following section.

3. Current trends of the Semantic Web

The survey carried out was divided into five categories: Demographics, Tools and Languages, Ontology, Ontology Size, and Production. The complete results of the survey can be found at (Cardoso, 2007) and are here presented as a summary of the most interesting points.

Ontology Editors. We asked respondents to tell us which ontology editors they were currently using in their organizations. The editor most frequently cited was Protégé with a market share of 68.2%. Approximately equal numbers of respondents use SWOOP (13.6%), OntoEdit (12.2%) (OntoEdit is now called OntoStudio), and Altova SemanticWorks (10.3%). A good survey of the most popular ontology editors can be found in (Escórcio and Cardoso, 07).

Ontology Languages. Our study revealed more than 75% of ontologists have selected OWL to develop their ontologies and that more than 64% rely on RDF(S). Curiously, Description Logic and FLogic are also being used with a penetration rate of 17% and 11.8%, respectively. A recent language, WSML (Web Service Modeling Language), has also gained some popularity (3.7%).

Reasoning Engines. We asked all respondents to indicate the reasoning engines they were using. The largest segment (53.6%) indicated that they were using Jena (McBride, 2002). Smaller groups indicated they were using Racer (28%) and Pellet (23.7%). FaCT++ (13.3%) and OWLJessKB (8.1%) have also gained preference by a small group of participants.

Ontology Domains. To determine the actual trend in the development of ontologies for particular domains, we asked all respondents to indicate for which industries they were representing knowledge with ontologies. Education and Computer Software are the best represented industries (31% and 28.5%), followed by Government (17%) and Business Services (17%).

Methodologies. We asked all respondents to indicate which methodology or method they were employing to develop their ontologies. Sixty percent develop ontologies without using any methodology. The methodologies with greatest adoption are METHONTOLOGY (13.7%) followed by On-To-Knowledge methodology (7.4%) and Uschold and King's method (4.2%).

Purpose of using ontologies. We asked participants to tell us the reasons that motivated them to use ontologies. The vast majority of participants (69.9%) answered "to share common understanding of the structure of information among people or software agents, so models can be understood by humans and computers".

Techniques used with ontologies. We asked respondents to tell us if they used any specific technique to manipulate ontologies. The largest segment of respondents (67.1%) indicated that they use ontology mapping. Roughly equal numbers of participants indicated that they were integrating ontologies (40.7%) and merging ontologies (33.9%). Twenty six percent stated that they align ontologies.

Ontologies size. We asked each respondent to indicate the average size of the smallest, typical, and biggest ontologies they were working with. A vast majority of respondents (72.9%) indicated that their smallest ontologies had less than 100 concepts. When asked about typical ontologies, forty four percent of respondents stated that such types of ontology had between 100 and 1000 concepts.

Production. Each respondent was asked to indicate if they would put their systems into production. More that 70% of all respondents indicated that they planned to adopt ontology-based systems, while 27.9% indicate that they do not have any plans to use such types of systems in the future.

4. Conclusions

Web 1.0 and Web 2.0 had, and still have, an important impact on society and electronic commerce. The next step for the evolution of the Web is the Semantic Web, or Web 3.0. The information presented in this article constitutes a checkpoint to frame the current status and trends in the Semantic Web. It depicts a paradigm change from an idea to the development and use of real and concrete semantic solutions.

5. References

Cardoso, J., "The Semantic Web Vision: Where are We?" IEEE Intelligent Systems, September/October 2007, pp.22-26, 2007.

Escórcio, L. and Cardoso, J. "Editing Tools for Ontology Construction", in Semantic Web Services: Theory, Tools and Applications, Idea Group, March 2007. ISBN: 1-59904-045-X .

Knowledge framework supporting semantic search of learning resources

Monique Grandbastien, Benjamin Huynh-Kim-Bang and Anne Monceaux

Abstract This chapter reports on a practical application of semantic technologies for retrieving learning resources. While most existing Learning Objects Repositories offer textual based search which fails in retrieving adequate resources if the words used in the query and in the metadata do not match, the proposed approach is entirely relying on several ontologies. Two use cases in industrial and academic contexts show how core ontologies based on LOM and competencies approach could be combined with specific representations to enable retrieving more resources better fulfilling learners' needs.

1 Introduction

Recent standardisation efforts in the area of learning technology have resulted in a considerable improvement of the interoperability of learning resources across different Learning Management Systems (LMS) and Learning Object Repositories (LOR). Indeed there are several international initiatives aiming at sharing Learning Resources, see for instance [1], [2], [3], [4]. An important feature in this evolving context is that a large number of providers will contribute with their resources and their resource descriptions. Thus we cannot hope the same coherence in descriptions as when they were performed in a centralized way by librarians. However existing systems using current metadata specification, such as MERLOT [5], which has been running for 10 years now, are still performing lexical based search. So during a query process the returned resources highly rely on the terms used in the query and the terms used for annotating the resources whereas recent Internet technologies can bring significant improvements for such tasks. These technologies include application communications via web services, distributed architectures and knowledge representation that can be processed by machines. The LUISA project [6] addresses

Monique Grandbastien, Benjamin Huynh-Kim-Bang
LORIA-UHP Nancy I, Campus Scientifique, BP 239 - 54506 Vandoeuvre-lès-Nancy Cedex, France
{Monique.Grandbastien, Benjamin.Huynh-Kim-Bang}@loria.fr

Anne Monceaux
EADS CRC, Avenue Didier Daurat - Centreda 1, 31700 Toulouse, France
Anne.Monceaux@eads.net

259

the development of a reference semantic architecture for improving the search, interchange and delivery of learning resources. The proposed solution is based on the use of distributed web services and on the provision of various ontologies and ontology based components. In this paper we only address knowledge description issues. In the context of Web learning resources, a rich conceptual representation of the domains is needed, so that search is performed through conceptual mapping and not only through textual mapping.

However, knowledge representation has been identified as a bottleneck [13] in knowledge engineering for many years since it is a very time consuming task requiring highly qualified people. Consequently an ontology based system can be an acceptable and scalable solution only if a common representation framework can be shared by many specific target applications. In this paper we present such a "knowledge framework" defined as a combination of ontologies and semantic tools allowing flexible implementation of different use cases while providing powerful semantic capabilities (section 2). Then we show how this framework can be extended and customized in order to fulfil the needs of industrial training requirements (section 3) and of an academic environment (section 4). In section 5 we compare this approach with some other ongoing projects and provide trends for future developments.

2   Common framework

Let us give a closer look at most existing querying processes for retrieving learning resources. First, as mentioned in the introduction, if you do not use the right term you have no chance to be returned the resource that would best suit your needs. Secondly the right term for one LOR is perhaps not the right term to use for querying another one. Finally, existing resources are more often described in terms of subject content than in terms of competency that a learner could acquire when using them, while there is a growing demand, especially in adult education and professional training, of filling specific competency gaps.

Given that context, we propose to include in a common knowledge framework a learning resource core ontology and a competency core ontology. The use-case sections will detail how these ontologies can be combined with subject and contextual ontologies.

2.1 Learning object core ontology: s-lom

One of the weaknesses of the LOM [7] specification is that it is not provided with a formal semantic description. The semantic interoperability is only performed through the meaning given to categories and through lists of values the semantic of which is often unclear, leading end-users to defining application profiles. In LUISA we propose a semantic version of LOM called s-lom [8].

This ontology is mostly based on the LOM schema to allow standard compliance as far as possible and is designed to provide richer computational semantics. The Learning Object concept is modelled as a class, then the metadata attached to a LO are represented as the property values of a class instance. For values set, the definition often relies on OpenCyc [14] in order to achieve more general semantic interoperability with other systems. For example, the context (field 5.6 in LOM) can be filled with an instance of the concepts ocGeographicalRegion, ocTimeInterval or ocAdministrativeUnit defined into OpenCyc. Moreover, the category 9 of LOM is used to extend and customise the schema. For example, by linking it to an ontology of competencies.

2.2 Competency core ontology: General Competency Schema (GCS)

As previously noticed there is a growing demand of acquiring new competencies either in higher and professional education or in company training whereas learning resources are not all indexed in terms of competency acquisition. So there is a need of sharing a competency ontology either for improving the description of resources and for performing competency based reasoning in order to fill competency gaps. The same ontology would also allow to move from a competency based search to a subject matter based search when needed. We provide hereafter a schema of the main classes of this ontology. A detail description can be found in [11] while the use-cases of the next sections will illustrate it.

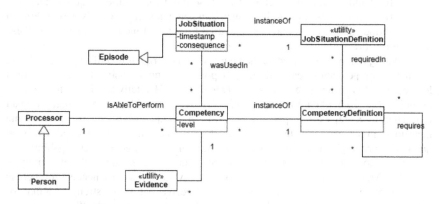

Fig. 1. Extract from the General Competency Schema

2.3 Flexible annotation tool: SHAME editor

The flexibility of the knowledge framework would not be possible without flexibility in the annotation. That is why the knowledge framework is completed with the flexible SHAME editor [15] based on Annotation Profiles. An Annotation Profile (AP) is a configuration of the metadata editor defining what to edit and how to edit it. Indeed, more and more users participate through different roles in the edition of complex metadata coming from different metadata structure. Thus, APs allow to easily define in the editor which pre-defined values (from taxonomies or ontologies) should show up in which style of field (drop-down list, cursor to move, …) or how data types have to be checked. An administrator can compose an AP by creating and aggregating some modular bricks of annotation. For example, s/he can create a brick for the "language" metadata by associating a view (display a field entitled "Language") and a model (linked this field to the field 1.3 of LOM). Then, the administrator can decide to ask the annotators for competencies by adding into the AP a brick displaying a drop-down list dynamically filled with some instances of the competency ontology and associated to another structure than LOM. When opening the annotation tool, the annotators will finally see in one page the Language and Competency fields to fill and quickly designed by the administrator.

3 An industrial use-case

We describe hereafter how the common knowledge framework is customised and extended in order to fulfil the needs of an industrial application.

The industrial case study in LUISA focuses on organizational knowledge gap analysis in terms of competences as the driver for learning object selection and composition, emphasizing the perspective of organizational learning. Therefore, the case study deals with metadata issued from some existing competency catalogue that were beforehand identified as relevant for describing job position requirements, and with learning resources for acquiring such competencies. It also deals with a domain and discipline classification that has been used for a long time for characterizing these learning resources.

Inside big companies indeed, some people are in charge of identifying and defining the main competencies required for job positions and of using them for Human Resources (HR) management activities. One of these HR activities is the formalizing of employees' individual competency profiles and gaps with regard to their assigned job. Therefore, gaps are expressed in terms of competencies and thanks to some measurement scales that state for expertise levels. These levels are defined involving qualitative criteria such as experience, autonomy or knowledge transfer capability.

For example in our context, for some 'Structural engineering' field of activity, a 'Metallic Materials & Technologies' competency is defined as needed for people working on metallic structures from the perspective of static strength. Kinds of activities are identified as typical "professions", e.g. in this example "Stress metal" is a profession in the 'Structural engineering' field.

The competency meaning must be clearly stated, and it might even be decomposed into skills and knowledge elements. In our example, the 'Metallic Materials & Technologies' competency is defined as follows: *"Knowledge of specific properties for all types of metallic materials and material conditions and the capability of advising on the correct material and condition to be used in a particular application. Production of material specifications and data sheets. Knowledge and experience of the various technologies associated with Metallic materials. Statistical analysis. Material testing"*. When a specific job position or a user's profile is described, this typical competency can be used along with a proficiency level that expresses the needed expertise degree.

All this descriptive work aims at organizing the HR management activities such as hiring, mobility and of course also training.

In order to prototype LUISA in this context, we built a local competency ontology that imports the GCS described above (Fig.2). This way, the GCS concepts are available for local competency domain description. Local concepts allow us conforming with the specific way to structure typical activities and competencies in our context, using a 'Function', 'Field' and 'Profession' tree, and specifying our company specific measurement scales. As we experimented, the GCS offers a suitable framework for describing many of the concepts needed.

In the prototype application, the Training Manager uses a subset of the ontology's concepts in addition to the already existing LOM metadata to annotate LOs. For example a LO may have a prerequisite that is a competency or a competency scaled with a particular measurement scale; a LO might target some outcome knowledge elements specified in our ontology; or a LO intended audience might match a population corresponding to a Field or to a set of typical Professions.

In fact several kinds of users might annotate LOs: the Author, the Training Manager, the Learner, etc. The SHAME editor allows for specifying several annotation profiles according to the user's role.

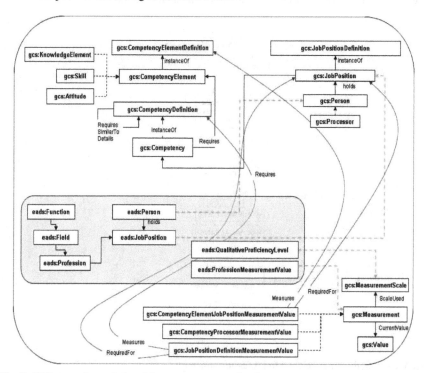

Fig. 2. GCS extension to industrial use case: concept level

The ontology also supports the LOR query mechanisms. If the learner's profile is available and his competency gap known from the system, then the LUISA system shall be able to select LOs that best fulfil the gap. When LO repositories are queried for the purpose of selecting LO, the relations stated inside the ontology between the concepts allows various query resolution strategies. For example the system might decompose a 'competency definition' into its knowledge elements and/or skills in order to refine an unsuccessful query. Or it can know about which typical profession's competencies were used to define the job position profile corresponding to user's position in order to identify and rank specific weaknesses with regard to a Profession.

The competency driven search function expected results are either a list or a combination of LOs in a sort of individual training program. It involves various query resolvers and composers to:

- Find all candidate LOs and rank them using levels
- Match LOs pre-requisites
- Use Similar Competencies
- Decompose Competencies into its Skill elements to refine search
- Cross Competencies with Domain LO metadata
- Relax some query criteria (constraints)

Besides the described annotation resources, we felt the need for integrating a small domain and discipline thesaurus (Fig.3) that people in charge of managing training resources traditionally use for characterising them. We integrated this classification by extending LOM thanks to the Classification metadata section.

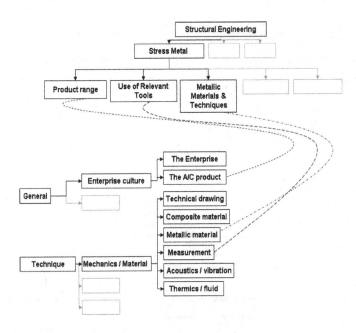

Fig. 3. Domain thesaurus relation to Profession structure

In addition to offer immediate search criteria (learning resources being systematically described using this classification in former internal training databases), we could then add a relation between 'Disciplines' or 'Specialities' and the Profession concepts in our competency ontology. In our example, the French thesaurus offers a coordinate entry 'Technique – Mécanique/Matériaux – Matériaux métallique' that is related to (although not equivalent to) the 'Stress Metal' profession mentioned above. These relationships offer additional potential for extending queries.

4 An academic use-case

We describe hereafter how to customise and extend the common knowledge framework in order to fulfil the needs of an academic application.

The academic use case deals with resources for acquiring basic competencies with Internet and Office software. Indeed, the French government created few years ago a structured list of nine major competencies decomposed in about forty refined competencies and validated by a diploma called C2I. For example, the major competency "Information Search" is detailed by the more refined competencies "Distinguishing different types of search engines", "Designing the query" and "Using the search results".

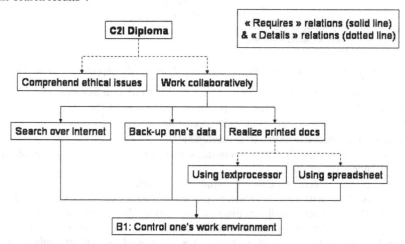

Fig. 4. GCS extension to academic use-case: instances of high-level competencies

As we experimented it, the GCS, described above, offers a suitable frame to implement the C2I competencies. Our case aims at gathering and offering C2I documents to the students through the university's LMS. GCS allows the competencies to be managed at two levels. A curricula manager manipulates Competency concepts and can express or visualise the different relations ('details' or 'requires') between them (see Fig. 4). At the course level, a professor manipulates CompetencyElement concepts and can detail a competency in finer grain as KnowledgeElement (see Fig. 5).

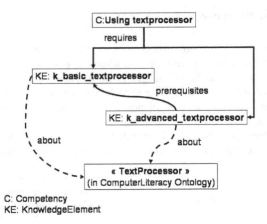

Fig. 5. GCS extension to academic use-case: Instances of low-level competencies (extract)

Conceptualizing competencies in the ontology allows different features as:
- Resolve dependencies between competencies and between LOs
- Decompose a competency into its sub-competencies
- Search over topics associated to competencies
- Basically map instances from our ontology with some instances of the ontology of the industrial use case.

Here are some details on how are applied these rules.

In the case of a search for "Using text-processor", the system was configured to decompose the query into smaller grains of competencies. If no documents are found at the high-level, the system can provide tentative compositions of documents annotated at the level of finer competencies. The goal is not to replace the instructional designer but to propose small possible aggregations validated or not by him/her.

As we saw it in section 2, LOM allows its extension through the field Classification. In our case we used it for three purposes: required and targeted competencies pointing to the GCS ontology and a Discipline purpose pointing to a basic ontology of disciplines in our university. The discipline ontology represents the different fields of study in our university. For historical reasons, these fields are different between universities. Beyond a basic classification, the ontology adds some links from a discipline to another one based on some common features. For example, Biology belongs to Life Sciences while Medicine belongs to the Health field. However Medicine is close to ("links_to" relation) Biology because of some common courses. In s-lom, we use the Discipline purpose as the discipline of the audience targeted by the resource. Indeed the students in sport science don't use a spreadsheet program in the same way as students in Biology. Each ones use tool's functions in a specific way or with specific data. But thanks to the ontology of disciplines, if the system doesn't find the right resource for a student, it can infer that a resource with the same characteristics and a close (thanks to the "links_to" relation) discipline is also correct.

The last point to mention is the "about" relation in Fig. 5. This relation should be seen as a link from a competency to a subject or contextual concept. In our case, the competencies are linked to instances in a Computer Literacy ontology. This last one is a formal representation of hardware and software generally used in C2I learning. For example, the ontology can expresses that "Microsoft Word" and "Open Writer" are "Text-processors" which belong to "Office Software" and that "Open Writer" can be launched on "Linux" and "Windows" operating systems but "Microsoft Word" can be launched just on Windows [16].

Thanks to this ontology and the link to GCS, a query over some competencies can be redirected, if necessary, over some other subjects or tools. If a learning object (LO) is annotated for learning "basic text-processing" on "Microsoft word XP", the system can found other LOs for the same tool but also infer that a LO about "Open Writer" is a LO with similar content.

5 Related work and further trends

The knowledge framework composed of ontologies and semantic tools proved its flexibility through its implementation in both use cases. We are currently testing the capabilities of semantic reasoning and will be able soon to compare it to related works as the ones presented below.

The need of a strong semantic-based layer and of a distributed architecture of semantic based services for supporting the sharing and reuse of learning resources has been acknowledged in several other on going projects. Among them, LORNET [2] is one of the more ambitious. TELOS, the integrating component of LORNET, is described as « an ontology driven eLearning Operating System » by its authors in [9]. In the same project, a LOM based ontology was also produced for supporting services in a Learning Design repository (IDLD) whereas several editors allow to associate metadata to resources. Some metadata are pointing to subject content knowledge which in turn can be associated to competencies.

Also based on a strong semantic layer, there are several attempts to partially automating the annotation process [12]. The results if successful could be used in the LUISA process.

The popularity of Web 2.0 websites (as for example YouTube for sharing videos) demonstrates the interest to consider collaborative approaches and to bridge them with semantic web technologies. In a future version of our prototype, we include the implementation of LO's ratings by users and then associate these evaluations to users's profiles. This ecological approach was developed by McCalla in [10]. For example, in the academic domain previously described, the system could observe that users studying Computer Sciences evaluate very well a LO while users in Medicine and Pharmacology are not satisfied with it. Then it could infer that this LO is not suitable for students in Health field and not recommend it to a student in Dentistry.

We already foreseen extensions for the common knowledge framework. We intend to use a part of the OpenCyc ontology about locations in order to describe where a training is delivered or where an exam can be passed for getting an academic certification. Other improvements to be investigated later include resource and service composition and defining criteria to be used when searching in several LORs.

Acknowledgments. The work reported here is part of the FP6-027149 LUISA project and benefited from all team members discussions.

References

1. ARIADNE Foundation, http://www.ariadne-eu.org
2. LORNET, http://www.lornet.org/
3. GLOBE, http://globe.edna.edu.au/globe/go
4. Open Courseware Consortium, http://www.ocwconsortium.org
5. MERLOT, http://www.merlot.org
6. LUISA Consortium: DoW, Document of Work (2005)
7. IEEE LOM specification: http://ltsc.ieee.org/wg12
8. LUISA Consortium: D4.9 A LOM based ontology of learning objects in WSML (2006)
9. Paquette, G.: An Ontology and a Software Framework for Competency Modeling and Management. Educational Technology & Society, 10 (3), 1-21 (2007) http://www.ifets.info/journals/10_3/1.pdf
10. McCalla, G.: The Ecological Approach to the Design of E-Learning Environments: Purpose-based Capture and Use of Information About Learners. Journal of Interactive Media in Education, 2004 (7). Special Issue on the Educational Semantic Web (2004) http://www-jime.open.ac.uk/2004/7/mccalla-2004-7-disc-t.html
11. Sicilia M.A. Ontology based competency management: Infrastructures for knowledge intensive learning organization. In M.D. Lytras & A. Naeve (eds) Intelligent learning infrastructure for knowledge intensive organizations: A semantic Web Perspective, 302-324, Hershey, PA, Idea Group pub (2005)
12. Cardinaels, K., Meire, M., Duval, E.: Automating Metadata Generation: the Simple Indexing Interface, International WWW conference, Chiba, Japan, ACM (2005)
13. Boicu, M., Tecuci, G., Stanescu, B., Balan, G.C., Popovici, E.: Ontologies and the Knowledge Acquisition Botteleneck, Proceedings of IJCAI-2001 Workshop on Ontologies and Information Sharing, pp9-18, AAAI press, Menlo Park, Ca (2001)
14. OpenCyc, http://www.opencyc.org
15. SHAME editor, http://kmr.nada.kth.se/shame/wiki/Overview/Main
16. LUISA Consortium: D7.2 Design and modeling of the specific metadata and models (2007)

Ontology-based tools for the management of customers' portfolios in a deregulated electricity market environment

Nikolaos Tilipakis[1], Christos Douligeris[1] and Aristomenis Neris[2]

Abstract. Electricity prices in the new deregulated electricity market across Europe are now formulated by market forces while the scarcity of infrastructure resources that are necessary in order to serve the steadily increasing demand is becoming more profound. An instrument to efficiently cope with this situation is demand side management, especially when applied to small electricity consumers. The efficient support of this task necessitates the utilization of efficient computation tools in order to manage the huge and heterogeneous amount of data involved in this process. A model based on the Semantic Web notions is proposed in this paper for the efficient modeling of customer characteristics, aiming to assist an electricity provider in the development of his customer's portfolio in order to participate in a demand side bidding process.

1 Introduction

During the last two decades, a transition towards a deregulated market environment is taking place in the European electrical power industry. The utilization of demand response, i.e. the persuasion of end-users to reduce consumption or disconnect appliances from the system in high demand periods,

[1]Department of Informatics,
University of Piraeus
80 Karaoli and Dimitriou,
18534 Piraeus, Greece
cdoulig@unipi.gr, ntilipakis@bankofgreece.gr

[2]Hellenic Transmission System Operator S.A.
Amfitheas 11
171 22 N. Smyrni, Greece
aneris@desmie.gr

can be a valuable tool for the   assurance of a reliable and economically optimum operation of a power system in such an environment.

Demand Side Bidding is a market mechanism, which enables final customers to actively participate in the electric power market, by offering to change their normal patterns of electricity consumption [1]. Today, only large customers such as power-intensive industries are participating while the smaller customers are kept out of this mechanism. The addition of domestic loads as a tradable power is expected to reduce the price for available power reserves and provide smaller customers with the opportunity to participate in the electricity market. This can be achieved through an aggregator, which could be, for example, the electricity provider of these customers. Even though aggregation of loads does not face any serious obstacles from the technical and legal sides, it requires software solutions, which will efficiently support all the parts of the process. In order to make such a system efficient, computer applications must be used in order to sort out potential customers by processing raw customer data so as to aggregate electric capacity into tradable blocks and optimise customer portfolios.

In this paper, a software model is presented that can actively assist an aggregator in the management of his customers' portfolio in order to construct his power reserve bid. The proposed modeling approach aims to efficiently treat this issue.

This model uses Semantic Web concepts to give information a well-defined meaning, thus better enabling computers and people to work in cooperation. The motivation of this approach lays in the idea that information modeling and processing, using ontologies, can facilitate the power industry so as to have a shared and common understanding of a domain that can be communicated between people and heterogeneous and distributed application systems.

2   Power system operation in a liberalised market environment

An electrical power system is comprised of the hardware that physically produces and transports electricity to customers, as well as the equipment that uses the electricity. Electricity is transported from the generators through the transmission and distribution grid to the loads (consumers).

The transition of the electrical power industry towards a deregulated market environment creates financial flows due to the transactions related to the physical power flows. These transactions and financial flows take place between the most important actors when they are completely unbundled. The list of actors includes [2]:

- *The producer* who is responsible for generating electricity;
- *The transmission system operator* (TSO) who is responsible for operating, maintaining and developing the transmission system. The TSO is also responsible for providing system services in his control area. Among them

power balancing is included, i.e. the compensation in real time of the difference in demand and supply;

- *The electricity provider* who is responsible for the sale of electricity to customers (retail);
- *The final customer* who purchases electricity for his/her own use and who is free to purchase electricity from the supplier of his/her choice.

The more elegant and efficient way of balancing the electricity system is the establishment of a separate balancing market, apart from the wholesale and retail markets. In many European power systems the ongoing liberalisation of the energy market has led to the establishment of these separate balancing markets [3].

This market is controlled by the TSO, who is the single buyer in this market. Access to the supply side of the balancing market is mainly limited to the large power producers and energy providers (whose offers consist of the demand response by their consumers, i.e. the curtailment or shift of electricity use). As soon as a situation of shortage arises, the TSO corrects this by buying the lowest price commodity offered in the balancing market. The TSO charges the energy suppliers that caused the imbalance on the basis of the relatively high price that he has paid on the balancing market. In case of a surplus of produced electricity, the TSO accepts and receives the highest bid in the balancing market for adjusting generating units downwards. Moreover in this case, the energy suppliers pay the TSO the relevant imbalance charges. To stimulate market players to make their forecasts of electricity production and demand as accurate as possible and to act in accordance with these energy programs, the price for balancing power (imbalance charges) must be above the market price for electricity. Because balancing power is typically provided by units with high marginal costs, this is in practice always the case.

3   The Option of Demand Side Bidding

As it was mentioned earlier, energy providers can join a balancing market through the offer of demand adjustments. An instrument for the implementation of such an action is demand side bidding (DSB). DSB is a process for formulating and delivering demand changes at customer premises in order to benefit TSOs, energy providers and customers. It allows demand changes to be predicted, made to happen on a reliable basis and be build into schedules as alternatives to generation in meeting system demand.

Customers willing to reduce demand, assist energy providers in a number of ways, including the provision of an alternative in order to avoid high prices and the assistance to avoid imbalance charges [1]. As a reward customers can be paid for their availability as well as for actually reducing their consumption. Looking at the structure of demand of many European countries, it can be observed that a considerable share of the electricity consumption is due to small domestic consumers. As an example, the share of low-voltage customers in Germany for the year 2001 is almost half of the total electricity consumption [4]. This issue motivated a number of pilot projects for the evaluation of technological solutions for the implementation of DSB in the small electricity customers sector. The most relevant outcome of this research effort is that the high complexity of information that should be processed in order to efficiently support the process necessitates efficient software solutions [5].

A lot of research effort has been devoted in order to cope with the several technical issues of demand side bidding aggregation. This effort was mainly focused in the utilisation of the Internet as a communication link between the aggregator and the numerous distributed end-users, as well as in the development of the necessary local communication and control infrastructure [4], [6].

The approach proposed in this paper, should be considered as an effort to contribute in the development of higher level aggregation services, necessary for the efficient treatment of the large and heterogeneous information coming from the end user level. It is based on ontologies, in order to assist an aggregator who can be the energy provider, to construct an optimised portfolio of customers for bidding in a balancing market.

4   Demand Side Bidding Implementation

In order to construct the portfolio, several restrictions based on the balancing market are taken into account, including among other the minimum volume of disconnectable power as well as well as the minimum time that this asset should be available to the TSO.

The characteristics used for the description of customers are:

> **Geographical location and zip code**: An important issue for the aggregation of demand response is related to the verification of the result. If all the customers are selected from the same geographic area, then the aggregated result of their response can be verified from centrally located grid meters. In addition, if consumers are selected in order to have the same zip codes, then it is easier to check which of them should not be disconnected in order to respect minimum comfort restrictions;

> **Consumer type** (residential, commercial or industrial): This characteristic is utilised because different marginal prices are used depending on the consumer type;

> **Type of activity:** It is assumed that the aggregator uses estimated power consumption profiles for each activity (households, shopping centers, offices, hospitals, schools, etc.) in order to estimate daily power consumption profiles;

> **Size of activity:** It is considered that customers are equipped with energy meters capable to provide hourly measurements. These measurements are transmitted to the aggregator a certain number of times per day and allow him/her to make a prediction of the customer's consumption as an indication of the size of activity;
> **Minimum and maximum disconnectable load:** This information is declared by each customer in order to describe the customer's capabilities of demand control.

5   A Semantic Approach for a Customer's Portfolio

Customer attributes mentioned in the previous paragraph, constitute a huge and complex volume of information, taking into account the large number of small electricity consumers. As a result, efficient management information solutions can assist the aggregator for an optimum decision making.

In our system, we want to take full advantage of all the information that describes the customers' characteristics and also the interrelations between customers because of the above characteristics, as these can be estimated from transactional histories and other available data. In order to develop our architecture we must discover the relations between customers. After that we use these relations to construct a semantic grid between them. Our target is to provide the aggregator with recommendations, in order to assist him in the management of his customers' portfolio for the construction of his power reserve bid. If the aggregator considers that a customer A is valuable for him in a specific period in a day, then we also propose consumers B, C and D because these four consumers have been tied together with one or more relations. This functionality constitutes the key element for an efficient treatment of information in our approach.

5.1 Prototype Customer's Portfolio Ontology

In order to construct a semantic grid linking the customers, we use the notion of ontologies [9] to present a prototype example which has been developed in a knowledge base dealing with customers and the relations between them. In addition, the biggest advantage is that all the information stored in the knowledge base can be represented in a standard format, in a widely used language like the Web Ontology Language (OWL) that has been developed by the Word Wide Web Consortium [7]. This is essential for the aggregator because it gives him the opportunity to manage a huge and heterogeneous amount of data and information about consumers and to interface with other systems or share this data with partners without software or hardware restrictions.

The proposed model is a system that aims to contribute in the fulfillment of the aggregator's management needs in an efficient way. The capability of clustering the whole set of customers according to similar characteristics gives aggregator's (as we will see in our example in section 7) the opportunity to easily, quickly and efficiently choose the appropriate customers for which he will reduce loads and finally to construct his/her power reserve bid. In order to gather knowledge for the knowledge base we can use raw customer data and customer's characteristics.

6   Partitioning the Product Space

In order to apply the necessary and appropriate relations between customers, we have to relate each other, to make "companions", "groups" or "clusters" of them. This can be achieved using the mathematical notions of equivalence relations which have the ability to partition the space in equivalence classes. When a number of items satisfy an equivalence relation, they form a subset of items which is named equivalence class.

For example, let X be a non-empty set and ~ an equivalence relation on X. The equivalence classes of ~ form a **partition** (a disjoint collection of non-empty subsets whose union is the whole set) of X. The result will be a partitioned space divided into sets (classes) of items. These items in each class are interrelated with equivalence relations between them.

In particular, we present the basic principles that allow the discovery of relations between consumers. At first we must propose some basic relations between consumers. Some of these relations can be the following: *is_analogous_to, same_region,   same_zip_code,   needed_with,   substitute_of, similar_consumption_pattern, equivalent_ min_disconectable_load, equivalent_ max_disconectable_load, same_customer_type, similar_pattern_of_activity,* and *shares_issues_with.*

Using concepts from set theory it can be proven that the above relations are equivalence relations [8]. In this sense, let us consider a set of consumers of electric power, which we can think of as vertices on a blackboard. If a consumer is strongly related with another one, then we say that he is connected through *"correlate_with"* and an edge is introduced to these vertices. Thus, a graph connecting the correlated consumers is produced. These correlations can be used as a clustering method.

6.1 Semantic Interrelation between Consumers

From the above we have seen that there can be equivalence relations between consumers. In order to extract results from the above interlinking of consumers, we need to find the relations between which exist in several classes of different equivalence relations.

This can be accomplished using the notion of intersection of equivalence relations [8]. Through this intersection, we can reach semantic similarities between consumers in order to cluster and introduce them to the aggregator in an efficient way, thus managing to grow his satisfaction. As we will see in the following, the capabilities of ontology languages, (like Web Ontology Language (OWL)) allow us to use logical and mathematical operations. Through them, we will able to enforce symmetric and transitive properties. We will then construct a grid, i.e. a semantic net between nodes (consumers). We can achieve an automatic semantic grid because if customers a, b, c are connected semantically with relations, we have to connect customer d (which has to be connected with the above) only with one of a, b, c. The connection with the others will be forced by the inference capabilities using properties such symmetry and transitivity.

7 An application example

We assume a power system, operating in a liberalised market environment, including a balancing market. In this market aggregators of demand side are allowed to participate. As mentioned in the previous paragraphs, when the portfolio of the aggregator includes a very large number of small customers, an efficient way of information management is needed.

Based on these issues, our model uses the interlinking between consumers through several relations. We use semantic dependencies among customers in order to achieve knowledge modeling and to implement a semantic network between them [9]. The exact relationships that can hold between two consumers are the important key points [10]. We have already discussed those specific relations within the set of customers like *is_analogous_to, same_region, same_zip_code, needed_with, substitute_of, similar_consumption_pattern, equivalent_min_disconectable_load, equivalent_max_disconectable_load, same_customer_type, similar_pattern_of_ activity, and shares_issues_with*, which can determine equivalence relations. Each time two consumers are connected with such a relation, they belong to the corresponding equivalence class. When the aggregator searches for consumers of electric power for his specific needs, depending for example on the geographical location, the size and the type of activity, the building characteristics, the maximum or minimum disconnectedly load of the consumer, he needs to have all these characteristics stored and available in an efficient manner in order to cope with the difficult issue of the management of all this critical data. Apart from the above, it would be very efficient for the aggregator; if there can be suggestions for clusters of customers with similar characteristics, customers similar or relevant to the one that the aggregator initially chooses. This would be very convenient for him in order to make the decisions about the sets of customers for which he will reduce loads.

For our purpose we have constructed a knowledge base dealing with consumers of electric power and their relations. We have constructed three classes, *Consumer_of_Ele_power*, *Geographical_Locations* and *Relations_of_Consumers*. This last class contains the set of the relations that we are going to use in order to interrelate the consumers. In the *Consumer_of_Ele_power* class, we have added instances of consumers with their characteristics as seen in table 1. In this table the consumers P1, P2, P3, P4, P5 and P6 have been joined with specific values in their attributes which have been described in section 4.

Table 1. Instances of consumers with their characteristics in the *Consumer_of_Ele_power* class. Here are the characteristics : Geo_location, Consumer_type, Building_characteristics, Zip_code, Type_of_activity, Size_of_activity.

Title of Consumer	Building Characteristics	Consumer type	Geo Location	Size of activity	Type of activity	Zip code
P1	A	residential	GL1	2	households	12345
P2	B	commercial	GL2	5	hospital	12346
P3	C	Small_industrial	GL3	8	offices	12347
P4	C	Shoping_center	GL1	8	commercial	12348
P5	B	commercial	GL2	6	hospital	12346
P6	B	commercial	GL2	5	hospital	12346

For example, let us assume that the aggregator has the need to provide a load reduction of size A and for this purpose, he has to find the consumers that are hospitals, of customer type commercial, in a specific location, having in mind a specific maximum and minimum disconnectedly load.

The aggregator has to take into consideration all the above characteristics, because these and the size of the load reduction are related. If a consumer has characteristics that suit to the specific need then it would be very convenient to find a number of others consumers with similar characteristics in order to reach the appropriate size of the requested demand reduction. The aggregator has to find an "initial" consumer; the interlinking through the specific relations will build up a cluster that contains the rest of the customers of the whole set who satisfies the exact relations. We can see in table 1 that consumer P2 has the characteristics that the aggregator is looking for. The same characteristics exist also in two more (P5,

P6) consumers from the whole set. These three consumers, as we can see in figure 7, are in the same cluster because they satisfy the relations *same_region*, *same_zip_code*, *similar_pattern_of_activity*, *same_customer_type* and *is_analogous_to*. If consumer P5 had a different value in the attribute Zip_code then the relation *same_zip_code* between P5 and the rest two, would be never satisfied. If the aggregator' need can be satisfied without the relation *same_zip_code* then the clustering with the others relations would give again (P2, P5, P6).

In this way the aggregator has the ability to choose the specific relations that satisfy his criteria for gathering the most convenient consumers for his purpose. He can choose the combinations of relations that he needs from the set of instances of the class *Relations_of_Consumers* , which he can enrich with new relations as the needs change and grow.

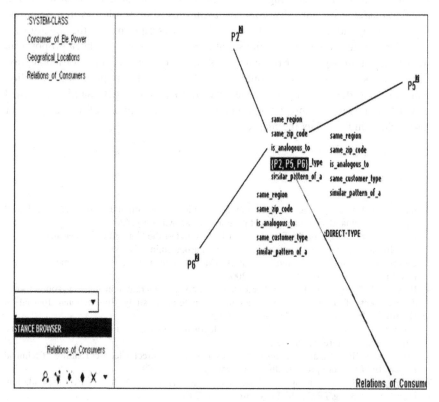

Fig. 1. Clustering of consumers.

8   Conclusions and Future Directions

In this paper, a solution has been proposed for the efficient construction of small electricity customers' portfolio, in order to assist their participation, via an aggregator, in the balancing market.

The aggregators of electric loads need an easy way to manage a huge and heterogeneous amount of data and information about consumers. However, data access is considered to be a difficult issue, because of the incompatibility of data structures. As the amount of information continues to explode, the need for efficient data capture and delivery is becoming more apparent. Without them in place, users in general will eventually spend more time searching for information than actually consuming it. There was only one way of enabling computers to deal with information in a meaningful way and that was to describe it in a precise, machine-readable format. This could be achieved using ontologies in a Semantic Web. Taking advantage of these tools, a description of the customer's characteristics as well as the relations that join them together has been proposed in order to assist an aggregator to manage his customer portfolio in an efficient way. Further work in this subject could take advantage of the proposed modeling approach in order to build the necessary management functionalities that will provide an integrated information platform for the support of the aggregator participation in the balancing market.

References

1. International Energy Agency: Demand Side Bidding for Smaller Customers. Technical report, IEA demand side management programme, www.iea.org, (2005)
2. Directive 2003/54/EC of the European Parliament and of the Council of concerning common rules for the internal market in electricity, http://europa.eu.int, (2003)
3. European Transmission System Operators: Current state of balance management in South East Europe, www.etso-net.org, June (2006)
4. Bendel, C., Nestle, D.: Decentralized electrical power generators in the low voltage grid-development of a technical and economical integration study. International Journal of Distributed Energy Resources. Vol 1, No.1, (2005)
5. Towards Smart power networks-Lessons learned from European research FP5 projects, http://ec.europa.eu/research/energy
6. Kofod, C.: DR by Danish Domestic Customers using Direct Electric Heating. Technical Report, EU Efflocom project, http://www.energinet.dk, (2007)
7. OWL Web Ontology Language Reference W3C Recommendation, http://www.w3.org/TR/2004/REC-owl-ref-20040210/
8. Radcliffe, Nicholas J.: The Algebra of Genetic Algorithms, Annals of Maths and Artificial Intelligence. Vol 10, 339--384 (1994)
9. Horrocks, Ian., Lei. Li.: A Software Framework for Matchmaking Based on Semantic Web Technology. International Journal of Electronic Commerce. Vol. 8, Iss. 4, 39--60 (2004)
10. Shum, S., Motta, E., Domingue, J.: ScholOnto: An Ontology-Based Digital Library Server for Research Documents and Discourse. International Journal on Digital Libraries. Vol. 3, Iss. 3, 237--248 (2000)

Semantic Navigation on the web: the LCSH case study

Ioannis Papadakis[1], Michalis Stefanidakis[2] and Aikaterini Tzali[2]

Abstract. In this paper, an innovative ontology-based, information seeking process is proposed, capable of aiding searchers in their quest to fulfill their information needs. Such a process supports multilinguality and concept disambiguation in a way that prevents overcrowding the screen while exposing the expressiveness of the underlying ontology. In order to assess the effectiveness of the proposed approach in a real-world scenario, a prototype web-based application is developed by utilizing the hidden knowledge existing within the authority records of the Online Public Access Catalog – OPAC located at the library of the Ionian University in Greece. More specifically, the underlying Library of Congress Subject Headings - LCSHs have been employed to formulate an ontology in OWL format. Interaction with library users is facilitated through an intuitive, web-based GUI implemented in AJAX technology.

1 Introduction

Information exploration on the web is always an open research agenda due to the diversity of the collections it contains. Such collections refer to various domains. Depending on the domain a collection refers to (e.g. domain: computer programming, collection: java), quite often a specific (formal or informal)

[1] Ionian University, Department of Archives and Library Sciences,
Plateia Eleytherias, 49100 Corfu – Greece

[2] Ionian University, Department of Computer Science,
Plateia Eleytherias, 49100 Corfu – Greece

{papadakis,mistral,ktzali}@ionio.gr

terminology is employed by the members of the domain. However, such terminology is usually 'foreign language' to people outside this domain that nevertheless wish to retrieve information from such collections.

This paper introduces a novel ontology-based information seeking process for medium to large collections on the web. Serving as an application of the semantic web [1], the proposed process is capable of bridging the gap between users' information needs (elsewhere defined as information goals or information retrieval context [2]) and the terminology that is usually employed to describe and index information assets within such collections.

More specifically, instead of relying on a typical static, predefined hierarchical navigation structure, which forces users to follow static, predefined paths, the proposed information seeking process relies on a dynamic, interactive graph-based structure. Such a structure visualizes the semantic structure of an underlying ontology (e.g. subject-based classification [3], thesauri [4], etc). The ultimate goal of the proposed work is to guide users in locating useful information as accurately and efficiently as possible.

The proposed process is capable of being integrated to common search interfaces as a query formulation tool. Users are able to express their information needs in search queries that are closer to the indexed terms of the underlying collection.

A prototype system has been developed in order to serve as a proof of concept for the proposed information seeking process. It combines interactive, user-centered searching and browsing in a rather intuitive manner. The prototype is based on an ontology deriving from existing LCSHs that are employed to provide subject cataloguing to the assets of the Library located at the Ionian University.

The rest of this paper is structured as follows: The next section summarizes similar projects aiming at providing information seeking alternatives on the web based on ontologies. Section three defines the proposed ontology-based, information seeking process. This section contains three subsections referring to a prototype web-enabled application that is based on the principles of the proposed information seeking process. More specifically, the prototype's architecture is presented, along with the GUI's functionality and the underlying ontology's structure. Finally, this paper draws conclusions and points directions for future work.

2   Ontology-based information seeking on the web

Ontology-powered information exploration is one of the most promising approaches to enhance existing search GUIs with features capable of enabling users to better express their information needs or to improve exploratory search styles [2]. The expressiveness of information within ontologies should find its way towards the GUI while at the same time the GUI should retain basic usability features [5] that constitute the whole information retrieval system appealing to its users. It should be also kept in mind, that GUIs based on ontologies should not only expose the concepts they contain. It is equally important to take advantage of the relations between concepts (i.e. properties-slots) in order to provide a more efficient interactive search tactic.

Several efforts have been made to employ ontologies within a broader information seeking system (for more information, see [6]). Among them, OntoQuery [7] employs a search interface where searchers are prompted to type terms that are fed into a Natural Language Processing – NLP system. Despite the promising results in certain occasions, such an approach can only be applied to a very strict number of domains were natural language is unambiguous.

Another interesting approach, OntoIR [8], provides a selection-based interface according to which searchers have the ability to engage themselves into an interactive process that ultimately leads to query refinement, based on the concepts of the underlying ontology. OntoIR manages to avoid exposing the complexity of the underlying ontology to the screen. Moreover, it takes advantage of the richness of information within the ontology to provide a rather efficient information exploration process to the searcher. Similarly to other information seeking efforts, direct access to the underlying repository is required, since the contained information assets should be annotated with the ontology.

In the following section, an ontology-based information seeking process is presented, aiming at aiding searchers expressing their information needs within the context of the formal terminology of the referring domain, as also suggested by Saracevic et al. in [9]. The proposed work combines searching and browsing within the context of interactivity between the system and the searcher.

3   Ontology-based information seeking process

The proposed approach aims at enabling searchers expressing the semantics of their information needs in an unambiguous fashion. This is achieved by providing certain search tactics that ultimately lead to the satisfaction of the searchers' information needs. According to Bates [10], tactics are defined as "one or a affordance handful of moves made to further a search" (e.g. query formulation, query refinement).

According to the proposed model, searchers take control over the search process through an interactive GUI. Interaction is generally appealing to searchers on the condition that the GUI provides straightforward interactions, as stated in [8].

The proposed GUI is comprised of boxes that correspond to concepts and labelled lines corresponding to the relations linking such concepts. Searchers may hop from one concept to a related one by selecting one of the various relations each concept is being involved. Such relations are outlined inside each box. Upon selection of a relation, a pop-up menu is presented containing the concept(s) that relate to the initial concept with the selected relation. Finally, by selecting an item within the pop-up menu, a new box is created together with a line that connects the two boxes. The whole iterative process is illustrated in Fig. 1.

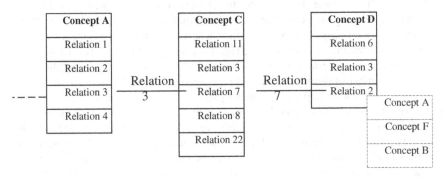

Fig. 1. Proposed information seeking process

As the searcher hops from concept to concept, hers/his information needs become formal terminology terms constituting the search query that will be ultimately addressed to the underlying search engine.

The aforementioned concepts and relations correspond to the classes and properties (or slots) of an ontology that manages to capture the conceptualization of the referring domain. It should be mentioned that the output of the proposed information-seeking process is essentially one or more concepts that may serve as query terms to the traditional search engine interface. Since the 'glue' between the information assets residing at the repository and the provided GUI are the concepts-terms, it is very important to design the ontology in a way that accurately corresponds to the terms being indexed by the search engine.

The proposed approach would have maximum effectiveness in the case of employing the ontology to annotate the underlying information assets. Although such a scenario would lead to much more relevant results and consequently greater satisfaction to the searcher, it is the authors' belief that serving as a complement to pre-existing search engines, the ontology-based information seeking process can be successfully applied to a wider range of real-world applications.

The proposed approach is capable of supporting many (if not all) of the search tactics proposed by Bates [10] provided that the corresponding relations are accordingly modelled in the ontology.

It is important to note that the GUI exposes the expressiveness of the ontology without cluttering the searcher's screen. This is accomplished by enabling the searcher to select which part of the ontology will be revealed to her/him. The searcher can expand and/or collapse the ontology through an interactive process at hers/his own will.

In order to narrow the interactions with the searcher and thus the overall time performance, it is very important to provide efficient entrypoints [8] to the system. Entrypoints are the concepts that the searcher confronts when the information seeking process is initiated. The closer the entrypoints are to the resulting concepts, the better for the searcher.

As stated in [7], the GUI of any ontology-based information seeking model should be web-browser based. In this context, the proposed approach should take advantage of semantic web standards for the encoding of the ontologies (e.g. Web Ontology Language – OWL) and new trends in web GUI design based on the most promising Ajax technology.

In the following section, a prototype system is presented based on the line of thoughts described throughout this section.

3.1 Prototype system Architecture

In order to test the proposed approach at the field, the academic library of the Ionian University in Greece was selected. Such library provides rich subject descriptions of the underlying information assets based on the widely employed LCSHs (available at: http://authorities.loc.gov/). Thus, each information asset corresponds to one to five subject headings corresponding to the formal LCSH.

Searchers are prompted to make use of the provided ontology-based prototype (fig. 2) in order to end up to the subject heading that best describe their information needs. Such a heading will seamlessly direct them to the desired information assets.

The interaction with the provided GUI results in the population of the search box of the traditional parametric search interface with terms corresponding to the various subject headings the searcher visits during the ongoing search process. From another point of view, the prototype system provides a list of assets corresponding to the subject heading the searcher has chosen.

The GUI is powered by an underlying ontology designed to capture the expressiveness of the formal LCSH structure. Each time a new heading is selected by the searcher, a new query is addressed to the underlying search engine. The whole process is concluded when the search results list contains information assets that match the searcher's information needs.

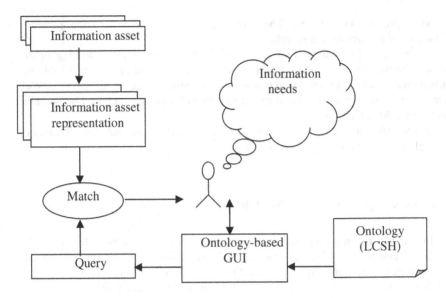

Fig. 2. Prototype system architecture

It should be mentioned that information assets within the library are linked to various indices apart from the index that contains subject headings. For the purposes of this research, the prototype GUI system interacts only with the subject headings index. In case of numerous search results, searchers are free to engage any other index (e.g. title, author) in order to narrow their search process.

The two main components of the proposed architecture, namely the underlying ontology and the ontology-based GUI are described in the following sections.

3.2 The underlying ontology

The Library of Congress Subject Headings catalogue (LCSH) is employed for building the class hierarchy of the underlying ontology. LCSH is used to classify books and other collections with a subject-based classification approach. The LCSH list classifies all existing disciplines into twenty-one basic classes, appearing in an alphabetical (rather than hierarchical) list. Most of these alphabetical classes are further divided into more specific subclasses. Each subclass includes a loosely hierarchical arrangement of the topics pertinent to the subclass, going from generic to more specific ones.

For the purposes of this work, from a total of 265,000 LCSH's records (terms), a subset of about 500 terms have been employed, corresponding to the subject headings of the Informatics subdivision of the Library at the Ionian University. The actual subjects (terms) that are used within the Library are Greek translations of the official LCSHs that have been modified according to restriction rules with respect to language, technical term and spelling.

LCSHs not only allow subjects to be hierarchically arranged, but also allow other statements to be made about such subjects (i.e. broader-than (BT), narrower-than (NT), RelatedTo(seeAlso), USE/UF relationships). The following paragraphs describe how the semantics of these statements are captured in the proposed ontology.

LCSH's BT and NT relationships are used to build an asserted hierarchical ontology, where terms are represented as classes and relationships as properties (also known as slots). A BT relationship refers to a superclass having a broader or less specific meaning than its descendant classes. The inverse relationship according to the LCSH system is known as NT and is implied by the BT. NT represents all subclasses having a narrower meaning. Classes may have many super – or subclasses according to the LCSH taxonomy. Hierarchical navigation through the class hierarchy constitutes the basic query refinement tool for the searcher.

The relationship 'seeAlso' refers to a term class related to another class, without being a synonym or a broader/ narrower term.

Moreover, according to LCSH, there are headings accompanied by a term in parenthesis, for example 'Programming (Mathematics)'. The existence of parenthesis signifies a term with a broader meaning, many times (but not all) referring to an authority record. Such a context term association is represented as the property 'in the context of'. Both 'seeAlso' and context association properties are exposed to the searcher by the GUI system, increasing the chances for serendipitous discovery of interesting terms.

According to the LCSH system, a USE/UF relationship implies that two terms are equivalent; one term refers to another (USE) that is to be preferred instead of this term (UF). In the proposed ontology such a relationship is represented as 'individual' or 'instance' of a collector LCSH term class, which groups all equivalent terms. Moreover, the role of individuals is expanded by adding the Greek versions of subject headings related to a formal LCSH term, as well as their UF terms.

The rdfs:label annotation property is employed to provide meaningful, human-readable labels to the underlying headings. USE/UF relationships facilitate non expert users to locate the concepts they are searching for.

Since the selected Library's repository indexes just the Greek version of the formal LCSH subject headings, instance labels serve as the keywords to be fed into the Ionian University Library's OPAC search engine.

3.3 The ontology-based GUI

The proposed GUI provides a web-based, user-driven visualization of the LCSH catalogue. Searchers interact with the GUI through a semantic-based process that enables them going from heading to heading according to predefined semantic criteria (see fig. 1). Such a search tactic is argued to bridge the gap between the searcher's information needs and the Library's formal terminology concerning the LCSHs. As stated earlier in this paper, the GUI attempts to sustain the expressiveness of the underlying ontology without compromising fundamental usability design guidelines.

Thus, the whole interface progresses linearly from left to right in accordance to the applied user interactions. The searcher's focus is most of the times at the right end of the interface, which corresponds to the most recent interactions. Since scrolling to the right is provided automatically, user-initiated scrolling is minimal and the active part of the screen is not overcrowded. At any time, searchers have the ability to scroll to the left and observe their complete navigation path.

Moreover, searchers do not have to type in anything, since the GUI clones each selected heading to the search engine's input box. This way, possible errors deriving from natural language interpretation are minimized. Searchers are capable of bypassing the GUI and type their own query terms, but such a scenario is beyond the scope of this paper.

The prototype also promotes serendipitous or casual discovery of interesting information connected to the current search process (see [8]). During the search process, searchers underpin their cognitive learning, since they are able to witness which information assets correspond to the formally defined subject headings they traverse.

Like any other search GUI, the proposed one should be assessed in terms of user's information needs fulfillment speed. The provision of suitable entrypoints located as close as possible to the resulting subject headings, is a key factor affecting such a criterion. Further research is required in terms of entrypoint selection, possibly in the context of personalized information retrieval, as suggested by Garcia and Sicilia in [2].

As a proof of concept, readers are prompted to visit the demo version of the working prototype, which is available at http://195.251.111.53/server/entry/index.html. The underlying ontology is encoded in OWL format, the gluing middleware is implemented in Python, and the provided GUI is based upon the most promising Ajax technology.

4   Conclusions – Future work

This paper presents a novel ontology-assisted information seeking process. Such a process utilizes not only the content but also the organizational schema of a domain ontology. This way, users may express their abstract needs to concrete concepts, subsequently indexed in digital collections. The presented interface can be seamlessly embedded into traditional search form interfaces, as a complementary query formulating tool.

According to the proposed method, a GUI exposes the hierarchy of the concepts included into a domain ontology, as well as all stated relations between different concepts, as links that the user can follow. Thus, searchers are able to effectively traverse the ontology and at the same time formulate the actual query to the underlying search engine. This act of interactive navigation through the domain collection helps searchers in accurately formulating their queries. This is achieved by offering broader or narrower concepts for selection or indicating alternative or related concepts that searchers might be initially unaware of. The augmented exposition of inter-relations between concepts provides multiple paths for information seeking and enables searchers to fulfill faster, more efficiently and in an intuitive manner their personal information needs.

The process of information seeking by traversing a domain ontology is demonstrated via a prototype web-based application, which aids users in searching/browsing the Ionian's Univesity library catalogue according to the subjects of the underlying information assets. Within the ontology, terms are arranged as a complete hierarchy of concepts, together with interconnecting relations (i.e. "seeAlso", "inContextOf") between concepts. Each concept class contains the equivalent and multilingual terms of a particular concept as instances.

The GUI of the prototype application visualizes the aforementioned information schema and allows for interactive traversal of the ontology. In each step of the information flow, corresponding terms are fed automatically into a search field of a typical search engine. Searchers may submit such terms to the library's OPAC, examine the results and redefine the query in subsequent steps by navigating to other parts of the ontology. The prototype GUI allows for a progressive expansion or reduction of the part of the ontology displayed, avoiding cluttering the interface with unneeded information.

In the proposed ontology-based traversing search process, the selection of strategic entrypoints is a critical aspect for it's speed and effectiveness. For the time being, entrypoints are fixed and manually selected from the underlying collection. While this approach is sufficient for a prototype system, future work includes research for automated entrypoint extraction or dynamic definition via personalized information retrieval methods. Moreover, a comparison with similar approaches is under way together with a qualitative evaluation of the working prototype.

References

1. Berners-Lee, T., Hendler J., and Lassila O.: The Semantic Web. Scientific American 284, no. 5, 34-38, 40-43 (May 2001)
2. García, E. & Sicilia, M.A. User Interface Tactics in Ontology-Based Information Seeking . Psychology e-journal 1(3):243-256, (2003)
3. Garshol, M.L.: Metadata? Thesauri? Taxonomies? Topic Maps! Making Sense of it all, Journal of Information Science, Vol. 30, No. 4, (2004), 378-391
4. Doerr, M.: Semantic problems of thesaurus mapping. Journal of Digital information, Vol. 1 No. 8, (2001), available at: http://jodi.ecs.soton.ac.uk/Articles/v01/i08/Doerr/#Nr.52
5. Krug, S. Don'T Make Me Think!: a Common Sense Approach to Web Usability. 1st. Que Corp., Indianapolis, isbn: 0789723107, (2000)
6. Papadakis, I and Stefanidakis, M. Semantic Web Browsing, Proc of WEBIST '07, pp 400-404, Barcelona, (March 2007)
7. Andreasen, T., Fischer-Nilsson, J. and Erdman-Thomsen, H. Ontology-based querying. In H. Larsen, editor, Flexible Query Answering Systems, Flexible Query Answering Systems, Recent Advances, pp 15-26. Physica-Verlag, Springer, 2000

8. García, E., Sicilia, M.A. Designing Ontology-Based Interactive Information Retrieval Systems. Proc. of the Workshop on Human Computer Interface for Semantic Web and Web Applications, Springer LNCS 2889, 223-234, (2003)
9. Spink, A., and Saracevic, T. Interaction in IR: Selection and effectiveness of search terms. Journal of the American Society for Information Science, 48(8), 741–761, (1997)
10. Bates, M.J. Where Should the Person Stop and the Information Search Interface Start?. *Information Processing & Management* 26, 575-591, (1990)

Ontologies and Ontology-Based Applications

Panorea Gaitanou

Abstract   This paper is a result of a thorough search and synthesis, aiming to provide an overall view of the application fields, where ontologies have already been deployed, presenting at the same time the benefits from their use in each field. In the following paragraphs, ontology applications in the fields of semantic web, knowledge management, e-commerce, multimedia and graphics, grid computing, pervasive computing environments are discussed, and in each field, an effort is made to outline the basic ontology features that deal with real or potential issues.

1. Introduction

Nowadays, the number of ontologies being developed and used by various applications is continuously increasing, as they become indispensable parts of many disciplines. Domain experts use ontologies to share and annotate information in their fields. An ontology is defined as a formal explicit specification of a shared conceptualization [18]. In other words, it is a shared understanding of some domain of interest, which is often realized as a set of classes (concepts), relations, functions, axioms and instances. Ontologies aim at capturing the semantics of domain expertise by deploying knowledge representation primitives, enabling a machine to understand the relationships between concepts in a domain [17]. Thus, they are complex knowledge representation artefacts intended for the development of intelligent applications, as well as social constructions for communication and crystallization of domain-specific knowledge [25].

Department of Archive and Library Sciences, Ionian University, Greece

rgaitanou@ionio.gr

2. Ontology application fields

2.1 Semantic Web and Upper Ontologies

The major challenge and research issue regarding the Semantic Web is information integration. Information integration is defined as the field of study of techniques attempting to merge information from disparate sources, despite differing conceptual, contextual and typographical representations. Information integration provides the basis for a rich "knowledge space" built on top of the basic web "data layer". This layer is composed of value-added services that offer abstracted information and mostly knowledge, rather than returning documents [22]. Consequently, the ability of ontologies to express semantics is of significant importance in this domain.

In this section, we mention some upper ontologies (also named top-level ontologies, foundational ontologies or universal ontologies), whose goal is to integrate heterogeneous knowledge coming from different sources. An upper ontology is a high-level, domain-independent ontology, providing a framework through which disparate systems may utilize a common knowledge base and from which more domain-specific ontologies may be derived [32]. The most frequently used ontologies in the existent literature are the Suggested Upper Merged Ontology[2] (SUMO), DOLCE[3] and Upper Cyc Ontology[4]. Our focus is to find out the similarities and the differences between these ontologies. SUMO aims at promoting data interoperability, information search and retrieval, automated inference and natural language processing. It was created by merging publicly available ontological content into a single, comprehensive and cohesive structure [26]. SUMO is multiplicative, meaning that aims to cover at a general level any concept that reality requires and also reductionist, as it attempts to be minimal rather than profligate. It is modular and relatively intermediate in size between smaller DOLCE and larger Upper Cyc [32]. DOLCE Ontology, developed in the WonderWeb project, aims at providing a common reference framework regarding WonderWeb ontologies, so as to ease information sharing [10] and is not intended to be a single standard upper ontology, as SUMO and Upper Cyc [32]. Finally, Upper Cyc Ontology is the largest and oldest ontology. It aims primarily at supporting AI applications. It is flexible and modular, like SUMO, divided into microtheories [32]. OpenCyc[5], part of Upper Cyc, contains over one hundred thousands atomic terms and is provided with an associated efficient inference

---

[2] http://www.ontologyportal.org
[3] http://www.loa-chr.it/DOLCE.html
[4] http://cyc.com
[5] http://www.opencyc.org

engine [29] and many formal definitions that are useful for knowledge management systems, such as time and date, terms descriptions and description of events and activities [30]. All three ontologies appear to be quite open and freely available to the public.

Researchers are actively working all these years on these challenges concerning information integration and specifically ontology integration. Nevertheless, one could support that they are only scratching the surface, as Semantic Web requires significant new advances to make integration possible on the Web scale.

2.2 KM and ontologies

Knowledge management (KM) deals with the representation, organization, acquisition, creation, usage, and evolution of knowledge in its various forms. It is defined as a discipline that promotes a collaborative and integrated approach as far as it concerns the identification, management and sharing of an enterprise's information assets [33]. KM is more than Knowledge Technology. First of all, it must be an enabler to achieve strategic business objectives. Nevertheless, knowledge model structures must be able to represent knowledge in a problem-solving usable manner. Thus, there is need for a modelling mechanism, which will be able to bridge the gap between the acquisition of knowledge and its use. Ontologies can help towards this direction, providing a framework for understanding how knowledge will be used [33].

In this paper, we mention two remarkable ontology-based applications applied in the context of KM Systems, the OntobUM and the Librarian-Agent application. OntobUM is a user modeling system that relies on a user ontology, using Semantic Web technologies and is integrated in an ontology-based KM, called Ontologging. It is a user-modeling server, which stores data in a RDF/RDFS format and, unlike other similar servers, it uses semantics [7]. Next, the Librarian-Agent application is a very interesting approach for the Information Science field. To be more specific, it is an ontology-based approach for the improvement of searching and retrieving data in an information portal. It plays the role of a human librarian in a traditional library. The system realizes a library scenario in which users search for information in a repository [14].

2.3 E-commerce

Ontologies may prove to be especially useful in the e-commerce field, where it is explicitly necessary to integrate applications from different enterprises and indefinable single web entities. In general, e-commerce can be divided in two fields, Business-to-Customer (B2C) and Business-to-Business (B2B). Ontologies could offer in both fields, for the increase of efficiency, increasing the efficiency while enabling cooperation at the same time.

In the B2C field, ontologies could be used for the implementation of the so-called shopbots [21]. A shopbot can compare specific characteristics, such as price, shipping costs, etc. for the same product from different merchants. With the use of ontologies by merchants, the shopbot agent could simply use the ontology of each merchant, or a mapping of its own ontology to the merchant's ontology. Consequently, we have simultaneous, integrated and automated query based procedures for the products from a number of merchants.

In the B2B field, a lot of work has already been done for the standardization of e-mails representation among several companies, such as the EDIFACT and XML applications. Furthermore, quite a few attempts have been made to describe the content of the e-mails, (e.g. RosettaNet, VerticalNet applications, which promote collaborative commerce). These content descriptions could be used in a vertical market and are unique for each market. How do we benefit from the use of ontologies in this area? First of all, it would be much easier for an e-market place to translate the different representations used among the companies. Moreover, it could manage the diverse ontology products and services from several e-businesses.

Generally, ontologies and especially ontology-based systems appear to be necessary for the development of efficient and profitable e-commerce solutions. An ontology-based application has the potential to accelerate the penetration of e-commerce, within vertical industry sectors, as it can enable interoperability at the business level, reducing at the same time the need for standardization at the technical level [15]. We refer to an interesting ontology based approach MKBEEM, a system that makes use of ontologies to mediate between languages and to infer answers to user questions in the multilingual e-commerce mediation [8]. MKBEEM emphasizes on the combination of human language processing and ontologies, showing how it can help three basic functions: multilingual cataloguing, processing customer language information requests and multilingual trading [15].

2.4 Multimedia and graphics.

Ontologies are adaptable to the demands of each Knowledge domain. In the multimedia field, ontologies can be expanded from their simple shape, where the concepts are represented with text, and multimedia ontologies can be created, in which each concept can be described as a multimedia entity (including image, video, sound, etc.). Multimedia ontologies cover a broad application field and especially [1]:

a.   Content visualization: for browsing and for the creation of tables of content.

b. Content indexing: improvement of indexing consistency in manual annotation systems and propagation of labels in automatic indexing systems.
c. Knowledge sharing: with the use of a common conceptual representation.
d. Learning: a collection annotated by different individuals using common ontologies leads to annotation consistency which is considered of extreme importance in applying approaches based on learning methodologies that use annotated collections for training.
e. Reasoning: not explicit information in data could be exported.

Many successful ontology-based applications could be enumerated in this field. OntoELAN was designed to deal with the lack of ontology-based annotation tools for linguistic multimedia data. It features: support of OWL ontologies, management of language profiles and storing OntoELAN annotation documents in XML format based on multimedia and domain ontologies. It is the first audio-video annotation tool in the linguistic domain providing support for ontology-based annotation [13]. The Large-Scale Concept Ontology is a remarkable step towards the goal of automatically tagging multimedia content for the support of end-user interactions (searching, filtering, personalization, summarization, etc). This application was designed to satisfy multiple criteria of utility, coverage, feasibility and observability and it aims at creating a framework for ongoing research on semantic analysis of multimedia content [20]. Finally, in the Reach Greek National Project, an ontology based approach is used in order to provide enhanced unified access to heterogeneous distributed cultural heritage digital databases. The project deals with new forms of access to multimedia cultural heritage material. In order to achieve this requirement, the CIDOC-CRM ontology is used, providing a global model able to integrate information (metadata) originating from different sources [23].

In graphics, the semantic enrichment of scenes can play an extremely important role in enabling viewers to query, understand and interact with the often complex and obscure visualized information in a simple, instinctive, user-friendly way. Thus, it allows user to identify 3D objects or sets, based on their graphic and semantic attributes and their relations with the other image objects, at a certain point of time [3]. In our research, we pinpointed OntoSphere, a rather new approach to ontology visualization, which uses a more than 3-dimensional space. This approach is especially effective in navigation and browsing, involving "manipulation-level" operations, such as zooming, rotating and translating objects and its scope is a graphical representation of the taxonomic and the not taxonomic links, as well as presenting information on the screen at an appropriate detail level, according to the user's interest [28].

2.5 Peer-to-peer networks and Grid Computing

The increase of use of semantic technologies has reached almost every computer science related field, including peer-to-peer (p2p) networks and the grid computing field. P2p networks rely primarily on the computing power and bandwidth of the participants in the network rather than concentrating it in a relatively low number of servers. They are typically used for connecting nodes via largely ad hoc connections. Such networks are useful for many purposes, such as sharing content files containing audio, video, data or anything in digital format including real-time data. A pure p2p network does not have the notion of clients or servers, but only equal peer nodes that simultaneously function as both "clients" and "servers" to the other nodes on the network. On the other hand, grid computing technologies cover location and allocation of resources, authentication for remote and community usage, data exchange, sharing, migration, and collaboration for distributed group of users. The idea of the grid is in fact the creation of an ideal, simple but at the same time powerful, self-administrated virtual computer, through a set of interconnected heterogeneous systems, which share several resources combinations. Grid technologies and p2p networks are supplementary. Grids can provide services to p2p networks, whereas applications concerning p2p could be used for the grid management.

One of the most significant sources that computer systems will share in these modern networks is knowledge, such as information for the existent networks and their current state, user profiles, concept definitions, optimum computer techniques, model descriptions etc. For this purpose, ontologies are especially useful, as they have the ability to facilitate the interoperability among computer systems. With the definition of a common vocabulary, errors among concepts are drastically reduced and the existent situation of several resources is described with accuracy and clarity.

As far as it concerns p2p networks, one of the most important problems regarding these networks is their scalability limitation. These networks cannot contain a large number of nodes because of the large amount of traffic that they have to handle. Local indexing is considered to be an efficient method, so as to avoid this problem and reduce the traffic. Rostami et. al. introduce a novel ontology based local index (OLI), which limits the size of local indexes without losing indexing information. This method can be implemented on many p2p networks and can be a base for future developments in this area [27].

Some remarkable ontology based implementations regarding grid technologies, are the OnBrowser, the Earth System Grid and OntoEdu. OnBrowser is an ontology manager that provides a simple and user friendly graphic interface and the ability to browse different ontology levels according to users' preferences. It is a Grid-aware tool, able to manage ontologies and integrate them with application-level and Grid-level metadata management systems and information systems [17]. Moreover, the Earth System Grid is developing a framework that integrates Grid technologies, to facilitate the analysis of the impacts of global climate change at national laboratories, universities and other laboratories. It supports a Web portal in which climate scientists and researchers may utilize distributed computing services to discover, access, select and analyze model data produced and stored on a daily basis on super computers across the US and aims to save time and bring more transparency to a scientific user [12]. Finally, OntoEdu, is a kind of a flexible educational platform architecture for e-learning. It aims at gaining concept reusability, device and user adaptability, automatic composition, function and performance scalability. In OntoEdu, an ontology is used to describe the concept of networked education platform and their relations and it includes two kinds of ontology: a content ontology and an activity ontology [24].

2.6 Pervasive Computing environments

Pervasive (or Ubiquitous) Computing Environments are physical environments enhanced with computing and communications integrated with human users. These environments require the construction of massively distributed systems, which implement a large number of autonomous entities or agents. These entities could be devices, applications, databases, users, etc. Several types of middleware have been developed so as to enable communication between different entities. Nevertheless, none of the existing middleware can offer semantic interoperability. The vision of these environments is that, the addition of computation and communication abilities to the artifacts that surround people will enable the users to set up their living spaces in a way that will minimize the required human intervention [16]. Six key requirements are dominant in ubiquitous computing: 1) distributed composition, 2) partial validation, 3) information richness and quality, 4) incompleteness and ambiguity, 5) level of formality and 6) applicability. Ontologies are able to incorporate these assets for context modeling and provide better modeling facilities than pure logic-based approaches. Ontological schemas and instances can be used by reasoners to infer additional knowledge, so that problems like ambiguity, incompleteness and validity of contextual data can be addressed. This additional knowledge may fill the information gaps (left by interruption or low quality measurements). All these highlight the benefits of the use of ontologies and, in addition to the right choice and implementation of ontology languages and tools, a significant number of issues could be handled [31].

The use of ontologies provides the ability to resolve several issues concerning the development and management of such systems:

- Semantic service discovery: In these environments, the concept of service is considered to be crucial, as each user selects the services he wants, in order to obtain certain service configurations. Therefore, a semantic service discovery method is indispensable so as to discover the semantically similar services [31].

- Context-awareness: relevant applications have to perceive the current context and adapt their behavior to different situations (by the word "context" we refer to the physical information, e.g. location, time, environmental information, personal information etc.) [32]. Therefore, there is need to have the ability to adapt to rapidly changing situations. The different types of contextual information must be well-defined, so that various entities can have a common understanding of context [4].
- Interoperability between different entities: in these environments, new entities edge in at any time. These entities interact with the existent and their interaction must be based on common, well-defined concepts, so that they are able to interoperate [4].

Three important approaches are mentioned in this domain. The first is ONTONAV, an indoor navigation system, which enables personalized path selection. This model exploits a User Navigation Ontology (UNO) developed for modelling users based on their individual characteristics that influence a) navigational decision (i.e. selection of the optimum path) and b) the form and the means that these navigational decisions are communicated to them [6]. Another interesting approach for the support of pervasive computing applications is the Standard Ontology for Ubiquitous and Pervasive Applications (SOUPA). This project is driven by a set of use cases and it is believed that it can help developers who are inexperienced in knowledge representation to quickly begin constructing ontology-driven applications using a shared ontology that combines many useful vocabularies from different consensus ontologies [9]. Finally, the GAS ontology provides a common language for the communication and the collaboration among ubiquitous computing devices, mentioned as eGets and addresses a number of key issues, such as the heterogeneity among the various systems and services, the demand for semantic interoperability, the dynamic nature of these environments, etc. [16].

3. Conclusions

Taking into consideration all the above, we come to the conclusion that ontologies are no longer only theoretical approaches; they are an established technology for knowledge collection and aim at fulfilling the need to facilitate the noble goals of sharing, reuse and interoperability. They are very powerful in managing semantic content and in delivering high quality services to end users, as they can really reveal and make available any information, from any source, and, additionally, assist each user in handling and using it more effectively and efficiently.

Nevertheless, we draw the conclusion that although a lot of ontology technologies have been implemented in many areas and fields and some remarkable results have already been achieved, however, still, there is neither an overall architecture, nor complete solutions that could cover a wide field. This does not imply that all the aforementioned efforts are not valuable. On the contrary, it is obvious that there is a lot of effort and research performed, with very interesting and precious results. However, it is common sense that all this work needs to be further explored, so as to proceed to more integrated applications, which will display all the benefits that ontologies have to offer to the semantic world.

References:

1. Xexeo G et al (2004): Collaborative Editing of ontologies in a Peer-to-Peer Framework. In: SEMPGRID'04, New York
2. Zhao Y, Sandahl K (2003): Potential advantages of Semantic Web for Internet Commerce. In: Proceedings of the 5th International Conference on Enterprise Information Systems, Angers, France, pp.151-160
3. Kalogerakis E, Christodoulakis S, Moumoutzis N (2006): Coupling Ontologies with Graphics Content for Knowledge Driven Visualization. In: Proceedings IEEE Virtual Reality Conference
4. Ranganathan A et al (2003): Ontologies in a Pervasive Computing Environment. In: Workshop on Ontologies in Distributed Systems at IJCAI, Acapulco, Mexico
5. Hovy E (1998): Combining and Standardizing Large-Scale, Practical Ontologies for Machine Translation and Other Uses. In: Proceedings of 1st International Conference on language resources and evaluation (LREC), Granada
6. Kikiras P, Tsetsos V, Hadjiefthymiades S (2006): Ontology-based User Modeling for Pedestrian Navigation Systems. In: ECAI 2006 Workshop on Ubiquitous User Modeling (UbiqUM), Riva del Garda, Italy
7. Razmerita L, Angehrn A, Maedche A (2003): Ontology-Based User Modeling for Knowledge Management Systems. In: User Modeling 9th International Conference, UM, Heidelberg, Germany
8. Heinecke J, Toumani F (2003): A natural language mediation system for e-commerce applications: an ontology-based approach. In: Proceedings of 2nd International Semantic Web Conference, Sanibel Island
9. Chen H et al: SOUPA (2004): Standard Ontology for Ubiquitous and Pervasive Applications. In: Proceedings of First Annual International Conference on Mobile and Ubiquitous Systems: Networking and Services MobiQuitous, Boston, MA
10. Noy NF (2004): Semantic Integration a survey of ontology based approaches. SIGMOD Record, Special Issue on Semantic Integration. 33(4)
11. What do we need for ontology integration on the semantic web? Position statement, http://ftp.informatik.rwth-aachen.de/Publications/CEUR-WS/Vol-82/SI_position_10.pdf
12. Pouchard L et al (2003): An ontology for scientific information in a grid environment the Earth System Grid. In: CCGrid (Symposium on Cluster Computing and the Grid), Tokyo, Japan
13. Chebotko A et al (2004): OntoELAN: an ontology-based linguistic multimedia annotator. In: Proceedings of IEEE Sixth International Symposium on Multimedia Software Engineering, Miami, USA, pp.329-336
14. Stojanovic N (2003): On the role of the Librarian Agent in ontology-based knowledge management systems. Journal of Universal Computer Science. 9(7), pp.697-718
15. IST Project IST-2000-29243 OntoWeb. OntoWeb: Ontology-based Information Exchange for Knowledge Management and Electronic Commerce. D21 Successful Scenarios for Ontology-based Applications v1.0, http://www.ontoweb.org/About/Deliverables/Deliverable1.2.1.pdf

16. Christopoulou E, Kameas A (2005): GAS Ontology: an ontology for collaboration among ubiquitous computing devices. International Journal of Human-Computer Studies. 62(5), pp.664-685

17. Cannataro M, Massara A, Veltri P (2004): The OnBrowser ontology manager: Managing ontologies on the Grid. In: International Workshop on Semantic Intelligent Middleware for the Web and the Grid, Valencia, Spain

18. Gruber TR (1993): Toward Principles for the Design of Ontologies Used for Knowledge Sharing. International Journal Human-Computer Studies. 43, p.907-928

19. Christopoulou E, Kameas A (2004): Ontology-driven composition of service-oriented ubiquitous computing applications. In: Third International Conference on Adaptive Hypermedia and Adaptive Web-Based Systems (AH2004), Eindhoven, the Netherlands

20. Naphade M et al (2006): Large-scale concept ontology for multimedia. IEEE Multimedia. 13(3), pp.86-91

21. Bruijn J de (2003): Using Ontologies: enabling knowledge sharing and reuse on the Semantic Web. DERI Technical Report DERI-2003-10-29

22. Doerr M, Hunter J, Lagoze C (2003): Towards a core ontology for information integration. Journal of Digital Information. 4(1)

23. Doulaverakis C, Kompatsiaris Y, Strintzis MG (2005): Ontology-based access to multimedia cultural heritage collection – the Reach Project. In: EUROCON, Serbia & Montenegro, Belgrado

24. Guangzuo C et al (2004): OntoEdu: a case study of ontology-based education grid system for e-learning. In: GCCCE2004 International conference, Hong Kong

25. Sicilia MA (2006): Metadata, semantics, and ontology: providing meaning to information resources. International Journal of Metadata, Semantics and Ontologies. 1(1)

26. Niles I, Pease A (2001): Towards a Standard Upper Ontology. In: Proceedings of the International Conference on Formal Ontology in Information Systems, Ogunquit, Maine, USA

27. Rostami H et al (2006): An ontology based local index in P2P networks. In: Second International Conference on Semantics, Knowledge, and Grid, Guilin, China

28. Bosca A, Bonino D, Pellegrino P (2005): OntoSphere: more than a 3D ontology visualization tool. In: SWAP, the 2nd Italian Semantic Web Workshop, Trento, Italy

29. Sanchez-Alonso S, Garcia-Barriocanal E (2006): Making use of upper ontologies to foster interoperability between SKOS concept schemes. Online Information Review. 30(3), pp.263-277

30. Sicilia MA et al (2006): Integrating descriptions of knowledge management learning activities into large ontological structures: a case study. Data and Knowledge Engineering. 57(2) pp. 111-121

31. Krummenacher R et al (2007): Analyzing the modeling of context with ontologies. In: International Workshop on Context-Awareness for Self-Managing Systems, Toronto, Canada

32. Semy SK, Pulvermacher, MK, Obrst, LJ (2004): Towards the Use of an Upper Ontology for U.S. Government and Military Domains: An Evaluation. MITRE Technical Report

33. Bhojaraju G. (2005): Knowledge Management: why do we need it for corporates. Malaysian Journal of Library & Information Science. 10(2) Dec 2005, pp.37-50

Semantic technologies for mobile Web and personalized ranking of mobile Web search results

Evangelos Sakkopoulos

Abstract The semantic Web has brought exciting new possibilities for informtion access. Semantic Web is already adopted in several application domains. Our main objective is to critically present solutions using semantic Web technologies to provide successful mobile Web services. Aim of this work is also to introduce a novel semantically enriched personalization technique for the accelerating market of mo-bile environment introducing an enhanced data structure and web algorithm. A prototype has been implemented and proved effective. Furthermore, performance evaluation is also both encouraging and promising

1 Introduction

The Web was designed to be a universal space of information and mainly offers unstructured and semi-structured natural language data. The Semantic Web (Berners-Lee et al 2001, Sicilia 2006,) is specifically a web of machine readable information whose meaning is well defined. The ontologies (Dogac et al, 2002) for the Semantic Web are an emerging technology which offers a promising infrastructure as far as the harmonization of the heterogeneous representations of web resources is concerned. In this direction, ontologies offer a common understanding of a domain that can be a mean of communication among application systems and people. Semantic web technology is already adopted in several web based applications and solutions (Makris et al 2006, Sakkopoulos et al 2006, Kanellopoulos et al 2007, Sicilia et al 2006) marking in this way a new era in the Internet technologies. However, the application of such Web oriented and

Computer Engineering and Informatics Dpt.
University of Patras,
GR-26504, Rio Patras, Greece

sakkopul@ceid.upatras.gr

semantic Web based techniques is not straight forward in the domain of mobile solutions.

Heterogeneous representations of web resources are common in the accelerating mobile web solutions area. In fact, according to the Gardner Group analysis (2004), there will be a high rate of change in the capabilities of mobile technology, infrastructure and telecommunications networks. No single technology will be suitable for all applications because each provides different trade-offs in terms of bandwidth, range and cost. Consequently, many types of short-range wireless networks will coexist in most organizations.

Enterprise users are already able to have personalized, seamless access to enterprise applications and services from any place and any time, regardless of the devices employed, in order to make contextualized decisions in behalf of the enterprises using vendor proprietary solution as in (Terziyan, 2001). However, there is a need to standardize views to commercial operations and help users to reach consensus between any buyer and any seller about general and specific features of their business relationships.

Towards this direction the multilevel profiling framework discussed in (Ericsson Enterprise, 2002) is able to manage ontologies, which are necessary for a semantic realization of mobile services. In this way it is possible to facilitate the concept of m-commerce as a public mobile electronic commerce, which is based on the assumption that every person in the society in some way more or less participates in public business process (public commerce or (p-commerce) in (Ericsson Enterprise, 2002).

The first objective of this work is to present a survey of promising approaches that unify semantic Web technologies with a number of different mobile operations. Furthermore, initial work on a novel approach that investigates the effects of semantic Web techniques for the personalization of mobile data centric solutions is presented. Aim of this work is to present an effective alternative that will provide limited and targeted searching/browsing results using semantics.

In the sequel, the paper will be organized in the following sections. In section 2, we critically present, categorize and compare a number of semantically enriched solutions for mobile applications and services, in the new semantic based context. In section 3, we introduce a novel algorithmic approach and a prototype that personalizes effectively the query results for mobile environments using an enhanced flavour of biased skip list data structure and ODP categorical metadata in the case of bursty access patterns. Finally, section 5 concludes the paper and presents future steps.

2 The new context of mobile web

There will be a high rate of change in the capabilities of mobile technology, infrastructure and telecommunications networks. No single technology will be suitable for all applications because each provides different trade-offs in terms of bandwidth, range and cost. Consequently, many types of short-range wireless networks will coexist in most organizations. (Gardner Group, 2004)

Important considerations on the path to mobility are wireless LAN access and roaming between wireless LAN and GPRS networks. These allow business users to wirelessly access corporate data at the office or at hotspots, such as airports or hotels, as well as in the wide area with GPRS access. (Ericsson Enterprise 2002)

Enterprise users are able to have personalized, seamless access to enterprise applications and services from any place and any time, regardless of the devices employed, in order to make contextualized decisions in behalf of the enterprises using vendor proprietary solution as in (Ericsson Enterprise 2002). However, there is a need to standardize views to commercial operations and help users to reach consensus between any buyer and any seller about general and specific features of their business relationships.

In a more technical paradigm, to deliver multiple copies of database information, partial broadcasting is usually adopted. When a broadcast session contains only a subset of the database items, a client might not be able to obtain all its items from the broadcast and is forced to request additional ones from the server on demand. Semantic-based broadcast approach (Lee et al 2000) attaches a semantic description to each broadcast unit, called a chunk. It allows a client to determine if a query can be answered entirely using a broadcast as well as defining the precise nature of the remaining items in the form of a "supplementary" query.

Furthermore, advances in spatially enabled semantic computing can provide situation aware assistance for mobile users. This intelligent and context-aware technology presents the right information at the right time, place and situation by exploiting semantically referenced data for knowledge discovery. (Carswell et al 2004). Semantic web technologies have already joined multiple implementations of current m-business reality. In the sequel, different services coupled with semantic technologies are presented.

Location-Based Services. Location-based services (LBS) are information services that exploit knowledge about where an information device user is located. The next-generation mobile network will support terminal mobility, personal mobility, and service provider portability, making global roaming seamless. A location-independent personal telecommunication number (PTN) scheme is conducive to implementing such a global mobile system (Mao et al 2004). There is a need for incorporation of design and performance of high-throughput database technologies into the forthcoming mobile systems to ensure that future systems will be able to carry efficiently the anticipated loads. Exploitation of the localized nature of calling and mobility patterns, the proposed architecture effectively reduces the database loads as well as the signaling traffic incurred by the location registration and call delivery procedures.

Time-Sensitive Information. M-commerce can be effective for information such as sports results, flight information and tourist information. An example of the latter is MoCHA (Mobile Cultural Heritage Adventures) that allows the mobile cultural heritage consumer to explore a personally tailored view of Dublin's treasured artefacts, historical events and districts in an interactive and intuitive way directly on their spatially enabled PDA (Carswell et al 2004). In order to boost delivery of such information, proposed mechanisms exist for transforming projection-selection queries to reuse cached data blocks (Ken et al 1999). This avoids transmitting unwanted data items over low bandwidth wireless channels. In WebCarousel (Nadamoto et al 2001) the search results are shown by synthesized speech synchronized with related images in a repeated manner by carousels.

Entertainment. Consumers can leverage m-commerce for uses such as downloaded games (mostly Java) and favourite web page links. Music and Video delivery have potentials but need at least 3G performance and lower prices to become attractive. Progressive delivery of Web documents in mobile Internet Services proposed in (Wagner et al 2002) allows focused delivery of entertainment data in a cost-effective sense. Use of XML technology documents that are automatically adapted to fit both personal user profiles and device constraints may enhance the web browsing entertaining experience.

Banking, Payment and Ticketing. A broad overview of mobile payment (micropayment and macropayment) and mobile banking services is presented in (Mallat et al 2004). Modest success has been realized in applications that have an element of mobility and immediacy, such as parking, road congestion charging.

3 Personalization for the mobile web searching

In this section, we introduce a new approach that personalizes the web searching results in mobile environments taking advantage of the web pages' categorical metadata (dmoz- ODP). We particularly focus on the case of bursty web search patterns. Our aim is to present a more effective algorithm to rank web search results for mobile environments. It is difficult for mobile gadgets to display ordinary the web search results, as they usually have limited dimensions in their displays. Our approach achieves to narrow down the possible and available results in order to facilitate the final choice made by the user. When the results matching a user's query are of a size, it is possible in most cases to complicate their manipulation. As a consequence the typical web search engine results should be further processed, so that they are presented in a way that can help users evaluate all available alternatives and perform relative comparisons before proceeding to further browsing. This is especially the case where the mobiles are utilized as shopping assistants while searching in the Internet and perform e-shopping (Haübl et al 2000).

Personalization on search results has already been studied previously in a number of cases (Jansen et al 2000, Henziger 2003). Successful cases also include techniques where semantic/ metadata pre-processing of the results has been utilized effectively. In the work of Makris et al 2007 a novel procedure has been introduced to personalize search results based on their semantic correlation as this derives from the ODP (dmoz.org) categorical metadata assigned to each web page result. The Open Directory (ODP) powers the core directory services for the Web's largest and most popular search engines and portals, including AOL Search, Google, Lycos, HotBot, and hundreds of others.(dmoz.org/about.html).

3.1 Bursty web category browsing pattern

In bursty cases, a few web pages results' categories get "hot" for short periods of time and are accessed very frequently in a limited temporal space. Such patterns have been also observed in various Internet applications in a number of studies (Zhou et al 2004, Ergün et al 2001, Lin et al 1997). In bursty web search pattern cases, the user attempts to find specific results that belong to limited categories of interest within a short time period. As a consequence an efficient retrieval and storing mechanism is needed to keep the users' personalized categories and frequent results.

3.2 The proposed algorithm

There are a number of self-adjusting or biased data structures (Sleator et al 1985) that are designed to exploit such biases, and provide similar (amortized) search times (eq. 2,3). These data structures perform complex balancing schemes which hinder their practical performance. In this work, we deploy and port a new flavour of the biased skip list by Ergün et al 2001 (BSL – section 3.3) that avoids such balancing operations, and employs a novel lazy maintenance scheme to provide fast insertion and deletion of categories in the preference list of the search results.

As a consequence, whenever we refer to bursty accesses to web search results, we implicitly detect the specific category (or group of categories closely related at the ODP graph) that the browsed page belongs to. (e.g. Retailers for Storage devices for which the ODP respective category is Top-Computers-Hardware-Storage-Retailers or Pizza in my neighbourhood -island Corfu- for which ODP categorizes the results in Regional-Europe-Greece-Prefectures-Corfu-Business and Economy-Restaurants and Bars). In order to construct our user profiles on the enhanced BSL logic, we utilize the idea of (Makris et al 2007) for a personalized graph of ODP categories per user.

Specifically, we refine the BSL approach introducing a "biasing category results in favour of latest frequently visited category" procedure (section 3.4). As a result, we achieve to narrow effectively the selection list whenever a user is actively searching repeatedly in semantically close category results.

The authors in (Makris et al 2007) proposed different methods for constructing the personalized subgraph G' of the ODP categorical metadata. The main idea is to keep a user-based personalized version of the ODP categories graph G carefully selected and as limited as possible. This subgraph can be constructed by tracking user preferences implicitly (using the visited web page results) or explicitly (asking the user to choose categories of interest per session). Every web page category v in the personalized G' graph is assigned a semantically based weight $\beta(v) > 0$. These weights are used in order to post-categorize pages returned to the end user. The most practical of the proposed approaches is called "semi-offline", where category weights are only updated after a number of web searching sessions (i.e. per day or per week). Category weights are updated according to the following:

$$\beta(v) = \beta(v) + \sum_{i=1}^{out\,deg\,ree(v)} d(v, v_i)\beta(v_i) + \sum_{i=1}^{in\,deg\,ree(v)} d(v_i, v)\beta(v_i) \tag{1},$$

where $d(u,v) = 1/outdegree(u,v)$ (Makris et al 2007).
The proposed algorithm includes the following steps depicted at figure 1.

1. While (!Categories of interest chosen == true)
2.   Implicitly or explicitly store in user profile the pages and respective categorical metadata of search results browsed
3. Construct personalized subgraph G' from the ODP categorical graph G assigning a weight $\beta(v)$ to each category v for each user utilizing function (eq. 1)
4. Store personalized subgraph on Biased Skip List data structure
5. While (Exists(bursty web category accesses pattern) == true)
6.   Bias category results in favour of latest frequently visited category utilizing (eq. 4)
7. If session == alive
8.   return to 3 and further update personalized G'
9. else //(session lifespan ends)
10.   return to 1 // for a new user session

Fig 1 Personalization algorithm for mobile devices in bursty access pattern cases.

3.3 Biased skip lists (BSL)

BSL require $O(n)$ space, and can be constructed in $O(n)$ expected time when categories are given in sorted order. The categories are ranked 1 through n according to how frequently or recently they have been accessed. Searching for a category k takes $(\log r(k))$ expected time (2), where $r(k)$ denotes the rank of the category in each user profile. Because the maximum rank is n, all operations have $O(\log n)$ expected worst case (3), as with Skip Lists and other efficient data structures – which is optimal.

In (Ergün et al 2001) the most recently accessed (MRA) scheme is utilized in the cases of highly bursty access patterns. Eq. 2,3 can be further improved in the cases where categories do not remain in the data structure for a long time, but instead have short lifespans. Once inserted, these categories are rapidly accessed a few times, then deleted after a short period. As a result, their MRA ranks always remain close to 1. To facilitate more efficient implementation of insertions and deletions, we adopt (Ergün et al 2001) who proposed a lazy updating scheme of levels and allow flexibility in class sizes.

The MRA implementation of BSL facilitates insertion or deletion of a category k in amortized $O(\log r_{max}(k))$ time, where $r_{max}(k)$ is the maximum rank of category k in its lifespan. In bursty patterns, when a category is hot, it is accessed a large number of times rapidly. This means that, according to the MRA scheme, the category maintains a small rank compared to the number of keys in the data structure. Thus, having the running times depend on the rank rather than the total number of categories yields significant gains.

3.4 Biasing category results in favour of latest frequently visited category

In our case the bursty event, the accessed category is ranked in the user profile biased according to the following weight β_{new}. When the category is already first in the rank no updates are needed.

$$\beta_{new_x} = \beta_{current_x} \frac{\sum_{i=1}^{k} \left(2^i \bullet exists\,\beta(i)\right)+1}{2^{k+1}-1} \quad (4)$$

where $exists(\beta(i))$ equals 1 if the category is chosen in the i_{th} access during the bursty pattern visits. Therefore, it exists whenever a new access is made to the category at the i_{th} visit, where $i \in [1,m]$ and m equals the total number of visits in the current bursty web access session.

3.5 Prototype on Personal digital assistants and initial results.

A prototype has been delivered at the Windows Mobile 5 platform and .NET and browser scripting technologies have been utilized. The proposed algorithm has been used to personalize the Google and Google Directory search results as shown in the figure 2 below. Notice that the re-ranked results include indication of original ordering/ranking delivered by Google search engine before personalization.

We have to mention that the presented approach is still on-going work. However the initial application performance results are promising (the inline browser re-ranking of results and implementation of the enhanced BSL is feasible and effective on the limited resources of a WM5 PDA) and evaluation is encouraging.

We have evaluated the performance of our approach as well as its effectiveness in personalizing the search results by measuring how higher the web page results of preferred categorical metadata are re-ranked with respect to their initial Google ranking. The evaluation has been performed using synthetic data according to the following bursty web access scenario parameters:

1. 8-10 categories from the top-3 ODP category levels were chosen for each user profile as preferred,
2. a two word query was randomly chosen (= a web page title randomly chosen from the pages listed in the categories chosen as preferred)
3. during the burst session, 10 web search results were chosen as preferred for each random query.

In the end, the proposed solution in the cases of bursty access patterns was overall promoted the relative results with 3.4 higher rankings on average in 10 users for 100 random queries each. This means that the user would have found the requesting results higher in the ranking list, easing in this way its browsing experience in the mobile device.

However, further evaluation is planned using real-life subjects/testers. For the overall evaluation of the proposed system, user testing is considered as the most appropriate method as in most web application evaluation cases only real end-users along with advanced users are in position to provide valuable feedback, identify problems and suggest modifications.

Fig 2 Personalization of Google Directory searching on Windows Mobile 5 for Pocket PC

4. Conclusions and Future Steps

Semantic web technologies have already served in a number of cases as a catalyst for improving the mobile application browsing experience. An analytic review of available semantic based solutions have been presented as well as categorized in location-based services, time sensitive service, entertainment services, small payment and ticketing.

Metadata can be considered the semantic web's cornerstone. In fact, categories-metadata is already available for a large number of web search results through the Open Directory Project. Our focus is to utilize the former metadata in order to provide improved experience in the limited display space and keyboard capabilities of the mobile environments. It is even more important than in desktop browsing, to be able to personalize effectively search results in mobile web. Personalization in this context means to narrow down the available search result choices using biased re-ranking based on the metadata and the users' preferences. We have introduced a novel approach that personalizes effectively the search results in the case of bursty web search access patters for the first time to the author's best knowledge. In our approach, we have deployed a new flavour of a biased skip list approach specialized for bursty access patterns in the case of re-ranking search results using their ODP based metadata-categories. A prototype has been introduced and initial results and performance evaluation have been promising.

Future steps include further experimentation and performance evaluation using subjects. A practical implication that has also to be considered is the presentation of long and overlapping names of ODP categorical metadata in the search results. Hashing techniques are investigated to overcome this implication. Furthermore, improving more the personalization combining ODP categories with user-preferred ontologies will be studied.

References

Berners-Lee, T., Hendler, J., and Lassila, O. (2001). *The Semantic Web*, Scientific American, Vol. 285, No. 5, pp. 34-43.

Carswell, J.D., Gardiner, K., Neumann, M. (2004): "Wireless spatio-semantic transactions on multimedia datasets", Proceedings of the 2004 ACM symposium on Applied computing, 2004, pp. 1201 – 1205

Dogac, A., Laleci, G., Kabak, Y., and Cingil, I. (2002). *Exploiting Web Services Semantics: Taxonomies vs. Ontologies*, IEEE Data Engineering Bulletin, Vol. 25, No. 4.

Ergün, F., Mittra, S., Cenk Sahinalp, S., Sharp, J., Sinha, R.K.: A Dynamic Lookup Scheme for Bursty Access Patterns. INFOCOM 2001, pp. 1444-1453

Ericsson Enterprise, (2002). *The path to the Mobile Enterprise*, Available at http://www.ericsson.com/enterprise/library/white_papers/Mobile_enterprise.pdf

Gardner Group, (2004), *The mobile business value scenario*, Winning in the Mobile and Wireless World, Strategic Planning Series, Chapter 2.

Haübl, G., and Trifts, V., "Consumer Decision Making in Online Shopping Environments: The Effects of Interactive Shopping Aids", Marketing Science 19 (1), 2000, pp. 4-21.

Henzinger, M., Algorithmic Challenges in Web Search Engines, Internet Mathematics 1, 1, 2003, pp.115-126

Hu, H., Lee, D.L. (2004): "Semantic Location Modeling for Location Navigation in Mobile Environment", Proceedings of the 2004 IEEE International Conference on Mobile Data Management (MDM'04), 2004

Jansen, B., Spink, A., and Saracevic, T., Real life, real users, and real needs: a study and analysis of user queries on the web. Information Processing and Management, 36(2) (2000), 207-227

Jung, J.J., Jo, G. (2003): Template-Based E-mail Summarization for Wireless Devices, ISCIS 2003, LNCS 2869, pages: 99-106

Kanellopoulos, D, Sakkopoulos, E., Lytras, M., and Tsakalidis, A., (2007), "Using Web-Based Teaching Interventions in Computer Science Courses", in IEEE Transactions on Education, special issue on "Mobile Technology for Education",in press

Lee , K.C.K., Leong, H. V., Si, A.(1999), Semantic query caching in a mobile environment, ACM SIGMOBILE Mobile Computing and Communications Review, v.3 n.2, pp.28-36, April 1999

Lee , K.C.K., Leong, H. V., Si, A. (2000) A Semantic Broadcast Scheme for a Mobile Environment based on Dynamic Chunking, the 20th International Conference on Distributed Computing Systems (ICDCS), pp. 522-529

Lin, S., and McKeown, N., "A simulation study of IP switching," in Proc. ACM SIGCOMM, 1997.

Makris, Ch., Panagis, Y., Sakkopoulos, E., and Tsakalidis, A. (2006). *Category ranking for personalized search*, in the Data and Knowledge Engineering Journal (DKE), Elsevier Science, Vol. 60 , No. 1, pp. 109-125.

Mallat, N., Rossi, M., Tuunainen, V.K., (2004) New architectures for financial services: Mobile banking services, Communications of the ACM, Vol. 47, No. 5, pp. 42 – 46

Mao, Z., Douligeris, Ch (2004): A distributed database architecture for global roaming in next-generation mobile networks. IEEE/ACM Trans. Netw. Vol. 12, No 1, pp. 146-160

Sakkopoulos, E., Kanellopoulos, D., and Tsakalidis, A. (2006a), *Semantic mining and web service discovery techniques for media resources management*, in Int. J. Metadata, Semantics and Ontologies, Vol. 1, No. 1, pp.66–75.

Sicilia, M.A.,(2006) Metadata, semantics, and ontology: providing meaning to information resources, in International Journal of Metadata, Semantics and Ontologies, Vol 1, No 1, pp. 83-86

Sicilia, M-A., Lytras, M-D, Rodríguez, E., Barriocanal, E.G. (2006) Integrating descriptions of knowledge management learning activities into large ontological structures: A case study, in Data Knowl. Eng., Elsevier, Vol. 57, No 2, pp. 111-121

Sleator, D. and Tarjan, R. "Self-adjusting binary search trees," Journal of the ACM, vol. 32, 1985.

Terziyan, V. (2001) Architecture for Mobile P-Commerce: Multilevel Profiling Framework. In Workshop Notes for the IJCAI01, Workshop on E-business & the Intelligent Web. August, 2001.

Wagner, M., Kießling, W., Balke, W.-T. (2002) Progressive Content Delivery for Mobile E-Services, in Proc. of the 3rd Int. Conf. on Advances in Web-Age Information Management (WAIM), LNCS 2419, Beijing, China.

Yu, Y.H., Jung, J.J., Noh, K.S., Jo, G. (2004): Mobile Q&A Agent System Based on the Semantic Web in Wireless Internet, Grid and Cooperative Computing GCC 2004, China, LNCS 3251, 2004, pp. 955-958

Zhou, B., Hui, S.C., and Chang, K., An Intelligent Recommender System Using Sequential Web Access Patterns, IEEE Conference on Cybernetics and Intelligent Systems. IEEE, Singapore, pages 393—398, 2004

A Web Classifier for Semantic Classification Between News and Sports Broadcasts

S. Voulgaris, M. Poulos, N. Kanellopoulos, and S. Papavlasopoulos

Abstract Lately, lot of work has been done in the area of content-based audio classification. In this paper we experiment on audio classification between sports and news broadcasts using the Average Magnitude Difference Function as the feature extractor and an LVQ1 neural network as classifier. The method proves robust and the results are reliable and could be further utilized in an automated web classifier.

1 Introduction

In recent years, developments in internet and broadcast technology have caused a rapid growth to the amount of web content which is published in multimedia form. Audio data is an essential part of most multimedia material and thus can be used for classification and indexing purposes. Audio classification raises new challenges compared to plain text. The most common method of classification and retrieval of audio files is the use of metadata and tags attached to the audio file manually usually by the creator of the original material. Originally automated

Spyros Voulgaris
Dept. Of Archives and Library Sciences, Ionian University, Palea Anaktora, 49100 Corfu, Greece, email: svoul@ionio.gr

Marios Poulos,
Dept. Of Archives and Library Sciences, Ionian University, Palea Anaktora, 49100 Corfu, Greece, email: mpoulos@ionio.gr

Nick Kanellopoulos,
Dept. Of Archives and Library Sciences, Ionian University, Palea Anaktora, 49100 Corfu, Greece, email: kane@ionio.gr

Sozon Papavlasopoulos,
Dept. Of Archives and Library Sciences, Ionian University, Palea Anaktora, 49100 Corfu, Greece, email: sozon@ionio.gr

methods of audio classification were based on speech recognition and the appliance of the same techniques used for text documents. On the other hand content-based classification utilizes specific features of the audio signal to extract numerical data and then performs the classification based on that data.

In this paper we investigate the possibility of creating online servers to which requests can be sent from remote clients in order to distinguish between news and sports audio files. The input data will be multimedia files gathered by an agent and the output will represent the classification. Inside the server classification will be performed by a neural network and the result of the classification procedure will be recorded as an appropriate XML file. Our proposed method helps automate the procedure of classification and metadata creation of audio files and thus facilitates structured electronic publication.

2 Method

A graphic representation of our proposed method is shown below:

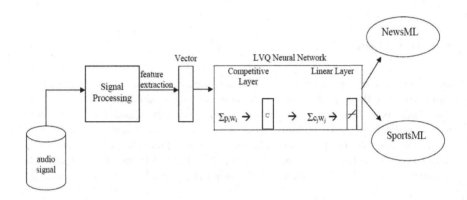

Fig. 1. An audio classifier based on an LVQ Neural Network

The input audio signal is processed by a feature extraction algorithm such as AMDF. The result of this process is a n-dimensional vector which is then fed to an LVQ (Learning Vector Quantize) neural network, which performs the classification between the two categories news or sports. The LVQ network consists of two layers. The competitive layer classifies input vectors dependent on the distance between and the linear layer performs a classification according to the classes defined by the designer. According to the classification a correspondent XML document is created (NewsML or SportsML). The content does not have to be embedded into the XML file, instead a pointer can be inserted which will identify the position of the original audio file to the publisher's web site

2.1 AMDF

AMDF (Average Magnitude Difference Function) is defined as

$$AMDF = \frac{1}{L}\sum_{t=1}^{L}\left|s(t) - s(t+m)\right|, \qquad 0 \leq m \leq t\text{-}1 \qquad (1)$$

where   s(t) is the audio signal
           m is the length of the analysis window
           L is the total number of the audio samples

The AMDF is a variation of Autocorrelation Function Analysis. The AMDF provides a faster alternative to the calculation of the autocorrelation function of a frame as it requires no multiplications. In the literature AMDF is considered as the most robust of the features extraction techniques [4, 11]. A key note that should be made about AMDF is the appropriate selection of the audio signal segmentation (L) and the analysis window (m).

2.2 LVQ

Neural networks are computer programs which simulate the behavior of human brain in order to solve a problem. Processing of information is done parallel and distributed and the neural network can be trained and learn to perform its task more accurately. Neural networks are widely used for classification and pattern recognition for the lat twenty years. There is a great variety of neural networks but they can be divided into two broad categories *supervised* (predefined classes) and *unsupervised* (group identification).

In this paper for the purpose of audio classification between *news* and *sports* we used an LVQ (Linear Vector Quantization) network, which can be described as a supervised classifier for an unsupervised network. LVQ was chosen for its robustness and for its capability of distinguishing between similar vectors and placing them into different classes.

An LVQ network has a first competitive layer and a second linear layer. The competitive layer learns to classify input vectors in subclasses and then the linear layer transforms the competitive layer's classes into target classifications defined by the user. The competitive layer classifies input vectors dependent on the distance between them while the linear layer performs a classification according to the classes defined by the designer, in our case these classes are *news* and *sports*.

2.3 Markup Language

In order to share or retrieve information through a vast and diverse network such as the internet it is very convenient if web content is published in a form that can be processed by software agents. The Extensible Markup Language (XML) is a general-purpose markup language whose primary purpose is to facilitate the sharing of data across different information systems and especially across the World Wide Web.

Based on XML there have been developed hundreds of different markup languages, used to express specialized material. NewsML and SportsML are two markup languages developed and supported by IPTC (International Press and Telecommunications Council). They can support data in various formats along with all the necessary metadata that enables the recipient to understand the relationship between components and understand the roles of each component.

3 Application

As an experimental set we used a database of 140 audio clips, half of them being news reports and the other half sports broadcasts. 20 audio clips from each category will be used for training purposes of the neural network while the remaining clips will be used for testing. Each audio clip is segmented into 6 smaller audio clips lasting one, two, three, four, five and six seconds respectively. In this way we have created an audio database containing 140x6=840 audio clips. That results in 6x20=120 audio clips totaling 1x20 + 2x20 + 3x20 + 4x20 + 5x20 + 6x20 = 420 sec. of training data and 6x50 = 300 clips totaling 1x50 + 2x50 + 3x50 + 4x50 + 5x50 + 6x50 = 1050 sec. for testing in each category .

Calculations were carried out in Matlab environment and the neural network was created with the Matlab Neural Networks Toolbox.

3.1 Feature extraction

For each audio file we extract the AMDF coefficients applying equation (1). According to bibliography and in compliance with the LVQ neural network we used for classification we set the analysis window m = 20. The total number of audio samples are 8,000 per second thus L is set to 8000, 16000, 24000, 32000, 40000 and 48000 for audio clips of 1, 2, 3, 4, 5 and 6 second duration respectively.

The function used to calculate the AMDF coefficients is

```
function y=amdf(x)
% AMDF function for one frame of signal
m=20;
l=length(x);
for i=1:m
    y(i)=mean(abs(x(1:l+1-i)-x(i:l)));
end
```

The AMDF [20x1] feature vectors of 12 different audio clips (6 news and 6 sports) are presented at the following tables. The 6 news audio clips are segments of the same original audio news clip and so does the sports clips.

Table 1a. AMDF feature vectors of news and sports audio clips

t=1sec.		t=2sec.		t=3sec.	
news	**sport**	**news**	**sport**	**news**	**sport**
0	0	0	0	0	0
0,004467	0,063915	0,021146	0,065831	0,027083	0,062844
0,005714	0,10475	0,032542	0,099939	0,043907	0,10067
0,007338	0,14467	0,041003	0,13662	0,055609	0,13792
0,007780	0,17158	0,046461	0,16148	0,063544	0,16555
0,007856	0,19688	0,052137	0,18880	0,070152	0,19252
0,008626	0,21154	0,058869	0,20393	0,077159	0,20866
0,008832	0,21894	0,065739	0,21317	0,084274	0,21835
0,010101	0,21483	0,073084	0,21296	0,093049	0,21922
0,010302	0,20304	0,077395	0,20725	0,10031	0,21388
0,010590	0,18337	0,078953	0,19427	0,10421	0,20125
0,010090	0,16152	0,078120	0,17824	0,10501	0,18551
0,009747	0,14210	0,077919	0,16289	0,10506	0,17088
0,009498	0,13122	0,078604	0,15104	0,10495	0,16103
0,009441	0,12823	0,079184	0,14484	0,10478	0,15612
0,009855	0,13515	0,078020	0,14504	0,10354	0,15641
0,009464	0,14770	0,075306	0,15001	0,10155	0,16000
0,009396	0,16362	0,072100	0,15661	0,098754	0,16449
0,008682	0,17910	0,070411	0,16512	0,096135	0,17057
0,009044	0,18971	0,071212	0,17137	0,09503	0,17464

Table 1b. AMDF feature vectors of news and sports audio clips

t=4sec.		t=5sec.		t=6sec.	
news	sport	news	sport	news	sport
0	0	0	0	0	0
0,028124	0,064676	0,029544	0,062626	0,028602	0,060853
0,046442	0,10313	0,048909	0,10119	0,047403	0,098156
0,059282	0,14120	0,061959	0,13833	0,059727	0,13311
0,068531	0,17024	0,070414	0,16762	0,067611	0,16098
0,075893	0,19937	0,076096	0,19652	0,07318	0,18870
0,083169	0,21731	0,082623	0,21532	0,079629	0,20726
0,090558	0,22944	0,090248	0,22819	0,087352	0,21976
0,099186	0,23263	0,099478	0,23283	0,09636	0,22460
0,10660	0,23026	0,10703	0,23199	0,10324	0,22388
0,11078	0,22015	0,11064	0,22381	0,10608	0,21661
0,11164	0,20652	0,11085	0,21185	0,10596	0,20582
0,11171	0,19219	0,11069	0,19827	0,10571	0,19344
0,11133	0,18030	0,11063	0,18641	0,10581	0,18207
0,11060	0,17071	0,11042	0,17624	0,10558	0,17172
0,10897	0,16504	0,10893	0,16936	0,10385	0,16457
0,10658	0,16337	0,10637	0,16601	0,10079	0,16073
0,10350	0,16429	0,10309	0,16535	0,097237	0,15959
0,10052	0,16787	0,10009	0,16751	0,094502	0,16149
0,098687	0,17156	0,098701	0,17005	0,093486	0,16425

3.2 Neural Network

For the classification between news and sports an LVQ1 neural network was created. Twenty news feature vectors (n1, n2, …, n20) and twenty sports feature vectors   (s1, s2, …, s20) were used for training. In fact we created 6 groups, consisting of 40 vectors each, for the audio clips segments of one, two, three, four, five and six seconds. For each group we perform a separate training and testing session.

We chose an LVQ1 neural network with four first layer hidden neurons and two target classes with equal a priori probabilities. The input vector is specified by
P = [n1, n2, ..., n20, s1, s2, ..., s20]
and the target vector
Tc = [1, 1, ,,, 1, 2, 2, ..., 2]
The training parameters were epochs = 300 and learning rate 0.001

3.3 Results

The results of the classification are presented at the next tables

Table 2a Classification Results

Audio Clip	Classification Class					
	t=1		t=2		t=3	
	sports	news	sports	news	sports	news
sports	42	8	44	6	45	5
news	5	45	6	44	6	44

Table 2b Classification Results

Audio Clip	Classification Class					
	t=4		t=5		t=6	
	sports	news	sports	news	sports	news
sports	47	3	49	1	50	0
news	4	46	2	48	1	49

To evaluate our classification method we ought to calculate the following probabilities:

Probability of classifying a sports audio clip into the sports category
Sport Predictive Value = 42 / 50 = 0.84 or 84%

Probability of classifying a news audio clip into the news category

News Predictive Value = 45 / 50 = 0.90 or 90%

Probability of an audio clip classified into sports category being indeed a sport clip

Sports Sensitivity = 42 / 47 = 0.89 or 89%

Probability of an audio clip classified into news category being indeed a news clip

News Sensitivity = 45 / 53 = 0.85 or 85%

The statistical evaluation of the classifications is presented at the following tables

Table 3a Classification Evaluation

	t=1		t=2		t=3	
	Predictive Value	Sensitivity	Predictive Value	Sensitivity	Predictive Value	Sensitivity
sports	84%	89%	88%	88%	90%	88%
news	90%	85%	88%	88%	88%	90%

Table 3b Classification Evaluation

	t=4		t=5		t=6	
	Predictive Value	Sensitivity	Predictive Value	Sensitivity	Predictive Value	Sensitivity
sports	94%	92%	98%	96%	100%	98%
news	92%	94%	96%	98%	98%	100%

REFERENCES

1. N. Adami, A. Bugatti, R. Leonardi, P. Migliorati: Low Level Processing of Audio and Video Information for Extracting the Semantics of Content. IEEE Fourth Workshop on Multimedia Signal Processing, 2001

2. E. Dellandria, P. Makris, N. Vincent,: Inner structure computation for audio signal analysis. Proceedings of the 3rd International Symposium on Image and Signal Processing and Analysis, 2003

3. R. Huang, J. Hansen: Advances in Unsupervised Audio Classification and Segmentation for the Broadcast News and NGSW Corpora. IEEE Transactions on Audio, Speech, and Language Processing, Vol. 14, No. 3, May 2006

4. Hae Young Kim, Jae Sung Lee, Myung-Whun Sung, Kwang Hyun Kim, Kwang Suk Park: Pitch Detection with Average Magnitude Difference Function Using Adaptive Threshold Algorithm for Estimating Shimmer and Jitter. Proceedings of the 20th Annual Znternational Conference of the ZEEE Engineering in Medicine and Biology Society, Vol. 20, NO 6,1998

5. N. Nitanda, M. Haseyama, H. Kitajima: Accurate Audio-Segment Classification Using Feature Extraction Matrix. IEEE International Conference on Acoustics, Speech, and Signal Processing, 2005

6. C. O'Leary, M. Humphrys : Lowering the entry level: Lessons from the Web and the Semantic Web for the World-Wide-Mind. 1st Int. Semantic Web Conf. (ISWC-02)

7. M. Poulos, S. Papavlasopoulos, G. Bokos: Specific Selection of FFT Amplitudes from Audio Sports and News Broadcasting for Classification Purposes.

8. M. De Santo, G. Percannella, C. Sansone, M.Vento: Classifying Audio of Movies by a Multi-Expert System. IEEE 11th International Conference on Image Analysis and Processing, 2001.

9. A. Selamat, S. Omatu,: Web page feature selection and classification using neural networks. Elsevier, Information Sciences—Informatics and Computer Science: An International Journal Vol. 158, No 1, 2004

10. G. Tzanetakis, M. Chen,: Building Audio Classifiers for Broadcast News Retrieval. 5th International Workshop on Image Analysis for Multimedia Interactive Services, WIAMIS'04

11. G. Ying, L. Jamiessen, C. Michell: A Probabilistic Approach to AMDF Pitch Detection. Proceedings., Fourth International Conference on Spoken Language, ICSLP'96

12. Jinjun Wang, Changsheng Xu, Engsiong Chng: Automatic Sports Video Genre Classification using Pseudo-2D-HMM. The 18th International Conference on Pattern Recognition, ICPR'06

A semantics-based software framework for ensuring consistent access to up-to-date knowledge resources in Public Administrations

Nenad Stojanovic[1], Dimitris Apostolou[2], Spyridon Ntioudis[3], Gregoris Mentzas[3]

Abstract Knowledge resources in public administrations are subject to continual change. These changes impose the need for keeping knowledge resources updated. In this paper we present an ontology-based approach for the systematic management of changes in knowledge resources in public administrations, which has been implemented in the SAKE semantics-based software framework. The current implementation allows management of explicit changes (i.e., alterations in the content of a document that have implications in the decision making process) and implicit changes (i.e., changes related to the usage of a document, the comments attached to it and related communication between users of the document).

1 Introduction

Changes in the environment cause frequent changes in the governments' regulations that may affect public administration (PA) processes, systems as well as knowledge resources needed to perform administrative processes or to deliver

[1]FZI at the University of Karlsruhe, Haid-und-Neu Strasse 10-14, 76131. Karlsruhe, Germany
nstojano@fzi.de

[2]University of Piraeus, Karaoli & Dimitriou 80, Piraeus, Greece 185 34,
dapost@unipi.gr

[3]Institute of Communication and Computer Systems, National Technical University of Athens, Iroon Polytechniou 9, Zografou, Athens, Greece 157 80,
{dioudis, gmentzas}@mail.ntua.gr

e-government services [2]. In particular, several factors make knowledge resources in public administrations subject to continual change:

- First, the environment in which an e-government system operates can change, thereby invalidating assumptions made when the system was built. For example, new laws and regulations require adaptation of tacit knowledge.
- Second, public servants' requirements often change after the e-government system has been built, warranting system adaptation. For example, hiring new employees might lead to low competencies and greater diversity in the government, which the system must reflect.
- Third, the processing of unpredictable requests and exceptions arises unanticipated "knowledge needs". Increasing citizen migration and movement across states creates complex cases for public administrations. For example, a request for issuing an EU driving licence based on an existing domestic driving licence demands a quite complex decision making process depending on many parameters like the origin country, driving experience etc.

In Europe in particular, the importance of supporting better management of continually changing knowledge is paramount due to the evolution of Europe towards a multicultural and multi-national society. The continuous accession of new member states in the European Union has paved the way for new legislation, regulations and corresponding changes that affect the way Public Administrations are organised and operate. These changes impose the need for updating the knowledge resources, which in turn are often heterogeneous and fragmented.

The SAKE project develops a system that aims to consistently manage changes in knowledge resources by introducing semantic technologies that can enable a formal and explicit representation of changes. Ontologies can enable efficient reasoning about effects of changes on the process of updating knowledge resources and transferring it between knowledge workers. Parallel to the monitoring of explicit and tacit changes, the SAKE system aims to manage the attention of public servants through the (sometimes overwhelming) information by monitoring knowledge resources, being aware of changes to them, evaluating changes and ensuring that public servants are notified accordingly. Moreover, the technical infrastructure of the SAKE system includes a content management system (CMS) and a groupware system (GWS) that are used as the primary sources of explicit and tacit knowledge resources. The CMS and GWS are used to illustrate the value added services of SAKE but they can be replaced by third-party systems containing knowledge resources (e.g. a database or a collaboration tool).

In this paper we present how the SAKE Information ontology models formally and explicitly the different kinds of knowledge resources with their respective structures, access and format properties and illustrate how the Change ontology supports systematic management of changes in knowledge resources. In the remaining of the paper, we give an analysis of knowledge resources in the e-Government domain and their changeability, we present our approach to change

management, and we give examples how the Change ontology can support
systematic representation of changes in knowledge resources.

2 Analysis of Knowledge Resources in Public Administrations

A main objective in developing the SAKE system is the ability to ensure
consistent access to up-to-date knowledge resources. To capture the concept of
knowledge resources in public administrations, we can proceed with the
W3C/IETF definition for resource, which is "anything that has identity". Familiar
examples include an electronic document, an image, a service (e.g., "today's
weather report for Paris"), and a collection of other resources. Not all resources
are network "retrievable"; e.g., human beings, corporations, and bound books in a
library can also be considered resources. A resource is "anything": physical things
(e.g., books, cars, people), digital things (e.g., Web pages, digital images),
conceptual things (e.g., colours, points in time).

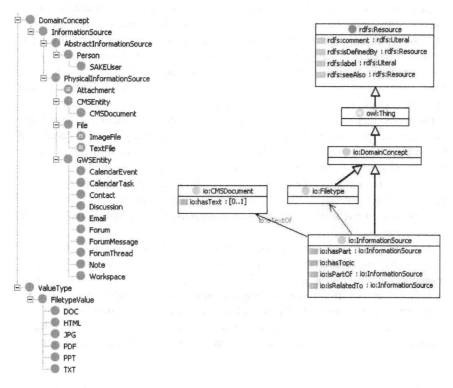

Fig. 1 Information ontology: a) Class hierarchy, b) Class diagram

The above resource set is too wide for our purposes. In order to manage knowledge resources in SAKE, we have to deal with the type of resources which can be captured and mapped into the SAKE system. Hence, we developed the Information ontology, that contains concepts and relations of which we want to express changes, such as documents of the CMS and forum messages of the GWS. Fig. 1 presents the Information ontology. In the DomainConcept subtree we differentiate between resources which are of an abstract nature (such as persons) and resources which physically exist in the SAKE system, such as documents, forums or e-mails. We further divided the resources into CMS specific and GWS specific entities. Fig. 1b depicts the internal organisation of the aforementioned classes.

3   Change Management via Ontology Evolution

Change management of knowledge resources is a key issue, from many aspects. Without proper change management the quality of knowledge resources can not be guaranteed. Change is the word used to describe the transition that occurs from same to different. Change in a knowledge resource is a change in its "identity", like change in its content, change in its metadata or change in its context. It is clear that an ad hoc management of changes in knowledge resources might work only for particular cases. Moreover, it can scale neither in space nor in time. Therefore, in order to avoid drawbacks in the long run, the change management must be treated in a more systematic way. It is especially important for the applications that are distributed over different systems, such as knowledge management applications that enable integration of various, physically distributed knowledge resources differing in the structure and the level of formality. In order to avoid unnecessary complexity and possible failures and to ensure the realization of a request for a change, the change management should deal with the conceptual model of such an application. Therefore in this paper we consider change management in the context of the management of the conceptual model of an application.

For ontology-based applications, to improve the speed and to reduce costs of their modification, changes have to be reflected on the underlying ontology. Moreover, as ontologies grow in size, the complexity of change management increases significantly. If the underlying ontology is not up-to-date, then the reliability, accuracy and effectiveness of the system decrease significantly [5]. For example, an obsolete classification of information objects in an ontology-based knowledge management system decreases the precision of the knowledge retrieval process.

Since the SAKE system is ontology-based, we consider ontology evolution as the focal point of our approach. This means that the notion of change will be interpreted as a basic characteristic of an ontology, i.e., a change is an ontology-related artifact and will be managed using ontology-based methods and tools. The task of the ontology evolution is to formally interpret all requests for changes coming from different sources (e.g. users, internal processes, business environment) and to perform them on the ontology and depending artifacts while keeping consistent all of them.

In our approach, the core ontology evolution process [10], [11], [12] starts with representing a request for a change formally and explicitly as one or more ontology changes (cf. Fig. 2). Then, the "semantics of change" phase prevents inconsistencies by computing additional changes that guarantee the transition of the ontology into another consistent state. In the "change propagation" phase all dependent artifacts (distributed ontology instances, dependent ontologies and applications using the ontology that has to be changed) are updated. During the change implementation phase required and derived changes are applied to the ontology in a transactional manner.

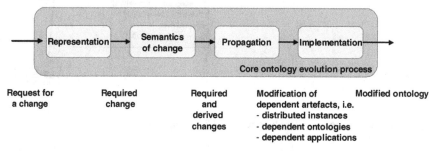

Fig. 2. Four elementary phases of the ontology evolution

In the remaining of the paper we focus on the Change ontology and we present how it can be introduced as a means to represent changes.

4   Representing Changes Using the Change Ontology

There are many sources of changes that can affect a knowledge resource, like adding, removing, deleting a new document or starting a new discussion. The Change ontology is used for representing these changes in a suitable format as shown in Fig. 3. There are four subclasses of Event: AddEvent, RemoveEvent, ChangeEvent and AccessEvent.

AddEvent is responsible for the creation of new events, e.g. a new document has been added to the SAKE CMS. It contains two subclasses (cf. Figure 3a): AddToCMSEvent, meaning the addition of a resource to the CMS and

AddToParentEvent, meaning the addition of an existing child to a parent element, e.g. posting a new message to a discussion thread (Fig. 4).

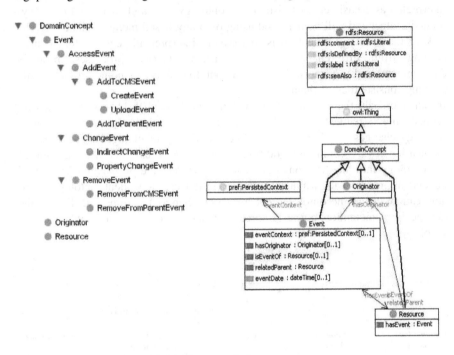

Fig. 3. Change ontology: a) Class hierarchy, b) Class diagram

RemoveEvent is dedicated to the deletion of the existing elements from the system, like the deletion of a document from CMS. It consists of RemoveFromCMSEvent, meaning the removal of a resource from the CMS and RemoveFromParentEvent, meaning the removal of a child from a parent element, but the child is still existent.

ChangeEvent is responsible for the modification of an existing individual, e.g., the change in the name of the author of a document. It consists of: PropertyChangeEvent, meaning that some properties of an individual have changed and IndirectChangeEvent, meaning a change caused by some other event.

AccessEvent is dedicated to the access of an existing individual. It represents a very broad class of events like reading a document, for which is very complicated to define the semantics clearly. For example, did someone who opened the document and closed it after five minutes, read the document or just opened, considered it as not interesting, but forgot to close it immediately?

We differentiate subclasses AddEvent and RemoveEvent by addition/removal of resources to/from the CMS and by addition/removal of a resource to/from a parent/child relationship using the isPartOf property. AddToCMSEvent is further differentiated by either creating a resource within the SAKE system or uploading an existing resource. For ChangeEvents, we distinguish between changes of the resource's properties (e.g. metadata) and changes which are caused by some other event.

Properties of an event are the resources the event relates to, the user who originated the event, a timestamp when the event occurred, an optional description of the event and a copy of the current runtime context. In the case of ChangeEvents we add the names of the resource's changed properties, and optionally link to another event which caused this ChangeEvent.

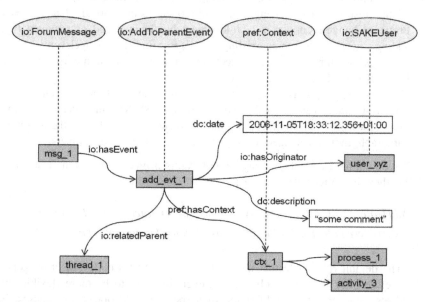

Fig. 4. AddToParentEvent for adding a new message to a thread

The following considerations are assumed:

- A knowledge resource is associated with multiple events, the first event is always an AddToCMSEvent (addition to the CMS). Then multiple events of different kinds can follow. After a RemoveFromCMSEvent (removal of the resource) no other events follow.
- In order to see which aspect of the resource has changed, we associate the names of the changed properties with the event.
- If the event has been caused by another event (e.g. the modification of a thread has been caused by the addition of a new message, see below), then an IndirectChangeEvent is generated which links to the original event via the causedBy property.

Special attention has to be paid if we define events for "compound" resources, i.e. resources which have child resources. Take a forum in the SAKE GWS for instance: There we have forums, which consist of multiple threads which consist of multiple messages. Now, imagine that someone adds a new message to a thread. It is clear that by adding a new message to a thread we can consider the thread as changed, thus creating an AddToParentEvent for the message and an IndirectChangeEvent for the thread.

In order to resolve this issue, we define the following as the default behaviour:

- Compound resources state their parent/child relationship by the property isPartOf or a sub-property thereof.
- For compound resources, a ChangeEvent will be generated if (i) the properties of the resource itself change (i.e. title of a forum thread changes) ==> PropertyChangeEvent; or if a child object has been added or removed (e.g. adding a new message to an existing thread) ==> IndirectChangeEvent.
- The modification of a child object does not result in a modification (i.e. IndirectChangeEvent) of the parent.
- The developers programmatically create only the most basic event, e.g. a PropertyChangeEvent or a AddToParentEvent. SWRL rules decide whether this event triggers an IndirectChangeEvent or not as described in the following paragraph. IndirectChangeEvents are never created by the developers.

We do not hard-code the propagation of events from child to parent, instead we define them in SWRL rules, such as:

$$AddToParentEvent(?e) \land hasEvent(?res,?e) \land relatedParent(?e,?res2)$$

$$\land swrlx : createIndividual(?e) \Rightarrow IndirectChangeEvent(?e2) \land hasEvent(?res,?e)$$

The default rules state that the addition/removal of a child object triggers a ChangeEvent for the parent object. However, in order to be more flexible, we could also state that the modification of a specific child object also causes the modification of its parent.

5   Related Work and Conclusions

Change management aims to ensure the integrity of the successor state of an environment after some changes have been performed. In the software engineering domain, there have been numerous efforts to develop change management or configuration control tools encompassing changes affecting every kind of software deliverable and artifact [4]; see for example change management tools for COTS-based systems [7], object-oriented systems [1] and business process management systems [13].

In the e-Government domain, several change management frameworks have been proposed, focusing mainly on supporting humans organize and systematically resolve requests for changes (see e.g. [14] [8]). In [9], requests for changes in an e-Government system have been modelled as cases using XML in an effort to represent changes in a broadly accepted standard and in order to preserve available knowledge about the ways requests for changes were handled so that this knowledge can be re-used in new governmental environments.

Although the importance of managing changes in systems that handle knowledge resources has been studied [3], to the authors' knowledge the corresponding methods and tools are still not yet realized at large. The primary reason has been the immaturity of the large-scale and long-living ontology-based applications in the industry, so that the long run pay-off could not be easily accounted for. The explosive development in the research and implementation of the Semantic Web has opened new challenges for the efficient development and the maintenance of ontologies that often underlie knowledge management systems.

A component-based framework for ontology evolution [6] based on the different representations of ontology changes covers the following tasks: (i) data transformation; (ii) ontology update; (iii) consistent reasoning; (iv) verification and approval; and (v) data access. Our system, although does not support data access provides means for the user-driven ontology evolution, allowing the ontology engineers to specify strategies for updating when changes in an ontology occur. Our approach is in-line with business approaches such as Prosci's change management model (www.change-management.com) in which strategy development for dealing with changes is a key step.

The Methontology [2] ontology engineering methodology addresses the ontology lifecycle based on evolving prototypes, not focusing, however, on the requirements for distributed, loosely controlled and dynamic ontology engineering. On the contrary, the evolution of dependent and distributed ontologies in a systematic way is one of main foci areas of our approach.

In this paper we presented an ontology-based approach for the systematic management of changes in knowledge resources in the e-Government domain. The approach has been implemented in the SAKE semantics-based software framework. A natural extension of the work presented herein is allowing expressive description of user preferences, which will enable matching changes in the available knowledge resources with the users preferences as well as alerting the user about the recent changes in the knowledge resources that are matching his/her preferences. To this end, we are developing a preference ontology along with a preference editor and a preference matching module responsible for matching the complete set of relevant information and ranking it based on the user's preferences.

Acknowledgements

Our thanks to the European Commission for partially funding the SAKE project.

References

1. Chaumun, M.A., Kabaili, H., Keller, R.K., Lustman, F.: A change impact model for changeability assessment in object-oriented software systems. In: Proceedings of the Third European Conference on Software Maintenance and Reengineering, pp. 130—138 (1999)
2. Fernandez-Lopez, M., Gomez-Perez, A., Sierra, J.P., Sierra, A.P.: Building a chemical ontology using methontology and the ontology design environment, IEEE Intelligent Systems, Volume 14, Number 1, pp.37-46, 1999.
3. Hardless, C., Lindgren, R., Nulden, U., Pessi, K.: The evolution of knowledge management system need to be managed. Journal of Knowledge Management Practice, Vol. 3 (2000)
4. Jones, C.: Software change management. Computer, Vol. 29, Issue 2, pp. 80 – 82 (1996)
5. Klein, M., Fensel, D.: Ontology versioning for the Semantic Web. In: Proceedings of the 1st International Semantic Web Working Symposium (SWWS), Stanford University, California, USA, pp. 75-91 (2001)
6. Klein, M., Noy, N.F.: A component-based framework for ontology evolution, In Proceedings of Workshop on Ontologies and Distributed Systems at 18th International Joint Conference on Artificial Intelligence (IJCAI-03), Acapulco, Mexico, CEUR-WS Volume 71, available as Technical Report IR-504, Vrije Universiteit Amsterdam, 2003.
7. Kotonya, G., Hutchinson, J.: Managing change in COTS-based systems. In: Proceedings of the 21st IEEE International Conference on Software Maintenance. ICSM'05, pp. 69 -- 78 (2005).
8. Nilsson, A., Josefsson, U., Ranerup, A.: Improvisational change management in the pubic sector., Proceedings of the 34th Annual Hawaii International Conference on System Sciences, (2001)
9. Papantoniou, A., Hattab, E., Afrati, F., Kayafas, E., Loumos, V.: Change management, a critical success factor for e-government. In: Proceedings of the 12th International Workshop on Database and Expert Systems Applications, pp. 402 – 406 (2001)
10. Stojanovic, L., Maedche, A., Motik, B., Stojanovic, N.: User-driven ontology evolution management. In: Proceedings of the 13th European Conference on Knowledge Engineering and Knowledge Management (EKAW'02), Siguenza, Spain, LNCS 2473, pp. 285-300 (2002)
11. Stojanovic, L., Maedche, A., Stojanovic, N., Studer, R.: Ontology evolution as reconfiguration-design problem solvin. In: Proceedings of the international conference on Knowledge capture (K-CAP'03), Sanibel Island, FL, USA, pp. 162-171 (2003)
12. Stojanovic, N., Stojanovic, L.: Usage-oriented evolution of ontology-based knowledge management systems. In: Proceedings of the 1st International Conference on Ontologies, Databases and Application of Semantics (ODBASE 2002), Irvine, CA, pp. 1186--1204 (2002)
13. Tripathi, U. K., Hinkelmann, K.: Change Management in Semantic Business Processes Modeling. In: Proceedings of Eighth International Symposium on Autonomous Decentralized Systems, ISADS '07, pp. 155 --162 (2007).
14. U.K. Cabinet Office, E-GIF: E-Government Interoperability Framework. Modernizing Government, London (2000)

Legislative meta-data based on semantic formal models

V. Bartalesi Lenzi, C. Biagioli, A. Cappelli, R. Sprugnoli, and F. Turchi

Abstract The Law Making Environment system for planning, wording and managing legislative sources is made up of editing and search supporting tools.

In order to handle the semantics of legislative sources, two interacting models have been developed: a rule model and a lexicon of concepts. Semantic draft and search supporting tools are based on both models, in a way that makes their interaction possible. A rule theory has been developed, which can describe the illocutionary profile of legislative texts through meta data. As far as concepts are concerned, a conceptual dictionary has been also created.

Through the search tool the user is enabled to query for instances of obligations related to particular actions or subjects, described in the query through the domain ontology. The metaSearch tool shows the related rules and additionally, if requested, finds implicit information, providing the user with a wide account on the subject and playing to some extent the role of an advice system.

1 Functional Framework: towards a formal disposition theory

The Italian NiR project has already promoted the standardization of legislative sources and its annotation by means of meta-data on acts and their

Valentina Bartalesi Lenzi, Amedeo Cappelli, Rachele Sprugnoli
CELCT, Via Sommarive 18 38050 Povo Italy, e-mail: bartalesi, cappelli, sprugnoli@celct.it

Carlo Biagioli, Fabrizio Turchi
ITTIG-CNR, Via dei Barucci 20 50127 Firenze Italy e-mail: biagioli, turchi@ittig.cnr.it

Amedeo Cappelli
ISTI-CNR, Via Moruzzi 1 56124 Pisa Italy e-mail: amedeo.cappelli@isti.cnr.it

contents, accepting our suggestion to add to the description of textual elements (partitions), the description also of their regulative functions (Biagioli 97).

"Semantics" of a text is the result both of its atomic components (terms), of their meaningful aggregations (normative micro-acts) and of the text as a whole (normative macro-act).

The functional elements suggested are called dispositions, or provisions, or rules and are intended as typical legislative statements. The formal profile has given place to DTD-NiR, while the functional to the analytical internal meta-data.

Although no linear relationship can be found between surface and functional patterns in a source, there is a consistent correspondence between text atomic items (paragraphs) and meaningful/functional units (dispositions), intended as normative speech acts. Based on this finding, it can be reasonably argued that this is no casual correspondence: indeed each provision is from a general standpoint the meaning of each basic text unit.

Functional structure includes classes and types of dispositions and their elements (arguments). This classification has been derived from legislative techniques and practices, by taking also into account, where necessary, of the bestknown theories on norms.

Dispositions are divided into two main class, "changes" and "rules" split those into the two major categories that are the subject of normative theories, often referred to as constitutive and regulatory rules, according to the well-known distinction drawn by J. Rawls (Rawls 1955): "justifying a practice and justifying a particular action falling under it", where practice stands for "any form of activity specified by a system of rules which defines offices, roles, moves, penalties, defenses, and so on, and which gives the activity its structure". Class also can be used in the semantic mark-up of complex partitions, having a more general meaning than dispositions.

Arguments are the main focus of dispositions and give them their logical structure. Its own arguments are always to be found in a provision of a certain type, to be regarded as such (see, for instance, the definiendum for a definition, or the addressee for an obligation). Arguments contents may be either single or multiple and appear in the texts in various forms: explicit direct, explicit indirect (e.g. "the aforesaid"), explicit variable (e.g. "any entity interested") and implicit (unknown).

In addition to the type of disposition, arguments contents typically make up the information of section/part titles in italian legislative sources: law maker uses provision typology and its arguments to inform about the ratio of the following partition.

Finally, the legislative text has been deeply modelled as a set of rules, while each provision has been modelled as a framework made of several well known internal components said arguments (slots). The contents of every argument are keywords that belong to a domain controlled vocabulary, organised into classes, as explained below. A double modeling approach has been in fact chosen. Disposition D-A model express the pragmatic side, how legislator organize and express rules about domain entities, while domain entities are classified and described ontologically.

The double modelling of the pragmatic and semantic profiles of texts meanings, is in tune with the Breuker-Hoekstra statement "an ontology is in the first place a set of terminological definitions built around a taxonomic backbone, while a framework is a an assembly of concepts or types of knowledge that reflect recurrent patterns of use" (Breuker and Hoekstra 2004).

1.1 Formalization of Disposition Theory

"The formal provision theory developed is a terminology (in the technical sense of description logic) for classifying fragments of legal texts. The domain of discourse is the set of textual fragments, that is to say, the formalization "talks about" textual fragments and it considers them as instances of meta-data, i.e., the dispositions structured in the terminology.

The terminology of dispositions presented here can be seen, therefore, as a theory of a possible set of meta-data that can be used for the mark-up of legal texts. Meta-data are isolated a priori and the logical relations holding between them are imposed axiomatically.

As such, the terminology of disposition presented cannot be properly considered a theory of normative concepts. The formalization of Biagioli's theory of provisions, amounts to a "logic of dispositions" and it can be viewed as an attempt towards a formal foundation of legistics (i.e. the set of techniques for legal drafting).

The description logic SHIF(D) has been used.

The formalism we propose is of a "modular" nature. We will first provide a sort of minimal theory of dispositions essentially corresponding to a taxonomy. Stronger logical relations could later on be imposed in order to enable richer inference patterns and to better characterize the dispositions at issue" (Biagioli and Grossi 2008).

For their effective employment arguments are to be synthetized and connected to structured dictionaries and terminological collections. In practice the model allows to evidence the terms of the dispositions that carry out a particular role, expliciting therefore theirs meaning in that context (disposition). The information on the general meaning of the term will be found in terminological collections.

The LME[1] system works with every classification of domain relevant keywords, from flat glossary to deeply structured ontology. More complex is the description of domain entities, more easy will be to express complex contents descriptions in the searching system queries (metaSearch). To test the LME

---

[1] Law Making Environment is the whole project of legislative drafting support, through a set of software tools and related knowledge management techniques.

system, a domain ontology has been developed, concerning the personal data protection Italian law.

2 The Role of Ontology: ontoPrivacy

Laws contain dispositions which deal with domain common sense entities (arguments contents), but they do not provide any general information on them, except the case of definitional provisions. The use of an ontology allows the possibility to acquire such additional general information. Moreover an ontology allows to obtain a normalized form of the terms by which entities are expressed, so that they can be indexed and used in the analytical meta data querying process of law document search and retrieval.

In recent years there have been several initiatives for the development of legal ontologies in order to offer a solid support for the acquisition, sharing and reuse of legal knowledge. In particular, we have taken into consideration two core ontologies: 1) LKIF Core Ontology (Breuker et al. 2007): it is inspired by the LRI Core ontology effort and it was developed within the Estrella project. 2) Core Legal Ontology (Gangemi et al. 2005): it organizes juridical concepts in classes of entities that are specializations of the DOLCE+ foundational ontology. At the same time, we have taken the LegalRDF Vocabularies as a reference. These Vocabularies have been developed by John McClure, Legal-RDF director, for the annotation of narrative legal documents in the Semantic Web perspective.

Our work focused on the study of the ontologies mentioned above in order to organize into classes the instances of a glossary of keywords extracted from the Italian Personal Data Protection Code (d.lgs. 196/2003). Therefore, ontoPrivacy can be considered a lightweight ontology consisting in a set of concepts and hierarchical relationships among them and not including axioms and constraints, peculiar of the heavyweight ontologies (Corcho et al., 2003).

The glossary, base for our experiment, has been manually created and it is made up of both specific terms of the Public Administration domain (e.g. *atto amministrativo*/administrative act), ruled domain words (e.g. *dispositivo elettronico*/electronic device) and generic words (e.g. *parere*/opinion). Synonymy, hyperonymy and hyponymy relations are identified among such terms (e.g. administrative act and judicial act are kinds of act).

Taking the relevant terms contained in the glossary as starting points, we have followed a bottom-up approach to create the ontology. Vocabulary and ontology are, in fact, closely tied with a two-way relation: a lexicon can be the basis for a well-built ontology and an ontology can serve as foundation to lexicon organization (Hirst 2003).

The classes in ontoPrivacy have been defined by analyzing the lexical entries of our glossary and the relations among them. ontoPrivacy has six main classes as described below.

Event. An event is a situation that happens or occurs, involving participants and it can be described as a change of state. There are many Event subclasses. Each Event subclass is named by a noun-phrase.

Scene. The Scene class defines places and times in which an event occurs. A Place may be either a boundary, a space, a structure, or a surface. A Temporal Expression (TE) can be a duration, a point, an interval or a set of times. At present, there are no TEs in our glossary but we intend to use an automatic annotation tool to recognize and normalize a broad variety of TEs which can be found within an input text.

Artificial Object. Artificial Objects can be tools, machines, pieces of furniture, and other artifacts intentionally made to serve a given purpose.

Mental Object. A Mental Object is a non-physical object, a thing we mentally manipulat. This class is divided in two subclasses: Information Object (IO) and Conceptualization. An IO is a reification of pure information as described in Shannon's communication theory. The IO subclass is further categorized in Juridical Information Object and General Information Object.

Legal Entity. A Legal Entity is "any natural person or any legal person, provided that it has been established under Community law or the applicable national law and has been given legal personality or has the capacity, in its own name, to hold rights and obligations of all kinds, to conclude contracts and to be a party to legal proceedings" (1999/65/CE). The Legal Entity class is divided into 2 subclasses: Natural Person and Legal Person. A Legal Entity always plays a role, that is a function performed by a certain entity, when it enters in relationships with other entities.

Role. A Role is a function played by a Legal Entity. The Role class is divided in two subclasses: Social Role played by some agent in the context of social activities and Judiciary Role played by some agent in the context of legal activities.

3 Semantic Mark-up: metaEdit

The main objective of our project is the Disposition-Argument model (D-A model) testing on a real legal domain, limited but meaningful. To such scope we have developed metaEdit, a web-based software program that allows the semantic mark up of drafted legal texts according to the provisions model and to the concepts model. The user can describe the semantic contents of each source partition, first qualifying its disposition type through the provisions model, thus capturing the basic intention of the legislator. Secondly the provision contents can be qualified through the available concept models, thus describing to some extent the content and details of each provision. metaEdit allow the user, before getting involved in the semantic mark-up process, to edit, modify and also create a dictionary of concepts to be used in the semantic mark up, if it is not already available from the beginning.

The semantic mark up includes the id partition, an unambiguous way to identify the partition of formal profile, that represents the gateway between the syntactic profile and the semantic profile. As example, we can see the following partition:

article 22, paragraph 8: *Data disclosing health may not be disseminate.*

In the semantic mark-up process, the previous paragraph is seen as a *prohibition*, with the "partition" set as "art22-par8" and the "action" argument set as "disseminate" and the "object" argument set as "data health".

When you assign the values to the arguments you rely on the ontological classes so that the available values belong to the appropriate ontological class. For example a "counterpart/addressee" argument belongs to the "Natural persons" class and the "action/activity" argument belongs to the "Events" class.

Mark-up strategies can range between two extreme ends. Documentalist can decide only explicit entities to be marked, so adopting a low degree of text interpretation. Otherwise also implicit information, detected tanks to an interpretative effort, can be added to the marked up entities. Obviously more complete is the mark-up, more wide will be the answer in the searching for norms.

The provisions belonging to the *Change* top class (*Derogations* and *Modifications* sub-classes), are dispositions acting on the other provisions belonging to the *Rule* top class. Somehow they belong also to the nature (logical structure) of the acted provisions: a derogation to a permission rule is part of the whole permission, deriving from the connection of the derogated provision and the derogating one. Then the derogating provision has typical contents (arguments) of the derogated one. Therefore derogations can be doubly marked up, as derogations and as provisions of the same type of the derogated provision.

4 Semantic Mark-up: metaSearch

The semantic mark is the condition to use metaSearch, an open source software tool to query the functional profile of legislative texts through D-A model and relied on the ontoPrivacy, the semantic domain ontology. This module allows the user to query a legislative information system on the base of two modalities of reasoning: a reasoning on provisions and their relations and/or on domain concepts and their relations.

Taking advantage of the knowledge deriving from ontoPrivacy, the searching software allows the user to formulate a better detailed query selecting a keyword from the structured vocabulary. Four simple steps are needed to create a query in metaSearch:

1. selecting the legal act having to be searched; it is possible to choose also the whole acts collection inherent the legal domain;
2. selecting the provision type: it's also possible to choose a class disposition. This selecting affects the arguments list showed in according to the D-A model. If the user choose a dispositions class the system shows the common argument among the dispositions belonging to that class;
3. selecting the specific argument. It is possible to choose the generic argument, any, to extend the query to all possible arguments of the disposition type chosen;
4. setting on the chosen argument by the legal vocabulary in two distinct manners:

   - the first approach is selecting from a semi-flat terms list comprehensive of the hierarchical linguistic relations (hyponymys/hyperonyms/synonyms)
   - the second one is browsing and selecting from the ontological classes and roles created in ontoPrivacy

The argument setting value process can involve more than one single term, generally tied to the previous ones through boolean operators.

A further choice consists in using the linguistic expansions throughout hyponymy, hyperonym and synonym relations between terms.

After preparing the query, clicking on run button, the system creates a new window, where are presented the results: the set of dispositions that satisfy the criteria set up in the query prepared. The result encompass the following information:

- disposition type
- formal partition (article and paragraph number)
- name argument
- value argument
- disposition text (on explicit user demand and extracted by a DOM parser that process the legal act in XML-DTD-NiR format)

The smallest information showed is the single disposition with all its associated arguments contents (meta-data).

5 Correlated dispositions

In the legistic tradition some kind of provisions, in some kind of situations, are linked with references. Let's call them syntactic relations (explicit links). For instance a derogation rule is usually linked to the derogated one, to make explicit this relation between the two provisions. The frequent lack of those explicit syntactic references makes harder legal order understanding.

The D-A meta-data model can, to some extent, to get round that difficulty, describing semantically relations and so allowing us to capture some correlations between several dispositions types. Therefore derogative provisions, for instance, can be further asked for in a query, founded tanks to the explicit reference, if existing, or also tanks to common arguments contents and to the type of provisions involved. Let's call them semantic relations (conceptual or implicit links).

Semantic relations between dispositions have basically two foundations, logic and technical (legistics).

Basic legal concepts, to which several dispositions belong, are related according logic rules. Constituives and Regulatives class are mainly concerned with those relations (logics of norms).

Those also are detectable through arguments contents. At present three logical relations have been individuated and activated. First one the well known logic relations between deontic concepts are used as relations between the homonymous provisions, allowing for example, when looking for obligations of a particular subject, to find also implicit obligations that take the form of claims of his counterpart. From those correlations implicit rules can be inferred.

According to legistics rules and legislative drafting practices, legislator can and uses establish explicit relations between several kind of disposition (syntactic relation).

Regulatives - Violations: Violation normally references to a functionally related Regulative disposition.

Rules - Changes: a whatever kind selected Rule can be influenced and changed by Modifications and Derogations; in this case it is normally referenced.

As explained before, provisions that belong to the *Derogations* sub-class (*Changes* class), can be marked up as *Changes* but also as *Rules*; this strategy allows us to capture and find derogations and modifications provisions also thanks to their semantic features. For instance a legistic relation lies regulative and violation type provisions: when they rule the same case in point, they have the same addressee and action arguments contents. In the Italian legistic practice regulative provisions and the connected violation dispositions are usually (but not systematically) also linked by a reference.

Related rules can be found activating syntactic or semantic (legistic/logic) relations. Those two kinds of connections, semantic and syntactic, allows an expansion of the answer, adding, if requested, new related provisions and so giving the answer more advice completeness. The metaSearch through the correlation dispositions request allows the user to retrieve further dispositions, to be added to the result of a query, and allow to show the complete result as union of the two sets: the first one extracted from the first query and the second one made by the correlated dispositions.

The aim is in general to turn as much as possible searching into advice, as a guide to the legislative sources consultation.

6 Queries Expansion: metaSearch

Starting from the results page, the system allows the user to search for the correlated dispositions. As we said, there are two correlation types:

- syntactic correlations;
- semantic correlations.

The syntactic correlation is based on the existence of an explicit normative reference between the involved dispositions, while the semantic relation relies on the corrispondence between common arguments contents (keywords).

The semantic correlation can be seen as a dyadic or 2-place relation: it puts together a number of pairs (Disposition, Argument), greater than or equal to 1, so defined:

(Dx, ax) $-correlation\!-\!\triangleright$ (Dy, ay)

where Dx is a x disposition type and ax is an argument belonging to Dx, Dy is a y disposition type and ay is an argument belonging to Dy.

The pairs can be put in relation between themselves, that is they can make part of the correlation, only if the associated arguments have in common the keywords. In other words the arguments involved in the relation contain the same terms extracted from the controlled legal vocabulary.

If the correlation pairs are greater than one, we can classify the correlation also according to the following types:

- strong: if all the pairs satisfy the equivalence between the arguments;
- weak: if at least a pair satisfies the equivalence betweens the arguments.

In this case the correlation is made by one single pair:

(*violation, action (k)*) $\longrightarrow$ (*obligation, action (k)*)

The first query+expansion example concerns the obligations about the assignment of personal data:

Query: *obligation* (*action*=assignment AND *object*=personal data).

Answer: art.16, par.1.

Then if we ask again the system for the violation dispositions syntactically correlated to the previous one, we'll get the new results page where the correlated violations are showed with a different color and listed above the disposition associated.

Second Query: (related) *violation*

Second global Answer: art.16, par.1 + art.162, par. 1.

A second example concerns the data controller obligations regarding the data subject.

Query: *obligation* (*addressee*=data controller AND *counterpart*=data subject);

Answer: art.52, par.4.

Starting from these result set, metaSearch allows the user to retrieve the claims semantically correlated (i.e. implicit obligations), according to a well known deontic relation between obligation and claim concepts.

Second Answer: art.52, par.4 + art.8, par. 2.
This type of correlations enable the user to catch different law maker's styles: in other words an obligation of someone can be expressed also as a claim of the counterpart.

A further question on related derogations will produce a final global answer:

Answer: art7, par.5 + art.10, par.5.

7 Conclusions: Searching for Rules rather than Documents

Surface descriptions of a source results into defining documentary units, such as articles and paragraphs. Pragmatic and semantic contents description models add virtual documentary units of substantive character to information systems: legislative rules and their arguments contents.

The traditional search for legal texts or articles will be coupled with the conceptual search by normative provisions and their contents. The system will be required to yield units (articles, paragraphs, etc.) including specific types of provision to be found in various laws at the same time.

This will allow easily identifying all the regulative contents provided for by all the laws regulating a given subject matter or case in point.

References

1. Biagioli, C.: Towards a legal rules functional micro-ontology. In: Proceedings of LEGONT'97. Melbourne (1997) Available via
   http://www.ittig.cnr.it/Ricerca/Testi/Biagioli97Legont.pdf
2. Biagioli, C., Grossi, D.: Towards a Formal Foundation of Meta Drafting. (To appear 2008)
3. Breuker, J., Hoekstra, R.: Epistemology and ontology in core ontologies: FOLaw and LRI- Core, two core ontologies for law. In: Proceedings of EKAW Workshop on Core ontologies. Northamptonshire (2004)
4. Breuker, J., Hoekstra, R., Boer, A., van den Berg, K., Rubino, R., Sartor, G., Palmirani, M., Wyner, A., Bench-Capon, T.: OWL ontology of basic legal concepts (LKIF-Core). Deliverable 1.4, Estrella (2007)
5. Corcho, O., Fernndez-Lpez, M., Gmez-Prez, A.: Methodologies, tools and languages for building ontologies. Where is their meeting point? Data & Knowledge Engineering 46(1) 41–64 (2003)
6. Gangemi, A., Sagri, M., Tiscornia, D.: Constructive framework for legal ontologies. In: Law and the Semantic Web. Springer Verlag (2005)
7. Hirst, G.: Ontology and the lexicon. In: Handbook on Ontologies in Information Systems. Springer Verlag, (2003)
8. Rawls J.: Two Concepts of Rule. Philosophical Review 64 3–32 (1955)

Enriching WordNet to Index and Retrieve Semantic Information

Angioni Manuela, Demontis Roberto, Tuveri Franco

Abstract. The work illustrated in this paper is part of the DART search engine. Its main goal is to index and retrieve information both in a generic and in a specific context where documents can be mapped or not on ontologies, vocabularies and thesauri. To achieve this goal, a semantic analysis process on structured and unstructured parts of documents is performed. The unstructured parts need a linguistic analysis and a semantic interpretation performed by means of Natural Language Processing (NLP) techniques, while the structured parts need a specific parser. Semantic keys are extracted from documents starting from the semantic net of WordNet and enriching it of new nodes, links and attributes.

1 Introduction

The work illustrated in this paper is a part of the DART [1, 2] search engine. The aim of the DART project is to realize a distributed architecture for a semantic search engine, facing the user with relevant resources in reply to a query related to a specific domain of interest. It focuses on geo-referencing features, in order to supply position based information strictly related to a user indicated area.

Our main goal is to index and retrieve information both in a generic and in a specific context whether documents can be mapped or not on ontologies, vocabularies and thesauri. To achieve this goal, a semantic analysis process on structured and unstructured parts of documents is performed. he first step of this process is to identify structured and unstructured parts of a document. The structured portions are identified by ontologies or structure descriptor

Angioni M., Demontis R., Tuveri F.
CRS4 - Center for Advanced Studies, Research and Development in Sardinia,
Polaris Edificio 1, 09010 Pula (CA), Italy
email: {angioni, demontis, tuveri}@crs4.it

as in the case of dynamic XML documents generated by Web services, RDF and OWL documents, if they are known by the system.

In the second step the semantic analysis is performed. The unstructured parts need a linguistic analysis and a semantic interpretation performed by means of Natural Language Processing (NLP) techniques, while the structured parts need a specific parser.

Finally, the system extracts the correct semantic keys that represent the document. These keys are defined starting from the semantic net of WordNet [3], a lexical dictionary for the English language that groups nouns, verbs, adjectives and adverbs into synonyms sets, called synsets, linked by relations, such as meronymy, synonymy or hyperonymy/hyponymy. The system uses a semantic net, called SemanticNet, derived from the WordNet semantic net by adding new nodes, links and attributes. For example the system geo-references the nodes by using the Geonames Database [4].

Section 2 describes how the system behaves in the general context while section 3 does it in specific contexts. Section 4 describes how the SemanticNet is obtained from WordNet and finally section 5 presents a use case related to a GIS (Geographical Information System) specific domain.

2 The generic context

Usually the system doesn't know the specific ontology or the thesaurus describing the context of the document. The main activity of the system is to index and retrieve web resources, by extracting semantic keys from a document or a user query through a syntactic and a semantic analysis and to identify them by a descriptor which is stored in a Distributed Hash Tables, DHT [1].

The semantic keys can be one of the following types of identifiers: a concept of WordNet represented by a synset ID; a category of WordNet Domains [5] represented by its name and a key composed by a category name and a word not included in the WordNet vocabulary. Semantic keys are extracted using the same procedure both in the indexing and in the searching phase, but different analysis are performed in structured and unstructured parts of the document identified in the first step of the document analysis.

Structured parts of a document related to an explicit semantic (XML, RDF, OWL, etc) and defined by a known formal or terminological ontology are parsed by the system. The results are concepts of the ontology, so that the system has to know their mapping onto a concept of the WordNet ontology [6].

This conceptual mapping could reduce the quality of the information, but in a generic context the concepts are evaluated using the WordNet point of view on the formal or terminological ontology which defines the structured part of the document. The goal of the conceptual mapping is to allow a better navigation between concepts defined in two ontologies, using a shared semantics. In this context, the more accurate the conceptual mapping will be, the better the response of the system. This process is managed by an external module of the system, which the user can add or remove. The module can also extract the specialized semantics keys from the structured part of a document and return the generic semantic key mapped to these keys by means of the conceptual mapping. Several instruments, such as SKOS (Simple Knowledge Organisation Systems) [7] a formal description, can be used into the specialized module in order to represent the conceptual mapping.

Unstructured parts need a linguistic analysis and a semantic interpretation to be performed by means of NLP techniques. The main tools involved are:

- the Syntactic Analyzer and Disambiguator, mainly composed by a syntactic analyzer, that uses the Link Grammar parser [8], a highly lexical, context-free formalism, in order to identify the syntactical structure of sentences, and to resolve the terms' roles ambiguity in natural languages;

- the Semantic Analyzer and Disambiguator analyzes each sentence identifying roles, meanings of terms and semantic relations in order to extract "part of speech" information, the synonymy and hypernym relations from the WordNet semantic net and to evaluate terms contained in the document by means of a density function based on the synonyms and hypernyms frequency [9];

- the Classifier is able to classifying documents automatically, applying a classification algorithm based on the Dewey Decimal Classification (DDC), as proposed in WordNet Domains [5, 10], a lexical resource representing domain associations between terms.

The semantic keys resulting from the analysis of structured parts, the linguistic analysis and the semantic interpretation of unstructured parts are of three types:

- a synset ID identifying a node of the WordNet semantic net

- a category name given by a possible classification

- a key composed by a word and a document category, i.e. when the semantic key related to the word is not included in the WordNet vocabulary.

Finally, all semantic keys are used to index the document whereas in searching phase they are used in order to retrieve document descriptors using the SemanticNet through the concept of semantic vicinity.

3 A specific context

In a specific context the system adopts a formal or terminological ontology describing the specific semantic domain. The semantic keys are the identifiers of concepts in the specialized ontology and the classification is performed using the taxonomy defined in it. The tools managing a specific context are in a separated module and can be added or removed from the system by the user. Different analysis are performed in structured and unstructured parts of the document, as identified in the first step of the document analysis. Moreover two types of indexing are performed: one with a set of generic semantic keys and the other with a set of specialized semantic keys.

If a document contains a structured part related to a specific context, all of the specialized semantic keys are directly extracted by the module. Otherwise the system performs the same analysis as in the general context and adds the result to the generic semantic keys set. Then, the extracted keys have to be mapped into specialized semantic keys. In this way a conceptual mapping between the specific semantics domain ontology and the WordNet ontology is needed in the design phase of the module. However, the conceptual map is not always exhaustive. Each time a concept can not be mapped into a synset ID, it is mapped into a new unique code.

The conceptual mapping of a specialized concept returns a WordNet concept or its textual representation as a code or a set of words. The main idea of such conceptual mapping is to represent the point of view of the specialized ontology about the WordNet ontology. The conceptual mapping defines the relation 'SAME_AS' that connects WordNet's synset IDs with concepts of the specialized ontology.

Using this relation, it is possible to build a specialized Semantic Net (sSN) that comply with the following properties:

1.   A sSN node represents a concept in the specialized ontology.
2.   A sSN node has at least one sSN relation with another sSN node or with a node in the SemanticNet with the 'SAME_AS' relation.
3.   A sSN relation has to be consistent to the same relation in the SN. A similar example could be the 'broader' relation described in SKOS, which identifies a more general concept in meaning. The 'broader' relation can be mapped to the "IS_A" if the mapping is consistent to the "IS_A" relation derived from WordNet 'hyponymy' relation.

In this way, a generic semantic key extracted from the unstructured parts of the document can identify a specialized semantic key if a mapping between the two concepts exists. After the extraction of the semantic keys, the system performs the classification related to the generic and specific context. So the document is indexed using two sets of keys and classifications: one related to the generic context and the other to the specialized context. The system can search documents using a specialized semantic key, for example a URI [11], or a generic semantic key and the other one with a semantic vicinity in the sSN or SN. An example of specific context module can be found in section 5 where the specific ontology is a terminological ontology for the GIS specific context.

4 The enriched Semantic Net

The difficulty to create a conceptual map of knowledge in an automatic way is a very relevant problem. In the specific context of DART, we think that the answer to a user query can be given providing the user with several kind of results, some not necessarily related in the standard way the search engines we use today do. It is very hard to build a conceptual map in an automatic way using documents coming from the Web, because the difficulty to distinguish between valid and invalid contents documents. Our goal was to identify valid and well-founded conceptual relations and links contained in documents in order to build a data structure, composed by concepts and correlation between concepts and information, to overlay the result set returned from the search engine. We therefore realized the importance of being able to access a multidisciplinary structure of documents, evaluating several solutions like language specific thesaurus or on-line encyclopedia.

In order to increase the semantic net of WordNet, a great amount of documents included in Wikipedia was used to extract new knowledge and to define a new semantic net enriching WordNet with new terms, their classification and new associative relations. In fact WordNet, as semantic net, is too limited with respect to the web language dictionary. For example, WordNet contains about 200.000 word "senses" whereas Wikipedia [12] contains about 1.900.000 encyclopedic information, the number of connections between words related by topics is limited, several word "senses" are not included in WordNet. These are only some of the reasons that convinced us to enrich the semantic net of WordNet, as emphasized in [13] where authors identify this and 5 other weaknesses in the WordNet semantic net constitution.

We call "SemanticNet" the enriched semantic net of WordNet.

We choose a multidisciplinary, multilingual, web-based, free content document encyclopedia, such as Wikipedia, excluding other solutions such as thesaurus or on-line encyclopedia available only in a specific language. A conceptual map built using Wikipedia pages allows a user to associate a concept to other ones enriched with some relations that an author points out. The use of Wikipedia guarantees, with reasonable certainty, that such conceptual connection is valid because it is produced by someone who, at least theoretically, has the skills or the experience to justify it. Moreover, the rules and the reviewers controls set up guarantee reliability and objectivity. In fact, an author of Wikipedia has to introduce data and opinions with the greatest possible neutrality, because people from various political and ideological extractions and different cultural background concur. The control activity also deals with the correctness of the inserted topics. The reviewers also control the conformity of the added or modified voices.

What we are more interested in are terms and their classification in order to build the enriched SemanticNet. The reason for this is that varied mental association od places, events, persons and things depend on the cultural backgrounds of the users' personal history. In fact, the ability to associate a concept to another is different from person to person. The enriched SemanticNet it is definitely not exhaustive but it is limited by the dictionary of WordNet, by the contents included in Wikipedia and by the accuracy of the information given by the system.

Starting from the information contained in Wikipedia about a term of WordNet, the system is capable of enriching the SemanticNet by adding new nodes, links and attributes, such as is-a or part-of relations. Moreover, the system is able to classify the textual contents of web resources, indexed through the Classifier that uses WordNet Domains and applies a "density function" able to assign a weight to each category related to the content.

Each term in WordNet has more than one meaning each corresponding to a Wikipedia page. We therefore need to extract the specific meaning described in the Wikipedia page content, in order to build a conceptual map where the nodes are the "senses" (synset of WordNet or term+category) and the links are given both by the WordNet semantical-linguistic relations and by the conceptual associations built by the Wikipedia authors.

To achieve this goal, the system performs a syntactic and a semantic disambiguation of the textual content of the Wikipedia page and extracts its meaning associating it to a node corresponding to the specific "sense" of a term in WordNet (synset) or, if it does not exists in WordNet, adding to the SemanticNet a new node (term + category). For example, the term *jellyfish* in WordNet corresponds to the Wikipedia page that has the same title as the term and URL *http://en.wikipedia.org/wiki/Jellyfish*. The text is analyzed and classified and animals and biology are the found categories. So the system is able to retrieve the synset related to the "sense" of the term *jellyfish* used in Wikipedia and corresponding to these categories and to associate to this node all the new relations extracted from the page itself, as well as the relation included in WordNet. Starting from the node jellyfish, the net is enriched with other nodes having a conceptual proximity with the starting node.

Such a conceptual map, allows the user to move on an information structure that connects several topics through the semantical-lexical relations extracted from WordNet but also through the new associations made by the conceptual connections inserted by Wikipedia users.

In order to extract the synonyms relations given by the use of similar terms in the document sentences, the *density function* is based on the computation of the number of synsets related to each term. Through the *density function,* the system is able to retrieve the most frequently used "senses" and to associate to the term the most correct meaning through the categorization of the document itself. From each synset a new node of the conceptual map is defined, containing information such as the synsetID, the categories and their weight. Through the information extracted from Wikipedia it is possible to build nodes, having a conceptual proximity with the beginning node, and to define, through these relations, a data structure linking all nodes of the SemanticNet. Each node is then uniquely identified by a semantic key, by the term referred to the Wikipedia page and by the extracted categories.

4.1 The data structure

Through the definition of new relations between the terms included in WordNet, we have enriched the semantic net with new terms extracted from Wikipedia. Wikipedia documents, each corresponding to a WordNet term, are classified using the same convention used for the mapping of the terms of WordNet in WordNet Domains. Such type of analysis was applied to about 60.000 Wikipedia articles independently from their content. The text of every article has been analyzed, in order to extract new relations and concepts, and classified assigning to each category a weight of relevance.

Only the categories having a greater importance are taken in consideration. Through the Wikipedia pages content classification, the system assigns them a synset ID of WordNet, if it exists. Through choosing a set of categories and analyzing manually the correctness of the resources classified under each category, the success in the assigning the categories has been evaluated to reach about 90%.

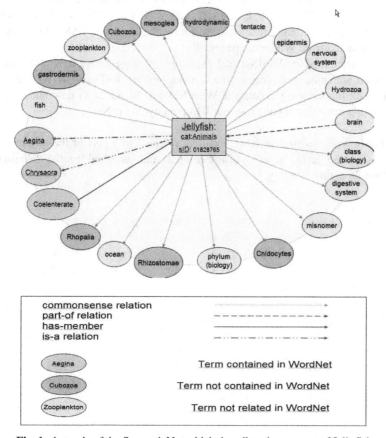

Fig. 1: the node of the SemanticNet which describes the concept of Jellyfish

Through the content of the Wikipedia pages, a new kind of relation named "COMMONSENSE" is defined, that defines the SemanticNet in union with the semantic relations "is-a" and "part-of" given by WordNet.

The *COMMONSENSE* relation defines a connection between a term and the links defined by the author of the Wikipedia page related to that term. These links are associations that the author identifies and put in evidence. From the document text content it is also possible, in some case, to extract *is-a* and *part-of* relations as new and different semantic relations, not contained in WordNet.

In the SemanticNet, relations are also defined as oriented edges of a graph. The inverse relations are then a usable feature of the net. An example is the Hyponym/Hypernym relation, labeled in the SemanticNet as a "is-a" relation with direction. The concept map defined is constituted by 25010 nodes each corresponding to a "sense" of WordNet and related to a page of Wikipedia. Starting from these nodes, 371281 relations were extracted, part of which are also included in WordNet, but in the most case they are new relations extracted from Wikipedia.

In particular 306911 COMMONSENSE relations are identified, where 48834 are tagged as IS_A_WN and 15536 as PART_OF_WN. The suffix WN indicates that they are WordNet semantic relations. Still now, the IS_A and PART_OF relations are not extracted from Wikipedia pages.

Terms not contained in WordNet and existing in Wikipedia are new nodes of the augmented semantic net. Terms which meanings are different in Wikipedia in respect with the meaning existing in WordNet will be added as new nodes in the semantic net but will not have a synset ID given by WordNet.

Here below you can find an XML example referred to a part of the semanticNet defined for the term "tiger", disambiguated and assigned to the "Animals" WordNet Domains category.

```
<node id = '52'>
    <data key='synsetID'>2045461</data>
    <data key='term'>tiger</data>
    <data key='desWikiID'>tiger. Tigers (Panthera
        tigris) are mammals of the Felidae family and
        one of four "big cats" in the panthera
        genus..</data>
    <data key='desWNID'>large feline of forests in
        most of Asia having a tawny coat with black
        stripes; endangered</data>
    <data key='category'>Animals</data>
    <port name='common_sense' />
    <port name='is_a' />
    <port name='part_of' />
</node>
<node id = '5589'>
```

```
      <data key='synsetID'>2041186</data>
      <data key='term'>cougar</data>
      <data key='desWikiID'>cougar. The puma (Puma
         concolor since 1993, previously Felis concolor)
         is a type of feline (cat)..</data>
      <data key='desWNID'>large American feline
         resembling a lion</data>
      <data key='category'>Animals</data>
      <port name='common_sense' />
      <port name='is_a' />
      <port name='part_of' />
</node>
<edge id='n032' source='5589' target='52'
      sourceport='common_sense'
      targetport='common_sense'>
   <data key='weight'>1</data>
</edge>
```

The SemanticNet allows users to navigate in the concepts through relations. The concept it is not an exhaustive map of all concepts of the human experience, but it guarantees a bigger amount of information and terms than WordNet.

Formulating the query through the search engine, the user can move through the SemanticNet and extract the concepts which really interest him, limiting the search field and obtaining a more specific result. The SemanticNet can also be used directly by the system without the user being aware of it. In fact, the system receives and elaborates the query by means of the SN. In this way the system extracts from the query the concepts and their related relations then shows the user a result set related to the new concepts found as well as the found categories.

The XML portion showed in fig.2 is referred to a part of the semanticNet defined for the term "tiger", disambiguated and assigned to the "Animals" WordNet Domains category. The XML structure is based on the GraphML [14] format, an "*easy-to-use file format for graphs*". The language core describes the structural properties of a graph and supports directed, undirected, and mixed graphs, graphical representations, references to external data, and other features.

5 The GIS Scenario

An example of a specific context is referred to a GIS context. In order to execute a coherent analysis of documents, two relevant problems have to be resolved. First the choice of the taxonomy and thesaurus describing the specific semantic domain. The multilingual 2004 GEMET (GEneral Multilingual Environmental Thesaurus, version 1.0) [15] was chosen. GEMET consists in 5.298 terms hierarchically ordered with 109 top terms, 40 themes, 35 groups and 3 super groups.

Then the problem of mapping GEMET concepts into the WordNet concepts. For example, the GEMET term "*topography*" has the right meaning in the WordNet semantic net, while the term "*photogrammetry*" does not appear at all. In such cases, and generally in all specialized contexts or specific domains, we need to define a new semantic key for this kind of term that is the identifier used in the GEMET thesauri.

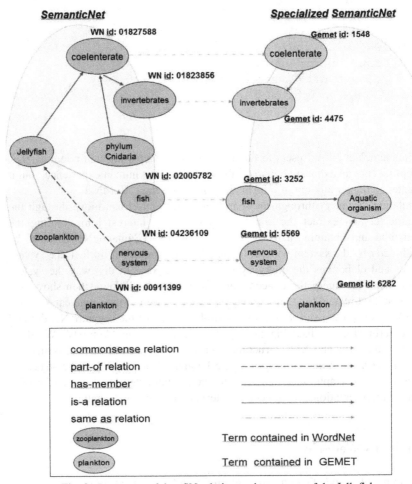

Fig. 2: A segment of the sSN relative to the concept of the Jellyfish.

In order to generate the conceptual mapping, a semi-automatic procedure was implemented. This procedure is very similar to the evaluation of the Wikipedia page for enriching the SemanticNet and it is based on two similar properties of GEMET and WordNet: GEMET and WordNet have a hierarchical structure. For example, the GEMET relations *"narrower"* and *"broader"* are similar to the *"hypernym"* and *"hyponym"* relations of WordNet. This similarity is also used to build the relation "IS_A" in the sSN. Another important property is the presence of textual description of concepts in both GEMET and WordNet.

Starting from top term in the GEMET thesauri, the semantic keys from the textual description of a concept are extracted and it is calculated its semantic vicinity with semantic keys extracted from the textual descriptions of concepts found in WordNet using the term related to the GEMET concept. The presence of some concepts such as the *"narrower/broader"* of the GEMET concept mapped to concepts *"hyperonymy/hyponymy"* of the concepts found in WordNet are also evaluated. The final evaluation of results was performed by a supervisor. A similar approach can be found at [16]. If the GEMET concept is not found in WordNet, the term related to the GEMET concept is used as the mapped semantic key.

Using such mapping makes it possible to classify the documents analyzed in the generic context with the GEMET taxonomy and to generate the sSN which contains the relations "IS_A", derived from the *"narrower"* and *"broader"* GEMET relations, and the 'SAME_AS' relation, described in the section 4, which is derived from the conceptual mapping and connects the sSN node with the SN nodes, an example is showed in figure 3.

The GEMET ontology is also used in geo-referencing of documents in the generic or the specific context. The system assigns locations to a document by geo-referencing concepts found in it. The procedure is very simple, for all of the concepts in the document the system evaluates the possible names related to it.

The names are used to query the Geonames gazetteer which returns locations with attributes: latitude, longitude, type and alternate names.

The Geonames ontology [17] contains a partial mapping between location's types and GEMET concepts.

Part of the Geonames ontology:

```
<ontology:Code rdf:about="#H.CNLI">
    <owl:sameAs                                    rdf:resource=
"http://www.eionet.europa.eu/gemet/concept/4507"/>
    <core:definition xml:lang="en">
        a canal which serves as a main conduct for
        irrigation water
    </core:definition>
    <core:inScheme rdf:resource="#H"/>
    <core:prefLabel xml:lang="en">
        irrigation canal
    </core:prefLabel>
</ontology:Code>
```

```
<core:Concept                                        rdf:about=
     "http://www.eionet.europa.eu/gemet/concept/4507">
   <owl:sameAs rdf:resource="#H.CNLI"/>
</core:Concept>
```

So by using the GEMET concept related to a type it is possible to determine the semantic of a location and to compare it with the classification of the document in the GEMET taxonomy. Moreover, using the latitude and longitude of found locations it is possible to evaluate if the content of a document is related to an area, for example a country and a continent. These informations are used to evaluate if the content of the document is related to a semantic theme, to an area or to both of them. This evaluation allows to perform the disambiguation in order to choose the right location for each name and to evaluate if the name is related or not to a location. The module is also capable to analyse structured documents that are based on the ISO 19115:2003 metadata schema standard [18], or are generated by a OGC (Open Geospatial Consortium) [19] Web Service.

6 Conclusions and future work

The SemanticNet is integral part of the project DART, Distributed Agent-Based Retrieval Toolkit, at present under development. The SemanticNet is structured as a highly connected directed graph. Each vertex is a node of the net and the edges are the relations between them. Each element, vertex and edge, is labeled in order to give the user a better usability in information navigation. For all that regards the user interface to the SemanticNet, a 3D Graphic user interface is under development in order to give users an alternative tool for the browsing of the Web resources by means of the map of concept described with the GraphML format.

Future works will include the measuring of the user preferences in the navigation of the net in order to give a weight to the more used paths between nodes.

Moreover the structure of nodes, as defined in the net, allows to access the glosses given by WordNet and Wikipedia contents. The geographic context gives the user further filtering elements in the search of Web contents. In order to make the implementation of modules of a specialized context easier, its conceptual mapping and the definition of the specialized semantic net, a future work will describe the SN with a simple formalism like SKOS. Therefore the system could be more flexible in indexing and searching of web resources.

References

1.   Angioni, M. et al.: DART: The Distributed Agent-Based Retrieval Toolkit.
      in Proc. of CEA 07, pp. 425-433 Gold Coast – Australia (2007)

2. Angioni, M. et al.: User Oriented Information Retrieval in a Collaborative and Context Aware Search Engine. WSEAS Transactions on Computer Research, ISSN: 1991-8755, vol. 2 issue 1, pp. 79-86 (2007)
3. Miller et al.: WordNet: An Electronic Lexical Database, Bradford Books, (1998)
4. Geonames, http://www.geonames.org/ Accessed 7 March 2008
5. Magnini, B. et al.: The Role of Domain Information in Word Sense Disambiguation. Natural Language Engineering, special issue on Word Sense Disambiguation, 8(4), pp. 359-373, Cambridge University Press (2002)
6. Wordnet in RDFS and OWL, http://www.w3.org/2001/sw/BestPractices/WNET/wordnet-sw-20040713.html Accessed 7 March 2008
7. SKOS, Simple Knowledge Organisation Systems (2004) http://www.w3.org/2004/02/skos/ Accessed 7 March 2008
8. Sleator, DD., Temperley, D.: Parsing English with a Link Grammar. Third International Workshop on Parsing Technologies (1993)
9. Scott, S., Matwin, S.: Text Classification using WordNet Hypernyms. COLING/ACL Workshop on Usage of WordNet in Natural Language Processing Systems, Montreal,
10. Magnini, B., Strapparava, C.: User Modelling for News Web Sites with Word Sense Based Techniques. User Modeling and User-Adapted Interaction 14(2), pp. 239-257 (2004)
11. Uniform Resource Identifier, http://gbiv.com/protocols/uri/rfc/rfc3986.html Accessed 7 March 2008
12. Wikipedia, http://www.wikipedia.org/ Accessed 7 March 2008
13. Harabagiu, Miller, Moldovan WordNet 2 - A Morphologically and Semantically Enhanced resource. Workshop SIGLEX'99: Standardizing Lexical Resources (1999)
14. GraphML Working Group: The GraphML file format. http://graphml.graphdrawing.org/ Accessed 7 March 2008
15. GEneral Multilingual Environmental Thesaurus – GEMET http://www.eionet.europa.eu/gemet/ Accessed 7 March 2008
16. Mata, E.J. et al. Semantic disambiguation of thesaurus as a mechanism to facilitate multilingual and thematic interoperability of Geographical Information Catalogues. Proceedings 5th AGILE Conference, Universitat de les Illes Balears, pp. 61-66 (2002)
17. Geonames, http://www.geonames.org/ontology/ Accessed 7 March 2008
18. ISO 19115 standard, http://www.iso.org/iso/en/CatalogueDetailPage.CatalogueDetail?CSNUMBER=26020 Accessed 7 March 2008
19. Open Geospatial Consortium – OGC, http://www.opengeospatial.org/ Accessed 7 March 2008

Adaptive Web Site Customization

Nikos Zotos, Sofia Stamou, Paraskevi Tzekou, Lefteris Kozanidis

Abstract. In this paper, we propose a novel site customization model that relies on a topical ontology in order to learn the user interests as these are exemplified in their site navigations. Based on this knowledge, our model personalizes the site's content and structure so as to meet particular user needs. Experimental results demonstrate that our model has a significant potential in accurately identifying the user interests and show that site customizations that rely on the detected interests assist web users experience personalized navigations in the sites' contents.

1 Introduction

The primary challenge of a Web personalization system is to *learn* the user interests and based on that knowledge to provide users with the information that they need, without expecting from them to ask for it explicitly. In this paper, we study how we can succinctly learn the user interests based on their navigational behavior and we investigate the insights of this knowledge into Web site customization. In a high level, our method proceeds as follows. Given a number of registered users in a web site, we collect their transaction logs and we pre-process them in order to extract information about the users' site visits as well as the navigational patterns exemplified in every visit. We then download the site's visited pages and we semantically process their contents in order to derive a set of topics for characterizing their thematic subject. For web pages' topical annotation, we rely on the use of a topical ontology which help us resolve word sense ambiguities and which also contributes towards capturing the semantic correlation between the pages' lexical items. Based on the combined analysis of the web pages' thematic content and visit patterns we model the user interests as a set of topics weighted by their degree of user interest. The modeled user preferences constitute the user profiles that our site customization system employs for supporting users' personalized navigations in their future site visits. To demonstrate the effectiveness of our approach in Web site customization, we carried out a user study where we measured the accuracy of our model in capturing the user interests

Computer Engineering and Informatics Department, Patras University,
26500 Patras, Greece
{zotosn, stamou, tzekou, kozanid}@ceid.upatras.gr

based on the semantic analysis of their navigation history. We also examined the potential of our recommendation technique in improving the sites' usability and hence in ameliorating the users' navigational experience. Obtained results indicate the effectiveness of our approach in learning the user interests automatically and prove the usefulness of this knowledge into modifying the sites' presentation.

The rest of the paper is organized as follows. We begin our discussion with a detailed presentation of our Web site customization model. In Section 2.1, we introduce our method for the automatic identification of the user interests. In Section 2.2 we describe how we exploit the identified user profiles for recommending site customizations and we show how our model adapts its functionality to volatile user interests. In Section 3 we evaluate the effectiveness of our model. In Section 4 we discuss related work and we conclude the paper in Section 5.

2   Adaptive Web Site Customizations

In our work, we introduce the use of a topical ontology for the semantic annotation of the visited pages' contents in order to derive the topics that characterize the user interests in their site visits. Following the user interests identification, we rely on the ontology's contents and the site pages' semantics in order to build recommendations that provide web users with customized site views.

2.1   Learning the User Site Interests

Based on the intuition that web site visitors are primarily interested in a small subset of topics discussed in the site's content, we designed a method that attempts to automatically derive the user interests based on their site navigational behavior. Our method operates upon the requirement that users register to a web site before its presentation is adjusted to their interests. Following user registration, the entire customization process is carried out automatically without asking for the user involvement. By requiring that users register to a Web site before this is customized, we at least ensure the user awareness of the data collection process through cookie technology. Following users' registration, a web transactions monitoring module is set into function which records for every site visitor her clickthrough data, the amount of time spent on every page, the frequency with which the user re-visits pages across her site visits, the user's click-stream, as well as the duration of every user's visit. Having collected data about the user's site accesses, we proceed with the analysis of the site's contents in order to identify their topical categories. Based on the combination between the site's thematic content and accessing patterns, we can estimate the user interests in the site's contents.

To automatically identify the topical categories of the site's contents, we proceed as follows. We download all the site pages that a user has visited in each of her site accesses and we pre-process them in order to extract a set of thematic terms for characterizing the pages' topics. Web pages' pre-processing accounts to HTML parsing, tokenization, POS-tagging and stop words removal. We then rely on the pages' content terms (i.e. nouns, proper nouns, verbs, adjectives and adverbs) and we try to annotate every content term inside a page with an appropriate sense. To enable that, we use WordNet [2] as our sense repository. That is, we map the page's content terms to their corresponding WordNet nodes and we resolve word sense ambiguities based on the Leacock and Chodorow similarity metric [16], which relies on the shortest path that connects two concepts, normalized by the maximum depth of the ontology. Formally, the similarity between two concepts is defined as:

$$LCsim(a, b) = -\log \frac{path\_length(a, b)}{2D} \tag{1}$$

Where *path_length* is the length of the shortest path that connects two concepts in the ontology and D denotes the maximum depth of the ontology. To achieve disambiguation, we pick the senses that maximize the LCsim. Following terms' disambiguation, our next step is to annotate the page's contents with one or more topics that represent the page's theme. To enable that we have labeled every WordNet node with an appropriate category tag that we have borrowed from the categories of the Dmoz [1] Directory. WordNet's topical enrichment has been performed in the course of an earlier study [19] in which we have semi-automatically annotated WordNet synsets with a set of 172 domain labels borrowed from the top two level topics of the Dmoz Directory. Given that page's terms have been assigned an appropriate WordNet sense and given also that WordNet senses are annotated with domain labels, we can rely on the above data in order to derive the topical categories that are the most likely to describe the page's theme. For our estimations, we rely on the Topic Relevance metric, which formally computes the probability that each of the ontology topics represents the page's theme and is formally given as:

$$Topic\ Relevance(P, T) = \frac{\left|\#of\ thematic\ terms\ in\ P\ matching\ T\right|}{\left|\#\ of\ thematic\ terms\ in\ P\right|} \tag{2}$$

Based on the above formula, we estimate the probability that each of the ontology topics that match one or more senses of the page's terms is expressive of the page's thematic content. Having estimated the probability with which the ontology topics represent the visited pages' thematic content, we now proceed with the description of how we utilize the user's navigational behavior, in order to estimate her degree of interest in each of the topics that describe the semantics of the visited site URLs.

To enable that, we process the user's log data in order to extract statistical information about the user's site visits. In particular, we compute for every visited site URL the frequency of the user visits. The URL visit frequency values are useful indicators for determining the user's degree of interest in particular site topics. Given that we know the topical categories of the pages the user has visited within a site and given also that we know the visit frequency of every page, we can put this knowledge together and estimate the user's degree of interest in each of the identified topics. In particular, we group the pages visited within a site by topic and we estimate for every topic the user's degree of interest as the product of the user's visits in pages relevant to the topic and the total visits in the site's pages. Formally, the user's degree of interest in topic T_A is determined by the fraction of pages in the user's site visits that are categorized under T_A as:

$$\text{User Interest}(T_A) = \frac{\left|\ \# \text{ of visits to pages assigned to } T_A\ \right|}{\left|\ \# \text{ of total visits}\ \right|} \tag{3}$$

Using the above formula, we estimate the probability that the user is interested in a particular topic while browsing the pages of a Web site. This topic preference probability coupled with the information extracted from the Web usage logs, i.e. the user's navigational behavior, constitute the user profile that our site customization model uses in order to recommend site views that match the given profile.

2.2 Building Recommendations

The objective of a recommendation system is to provide Web users with a list of recommended hypertext links (URLs) that are deemed related to their interests. A recommendation system is responsible for deciding which site URLs correlate to the user interests and, based on this decision, to present the site's content accordingly. In this section, we present the insights of our recommendation mechanism and we describe the way in which recommendations are generated and presented to the user.

Considering that we can annotate every page in a site with an appropriate topic from the ontology and given also that we can represent the user interests as a set of the ontology's topics, we can easily detect the site URLs that relate to the user interests simply by picking the pages that are annotated with the same topic in the user interests. In such scenario, our system would recommend the user a set of URLs that are characterized by the same topical category that describes the user interests. Although this approach is straightforward and could work well in the ideal situation that a user is interested in a single topic every time she visits a particular Web site; in a practical setting though this is rarely the case, since users might visit Web sites for various reasons therefore having varying interests. Moreover, the user interests might change over time, while the site's contents remain relatively stable or conversely the site contents might change and the user interests remain the same. Apparently, recommendations that rely exclusively on the matching between the user interests and the site semantics are insufficient for handling such complex situations.

To address such difficulties, we equipped our site customization model with a powerful recommendation mechanism, which considers the user's degree of interest in specific topics, as well as the pages' semantic correlation with these topic interests. More specifically, our mechanism orders the topics that the user deems interesting within a site in terms of the values computed by our *User Interest* formula. This implies that the higher a topic is in the interests' list, the more the user's interest in that topic. Additionally, our mechanism groups the pages within a site into topic clusters and sorts the pages in very cluster according to their *Topic Relevance* values. It then explores the correlation between the user interesting topics, weighted by their degree of interestingness, and the pages' semantics, weighted by their degree of topic relevance, in order to decide which pages are the best matches to that user interests. Formally, the correlation between users and pages with respect to some topic T is:

$$\text{Correlation}\big(U,(P \mid T)\big) = \text{User Interest}(T) \times \text{Topic Relevance}(P, T) \qquad (4)$$

Where, User Interest(T) denotes the user's degree of interest in topic T, Topic Relevance (P, T) denotes the relevance between the semantics of page P and topic T and Correlation (U,(P | T)) gives the probability that page P that relates to topic T will be of interest to the user who has some interest in T. Based on the above formula, our system orders the pages that match the user interests according to their user correlation values and recommends them to the site visitors. Ordering recommendations according to the probability that they might be of interest to the user, ensures that the customized site views suggested to the users facilitate personalized navigations in the site's contents. Moreover, offering recommendations that rely not only on the user's topic preferences but also on the pages' relevance to particular topics, ensures that our model can accommodate changing user interests in the sense that even if the user changes her interests in one of her site visits, she will still be offered with pages that are highly relevant to her newly detected interest. Unlike traditional recommendation systems that rely on the user ratings (explicit or implicit), our recommendation mechanism is transparent since it does not require any effort from the user and offers the latter the ability to experience personalized site browsing.

3 Experiments

To evaluate the effectiveness of our site customization approach, we implemented a browser plug-in that records the users' navigational behavior in their Web site visits. We then recruited 15 postgraduate students from our school, who were informed about our study and volunteered to install the plug-in and supply us with information about their Web transactions. We collected the log files of our subjects for a period of one month, we cleaned them from hits that were redirected or caused errors, we removed records accounting to non-textual Web accesses (e.g. video, images) and we supplied the cleaned log files as input to our site customization system. Table 1 summarizes the statistics on our experimental data.

Table 1. Statistics on the experimental dataset.

Collection period	March 1-31 2007

Number of users	15
Number of sites visited	57
Number of log files	128
Average number of visited pages per site	8.3
Average number of hits per day	156
Average number of topics per site	5.7
Average number of visited pages per topic	3.9
Average number of interesting topics per user	4.1

Specifically, we downloaded the Web site pages that our participants visited during the recording period; we pre-processed them and categorized them in the ontology's topics, as described above. We then processed the collected log files in order to identify the topic interests that are hidden behind the users' site navigations. For evaluating the performance of our system, we asked our subjects to write down for every site they visited during the recording period, their general topic interests, using the text descriptors of the 172 Dmoz categories. Note that the respective topics have been employed for annotating WordNet synsets with a domain label.

In our evaluation, we compared the topics that our participants denoted as interesting for each of their site accesses to the topics that our system identified as interesting for the respective user visits. Based on this comparison we measured the accuracy of our system in automatically detecting the user interests from their site navigations. Finally, we used the learnt interests in order to recommend customized site views to each of our participants. To evaluate the effectiveness of our site customization approach, we relied on the correlation between the actual user interests and the pages recommended by our system. Obtained results are reported and discussed in the following sections.

3.1 Accuracy of User Interests Learning

To evaluate the performance of our user interests detection technique, we relied on the actual topic interests that our subjects indicated for their site navigations, which we grouped into site clusters, with one cluster of topics for every site. We then presented the topic clusters to our participants and asked them to rank the topics in every cluster according to their interestingness for each of the topics in their respective site visits. Their rankings were indicated on a 10-point scale, with 10 indicating the most interesting and 1 the least interesting topic and were subsequently normalized so that all values range between 1 and 0. Furthermore, we applied our *UserInterest* formula to measure the degree of interest to the topics identified by our system for each of the participants. Thereafter, we employed the Kendall's distance metric [10] to evaluate the accuracy of our model in providing users with the most useful recommendations. Formally, the Kendall's distance metric (τ) between two ordered lists of recommendations is given by:

$$\tau\,(E_K, A_K) = \frac{\left|(i, j) : i, j \in R, E_K(i) < E_K(j), A_K(i) > A_K(j)\right|}{|R| * |R - 1|} \tag{5}$$

Where A_K denotes the ranked cluster of actual topic interests indicated by our study participants, E_K denotes the ranked cluster of the learnt topic interests, R is the union of A_K and E_K, and (i, j) is a random pair of distinct topics. Values of τ range between 0 and 1 and take 0 when the two rankings are identical. Obtained results are reported in Table 2.

Table2. Learning accuracy (lower is better).

User	KSim	User	KSim
1	0.1667	9	0.0666
2	0.2809	10	0.0667
3	0.1000	11	0.1065
4	0.1857	12	0.2222
5	0.2762	13	0.2122
6	0.1667	14	0.2328
7	0.2098	15	0.1809
8	.02166		
Total Average: 0.1794			

Results demonstrate the potential of our method in automatically identifying the user interests based on little data about the user's navigation history. Specifically, we observe that our approach has an overall accuracy of 0.1794, which practically means that our mechanism can successfully detect the user preferences in their site navigations in nearly 82% of the cases. As such our method can be fruitfully explored for customizing the presentation of Web sites. Next we investigate how the learnt user interests can be explored for providing useful recommendations.

3.3 Effectiveness of Site Customizations

To measure the effectiveness of our recommendation mechanism in offering customized site views to specific users, we compared the following ranking recommendation schemes: (i) **Actual Interests Recommendations (AIR)**: given the user scored interests, we compute for every page in the sites our participants have visited their *Correlation* values to the user defined interests and we rank the site pages accordingly. We finally employ the 5 most correlated pages and recommend them to our subjects. (ii) **Learnt Interests Recommendations (LIR)**: given the learnt user interest values, we compute for every page in the sites our users have visited their *Correlation* to the learnt interests and we rank the site pages accordingly. We again select the 5 most correlated pages to recommend them to our participants.

Thereafter, we asked our participants to indicate in each of the sites they have visited during the reporting period which of the pages they considered the most relevant to their specific site interests. Then for each of our subjects and interests we computed the average rank of the recommended pages, as:

$$\text{Avg Correlation}(U_i, T_k) = \frac{1}{P} \sum_P \text{Correlation}(P_j \mid T_k) \qquad (6)$$

where P denotes the pages recommended for topic T_k, Correlation($P_j \mid T_k$) denotes the total correlation values of the pages recommended for T_k and Avg. Correlation (U_i, T_k) denotes the average correlation of the recommendations offered to the ith user with some interest in topic T_k by the given recommendation mechanism, i.e. AIR or LIR. Higher Avg.Correlation values indicate better recommendations. Figure 1 aggregates the results by users and demonstrates the overall effectiveness of our recommendations for each participant.

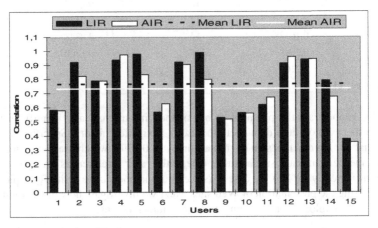

Fig. 1 Recommendation effectiveness.

As we can see our recommendation mechanism has a strong potential in improving the sites' usability for specific users. In particular, we observe that the recommendations offered by our system are highly correlated to the actual user interests. Moreover, results augment our findings on the learning accuracy of our user profiling method as this is attested by the comparable correlation values between the recommendations offered for the user-defined and the system-learnt interests. An interesting finding is that in some cases the recommendations offered for the learnt user interests are valued higher (i.e. have increased correlation scores) compared to the recommendations offered for the user defined interests. This might be due to the users' difficulties in detecting the pages that are the most correlated to their interests during their site visits. Such difficulties arise in case of deep site structures that hinder the visibility of some pages or in case of poor contents' representation in the site's main pages.

Alternatively, we may speculate that higher valued recommendations for the learnt interests are attributed to vague user interests in their site visits, which practically translates into the users' difficulty in attributing their interests to the sites' contents. Although, further investigation is needed before we can safely conclude on why in some cases the learnt user interests give better recommendations, compared to the actual user interests; nevertheless it is important to underline the potential that our technique has in enhancing the users' site navigations by suggesting pages that are closely related to the user interests.

4 Related Work

Many researchers have proposed ways of customizing Web sites to the needs of specific users [4, 5, 6, 7, 8, 14, 17, 18, 20]. For a complete overview we refer the reader to the work of [22]. Most of these efforts use data mining techniques in order to extract useful patterns and rules from the users' navigational behavior and based on these patterns they modify the site's content and structure so as to meet specific user interests. Moreover, there exist studies [11] [15] that examine the sites' content in order to extract specific features. Such features are integrated in the customization process, so as to retrieve similarly characterized content. In this direction, researchers have investigated the problem of providing Web site visitors with recommendations that relate to their interests [3]. Recommendation systems essentially match user activity against specific profiles and provide every user with a list of recommended hypertext links. In the last years, there has been a surge of interest into enabling semantically-driven site modifications [7] [13]. In this respect, researchers have explored the use of ontologies in the user profiling process. We refer the reader to the work of [9] for a complete overview on the role of ontologies in the site customization process. Recently, [12] used an ontology and utilized the Wu & Palmer similarity measure [21] for estimating the impact of different concepts on the users' navigational behavior. However, there are no results reported on the impact of the recommendation process. In our work, we experimentally evaluate the impact of our semantically-driven recommendations and as such we perceive our work to be complementary to existing studies.

5 Concluding Remarks

In this paper, we presented a novel site customization approach, which explores a subject hierarchy and Web mining techniques for accumulating knowledge about both the user interests and the site semantics. The innovative features of our approach are: the handling of varying user interests, through our User Interest evaluation formula as well as the exploitation of the semantic correlation between the site users and the site contents for recommending interesting pages. Experimental results of a human study indicate that our approach has a significant potential in customizing sites to specific users, by supplying the latter with recommendations that strongly correlate to their interests. In the future, we plan to extend our model so as to account for rich user profiles and thereafter evaluate it against other site customization approaches. However, in the course of the present study we seek to acquire perceptible evidence about our model's effectiveness before we deploy it to a practical setting.

References

1. Open Directory Project (ODP): http://dmoz/org
2. WordNet: http://wordnet.princeton.edu
3. Baraglia, R., Silvestri, F. An Online Recommender System for Large Web Sites. In Proceedings of the ACM/IEEE Web Intelligence Conference, 2004.
4. Berednt, B., Spiliopoulou, M. Analysis of Navigation Behavior in Web Sites Integrating Multiple Information Systems. In the VLDB Journal, 9: 56-75, 2000.
5. Chakrabarti, S., Dom, B., Gibson, D., Kleinberg, J., Kumar, R., Raghavan, P., Rajagopalan, S., Tomkins, A. Mining the Link Structure of the World Wide Web. In IEEE Computer, 32(6), 1999.
6. Coenen, F., Swinnen, G., Vanhoof, K., Wets, G. A Framework for Self Adaptive Websites: Tactical versus Strategic Changes. In Proceedings of the WEBKDD Workshop, 2000.
7. Dai, H., Mobasher, B. Using Ontologies to Discover Domain-Level Web Usage Profiles. In Proceedings of the 2nd Workshop on Semantic Web Mining at PKDD, Finland, 2002.
8. Eirinaki, M., Vazirgiannis, M., Varlamis, I. SeWeP: Using Site Semantics and a Taxonomy to Enhance the Web Personalization Process. In Proc. of the SIGKDD Conference, 2003.
9. Eirinaki, M., Mavroeidis, D., Tsatsaronis, G., Vazirgiannis, M. Introducing Semantics in Web Personalization: The Role of Ontologies. In LNAI 4289, pp. 147-162, 2006.
10. Haveliwala, T. Topic-Sensitive PageRank. In Proceedings of the WWW Conference, 2002.
11. Jin, X., Zhou, Y., Mobasher, B. A Maximum Entropy Web Recommendation System: Combining Collaborative and Content Features. In Proceedings of the 11th ACM KDD Conference, 2005.
12. Kearney, P., Anand, S.S. Employing a Domain Ontology to Gain Insights into the User Behavior. In Proceedings of the 3rd Workshop on Intelligent Techniques for Web Personalization, 2005.
13. Middleton, S.E., Shadbolt, N.R., De Roure, D.C. Ontological User Profiling in Recommender Systems. In ACM Transactions on Information Systems, 22(1): 54-88, 2004.
14. Mobasher, B., Dai, H., Luo, T., Sung, Y., Zhu, J. Discovery of Aggregate Usage Profiles for Web Personalization. In the Web Mining for E-Commerce Workshop, 2000.
15. Perkowitz, M., Etzioni, O. Adaptive Web Sites. In Com. of ACM, 43(8):152-158, 2000.
16. Leacock, C., Chodorow, M. Combining Local Context and Wordnet Similarity for Word Sense Identification. In WordNet: An Electronic Lexical Database, MIT Press, 1998.
17. Spiliopoulou, M. Web Usage Mining for Web Site Evaluation. In Communications of the ACM, 43(8): 127-134, 2000.
18. Srivastara, J., Cooley, R., Deshpande, M., Tan, P.N. Web Usage Mining: Discovery and Applications of Usage Patterns from Web Data. In SIGKDD Explorations,1(2):12-23, 2000.
19. Stamou, S., Ntoulas, A., Krikos, V., Kokosis, P., Christodoulakis, D. Classifying Web Data in Directory Structures. In Proceedings of the 8th APWeb Conference, pp. 238-249, 2006.
20. Sugiyama, K., Hatano, K., Yoshikawa, M. Adaptive Web Search Based on User Profile without any Effort from Users. In Proceedings of the WWW Conference, 2004.
21. Wu, Z., Palmer, M. Web Semantics and Lexical Selection. In the 32nd ACL Meeting, 1994

22. Eirinaki, M., Vazirgiannis, M. Web Mining for Web Personalization. In ACM Transactions on Internet Technology, Vol.3, No.1, pp. 1-27, 2003.

Social and Domain Knowledge Management through the Integration of Storytelling and Case Based Reasoning

Stefania Bandini[1], Federica Petraglia[1], and Fabio Sartori[1]

Research Center on Complex Systems and Artificial Intelligence
Department of Computer Science, Systems and Communication (DISCo)
University of Milan - Bicocca
via Bicocca degli Arcimboldi, 8
20126 - Milan (Italy)
tel +39 02 64487857 - fax +39 02 64487839
{bandini, sartori, federica}@disco.unimib.it

Summary. The complexity reached by organizations over the last years has deeply changed the role of Knowledge Management. Today, it is not possible to take care of knowledge involved in decision making processes without taking care of social context where it is produced. In this paper a conceptual and computational framework to acquire and represent both social and know-how knowledge is presented based on an integration of case–based techniques and storytelling methodology. The result is the possibility to exploit a unique knowledge structure, named Complex Knowledge Structure (CKS) to model knowledge about a decisional process to solve a problem (i.e. the story) from both the problem solving and communication among people involved viewpoints.

1.1 Introduction

Since the end of 1980's, several works (see e.g. [12] [13] [7]) have pointed out the importance of social context on learning, knowledge generation and sharing processes. In these approaches, it emerges the vision of knowledge as a complex entity, that is the result of the interaction between the individuals involved and the environment where they live and work. This situated approach (see e.g. [11] [5]), that is inspired by Vigostskij (see e.g. [14]), highlights that knowledge is characterized by the nature of the specific situation in which it is produced. A typical example of such situations is given by Communities of practice [15], where knowledge production and dissemination is the result of a possibly complex negotiation and reification process among their members (see e.g. [3]).

In this context, knowledge becomes an active entity: a piece of knowledge cannot be considered a fact that is used to generate other facts, but the result of a social process that possibly generates other social processes. Thus, a modern approach to Knowledge Management should focus on the development of methodologies and tools for properly representing social interactions among people involved in knowledge creation.

In this paper, we present a conceptual and computational framework for the acquisition and representation of knowledge involved in complex decision making processes, both from the domain know–how and social interchanges between experts perspective. This approach is based on the integration of storytelling and case–based reasoning [10] methodologies: the former allows to manage a decision making process like a story that describes problem characteristics and what kind of communications among people and problem solution strategies can be applied to solve it; the latter is a very useful and efficient mean to compare stories (i.e. cases) finding solutions to new problems by reusing past experiences. The result is a Complex Knowledge Structure (CKS) that allows to describe at the same time all the aspects of a problem, its solution and how the solution has been found, and that can be compared to other CKSs in order to improve knowledge formalization and sharing within organizations.

In this paper, we present Complex Knowledge Structures from the conceptual point of view: in Section 1.2 and Section 1.3, after a brief introduction to storytelling for motivating its adoption in the CKS definition, the paper describes CKSs as useful means to support CoP in the generation and reuse of negotiation and reification processes. To better explain the aims of CKSs, the intuitive example of dinner preparation is used in Section 1.4. Section 1.5 briefly introduces how CKSs can be used within a framework based on Case–Based Reasoning. Finally, conclusions and future work are briefly pointed out.

1.2 Storytelling and Complex Knowledge Structures: a Knowledge Management Conceptual Framework

Storytelling [1] is a short narration through which an individual describes an experience on a specific theme. In this way, the human being is motivated to focus the attention on his/her own knowledge about the specific theme that is the subject of narration [6]. Storytelling allows to bring order and meaning to the event to be told, with benefits for both who tells and who listens.

Within organizations, this method can be considered an effective way to capitalize the knowledge that is produced from the daily working activities. For example, Roth and Kleiner [9] have analyzed how the adoption of storytelling allows an organization to be more conscious about its overall knowledge, to share knowledge among all the people involved in its generation and to capitalize and disseminate new knowledge originated through the sharing of different stories.

The adoption of storytelling can promote the development of new professional contexts where different professionals collaborate to solve common problems, share experiences, explicit and implicit assumptions and understandings in order to improve the global capability of the organization to transform, create and distribute knowledge.

In this sense, Knowledge Management can profitably exploit storytelling as a way to make explicit the individual experiences, skills and competencies, to promote the negotiation processes through dialogues among people involved, to support the reification of new knowledge in order to make it available for the future and to help newcomers in the learning process about his/her job through the analysis of the problem–solving strategies and social context represented by the stories.

Doing so, according to [1], Knowledge Management can become "*a way to better understand the past and the present and the way to leave a personal legacy for the future*".

For this reason, the development of tools and methodologies for acquiring and representing properly knowledge involved in complex human activities also from the social context point of view is becoming a very important aspect of Knowledge Management. In the following, the Complex Knowledge Structure will be presented as an example of how this KM aspect can be captured into a conceptual framework based on the definition of Complex Knowledge Structures. CKS has been thought and designed to support the knowledge acquisition, representation and use in organizational contexts where Communities of Practice emerge and operate.

CoPs are groups of people sharing expertise and passion about a topic and interacting on an ongoing basis to deepen their learning in this domain [15]. One of the most interesting feature of CoPs is their informal nature: a CoP is typically transversal with respect to the formal structure of an Organization. Each member is bounded to others by common interests, friendship and other social relationships different from the normal day by day working activities. A CoP is an excellent vehicle for the circulation of ideas, information and knowledge within Organizations, thus they should be able to promote the development of CoPs.

When a new problem arises that a CoP member should solve, an immediate and deep communication process starts, involving all the people belonging to the CoP and eventually other CoPs. The process is typically iterative, ending when the problem is solved and generating new knowledge that will be useful in the future. This process is called *negotiation–reification* and represents the way how CoPs are able to manage their core competencies, characterizing themselves as important centers for finding innovative solutions to a wide variety of problems in a lot of domains. The term Complex Knowledge Structure (CKS) has been coined to indicate a way to represent all the features of the negotiation–reification process inside CoPs. The reason why the knowledge structures related to a negotiation and reification process are considered "Complex" is that a CKS is not only a representation of a simple piece of knowledge owned by CoP members, but also of the social relationships established among the people belonging to the Community during its generation:

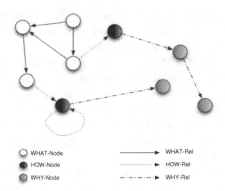

Fig. 1.1. *The representation of CKSs in the CKS–Net Framework*

Definition 1 (Complex Knowledge Structure) *A Complex Knowledge Structure is a mean to acquire and represent in a uniform fashion both the domain and social knowledge involved in a CoP negotiation–reification process.*

Domain knowledge concerns the problem–solving activity, while social knowledge is related to what kind of communications and relationships are established among CoP members in order to solve critical situations. Domain and social knowledge involved in a negotiation–reification process should describe three main features of it:

1. *WHAT* are the main elements of a negotiation–reification process, i.e. what is the structure of a problem to be solved in terms of *entities* that are considered by CoPs' members and relationships are established among them?
2. *WHY* CoPs' members work on the structure defined by the previous point, i.e. what are the goals of the negotiation–reification process?
3. *HOW* CoPs' members exploit their experience to modify or change the problem structure according to the wished aims?

In this sense, a Complex Knowledge Structure can be considered as a mean to describe the narration of a story represented by a negotiation–reification process.

1.3 Representing CKSs

A CKS is represented (see Figure 1.1) as a graph with three kinds of nodes and relationships among them: WHAT–Nodes are used to describe entities involved in the problem description. They could be a representation of people or pieces of knowledge. HOW–Nodes are exploited to identify what kind of

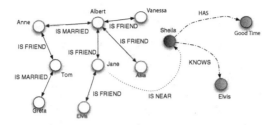

Fig. 1.2. The representation of social relationships among people invited to Philip and Tamara dinner. Sheila is a HOW–Node, since she doesn't know anyone and Philip and Tamara wish she has a good time. The solution adopted is to place Jane near Sheila, in order to make possible that Sheila knows Elvis. Moreover, Jane has a many direct or indirect connections to other nodes.

entities helps in the definition of a solution to a problem. Finally, WHY–Nodes can explain the result of the solution application to the problem. Relationships among these nodes are used to express in a completely way the negotiation-reification process. WHAT–Relationships (WHAT–Rels) bind a WHAT-Node to another one and represent a social or knowledge link between them in the description of a problem. HOW–Relationships (HOW–Rels) are established between a WHAT–Node and a HOW–Node, in order to point out that the HOW–Node can be linked to a WHAT–Node representing a part of the problem description.

Finally, a WHY–Relationship (WHY–Rel) can be drawn from a HOW–Node to a WHY–Node in order to highlight what kind of aim could be reach exploiting the solution or from a WHY–Node to another one to make clear some causal relation between an aim of the problem solution and a possible side-effect. Relationships are generic and labelled: this means they can be utilized to describe CoPs and, in particular, the negotiation-reification process, from different point of views.

For instance, WHAT–Rels could be used to illustrate a negotiation-reification process in terms of: *Social relationships* among CoP members; *Know-How relationships* among the parts of a product or the phases of a production process; *Interactions* among different CoPs.

To show how a CKS can be constructed, a very simple and intuitive problem will be exploited: the organization of a dinner. This relatively trivial case study allows to take care of all the issues reported above. From the social relationship point of view, a dinner can be viewed as a net of people and relationships among them. From the know-how relationship stand point the dinner can be considered as a set of different meals, each one prepared according to precise rules. Finally, a dinner can also be exploited to analyze interactions among different people involved in its configuration.

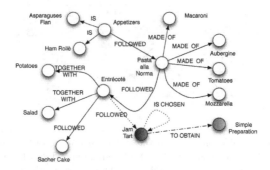

Fig. 1.3. The representation of know-how relationships owned by Tamara about the dinner menú. In particular, Tamara decided to prepare a jam tart instead of a Saker Cake due to lack of time. Thus the jam tart node is a HOW-Node

1.4 Telling Stories by Means of CKSs: An Example

Philip and Tamara are married. They have no sons, but a lot of friends. A day, Tamara decides to invite them for a dinner: unfortunately, many friends are already busy, thus the dinner becomes a very restricted event. People accepting the invitation are Albert, Anne, Tom, Greta, Jane, Sheila, Tracy and Elvis. Albert and Anne were schoolmates of Philip and Tamara and, as well as them, they are married. Anne and Tom are colleagues: they are friends, but Tom doesn't know Anne's husband Albert. Greta is Tom's wife: they married in a while after they knew, a very simple ceremony with few guests. Thus, Greta doesn't know anyone. Jane is single and she is a very close friend of Albert as well as Tracy. Elvis only knows Philip and Tamara and Jane. Finally, Sheila is a friend of Philip and Tamara they knew during a trip. She is very nice but shy and she doesn't know anyone. Philip and Tamara would be happy if Sheila will have a good time. Moreover, they wish Sheila knows Elvis.

The situation depicted above is shown in Figure 1.2, where Sheila has been drawn as a HOW-Node. In fact, the solution adopted by Philip and Tamara is to place Jane near Sheila during the dinner. This is due to the following reasons: Jane is a friend of Albert, that is a friend of Tracy and married to Anne. Thus, Jane has also the possibility to be introduced to Anne and Albert friends; Jane is the only person that knows Elvis; with respect to Albert, who could be the other candidate to sit near Sheila, Jane is a female. Since Sheila is very shy, it will probably be simpler for her to talk to another woman rather than a man.

Tamara has just solved the problem of finding a place to Sheila, but she has a new critical situation to think about: the menú configuration. She would organize a four-course Italian style dinner: a cold appetizers, made of asparagus flan and ham rollé; pasta alla Norma, that is macaroni with mozzarella,

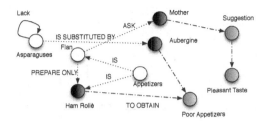

Fig. 1.4. The representation of interaction relationships between two people to solve a problem. Tamara's mother suggests to her daughter to substitute asparaguses with aubergines in order to prepare the flan. Doing so, Tamara will be able to preserve consistency and pleasant taste of appetizers. There is a causal relationship between the WHY–Node Suggestion and the WHY–Node Pleasant Taste since the second one is a direct consequence of the first one.

pomodoro, aubergine and basil; entrécóte with mixed salads and oven-roasted potatoes; jam tart with mixed fresh fruit; coffee and tea. Tamara has not much time. Thus, she has chosen courses characterized by ingredients easy to be bought and simple in preparation, light but with a pleasant taste too.

Figure 1.3 shows the representation of the dinner menú as a Complex Knowledge Structure. It is possible to notice how the decision to offer a jam tart has been guided by the lack of time: in fact, Tamara decided to discard the Sacher Cake, too difficult and time–consuming to be prepared.

The dinner day is arrived. Tamara has just come back home from the office and she has to prepare the decided menú. Unfortunately, she notices that asparaguses are not present at home. Thus, she cannot prepare the asparagus flan. As a first solution to this problem, Tamara decides to present ham rollé as the unique appetizer. But she immediately discards this possibility. Then, she thinks to ask her mother how to prepare an asparagus flan without asparaguses: "Use aubergines instead of asparaguses" - the mother says - "Do you have aubergines, don't you? Aubergines are good and you can prepare a very good cream using them. Substitute the asparagus flan with an aubergine one in your appetizer list and you'll be able to preserve the pleasant taste of your dinner." Tamara thanks her mother for the important suggestion and comes back to work on the menú.

The diagram shown in Figure 1.4 contains three HOW–Nodes: mother, aubergine and ham rollé. The first node represents how Tamara solves her problem (i.e. what can I prepare instead of asparagus flan?), the second one is the solution to the effective problem represented by the CKS (i.e. in what way can lacking asparagus be substituted?). The third HOW-Node is a representation of the initial solution found by Tamara, that was to offer a unique appetizer to invited people. This solution, that makes the ham rollé change from the WHAT-Node to the HOW-Node status, would have produced the Poor Appetizers WHY-Node, that is the representation of a drawback rather

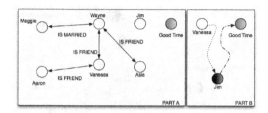

Fig. 1.5. An Unsolved Complex Knowledge Structure representing the new problem of Tamara in organizing a lunch with her colleagues (Part A) and the solution obtained by comparing the new situation with the past dinner (Part B).

than a benefit. The Pleasant Taste WHY-Node is the final state of the CKS: there is a direct consequence between the solution to Tamara's problem and to the problem represented by the CKS: asparaguses have been substituted by aubergines because Tamara asked her mother what she had to do. This consequentiality between the two WHY-Nodes is highlighted by the presence of a causal relationship starting from the Suggestion node and ending into the Pleasant Taste node.

1.5 Comparing Stories: Unsolved Complex Knowledge Structures

This representation can be used in a Case-Based Reasoning framework to compare negotiation–reification processes from both the social and know-how standpoints: let's suppose that a new problem arises that should be tackled by a CoP. CoP members starts a negotiation to find a solution, maybe exploiting past experiences that could have been stored into another CKS. In this way, it could be possible to establish analogies between a solved CKS and an *unsolved* (UCKS) one, that is a CKS without HOW–Nodes and HOW–Rels, and use the lessons learned in the past to solve a current critical situation. To better explain how, let us tell another story about a dinner configuration.

After the first successful dinner, Tamara decides to invite her colleagues for a lunch on Sunday. Invited people are completely different, but Tamara has a similar problem: how to make Jim be happy during the lunch, since he is a newcomer who doesn't know anyone but Tamara. The representation of this problem is shown by the Unsolved Complex Knowledge Structure in part A of Figure 1.5: the situation is very similar to the previous one (see Figure 1.2). Jim, as Sheila, is an isolated node in the problem description. The aim of a possible solution is to create a link to the Good Time WHY-Node: to do this, it is important to notice that Wayne and Vanessa, indeed, are similar to Jane and Albert in Figure 1.2. Thus, it is possible to state that: Vanessa and Jane are equivalent; Wayne and Albert too. It is reasonable to suppose that the application of the old solution to the new problem could be a good step. Thus, Jim is transformed into a HOW-Node through the creation of a IS NEAR link from Vanessa to him, as shown in the part B of Figure 1.5.

Through a generalization of the simple problem solving method above it has been possible to obtain an effective retrieval algorithm for Complex Knowledge Structures, based on the identification of the so called *critical nodes* (e.g. Vanessa, Jim, Wayne and Albert) in the UCKS and CKS descriptions, acting on the set (rather than one as in the example) of all the past Complex Knowledge Structures. The definition of criticality of nodes in the Complex Knowledge Structures has been inspired by the concept of *centrality of nodes* in the Social Network Analysis [8]: Further details about the algorithm are out of paper scope and they can be found in [2].

1.6 Conclusions and Future Work

This paper has presented a way to describe social and domain knowledge relationships involved in a negotiation reification process within organizational contexts where communities of practice are active, based on the Complex Knowledge Structure artifact.

According to the conceptual model described in this paper, a computational framework prototype, named CKS–Net, has been designed and implemented exploiting the Java technology, as a first step in the development of a complete software platform for supporting CoPs.

The development of this prototype has allowed to test the effectiveness of the CKS–Net framework in the context of the P–Truck Tuning project [4], a collaboration between the University of Milan–Bicocca and the Business Unit Truck of Pirelli to support experts in the analysis and solution of process anomalies that can arise during the manufacturing of truck tires (i.e. the *tuning problem*): The work has shown that the representation of expert decision making processes as *comparable stories* described by CKSs and the retrieval algorithm described could be a good approach, but this should be investigated at a deeper level of detail.

In fact, the tuning problem is characterized by few possible anomalies, representable by CKSs with few nodes and relationships. Thus, the CKS–Net framework must be necessarily tested on larger CKS–Bases than the P–Truck Tuning one.

Moreover, CKS–Net presents some other drawbacks that could represent possible limitations to its employment in solving general configuration problems: (1) the syntax is not simple to be managed. The adoption of three sets of nodes and relationships could result difficult to be understood. Despite of the prototype development with its graphical user interface, differences among nodes and relationships and how to describe them into a CKS could be not simple; (2) the definition of the conceptual model of the framework has been given in a specific domain.Thus, it is possible that it cannot be applicable to other kinds of domains; (3) from the negotiation–reification process point of view, the unification of problem description, solution and outcome into a story is indeed useful for fully understanding how core knowledge is produced inside CoPs. Anyway, this could be not true outside the CoP context, where negotiation typically doesn't exist. The analysis of the three points above will be subject of future work to verify its applicability in building supporting systems for knowledge sharing and learning.

References

1. Atkinson, R., *The Life Story Interview*, Sage University Papers Series on Qualitative Research Methods, vol. 44, SAGE Publications, Thousand Oaks, CA, 1998.
2. Bandini, S. and Sartori, F., *CKS–Net, a Conceptual and Computational Framework for the Management of Complex Knowledge Structures.*, In Bhanu Prasad (ed.), Proceedings of the 2nd Indian International Conference on Artificial Intelligence, Pune, India, December 20-22, 2005. IICAI 2005, pp. 1742–1761.
3. Bandini, S., Simone, C. Colombo, E. Colombo, G. and Sartori, F., *The Role of Knowledge Artifact in Innovation Management: the Case of a Chemical Compound Designers' CoP*. In C&T 2003 –International Conference on Communities and Technologies, Amsterdam, Kluwer Press, 2003, pp 327-346.
4. Bandini, S., Manzoni, S., and Simone, C.,*Tuning Production Processes through a Case Based Reasoning Approach*, Advances in Case Based Reasoning, LNCS 2416, Springer-Verlag, Berlin, 2002, pp. 475-489.
5. Brown, J. S. and Duguid, P., *Organizational Learning and Communities of Practice: Toward a Unified View of Working, Learning and Innovation*, Organization Science, 2/1, February 1991, pp 40–57.
6. Bruner, J., *The Narrative Construction of Reality*, Critical Inquiry, 18, 1991, pp. 1–21.
7. Cole, M., *Situated Learning. Legitimate Peripheral Participation*, Cambridge University Press, Cambridge, MA, 1991.
8. Hannemann, R. A., *Introduction to Social Network Methods*, Department of Sociology, University of California - Riverside, 2001.
9. Kleiner, A. and Roth, G. *How to Make Experience Your Company's Best Teacher.*, Harvard Business Review, Vol. 75, No. 5, September-October, 1997, p 172.
10. Kolodner, J. *Case-Based Reasoning*, Morgan Kaufmann, San Mateo (CA), 1993.
11. Lave, J. and Wenger, E., *Situated Learning. Legitimate Peripheral Participation*, Cambridge University Press, Cambridge, MA, 1991.
12. Rogoff, B. and Lave, J., *Everyday Cognition: Its Development in Social Context*, Harvard University Press, Cambridge, MA, 1984.
13. Suchman, L., *Plans and Situated Actions: The Problem of Human–Machine Communication*, Cambridge University Press, 1987.
14. Rieber, R. W. and Carton, A. S. (eds.), *The Collected Works of L. S. Vygotsky*. (Trans. by N. Minick.), New York, Plenum Press, 1987.
15. Wenger, E., *Community of practice: Learning, meaning and identity*, Cambridge University Press, Cambridge, MA, 1998.

Analysis of XBRL documents containing accounting information of listed firms using Semantic Web Technologies

Sheila Méndez, Jose Labra, Javier de Andrés, Patricia Ordóñez

Abstract This paper presents an approach to analyze XBRL documents using semantic web technologies. XBRL is an XML-based standard widely used in the exchange and representation of accounting and business information between different organizations. The proposed system takes an XBRL document and converts its information into RDF files. The obtained files are merged with an OWL ontology describing financial information domain. The system enables the formulation of SPARQL queries over the generated data which facilitate the analysis of the financial information. Currently the system has been applied to the XBRL reports generated by the Spanish Securities Commission on the basis of the accounting information submitted by listed societies with shares admitted to quotation.

1 Introduction

XBRL (eXtensible Business Reporting Language) is an XML based standard developed by a not-for-profit international consortium of approximately 450 organizations including regulators, government agencies and software vendors. It has successfully been applied in the exchange and representation of accounting and business information between different organizations. XBRL employs XML Schema and XLink technologies to describe different taxonomies for specific domains so that each XBRL document is an instance of an specific XBRL taxonomy.

Sheila Mendez
University of Oviedo. C/ Valdés Salas s/n 33007 Oviedo, sheilamendeznunez@gmail.com

Jose Labra, Javier De Andrés, Patricia Ordóñez
University of Oviedo. C/ Valdés Salas s/n 33007 Oviedo {labra, jdandres, patriop}@uniovi.es

In Spain, XBRL adoption was leaded by the Bank of Spain (*Banco de España*) and by the Spanish Securities Commission in 2005 (www.cnmv.es). In the case of the Spanish Securities Commision (*Comisión Nacional del Mercado de Valores –* CNMV), it publishes periodically via web, in XBRL format, accounting information regarding the listed firms. In our paper we will concentrate in the IPP (*Información Pública Periódica* - Periodic Public Information) taxonomy, which contains the main items of the quarterly and semester accounting reports.

On the other hand, the semantic web can be defined as a long-term vision which pursues the development of technologies that facilitate the automatic manipulation of data published on the Web. Leaded by the World Wide Web consortium (www.w3c.org), a number of semantic web technologies have appeared, like RDF to describe resources using a graph model, OWL to define ontologies based on description logics, and SPARQL, to define queries over data RDF graphs. One important aspect of these technologies is that they can be neatly combined using several tools and even allowing the system to infer new knowledge using description logics capabilities.

The remainder of the paper is structured as follows: the next section briefly describes the accounting standardization using XBRL. Section 3 explains the supervising function of the CNMV and why XBRL is important for the fulfillment of this function. Section 4 details the architecture of the proposed system for the analysis of the accounting information in XBRL format which can be downloaded from the CNMV website. Finally, sections 5 and 6 outline related works and the main conclusions of our research.

2 The XBRL standard

XBRL is a language for the electronic communication of business data. It is especially suitable for the standardization of accounting reports. It provides major benefits in the preparation, analysis and communication of financial information. It offers cost savings, greater efficiency and improved accuracy and reliability to all those involved in supplying or using accounting information.

XBRL stands for eXtensible Business Reporting Language. It is one of a family of "XML" languages which is becoming a standard means of communicating information between businesses and on the internet. XBRL is being developed by XBRL International, which is an international non-profit consortium (http://www.xbrl.org) of approximately 450 major companies, organisations and government agencies (march 2008). It is an open standard.

XBRL International is comprised of jurisdictions which represent countries, regions or international bodies and which focus on the progress of XBRL in their area. By now (march 2008) the following countries have established a XBRL juristiction: Australia, Belgium, Canada, Denmark, France, Germany, Ireland, Japan, Korea, Netherlands, New Zealand, Poland, South Africa, Spain, Sweden,

United Arab Emirates, United Kingdom and the United States. There is also a jurisdiction for the standards issued by the International Accounting Standards Board (IASB)

We must also mention XBRL Europe which is a two-year project financed by the European Commission within the 6th Framework Programme to accelerate the use of XBRL in Europe by increasing awareness and assisting EU member states in forming local jurisdictions.

Regarding the Spanish jurisdiction, XBRL Spain (www.xbrl.org.es) was formed in March 2004. By now (March 2008) it comprises more than 40 members. Its outstanding projects are the use of XBRL for the stantardization of the information that listed companies must submit to the CNMV and the use of XBRL for the standardization of the financial statements that banks must submit to the Bank of Spain.

Through the use of XBRL-standardized reports financial analysts and other external users of accounting information can obtain data quickly and reliably via automated reporting, reduce costs in processing data, and compare and analyse financial information much more reliably, fully and effectively. These advantages have been empirically tested by several authors (Hodge et al. 2004).

3 The Spanish Securities Commission

The Spanish Securities Commission (CNMV) is the agency in charge of supervising and inspecting the Spanish Stock Markets and the activities of all the participants in those markets. It was created in 1988. In 1998 a regulatory framework that is fully in line with the requirements of the European Union was established.

The actions of the Commission relate to companies which issue securities for public placement, to the secondary markets in securities and to investment services companies. The Commission also exercises prudential supervision over the last two in order to ensure transaction security and the solvency of the system. These entities are the following:

- Collective Investment Schemes, a category which includes: investment companies (securities and real estate), investment funds (securities and real estate) and their management companies.
- Broker-Dealers and Dealers, which are entities engaging primarily in the purchase and sale of securities.
- Portfolio Management Companies, i.e. entities focusing primarily on managing individuals assets (principally securities).

XBRL has several advantages for supervising institutions. Among those cited by XBRL International (2008) we must highlight the following:

- Obtain data which can be entered automatically into systems.
- Dramatically reduce costs by automating routine tasks.
- Quickly and automatically identify problems with filings.
- Analyse and compare data much more quickly, efficiently and reliably.
- Focus effort on analysis, decision-making and dealing with counterparties rather than on data manipulation.
- Provide a much faster and focussed response to counterparties.

The CNMV is founding partner of XBRL Spain. From July 1 2005 onwards, the CNMV requires listed societies with shares admitted to quotation to submit their quarterly and semester information in XBRL format. This information is publicly available to every user of financial information through the CNMV website (www.cnmv.es).

The XBRL reports prepared by the emitting societies are based on a XBRL taxonomy which was developed for this purpose. This taxonomy is called IPP (*Información Pública Periódica* - Periodic Public Information). IPP was approved the 30 of June of 2005 by XBRL Spain. It gathers the models of financial statements regulated by the CNMV Circular 1/2005 for the introduction of the International Financial Reporting Standards (IFRS) and the International Accounting Standards (IAS). The following section describes the architecture of a system for the analysis of this information.

4 Architecture of the system

The architecture of the system is depicted in figure 1.

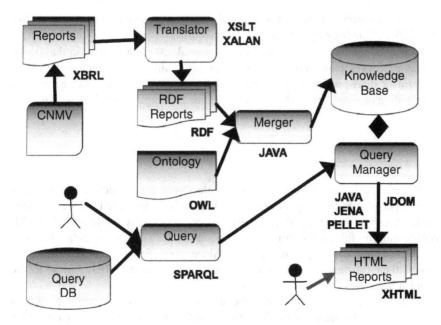

Figure 1: Architecture of the System

The main components are:

- **Translator:** It takes the XBRL reports produced by listed firms which are available at the CNMV website and converts them to RDF reports. We use XSLT to carry on the conversion. Each XBRL concept is transformed into a OWL class or property.
- **Merger:** It combines the RDF reports obtained from the translator with an domain specific OWL ontology. The ontology defines over 100 concepts from the IFRS/IAS. The results of the merger are stored in the knowledge base of the system.
- **Query Manager:** This module executes SPARQL queries over the knowledge base and generates HTML reports of the results. The queries can be defined by the end user or they can also be stored and retrieved from a query store.

The system has been implemented as a standalone Java application, although we are planning to develop a web based interface.

5 Related Work

The XBRL approach to define taxonomies using XML Schema and XLink has already been criticized by semantic web practitioners, and there have been several proposals to combine both technologies. Recently, a group has been created to that end (XBRL Ontology Specification Group, 2006).

Our approach has been inspired by (Lara et al. 2006), however, in that paper, the authors develop an ontology over the financial information which is specific of investment funds, while we concentrate in the quarterly and semester accounting information of listed firms which can be obtained through the CNMV website.

6 Conclusions

XBRL is a XML-based language for the electronic communication of business data, especially accounting information. XBRL is widely used in the financial world and many XBRL applications have been successfully implemented. XBRL is especially useful for Securities Commissions, as they can obtain data which can be entered automatically into systems. Since 2005 Spanish listed firms must submit their quarterly and semester accounting reports in XBRL format to the Spanish Securities Commission (CNMV).

In this paper we have presented the architecture of a system which facilitates the analysis of this information. This system relies upon the use of Semantic Web Technologies. Specifically, RDF is used to describe resources using a graph model, OWL is used to define ontologies based on description logics, and SPARQL to define queries over data RDF graphs.

The system has already been implemented and can be used to obtain several practical results. As an example, it can be used to assess the financial health of an enterprise, to assess its future profitability, or to search enterprises by a given profile.

The proposed system offers a great flexible way to adapt to other domains and we are planning to apply it to other XBRL taxonomies. At the same time, we are also considering to develop a web site which could offer several services for the accounting community.

References

Hodge FD, Kennedy SJ, Maines LA (2004) Does search-facilitating technology improve transparency?. Accounting Review 79(3): 687-704.
Lara R, Cantador I, Castells P (2006) XBRL taxonomies and OWL ontologies for investment funds. First International Workshop on Ontologizing Industrial Standards at the 25th International Conference on Conceptual Modeling (ER2006), Tucson, Arizona, USA, November 6-9, 2006
Spanish Securities Comission (CNMV) (2005) Circular 1/2005, de 1 de abril, de la Comisión Nacional del Mercado de Valores, por la que se modifican los modelos de información

pública periódica de las entidades emisoras de valores admitidos a negociación en Bolsas de Valores. Spanish Official Bulletin April 6, 2005.

XBRL International (2008) XBRL and Business. http://www.xbrl.org

XBRL Ontology Specification Group (2006) XBRL Ontology Specification Group. http://groups.google.com/group/xbrl-ontology-specification-group.

XBRL Spain (2005) Taxonomía IPP. http://www.xbrl.es/informacion/ipp.html

Guidelines for Web Search Engines: From Searching and Filtering to Interface

Markos Papoutsidakis , Stavroula Sampati , Ioannis Ledakis , Afroditi Sotiropoulou and Stavros Giannopoulos

Abstract In this paper we address a set of important guidelines that web search engines should follow in order to become effective. We refer to the importance of semantic web in the section of search engines which comes up from the better set-up that ontologies offer. Moreover, some of the most known and adaptive learning techniques are described in order to personalize web search engines, including methods for implicit and explicit feedback. In addition, we focus on how these methods can coexist so as to achieve high performance and we investigate the role of metadata in web searching in order to detect user interests and improve the information filtering procedure. Finally, we propose how these can be combined and presented into an interface, which will be considered as user friendly.

1 Introduction

Information Retrieval is considered nowadays of great interest in research society. This interest is focused especially on the web search engines, which are continually developed as regards their efficiency, but also concerning their usability. As the

Papoutsidakis Markos
Computer Engineering and Informatics Department, University of Patras, 26500, Patras, Greece
e-mail: papoutsi@ceid.upatras.gr

Sampati Stavroula
Computer Engineering and Informatics Department, University of Patras, 26500, Patras, Greece
e-mail: sampati@ceid.upatras.gr

Ledakis Ioannis
Computer Engineering and Informatics Department, University of Patras, 26500, Patras, Greece
e-mail: ledak@ceid.upatras.gr

Sotiropoulou Afroditi
Computer Engineering and Informatics Department, University of Patras, 26500, Patras, Greece
e-mail: sotiropu@ceid.upatras.gr

Giannopoulos Stavros
Open Research Society, N.G.O e-mail: stavrosgian@gmail.com

volume of information in World Wide Web grows permanently, more and more people make use of these engines, having different interests and familiarization with systems' environments. Thus, the development of such systems, with a way that they would satisfy the needs of all users, is rendered difficult but seductive. For this reasons, researchers have turned their attention in the exploitation of methods and technologies that can improve engines' efficiency by far. Certain of those, which will be reported below, are the promising semantic web and metadata. Moreover, nowadays, there is a huge challenge for research of how such systems could understand the users' interests, either with their help (explicitly), or without any effort from them (implicitly) [12]. Concerning both ways, we should emphasize the importance of metadata. Furthermore, technologies such as query expansion, context-sensitive retrieval [6, 16] etc, are considered of great importance too. All of them, are kinds of personalization. We believe that semantic web and personalization are the keys for the accuracy of retrieval in web search engines and will be studied below.

Last but not least, we should emphasize on the importance of the interface of such systems and the way the users interact with them. Although efficiency plays the most important role, however, only small importance is given in the interaction environment, even less if the tools that a search engine has, are many and complicated.

The paper is organized as follows: We begin by giving a short overview of semantic web and we focus on its role in the efficiency of web search engines. In Sect. 3 we make an introduction in personalized web search and we mention the creation and maintenance of user profiles. Furthermore, we analyze the concept of relevance feedback and implicit feedback, the benefits and the disadvantages of these methods and how they can coexist so as to improve the system's effectiveness. Moreover, we discuss how we can use metadata to build vector profiles and why these vectors may cause high complexity. We then refer to the issue of query expansion, how filtering and re-ranking can improve the results that appear to the users and we underline the role of metadata in these procedures. Finally, Sect. 4 refers to the importance of the interface, especially when search engines include many tools and options for the user, like the technologies we present on the other sections and then we come up with conclusions.

2 The Role of Semantic Web

The Internet and the World Wide Web comprised a revolution of the information technology but also of the daily life of person. It is an effort that achieved to exceed the geographic barriers and to connect the entire planet in a common network of distribution of information. It is obvious however, that this kind of information, after it is produced and published practically by anyone, does not have a single form. Moreover, it does not exist a single way of organisation, so that each one could retrieve. As far as the search engines are concerned, many problems are presented with regard to the excessive supply of results of low affinity with the asked, low or no offer of results, while the current technology of search engines is sensitive in the vocabulary and without taking into account the implied content. All these are considered to be exceeded with semantic web because of the different layout of information that this provides. According to the Architecture of Semantic Web Activity that Tim Berners-Lee has defined [19], we can say that for the growth of semantic web, it is essential the resources in the web to be presented or commented with structured descriptions of the content and their relations, comprehensible from PCs. This is feasible with the use of vocabularies and fabrications that are declared expressly in the region of ontologies. According to the Tim Berners-Lee: "The concept of machine understandable documents does not imply some magical artificial intelligence which allows machines to comprehend human mumblings. It only indicates a machine's ability to solve a well defined problem by performing well-defined operations on existing well-defined data. Instead of asking machines to understand people's language, it involves asking people to make the extra effort".

2.1 Web Search Engines and Semantic Web

In the sector of search engines the semantic web will offer lots of innovations.

Table 1 Comparison between content-based and semantic web search engines.

Current technology of search engines	Search engines in the semantic world wide web
high rate of repetition of retrieval, small precision	search based on meanings instead of key words
sensitive in the vocabulary	semantic focus/enlargement of questions
they do not take into consideration the implied content	use of operands for text transformation

With better organisation of information via ontologies, better and more qualitative results can be provided, without charging so much the network. In addition, the user will be henceforth capable to modulate/shape more freely his questions, no necessarily using key words or Boolean operands, and the search engine to bring him satisfactory results. This will be achieved obviously by the use of XML and ontologies, with which the machine might comprehend and evaluate logically the content of a page. Also, it will be able to comprehend the questions semantically and no simply as key words. Consequently, all these mean bigger precision to retrieval, and as a result more qualitative search results. Doulaverakis et al. [17] made an investigation about content-based and ontology-based multimedia retrieval. The experiments showed that the ontology-based retrieval is more efficient and much faster than the content-based one. Thus, in this paper one of the recommendations that we make is search engines using semantics.

3 The Need for Personalized Web Search

In traditional web search engines, searchers specify their information needs by just typing some keywords. The information overloading on the internet leads searching of this kind to a restricted effectiveness. There are two basic reasons for this. First, the interests of a user cannot be represented by a single query, because its terms are limited. Second, the user may not have the ability to clearly express what he wants to find, not only because he may not knows how to syntax a query, but also due to the ambiguity that terms have. Thus, the system should have the ability to understand somehow the interests of the user in order to return searching results that will correspond to them.

For all the above reasons, the usage of personalization could improve the effectiveness of the system, by filtering and re-ranking search results or by reformulating the given query, making the information retrieval more accurate and satisfying the users.

3.1 Definition of User Profiles

The creation of user profiles is a very important part of every modern search engine and there are several techniques that can be used for it. A user profile can be a vector, or a group of vectors of terms that represent user interests. Nevertheless, a search engine should work without user profiles as well, as it should be more flexible. There are several kind of techniques and methods that construct such vectors for a user, but in this paper we focus on the most known and adaptive.

3.1.1 Relevance Feedback

Relevance Feedback is one of the most powerful methods for improving IR performance. This technique is used comprehensively for user profiling, during short-term modeling of a user's immediate information need or for long-term modeling of user interests [2], so that the best retrieval accuracy could be achieved. The techniques of Relevance Feedback, also known as *explicit feedback techniques*, usually named so those which users explicitly provide feedback in the system by rating the articles that they read, by choosing which search results are closest to their interests and which aren't, either by typing each keywords or by filling questionnaires, to form query or profile vectors. For search engines, the method which is suggested is that of the definition from the user of relevant and irrelevant documents which are returned, sometimes by giving relative scores. By this way, the profile vectors are constructed and refreshed by inserting or removing terms and adjusting existing term weights, using the terms in the relevant or irrelevant results.

3.1.2 Implicit Feedback

The technique of the explicit feedback which was described has the important disadvantage of requiring from the users to spare time in order to rate the search results, although this helps the system to build a better representation of their needs [4]. In most cases, users are reluctant to provide this kind of feedback. For this reason, the last years, the interest of researchers is turned in the finding of methods and techniques that function without the intervention of user in the process feedback. Thus, Implicit Feedback (IF) has been proposed as a way in which profile vectors or search queries can be improved by observing and monitoring the searchers' behavior as they interact with the system [2]. Thus, the system attempts to estimate what the user may be interested in.

The techniques of IF that have been suggested through time are enough and most of them were efficient. Fabio Gasparetti [4] proposed an algorithm with which the system could identify the users' interests by exploiting Web Browsing Histories. These kinds of methods have the disadvantage of negative affection on menus, advertisements or pages that cover multiple topics that the browser has collected. In these cases, we can include also different approaches to extract information from Web pages, e.g., advertisement removal techniques. Claypool et al. [5] investigated different kinds of user behaviors, such as scrolling, mouse clicks, and time on page. The investigation showed that the amount of scrolling on a page, the combination of scrolling and time spent on a page, were good indicators for the interests of a user. Also, Joachims et al. [14] showed that clicks are informative but biased. Granka et al. [15] investigated how users interact with the page results of a web search engine using eye-tracking, in order to have a better understanding of their behavior and have more accurate interpretations of implicit feedback like click through and while reading time. Their purpose was to find some parameters that could affect the implicit feedback. Generally, they have been researched many users' behaviors by which only a few are those who could approach satisfying their interests. But even for these behaviors there should be a relevant reservation. For instance, the amount of time that an object is displayed does not necessarily correspond to the amount of time that the object is examined by the user, so it is not coincident with the reading time [2]. White et al. [18] investigated how search task complexity, search experience of the user and the stage in the search, affect the use and effectiveness of implicit feedback. What they found was that all factors appear to have some effect on these measures. It deserves however to mark that implicit measures are less accurate than explicit measures, as the users' interests change continuously.

3.1.3 Coexistence of Feedback Methods

Several researchers, suggest the conjunction of both techniques for the construction and the continuously refreshment of the profile vectors for a better representation of user interests [2]. In this case, we believe that explicit feedback should be influenced more by search results, because in contrast with the implicit, this kind of feedback expresses more efficiently what a user wants. In order to achieve this we can correlate with bigger weights in terms which come from web pages that have been regarded as relevant by explicit way from the user.

3.1.4 The Role of Metadata

Due to the increasingly amount of data which exist in the web the last years, the use of metadata, which means data about data, is considered as a very useful tool for the definition of web pages and not only. Metadata can be used to describe various aspects of the document content. As regards personalized web search, metadata could be used for the construction of the profile vectors, in order to improve the efficiency of a search. This could be achieved by inserting the metadata of the web pages which have been regarded as relevant, in these vectors. Relevant documents came up through explicit or implicit feedback from the system, by methods which were described. We would suggest the terms of profile vectors which coincide to metadata to take bigger weights, in order to influence more the results from the users' search, as metadata are regarded that represent better the content of web pages, according to the terms that are extracted automatically by several techniques. Moreover, the user should have the chance to insert metadata manually, by selecting predefined topics-ontologies from Open Directory Project (ODP) [13] or other web directories or even defining several keywords of his interests. ODP uses a hierarchical ontology scheme for organizing site listings that, on a similar topic, are grouped into categories which can then include smaller categories. The advantages of ODP are its extensive categorization, the large number of listings, and its free availability for use by other directories and search engines but also multilingual capability. Moreover, the user can define relevance weight for every keyword in the vector by such way that could reflect its importance.

3.1.5 Problems with User Profile Vectors

Although the creation of user profiles is a very avant-garde way for the improvement of the personalized web search, there are also enough disadvantages in its application, as regards efficiency. For instance, maintaining a single profile vector for a user reduces the effectiveness of filtering, since the most times it is not able to represent all its interests in order to make all the searches efficient. For this problem there have been suggested many resolution methods, such as the creation of many profile vectors for one user, with each vector representing only a portion of a user's information needed, with the precondition that the number of vectors which will be refreshed would be set. The solution into this problem gave the *multi-modal* representation of users' profiles [1]. According to this, there was suggested an algorithm of constructing and maintaining user profiles with multiple vectors, based on user feedback, with the difference that size and elements of these vectors change adaptively. Experiments showed that this algorithm is efficient enough. However, only the existence of many interests for each user demands high complexity for the system, when the response time of search engines is a major parameter.

3.2 Query Expansion

Query expansion is a process of reformulating a query that a user gives to the system, in order to improve retrieval performance. As users usually do not know the retrieval environment within they interact, the most times it is hard for them to formulate the query in that form that the system could return useful and satisfying results to them. As a result, after explicit feedbacks that users give by determining the relevant and irrelevant results that the engine returned, the query is reformulated in the base of those feedbacks [8]. The aim of this method is not only to improve the syntax query, but also to tackle problems of polysemy. For instance, if a particular user types "java", it would be impossible for the system to know if the user wants to find information about the "java" island or the programming language, as the user is unlikely searching for both types of documents at the same time. Xuehua Shen et al. [6] showed that such problems were solved with *Implicit Relevance Feedback (IRF)*, by exploiting history information. Thus, if the user typed the words "programming with php" in the previous query, then we would understand that he wants to learn about the programming language "java". Query expansion analyzes the most recent queries of the user, thus it can be used even if there is no profile.

3.3 Filtering, Re-ranking and the Contribution of ODP

An effective web search engine is supposed to have an efficient ranking algorithm, so as to make it easier for users to find the information that they ask for and maybe an adaptive filtering subsystem which will present them only the information that corresponds to their interests. Personalized web search would have been more effective if search algorithms had the personalization aspect already included in the initial rankings. However, this seems to be difficult to implement [11, 7]. For instance, PageRank is an efficient algorithm that has been proposed years ago and implemented in Google, so as to rank the results of search depending on their relativity with the given query. Recently, various variants of this famous algorithm have been proposed, for the inclusion personalization, aiming at redefining the importance of search results according to user interests. Initial steps to this direction have been made by Page and Brin [9], however it is impossible to compute one PageRank vector for each user profile. Since then, enough researchers proposed alternative methods with Personalized PageRank [10, 11]. Despite this, personalization is better achieved by procedures like filtering and/or re-ranking.

In the filtering task, the system is required to make a *binary* decision in order to find out which document is relevant or irrelevant to user interests. Thus, the search results will be less, without however this to constitute important advantages, as the user should have access to all the results that the engine returned , either these were judged as relative or not. This is also one of the reasons why the use of filtering in the search in internet is not judged essential. In any case, the results must be re-ranked, based on profile users, so as to be present in an appropriate order.

Re-ranking and filtering are achieved by the comparison of user profile vector and the vector that corresponds to each web page which is created with use of suitable techniques, like tf-idf etc. In the filtering process, we can use metadata that exist in categories as those of ODP. Chirita et al. [13] proposed a method for the improvement of this process, by taking into account the tree taxonomy of ODP categories. Calculating distances between metadata of user profile and metadata of the vector which corresponds to the web page, we can make an approximation on how relevant this page is to users' interests. Moreover, query expansion can also be applied, by exploiting history information, for better results.

4 Interface

The interface of a web search engine is an equally important and interesting field of research which, however, hasn't received enough attention. Even though they return desirable results to users, very often the latter are dissatisfied with the interface and the way they interact with the system, as most of them are not familiarized with computers and internet. For this reason, a user friendly environment is required, that would address to every person who wants to retrieve information, even for visually impaired users [3]. An important task is how these methods that were mentioned before can be applied, so that users would be able to use easily all the features that can help them. Furthermore, search and results will be supposed to be on a distinguished place on web page. The subject of the interface in a web search engine is considered to be very complex. Thus, we will focus on how the solutions we gave in the above sections can be included in such an engine.

4.1 A User Friendly Interface

A successful search engine should address to all kind of users, from beginners to the most adept. So, to ensure this sense, engine must have a simple and easy to use interface for simple searching and also, the tools that focus on the experienced users must be visible and distinctive. There are many different approaches of this issue that are applied by the existing web search engines, for example the simplified interface of "Google" and of "Live Search" engines or the more complex and with more options "Allth.at" and "Excite.com" which are considered metasearch engines. In each case, the text field of queries should be obvious in the first page, so as in case engine offers personalized search, users should be able to log in to the system.

In case we use explicit feedback, the interface of search engine is even more important as it is required extra interaction with user when he defines the relevance of each retrieved result. In "Searchbots.net", when user selects a page from list, then the browser opens a new window while a pop-up window opens too, this asks the user to score the relevance of the result, by clicking on a specific bar. This method is considered to be efficient but it is also hard to be used, because the user has to manage with too many windows in the browser. We propose as a solution to this problem the appearance of a special frame for explicit relevance judgments, in the upper part of the page. This can be implemented with modern internet technologies like A.J.A.X. while we can add even more options in this frame. Furthermore, the user will have the possibility to close it, whenever he wants. Moreover, as we mentioned in Sect. 3.1.5, if we make use of multi-modal representation of user profiles, it would be easy for user to choose the desired profile, for instance, by selecting it from a drop-down list that would be next to the text field of queries.

As we mentioned in Sect. 2, ontologies can improve the effectiveness of a search engine. Thus, we make use of this feature to present to user several results that our engine returns after a semantic process of the given query. This is to help the user to select the appropriate lexical meaning, so that the system could automatically reformulate the query.

5 Conclusions

In this paper, we presented a generalized guideline for web search engines, proposing some important technologies that such engines should include so as to improve effectiveness and manageability. Thus, we mentioned many of the most known and efficient methods of each technology, such as semantic web, personalization and metadata, in order to indicate the possibilities of a web search engine and underline the necessity of the existence of such technologies in existing and future engines. Moreover, we proposed their coexistence for better results, even though further research is needed, as regards specific methods of these technologies, which have been proposed by many researchers, by making several experiments. Finally, we pointed out the necessity of existence of a user-friendly interface for a web search engine, which would combine the output with simplicity and manageability, by presenting the above features to users in order to satisfy them with the system's performance.

References

1. Cetintemel U., Franklin M. and Giles L.: Flexible user profiles for large scale data delivery. *Technical report* CS-TR-4005, Computer Science Department, University of Maryland, (1999)
2. Kelly D. and Teevan J.: Implicit Feedback for Inferring User Preference: A Bibliography. *SIGIR Forum*, vol. 37 (2003) 18-28
3. Leporini B., Andronico P. and Buzzi M.: Designing search engine user interfaces for the visually impaired. *ACM International Conference Proceeding Series. Proceedings of the international cross-disciplinary workshop on Web accessibility* (2004)
4. Gasparetti F. and Micarelli A.: Exploiting Web Browsing Histories to Identify User Needs. In: *Proc. International Conference on Intelligent User Interfaces* IUI 2007, Hawaii, January (2007) 28-31
5. Claypool, M., Le, P., Waseda M. and Brown D.: Implicit interest indicators. *In: Proceedings of the 6th International Conference on Intelligent User Interfaces* (IUI '01), USA, (2001) 33-40
6. Shen, X., Tan, B., and Zhai, C.: Context-sensitive information retrieval using implicit feedback. In: *Proc. of the 28th annual international ACM SIGIR conference on Research and development in information retrieval (SIGIR 2005)*, Salvador, Brazil (2005) 43-50
7. Paul–Alexandru Chirita, Claudiu Firan and Wolfgang Nejdl: Summarizing Local Context to Personalize Global Web Search. In: *Proceedings of the 15th ACM International CIKM Conference on Information and Knowledge Management*, Arlington, United States
8. Salton G. and Buckley C.: Improving retrieval performance by relevance feedback. *JASIS* 41, 4 (1990) 288-297
9. Page L., Brin S., Motwani R. and T. Winograd. The PageRank citation ranking: Bringing order to the Web. *Technical report*, Stanford University Database Group (1998)
10. Haveliwala T.: Topic-sensitive pagerank. In: *Proceedings of the Eleventh International World Wide Web Conference*, Honolulu, Hawaii (2002)
11. Jeh G. and Widom J.: Scaling personalized web search. In: *Proceedings of the 12th Intl. World Wide Web Conference* (2003)
12. Sugiyama K., Hatano K., and Yoshikawa M.: Adaptive web search based on user profile constructed without any effort from users. In: *Proceedings of the 13th international conference on World Wide Web* (2004) 675–684
13. Chirita P.-A., Nejdl W., Paiu R. and Kohlschütter Chr.: Using ODP metadata to personalize search. In *Proc. of the 28th Intl. ACM SIGIR Conf.* (2005)
14. Joachims T., Granka L., Pan B., Hembrooke H. and Gay G.: Accurately interpreting clickthrough data as implicit feedback. In: *Proceedings of SIGIR* (2005)
15. Granka L., Joachims T., and Gay G.: Eye-Tracking Analysis of User Behavior in WWW Search. In: *Proceedings of the Conference on Research and Development in Information Retrieval (SIGIR)* (2004)
16. Shen Xuehua: User-Centered Adaptive Information Retrieval. In: *Proceedings of ACM Conference on Research and Development on Information Retrieval (SIGIR)* (2006)
17. Doulaverakis C., Nidelkou E., Gounaris A. and Kompatsiaris Y.: An Ontology and Content-Based Search Engine For Multimedia Retrieval, *10th East-European Conference on Advances in Databases and Information Systems*, ADBIS 2006, Thessaloniki, Hellas (2006)
18. White R.W., Ruthven I. and Jose J.M.: A study of factors affecting the utility of implicit relevance feedback. In: *Proceedings of the 28th Annual International ACM SIGIR Conference on Research and Development in Information Retrieval*, Salvador, Brazil (2005)
19. W3C http://www.w3.org

An Adaptive Complex Data Investigation Methodology using Interactive Multi-Menus

Ioannis Deliyiannis, Andreas Floros and Michael F. Webster

Abstract Multimedia presentation of dynamic rheological experimental and simulated data sets is a complex process, due to the dynamic interrelation of the data. In this work we address the problem of direct data interaction, focusing particularly on the case where the application has to dynamically handle changes at runtime. Interactivity modeling relies on visual metadata representations, which are both used to relate directly to the underlying system-graph and formally describe content-connectivity. Under this context a novel user-interaction structure (Multi-Menu) is introduced, allowing valid-only data comparison across the vast number of possible results combinations, supporting discussion-based data combinations and user-driven scenarios, which can in turn trigger automated simulation execution to generate missing data. The proposed methodology applies to other complex data investigation scenarios and systems with adaptive interactivity and automatic system-adjustment requirements.

1 Introduction

This work introduces a user interface construction methodology used for interactive multimedia investigation of scientific and rheological data. The multimedia content used under the case-study is the end-result of simulation or experimental studies and is provided in visualised post-processed form. Under the current case study, results are generated for model fluids in a two-dimensional (2D) setting. Further investigations included 3D and free-surface modeling, validated against results obtained from actual kneading experiments. Fully and part-filled cases were considered, in vertical and horizontal mixer orientations. The main objectives of this work is to demonstrate the navigation flexibility through the vast content-domain of the selected case study, under various

Andreas Floros
Dept. of Audiovisual Arts, Ionian University, Corfu, Greece, e-mail: floros@ionio.gr

Ioannis Deliyiannis
Dept. of Audiovisual Arts, Ionian University, Corfu, Greece, e-mail: yiannis@ionio.gr

Michael Webster
Computer Science, University of Wales, UK, e-mail: m.f.webster@swan.ac.uk

presentation modes and to identify the principal factors, which lead to the reduction of time and cost of mixing by appropriate adjustment of stirrer design. This is achieved through extensive data visualisation, supported by a graphical interaction mechanism. Added complication is introduced as data are calculated and delivered by multiple research groups, working in parallel, particularly as each group employs individual methods to represent the data. Experimental and simulation results generate a variety of investigation areas, introducing a large number of variables.

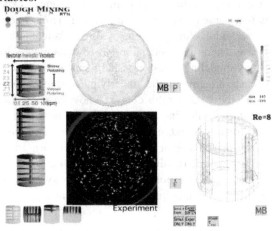

Fig. 1 Multi-menus indicating rheological settings (left) with animated motion-blur, pressure, laser-scatter and three-dimensional extension data, for an inelastic fluid with mixing speeds between 12.5 to 100 rpm, Z2 plane, rotating vessel.

Visual metadata are employed to build the human-computer interaction subsystem, enabling complete, direct and meaningful presentation of the associated data. This is achieved by creating an XML-based multimedia visualisation database and a controlling interface, supporting interactive user-driven interrogation and illustration scenarios of the key factors that affect the process of dough kneading. Combinations of novel interaction techniques are realised, together with pre-determined modes of interaction (cruise-control/data-navigation). The current industrially-related case study combines a non-linear access mechanism, where system attributes (such as pre-defined cruise-control paths and hierarchical presentation orders) may be dynamically multiplexed, enabling various abstract data-investigation levels to be activated. The sheer size of data introduces storage/retrieval limitations, particularly as non-linear access is supported by the end-system. Synchronous display of multiple streams results in system/network-bottlenecks, particularly as delivery over Internet communication channels is required. In addition, presentation of the data in a meaningful manner has triggered the need for advanced and multiplexed navigational routes, which permit various investigative scenarios, alongside pre-determined presentation-paths. In Fig. 1 for example, various animated data are presented simultaneously, while the system permits either the selection of a deterministic presentation path, or direct interaction via option-selection of the multi-menu icons displayed on the left.

MMS data integration ([7]), [13]) has enabled effortless navigation through vast volume of information, dispensation of data-duplication, and interactive comparison of experimental and simulation animations, within a single MMS frame. A frame may be described as a holder for meta-data information, enabling multimedia data-instances to be grouped, categorised, synchronised, positioned, indexed, cached and displayed on-demand. For example, when two animations are to be displayed simultaneously, the interaction mechanism reads the metadata stored in both frames and subsequently adjusts appropriately the frame-rate, to display the data in synchronisation. In Fig. 1, four data frames are resized, synchronised and positioned automatically for the user to contrast fluid characteristics in both experimental and simulated settings. In addition, the MMS may be programmed to simulate common interaction modes [8].

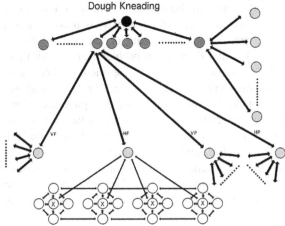

Fig. 2 Representation of the wide variety of research modes. V indicates vertical mixer orientation used for bread mixing, H horizontal for biscuits, P for part-filled and F for fully-filled container.

The visualised content consists of experimental, 3D simulated and transient rheological data. This is accessed through parameter-adjustment and customised-menus, reflecting design-choice and parameter-setting. Interface-design is based on the mixing-vessel design/orientation/fill and process parameters, as shown in Fig. 2. Comparison against experimentation introduces greater content-complexity. User-defined data-organisation, presentation and interaction-paradigms are combined, to cover multiple levels of presentation-requirements. New interface styles for MMS data-presentation have been developed, using an hierarchical organisation, based on model adjustment and navigational graphs, introducing intelligent navigation [3], [4].

Under the current case study, results are generated for Horizontal or Vertical Mixer Orientation; Incremental Stirrer Complexity for One Stirrer Concentric, One Stirrer Eccentric, Two Stirrers Eccentric (with/without) Baffles; Viscous and Viscoelastic Fluid-types; Speed of Kneading of 12.5, 25, 50 and 100 rotations per minute; 3D Investigation of the flow across depth for multiple planes; Fully and part-filled mixing; Free-surface in two and three dimensions, including transient development of the free surface; Stirrer shapes that include Full-Stirrer, Half-Stirrer Horizontal, Half-Stirrer Vertical. Experimental fluids cover: model-fluids (for transparency), model-doughs (for material time-independency), to actual industrial doughs. Each of the above considerations consists of various geometrical and parameter adjustments of incremental complexity. Fluid model representation ranges from Newtonian to inelastic, and finally, to viscoelastic. Adjustment of geometry and modelling complexity transcends from one stirrer, concentric to the final case of two stirrers, eccentric, free surface. Incrementation through experimental studies is outlined.

Frequently, calculations may be repeated with algorithm adjustments. Thus, each time data are received, increased complexity is introduced as it is necessary to identify unique, fresh data to be categorised and inserted, appropriately. Categorisation, ordering and duplication problems arise with propriety software and new data. The above deficiencies are amplified, as their inability to impose specific content-quality criteria, such as colour-depth and resolution, may introduce further comparison and conversion complexities. Within MMS, new data are inserted, or replaced, straightforwardly to the system without-preferred order. Some initial practical problems to be tackled include the collection, categorisation, visualisation and presentation of simulation results, having established data-sharing practice. This minimises data conversion, and as a consequence, the visualisation workload. The plethora and diversity of data, demands MMS techniques, relating to efficient content-updates and direct data-insertion.

2 Scientific Interactive Multimedia Framework and Model

Previous research has introduced a combined multimedia organisation and presentation framework [3], where interaction is classified between developers, users and observers in an MMS production and use stages . An overlapping set-diagram representation describes the relationships between the various groups, while a model describes content-connectivity using dynamically adapted graphs [3]. Framework-areas may be colored, to indicate individual and overlapping party-roles. Arrows may indicate group-interaction across the system. Set unions (A, B, C, D) indicate higher-order interaction, say between groups in construction-mode for a single-MMS, or indeed, a super-MMS, as in Fig. 3, right. Such a system is an implied product of the developer's domain.

Various interaction instances may be considered covering a wide range of scenarios. The area-exclusive scenario, which implies only limited interaction between the groups, where there are clearly defined expertise-boundaries. Each group describes its' requirements according to its' individual constraints. A common agreement across groups specifies the resulting MMS. For each group this is achieved without a detailed understanding of the mechanics of other groups. This is a typical scenario when, for example, a Multimedia company is employed to design an MMS. Line-diagrams may be used to specify relationships between these clearly defined groups in detail.

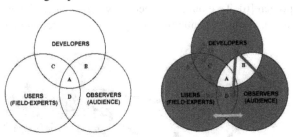

Fig. 3 The Scientific Interactive Multimedia Framework in various modes

A second scenario describes the instance where only "A" is colored. Here, the development group possesses knowledge that transcends all three groups. This would encompass the single-developer instance, where one has understanding of MM-development, expertise on the subject-matter and appreciates audience expectations. A third interaction scenario is identified when "C" and "D" only are highlighted. This setting implies that users/field-experts assume an active role in development (indicated by arrow), and commute between roles as user/audience. This accurately describes the development scenario of various scientific-level multimedia presentations. Bi-directional relationships may be indicated by double-arrows. In this manner, interaction between the parties involved may be described in a highly informative manner. The fourth instance describes a complex setting [Fig. 3, right], combining users (field-experts), developers and various audience-types (both versed and unversed in the subject matter). Here, the proposed framework achieves a higher-order description of the relationship between the parties involved. Varying levels of expertise may be described of increased complexity on-demand: users/field-experts (aware of development constraints), developers (aware of scientific context) and their interrelations. In such respect, traditional frameworks have been found lacking. By design, they were never intended to describe diverse configurations, in terms of expertise, content and development for an MMS. Instead, they assign further workload to a single party (usually the developer) to evaluate the quality of information. To interpret J. Carter [2] '...developers must understand the intended meaning of the data from the information providers, in order to evaluate its quality'. This is a particularly pertinent issue when considering research-content.

MM development relies on the Scientific Interactive Multimedia Model (SIMM), which addresses the issue of content / context connectivity through advanced representation means. The model transforms the system specification into an MMS by accommodating the multifaceted presentation requirements introduced with complex scientific-data. Indexes encapsulating multimedia frames are used instead of individual media components and interrelationships between them. Each frame contains multiple media elements, such as text, sounds, images and meta-data, which are created automatically or may be inserted manually in XML format. Similar ideas have been cited in the literature, utilising a complex rule-based approach [6]. To emulate connectivity across lower-level content (such as single-streams), frames containing only a single media-element may be employed.

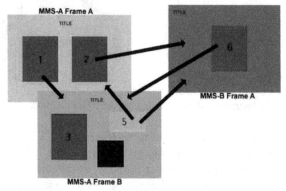

Fig. 4 Various linking scenarios for multimedia frames and streams

This approach poses multiple advantages, when compared to other cited in the literature [1]. First, low-level content connectivity is abstracted, as direct comparison is activated between two or more streams. In-turn, the volume of links is reduced. A second advantage is that individual media-components may be referenced separately, despite being organised within a more general structure. In addition, their ability to form further combinations is not reduced. This may be achieved separately, by being linked to other frames. Furthermore, a frame containing a title, and a set of streams provides immediate identification and categorisation of content. This introduces an advanced indexing mechanism, consisting of a frame-index, media-indexes (contained within each frame), and a set-of-states (in which a frame and a set of media are active). Content-linking is addressed using a "media-element to frame" referencing procedure. Each media-element may be employed as a user-interface construct. Fixed links may be programmed directly, or copied across other media-elements, reducing re-programming. Additionally, case-based links may be programmed locally (within frames of a single-MMS), unless external frame-access is necessary. Use of a knowledge-based approach (to dictate link-behaviour) is supported within the model via scripting.

Mathematical representation is used to formally describe the proposed model. From the computer science perspective, it is common to use mathematical constructs in system specification, automated verification and development [9]. Typical formal specification tools employ algebras, signatures and rules [11]. As a consequence, the functional representation chosen may be modeled directly through computer algorithms to enable automated presentation-construction and verification.

3 Multi-Menus, Graphs, Metadata and System Programming

Multi-Menus are classified as a user-interface construction structure. These are linked directly to the underlying SIMM of an MMS. In this respect, visual media components such as icons, video-segments, complete video clips and text are used for frame-linking, which essentially is mapped to content-linking (see Fig. 4). When large content-domains are involved, complications are introduced, due to their unmanageable size and complexity in connectivity. This may result in multiple system-deficiencies, such as link- or interface-inconsistency. Therefore, link-management protocols are introduced (at developmental stages), designed to allow consistent replication of frame-connectivity. This is achieved through the deployment of MM-templates, featuring fully functional external connectivity. When fresh data-content is appended, use of an appropriate template, with external links already earmarked, reduces programming to amending local-links.

Multi-Menus do not impose constraints in terms of the underlying development environment. The developer is allowed the flexibility to implement similar system-functionality, through a pick-and-mix approach. Hence, many non-MME technologies may be utilised. Examples include document-based construction tools (such as HTML pages utilising java applets), and hybrid combinations with other technologies, involving XML [10], ASP, JAVA, JSP, etc. The only requirement is dynamic-linking support. For example, plain HTML-pages cannot support Multi-Menus, since links point to a fixed address.

For MM-based user-interface development it is important to establish a detailed view of content interdependencies. The subsequent building step involves construction of user-interface structures. Here, these act as building blocks for user-interface/interaction. Having prepared all necessary media-components, one must develop the principal frames involved. In order to create a consistent user-interface for all sections, a single instance is developed by programming all the relative links once to all other relevant addresses. This reduces the programming effort as a copy of the complete interface is used as a template for new content. Current selection indication is achieved via setting particular icon-attributes to high-visibility. Visual icon-attributes such as low-visibility are also supported, where reduced visibility implies unavailable links. Having obtained a basis that is fully linked to the other instances, it remains to clone the completed frame.

Copying or expanding the convoluted icons to share functionality across distinct frames achieves this. Adding the media-components themselves completes the task. Compared to the re-programming effort required when each multimedia instance is completed separately this is a speedy task. Also, it provides consistent icon-placement.

In addition, SIMM may be actively employed in the construction and functional extension of an MMS. In this manner, one aims to model content-connectivity [5] and interactivity. An additional user-interface structure is deemed necessary, in the construction of a front-end to underlying content. In that respect, "Multi-Menus", are employed to specify interface-component functionality, whilst relating to underlying content-frames. The principal reasons for using a Multimedia building-environment include: encapsulation of content, support for cross-platform delivery, system-extendibility and provision for fully functional scripting.

Multi-Menus Development using Underlying Graph Structure

Within the current case study, extensive use of graphs and related representation structures have been utilised for the rigorous implementation of interactive navigation. The type of graph used with this case study is a multi-connected graph [Fig. 2] For the organisation of simple slide-based presentations, a dynamic linked-list structure is employed. Each branch is itself a presentation, linked to external data (such as experimentally-captured and simulation-generated animations). This data categorisation is followed within the Multimedia organisation, but in a more liberal manner. Replacing strict-ordering of frames, data are retained locally to one instance in the MME. Links join the top-level to the case-study introduction, flyer-animation and project-plan slide-sorter. The second-level (indicated by dark-grey intensity) consists of the menus organised across geometry and setting-complexity (one-stirrer, concentric to two-stirrers, eccentric with baffles). Subsequent levels branch out from the second-level options, providing links to individual frames and their related information.

Fig. 5, left, shows a section snapshot of organisation for links to MMS-components. Varying parameters represent settings which trigger the display of content components, animations and sounds. Adjacent settings represent related MM-frames. To represent this hierarchy using a graph, each node must represent a MM-frame. Each such node can inherit attributes from another; new attributes/behaviours may be appended, or replace those previously. This organisation is adaptive and flexible and can be utilised to develop interfaces which may simultaneously employ direct manipulation and adaptation [12]. Attributes and metadata need not be programmed for each frame, being inherited for a copy-object of an existing frame. When an attribute is programmed, it generates a new database object that may be associated with any component of a frame. Frame components are stored uniquely within the database and are referenced to the same item, when multiple instances are on display. Instead, a link is employed, if many instances of the same data element are required. The user may select when the memory is flushed of that particular element.

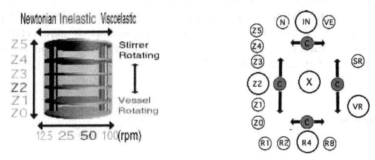

Fig. 5 Multi-menu graph representation for two-stirrer design, contrasted to the user-interface component used under the dough-kneading multimedia system.

Up to this point, user-driven investigation was implemented through the use of visual database queries. Parameter selection triggered a series of events where with the use of metadata encapsulated under each frame, appropriate streams were selected, pre-cached, positioned and ultimately displayed. Dynamic and adaptive linking may be implemented via Multi-Menus, even with primitive programming tools provided under propriety interactive multimedia environments. This involves the specification of an external mechanism (for example a knowledge-base), which SIMM accesses when multiple-links are encountered. The full complexity of such external decision-making may be implemented within a MME. One method to integrate decision-making procedures, within the MME, is through the use of global data-structures. These may be tables or linked-lists and may be employed to store information at runtime. Multi-Menus may access these global structures directly, by reference to structure-name.

4 Conclusions

Multi-Menus are an interaction structure that beyond the support for advanced, automated and user-defined interaction, offers the ability to present results comparatively, from case to case, or via interactive mode-switching, a highly desirable presentation characteristic. Research in this interdisciplinary area of interactive multimedia has resulted in the development of a wide range of MMS, destined for courseware, research and industrial applications [3]. We have shown that combined use of the framework, model, metadata-based multi-menus and internal or external rule-based reasoning may be used as an effective method to create useful research and presentation tools for customised fields of research, where propriety presentation software has been found lacking. The system thus developed has been used actively to cover wide-ranging presentation requirements, addressing, in particular, industrial and academic audiences. Also, it displays the potential to reach more general/school audiences. The choice of a fully programmable Multimedia-development platform for the Internet (Adobe Director) prevented presentation deficiencies and limitations introduced with proprietary software, enabling web-delivery to be implemented without the need for additional end-system re-programming.

References

1. Botafogo RA, Mossé D (1996) The Capoeira Model for Distributed and Reconfigurable Multimedia Systems. Technical Research Report, Computer Science Department, Universidade Federal Fluminense, Brazil
2. Carter J (2000) Developments in Web Research and Practice. In Proc. Motivating Multimedia. San Diego, California, US
3. Deliyannis I (2002) Interactive Multimedia Systems for Science and Rheology. In: Computer Science. Ph.D Thesis, University of Wales, Swansea, p 285
4. Deliyannis I, Harvey J, Webster MF (2003) Content-Based Interactive Multimedia Systems for Rheological Science. In Proc. e-Society. Lisbon Portugal, p 181-186
5. Doherty G, Harrison MD (1997) A Representational Approach to the Specification of Presentations. In Proc. 4th Eurographics Workshop on the Design Specification and Verification of Interactive Systems (DSV-IS '97). Granada, Spain
6. Geurts JPTM, Ossenbruggen JRv, Hardman HL (2001) Application-specific constraints for multimedia presentation generation. In Proc. Eighth International Conference on Multimedia Modeling (MMM01). Amsterdam, Netherlands
7. ISO-Standard (1988) *Information technology - Computer graphics and image processing - Presentation Environment for Multimedia Objects* (PREMO).
8. J. Dakss, S. Agamanolis, E. Chalom, Bove MVJ (1998) Hyperlinked Video. In: Proc. SPIE Multimedia Systems and Applications.
9. Martinez OR (2002) Design Dependencies within the Automatic Generation of Hypermedia Presentations. Technical University of Catalonia, Catalonia
10. Pittarello F, Celentano A (2001) Interaction locus: a multimodal approach for the structuring of virtual spaces. In Proc. HCItaly. Firenze, Italy
11. Rees DLL, Stephenson K, Tucker JV (2000) Towards an Algebraic Structure of Interface Definition Languages and Architectures. Computer Science Department Research Report, University of Wales Swansea, Swansea
12. Tsandilas T, Schraefel MC (2004) *Usable adaptive hypermedia systems*. New Review of Hypermedia and Multimedia J 10:5-29
13. Vazirigiannis M, Theodoridis Y, Sellis T (1998) Spatio-temporal composition and indexing for large multimedia applications. Multimedia Systems J 6:284-298

Reference Ontology Design for a Neurovascular Knowledge Network

Gianluca Colombo, Daniele Merico and Giancarlo Mauri

Abstract In this paper we describe the ontological model developed within the NEUROWEB project, a consortium of four European excellence centers for the diagnosis and treatment of the Ischemic Stroke pathology. The aim of the project is the development of a support system for association studies, intended as the search for statistical correlations between a feature (e.g., a genotype) and the clinical phenotype. Clinical phenotypes are assessed through the diagnostic activity, performed by clinical experts operating within different neurovascular sites. These sites operate according to specific procedures, but they also conform to the minimal requirements of international guidelines, displayed by the adoption of a common standard for the patient classification. We developed a central model for the clinical phenotypes (the NEUROWEB Reference Ontology), able to reconcile the different methodologies into a common classificatory system. To support the integrative analysis of genotype-phenotype relations, the Reference Ontology was extended to handle concepts of the genomic world. We identified the general theory of biological function as the common ground between the clinical medicine and molecular biosciences; therefore we decomposed the clinical phenotypes into elementary phenotypes with a homogeneous physiological background, and we connected them to the biological processes, acting as the elementary units of the genomic world.

Gianluca Colombo
Department of Computer Science Systems and Communication (DISCo), University of Milano-Bicocca , viale Sarca, 336 20126 - Milan (Italy), e-mail: giacolos@gmail.com; gianluca.colombo@disco.unimib.it

Daniele Merico
Terrence Donnelly Centre for Cellular and Biomolecular Research (CCBR) Banting and Best Department of Medical Research, University of Toronto, 160 College St M5S 3E1 - Toronto (Ontario, Canada) e-mail: daniele.merico@gmail.com

Giancarlo Mauri
Department of Computer Science Systems and Communication (DISCo), University of Milano-Bicocca , viale Sarca, 336 20126 - Milan (Italy), e-mail: giancarlo.mauri@disco.unimib.it

1 Overview

Ontologies are a popular research topic in various communities such as knowledge engineering [1, 10], natural language processing [4], cooperative information systems [12], [5], intelligent information integration [2], and knowledge management [6]. In computer science, ontologies can be defined as computational models which describe the kind of entities, properties of entities, and relations between entities that exist in a specified domain of knowledge; under an AI perspective, they can be regarded as *content theories*, in opposition to *mechanism theories* [8].

One of the most popular end-use of ontologies in information technology is to create an agreed-upon vocabulary for information exchange within a domain. For instance, interoperability among autonomously-developed DBs can be significantly hindered by the absence of uniform semantics; reconciliation can be accomplished through the use of a reference ontology to which the semantics of the individual resources can be related [5].

Standard interchange languages (XML, OWL, RDF) were developed to enable the establishment of web services to retrieve and exchange ontology-encoded information through the web (W3C, Web Ontology Language). Nonetheless, the choice of specific representation languages for the formal ontology encoding, and the technological issues of database interoperability, do not wear out the whole range of problems concerning ontological modeling [27, 24, 25, 26]. Despite the effort for defining a standard semantic, experts seem to resist to any attempt of homogenization. Partly, this is due to practical problems, but there are also theoretical reasons why this is not easily accepted and not even desirable. In fact, lots of cognitive and organizational studies show that there is a close relationship between knowledge and identity. Knowledge is not simply a matter of accumulating "true sentences" about the world, but it is also a matter of interpretation schemes [9], contexts [34], mental models [32], perspectives [33], which allow people to make sense of what they know. All these mental structures are an essential part of what people know, as each of them provides an alternative lens through which reality can be read.

2 The NEUROWEB project: problem analysis

NEUROWEB is a EU-funded, health-care oriented project. Its aim is the development of an IT infrastructure to support association studies in the neurovascular domain. As their name suggests, association studies consist in the assessment of the statistical significance of association (i.e. co-occurrence) between a phenotype and genetic, environmental or demographic factors; typical examples are the search for genetic markers associated to an increased susceptibility to Type-2 Diabetes, or the discovery of a relation between the average number of daily-smoked cigarettes and the incidence of lung cancer. In these examples, the phenotype is always a pathology (Type-2 Diabetes, lung cancer); however, the notion of phenotype is commonly used also in non-pathological contexts (e.g. blood groups, somatic traits): according to a more general definition, a phenotype is an observable state of an individual organism [22].

Phenotypes can consist of a single parameter (e.g. glycemia, the level of glucose in venous blood), or a structured ensemble of inter-related features (e.g. diabetes is a complex pathological state, comprising abnormal glycemia). Within NEUROWEB project, the phenotype is intended as a pathological state, due to the occurrence of a neurovascular lesion, and diagnosed by a clinical expert; this specific declension will be referred as *clinical phenotype* throughout the paper.

Association studies require large patient cohorts to be effective. For that reason, the NEUROWEB consortium is constituted by four clinical sites from different EU-member countries, which are recognized excellence centers in the field of neurovascular disorders, with a particular focus on ischemic stroke. However, the amount of available data is not a valuable asset itself, unless data quality and methodological coherence are carefully preserved. Considering the specific NEUROWEB context, the critical point is whether phenotypes are defined and assessed homogeneously across different sites. Indeed, although all sites comply with international guidelines, they also have developed specific diagnostic procedures, and in-depth competencies in different areas of stroke diagnosis (such as imaging, biochemical essays, etc...)[1]. This situation is mirrored by the clinical repositories, which were independently developed in each local site to store patient profiles. Clearly, enforcing a top-down standardization of phenotype assessment is neither practicable nor desirable in the applicative context outlined [11]. Therefore, to address the problem of methodological coherence, the phenotypes were encoded in a specific Reference Ontology, which will be referred as the *NEUROWEB Reference Ontology* (or, shortly, the NEUROWEB ontology); the NEUROWEB ontology enables the NEUROWEB system to operate on different clinical repositories, and to retrieve patients characterized by a given (set of) phenotype(s), formulated according to negotiated criteria.

General-purpose medical ontologies [19, 18, 17, 15, 14, 13] could not be used to meet that end, as they proved unsuitable to represent the specific expert knowledge of the NEUROWEB neurovascular communities [16, 22]. The diagnostic process has traditionally resisted many efforts to be fully automatized [28, 35]; it is important to point out that the aim of the NEUROWEB infrastructure is not to replace the clinical expert in the diagnostic activity, but rather to reconstruct the patients' clinical phenotypes, according to the evidences collected - and interpreted - by the medical experts during the diagnostic process; the rationale of using explicit and analytical phenotype formulations is to integrate data from different sources preserving methodological coherence.

Association studies within the NEUROWEB project have a special commitment to genotype-phenotype relations [A, B]; specifically, the genotypic component assessed is the value of Single Nucleotide Polymorphisms (SNPs) [C, D] in the patients' genome. Beyond the search for statistically relevant SNPs-phenotype associations, there are valuable functionalities requiring to extend the NEUROWEB Ref-

---

[1] International guidelines should not be regarded as exhaustive formulations of diagnostic procedures, but rather as minimal requirements to be met in order to formulate correct diagnoses.

erence Ontology to gene functions, and enabling it to treat phenotype formulations as provided by genomic resources. Conjugating phenotypes, as conceived within neurovascular medicine, with entities belonging to the genomic world, clearly requires to bridge two knowledge domains belonging to different disciplines; whereas clinical medicine is committed to the identification of pathological states (diagnosis) and their treatment (or prevention), molecular biology and molecular genetics are committed to the study of biological mechanisms at the molecule level and to the study of the information encoded by the genome.

3 The NEUROWEB Reference Ontology

The core concept of the NEUROWEB Reference Ontology is the phenotype. The ontology is primarily committed to the representation of clinical phenotypes, federating the different clinical communities without compromising methodological coherence. Decomposing the clinical phenotypes into general domain components enables to extend the NEUROWEB Reference Ontology to genomic entities, bridging two different knowledge domains.

The NEUROWEB Project is committed to associations studies, and the primary computational task is the retrieval of patients sharing a common phenotype. As we discussed in the previous sessions, this task is not straightforward. On the one hand, each site independently collects and organizes the clinical evidences required to formulate a phenotype, mirroring the methodological specificities of the local Clinical site. On the other hand, however, the clinical communities accept the federation under a common standard for phenotype classification, the TOAST[2]. All in all, the solution we adopted is an ontological model formulating clinical phenotypes on the basis of clinical evidences stored in the repositories. Given an input phenotype, the ontological model enables the query system to retrieve patients from different repositories; the adoption of an ontological phenotype formulation, opposed to a looser query system, grants the application of coherent criteria for phenotype formulation across different repositories. In the beginning, we devised an initial two-layered model. The lower layer is the Core Data-Set (CDS), a set of common indicators from the local repositories, which clinicians consider essential for stroke diagnosis (e.g. Anterior cerebral artery lesion, Blood pressure). The CDS enables to connect clinical evidences having the same semantic across the different communities. The CDS is the result of an iterative negotiation process among the NEUROWEB clinical communities, supervised and aided by the NEUROWEB Knowledge Engineers and IT personnel.

Under an IT perspective, the CDS alone would be enough to support a query system, operating on the integrated ensemble of the four clinical repositories; in that setting, the task of phenotype formulation would be executed by the user by assem-

---

[2] The TOAST classificatory system [30, 31, 29] was developed by the international neurovascular community to classify stroke patients on a diagnostic basis, and it was already adopted by most of the clinical sites before the existence of the NEUROWEB consortium.

bling different CDS indicators into a query formula. We can reasonably expect that there is a set of clinical phenotypes used on a regular basis for association studies - the TOAST phenotypes, in the case of the NEUROWEB consortium, as previously discussed; a query system relying only on the CDS would oblige the user to reformulate the phenotypes for every new access to the system, a solution which would be time-consuming and error-prone. For that reason, we collect the TOAST phenotypes in a taxonomy of stroke types and subtypes, termed Top Phenotypes. The Top Phenotypes constitute the second layer of the model, and they are connected to the CDS indicators via a definition formula. The formula is structured as a conjunction/disjunction of criteria on the CDS indicators, expressed as equality / inequality bounds, or quantitative ranges to be satisfied. An example is: (Cholesterol Level > 110) AND (Posterior cerebral artery lesion = yes). The existence of a negotiated, but centrally encoded, phenotype formulation establishes a methodologically-coherent federation of the different communities' resources. Local practices are reconciled within this model, as different sets of CDS indicators can be used to identify a common phenotype. The easiest case occurs when the same clinical evidence can be assessed using different technologies but achieving the same degree of probatory strength (e.g. Severe Stenosis in the Internal Carotid Artery can be determined by a Duplex AND a Computed Tomography Angiography Scan, OR by a Duplex AND a Magnetic Resonance Angiogram Scan). The way phenotypes are encoded strictly resembles the typical formulation of a query, and thus can be easily handled by a clinical expert; for that reason, the two-layered model was successfully used for the Knowledge Acquisition activity.

The two-layered model is a simple and effective model to encode a set of given phenotypes, organized according to homogeneous classificatory criteria, as in the case of the TOAST. The NEUROWEB Consortium accepts the TOAST as a federation standard, but the ontology should be flexible enough to manage the existence of alternative neurovascular schools, adopting a classification alternative to the TOAST. The introduction of stroke types organized according to different classificatory criteria would be managed in the two layer model by introducing an additional taxonomy, besides the TOAST taxonomy. However, the exploitation of clinical phenotypes for association studies requires to dynamically redefine the phenotypes, going beyond the categories of a specific classificatory system; in this scenario, the TOAST is a source of robust clinical phenotypes, grounded onto the diagnostic practice, which can be refined or modified to meet at best the ends of association studies. We argue that to enable at best the manipulation of Top Phenotypes it is necessary to introduce an additional layer, in which the Top Phenotypes are decomposed into their *building blocks*, according to the classification criteria. We will also show that decomposing the Top Phenotypes according to classification criteria enables to identify general domain concepts, supporting the bridging to genomic entities. The CDS indicators are not suitable building blocks, as

- the formulation of Top Phenotypes using the CDS indicators does not explicitly represent the classificatory criteria;
- CDS indicators do not represent general concepts of the medical domain; instead, they are the minimal elements of the diagnostic practice, as it is exerted in the

NEUROWEB clinical communities. For example, anatomical parts are often referred in the CDS indicators, but they are not represented as stand-alone entities of the CDS.

The Top Phenotypes taxonomy enables to represent the characterizations of the stroke types with increasing specificity from the root to the leaves (e.g. Ischemic Stroke, Atherosclerotic Ischemic Stroke, Atherosclerotic Ischemic Stroke Evident, Atherosclerotic Stroke Evident with Intracranial Cerebral Artery Stenosis); however, the taxonomy is intrinsically incapable of representing the notion of part, as required by the identification of the building blocks. To identify the building blocks of the TOAST Top Phenotypes, it is necessary to consider what are the TOAST classification criteria:

- etiology (i.e. Atherosclerotic, Cardioembolic, Lacunar Stroke);
- confidence of the etiological assessment (i.e. Evident, Probable, Possible), depending on the probatory strength of the diagnostic evidence;
- anatomy (i.e. the location of the lesion, e.g. left carotid artery).

The TOAST classification criteria suggest the use of specialized relations[3] to deconstruct the Top Phenotypes into building blocks (see Figure 1):

- Has-Cause (pointing to the specific etiology);
- Has-Evidence (pointing to diagnostic evidences);
- Has-Location (pointing to the anatomical site of the neurovascular lesion).
- Has-Side (pointing to the side of the neurovascular lesion).

To account for the anatomical criterion, we add to the ontology the Anatomical Parts; the Anatomical Parts of interest for the NEUROWEB project are typically vascular territories, such as the Intracranial Cerebral Artery (ICA). These concepts are not phenotypes, since phenotypes are generally defined as observable properties of an organism; on the contrary, Anatomical Parts are physical entities bearing observable properties. We also add to the ontology a set of Topological Concepts, to manage the side of the lesions (including the notions of spatial coaxiality and symmetry). Whereas the CDS indicators derive from the community-level diagnostic knowledge, and the TOAST Top Phenotypes derive from the school-level diagnostic knowledge, the Anatomical Parts and the Topological Concepts are general domain concepts (i.e. on the Biomedical Knowledge level).

The etiological criterion implicitly assumes a partition between:

- the Stroke as a neurovascular occlusive event, causing a brain lesion, and
- the pathophysiological factors causing the occlusive event.

This difference implicitly organizes the diagnostic activity, yet it essentially relies on the physiological nature of stroke as conceived in the general biomedical knowledge. Ischemic stroke literally means a sudden alteration of neurological functions due to an ischemic (i.e. absence of blood flow) event in a brain area. With more details, there is a cascade of sequential events: the initial trigger is the generation of the

---

[3] As these relations express the partonomy of the phenotype (i.e. its constitutive parts), they can be regarded as specialized mereological relations [3]

occluding body or structure, which stochastically leads to vessel occlusion; as a consequence, the brain area downstream the occluded vessel suffers a severe restriction in blood supply (i.e. there is a *local ischemia*); that leads to tissue damage, partial functional impairment at organ and system level (brain and nervous system), and finally behavioral and cognitive anomalies. The stroke can be diagnosed by looking for clinical evidences of these events: the brain region affected by ischemia and necrosis can be identified by means of imaging techniques (i.e. Relevant Lesion); behavioral and cognitive anomalies are typical symptoms exhibited by the stroke patient. The initial trigger, that is the generation of the occluding body, has causal roots in a specific pathological background; the TOAST assumes three etiological groups:

- Atherosclerotic
- Cardioembolic
- Lacunar

Each of these groups refers to a *durative* pathological background, eventually leading to the generation of the occlusive body. For instance, *Atherosclerosis* is a systemic blood vessel pathology, affecting multiple sites in the circulatory system; it consists in the deposition of cholesterol on the blood wall, contextual to the establishment of an inflammatory process, eventually leading to the formation of an atherosclerotic plaque; if the inflammatory process override the wound healing process, the plaque ruptures, thus triggering the coagulation process and the generation of a clot on the inner side of the blood wall; if the clot detaches from the wall (i.e. embolization), it circulates until it behaves as an occluding body. Atherosclerosis is diagnosed by the observation of stenosis in the brain afferent arteries, altogether with other diagnostic evidences. For these reasons, we introduce the concept of *Durative Background* and *Diagnostic Evidences*; Diagnostic Evidences are further specified into *Durative* and *Point Event*, to distinguish the diagnostic evidences for the events triggered by the occlusion, and the ones enabling to recognize the durative background (see Figure 1).

The decomposition according to these criteria leads to the identification of concepts we term Low Phenotypes. Altogether with Anatomical Parts and Topological Concepts, the Low Phenotypes constitute a new middle layer, connected to the Top Phenotypes and the CDS indicators. We argue that the criteria adopted to identify the Low Phenotypes are implicitly guided by the separation of different pathophysiological processes; in other words, Low Phenotypes are characterized by different underlying pathophysiological processes. For instance, Atherosclerotic Ischemic Stroke Evident (AISE) is caused by Atherosclerosis, whereas Lacunar Ischemic Stroke Evident (LISE) is caused by Small Vessel Disease; however, Atherosclerotic Ischemic Stroke Possible (AISPo) is caused by Small Vessel Disease and Atherosclerosis, thus there is a situation of two concurring causes. Therefore, LISE and AISPo share a common pathophysiological process, Small Vessel Disease. That information was not encoded by Top Phenotypes alone, and it would have been cumbersome to reconstruct it from the CDS-based definition formulas. Decomposing clinical phenotypes in terms of processes implies a shift from a clinical understanding - rooted

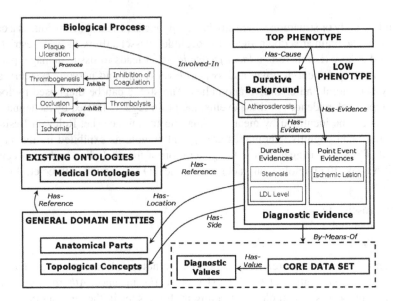

Fig. 1 The figure depicts the NEUROWEB Ontology components, and their relations.

onto diagnostic evidences, methods and theories - to the general theory of biological function, which belongs to the corpus of biomedical knowledge. That is the common ground between medicine and molecular biosciences, providing the basis for the cross-domain bridging.

4 The genomic extension of the Reference Ontology

Clinical Phenotypes were encoded in order to conceive the diagnostic knowledge of the NEUROWEB clinical communities, and then decomposed to extrapolate general domain concepts. In order to specifically support genotype-phenotype association studies, it is necessary to establish relations between the clinical phenotypes and genomic entities. Specifically, two functionalities can be addressed:

- represent relations between gene functions and clinical phenotypes
- integrate phenotypes from the clinical and genomic domains, managing

  - the different aims and methodologies
  - the different granularities (spanning single molecules, biomolecular processes, cell types, tissues, organs, systems, body).

The first task was accomplished by introducing new relations and entities to connect the Low Phenotypes to the reference gene functions, as they are provided by the controlled vocabulary Gene Ontology[4]. As we argued in the previous section, the decomposition into Low Phenotypes (see Figure 1) is implicitly guided by the separation of different pathophysiological processes. We add to the NEUROWEB Reference Ontology specific Biological Processes[5], relevant for the stroke and its causal backgrounds (e.g. Atherosclerotic Plaque Ulceration, Thrombogenesis). These concepts are connected to through the Low Phenotypes via the Involved-In relation (e.g. Atherosclerotic Plaque Ulceration Involved-In Atherosclerosis). NEUROWEB Biological Processes are then connected to their Gene Ontology counterparts via the Has-Reference relation. We argue that decomposing the clinical phenotypes into Low Phenotypes, associated to different processes, enables to overcome the discrepancy between the clinical and genomic phenotype representation, due to the different aims and methodologies of the two disciplines. For instance, the association between a genotype and the equivalent of the Low Phenotype Atherosclerosis is significantly more frequent than the association with the corresponding Top Phenotype, Atherosclerotic Ischemic Stroke. Indeed, the decomposition of Top Phenotypes into Low Phenotypes supports the analytical treatment of the context factor: Atherosclerotic Ischemic Stroke (Top Phenotype) is a stroke event (Low Phenotype: Relevant Scan Lesion) in the causative context of Atherosclerosis (Low Phenotype), but the notion of Top Phenotype alone does not enable to recognize these two separate elements.

As far as the second task is concerned, a granularity discrepancy arises when phenotypes - as represented in genomic resources - refer to entities spanning different level of organization (ranging from single molecules to the whole body); for instance, a phenotype can be expressed as the altered level of a protein or a molecular complex (e.g. increased level of LDL). Granularity can be fully managed only in presence of a general-purpose content theory of biological parts and functions; since there is no such reference ontology available for the biological domain, it was not possible to accomplish this task, as out of the project reach. Although the task of managing the different granularities is not presently supported, the ontology can be suitably extended to handle it, just by adding more modules and relations to the existing structure: as we have already shown, the NEUROWEB Low Phenotypes can be put in relation with biomolecular processes; we argue that it is possible to establish relations also with other general domain concepts, such as cell types, tissues and organs. For instance, a greater resolution in the representation of the Atherosclerotic processes and physical parts can provide the groundwork for the detailed acquisition and elaboration of genomic data. For instance, Atherosclerosis is a pathology with multiple facets, including molecular functions, biomolecular

---

[4] Gene Ontology is regarded in the genomic community as the standard resource for the annotation of gene functions. It is a general purpose domain ontology - in the genomic community, the use of community-specific or school-specific bio-ontologies is not a common practice. Gene functions are categorized into three separate classifications: Molecular Function (the biochemical activity of the gene product), Cellular Component (the cellular structure of which the gene product is a component), Biological Process (the process to which the gene product takes part).

[5] We adopt the term "Biological" Process instead of "Pathophysiological" in analogy to the Gene Ontology Biological Processes

processes, cell types, anatomical sites and parts, systems; the liability to trigger a stroke cascade depends on the state of all these components, organized at different level of granularity; different evidences from the genomic research (e.g. gene expression patterns, genotypic profiles, phenotypes) can be related to the clinical phenotypes, only in presence of a content theory organizing them accordingly. Finally, the NEUROWEB Reference Ontology has been formalized through OWL-DL [20]. The editor adopted for the OWL files generation is Protégé [21], a well known tool developed and distributed by the Stanford University, where the Reference Ontology concepts are represented as T-Box (Terminological Box) entities.

5 Conclusion and future directions

The NEUROWEB project posed relevant challenges to the ontological modeling effort. On the one hand, it was necessary to take into account the specific methodologies adopted by different clinical communities of practice, and reconcile them it into a common classificatory system (the TOAST), developing an ontology for the clinical phenotypes; the resulting ontology supports a query system operating across the different repositories. As an explicit ontology design principle, we represented the classification criteria using specialized mereological relations; we argue that this feature enables to reconcile in a common representation frame different classificatory system, adopted by different neurovascular communities. On the other hand, a greater challenge was posed by the bridging of clinical phenotypes, belonging to the world of diagnostic medicine, onto gene functions and phenotypes belonging to the field of genomics. The strategy adopted was to identify a common ground, the general theory of biological function, and accordingly decompose the concepts from the different disciplines into common elementary units (i.e. building blocks). Specifically, we identified clinical phenotypes having a homogeneous physiological background, the Low Phenotypes, and we established connections to the biomolecular processes.

Acknowledgements The work presented in this paper reflects the initial activities in the NEUROWEB project (project number 518513). The authors wish to thank the clinical partners: Istituto Nazionale Neurologico Carlo Besta (INNCB, Milan - Italy), Orszagos Pszichiatriai es Neurologiai Intezet (AOK-OPNI, Budapest - Hungary), University of Patras (UOP, Patras - Greece), Erasmus Universitair Medisch Centrum Rotterdam (MI-EMC, Rotterdam - Holland). In particular we wish to thank Dr. Yiannis Ellul and Dr. Stella Marousi from UOP, Dr. Zoltan Nagy and Dr. Csaba Ovary from AOK-OPNI, Dr Aad Van Der Lugt and Dr. Philip Homburg from MI-EMC, and Dr. Giorgio Boncoraglio from INNCB, for the valuable contributions during the knowledge acquisition campaign and model refinement process.

References

1. Y. Kitamura, R. Mizoguchi. 2003. Ontology-based description of functional design knowledge and its use in a functional way server. *International Journal of Expert System with Application* 2:153–166.
2. Bouquet, P., Don, V., Serafini, A. 2002 *ConTeXtualizedlocal ontology specification via ctxml.* Proceedings of AAAI workshop on Meaning Negotiation, Edmonton Alberta, Canada, 2002.
3. Simons, P., 1987, *Parts: A study in ontology*, Oxford University Press, Oxford, 1987.
4. Zaihrayeu, I., Sun, L., Giunchiglia, F., et al. 2007 *From Web Directories to Ontologies: Natural Language Processing Challenges.*In proceedings The 6th International Semantic Web Conference and the 2nd Asian Semantic Web Conference, 2007, Busan, Korea, 11 - 15 November, 2007, pp 623–636.
5. Benassi, R., Beneventano, D., Bergamaschi, S., Guerra, F., Vincini, M., 2004, *Synthesizing an Integrated Ontology with MOMIS*, International Conference on Knowledge Engineering and Decision Support (ICKEDS). Porto, Portugal, 21-23 July 2004.
6. Bergamaschi, S., Guerra, F., Orsini, M.,Sartori, C., 2007 *Extracting Relevant Attribute Values for Improved Search*, IEEE Internet Computing, vol. 11, no. 5, pp 26–35, Sept/Oct, 2007.
7. ueg, C., 2002, *Knowledge Management and Information Technology: Relationship and Perspective*, Upgrade - Knowledge Management and Information Technology, 2002.
8. Chandrasekaran, B., Josephson, J.R., Benjamins, V.R., 1999, *What are ontologies, and why do we need them? Intelligent Systems and Their Applications*, IEEE Volume 14, Issue 1, Jan/Feb 1999, pp 20–26.
9. Kuhn, T., 1970 *The Structure of Scientific Revolutions*, 1970, Chicago, University of Chicago Press, 1970.
10. Gomez-Perez, A., Corcho-Garcia, O., Fernandez-Lopez, M. 2003, *Ontological Engineering*, New York, Springer-Verlag, 2003.
11. Van der Vet, P.E., Mars, N.J.I., 1998, *Bottom-Up Construction of Ontologies*, IEEE Trans. Knowl. Data Eng. 1998, 10(4), pp 513–526.
12. Guizzardi, G. 2007, *On Ontology, ontologies, Conceptualizations, Modeling Languages, and (Meta)Models*, Frontiers in Artificial Intelligence and Applications, Databases and Information Systems IV, IOS Press, Amsterdam, 2007.
13. Galen, $http://www.openclinical.org/pr j_galen.html$
14. PATO, $http://www.obofoundry.org/$
15. SNOMED-CT, $http://www.snomed.org/$
16. Bodenreider, O., Smith, B., Kumar, A., Burgun, A., 2007, *Investigating Subsumption in DL-Based Terminologies: A Case Study in SNOMED CT*, Artif. Intell. Med. 2007, 39(3), pp 183–195.
17. OBO, Open Biomedical Ontologies $http://obo.sourceforge.net/$.
18. The Gene Ontology Consortium, $http://www.geneontology.org$.
19. The National Center for Biomedical Ontologies, $http$: $//www.bioontology.org/wiki/index.php/Main_page$.
20. W3C - Web Ontology Language $http://www.w3.org/TR/owl - guide/$.
21. Protg, User Documentation $http://protege.stanford.edu/doc/users.html$.
22. Bard, J. B., Rhee, L., Seung, Y., 2004 *Ontology in Biology: design, application and future challanges*, Nature Reviews Genetics, 2004/3, pp 213–222.
23. Smith, B., 2004, Beyond Concepts: Ontology as reality represenation, 2004, in Procedeengs FOIS 2004.
24. Guarino, N., 1995, *Formal Ontology, Conceptual Analysis and Knowledge Representation*, in International Journal of Human and Computer Studies, 43(5/6), pp 625–640.
25. Guarino, N., 1998, *Formal Ontology in Information Systems, In Formal Ontology in Information Systems*, Proceedings of FOIS'98, Trento, Italy, June 6-8, 1998. IOS Press, Amsterdam, pp 3–15.

26. Gruber, T. R., 1995, *Toward principles for the design of ontologies used for knowledge sharing*, International Journal of Human-Computer Studies, Vol. 43, Issues 4-5, November 1995, pp 907–928.

27. Amie L., Thomasson, 2004, *Methods of Categorization*, Proceedings of the third International Conference (FOIS-2004) IOS Press, pp 3–16, 2004.

28. Szolovits, P., Patil, R.S., Schwartz, W.B., *Artificial intelligence in medical diagnosis*, 1988, Annals of internal medicine, 1988.

29. Goldstein, L.B., Jones, M.R., Matchar D.B., et al., 2001 *Improving the reliability of Stroke subgroup classification using the Trial of ORG 10172 in Acute Stroke Treatment (TOAST) criteria*, Stroke 2001; 32: 1091–1097.

30. Adams, H.P. Jr., et al., 1993 *Classification of Subtype of Acute Ischemic Stroke, Definition for Use in a Multicenter Clinical Trial, TOAST. Trial of Org 10172 in Acute Stroke Treatment*, Stroke 1993, 24, pp 35–41.

31. Ay, H., Furie, K.L., Singhal, A., Smith, W.S., Sorensen, A.G., Koroshetz, W.J., 2005 *An evidence-Based Causative Classification System for Acute Ischemic Stroke*, Annals of Neurology, 2005, (58), pp 688–697.

32. Johnson-Laird, P. N. 1983, *Mental models: Towards a cognitive science of language, inference, and consciousness*, Cambridge, MA, Harvard University Press, 1983.

33. Boland, J., Tenkasi, R.V., 1995, *Perspective making and perspective taking in communities of knowing*, Organizational Science 6(4) pp 350–372.

34. Benerecetti, M., Bouquet P., Ghidini C., 2000, *Contextual Reasoning Distilled*, Journal of Theoretical and Artificial Intelligence (JETAI), 12(2000), pp 279–305.

35. Sicilia, J.J., Sicilia, M.A., Snchez-Alonso, S., et al., 2007, *Knowledge Representation Issues in Ontology-based Clinical Knowledge Management Systems*, International Journal of Technology Management, 2007.

Rules for Mapping SQL Relational Databases to OWL Ontologies

Irina Astrova

Abstract This paper proposes an approach to automatic transformation of relational databases to ontologies, where constraints CHECK are also considered. A relational database is written in SQL and an ontology is written in OWL. The proposed approach can be used for integrating data that are scattered across many different domains and that reside in many separate relational databases.

1 Introduction

Today it is common to get data from a relational database whose structure is defined by a relational database schema. However, relational databases are generally separate and not easily used as merged data sources. Relational database schemas are created independently for each relational database. Even if a million companies clone the same form of relational database, there will be a million relational database schemas, one for each relational database.

On the other hand, many in the science of data integration search for ways to unify the description and retrieval of data in relational databases, by using ontologies. There are several benefits of using ontologies for data integration; e.g.:

- Ontologies provide the ability to recognize inconsistency and redundancy of data in relational databases [1].
- Ontologies are sufficiently comprehensive to support shared common understanding and mapping of data in relational databases [1].
- Ontologies provide a rich predefined vocabulary of the terms used in relational databases. This vocabulary serves as a stable conceptual interface to relational databases and is independent of relational database schemas [1].
- Ontologies provide the ability to express the equivalence of the terms used in relational databases [2].

Tallinn University of Technology, Akadeemia tee 21, 12618 Tallinn, Estonia

irinaastrova@yahoo.com

415

Since ontologies are important to data integration, there is a need to transform relational databases to ontologies. However, manual transformation is hard to do and often takes a lot of time. Thus, there is also a need to automate this transformation. Therefore, this paper proposes an approach to automatic transformation of relational databases (written in SQL [3]) to ontologies (written in OWL [4]).

2 Approach

While there are several approaches to transforming relational databases to ontologies (e.g. [5], [6], [7] and [8]), many data integration scenarios are too complex or require more flexibility than the existing approaches enable. E.g. none of the existing approaches can identify (inverse) functional properties, value restrictions and enumerated data types.

Fig. 1 illustrates the basic idea behind the proposed approach. A relational database is transformed to an ontology using a set of rules called *mapping rules*. These rules relate constructs of a relational model (i.e. tables, columns, constraints, and rows) to those of an ontological model (i.e. classes, properties, inheritance, restrictions, and instances). The mapping rules are then applied to the relational database (source) to produce the ontology (target). Since the mapping rules are specified on the model level, they are applicable to any relational database that conforms to the relational model.

Next the mapping rules will be illustrated by example. An example is the relational database of a company.

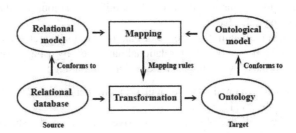

Fig. 1. Transformation of relational databases to ontologies.

2.1 Mapping Tables

A table is mapped to a class unless all its columns are foreign keys to two other tables. Then it is mapped to two object properties (one is an inverse of another).

The primary key of a table `Involvement` in Fig. 2 is composed of foreign keys to two other tables `Project` and `Employee`, indicating a binary (many-to-many) relationship. Therefore, this table is mapped to two object properties: `EmployeeID` (that uses classes `Project` and `Employee` as its domain and range, respectively) and `ProjectID`. The latter is an inverse of the former, meaning that the relationship is bidirectional (i.e. a project involves employees and an employee is involved in projects).

```
CREATE TABLE Involvement (
 EmployeeID INTEGER REFERENCES Employee,
 ProjectID INTEGER REFERENCES Project,
 PRIMARY KEY (EmployeeID, ProjectID))
                          ↓
<owl:ObjectProperty rdf:ID="EmployeeID">
 <rdfs:domain rdf:resource="#Project"/>
 <rdfs:range rdf:resource="#Employee"/>
</owl:ObjectProperty>
<owl:ObjectProperty rdf:ID="ProjectID">
 <owl:inverseOf rdf:resource="#EmployeeID"/>
</owl:ObjectProperty>
```

Fig. 2. Table is mapped to two object properties (one is an inverse of another).

The primary key of a table `Involvement` in Fig. 3 is composed of foreign keys to two other tables `Employee` and `Project`, indicating a binary relationship, again. However, since this table now has an additional column `hours`, it is mapped to a class `Involvement`.

```
CREATE TABLE Involvement (
 EmployeeID INTEGER REFERENCES Employee,
 ProjectID INTEGER REFERENCES Project,
 hours INTEGER,
 PRIMARY KEY (EmployeeID, ProjectID))
                          ↓
<owl:Class rdf:ID="Involvement"/>
```

Fig. 3. Table is mapped to class.

The primary key of a table `Involvement` in Fig. 4 is composed of foreign keys to three other tables `Employee`, `Project` and `Skill`, indicating a ternary relationship. Since only binary relationships can be represented through object properties, this table is mapped to a class `Involvement`.

```
CREATE TABLE Involvement (
 EmployeeID INTEGER REFERENCES Employee,
 ProjectID INTEGER REFERENCES Project,
```

```
SkillID INTEGER REFERENCES Skill,
PRIMARY KEY (EmployeeID, ProjectID, SkillID))
                                      ↓
<owl:Class rdf:ID="Involvement"/>
```

Fig. 4. Table is mapped to class (contd.).

2.2 Mapping Columns

A column is mapped to a data type property with a maximum cardinality of 1 unless it is (part of) a foreign key; i.e. there is a constraint REFERENCES or FOREIGN KEY on it. (For mapping foreign keys, see Section 2.3.4.)

A column ssn in a table Employee in Fig. 5 is not a foreign key. Therefore, this column is mapped to a data type property ssn that uses a class Employee as its domain. This property has a maximum cardinality of 1, because the column ssn may have at most one value for each row in the table Employee (atomicity). Alternatively, the property ssn could be defined as functional, which is the same as saying that the maximum cardinality is 1. It should be noted that if the column ssn were a surrogate key, it would be ignored. A surrogate key is internally generated by the relational database management system using an automatic sequence number generator or its equivalent; e.g. an IDENTITY in SQL Server and Sybase, a SEQUENCE in Oracle and an AUTO_INCREMENT in MySQL.

```
CREATE TABLE Employee(
  ssn INTEGER CHECK (ssn > 0))
                                      ↓
<owl:DatatypeProperty rdf:ID="ssn">
 <rdfs:domain rdf:resource="#Employee"/>
 <rdfs:range rdf:resource="&xsd;positiveInteger"/>
</owl:DatatypeProperty>
<owl:Class rdf:ID="Employee">
 <rdfs:subClassOf>
  <owl:Restriction>
   <owl:onProperty rdf:resource="#ssn"/>
   <owl:maxCardinality rdf:datatype="&xsd;nonNegativeInteger"1/>
  </owl:Restriction>
 </rdfs:subClassOf>
</owl:Class>
```

Fig. 5. Column is mapped to data type property with maximum cardinality of 1.

Most of the mapping of columns has to do with the mapping of data types from SQL to XSD. Unlike SQL, OWL does not have any built-in data types. Instead, it uses XSD (XML Schema Data types).

A column `ssn` in Fig. 5 uses `INTEGER` as its data type. Therefore, a data type property `ssn` could use `integer` as its range. However, there is a constraint `CHECK` on the column `ssn`. This constraint further restricts the range of values for the column `ssn` to integers greater than 0 (i.e. positive integers). Therefore, the data type property `ssn` uses `positiveInteger` as its range.

2.3 Mapping Constraints

SQL supports constraints `UNIQUE`, `NOT NULL`, `PRIMARY KEY`, `REFERENCES`, `FOREIGN KEY`, `CHECK`, and `DEFAULT`. However, not all the constraints can be mapped to OWL. E.g. a constraint `DEFAULT` (that defines a default value for a given column) has no correspondence in OWL. Therefore, it is ignored.

2.3.1 Mapping Constraints UNIQUE

`UNIQUE` is a column constraint. It is mapped to an inverse functional property.

A constraint `UNIQUE` in Fig. 6 specifies that a column `ssn` in a table `Employee` is unique, meaning that no two rows in the table `Employee` have the same value for the column `ssn` (i.e. social security numbers uniquely identify employees). Therefore, this constraint is mapped to an inverse functional property.

```
CREATE TABLE Employee(
  ssn INTEGER UNIQUE)
```
                              ↓
```
<owl:InverseFunctionalProperty rdf:ID="ssn"/>
```
Fig. 6. Constraint UNIQUE is mapped to inverse functional property.

2.3.2 Mapping Constraints NOT NULL

`NOT NULL` is a column constraint. It is mapped to a minimum cardinality of 1.

A constraint `NOT NULL` in Fig. 7 specifies that a column `ssn` in a table `Employee` is not null, meaning that all rows in the table `Employee` have values for the column `ssn` (i.e. all employees are assigned social security numbers). Therefore, this constraint is mapped to a minimum cardinality of 1.

```
CREATE TABLE Employee(
  ssn INTEGER NOT NULL)
```
                              ↓
```
<owl:Class rdf:ID="Employee">
 <rdfs:subClassOf>
```

```
<owl:Restriction>
 <owl:onProperty rdf:resource="#ssn"/>
 <owl:minCardinality rdf:datatype="&xsd;nonNegativeInteger"1/>
 </owl:Restriction>
 </rdfs:subClassOf>
</owl:Class>
```

Fig. 7. Constraint NOT NULL is mapped to minimum cardinality of 1.

2.3.3 Mapping Constraints PRIMARY KEY

There are two forms of constraint PRIMARY KEY: using it as a column constraint (to refer to a single column) and using it as a table constraint (to refer to multiple columns). A column constraint PRIMARY KEY is mapped to both an inverse functional property and a minimum cardinality of 1.

A constraint PRIMARY KEY in Fig. 8 specifies that a column ssn in a table Employee is a primary key, which is the same as saying that the column ssn is both unique and not null. Therefore, this constraint is mapped to both an inverse functional property and a minimum cardinality of 1.

```
CREATE TABLE Employee(
  ssn INTEGER PRIMARY KEY)

                              ↓
<owl:InverseFunctionalProperty rdf:ID="ssn"/>
<owl:Class rdf:ID="Employee">
 <rdfs:subClassOf>
  <owl:Restriction>
   <owl:onProperty rdf:resource="#ssn"/>
   <owl:minCardinality rdf:datatype="&xsd;nonNegativeInteger"1/>
  </owl:Restriction>
 </rdfs:subClassOf>
</owl:Class>
```

Fig. 8. Constraint PRIMARY KEY is mapped to both inverse functional property and minimum cardinality of 1.

2.3.4 Mapping Constraints REFERENCES and FOREIGN KEY

REFERENCES is a column constraint, whereas FOREIGN KEY is a table constraint. Both constraints are used for specifying foreign keys. A foreign key is mapped to an object property unless it is also a primary key. Then it maps to class inheritance.

A constraint REFERENCES in Fig. 9 specifies that a column ProjectID in a table Task is a foreign key to another table Project, indicating a binary (one-to-zero-or-one, one-to-one or many-to-one) relationship. Since the foreign key is not (part of) the primary key, it is mapped to an object property ProjectID that uses classes Task and Project as its domain and range, respectively. This property is restricted to all values from the class Project, because the foreign key implies that for each (non-null) value of the column ProjectID there is the same value in the table Project.

```
CREATE TABLE TASK(
 TaskID INTEGER PRIMARY KEY,
 ProjectID INTEGER REFERENCES Project)
                              ↓
<owl:ObjectProperty rdf:ID="ProjectID">
 <rdfs:domain rdf:resource="#Task"/>
 <rdfs:range rdf:resource="#Project"/>
</owl:ObjectProperty>
<owl:Class rdf:ID="Task">
 <rdfs:subClassOf>
  <owl:Restriction>
   <owl:onProperty rdf:resource="#ProjectID"/>
   <owl:allValuesFrom rdf:resource="#Project"/>
  </owl:Restriction>
 </rdfs:subClassOf>
</owl:Class>
```

Fig. 9. Foreign key is mapped to object property.

A constraint REFERENCES in Fig. 10 specifies that a column ProjectID in a table Task is a foreign key to another table Project, indicating a binary relationship, again. However, since the foreign key is now part of the primary key, it is mapped to an object property ProjectID with a cardinality of 1.

```
CREATE TABLE TASK(
 TaskID INTEGER,
 ProjectID INTEGER REFERENCES Project,
 PRIMARY KEY (TaskID, ProjectID))
                              ↓
<owl:ObjectProperty rdf:ID="ProjectID">
 <rdfs:domain rdf:resource="#Task"/>
 <rdfs:range rdf:resource="#Project"/>
</owl:ObjectProperty>
<owl:Class rdf:ID="Task">
 <rdfs:subClassOf>
  <owl:Restriction>
   <owl:onProperty rdf:resource="#ProjectID"/>
   <owl:cardinality rdf:datatype="&xsd;nonNegativeInteger"1/>
  </owl:Restriction>
 </rdfs:subClassOf>
```

```
</owl:Class>
```

Fig. 10. Foreign key is mapped to object property (contd.).

A constraint FOREIGN KEY in Fig. 11 specifies that a column ProjectID in a table SoftwareProject is a foreign key to another table Project, indicating a binary relationship, again. However, since the foreign key is now the primary key, it is mapped to class inheritance: SoftwareProject is a subclass of Project (i.e. a software project is a project).

```
CREATE TABLE SoftwareProject(
  ProjectID INTEGER PRIMARY KEY,
  FOREIGN KEY (ProjectID) REFERENCES Project)
                                    ↓
<owl:Class rdf:ID="SoftwareProject">
  <rdfs:subClassOf rdf:resource="#Project"/>
</owl:Class>
```

Fig. 11. Foreign key is mapped to class inheritance.

2.3.5 Mapping Constraints CHECK

There are two forms of constraint CHECK: using it as a column constraint (to refer to a single column) and using it as a table constraint (to refer to multiple columns). A column constraint CHECK is mapped to a value restriction unless it has enumeration. Then it is mapped to an enumerated data type. It should be noted that OWL is not powerful enough to express all the value restrictions that can be imposed by a constraint CHECK (e.g. an employee's age as an integer between 18 and 65).

A constraint CHECK in Fig. 12 specifies that a column type in a table Project may have only a value Software. Therefore, a data type property type is restricted to have the same value for all instances in a class Project.

```
CREATE TABLE Project(
  type VARCHAR CHECK (type='Software'))
                          ↓
<owl:Class rdf:ID="Project">
  <rdfs:subClassOf>
    <owl:Restriction>
      <owl:onProperty rdf:resource="#type"/>
      <owl:hasValue rdf:datatype="&xsd;string">Software
      </owl:hasValue>
    </owl:Restriction>
  </rdfs:subClassOf>
</owl:Class>
```

Fig. 12. Constraint CHECK is mapped to value restriction.

A constraint CHECK in Fig. 13 specifies the range for a column sex in a table Employee through a list of values Male and Female. Therefore, this constraint is mapped to an enumerated data type, with one element for each value in the list.

```
CREATE TABLE Employee(
 sex VARCHAR CHECK (sex IN ('Male', 'Female')))
                             ↓
<owl:DatatypeProperty rdf:ID="sex">
 <rdfs:domain rdf:resource="#Employee"/>
 <rdfs:range>
  <owl:DataRange>
   <owl:oneOf>
    <rdf:List>
     <rdf:first rdf:datatype="&xsd;string">Male
     </rdf:first>
     <rdf:rest>
      <rdf:List>
       <rdf:first rdf:datatype="&xsd;string">Female
       </rdf:first>
       <rdf:rest rdf:resource="&rdf;nil"/>
      </rdf:List>
     </rdf:rest>
    </rdf:List>
   </owl:oneOf>
  </owl:DataRange>
 </rdfs:range>
</owl:DatatypeProperty>
```

Fig. 13. Constraint CHECK is mapped to enumerated data type.

2.4 Mapping Rows

A row is mapped to an instance. A row in a table Project in Fig. 14 has a value Software for a column type. Therefore, this row is mapped to an (anonymous) instance in a class Project that has the same value for a data type property type.

```
INSERT INTO Project (type) VALUE ('Software')
                             ↓
<Project>
 <type rdf:datatype="&xsd:string">Software
 </type>
</Project>
```

Fig. 14. Row is mapped to instance.

3 Conclusion

This paper has proposed a set of rules for mapping relational databases (written in SQL) to ontologies (written in OWL). These rules can map all constructs of a relational database to an ontology, with the exception of those constructs that have no correspondences in the ontology (e.g. a constraint DEFAULT).

References

1. Buccella A, Cechich A (2003) An Ontology Approach to Data Integration. JCS&T, 3:62 68
2. Berners-Lee T (1998) Relational Databases on the Semantic Web. http://www.w3.org/DesignIssues/RDB-RDF.html. Accessed 17 January 2008
3. SQL (2002) Database language SQL. ANSI X3.135. http://www.contrib.andrew.cmu.edu/~shadow/sql/sql1992.txt. Accessed 17 January 2008
4. OWL (2004) OWL Web Ontology Language Reference. http://www.w3.org/TR/owl-ref. Accessed 17 January 2008
5. Li M, Du X, Wang S (2005) Learning Ontology from Relational Database. Proceedings of the 4th International Conference on Machine Learning and Cybernetics. 6:3410 3415
6. Shen G, Huang Z, Zhu X, Zhao X (2006) Research on the Rules of Mapping from Relational Model to OWL. Proceedings of the Workshop on OWL: Experiences and Directions. 216
7. Astrova I, Kalja A (2006) Towards the Semantic Web: Extracting OWL Ontologies from SQL Relational Schemata. Proceedings of IADIS International Conference WWW/Internet. 62 66
8. Buccella A, Penabad M, Rodriguez F, Farina A, Cechich A (2004) From Relational Databases to OWL Ontologies. Proceedings of the 6th National Russian Research Conference

Ontology Oriented Support for the Teaching Process in the Greek Secondary Education

V. S. Belesiotis

Abstract In this paper we present the advantages of ontology based assistance in teaching, particularly regarding the Greek Secondary Education System, and especially Informatics related courses. We propose the use of ontologies as a tool for better organizing the learning subject, for supporting the teaching process and enhancing the evaluation procedure. More specifically, we present a methodology for the development of teaching ontologies following the aim and goals of the Educational System, the latest theories about learning, the relevant textbooks and the students' educational level.

1. Introduction

The science of Didactics is primarily focused on two concepts; the concept of teaching and the concept of learning, with the teaching process comprised by the student, the teacher and the learning subject [1]. The success of the learning process depends on the effectiveness of the teaching process, which does not only depend on teaching, but also on the design and development phase of the teaching process. The Design and Development phase is extremely crucial to the students' learning performance. During this phase, the teacher decides upon the goals, the teaching activities, the relevant educational material, the supportive teaching techniques and a timetable. The teaching process may be supported by Information and Communication Technologies (ICT) [2], that incorporate elements of the science of teaching and the learning theories, as for instance the didactic concept of representation (believement - conception), adjusted according to the curriculums and the students' level, in order to increase the quality of the educational output and enhance critical thinking. There are many representation techniques for visualizing the relations between concepts that can be used during the teaching process to enhance the learning output. These representation techniques have several limitations, primarily because of the static nature of the

Department of Informatics, University of Piraeus, 80 Karaoli & Dimitriou str., Piraeus 18534, GREECE, vbel@unipi.gr

visualization and their lack of formal organizational structure. In order to overcome these limitations, we propose a methodology for the use of ontologies in the teaching process.

The structure of this paper is organized as follows. Section 2 provides a didactic related Theoretical Frame, and in section 3 we introduce representation technologies for teaching support. Furthermore, in section 4 we present a methodology for the development of teaching ontologies and in section 5 we provide an example along with the methodology. Finally, in the last section conclusions along with future work are discussed.

Keywords for this paper: Didactics, Ontology, Knowledge representation, ICT, Intelligent teaching support systems, Education

2. Didactic's Theoretical Frame

The teacher, during the teaching designing and development phase, has to bear in mind several factors that can improve the learning process. These factors include the introduction of ICT technologies, which can be used, alongside textbooks, to support the teaching process of the learning subject, providing the students an environment suitable to discover, search and enhance of their thinking abilities.

The textbooks have a linear structure, and evidently cannot provide a multidimensional representation of the relations among the concepts they describe, nor categorize these concepts in complex multidimensional structures.

Technologies for the organization and presentation of the learning subject can be used during the teaching designing and development phase, as well as during the actual teaching process. Several factors should be considered in order such methodologies to be successfully incorporated in the teaching process:

- The modern theories about learning.
- The rules of the Educational System and the revalent curriculums.
- The textbooks.
- The students' level.

The teachers must select the most relevant software, and additionally be able to modify it according to their didactic choices, since every learning subject must be taught with respect to the corresponding students. For instance, in Greek Education that is used as a reference for this paper, the concept "structure of the computer" appears in different Informatics courses in the Lower Secondary Education (in Greek Gymnasio), in the Upper Secondary Education (in Greek, Geniko Lykeio-GE.L) and the Technical Vocational Educational Schools (in Greek Epaggelmatiko Lykeio-EPA.L), and as a result is taught to students of different age, educational level and learning purpose. Therefore, the Greek Pedagogical Institute has determined the aim and goals for every educational curriculum [3, 4], and proposed different textbooks for each grade. According to our experience, most of the aforementioned guidelines are not really used in the teaching process at the level in question. Therefore, more feasible proposals are vital.

3. Representation technologies and teaching support

The concept of representation (believement) is a significant factor of the educational process and the enhancement of critical thinking. There are many methodologies for the support of this process as, mind maps, conceptual diagrams, concept Maps [5, 6]. These techniques may be either used by the teacher to present the concepts and their relations during teaching (visualizing the relations between concepts), or even to evaluate the learning level. The student may either construct the map from scratch, or rectify it by introducing or deleting nodes and relations.

The following characteristics of such category representation techniques result in several limitations:

- Only one "view".
- Limited reusability.
- No formal organization of concepts.

The teachers, during the teaching designing and development phase, have to develop different versions of the same didactic entity, and use the most appropriate version with respect to the students' educational level, in the classroom, as it is formed at this point. The teacher can overcome this limitation, if the representation of concepts and relations is stored in a structure which follows specific rules, and enables the controlled modification of the stored knowledge, combined with a series of relevant visualizations.

According to Gruber 1993 [7], "An ontology is a specification of a conceptualization", and can be employed to formally describe the concepts of a given domain and their properties. Ontologies include concepts, slots (properties) on these concepts and restrictions on the properties. A knowledge base is an ontology together with individual instances of its concepts. The concepts (or classes) of an ontology describe the most significant concepts in the domain. For instance the classes of an educational ontology may include the concepts student, subject and teacher. Slots illustrate properties of the concepts of the ontology. For instance a slot for a subject may be if it has any prerequisite knowledge. An individual (or instance) of the concept "student" can be a specific student of the class.

According to [8] the development of ontology includes the following:

- Define classes in the ontology.
- Arrange the taxonomy of classes (i.e. hierarchical organization).

- Define slots and restrictions.
- Create instances.

Some relevant benefits of ontology engineering are: Formal Rules, Existance of several Knowledge Engineering Tools and Methodologies aiding the development and visualization process, Reusability, and Coherent organization. According to [8] some reasons behind the development of ontologies may be: Sharing of common understanding of the structure of information, Reuse of domain knowledge, Analysis domain knowledge.

First of all, by developing a domain ontology conceptualizing the knowledge behind the concepts teaching, we aim in capturing the knowledge of the most experienced teachers, regarding the teaching process for specific subjects and educational levels, and share this knowledge with the teacher community. Given this knowledge, less experienced teachers will have a concise organization of the teaching material. Our goal is to manage and organize the teaching material in a commonly accepted manner. The knowledge captured in the ontology may be used by teachers in the process of organizing their teaching material, as a concise conceptualization of the domain that the students must be taught. In addition, the ontology can be utilized for the visualization of the taught concepts and their relations. As a result, the knowledge of the teaching ontology can be reused and even be extended or modified to reflect changes in the curriculum.

Moreover, current research in ontological engineering has provided many interesting methodologies and systems, e.g. Protégé [9], that can assist in developing ontologies and presenting them in different forms.

4. A methodology for the development of teaching ontologies

In this section we present a methodology for the development of teaching ontologies that can be used in the teaching process, and particularly in the Greek secondary education in Informatics.

The development of an ontology for the aforementioned educational role must differ from the general case of the development of an ontology for a specific subject, as for instance the human body or the computer in general. In order to develop an ontology that can be used for educational purposes the following must be taken into consideration:

- The aims and goals for the specific educational level, as stated in the correspondence curriculum.
- The age of the students.
- The relevant textbooks.
- The educational level of the students.

The learning subject must be organized in a manner that enables the possibility of a multidimensional approach, contributing this way in the development of knowledge as well as to the enhancement of the critical thinking.

Moreover, the ontologist must take into account:

- The latest educational theories in learning [10] with respect to the students' age.
- The functions of the human cognitive systems, which is considered a current research field of neuroscience [11], and that according to traditional psychology can be hierarchically organised as: perception, memory, thought, representation and imagination; with memory to be considered the most significant function with respect to teaching, which can be broken into [12] critical, stochastic-critical and creative thinking.
- The function and nature of the human brain/intelligence and the theories regarding the emotional intelligence [13] and multiple intelligence [14].

The methodology behind the development of an ontology with respect to the aforementioned scope must follow the following phases.

Phase A: Development of a pilot ontology
Step 1: Research-Design-Implementation

- A workgroup is assembled from the selected educational level, including ontologists and experienced teachers.
- The educational units that will be included in the ontology are defined and the relevant educational theories and the means of their successful incorporation are specified.
- The ontology is designed.
- The ontology is implemented.

Step 2: Pilot use

- A group of teachers is selected to participate in the initial use of the ontology. They are prepared and trained by the work group, both technically and educationally, for the appropriate usage of the educational environment. The ontology is delivered to the group for pilot use.
- The ontology is modified by the teachers, with respect to the level of their students and their didactic approaches.
- Teachers utilize the modified ontologies to automatically produce a series of diagrams.
- The ontology and especially the resulting diagrams are used in classroom to support the teaching process.

Step 3: Evaluation of the pilot ontology

- The ontology is evaluated with respect to both the teacher and the student.

- The findings of the evaluation are analysed and the ontology is modified accordingly be the working group.
- Technical and didactic documentation is created.
- A forum for the gathering of the teachers' commends and ideas, is created.
- The ontology is adapted according to the gathered information, and delivered for use.

Phase B: Utilization of the ontology to support teaching

- The ontology is utilized during the teaching process
- The forum is used in order to gather ideas about further possible uses and the modification of the ontology. The resulting environment will be adapted to the average level of the educational rung in question.
- The ontology must be iteratively modified, extended and adjusted, both educationally and technically, following all the latest advances; with latest version will be used and revaluated.

5. A paradigm

We will demonstrate the modeling of the concept of Computer Memory. This concept can be related to other relevant concepts such as   main memory, secondary memory, BIOS, RAM, ROM, flash memory, volatile, static, flip-flops, magnetic disk, optical disc, magnetic tape, hard disc, floppy disk, CD, DVD, access time, byte and word. These concepts may be represented in the ontology as classes. The relations among these concepts, with respect to the aforementioned theory about the kinds of human intelligence [14], may be modeled in the ontology as relationships among the relevant classes.

Therefore, the following relationships may be introduced:

- Linguistic intelligence: part-of, consists-of
- Logical-mathematica: intelligence: quantitative, dimensions
- Spatial intelligence: is-positioned-on.
- Bodily-kinesthetic intelligence: The series of operations needed to mount the main memory to the motherboard.

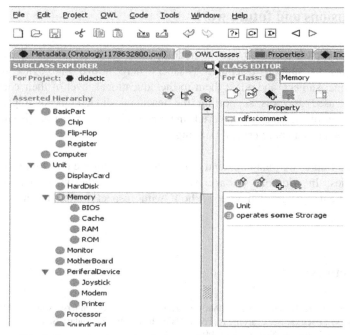

Fig. 1. Screenshot from the Software Environment, Protégé [9]

This ontology has been created to organize the concepts and their relations as they appear in the relevant textbooks for the Greek GE.L. Accordingly, the didactic scope of the ontology is relevant to the educational level of the GE.L students. For the implementation of the ontology, Protégé [9] was employed (Fig1). The concept maps were automatically created through the Jambalaya protégé plug-in (Fig2).

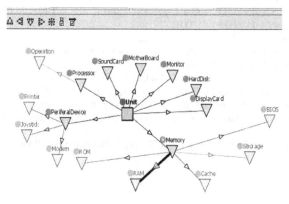

Fig. 2. Screenshot from Protégé Jambalaya plug in [9], for the concept 'Unit'

Conclusions and future work

In this paper we proposed our methodology for the development of educational ontologies to support teaching. Teachers may utilize ontologies for every educational subject, and adapt them to the educational level of their class. These may be used as tools supporting the teachers' didactic needs regarding the preparation of the teaching material, the automatic production of visual stimulus and the enhancement of critical thinking.

In the future, we plan to extend our methodology for the development of richer ontologies. In addition, we are working on the extensive evaluation of the employment of our methodology both with respect to the teachers' and the students' needs.

References

1. Ματσαγγούρας, Η.: Θεωρία της Διδασκαλίας, pp. 136-140, Gutenberg, Αθήνα (2003)
2. Leask, M., Pachler, N.: Learning to Teach Using ICT in the Secondary School, Routledge, London; New York (1999)
3. Δ.Ε.Π.Π.Σ.: Διαθεματικό Ενιαίο Πλαίσιο Προγραμμάτων Σπουδών, Παιδαγωγικό Ινστιτούτο, Αθήνα (2002)
4. Ε.Π.Π.Σ.: Ενιαίο Πλαίσιο Προγραμμάτων Σπουδών Ενιαίου Λυκείου, Αθήνα: Παιδαγωγικό Ινστιτούτο (1998)
5. Novak, J., Gowin, B.: Learning How to Learn, Cambridge University Press (1984)
6. Novak, J.: Learning, Creating, and Using Knowledge, Erlbaum, Lawrence Associates, Inc. (1998)
7. Gruber, T.R.: A Translation Approach to Portable Ontology Specification. Knowledge Acquisition (1993)
8. Noy, N.F., McGuinness, D.L.: Ontology Development 101: A Guide to Creating Your First Ontology, Stanford University (2001)
9. Protégé, Stanford, http://protege.stanford.edu/
10. Bransford, .D., Brown A.L., Cocking, R.R.: How People Learn: Brain, Mind, Experience and School. National Academy Press (1999)
11. Posner, M. & Raichle, M.: Images of Mind, Freeman, New York (1995)
12. Nickerson, R.: Dimensions of Thinking: A Critique, in Jones, B.F.,& Idol, L., Dimensions of Thinking and Cognitive Interaction, Hillsdale, N.J., Erlbaum (1990)
13. Goleman, D.: Emotional Intelligence: Why it Can Matter More than IQ, Bantam Books, New York (1996)
14. Gardner, H.: Multiple Intelligences. The Theory in Practice. Basic Books, New York (1993)

A new Formal Concept Analysis based learning approach to Ontology building

Haibo Jia, Julian Newman, Huaglory Tianfield

Abstract: Formal Concept Analysis (FCA) is a concept clustering approach that has been widely applied in ontology learning. In our work, we present an innovative approach to generating information context from a tentative domain specified scientific corpus and mapping a concept lattice to a formal ontology. The application of the proposed approach to Semantic Web search demonstrates this automatically constructed ontology can provide a semantic way to expand users' query context, which can complement a conventional search engine.

1 Introduction

Development of web technology provides a networked platform for a distributed research community to disseminate their research contributions and acquire others' research findings. Digital libraries, E-Journals, E-Prints, scholarly websites and search engine tools offer researchers great capability to obtain online information. However massive amounts of information, lack of formalized domain knowledge representation and non-unified terminology bring about either an "information explosion" as result of polysemy or "information loss" where synonymy is overlooked. This inevitably affects the efficiency and effectiveness of researchers' information searching and browsing.

Current search engines employ user–specified keywords and phrases as the major means of their input. Digital libraries, such as ACM DL[2], add a metainformation layer, so that from a given author, journal, conference proceedings and predefined topic description, publications can be found. Google

Haibo Jia, Julian Newman, Huaglory Tianfield

School of Engineering and Computing, Glasgow Caledonian University, Glasgow UK
{Haibo.Jia, J.Newman, H.Tianfield}@gcal.ac.uk

---

[2] http://portal.acm.org/dl.cfm

also use document similarity to extend the result of users' query. However, these services are not able to augment context in the process of search. They cannot assist the user to generate a proper query term according to the topics of interest and even cannot expand query terms according to semantic similarity and different semantic generality.

Semantic web provides a knowledge-based environment in which information can be well defined by ontology and intelligent application can better process linked data to improve the interactions between the user and computer system. Ontology is a conceptualization of a domain into human understandable but machine readable format consisting of entities, attributes, relationship and axioms [1]. In the document query scenario, factors in the ontology could be used to expand the users' understanding of query term so that an extended query context will be provided.

In this paper, a new concept clustering based learning approach is proposed for ontology building. The application using the constructed ontology for query expansion is also demonstrated. The rest of this paper is organized as follows. Section 2 discusses related work. Section 3 discusses the detail of using formal concept analysis to extract ontology from a scientific corpus. Section 4 discusses the application of using semantic web technology to expand query context. Conclusion is given in the Section 5.

2 Ontology building by machine learning: states of the art

Ontology building is the process by which concepts and their relations are extracted from the data which can be free-text, semi-structured or data-schema. In general, it is unrealistic to use general-purpose ontologies for guiding such learning in a specific scientific or research domain. Krovetz & Croft [2] points out that 40% of the words in canonical form in the titles and abstracts of the Communications of the ACM are not included in the LDOCE (Longman Dictionary of Contemporary English). Recently, some researchers have looked for possible ways to automatically build domain ontology from scientific corpus and develop scholarly semantic web based on this ontology [3][4][5][6]. Consequently, a number of machine learning approaches are applied to ontology building, including scientific text structure based learning, syntactic pattern based learning and conceptual clustering based learning etc.

In [7], Makagonov observes that scientific text is highly hierarchical text so that words at different levels of abstraction are located in different parts of a scientific document. In most cases concepts in the domain description are more general than concepts in the conference or journal name and the later are more general than concepts in the individual document title and so on. Based on this observation, a level-by-level automatic ontology learning is proposed for ontology building. This approach is simple but quite efficient for ontology building when learning from small corpus. However, the learning result could be negatively affected due to the authors giving their documents an inexplicit title (for example, a PhD thesis entitled "who are the Experts? E-Scholars in the Semantic Web"). This is, unfortunately not unusual in scientific publication. Furthermore, the amount of generality level has been decided before the learning, which may not be consistent with real concept structure.

In [3], an approach of extracting taxonomy using syntactical patterns is discussed, which is based on the work presented by Hearst [8]. In this approach, linguistic syntactical patterns such as "NP such as NP", "NP including NP" etc are used to recognize the concept and semantic relation namely is-a relation, here NP refer to "Noun Phrase". It has been proved that this approach can result in quite high quality ontology. However, Hearst's patterns appear relatively rarely even in big corpora [9], So many useful concepts could be neglected.

Clustering algorithms have been broadly studied within the Machine Learning and Data Analysis community. Hierarchical concept clustering has been applied in the learning to build ontology. In [10], Bisson et al design general framework and a corresponding workbench –Mo'k- for user to integrate concept cluster methods to build ontology. An agglomerative clustering algorithm is also used to present the result. In [11], Philipp compares Formal Concept Analysis (FCA), Divisive and Agglomerative Clustering for learning taxonomies from text. The result shows FCA has low efficiency but very good traceability compared to other two methods. The clusters learnt by FCA also have their own intentional meaningful descriptions, thus facilitating users' understanding of generated clusters. Another advantage of FCA is that its final outcome is concept lattice rather than tree like forms produced in other two methods. Lattice form assures a concept may have more than one super or sub concept, which reflects real-life concepts organisation. Generally, the principle paradigm in most of these approaches is based on a distributional hypothesis, which assumes that terms are similar to the extent to which they share similar linguistic contexts and similar terms can be clustered together to form a concept. Thereafter according to various linguistic contexts, corresponding ontology can be developed.

In learning from scientific corpus to build scholarly ontology, the topical context rather than linguistic context is more widely considered. In [4], Quan proposes a Fuzzy Formal Concept Analysis (FFCA) framework to automatically generate ontology for scholarly semantic web. The information context is built by scientific documents (object) and keyphrase (attribute). The most frequent keyphrases occurring in the same papers are clustering to form hierarchical clustered concept to represent different research areas in a particular domain. However, Zhang [5] argues that document-keyword context allows a keyword that only occurrs in one document to be selected to compute concept lattice, which could result in large noisy information due to the authors' misuse of a keyword. He points out that information context should be built from the viewpoint of collection rather than an individual. So Zhang builds information context using keywords as both objects and attributes, where each object has particular keywords as attributes if that keyword occurs along with the object keyword in a document and meets a specified support threshold in the whole collection. The concept hierarchies learnt from this information context can bring improved precision for document classification.

3 Formal Concept Analysis based Learning approach to Ontology building

Different methods have been proposed in the literature to address the problem of (semi-) automatically deriving a concept hierarchy from scientific text. Our motivation is that this concept hierarchy should be applied in the users' query to expand query context. Users' query term should be identified in this structure; topical similar terms should be clustered into the same concept and the intentional description of the concept should be better understood and commonly accepted by the practice of community. The previous research has shown FCA is an effective technique that can formally abstract data into a hierarchical conceptual structure with good traceability and understandability. In our research, the selection of context and the mapping from formal concept lattice to formal ontology representation are major consideration. The work flow of our proposed approach can be depicted as in Figure 1.

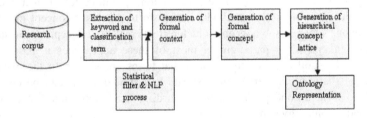

Fig.1. Ontology Learning Work Flow

3.1 Formal Concept Analysis

In order to better interpret our approach, we briefly recall some basic terminologies and definition of FCA and further detail can be found in [12].

Definition 1. A Formal Context is a triple *(G, M, I)*, where G is a set of objects, M is a set of attributes, and I is a binary relation between G and M (i.e $I \subseteq G \times M$). *(g, m)* $\in I$ can be read as object g has attribute m.

Definition 2. Formal Concept of context *(G, M, I)* is a pair *(A, B)* with
$A \subseteq G$, $B \subseteq M$, $A\acute{} =B$, $B\acute{} =A$ where iff $A \subseteq G$ we define
$A\acute{} :=\{m \in M \mid \forall g \in A:(g,m) \in I\}$ and iff $B \subseteq M$ we define
$B\acute{} := \{g \in G \mid \forall m \in B:(g,m) \in I\}$

Definition 3. Sub-Super concept relation: $(A_1,B_1) \le (A_2,B_2) \Leftrightarrow A_1 \subseteq A_2 \ (\Leftrightarrow B_2 \subseteq B_1)$
is defined as (A_2,B_2) is superconcept of (A_1,B_1).

FCA uses order theory to analyze the correlations between objects, G, and their attributes, M. A concept is composed by a set of objects which are similar according to the interpretation of attributes. Inclusion relation between the object sets can reflect the sub-super relation between different concepts. The concepts and their relations can construct a concept lattice which will finally be converted to domain ontology; in this ontology only subsumption relation can be extracted rather than other enriched relation. The selection of object and attribute will vary based on different application.

3.2 Information Context Construction

In FCA, the selection of formal context is a crucial step. Different formal context will model different aspects of the information and result in different applications to consume the information. For our case, we intend to model keywords in a research domain by topical similarity and subsumption which should expand users' search context and improve the interactive capability of traditional search engines.

In [5], information context is developed based on keyword-keyword pairs. If two keywords are correlated with the same keyword set, these two keywords are assumed to be semantically similar. The correlation is determined by cooccurence of keywords in the same document. In the concept lattice, a concept will be described by a set of keywords. However, in our point of view concept descriptors should be more intensively meaningful and controlled terms, which should be more easily understandable for users. On the other hand, the large number of keywords in the corpus will increase the size of attribute list so that the efficiency of FCA is to be affected. The candidate of attribute in the information context should be common topical terms in a domain which should be easily understandable and have suitable level of generality. In addition, its size should be restricted in a controlled range.

In ACM digital library, a Computing Classification System (CCS) [3] is well defined. It is an existing knowledge base in computer science discipline to assist the author to classify their works. In CCS, the tree structure of topical terms normally used to classify the paper could be used to describe the keywords

---

[3] http://www.acm.org/class/

clustered within such topic because a set of keywords can be regarded as the representative of the paper. In most papers from ACM, author defined keywords and classifiers (i.e., classification terms) from CCS may occur explicitly. We propose a novel approach to utilising these resources to construct keyword-classification term context in computer science. In this context, keywords are explicit definition from author, which are also widely used by user to raise queries in routine search, and classification terms are from the controlled terms defined in CCS. Moreover the correlation between keywords and classifier can be implicitly discovered from the real classification of the paper made by authors themselves.

In order to implement our approach, we have downloaded 900 papers from ACM digital library to construct a tentative domain-dependent scientific corpus. Every paper's primary classification is below "**H.3 INFORMATION STORAGE AND RETRIEVAL**". The selection of a specified domain can avoid the sparse distribution of the keyword in the corpus. All the metadata information is parsed from the information page of the paper and then they are fed in predefined database; the data schema is depicted in Figure 2. The 8 keyword fields are defined, which basically cover the maximum number of author defined keyword in a paper.

source	
Paper_ID	int unsigned
File_ID	int
Paper_title	varchar(200)
Author1	varchar(45)
Author2	varchar(45)
Author3	varchar(45)
Journal_conference_name	varchar(200)
Page	varchar(11)
Year_of_pub	year
URL_link	varchar(45)
Keyword1	varchar(45)
Keyword2	varchar(45)
Keyword3	varchar(45)
Keyword4	varchar(45)
Keyword5	varchar(45)
Keyword6	varchar(45)
Keyword7	varchar(45)
Keyword8	varchar(45)
Primary_class	varchar(45)
Additional_class	varchar(100)
Abstract	longtext (2147483647)

Fig.2. metadata table schema

Due to existence of the multidisciplinary nature of the papers, it is very common that a series of classification terms are used to classify the paper. So in this scheme, we define two classification fields for each document. In a record of the data table, all keywords and corresponding classification term are calculated and the relation weight between them is incremented. The pseudo-code of the corpus-wide method which, given a metadata data table of the corpus, returns the information context is presented in List 1. The snippet of the context with weighted relation is shown in List 2.

```
HashMap <String, HashMap> Context=new HashMap<String,HashMap>();
HashMap <String, Integer> Relation;
```

```
for-each Record in Recordset
    for-each Classification in Record
        for-each Keyword in Record
            if (context.containKey(Keyword)==null)
                Relation=new HashMap<String,Integer>;
                Relation.put(Classification,1);
                Context.put(Keyword,Relation);
            else
                Relation=Context.get(Keyword);
                if (Relation.containKey(Classification))
                    Integer weight=Relation.get(Classification)++;
                    Relation.put(Classification,Weight);
                else Relation.put(Classification, 1);
                end if-else
            end if-else
        end for
    end for
end for
```

List.1. Pseudo-code of the context construction

personal agents----{Information Search and Retrieval=1, Distributed Artificial Intelligence=1, Learning=1}
web searching----{Information Search and Retrieval=1, Systems=1, CODING AND INFORMATION
THEORY=1, Online Information Services=1, Content Analysis and Indexing=1}
scorm - lom----{Systems and Software=1, Online Information Services=1, Document Preparation=1}
replication----{Systems and Software=1, PERFORMANCE OF SYSTEMS=1}
computer mediated communication----{Information Search and Retrieval=1, Public Policy Issues=1}
edit distance----{Online Information Services=1}
ontology----{Systems and Software=4, Information Search and Retrieval=14, Interoperability=1, Library
Automation=1, Formal Definitions and Theory=1, Models=1, User Interfaces=1, Distributed Artificial In
telligence=1, SOFTWARE ENGINEERING=1, Online Information Services=9, Information Storage=1
Learning=1, Knowledge Representation Formalisms and Methods=2}
daily delta----{INFORMATION STORAGE AND RETRIEVAL=1, Hypertext/Hypermedia=1}
order of insertion----{DATA STORAGE REPRESENTATIONS=1, DATA STRUCTURES=1, Content
Analysis and Indexing=1}
service composition----{Online Information Services=1} ....

List.2. Information Context snippet

3.3 Statistic filter and Natural Language Processing

The initial information context consists of 2201 keywords and 107 corresponding classification terms. According to FCA, a set of keywords will be clustered to the concept and the associated classification terms will be description of the concept. To some extent, ontology is consensus in a domain. So it is necessary to assure that the keywords and their associated classification terms are reasonable and commonly acceptable. Here we propose an empirical statistic approach to filtering out uncommon accepted keywords and associated keyword-classifier relations, which could be caused by author's individual preference, their error prone definition or correlation approach we use to construct information context. In this approach, we are mainly concerned about the occurrence frequency of the relation between keyword and associated classification term. We assume that in our corpus if the number of associated relations between a keyword and a corresponding classification term is higher than a threshold, this relation will be retained for final ontology construction. Otherwise this relation will be deleted from the context; furthermore if there is no relation between a keyword and any classification term, the keyword will be deleted. Likewise, if no keywords are related with a specified classification term, this term will be removed from the context. The thresholds n=1,2,3,4,5 respectively are used to this information context, empirical study shows n=3 is the idealist threshold value, which can give a good trade-off between the quality of keywords and the quantity of classification. After filtration 173 keywords and 12 classification terms are kept in the context, the new binary information context is shown as in Figure 3.

Context Table	Natural Language Proc...	Information Search an...	Learning	Content Analysis and L...	Knowledge Represent...
indexing		X		X	
wordnet		X		X	
latent semantic indexing		X		X	
content-based image r...		X		X	
text categorization		X		X	
text mining		X		X	
similarity search		X		X	
data mining		X		X	
natural language proce...	X	X		X	
machine learning		X	X	X	
information retrieval	X	X		X	
xml retrieval		X		X	
information extraction	X	X	X	X	
language modeling		X			
automatic topic search		X			

Title: Scholar

Fig.3. Information context with binary relation

3.4 Formal concept generation

After constructing the context the concepts and concept lattice can be generated using Formal Concept Analysis. Here we use ToscanaJ [13] –a classical FCA tool. Constructed context is input; an extracted concept lattice is produced shown as in Figure 4. In the concept lattice, each node represents a concept that has object (white box) and attribute (grey box). In this case, object is represented by a set of keywords and attribute is represented by classification terms. The link between two concepts represents super-sub concept relation. The object of each concept is a union of all the objects from the subconcept and itself, likewise each attribute is an intersection of all the attributes from superconcept. Obviously the subconcept has fewer keywords and more restrictive classifier than superconcept. This structure can be used to expand users' query.

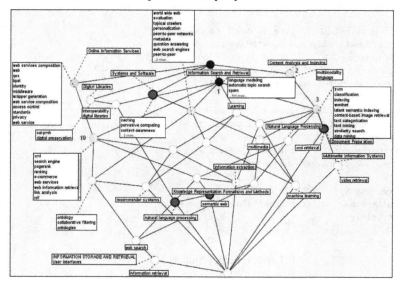

Fig.4. Concept Lattice

3.5 Formal Ontology Representation

Ontology is formalization of concepts and their relations between concept, which can be utilized by agent to better interpret and consume the information. Generally ontology can be formally defined by <C,P,I,S,E>, where C refers to Class; P refers to property of Class; I refers to instance of Class; S refers to subsumption relation and E refers to other Enriched relation. In our case, only subsumption relation is considered. In the above concept lattice, the concept can be mapped to class in the ontology definition; the keywords in each concept can be mapped to the instance of ontology; the element of attribute will be mapped to the property of ontology and finally sub-super concept relation is equivalent to subsumption relation in ontology. This ontology can easily be represented by standard ontology language RDF/RDFS. The snippet of ontology is shown as in List 3.

```
<rdfs:Class rdf:ID="Concept1"/>
<rdfs:Class rdf:ID="Concept2"/>
<rdfs:Class rdf:ID="Concept3"/>
<rdfs:Class rdf:ID="Concept4"/>
<rdfs:Class rdf:ID="Concept6">
    <rdfs:subClassOf rdf:resource="#Concept4"/>
    <rdfs:subClassOf rdf:resource="#Concept2"/>
</rdfs:Class>
.........
<rdf:Property rdf:ID="Online_Information_Services">
    <rdfs:domain rdf:resource="#Concept1"/>
</rdfs:Property>
<rdf:Property rdf:ID="Digital_Libraries">
    <rdfs:domain rdf:resource="#Concept2"/>
</rdf:Property>
<rdf:Property rdf:ID="System_and_Software">
    <rdfs:domain rdf:resource="#Concept3"/>
</rdf:Property>
<rdf:Property rdf:ID="Information_Search_and_Retrieval">
    <rdfs:domain rdf:resource="#Concept4"/
</rdf:Property>
<rdf:Property rdf:ID="Learning">
    <rdfs:domain rdf:resource="#Concept8"/>
</rdf:Property>
```

List.3. Ontology Snippet

4 Query Expansion Application

The concept in the above ontology can be regarded as the query context, the expansion within a context and among the context provides a solid mechanism to expand users' query. In our work, we intend to build ontology driven expansion functionality on the top of search engine rather than replacing it.

In this application, SPARQL can be used to express queries across RDF data sources to discover the relevant concept. If a user raises the initial query using keyword "xml", the narrowest concept including this keyword can be located by SPARQL statement (1) in List 4. In our example corpus, concept 10 will be returned (cf. Figure 4). "search engine" "pagerank" "ranking" "RDF" "web service" "link analysis" etc keywords list in this concept can also be recommended by statement (2). By executing statements (3), all the classification terms associated with this concept and its super concept can be obtained. As there is no inference function in the SPARQL itself, so a program model is needed to trace all the super concepts. Here classification terms {Online Information Services}^{Information Search and Retrieval} can be obtained as the description of this query context. If this query context is too narrow to user's requirement, user can filter this classification term set. Statement (4) can be used to relocate new concept which implicitly represent a new query context, thereafter more relevant keywords will be recommended. Likewise if the user wants to narrow his query to obtain more pertinent query context and keywords, he can navigate the subconcepts to relocate new query context and keyword list. After this process, the selected keywords will be utilized by search engine to return documents.

```
Prefix :<http://www.owl-ontologies.com/scholar.owl#>
Prefix rdf: <http://www.w3.org/1999/02/22-rdf-syntax-ns#>
Prefix rdfs: <http://www.w3.org/2000/01/rdf-schema#>
(1) Concept= SELECT  ?Concept
               WHERE {:xml  rdf:type  ?Concept.}
(2) KeywordList= SELECT ?keywords
               WHERE {?keywords rdf:type :Concept}
(3) SuperConcepts= SELECT ?SuperConcept
               WHERE {:Concept rdfs:subClassOf ?SuperConcept}
    Classifications= SELECT ?Classification
               WHERE{
               {?Classification rdfs:domain :Concept} UNION
               {?Classification rdfs:domain :SuperConcept1} UNION
               ...UNION{?Classification rdfs:domain :SuperConceptn}}
(4) Concept= SELECT ?Concept
            WHERE {
            {:Classification1 rdfs:domain  ?Concept} UNION
            {:Classification2 rdfs:domain ?Concept} UNION
            ….. UNION {:Classficationn rdfs:domain ?Concept}}
```

List.4. SPARQL Statements Example

5 Conclusion

In this paper, we have presented a Formal Concept Analysis based learning approach to building domain specific ontology from scientific corpus. The keyword-classifier context has been utilized to generate information context. The semantic web technology has been adopted to demonstrate function of query expansion driven by this ontology, which can be applied to complement the capability of search engine in digital library.

References:

[1] Guarino, N., Giaretta, P.: Ontologies and Knowledge Bases: Towards a Terminological Clarification. IOS Press, Amsterdam (1995)

[2] Krovetz, R., Croft, W.B.: Lexical Ambiguity and Information Retrieval. Lexical Acquisition: exploiting on-line resources to build a lexicon, pp.45-65. Hillsdale, New Jersey, Lawrence Erlbaum Associates (1991)

[3] Novacek, V., Smrz, P., Pomikalek, J.: Text Mining for Semantic Relations as Support Base of a Scientific Portal Generation. In Proceedings of 5th International Conference on Language Resources and Evaluation, pp1338-1343. ELRA, Genova (2006)

[4]Quan, T., Hui, S., Fong., A., Cao,T.: Automatic Generation of Ontology for Scholarly Semantic Web. In The Semantic Web – ISWC 2004, LNCS, pp726-pp740. Springer, Hiroshima (2004)

[5]Zhang, G., Troy,A., and Bourgoin, K.: Bootstrapping Ontology Learning for Information Retrieval Using Formal Concept Analysis and Information Anchors. In 14th International Conference on Conceptual Structures. Alborg (2006)

[6]Zhao, P., Zhang, M., D., Tang, S.: Finding Hidden Semantics behind Reference Linkages: an Ontological Approach for Scientific Digital Libraries. In The Database Systems for Advanced Applications, 10th International Conference, LNCS, pp699-710. Springer, Beijing (2005)

[7]Makagonov, p., Figueroa, A., Sboychakov, K., Gelbukh, A.: Learning a Domain Ontology from Hierarchically Structured Texts. In Proc. of Workshop "Learning and Extending Lexical Ontologies by using Machine Learning Methods". At 22nd International Conference on Machine learning. Bonn (2005)

[8]Hearst, M., A.: Automatic acquisition of hyponyms from large text corpora. In Proceedings of the 14th conference on Computational linguistics, pp539-545. Morrisotown, NJ, USA (1992)

[9]Cimiano,P., Pivk,A., Thieme,L.: Learning Taxonomic Relations from Heterogeneous Sources of Evidence. Ontology Learning from Text: Methods, Evaluation and Applications Volume 123 of Frontiers in Artificial Intelligence, pp 59-73. ISO Press (2005)

[10]Bisson, G., Nédellec, C., Cañ amero, L.: Designing clustering methods for ontology building – The Mo'k workbench' in proceedings of the ECAI Ontology Learning Workshop. Berlin (2000)

[11]Cimiano, P., Hotho, A., Staab, S.: Comparing conceptual, divisive and agglomerative clustering for learning taxonomies from text. In Proceedings of the European Conference on Artificial Intelligence (ECAI), pp 435-439. Valencia (2004)

[12]Carpineto, C., Romano, G.: Concept Data Analysis – Theory and Applications. John Wiley & Sons Ltd, England. (2004)

[13] ToscanaJ Suite, http://toscanaj.sourceforge.net.

Creating and Querying an Integrated Ontology for Molecular and Phenotypic Cereals Data

Sonia Bergamaschi and Antonio Sala

Abstract I
n this paper we describe the development of an ontology of molecular and phenotypic cereals data, realized by integrating existing public web databases with the database developed by the research group of the CEREALAB project (www.cerealab.org). This integration is obtained using the MOMIS system (Mediator envirOnment for Multiple Information Sources), a mediator based data integration system developed by the Database Group of the University of Modena and Reggio Emilia(www.dbgroup.unimo.it). MOMIS performs information extraction and integration from both structured and semi-structured data sources in a semi-automatic way. Information integration is performed in a semi-automatic way, by exploiting the knowledge in a Common Thesaurus (defined by the framework) and the descriptions of source schemas with a combination of clustering and Description Logics techniques. The result of the integration process is a Global Virtual Schema (GVV) of the underlying data sources for which mapping rules and integrity constraints are specified to handle heterogeneity. Each GVV element is annotated w.r.t. the WordNet lexical database(wordnet.princeton.edu). The GVV can be queried transparently with regards to integrated data sources using an easy to use graphical interface regardless of the specific languages of the source databases.

1 Introduction and Motivation

In the last few years numerous public data sources have been realized and are now available for researchers in the field of molecular biology. The main problem is that these data sources have different and heterogeneous structures and interfaces,

Dipartimento di Ingegneria dell'Informazione
Università degli Studi di Modena e Reggio Emilia
e-mail: bergamaschi.sonia@unimore.it, sala.antonio@unimore.it

and a different way of presenting their data. Moreover, the users are typically biology researchers with low information technology skills. For all the above problems, sometimes a simple information search can take long time and eventually fails, even because of the number of different data sources to be accessed. What is needed by users is, thus, to have access to the information available in different data sources in a transparent and easy way, independently from the format of the different sources.

There are different public reference databases regarding cereals molecular data: Graingenes[1], for wheat and barley, and Gramene[2] for rice. These databases present also descriptions of phenotypic characters, but no quantitative evaluation of such traits is available. On the other hand, the American Germplasm Resources Information Network (GRIN)[3] provides phenotypic information about many germplasms, but no molecular data.

The aim of our work is thus to create a unique ontology with a global interface, that integrates the above mentioned public data sources providing both molecular and phenotypic data about wheat, barley and rice. Moreover, the ontology has to easily integrate new molecular data coming from the research activity of the CEREALAB project.

The integration process of the public databases and the CEREALAB database is performed with the MOMIS system[4](for further details on the integration process, see [7, 8, 5]).

The work presented in this paper has been conducted as a joint collaboration between the DBGroup and the Agrarian faculty of the University of Modena and Reggio Emilia within the CEREALAB project. As far as we know, no resource is available containing both these two kinds of data for the purpose of this project. For this reason, we developed a Global Virtual View (GVV) which is the integration of existing molecular and phenotypic data sources with data provided by the CEREALAB project. The GVV can be seen as an ontology of the underlying sources.

Other ontologies about these domain exist, but none of these correlates phenotypic data with molecular data. For example the Trait Ontology (TO)[5] is a controlled vocabulary that describes each trait as a distinguishable feature, characteristic, quality or phenotypic feature of a developing or mature individual. The TO partially covers our domain of interest, and thus has been used as a reference.

Our ontology overcomes the TO as it integrates the trait ontology with molecular data related to phenotypic data.

Moreover, an important requirement we addressed in our work is usability: as this ontology is a working tool for users with high domain knowledge and low IT expertise, it follows that the usage of the system has to be as much user-friendly as possible, and it is necessary to provide the users with a graphical interface to query this ontology.

---

[1] http://wheat.pw.usda.gov/GG2

[2] http://www.gramene.org

[3] http://www.ars-grin.gov/

[4] http://www.dbgroup.unimo.it/Momis

[5] http://www.gramene.org/plant_ontology/

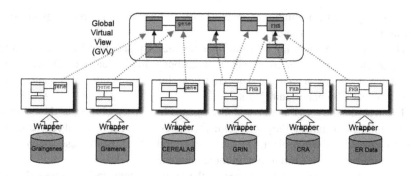

Fig. 1 Creating the GVV with the MOMIS System

The goal of this work is to present the ontology with its interface and sketch the translation of graphical queries into queries executable by the MOMIS system.

The rest of the paper is organized as follows: Section 2 describes the domain of the CEREALAB project to clarify the terms used and the data sources involved in the integration process. Section 3 briefly presents the MOMIS system and the approach used for the integration. Section 4 describes the integrated ontology obtained while Sect. 5 sketches out the querying process with the MOMIS Query Manager and presents the graphical interface developed to graphically formulate SQL queries over the integrated ontology. Finally, Sect. 6 presents some related works while Sect. 7 gives conclusions.

2 Description of the Domain and of the Data sources

To facilitate the comprehension of the terms involved in our project, in this section we provide a brief description of the domain of the CEREALAB project and of the data sources integrated. The main entities about molecular data are three:

- **Gene:** it is the unit of heredity in living organisms, which controls the physical development of the organism. An allele is any one of a number of viable DNA codings of the same gene occupying a given locus (position) on a chromosome.
- **QTL:** a quantitative trait locus, it is a region of DNA that is associated with a particular trait. Though not necessarily genes themselves, QTLs are stretches of DNA that are closely linked to the genes that underlie the trait in question.
- **Marker:** it is a known DNA sequence (e.g. a gene or part of gene) that can be identified by a simple assay, associated with a certain phenotype. A genetic marker may be a short DNA sequence, such as a sequence surrounding a single base-pair change, or long one, like microsatellites.

All these entities have their own specific attributes, such as its chromosome, which is physically organized piece of DNA that contains Genes or QTLs; or its Allele, which is any one of a number of viable DNA codings that occupies a given locus (position) on a chromosome.

The term Germplasm identifies an assemblage of plants that has been selected for a particular attribute or combination of attributes and is clearly distinct, uniform and stable in its characteristics. The Trait is an inherited feature of a plant, and is thus influenced by genes and QTLs.

The web databases Gramene and Graingenes have been chosen as data sources for the molecular data as they were indicated to be the most relevant regarding the species involved in the project, i.e. rice, barley and wheat. Both these sources provide a traditional web form to obtain molecular data.

Moreover, Gramene is the developer of the Trait Ontology and it allows to browse this ontology, which is only a controlled vocabulary and a taxonomy of phenotypic traits. As no molecular data are related to the terms of the TO, it results to be incomplete for the purpose of the CEREALAB project.

These two data sources have been integrated with molecular data obtained from a systematic genotyping work performed by the CEREALAB research group.

Phenotypic evaluations can be found in the GRIN database, which provides quantitative evaluations of numerous traits for many germplasms. Other phenotypic data have been collected by the CEREALAB research group from specific literature for regional germplasms (Emilia Romagna Data, ER Data) and from the italian National Council of Research in Agriculture (CRA), creating a local repository of these data to be integrated in our ontology.

All these data sources, if considered separately, present incomplete information for the purpose of the CEREALAB project and are sometimes overlapping.

3 The Momis Integration Process

MOMIS performs information extraction and integration from both structured and semistructured data sources. In this case, all the data sources involved are relational databases, but the system can deal also with XML and XSD sources and existing ontologies expressed in OWL. The GVV realized with the MOMIS system is expressed using the ODL_{I3} language, an extension of the ODL language, an object-oriented language developed by ODMG[6]. ODL_{I3} is transparently translated into a Description Logic [4, 2, 8]. ODL_{I3} allows to represent in a common data model different kinds of data sources and the view resulting from the integration process. The GVV is composed of Global Classes. Each Global Class includes several Global Attributes. Moreover, the GVV elements are annotated according to the WordNet lexical reference system[7], which provides an easily understandable meaning for each GVV element.

---

[6] http://www.odmg.org/

[7] http://wordnet.princeton.edu/

The MOMIS integration process for building the GVV, shown in Fig. 2, has five phases:

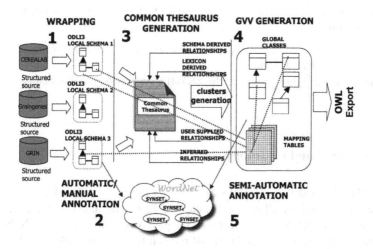

Fig. 2 Integration Process Overview

1. **Local source schemata extraction**. Wrappers automatically extract sources schemas. Such schemas are then translated into the common language ODL_{I3}.
2. **Local source annotation with WordNet**. The integration designer selects a meaning for each element of a local source schema, according to the Word-Net lexical ontology. A tool supports the integration designer: some WordNet synsets are suggested for each source element. Annotation is semi-automatically performed [10, 9].
3. **Common thesaurus generation**. Starting from the annotated local schemas, MOMIS extracts relationships describing inter- and intra-schema knowledge about classes and attributes of the source schemata that are inserted in the Common Thesaurus. The Common Thesaurus is incrementally built starting from schema-derived relationships, automatically extracted intra-schema relationships from each schema separately. Then, the relationships existing in the WordNet database between the annotated meanings are exploited to generate relationships between the respective elements (classes, attributes), called lexicon-derived relationships. The Integration Designer may add new relationships to capture specific domain knowledge, and finally, by means of a Description Logics reasoner, ODB-Tools [6](which performs equivalence and subsumption computation), infers new relationships and computes the transitive closure of Common Thesaurus relationships.
4. **GVV generation**. MOMIS exploits the relationships included in the Common Thesaurus to generate an affinity matrix showing the similarity measure of the elements of the sources. A hierarchical clustering technique applied to this affin-

ity matrix groups similar elements of different sources in clusters, then generating a global schema (GVV) and sets of mappings with local schemata [8].

5. **GVV annotation**. Exploiting the annotated local schemata and the mappings between local and global schemata, the MOMIS system semi-automatically assigns name and meaning to each element of the global schema.

The GVV obtained at the end of the integration process can be translated and exported in the OWL language.

A more detailed description of the MOMIS integration process can be found in [3, 5].

4 The integrated Ontology

The GVV obtained with MOMIS can be seen as an ontology of the underlying sources. This ontology allows to correlate the molecular data of Gramene, Graingenes and the CEREALAB project with the phenotypic data of the GRIN database and those collected by the CEREALAB project. In this way, molecular data about genes and QTLs and information about their associated molecular markers are available. For each gene and QTL it is possible to retrieve its associated germplasms, i.e. the cultivars where that gene/QTL has been identified. Genes and QTLs are also associated with traits, and phenotypic evaluations of each of these trait are available for many germplasms.

The ontology is thus divided in two parts (see Fig.3): the first containing genotypic data, and the second one containing phenotypic data. Genotypic data are divided into the classes `Gene`, `QTL`, `Markers` and `Traits`. The markers can be `marker_for` instances of the classes `Gene` or `QTL`. Each trait can be affected by one or more genes or QTLs.

Phenotypic data are divided into six categories chosen among those of major interest for the cereal breeders: Abiotic Stress, Biotic Stress, Growth and Development related traits, Quality traits and Yield traits. For each trait the specific value of a germplasm for that trait is available.

Genes and QTLs are related to phenotypic data indicating their presence in a germplasm for which a quantitative phenotypic evaluation is available.

Thanks to the combined information available in our ontology, it is possible to find the specific molecular markers that can identify genes or QTLs that express a particular phenotypic trait. In this way genotypic selection of cereals cultivars can be performed starting from phenotypic data.

5 Querying the Integrated Ontology

The MOMIS Query Manager allows the user to pose a query expressed in the SQL language over the ontology and to obtain a unified answer from all the data sources integrated in the GVV (see [1] for a technical description). When the MOMIS Query Manager receives a query, it rewrites the global query as an equivalent set of queries expressed on the local schemata (local queries); this query translation is carried out by considering the mapping between the GVV and the local schemata. Since MOMIS follows a Global as View (GAV) approach [16], where the contents of the mediated schema is expressed in terms of queries over the sources, this mapping is expressed by specifying, for each global class C, a mapping query QC over the schemata of the local classes belonging to C. The system automatically generates the mapping query QC, by extending the Full Disjunction (FD) operator [13] and exploiting the Data Transformation Functions, which are defined by the user and represent the mapping of local attributes into the attributes of the GVV. The query translation is thus performed by means of query unfolding, i.e. by expanding a global query on a global class C of the GVV according to the definition of the mapping query QC. Results from the local sources are then merged exploiting reconciliation techniques and proposed to the user [1].

In order to assure full usability of the system even to users who do not know the SQL language, a graphical user interface has been developed to compose queries over the GVV. This interface, shown in Fig.3, presents in a tree representation the

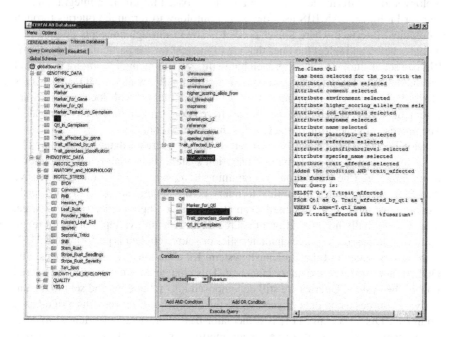

Fig. 3 The Graphical User Interface for querying the Integrated Ontology

ontology, showing ISA relationships among the classes. The user can select the global classes to be queried and their attributes are shown in the "Global Class Attributes" panel with a simple click. Then the attributes of interest can be selected, specifying, if necessary, a condition in the "Condition" panel with the usual SQL and logic operators. More than one global class can be joined just choosing one of the "Referenced Classes" of the currently selected class with no need to specify any join condition between the classes as it is automatically inserted. Selections and conditions specified by the user are then automatically translated into an SQL query and sent to the MOMIS Query Manager.

Once the query has been executed, the result is presented to the user in a table format.

6 Related Work

In the last few years the problem of data integration for biology has become really important both due to continuous increases in data volumes and the growing diversity in types of data that need to be managed. For example the Transparent Access to Multiple Bioinformatics Information Sources project, known as TAMBIS [17], is a mediator-based integration system in which a domain ontology for molecular biology and bioinformatics is used in a retrieval-based information integration system for biologist. TAMBIS uses the global ontology to formulate queries through a graphical interface where a user needs to browse through concepts defined in a global schema and select the ones that are of interest for the particular query. TAMBIS can seem similar to our approach but in this system mappings among the global schema and the local sources are constructed manually, while in MOMIS clusters of similar classes and mappings of global schema classes with local schemas are automatically generated once the sources have been semi-automatically annotated. The process of generation of the GVV is thus semi-automatic.

BioKleisli [11] is primarily a loosely-coupled federated database system. The mediator on top of the underlying integration system relies mainly on a high-level query language (the Collection Programming Language, or CPL) more expressive than SQL that provides the ability to query across several sources. In BioKleisli, a query attribute is usually bound to an attribute in a single predetermined source; there is essentially no integration of sources with content overlap. Furthermore, no optimization based on source characteristics or source content is performed. K2 [12] is the newer version of the BioKleisli system. K2 abandons CPL and replaces it by OQL, a more widely used query language. This change does not modify the overall flow of the system. Queries are still decomposed into subqueries and sent to the underlying sources using data drivers, while the query optimizer remains a rule-based optimizer. DiscoveryLink [14] is a mediator-based and wrapper-oriented middleware integration system. It serves as an intermediary for applications that need to access data from several biological sources. Applications typically connect to DiscoveryLink and submit a query in SQL on the global schema, not necessarily aware of the underlying sources. These two systems offer format and location transparency but do not hide the sources and do not offer schema or data reconciliation.

A survey of these and some other well-known systems that are currently available can be found in [15].

As it can be seen, the data integration problem for biology has been addressed in numerous way, but as far as we know the approach presented in this paper is the first one that combines molecular and phenotypic data in an integrated ontology. All the other systems integrates only molecular data sources, while our combines molecular and phenotypic data. Moreover, except TAMBIS, usually the existing systems uses the SQL language to formulate queries, while in our system we developed a graphical interface for query formulation which is considered a necessity as the users of this kind of systems have low IT expertise and thus need a user-friendly system.

7 Conclusions

We created a unique ontology providing both molecular and phenotypic data about wheat, barley and rice, integrating existing molecular and phenotypic data sources and data provided by the CEREALAB project. In this paper we presented this ontology and the graphical user interface available to compose queries over the integrated ontology. The main advantage of our system is that retrieving data coming from numerous data sources requires only the use of a single interface instead of navigating through numerous web databases, querying them and then manually fusing the information obtained.

This integrated ontology can improve the breeding process as it allows cereal breeders to find the right molecular markers to be used to intentionally breeds certain traits, or combinations of traits, over others. To do this, access both to molecular data and phenotypic evaluation of traits is required. No resource was available so far that combined both these two kind of data and thus many data sources had to be accessed and the information obtained had to be combined manually. With our system both molecular and phenotypic data are available through a single graphical interface. Our integrated ontology thus overcomes the Trait Ontology as it combines molecular and phenotypic data and associates quantitative evaluations of the phenotypic traits of the TO with molecular data.

Acknowledgements The work presented in this paper was partially supported by MUR FIRB NeP4B - Network Peer for Business project (http://www.dbgroup.unimo.it/nep4b) and by the IST FP6 STREP project 2006 STASIS (http://www.dbgroup.unimo.it/stasis).

References

[1] Beneventano D, Bergamaschi S (2007) Semantic Web Services: Theory, Tools and Applications, Idea Group Publishing, chap Semantic Search Engines based on Data Integration Systems

[2] Beneventano D, Bergamaschi S, Lodi S, Sartori C (1998) Consistency checking in complex object database schemata with integrity constraints. IEEE Trans Knowl Data Eng 10(4):576–598

[3] Beneventano D, Bergamaschi S, Guerra F, Vincini M (2003) Synthesizing an integrated ontology. IEEE Internet Computing 7(5):42–51

[4] Beneventano D, Bergamaschi S, Sartori C (2003) Description logics for semantic query optimization in object-oriented database systems. ACM Trans Database Syst 28:1–50

[5] Bergamaschi S, Sala A (2006) Virtual integration of existing web databases for the genotypic selection of cereal cultivars. In: Meersman R, Tari Z (eds) OTM Conferences (1), Springer, Lecture Notes in Computer Science, vol 4275, pp 909–926

[6] Bergamaschi S, Beneventano D, Sartori C, Vincini M (1997) Odb-qoptimizer: A tool for semantic query optimization in oodb. In: Gray WA, Larson PÅ (eds) ICDE, IEEE Computer Society, p 578

[7] Bergamaschi S, Castano S, Vincini M (1999) Semantic integration of semistructured and structured data sources. SIGMOD Record 28(1):54–59

[8] Bergamaschi S, Castano S, Vincini M, Beneventano D (2001) Semantic integration of heterogeneous information sources. Data Knowl Eng 36(3):215–249

[9] Bergamaschi S, Po L, Sala A, Sorrentino S (2007) Automatic annotation for p2p data integration systems: the wordnet domains disambiguation approach. In: Fifth International Workshop on Databases, Information Systems and Peer-to-Peer Computing (DBISP2P 2007) to be held at VLDB 2007 33st International Conference on Very Large Data Bases. University of Vienna, Austria, September 24, 2007

[10] Bergamaschi S, Po L, Sorrentino S (2007) Automatic annotation for mapping discovery in data integration systems. In: Meersman R, Tari Z (eds) OTM Conferences (1), Springer, Lecture Notes in Computer Science

[11] Davidson SB, Overton GC, Tannen V, Wong L (1997) Biokleisli: A digital library for biomedical researchers. Int J on Digital Libraries 1(1):36–53

[12] Davidson SB, Crabtree J, Brunk BP, Schug J, Tannen V, Overton GC, Jr CJS (2001) K2/kleisli and gus: Experiments in integrated access to genomic data sources. IBM Systems Journal 40(2):512–531

[13] Galindo-Legaria CA (1994) Outerjoins as disjunctions. In: Snodgrass RT, Winslett M (eds) SIGMOD Conference, ACM Press, pp 348–358

[14] Haas LM, Schwarz PM, Kodali P, Kotlar E, Rice JE, Swope WC (2001) Discoverylink: A system for integrated access to life sciences data sources. IBM Systems Journal 40(2):489–511

[15] Hernandez T, Kambhampati S (2004) Integration of biological sources: Current systems and challenges ahead. SIGMOD Record 33(3):51–60

[16] Lenzerini M (2002) Data integration: A theoretical perspective. In: Popa L (ed) PODS, ACM, pp 233–246

[17] Stevens R, Baker PG, Bechhofer S, Ng G, Jacoby A, Paton NW, Goble CA, Brass A (2000) Tambis: Transparent access to multiple bioinformatics information sources. Bioinformatics 16(2):184–186

A Notification Infrastructure for Semantic Agricultural Web Services

Brahim Medjahed and William Grosky

Department of Computer and Information Science, University of Michigan – Dearborn, 4901 Evergreen Road, Dearborn, MI 48120, USA {brahim,wgrosky}@umich.edu

Abstract The Emerald Ash Borer (EAB) has killed or infested millions of ash trees in Michigan and is fast spreading to neighboring states. The US Department of Agriculture (USDA) estimates that if EAB went unchecked in the rest of the country, the loss to the nation could range from $20 billion to $60 billion. One key requirement for the success of EAB containment programs is the underlying information sharing infrastructure. EAB partners are maintaining Web sites to publish information about the borer. However, this approach for sharing information is ad hoc and requires intensive human intervention. In this paper, we propose a service-oriented infrastructure, called Sentinel, for the intelligent and timely sharing of EAB-related information

1 Introduction

The Emerald Ash Borer (EAB) is a shiny and invasive green beetle known for killing Ash trees in the United States (US) [8,9]. The borer is native to Asia and is widely believed to have arrived from China through wooden crates used for packing auto parts. It has the potential to decimate Ash as a component of North American forests, which will have dramatic ecological and economic effects. Ash wood is used for all traditional applications of hardwood from flooring and cabinets to baseball bats. In addition, ash trees are beautiful shade giving trees and one of the commonly used landscaping trees in most cities of North America. EAB has already killed or infested ten million ash trees in Michigan alone and fast spreading to adjoining states. The USDA (US Department of Agriculture) esti-

Brahim Medjahed and William Grosky

Department of Computer and Information Science, University of Michigan – Dearborn, 4901 Evergreen Road, Dearborn, MI 48120, USA {brahim,wgrosky}@umich.edu

mates that at the national level, if the EAB went unchecked, the loss to the nation could range from 20-60 billion dollars [8,9].

Realizing the importance, the US Congress approved for the year 2006, about two and half times higher support funding for eradication of EAB. The USDA Animal and Plant Health Inspection Service (APHIS), the USDA Forest Service and the Canadian Food Inspection Agency, in cooperation with State Departments of Agriculture and Natural Resources, have joined forces to implement a long-term program to contain and eventually eradicate EAB from North America. The plan, which is in the early stages of implementation, combines efforts at different levels: *research*, *prevention*, *detection*, and *legal*. At the research level, scientists are working round the clock to understand the beetle's life cycle, find ways to detect new infestations, control EAB adults and larvae, and produce new insecticides. At the prevention level, mass awareness campaigns (e.g., via multimedia publicity on television, radio, and newspaper ads, fliers, press releases, and posters) are regularly launched to spread the word about EAB and the dangers posed by transporting firewood. At the detection level, federal, state, and local agencies promptly locate and eradicate outlier infestations (e.g., by cutting ash trees in infected areas). At the legal level, aggressive enforcement of state and federal quarantines is implemented. For instance, inspection and enforcement programs are targeting rest areas, highways and campgrounds at critical times of year such as major holidays and hunting season.

One key requirement for the success of the aforementioned EAB containment programs is the underlying information sharing infrastructure. EAB-interested partners (e.g., governments, universities, and news outlets), are continuously publishing information (e.g., quarantine procedures and areas, need for cutting Ash trees, research results) on their Web sites about the borer. Multi-state efforts are being made to bring the latest information about the insect (e.g., http://www.emeraldashborer.info). However, the current process for sharing EAB information is *ad hoc* and requires intensive human intervention which may hinder EAB containment plans. For example, Web sites include lists of phones numbers that can be used to report infestations. The called agencies generally process such information in a manual fashion; for instance, they need to figure out which other EAB partners need to be notified, *how* (fax, letter, etc.), and *when*. In this paper, we propose a novel infrastructure, called *Sentinel*, for the *intelligent* and *timely* sharing of EAB-related information. *Sentinel* provides support for EAB partners in the following tasks:

1. *Dissemination*: Identify the partners that need to be notified about any given type of relevant EAB information; and
2. *Decision Making*: Determine the actions to be performed (e.g., launch an awareness campaign) at the reception of EAB.

The proposed approach seeks to achieve the following three objectives: (i) model information sharing patterns among EAB partners; (ii) enable the automatic and intelligent dissemination of EAB information; (iii) facilitate the decision making process for EAB containment. In the rest of this paper, we overview the techniques proposed in Sentinel to achieve the aforementioned objectives.

2 Ontology for Modeling EAB Interaction Patterns

An ontology is a formal and explicit specification of a shared conceptualization [2,4]. This concept is increasingly seen as key to facilitate knowledge sharing and reuse. In *Sentinel*, we propose an ontology, called *EAB ontology*, to model the different patterns through which EAB partners exchange EAB-related information. We defined two taxonomies, namely *EAB Info (Fig 1) and EAB Partners (Fig 2)* taxonomies, to enable the specification of the EAB ontology.

```
1.    Origin/History
      1.1 types of trees affected
      1.2 symptoms
      ...
2.    Biological Information
      2.1 physiology
      2.2 life cycle
      ...
3.    Potential Damage
      3.1 economic impact
      ...
4.    Regulatory Information
      ...
5.    Quarantine Information
      ...
...
```

Fig. 1. EAB Info Taxonomy.

The EAB Info taxonomy gives the various types of messages that may be exchanged among EAB partners. The following are the various types of information on EAB (Fig 1): "Origin/History", "Biological Information", "Potential Damage", "Surveying an Area", "Regulatory/Quarantine Information", "Steps to be taken at the First, Identification of the Borer", "General Control Information", "Research Information/ Results", and "Campaign to Create Mass Awareness". Each entry in the taxonomy corresponds to a type of EAB message and has a unique ID (e.g., 1, 2, 1.1, 2.1.2). An EAB message M is define by (T,D) where T is an ID from the EAB Info Taxonomy and D is the actual data to be sent.

The EAB Partners taxonomy gives the categories of partners that may need to exchange EAB-related information (Fig 2). We identify twelve (10) categories of partners: "Federal and university research departments", "State department of agriculture", "US Department of Agriculture", "legislators/law makers", "local government", "voluntary agencies", "private research", "field personnel", "farmers/

farmer groups", and "media". Each EAB partner has a category and is exposed as a Web service. Details about modeling EAB partners as Web services are given in Section 3.1.

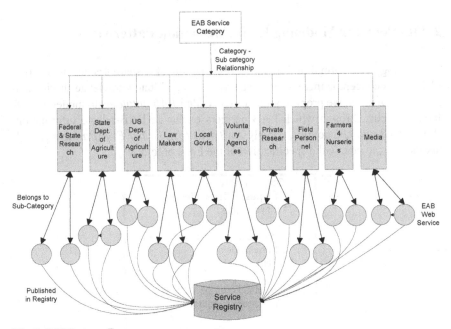

Fig. 2. EAB Partners Taxonomy.

The EAB ontology can be depicted as a labeled directed graph; nodes represent concepts and labeled edges represent relationships between concepts. Concepts refer to different categories of EAB partners as defined in the EAB Partners taxonomy. An edge from E_1 to E_2 labeled with T_1 means that partners that belong to category E_1 shares information of type T_1 (as defined in the EAB Info taxonomy) with partners that belong to category E_2. Fig 3 gives an example of EAB ontology. For instance, it shows that local governments send EAB quarantine information to media agencies.

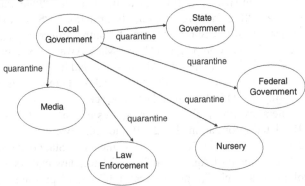

Fig. 3. Example of EAB Ontology.

3 The Sentinel Framework: an Overview

Sentinel uses the EAB ontology as a basis for disseminating EAB-related information and providing assistance during decision making. In the rest of this section
we overview the major techniques proposed in *Sentinel*.

3.1 Modeling EAB Partners as Web Services

One important feature of *Sentinel* is the automatic interaction among EAB partners (i.e., sending/receiving information). EAB partners belong to heterogeneous,
autonomous, and geographically distant organizations (e.g., the USDA APHIS,
nursery operator). To enable such interactions, we represent each EAB partner by
a *Web service*, called EAB Web service (Fig 4). A Web service is an application
accessible on the Web via programmatic means [1]. Web services adopt standard
technologies such as XML and HTTP for the exchange of messages. We use
software design patterns to define a toolbox that can be used by EAB partners to
easily create EAB Web services [5]. In a nutshell, a *software design pattern* is a
general solution to a recurrent design problem. EAB partners simply need to use
the toolbox (via a friendly user interface) to instantiate their Web services. All
Web services related to EAB are registered in the service registry (UDDI in our
case) under the category "Emerald Ash Borer" (Fig 2). The Web service will further be categorized based on the type of partner to which the Web service belongs
(as defined in the EAB Partners taxonomy).

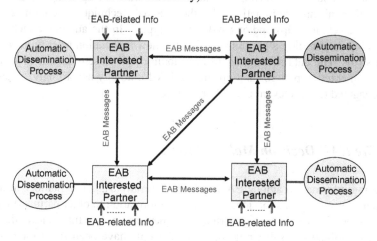

Fig. 4. Interactions among EAB Web Services in Sentinel

3.2 Dissemination Techniques for EAB Web Services

Information dissemination involves two types of EAB Web services: *producers* (send messages) and *consumers* (receive messages). The same EAB Web service may act as a producer and consumer. We design two classes of dissemination techniques: *pull* and *push*. In the *pull* class, information is delivered by producers as a reply to specific requests submitted by consumers. We identify two pull techniques: *explicit* and *implicit*. The *pull explicit* mechanism is the most common Web service exchange pattern; a consumer submits a request for information to a producer which sends back a reply to the consumer. The *pull implicit* technique corresponds to the well-known publish/subscribe interaction scheme [3]. Consumers explicitly register their interest (via subscription) in receiving messages that belong to certain information types (as defined in the EAB Info Taxonomy) with potential producers. The *push* technique uses the EAB to enable the sharing of information with EAB partners that did not request or subscribe to it, but would benefit from receiving it. Issues such as double notifications and notification loops are addressed.

3.3 EAB Ontology Evolution

The EAB ontology is initially created based on domain expertise. However, this ontology is dynamic and can evolve over time; relationships and EAB partner types may be added or removed. We identify two ways for updating the EAB ontology: manual and automatic. In the manual technique, domain experts add/remove relationships and/or EAB partner types. In the automatic technique, we develop data mining algorithms to discover new association rules among EAB partners [6]. The data mining algorithms monitor pull disseminations to identify frequent interaction patterns and update the EAB ontology accordingly. Updates are propagated to all relevant EAB Web services.

3.4 The EAB Decision Making Process

Sharing information among EAB partners generally triggers a number of internal decisions and actions (besides forwarding information to other partners) within each partner. For example, a government agency may notice that, during the past two major holidays, a substantial number of people have been fined for moving firewood outside a certain quarantine area. It may decide to improve its publicity campaign in that area in the coming holiday. We develop *machine learning* techniques to generate decision rules. Machine learning is concerned with the development of algorithms and techniques that allow computers and programs to "learn" [7]. We use several learning approaches such as supervised, unsupervised, semi-supervised, and reinforcement.

4 Conclusion

We presented in this paper our ongoing research in the *Sentinel* project. As of today, we developed the EAB ontology and the proposed techniques for dissemination among EAB services. We also implemented these techniques in *Sentinel* prototype. As a proof of concept, we deployed representative EAB Web services in the university's local network. We are currently investigating techniques for EAB ontology evolution and facilitating the EAB decision making process.

Acknowledgments Brahim Medjahed's work is supported by a grant from the University of Michigan's Office of the Vice President for Research (OVPR).

References

1. G. Alonso, F. Casati, H. Kuno, V. Machiraj, Web Services: Concepts, Architecture, and Applications, Springer Verlag (ISBN: 3540440089), June 2003
2. T. Berners-Lee, J. Hendler, O. Lassila, The Semantic Web. Scientific American, 284(5):34-43, May 2001
3. P. T. Eugster, P. A. Felber, R. Guerraoui, A.-M. Kermarrec, The Many Faces of Publish/Subscribe, ACM Computing Surveys, 35(2):114–131, June 2003
4. D. Fensel, Ontologies: A Silver Bullet for Knowledge Management and Electronic Commerce, Springer Verlag (ISBN: 3540003029), September 2003
5. E. Gamma, R. Helm, R. Johnson, J. Vlissides, Design Patterns: Elements of Reusable Object-Oriented Software, Addison-Wesley (ISBN: 0201633612), January 1995
6. H. Mannila, Local and Global Methods in Data Mining: Basic Techniques and Open Problems, In 29th International Colloquium, on Automata, Languages and Programming, 57-68, 2002
7. T. M. Mitchell, Machine Learning and Data Mining, Communications of the ACM, 42(11):30-36, 1999
8. C. Schuster, Invasive Insects. Maryland Cooperative Extension. Newsletter. 7(1):3-5, 2005
9. D. Smitley, Emerald Ash Borer: Late Summer and Fall Management Strategies, Landscape Alert, Michigan State University. 8(15), August 2002.

agroXML
Enabling Standardized, Platform-Independent Internet Data Exchange in Farm Management Information Systems

Mario Schmitz, Daniel Martini, Martin Kunisch, and Hans-Jürgen Mösinger

Abstract agroXML is a standardized language for data exchange in agriculture. It is based on the eXtensible Markup Language (XML) using XML Schema as its definition language. agroXML is used to submit data from farm management information systems to external partners, like e. g. product processing industries in the food supply chain or agricultural service providers. In addition, data about operating supplies like fertilizers or pesticides can be made available to the farmer by their respective suppliers. In the future, using XML linking technologies might provide a dynamic and flexible mechanism to link documents to such external information sources.

1 Introduction

Documentation of agricultural practices is becoming more and more of an issue for farmers. On the one hand, they are increasingly obliged to it by legislation, on the other hand, integrative planning of agricultural production requires thourough information about measures and events in the past. In many cases, documentation has to be handed on to external partners, like e. g. government agencies or agricultural service providers. The demand for appropriate technical solutions for this purpose has become obvious. For data exchange processes in agriculture up to now only individual interfaces between different communication partners were available. Even if the farmer had electronic systems to record production data, the required data had to be transferred by hand from one software to another or from screen into

Mario Schmitz · Daniel Martini · Martin Kunisch
Association for Technology and Structures in Agriculture, Bartningstraße 49,
64289 Darmstadt, Germany
e-mail: m.schmitz@ktbl.de, d.martini@ktbl.de, m.kunisch@ktbl.de

Hans-Jürgen Mösinger
Software AG, Uhlandstraße 9, 64297 Darmstadt
e-mail: Hans-Juergen.Moesinger@softwareag.com

paper forms. A standardized system for electronic data exchange offers new possibilities for information-directed agricultural production increasing sustainability
and keeping adversary effects to the environment at a minimum. By allowing for
an integrated view of farm production data and other data like e. g. climate or geographic data, measures can be adapted to different conditions, optionally leveraging
algorithms or expert systems provided by third parties. Using agroXML as a data
exchange language, these procedures are facilitated and the individual interfaces between communication partners are substituted by universally usable data exchange
processes.

2 The agroXML Schema, Profiles and Content Lists

The agroXML schema is a model of the real-world objects and their attributes and of
the processes in agricultural production. It is based on eXtensible Markup Language
[2]. Definition of document structures is done using the XML Schema Language
from the W3C [5]. Its architecture is data-centric and currently monolithic. At the
moment, agroXML can describe data for plant production. An agroXML document
is divided into four parts: A header providing information about the farm in general
like e. g. address, name of farm manager etc., a block of data about the fields, like
e. g. area and geographic coordinates, a further block of data about the cultivation
on different fields, like e. g. the plant species, catch crops etc. and finally, data about
the individual measures carried out: fertilization, seeding, pest control, tillage etc.
A schematic representation of this is given in Figure 1.

On the one hand, agroXML can be used to generate consistent stand-alone XML
documents. But following the extensibility paradigm of XML, it also offers a collection of data types and elements reuseable and embeddable in other documents.

To facilitate integration with geographic services, spatial vector data are modeled in agroXML reusing constructs from the Geography Markup Language (GML).
Several factors were taken into account when choosing GML as the representational
format. While there are other XML-dialects available for vector image data – like
e. g. Scalable Vector Graphics (SVG) [6] – GML is the only widely acknowledged
format offering support for geographic coordinate reference systems. Whereas other
more or less open binary formats (like e. g. Shapefiles or TIGER in the U. S.) for
geographic data exist, they are not easy to integrate in a manner allowing tight inter-
connections and references between the data contained within and agricultural data
represented in agroXML. The existance of service interfaces and respective reference implementations for GML like the Web Feature Service facilitates creation of
web applications handling the data. Technically, the reuse of GML datatypes and
elements is achieved by creating a profile of GML according to [3] and importing
this profile together with the GML-namespace into agroXML. As a profile is only a
subset of elements from a larger schema, this has the advantage, that the code necessary to fulfill the requirements of the format given by the schema stays small and
lightweight. Other methods of inclusion, like importing the whole GML schema

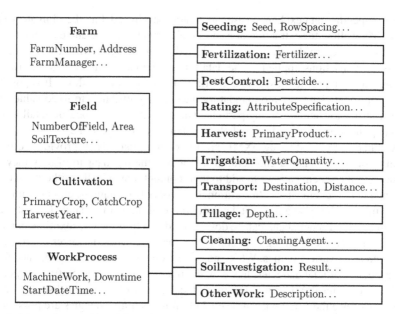

Fig. 1 Schematic overview of the objects and the issues represented in agroXML. Everyone of the four basic blocks expands with further subelements. Shown are only example subelements of WorkProcess.

have been evaluated. However, it was found that this particular solution pushes standard code generation tools for XML schema to their limits. If one additionally takes into account, that only the point, linestring and polygon datatypes and associated subelements have actually proven to be required by current use cases, it becomes obvious that importing the whole of GML is not the proper way of integrating it into other standards requiring only a limited amount of spatial data representation.

These kind of issues concerning practical feasibility in different computing environments are an important factor while developing models to integrate other XML vocabularies. Farm management information systems are written in different programming languages. Components of these management systems providing certain functionality run on a variety of hardware platforms from handhelds to powerful servers for web applications. While in theory combination of different vocabularies seems desirable, in practice it often leads to large, bulky constructs unmanageable by common XML tools. Simplicity, clarity and generality are key properties of well engineered IT systems [9]. For these reasons, vocabularies, which are too extensive and do not allow restriction like e. g. GML does, are currently out of scope for agroXML.

The schema is available at http://www.agroxml.de/schema under the W3C open source licence. Since June 2007, Schema development is carried out in the English language, so that further versions will be accessible and understandible to developers from non-germanspeaking countries.

For a specific data exchange case, application profiles define the obligatory elements. They allow for extraction of a subset of a larger datatype and element collection. To create a profile, elements are selected from the agroXML schema and the necessary restrictions applied to the data types. The basic rule is, that an instance conforming to a profile must also conform to the schema as a whole. It is possible to turn optional elements into mandatory ones, to set attributes to fixed values and to restrict the cardinality of any particle. The process is described in detail in [3]. Using application profiles, lean and clear instances can be generated.

Another component of agroXML are the content lists. They provide the functionality of XML Schema enumerations, however the mechanism of how they are included in the schema allows to add to their content dynamically without effecting a change in the schema itself. In addition, they not only contain the enumeration values themselves but also a name and a description of the item at hand. The lists conform to a unified schema and can be downloaded at http://www.agroxml.de/content. Several lists exist containing e. g. soil types, machine types, fertilizer types, pesticides and plant variety names. Where possible, content for the lists is obtained from the respective official agencies, like e. g. the plant variety offices. Software systems implementing agroXML can either use a local copy of the content lists for filling instances or use the version on the web. Different caching strategies are possible to ensure a recent data pool even if the internet connection is only intermittent. Technological details concerning integration of list content into instances and provision of recent lists are described in [11].

It is important to note, that due to the dynamic integration into an XML instance (lists are referenced by their Uniform Resource Locator), it is possible to include different lists than the ones provided at http://www.agroxml.de/content for special purposes or containing language- or country-specific content.

3 Applications

An interface which can write (at the sender) or read (at the receiver) agroXML is the prerequisite. The transport of an instance on the internet can be conducted using standard protocols like the hypertext transfer protocol (HTTP), the file transfer protocol (ftp) or the simple mail transfer protocol (SMTP). Exchange is currently done in a document-oriented manner: a complete agroXML document is transferred in a single file. For the transfer of only selected items in a dialog-enabled system, query mechanisms are needed. For this purpose, web services based on a service oriented architecture (SOA) can be used. But such systems are complex and resource-hungry during runtime. A lightweight alternative would be to use a standardized XML query language, e. g. XQuery [1] or using services following the paradigm of representational state transfer (REST) [7].

An example of an application using agroXML in association with geo-data is the system developed by the KTBL in the course of a feasibility study supported financially by the Federal Ministry of Agriculture and the Landwirtschaftliche Rentenbank [8]. The prototypical application provides a catalogue with a set of adresses of mapservers which provide useful data like outlines of areas with land use restrictions. It enables farmers to collect geospatial data associated to their fields from official authorities and transform the data from different formats into the agroXML format readable by farm management information systems.

4 Organizational Setup

Most of the development work of agroXML is done at the Association for Technology and Structures in Agriculture in Germany. However, agroXML is open to contributions from other stakeholders. The Association for Technology and Structures in Agriculture is providing and maintaining an infrastructure consisting of a source code management system and documentation. Coordination is done in a working group consisting of the major producers of farm management information systems in Germany. Recently, an effort is going on to lift the developed XML technology onto a broader international level. During a workshop in Hamburg in November 2007 members from organisations, governmental agencies and research institutes from the Netherlands, France, Italy, Finland, Sweden and the Czech Republic agreed to start a joint initiative to bring together the work already done in the different countries. A roadmap involving several use cases from different subdomains of agriculture has been developed. There are different requirements concerning data exchange in agriculture in the different countries. This is mostly due to distinct regional agricultural practices but also due to different legislation. So, a lot of basic development work will have to be done, as the current monolithic approach will probably reach its limits, when it comes to integrating these different requirements.

5 Outlook

Currently, further upgrading of geo-data (also raster data) functionality as well as addition of elements for livestock farming and cultivation of vegetables and fruit are worked upon. This increasing demand from agricultural sectors other than only plant production leads to technological issues, which are currently dealt with. Especially, a schema architecture and design to allow modularization and extensibility while at the same time keeping internal consistency, is needed. The goal of the work is to provide a schema which can be used only in part to implement the datatypes needed for a specific application, while not breaking application interoperability.

Data about operating supply items, like e. g. fertilizers or pesticides are copied directly into XML instances by the farm management information systems. Suppose a company changes the nitrogen content of a certain fertilizer. With the current model of information integration, the farmer has to update this value in his farm management information system. If he is not aware of the change, he will transmit incorrect data in further transactions. So, in most cases, a better model would be to leave this information at the place where it is produced, i. e. in the example above on a web server at the fertilizer producer, and use generic link mechanisms like the XLink Standard [4], to only reference the information. URIs offer an excellent system to provide globally unique identifiers. Ressources like fertilizers could be described using agroXML element hierarchies. Another possibility would be to use the Resource Description Framework (RDF) [10] to represent relationships between objects used in agriculture. Not only would this enable real distributed data storage and ensure recent information, but would also enhance the possibilities to harvest and link data to build real knowledge bases. Key factor for the success of such an architecture is a simple and easily adoptable standard.

References

[1] Boag S, Chamberlin D, Fernández MF, Florescu D, Robie J, Siméon J (2007) XQuery 1.0: An XML Query Language. World Wide Web Consortium, http://www.w3.org/TR/xquery/

[2] Bray T, Paoli J, Sperberg-McQueen CM, Maler E, Yergeau F, Cowan J (2006) Extensible Markup Language (XML) 1.1. World Wide Web Consortium, 2nd edn, http://www.w3.org/TR/xml11/

[3] Cox S, Daisey P, Lake R, Portele C, Whiteside A (2004) OpenGIS Geography Markup Language (GML) Implementation Specification. Open GIS Consortium, Inc.

[4] DeRose S, Maler E, Orchard D (2001) XML Linking Language (XLink) Version 1.0. World Wide Web Consortium, http://www.w3.org/TR/xlink/

[5] Fallside DC, Walmsley P (2004) XML Schema Part 0: Primer. World Wide Web Consortium, 2nd edn, http://www.w3.org/TR/xmlschema-0/

[6] Ferraiolo J, Jun F, Jackson D (2003) Scalable Vector Graphics (SVG) 1.1 Specification. World Wide Web Consortium, http://www.w3.org/TR/SVG11/

[7] Fielding RT (2000) Architectural styles and the design of network-based software architectures. PhD thesis, University of California, Irvine

[8] Geißner G, Grimm S, Frisch J (2007) Geodaten in der Landwirtschaft – Bereitstellung mit agroXML. In: agroXML – Informationstechnik für die zukunftsorientierte Landwirtschaft, Munich, KTBL-Schrift, vol 454, pp 103–118

[9] Kernighan BW, Pike R (1999) The Practice of Programming. Professional Computing Series, Addison-Wesley

[10] Manola F, Miller E (2004) RDF Primer. World Wide Web Consortium, http://www.w3.org/TR/rdf-primer/

[11] Martini D, Frisch J, Kunisch M (2007) agroXML-Inhaltslisten – Konzeption und Inhalte. In: Proceedings 27. GIL-Jahrestagung, pp 139–142

Comparing Different Metadata Application Profiles for Agricultural Learning Repositories

Nikos Manouselis , Gauri Salokhe , Johannes Keizer

Abstract. Agricultural learning repositories can provide new opportunities for sharing, accessing, using and reusing learning resources online. Metadata plays a crucial role in such systems: apart from simply indexing resources, metadata makes it easier to discover a learning resource in a repository, as well as to decide about ways to use it for teaching or learning purposes. In the context of agricultural education and training, a variety of appropriate metadata standards may be selected, adapted and implemented for a learning repository. In this paper we introduce the concept of metadata for agricultural learning resources, and compare two particular cases: one application profile based on the Dublin Core Metadata Element Set (DCMES) and the other based on the IEEE Learning Object Metadata (LOM). The paper attempts to identify similarities and differences between the two case studies and to outline issues that have to be resolved in order to harmonize such efforts.

1 Introduction

The rapid evolution of Information and Communication Technologies (ICT) creates numerous opportunities for providing new services for education and training. Internet increasingly becomes a dominant medium for making resources available online in a digital format, in order to be accessed, used and reused by interested

Nikos Manouselis
Informatics Laboratory, Agricultural University of Athens, 75 Iera Odos Str., 11855, Athens, Greece,
e-mail: nikosm@ieee.org

Gauri.Salokhe, Johannes.Keizer
Food and Agriculture Organization of the United Nations, Viale d. Terme di Caracalla, 00153 Rome, Italy
e-mail: gauri.salokhe@fao.org

Johannes.Keizer
Food and Agriculture Organization of the United Nations, Viale d. Terme di Caracalla, 00153 Rome, Italy
e-mail: johannes.keizer@fao.org

audiences. In education and training, the central paradigm of this reuse-oriented technology is the notion of learning resources (sometimes referred to as learning objects) as reusable pieces of digital content. Very often learning resources are organized in learning repositories (LRs), which are systems for the storage, location and retrieval of content. In LRs, resources are being described using appropriate metadata that helps users discover them online and decide if/how they can put these resources into new educational uses.

Thus, in the education and training context, metadata interoperability has been judged as an essential issue. It allows the exchange and preservation of crucial learning and teaching information (such as competency profiles, learning activities, and descriptions of learning resources), as well as its future reuse among a large number of different systems and repositories. Recent standardization and specification efforts in the area of learning technologies have contributed to this direction. At the level of sharing, exchanging and reusing learning resources among different Learning Management Systems (LMS) and Learning Repositories (LRs), learning technologies aim to preserve a high level of interoperability by implementing relevant standards and specifications such as the Institute of Electrical and Electronics Engineers Learning Object Metadata (IEEE LOM [6]), Dublin Core (DC [4]) and its educational element set, and the recently introduced ISO Metadata for Learning Resources (ISO/IEC MLR [8]).

On the other hand, in the field of agricultural education and training, learning technologies' specifications and standards have not yet been widely adopted. Few initiatives have reported implementing them, and in most cases only to describe learning resources by using IEEE LOM or DC. In addition, efforts until now have been distributed and dispersed, leaving space to approaches with significant differences between them. This paper attempts to report such an experience from two initiatives that used different metadata standards for describing agricultural learning resources. It aims to identify commonalities and variations in the two approaches, and in this way gives interesting feedback to other implementers. Overall, this could serve as an initial step towards a potential harmonization of similar/competing approaches as far as the implementation of learning technologies in agricultural education and training applications is concerned.

More specifically, the paper examines how two widely accepted metadata standards (DC and IEEE LOM) have been used as the basis for the development of specialized metadata that will describe agricultural learning resources in two different application domains. The concept of metadata application profiles is introduced, representative related work on application profiles for agricultural learning resources is described, and then the two particular case studies are presented. Finally, based on a comparison of the two schemas, an identification of major similarities and differences is attempted in order to outline a number of issues that have to be resolved so as to bring closer such initiatives in the future and facilitate information sharing.

2 Background

Metadata is usually termed as 'data about data' or 'information about information' [11, 14]. It is generally engaged for describing the properties of information resources, in order to facilitate their categorization, storage, search and retrieval in digital collections. If metadata is stored in a structured and standardized manner, it may generally support the automation of search and retrieval mechanisms, the comparison between descriptions of different resources, the reusability of descriptions in different applications, as well as the interoperability between different storage systems. Metadata is made up of data items that are associated to the resource, the so-called metadata elements. Metadata schemas (or metadata models) are sets of metadata elements designed for a specific purpose, such as describing a particular type of resource [11]. Metadata specifications are well-defined and widely agreed metadata schemas that are expected to be adopted by the majority of implementers in a particular domain or industry. When a specification is widely recognized and adopted by some standardization organization, it then becomes a metadata standard.

Despite the existence of numerous metadata standards, there is no one all-encompassing one to be used in every application. Rather, there are various metadata standards or specifications that can be adapted or "profiled" to meet community context-specific needs [9]. This conclusion has lead to the emergence of the application profile concept. An application profile (AP) is an assemblage of metadata elements selected from one or more metadata schemas, and its purpose is to adapt or combine existing schemas into a package that is tailored to the functional requirements of a particular application, while retaining interoperability with the original base schemas [5].

Many institutions are currently engaged in developing LRs that can be searchable and accessible for wider audience [16]. In this context, metadata plays an important role, since it makes access to the learning resources faster, easier and more effective. Towards this direction, standardization efforts around the world such as the IEEE Learning Technology Standards Committee[4] (IEEE LTSC), the Education Working Group of the DC metadata initiative[5], and ISO's sub-committee on Information Technology for Learning, Education and Training[6] (ISO/IEC JTC1 SC36) have focused on the study and implementation of metadata element sets for describing learning resources, based on existing standards such as IEEE LOM and DC. Using such recognized metadata standards is important for a variety of reasons: metadata descriptions (records) of learning resources may be exchanged among different LRs; search queries may be propagated among different (and interconnected) LRs; and generally the integration of data from different sources is facilitated. For instance, this is the reason behind the extensive implementation and study of numerous APs of the LOM standard in LRs around the world [16, 7].

---

[4] http://ieeeltsc.org/
[5] http://www.dublincore.org/
[6] http://jtc1sc36.org/

3 Metadata for agricultural learning resources

There have been several interesting approaches in creating metadata sets (or APs) for describing learning resources for the education and training of agricultural or rural stakeholders using the IEEE LOM. For instance, the CG LOM Core [18] has been created by the Consultative Group on International Agricultural Research (CGIAR) in order to describe its learning resources in a manner that best suits the content, purpose and audience of CGIAR's Online Learning Resources project[7]. This involves the development of a LR that will support an international community of trainers, educators, researchers and learners in agriculture and natural resources management. CGIAR defined a core set of metadata elements that describes, documents and registers the CG learning object metadata core (which is termed as CG LOM Core). The goal of applying a shared set of core metadata elements is to allow the federated search of training related documents across all CGIAR centers, as well as to achieve interoperability across the centers and with external entities. Because most centers have based the metadata of their Web resources on DC, the CG LOM core also includes a mapping with the DC metadata element set.

Another interesting LOM AP is the one developed by the European e-Content project Bio@gro[8] for information dissemination and increasing public awareness regarding organic agriculture. This was created in order to categorize online educational resources that are related to organic agriculture [2]. The Bio@gro LOM AP has adopted a number of LOM elements, appropriately selecting vocabularies of values in such a way that the metadata descriptions reflect the particularities of the application area (i.e. organic agriculture). It will also be used as a basis for the development of a revised AP for the description of learning resources for organic agriculture and agroecology in the context of the Organic.Edunet initiative[9] [13].

A similar AP has been developed to support the Turkish Agricultural Learning Objects Repository (TrAgLor) [3]. The main objective of this multilingual repository is to store digital learning objects developed for agriculture, veterinary, food, environmental and forestry sciences as well as all other agriculture related basic and applied sciences. TrAgLor, which is still work in progress, has been designed and developed based on a LOM AP. At present, this is a LR promoted to faculties of agriculture, veterinary, food and forestry around Turkey, where resources are being contributed by academic staff and students.

Other initiatives implementing a LOM AP for their LRs have been developed in the general life sciences domain. A characteristic example is the Biosci Education Network (BEN) repository[10]. This has been funded by the American National Science Foundation's National science, mathematics, engineering and technology education (SMETE) Digital Library program, the American Association for the Advancement of Science (AAAS), as well as other professional societies and coalitions for biology education. A BEN metadata specification based on LOM has been developed [1], in

---

[7] http://learning.cgiar.org/
[8] http://www.bioagro.gr
[9] http://www.organic-edunet.eu
[10] http://www.biosciednet.org/

order to facilitate BEN partners in making their collections of online biological sciences teaching and learning resources searchable through the BEN repository site.

Apart from the LOM-based approaches, other schemas are also used for the description of learning resources. For instance, a recent survey indicated that although 54% of surveyed LRs use LOM-based metadata, approximately 22% use DC-based metadata [16]. In this paper, we explore two characteristic representatives of these different approaches for agricultural education and training, and attempt a comparison.

4 Case studies

The two case studies of this paper are two metadata APs for learning resources that have been presented during the Special Session on Agricultural Metadata and Semantics of the 2nd International Conference on Metadata and Semantics Research (MTSR'07), which took place during October 2007 in Corfu, Greece[11]. These APs have been developed following different philosophies:

- The first one, the FAO Ag-LR AP, has been developed by the Food and Agriculture Organization (FAO) of the United Nations, and is based on DC. It aims to support its Capacity and Institution Building Portal, which provides structured access to information on FAO's capacity and institution building services and learning resources [15].
- The second has been developed by the Informatics Laboratory of the Agricultural University of Athens, Greece, and has been built upon LOM. It describes training resources for rural development in the context of the Rural-eGov project [10].

4.1 FAO's Agricultural Learning Resources Application Profile

The United Nations General Assembly (A/RES/59/250) recognizes the crucial role of capacity building for achieving the Millennium Development Goals and calls upon the United Nations organizations to increase their support to developing countries' own efforts [17]. Capacity and institution building is a core function of FAO. In order to provide structured access to FAO's agricultural learning resources and capacity and institution building services, the "Capacity and Institution Building Portal" (*hereafter referred to as the CIB Portal*) project was started in 2006. When completed, the CIB Portal will provide direct access to learning resources, such as training materials, guidelines, tool kits, available in any media, which are usable in or prepared in support of a learning process by which individuals, groups and organizations can enhance their skills, and develop associated knowledge, attitudes and values, to improve their performance and solve problems in order to achieve their objectives. It will also facilitate access by external users, as well as FAO staff, to the Organization's learning resources and services, thus enhancing member countries' capacities.

---

[11] http://www.mtsr.ionio.gr/

To ensure that the CIB Portal can be searched by users and to enable interoperability with other LRs, one of the core activities of this project was to design an AP which adheres to standard nomenclature to describe agricultural learning resources. An important consideration when developing the AP for FAO's agricultural learning resources was the conformance with existing standards so as to assure that metadata records can be shared with other repositories, especially with those providing agricultural learning resources. Although the tendency of most LRs is to use LOM as the basis schema, FAO decided to base its standard on DC, for two main reasons:

- A considerable amount of FAO's learning resources already have a metadata record in one of FAO's repositories. These resources are currently described using the AGRIS AP, which is based on DC and the Agricultural Metadata Element Set (AgMES) [12]. This specification is widely used by FAO and its partner organizations. To be able to reuse these records would imply immense cost-savings, so an AP based on DC and AgMES was considered the optimal solution.

- Because the AP would be promoted to FAO's member countries, who wish to establish similar LRs, it was important to ensure that it would be easy to use and implement. Thus, it was also important to identify a balanced number of data elements to keep the metadata creation effort manageable and to ensure a high return on investment. An AP which uses the complete set of 76 LOM elements was, therefore, not practical. A survey on the usage of LOM shows, that in practice most communities use only parts of the complete set [7].

Table 1 DC, AgMES, and LOM elements that have been further specialized in Ag-LR AP.

Title	Description	Use in Ag-LR	Vocabulary
Subject / FAO categories	The topic of the resource.	Focusing on the particular subject categories of interest to FAO.	FAO Categories [15]
Type	The nature or genre of the resource.	Using an AgMES-based controlled vocabulary.	Type vocabulary [15]
Format – Type	The file format, physical medium, or dimensions of the resource.	Using an AgMES-based controlled vocabulary.	Format vocabulary [15]
Relation	A related resource.	Relating resource to the collections it belongs to and to its other translations.	'collections', 'translations'
Intended End User Role	Principal user(s) for which this resource was designed.	Limiting original LOM vocabulary to desired values.	Adapted version of LOM's [15]

Given the above circumstances, the most cost effective solution in the case of FAO resources was to set up an exchange profile with Dublin Core, AgMES and LOM elements. The needs analysis and the evaluation of existing standards resulted in an Agricultural Learning Resource AP (Ag-LR AP) which is created by taking elements from DC, IEEE LOM and AgMES. Twelve elements were taken from the DC Metadata Element Set namespace. Additional, seven elements from LOM were added to fulfill the task of fully describing a "learning resource".

Another requirement of describing FAO learning resources has also been the use of standard terminologies such as FAO's multilingual agricultural thesaurus AGROVOC[12]. To allow consistent description of the learning resources in the CIB Portal, it was important to provide the possibility to index resources using terms from the AGROVOC thesaurus. Therefore, elements from the AgMES, namely subject refinements and the possibility to explicitly indicate AGROVOC (or any other agricultural thesaurus) were included in the AP. This will allow FAO resources (learning and other types) to be searched simultaneously using the same keywords.

An overview of the elements of DC, LOM and AgMES that have been specialized for the needs of Ag-LR AP is presented in Table 1. The original description of each element as well as the way it has been used in Ag-LR AP are included. More details about the Ag-LR AP and its elements are available in Stuempel et al. [15] and via the Agricultural Information Management Standards (AIMS) Web site[13].

Table 2 LOM elements that have been further specialized in ReGov LOM.

Title	Description	Use in ReGov	Vocabulary
Language	The primary human language(s) used within this resource to communicate to the intended user.	As LOM, focus on languages of Rural-eGov regions.	ISO 639-2
Keyword	Keyword or phrase describing the topic of this resource.	Resource classification based on agricultural subject category.	AGRIS Subject Categories[14]
Coverage	Geography or region to which this resource applies.	Include coverage of specific European regions.	ISO – 3166-1 and NUTS Codes[15]
Intended End User Role	Principal user(s) for which this resource was designed, most dominant first.	Extending original vocabulary with "vocational learner".	Adopted from LOM
Context	The principal environment within which the resource and use of this resource is intended to take place.	Extending original vocabulary with "vocational training".	Adopted from LOM
Language	The human language used by the typical intended user of this resource.	As IEEE LOM, focus on languages of Rural-eGov regions.	ISO 639-2

4.2 Rural e-Gov IEEE LOM Application Profile (ReGov LOM)

Regional as well as centralized authorities around Europe develop and offer an increased variety of online public services, which may be particularly useful for agricultural professionals in rural areas. Nevertheless, a major barrier towards their

---

[12] http://www.fao.org/aims/ag_intro.htm
[13] http://www.fao.org/aims/
[14] http://www.fao.org/scripts/agris/c-categ.htm
[15] http://ec.europa.eu/comm/eurostat/ramon/nuts/codelist_en.cfm?list=nuts

adoption has been identified to be the low degree of ICT penetration that is usually recorded in these areas. Addressing such shortcomings, a recently deployed initiative titled 'Rural-eGov: Training SMEs of Rural Areas in using e-Government Services'[16] focuses on SMEs in five European regions (namely Wales in UK, Brandenburg in Germany, Aegean islands in Greece, Koscierzyna community in Poland, and Moravske Toplice in Slovenia). It builds on relevant experience from similar initiatives and bases its training activities around an online point of reference (the Rural e-Gov Observatory) which rural SMEs can access to find relevant information and learning resources.

Through the Rural-eGov Observatory, agricultural professionals will be able to find digital training resources about how to reap maximum benefits from the use of e-Government services that cover their region. Thus, the Observatory includes a LR with training resources for rural stakeholders. To facilitate interoperability with other LRs, it has been decided that the metadata to be used in this LR should be based on LOM. Since it was not possible to locate other LOM-based schemas that are particularly developed for training resources and rural SMEs, a new AP was judged necessary.

To facilitate searching, locating and downloading appropriate resources, the important characteristics of the Rural-eGov training resources had to be reflected in their metadata. Metadata records had to also be available in the language of the users (that is, multilingual descriptions will be necessary). Since LOM has been chosen as a basis, the new AP has been termed as the Rural-eGov LOM (or simply, ReGov LOM) AP. ReGov LOM adopts many of the LOM elements as they are recommended by the standard, but also specializes several of them in order to best match the needs of the particular LR. In Table 2, the elements that have been specialized for Rural-eGov are described.

5 Comparison

The following paragraphs compare the overall characteristics of the two APs and discuss issues related to their educational and agricultural aspects. On the long run, this comparison aims to identify a set of issues that have to be clarified in order for such APs to be developed in a harmonized manner.

The Ag-LR AP of FAO consists of 23 elements, 9 of which are mandatory (M), 13 optional (O) and 1 automatically created (A). On the other hand, ReGov LOM AP consists of 48 elements, 16 of which are mandatory (M), 21 optional (O) and 11 automatically created (A). As it is expected, the Ag-LR AP seems to be considerably easier for metadata authors to complete, compared to ReGov LOM AP.

In Ag-LR AP, 8 elements are used for the representation of general resource properties, 4 for classification purposes, 7 to reflect educational properties, 2 to represent copyrights and cost (Rights, Cost) information, and 2 (Identifier, Relation) to facilitate archiving/accessing of related materials (including language versions). Similarly, in the ReGov LOM AP 15 elements are used for the representation of

---

[16] http://rural-egov.eu

resource properties, 6 for classification purposes, 14 to reflect educational properties, 3 to represent copyrights and cost information, and 15 to facilitate archiving/accessing a resource. We note that the major difference between the two APs is that the ReGov LOM uses significantly more elements to describe general properties (e.g. Duration), educational properties (e.g. Difficulty), and to facilitate archiving/accessing (e.g. the Meta-Metadata category). This observation illustrates clearly the intrinsic difference in the philosophy of the LOM and the DC standards.

The elements that may be used for educational purposes in FAO's Ag-LR AP are the following: Notes, Aggregation Level, Type, Intended End User Role, Context, Interactivity Level, and Typical Learning Time. All but the Notes and Type elements are purely from LOM, and may be mapped to the corresponding ones of ReGov LOM AP, which include: Aggregation Level, Interactivity Type, Learning Resource Type, Interactivity Level, Typical Age Range, Difficulty, Typical Learning Time, Intended End User Role, Context, Language (of the targeted learners). Ag-LR Type element is used in a similar manner as the Learning Resource Type, where as Notes is used as the Description sub-element of the Annotation category in ReGov LOM AP. Since most of the educational elements in both APs are optional, we could say that ReGov LOM provides the possibility to express educational properties in a richer manner. But on the other hand, this makes the process of authoring a full record more time consuming and complex for a metadata author who is not an expert in classifying learning resources.

It is also interesting to examine the choice of elements in the two APs to classify resources according to their agricultural characteristics, e.g. using an agricultural classification scheme or vocabulary. In FAO's Ag-LRM AP only two elements use such a scheme: Subject/FAO Categories and Subject/Keywords. Similarly, in ReGov LOM AP the following two elements engage some agriculture-related vocabulary for resource classification: Keyword and Coverage (which is expressed in terms of particular regions in each country).

Overall, we can say that the development of the two APs for describing agricultural learning resources reveals differences that are more related to the different philosophies of the base schemas (i.e. LOM and DC) rather than the way these two are specialized for agricultural education and training. The main difference is in the number of elements that the two APs use for the description of non-agricultural properties such as general, educational and archiving ones. On the contrary, both APs use between 4-6 elements for classification purposes. From these, two are appropriately specialized for categorization according to some agriculture-related taxonomy or thesaurus. These two are not the same though for each schema, since Ag-LR is using an enhanced Subject classification using FAO Categories and Keywords (e.g. from AGROVOC); whereas ReGov LOM is using Keywords from the AGRIS categories, as well as a Coverage classification that goes to the level of individual regions (NUTS regions codes). If a common way of using such elements could be found, so that they can be easily mapped to one another, metadata interoperability on agricultural elements would be greatly facilitated.

6 Conclusions

The development of an appropriate metadata schema can greatly facilitate the search and retrieval tasks of the users that are accessing an online agricultural LR, and several initiatives have produced their own APs of popular metadata specifications or standards like DC and IEEE LOM. On the other hand, the adoption of standards that have such different philosophies, might lead to the development of APs that have important differences, and are, therefore, impossible to combine through simple mappings. The examination of these two case studies, the DC-based Ag-LR AP and the LOM-based ReGov LOM AP, has clearly illustrated this. But it has also been observed that both schemas represent agriculture-related properties of the resources (mostly for classification purposes) in a similar manner. Therefore, it seems reasonable to head first for some consensus about the way such elements are defined and used in APs for agricultural learning resources. Appropriate guidelines and/or best practices could be devised and suggested.

As far as the rest of the elements are concerned, our study indicated that they are generally used for purposes that seem to be closely linked to the needs of the application domain (e.g. archiving/accessing, educational, etc.). A more extended study of similar APs will reveal if any concurring patterns exist in the use of such systems in agricultural education and training initiatives, or if those elements should be treated depending on the application.

Acknowledgments

The authors would like to thank their colleagues from FAO and the Rural-eGov project that have contributed in the development of Ag-LR AP [15] and ReGov LOM AP [10], respectively.

References

1. BEN (2003) Biosci Education Network (BEN) Metadata Specification. AAAS for the Biosci Education Network Collaborative, Version 1.2.
2. Bio@gro (2005) Metadata Models for Bio@gro Content Objects (BCOs) Description. Bio@gro Technical Report.
3. Cebeci Z., Erdogan Y., Kara M. (2008) TrAgLor: A LOM-Based Digital Learning Objects Repository for Agriculture. In: Proc. of the 4th Int. Scientific Conference "eLearning and Software for Education (eLSE'08)". 17-18 April 2008, Bucharest, Romania.
4. DC (2004) Dublin Core Metadata Element Set, Version 1.1: Reference Description. Dublin Core Org.
5. Duval E, Hodgins W, Sutton S, Weibel SL (2002) Metadata Principles and Practicalities. D-Lib Magazine, 8. http://www.dlib.org/dlib/april02/weibel/04weibel.html. Accessed 18 January 2008.
6. IEEE LOM (2002) Draft Standard for Learning Object Metadata. IEEE Learning Technology Standards Committee, IEEE 1484.12.1-2002.

7. ISO (2004) Final Report on the "International LOM Survey". ISO/IEC JTC1 SC36. http://jtc1sc36.org/doc/36N0871.pdf. Accessed 18 January 2008.
8. ISO/IEC (2005) Working Draft for ISO/IEC 19788-2 – Metadata for Learning Resources – Part 2: Data Elements. ISO/IEC JTC1 SC36.
9. Kraan W (2003) No one standard will suit all. The Centre for Educational Technology Interoperability Standards. http://www.cetis.ac.uk/content/20030513175232. Accessed 18 January 2008.
10. Manouselis N, Kastrantas K, Tzikopoulos A (2007) An IEEE LOM application profile to describe training resources for agricultural and rural SMEs. In: Proc. of the 2nd International Conference on Metadata and Semantics Research (MTSR'07), Corfu, Greece.
11. NISO (2004) Understanding Metadata. National Information Standards Organisation, NISO Press.
12. Salokhe G, Onyancha I, Weinheimer J, Richards B, Le Hunte Ward F, Keizer J (2005) The AGRIS Application Profile for the International Information System on Agricultural Sciences and Technology. Food and Agriculture Organization of the United Nations, Italy. http://www.fao.org/docrep/008/ae909e/ae909e00.htm. Accessed 18 January 2008.
13. Sanchez-Alonso S, Sicilia M-A (2007) Using an AGROVOC-based ontology for the description of learning resources on organic agriculture. In: Proc. of the 2nd International Conference on Metadata and Semantics Research (MTSR'07), Corfu, Greece.
14. Steinacker A, Ghavam A, Steinmetz R (2001) Metadata Standards for Web-Based Resources. IEEE Multimedia, 70-76.
15. Stuempel H, Salokhe G, Aubert A, Keizer J, Nadeau A, Katz S, Rudgard S (2007) Metadata Application Profile for Agricultural Learning Resources. In: Proc. of the 2nd International Conference on Metadata and Semantics Research (MTSR'07), Corfu, Greece.
16. Tzikopoulos A, Manouselis N, Vuorikari R (2007) An Overview of Learning Object Repositories. In: Northrup P (ed) Learning Objects for Instruction: Design and Evaluation, Hershey, PA: Idea Group Publishing, 29-55.
17. UN (2005) Triennial comprehensive policy review of operational activities for development of the United Nations system (59/250). United Nations General Assembly: Resolution adopted by the General Assembly on the report of the Second Committee. http://daccessdds.un.org/doc/UNDOC/GEN/N04/491/26/PDF/N0449126.pdf. Accessed 18 January 2008.
18. Zschocke T, Paisley C, Duval E, Beniest J (2005) CG Learning Object Metadata (LOM) Core. CGIAR ICT/KM OLR Project.

Using an AGROVOC-based ontology for the description of learning resources on organic agriculture

Salvador Sánchez-Alonso and Miguel-Angel Sicilia

Abstract. Education is a critical requirement for the development of sustainable agriculture. Learning resources available through the Web can be described with metadata for enhanced availability. The provision of semantic metadata describing these resources further facilitates retrieval and selection of resources based on richer annotations that use ontologies. This paper sketches the potential use of ontologies related to organic agriculture for the description of learning resources.

1 Introduction

Organic agriculture is a form of agriculture whose main objective is obtaining food efficiently while respecting the environment and preserving Earth's natural fertility, which is attained through the optimization of the resources available as well as avoiding synthetic pesticides and fertilizers. Although organic farming is nowadays widespread in most developed countries, the promotion of the ecological practices in agriculture requires much effort in terms of education. Different institutions and organizations provide educational resources on the topic, some of them openly available through the Web. However, locating those resources with conventional

Salvador Sanchez Alonso and Miguel-Angel Sicilia

Computer Science Dep. University of Alcalá
Ctra. Barcelona km. 33,600. 28871, Alcalá de Henares, Spain.
{salvador.sanchez, msicilia} @uah.es

search engines is complicated, mainly due to noise in the results of common input terms. Learning object repositories provide an alternative – which can be seen as an extension–, which enables more relevant results at the cost of developing (and packing together with the learning objects) a few metadata records. The IEEE LOM standard[2] can be used to provide metadata to learning resources thus facilitating their retrieval.

There exists, however, an additional extension that would provide richer means of browsing, navigating and searching for educational resources: the use of formal annotation based on (formal) ontologies. This approach is specially suited to the field of agriculture, since the large and mature thesaurus AGROVOC[3], a vocabulary covering the terminology of subject fields in agriculture, forestry, fisheries, food and related domains, is widely used in practice, which represents a degree of consensus regarding terminology.

Moving to a Semantic Web practice requires essentially three elements: (i) the elaboration of a formal ontology from the thesaurus, (ii) the provision of specialized semantic search software and (iii) the change in current indexing practices, from the traditional use of thesauri to the new semantic annotation. This paper focuses on element (i), providing a tentative mapping technique for the specifics of AGROVOC. The technique is targeted to the annotation of learning objects, reusing the effort carried out in ontologies for learning resources (Sicilia et al., 2004).

AGROVOC is a structured, controlled vocabulary used for indexing and retrieving data in agricultural information systems. It consists of organized terms (in different languages) covering not only the terminology of agriculture, but also terms in forestry, fisheries, food and other related domains. These terms are used to unambiguously identify resources. Indeed, the knowledge contained in the vocabulary allows standardizing indexing processes, making searching simpler and more efficient.

As in other thesauri, terms are related in AGROVOC, but the even though the kind of relationships supported in thesauri is generally very limited, AGROVOC includes a richer set of relationships classified in "traditional thesaurus relationahisps", "concept-to-concept relationships", "term-to-term relationships" and "String-to-String relationships". The most important among traditional relationships in AGROVOC are:

- *Broader term* (BT) relationships link a general term to other(s) more specific. Thus, the concept Soil is BT related to more general terms such as Land cover.

---

[2] http://ltsc.ieee.org/wg12/
[3] http://www.fao.org/agrovoc/

- *Narrower term* (NT) relationships represent the opposite of BT. The concept Soil is NT related to the three more specific concepts Top soil, Rhizosphere and Subsoil.
- *Related term* (RT) relationships link any two concepts holding a non hierarchical relationship. The term Fish, for instance, is RT related to terms as varied as Foods, Perishable products, Seafoods, Fresh products or Postmortem changes.

Other less relevant relationships in AGROVOC are: *Is Referenced in Scope Note* (SNX), *Scope Note Reference* (SNR), *See* (SEE), *Seen for* (SF), *Use* (USE) and *Used for* (UF). But despite the interesting set of relationships included in the thesaurus (those classified as "concept-to-concept relationships", "term-to-term relationships") if resources are to be meta-tagged using the terms and relationships in AGROVOC, these relationships should be unambiguously defined for data to be the basis of advanced management processes based on computational semantics. This unambiguous definition is possible only through a formal representation in an ontology language.

AGROVOC was developed by FAO (*Food and Agriculture Organization of the United Nations*) and the *Commission of the European Communities* in the early 1980s, being updated since then on a regular basis and extensively used for indexing and retrieving data in agricultural information systems. Understanding that similar efforts such as the European GEMET exist (de Lavieter, 1995), the number of terms included (up to 40.000 terms per language), the continuous support and funding from FAO, as well as its generally acceptance, number of active partners and widespread use, make of AGROVOC an outstanding resource in the field of vocabularies and certainly a point of reference for the subject fields covered.

The maturity of AGROVOC makes it a good candidate to become a point of departure for an effort of formalization. In fact, this has already been approached; see for example (Soergel et al., 2004). However, this paper focuses on semantic annotation for learning resources, which would be a particular application of the development of an AGROVOC-based ontology.

The rest of this paper is structured as follows. Section 2 reviews previous work in the field, before section 3 exemplifies the extension of AGROVOC to formal ontology focusing on a particular aspect of organic agriculture, fertilization, which is covered by the thesaurus. Then, section 4 sketches some guidelines on how annotation of learning resources on organic farming can be annotating by making use of the ontology. Finally, conclusions and outlook are provided in section 5.

2 Timeline for the creation of an AGROVOC ontology

From 2003, several efforts have attempted to convert the AGROVOC thesaurus into an ontology. And even though the full conversion of AGROVOC to a formal ontology is currently ongoing work, probably due to the massive effort necessary to properly address this issue, it is fair to recognize that some interesting work has been done during the years.

In 2003, the thesaurus was converted into an RDFS file. Later on, several efforts coordinated to redesign the traditional thesaurus into an ontology-based relational database available to download. Subsequent efforts used AGROVOC in the design of ontologies specific to given domains, such as food safety (Lauser, 2001), or bibliographic information on agriculture (Wildemann, Salokhe and Keizer, 2004), among others. In a more general domain, Kashyap (1999) proposed an approach for designing an ontology for information retrieval based on databases' schemas and a collection of queries that are of interest to the users. However, advanced semantic inference is not considered an issue and thus not dealt with in depth, as the main goal is to reduce the involvement of domain experts. Closer to AGROVOC, an interesting effort by Gangemi et al. (2002) aims at building a fishery ontology by reengineering and integrating the fisheries terminologies from the several systems, one of which is AGROVOC. On the other hand, Fisseha, Liang, and Keizer (2003) sketched some ideas to transform AGROVOC to an ontology, while created a root application ontology based on an application profile addressing the problem of heterogeneity due to differences in terminologies (Liang et al., 2006). These were important moves towards a proper ontology of AGROVOC, even though important issues such as providing "intelligent behind-the-scenes support for query expansion" (in their own words), or creating the complete inventory of domain-relevant entity types and relationship types, to name a few, remain unattained.

In spite of the several ongoing works on developing agriculture ontologies, and the existence of several application profiles and other IEEE LOM-based schemas specific to agriculture such as CGIAR's LOM Core (Beniest & Zschocke, 2005), FAO's learning resources application profile (FAO 2006), Rural-eGov's LOM application profile (Tzikopoulos et al., 2007) and others, there are no reports on the development of specific schemas for the semantic annotation of learning resources for agriculture education.

3 Converting AGROVOC to ontological languages: the case of fertilization

At present, AGROVOC contains close to 30,000 descriptors and more than 10,000 non-descriptors called synonyms (terms which help the user to find a specific descriptor). Given the size and scope of AGROVOC, any ontology created from it will likely include thousands of concepts and relationships, and consequently will not be feasible to manage. Here we will focus on the concrete case of fertilization in organic agriculture as a simple application of a part of the thesaurus.

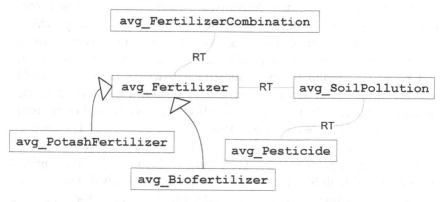

Figure 1. A fragment of the terms in AGROVOC related to fertilization.

Fertilization, understood as *"any aspect of the use of fertilizers to improve crop growth and soil fertility"*, is a central concept in organic agriculture. It is a fact that no farming exploitation can be considered –and consequently certified as– *organic,* unless a strict use of fertilizers and fertilizing techniques, specific to organic agriculture, is followed. In Europe, for instance, regulation on organic certification enforces fertilizers and soil conditioners to be composed only of substances listed, which particularly involves varied cultivation practices, and the rigorous limitation on the use of non-synthetic fertilizers. In AGROVOC, the term

Fertilization[4] is considered a physiological concept, so the AGROVOC term defining the application of fertilizers to soil or plants that should be used is, instead, Fertilizer application. This latter term is related to (RT) Fertilizers, a concept which includes any natural or synthetic compound spread on the plant or worked into soil to increase the plant's natural capacity to grow.

A particular kind of fertilizers is Biofertilizers, a NT related concept describing "any naturally occurring organic substances applied to soil for the purpose of maintaining or improving fertility". As Biofertilizers are exclusively composed of natural substances such as animal manures, composts, nitrogen fixing bacteria and mycorrhizae, it is suitable (from the point of view of current regulations) for organic farming practices. On the contrary, other types of NT related Fertilizers such as Nitrogen fertilizers and Phosphate fertilizers —and their derivatives Superphosphate and Rock phosphate— are generally prohibited for organic farming. This is because they have been named as factors in the over enrichment of surface waters (excessive nutrients in ponds and lakes cause over growth of algae) and phosphate accumulation in subterranean waters (extremely soluble nitrogen in its nitrate form not sufficiently absorbed by plants can leach into groundwater). Others types of Fertilizers (i.e. NT related to this term) are Biofertilizers, Calcium fertilizers, Inorganic fertilizers, Liquid gas fertilizers or Organic fertilizers, among others (see Figure 1). Figure 1 shows a fragment of AGROVOC with NT/BT relations interpreted as class/subclass.

An interesting term in AGROVOC is Fertilizer combinations. It represents any fertilizer mixture with agents such as herbicides, plant growth substances or pesticides. This is obviously not suitable for organic agriculture according to the definition provided at the beginning of this article. At the moment, this is one of the many terms related to Fertilizers (i.e. Fertilizer combinations is NT related to Fertilizers). Another interesting concept to note is that of Soil pollution, a general concept RT related to Soil degradation which is not certainly applicable to given types of Fertilizers such as Biological fertilizers, a powerful

---

[4] To enhance readability, AGROVOC terms are in courier font. In figures, agrovoc terms are prefixed by agv_ as a form of classifying terms from different sources.

reason to better profile the relationship holding between `Fertilizers` and `Soil Pollution`.

Current relationships in AGROVOC suggest the following:
- All kinds of `Fertilizers` can be involved in `Soil degradation`, a concept RT related to `Soil Pollution` which is in turn related to `Fertilizers`.
- Any instance of `Fertilizers` can be part of `Fertilizers combinations`, which is probably false for some kinds of `Biological fertilizers`.

Figure 1 shows the abovementioned concepts and the relations holding between them as a previous step for its formulation and clarification in ontological terms.

In AGROVOC, four relationships showing the hierarchical links between terms exist: BT (broader term), NT (narrower term), RT (related term) and UF (non-descriptor). These relationships are specific to thesauri and, as such, can not be considered a limitation or disadvantage. However, an ontology takes this conceptual framework one step further by structuring the terms more formally, and by providing richer relationships between concepts than what is currently provided in thesauri. An AGROVOC ontology should ideally clarify the hierarchies defined to better prepare the knowledge base for inferences. Thus, a number of basic actions should be taken such as:
- Creating two new sub-concepts of `Fertilizer applications` namely `General fertilizer applications` and `Specific fertilizer applications`. `General fertilizer applications` would give support to fertilizer techniques suitable for all kinds of farming practices (organic and non organic). These techniques will likely include the utilization of permitted Fertilizers and will explicitly avoid non permitted compounds. On the other hand, `Specific fertilizer applications`, would provide support to techniques suitable for specific forms of agriculture. This can be subsequently divided into `Organic agriculture fertilizers applications` (for organic agriculture techniques), extensive agriculture techniques, etc.

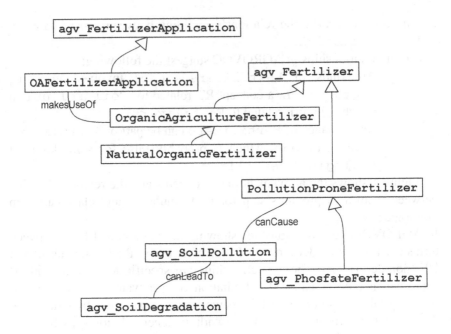

Figure 2. Fragment of an AGROVOC-based ontology for fertilization.

- A subclass of `Fertilizers`, should be created to give support to the concept of Organic agriculture-suitable fertilizer. Let us name this term `Organic agriculture-suitable fertilizers`.
- Remove the relationship between `Fertilizer application` and `Fertilizers`, as in its current for it provides room for errors in selecting the appropriate resource if the selection is based on the ontology knowledge. A good solution (but more complex than current situation) is to link `Organic agriculture fertilizer applications` to `Organic agriculture-suitable fertilizers` through an ontology property named `makesUseOf`.
- Link `Soil pollution` only to those fertilizers which might be cause of pollution; let us name them `Pollutant-prone fertilizers`. In this manner, the rest of the different types of `Fertilizers` will no longer be able to be associated to `Soil degradation` through `Soil pollution` as this relationship will not hold to all the `Fertilizers` but only to those *pollution-prone*.

Figure 2 summarizes all the above discussion.

4 Case study: annotating resources on fertilization

Learning resources on organic agriculture may be targeted to different kinds of learners. Here we will provide two cases that illustrate such diversity of needs. The first will be a scientific paper while the second is a resource oriented to dissemination of technical practices.

Annotating technical resources

In general, any digital resource can be explicitly declared as an instance of a LearningObject class –or any of its subclasses. Then, there is a family of properties (and sub-properties) starting from a generic about that connects them to any other concept. The about predicates play the same role of a "keywords" marker, but it can be specialized. One important educational issue is the production of organic agriculture fertilizers. However, the notion of what an OA fertilizer is can be defined in several ways. A possible definition can be provided by the next two SWRL rules:

```
NaturalOrganicFertilizer(?x)                            →
OrganicAgricultureFertilizer(?x)

agv_Fertilizer(?x)
∧ defines(?y, ?x)
∧ OrganicAgricultureStandard(?y)
      → OrganicAgricultureFertilizer(?x)
```

Rules in SWRL (Horrocks et al., 2004) are of the form of an implication in the form antecedent → consequent, so that each rule can be read as: "whenever the conditions specified in the antecedent hold, then the conditions specified in the consequent must also hold". In the examples above, natural organic fertilizers are suitable to organic agriculture but also any fertilizer defined as such by standards or recommendations is.

Composting is one of the most widespread of these production techniques. The *Compost happens!* tutorial (CHT[5]) is an online resource with a common sequential structure. This resource can be declared as an

---

[5] http://www.compostinfo.com/main/intro.htm

instance `TutorialLearningObject(cht)`. The tutorial can be annotated as `describes(cht, composting)` where `OAFertilizerProductionTechnique(composting)`.

A user searching for techniques for producing organic agriculture fertilizers (anything about `OAFertilizerProductionTechnique`) will match the resource since `produces(composting, compost)` and `compost` will be classified as OA, for example, because it is defined by the BSI's[6] `BSI_PAS_100` standard.

Annotating scientific literature

Palomäki et al (2002) reported a typical comparative study of organic versus traditional techniques, in this case for the particular kind of *Elsanta* strawberries, a variety of strawberry with a particular flavour. This kind of resources considered as LO are regarded as `ScientificReportLO`, and they can be annotated with respect to the concrete research methods employed.

A user might first search for reports regarding `StrawberryPlantType` that report on `Experiments` (specified in the `researchMethodUsed` property). The report mentioned will be of the kind `ComparativeExperiment`. A more detailed specification may specify as `measuredVariable fruitProductivity`. This kind of measures can be used for a systematization of research evidence, but it also can be retrieved as supplementary material for expositive or tutorial learning objects, which are related to the learning topics underway.

5   Conclusions and outlook

An example on how an ontology fragment derived from AGROVOC can be used to annotate resources has been provided. Further work will deal with advancing the conversion of AGROVOC to formal ontology, and with the provision of tools and improved techniques for semantic annotation specific to learning resources.

---

[6] http://www.bsi-global.com/

Acknowledgements

This work has been supported by EU funded projects LUISA (Learning content management system Using Innovative Semantic web services Architecture, FP6–2004–IST–4 027149), and Organic.Edunet (ECP-2006-EDU-410012).

References

Beniest, J. & Zschocke, T. (2005). Developing a learning object repository for international agricultural research. In Proceedings of World Conference on Educational Multimedia, Hypermedia and Telecommunications 2005 (pp. 4553-4555).

FAO (2006). Metadata Application Profile for FAO's Learning Resources (draft). Online at: ftp://ftp.fao.org/gi/gil/gilws/aims/metadata/docs/learnap.doc

Fisseha, F., Liang, A. and Keizer, J. (2003). Reengineering AGROVOC to Ontologies Step towards better semantic structure. In *Proceedings of the NKOS Workshop, Rice University, Houston, Texas, USA.*

Gangemi, A., Fisseha, F., Pettman, I. Jand Keizer, J. (2002). Building an Integrated Formal Ontology for Semantic Interoperability in the Fishery Domain. In *Proceedings of the First International Semantic Web Conference, ISWC 2002.*

Horrocks, I., Patel-Schneider, P.F., Boley, H., Tabet, S., Grosof, B. and Dean, M. (2004) SWRL: A Semantic Web Rule Language Combining OWL and RuleML. W3C Member Submission, http://www.w3.org/Submission/SWRL/

Kashyap V. (1999) Design and creation of ontologies for environmental information retrieval. In *Proceedings of the 12th Workshop on Knowledge Acquisition, Modeling and Management (KAW'99)*, Banff, Canada.

Lauser, B. (2001). From thesauri to Ontologies: A short case study in the food safety area in how ontologies are more powerful than thesauri - From thesauri to RDFS to OWL. In proceedings of the ECDL 2001 OAI Workshop.

de Lavieter, L. (Ed.) (1995). Multilingual Environmental Thesaurus. Part 1, English; Part 2, Français; Part 3, Deutsch; Part 4, Nederlands; Part 5, Italiano; Part 6, Norsk; Part 7, Dansk; Part 8, Español. NBOI, Nederlandse Bureau voor Onderzoek Informatie / EEA-TF - European Environment Agency - Task Force, Amsterdam, November 1995, pp. (English) vi + A-78; B-112; C-56; D-199, total 445.

Liang, A., Salokhe, G, Sini, M. and Keizer, J. (2007). Towards an infrastructure for semantic applications: Methodologies for semantic integration of heterogeneous resources. In *Cataloging & Classification Quarterly*, 43 (3/4).

Palomäki, V., Mansikka-aho, A.-.M. and Etelämäki, M. 2002. Organic fertilization and cultivation technique of strawberry grown in greenhouse. Acta Hort. (ISHS) 567:597-599 http://www.actahort.org/books/567/567_129.htm

Sicilia, M.A., García, E., Sánchez-Alonso, S. and Rodríguez, E. 2004. Describing learning object types in ontological structures: towards specialized pedagogical selection. In *Proceedings of ED-MEDIA 2004 - World conference on educational multimedia, hypermedia and telecommunications*, pp. 2093-2097.

Soergel, D., Lauser, B., Liang, A., Fisseha, F., Keizer, J. and Katz, S. (2004). Reengineering thesauri for new applications: the Agrovoc example. *Journal of Digital Information*, 4(4).

Tzikopoulos, A., Manouselis, N., Yialouris, C.P., Sideridis, A.B. (2007). Using educational metadata in a learning repository that supports lifelong learning needs of rural SMEs. In *Proceedings of the 2007 EFITA Conference*, Glasgow, UK.

Wildemann, T., Salokhe, G. and Keizer, J. (2004). Applying new trends to the management of bibliographic information on agriculture. *Zeitschrift für Agrarinformatik*, 12(1), 9-13.

Using Agricultural Ontologies

M. T. Maliappis

Abstract. Despite the growing number of ontologies online available, their range of application in real world projects is comparatively limited. This paper describes the construction of an ontology, concerning the horticultural domain of Agriculture, and examine its usage in particular application areas. The proposed ontology is used, (a) as a refine and classification tool facilitating searching process in a repository environment, and (b) as a domain model for rule knowledge base construction. A prototype web application has been developed to investigate the usefulness of ontology and examine several software development tools.

1 Introduction

Knowledge collection and representation in a usable and efficient way is a cumbersome, time consuming and expensive process. Sharing of the same knowledge in different applications and its reuse without or little modifications in solving separate problems is a critical factor in knowledge dissemination. Among knowledge representation techniques, ontology formalization can be used to model real world in a consistent, formal, manageable and reusable way. Ontologies can be used to facilitate several aspects of knowledge management such as knowledge representation, knowledge sharing and reuse, knowledge classification and knowledge search and retrieval.

There are several efforts towards construction and usage of ontologies in several fields. In Agriculture domain, there is a number of initiatives towards the development of specific ontologies[1,5]. Among the most interesting and promising endeavors is the work carried on in FAO [2]. FAO started several initiatives towards the construction of agricultural domain ontologies based on FAO's Multilingual Agricultural Thesaurus (AGROVOC) [3,9] and through the Agricultural Ontology Service (AOS) project [4].

Michael T. Maliappis

Informatics Laboratory, Agricultural University of Athens, 75 Iera Odos, 11855, Athens, Greece, e-mail: michael@aua.gr

Despite the growing number of ontologies online available, their range of application in real world projects is comparatively limited [8]. A major objective of this paper is to construct an ontology targeting horticultural domain of Agriculture and examine its usage in particular application areas. The proposed ontology describes production of horticultural crops in low technology greenhouses and includes several financially important vegetable crops in the area of Mediterranean basin, such as tomato, pepper and aubergine. Among the objectives of the proposed ontology is the systematic organization and representation of knowledge and terminology, concerning all stages of horticultural production and marketing.

The developed ontology has been used in two specific applications. In the first, application ontology has been incorporated as controlled vocabulary into DSpace repository. The provided by DSpace indexing mechanism has been modified to use synonyms from ontology structure and to handle Greek language intricacies such as term stemming. Since DSpace uses Apache Lucene search engine as its underlying search and indexing mechanism most of the work targets to modifications of Lucene functions.

The second application is trying to incorporate ontology into a traditional rule based expert system. The initial system [7] was a diagnostic expert system which could be used to identify the principal pests, diseases and nutritional disorders of some common vegetable crops and provide guidance for their control in plastic covered greenhouses. Ontology is used to provide the facts and the attributes of the fact-attribute-value structure of the rules.

2 Ontology Construction

Usage of traditional IF-THEN rules in expert system applications is a predominant way in knowledge base construction, since they offer a rich expressive environment accompanied with a freedom in expression and design. During development of several knowledge bases and specific expert systems [6, 7, 10] was recognized that formalization and standardization of the needed knowledge is an absolute necessity towards the construction of efficient and robust expert system applications. Lack of formal and disciplined way of knowledge representation made development and maintenance process a difficult task.

Starting from these observations, an effort was started to investigate other possible knowledge representations which, keeping the same expressive power, will offer more discipline in knowledge representation and opportunities for knowledge reuse, allowing easy reengineering of expert system applications developed so far. Ontologies were identified as the knowledge structure filling these requirements.

OntoCrop ontology was the result of this endeavor. It covers a portion of the horticultural domain and the cultivation of vegetable crops in low-technology greenhouses. Since ontology construction is an evolutionary process and goes through several stages until its completion, its development started from the part needed for reengineering the already existed applications. Emphasis has been set to a clear and consistent description of the domain under investigation. Other objectives of this attempt were to describe the specific domain taking into consideration the usage of the ontology and to provide enough information to use ontology in a multilateral and multilingual environment. Identification of unique, with well-defined semantics, relationship types between concepts in the investigated domain were another desired goal [9].

At a second stage, ontology augmented with characteristics to assist its usage in organizing and searching for information. For this purpose, ontology enriched with synonyms, and in some cases with antonyms, of the main terms in English and Greek. Multilanguage dimension is an important issue in countries with native languages different than the dominant languages and more specifically than English. So, the capability for knowledge indexing and searching in native language, in parallel with English, is a crucial factor in application usefulness. OntoCrop has been constructed using Protégé[2] ontology editor.

OntoCrop contains knowledge concerning cultivation techniques, pest management and crops' physiology. OntoCrop has, also, been extended to include knowledge about propagation, post-harvest physiology, consumption and marketing.

3 Using Ontology in Rule Reasoning

OntoCrop ontology has been used to investigate effectiveness of ontology usage in expert system development using IF-THEN rule reasoning structure This application is a reengineering of a previous developed application [7] which was using traditional IF-THEN rules to construct its knowledge base. The initial system was a diagnostic expert system which could be used to identify the principal pests, diseases and nutritional disorders of six common vegetable crops (aubergine, bean, cucumber, lettuce, pepper and tomato) and provide guidance for their control. In its reengineering form the application incorporates OntoCrop in the construction of its rules providing facts and attributes of the fact-attribute-value structure of the rules.

Reengineering of the expert system application started from the construction of OntoCrop describing the set of concepts covered by the rules. During the process were identified duplications in concepts and relationships between them. The rules were rewritten using the refined concepts of ontology. Access to ontology contents had been accomplished using Protégé API. Application's front end accepts input data through special forms, converts them in XML format and forwards them to

---

[2] http://protege.stanford.edu

the server. The reverse process is followed to present the results with system suggestions to the user.

4 Using Ontology in Indexing and Searching

The second application uses ontology to assist indexing and searching of information material relevant to crop cultivation domain. Information material is stored in a DSpace[3] repository which uses Apache Lucene[4] as search engine. DSpace is able to use a controlled vocabulary for indexing and searching purposes. This vocabulary has a specific XML structure in which OntoCrop is converted using Castor software. Having the proper controlled vocabulary the user is able to select terms from this structure to index the submitted material. DSpace provides a reverse mechanism to search the stored material using terms of the controlled vocabulary.

Apart from the simple incorporation of OntoCrop as controlled vocabulary into DSpace a major modification of Lucene Java classes is needed to be able to handle synonyms in indexing and searching. Two Java classes of Lucene have been modified to handle customized indexing and searching processes. The class used for indexing modified to be able to search, find and use the synonyms of the terms selected for indexing and handle peculiarities of Greek language. Synonyms can be in the same or different language, English or Greek. A similar modification made to the Java class used for searching to return material corresponding to the synonyms of searching term. Protégé API used to access OntoCrop to get synonyms of specified terms.

5 Conclusion

This paper describes the initial endeavors for the development of an ontology concerning the horticultural domain. Through its usage the proposed ontology passed several rounds of refinement. At its current stage of development it contains useful knowledge targeted to several kinds of users. Students can consult the ontology to identify and learn concepts and relationships between them for the horticultural domain. Growers are able to search for useful knowledge concerning specific cultivation techniques in the field.

A major objective of this work is the investigation of the usage of the same ontology in different situations and the identification of the difficulties of this endeavor in order to modify ontology structure or to enhance the used software

---

[3] http://www.dspace.org
[4] http://lucene.apache.org

tools. Ontology was proved a valuable tool in development of rule-based expert systems, offering concrete structure and discipline which are missing from these systems.

A guided searching process with the help of domain representation structures, such as domain ontologies, would be able to direct the user to find more clearly and easily the desired information or knowledge and help in proper application of knowledge in the daily activities of farms. Quality, precision and accuracy of the searching results are heavily depended on the quality of domain ontology and indexing process.

In the future, OntoCrop ontology is going to be augmented to include more portions of the horticultural domain. Furthermore, an application is going to be developed offering access, searching and navigation, to OntoCrop ontology using web services technology.

Acknowledgments This work is supported by the "PYTHAGORAS-II" research project, which is co-funded by the European Social Fund and Greek national resources (EPEAEK II).

References

1. Beck, H. W., Kim, S., Hagan, D.: A Crop-Pest Ontology for Extension Publications. In: Proceedings of 2005 EFITA/WCCA Joint Congress on IT in Agriculture, Vila Real, Portugal (2005)
2. Beck, H., Pinto, H. S.: Agricultural Ontology Service. UN FAO (2002)
3. Fisseha, F.: Towards better Semantic Standards for Information Management AGROVOC and the Agricultural Ontology Service (AOS). UN FAO, Rome, Italy (2002)
4. Hagedorn, K., Fisseha, F.: Agricultural Ontology Service (AOS). A tool for Facilitating Access to Knowledge. UN FAO, Rome, Italy (2001)
5. Koenderink, N. J. J. P., Top, J. L., van Vliet, L. J.: Expert-Based Ontology Construction: A Case-Study in Horticulture. In: 16th International Workshop on Database and Expert Systems Applications (DEXA'05) (2005)
6. Mahaman, B. D., Passam, H. C., Sideridis, A. B., Yialouris, C. P.: DIARES-IPM: a diagnostic advisory rule-based expert system for integrated pest management in Solanaceous crop systems. Agricultural Systems, vol. 76, pp. 1119--1135 (2003)
7. Passam, H. C., Sideridis, A. B., Yialouris, C. P., Maliappis, M. T.: Improvement of Vegetable Quality and Water and Fertilizer Utilization in Low-Tech Greenhouses through a Decision Support Management System. Journal of Vegetable Crop Production, vol. 7, pp. 69--82 (2001)
8. Simperl, E. P. B., Tempich C.: Ontology Engineering: a Reality Check. In: 5th International Conference on Ontologies, Databases, and Applications of Semantics ODBASE2006 (2006)
9. Soergel, D., Lauser, B., Liang, A., Fisseha, F., Keizer, J., Katz, S.: Reengineering Thesauri for New Applications: the AGROVOC Example. Journal of Digital Information, vol. 4 (2004)

10. Yialouris, C. P., Passam, H. C., Sideridis, A. B., Metin, C.: VEGES: A multilingual expert system for diagnosis of pests, diseases and nutritional disorders of six greenhouse vegetables. Computers and Electronics in Agriculture, vol. 19, pp. 55--67 (1997)

Metadata Application Profile for Agricultural Learning Resources

Hilke Stuempel[1], Gauri Salokhe[1], Anne Aubert[1], Johannes Keizer[1], Andrew Nadeau[1], Stephen Katz[1], Stephen Rudgard[1]

Abstract. Capacity and institution building is a core function of the Food and Agricultural Organization of the United Nations (FAO). FAO has recently started the "Capacity and Institution Building Portal" to provide structured access to information on FAO's capacity and institution building services and learning resources. To ensure that the Portal can be searched by users and to enable interoperability with other recognized educational repositories, an Application Profile (AP) was created conforming to available and commonly used standards, to describe agricultural learning resources. This article presents the AP, provides an example of an FAO learning resource described and displayed using FAO Learning Resource AP, and presents the lessons learned.

1 Background – Capacity and Institution Building Portal

The United Nations General Assembly (A/RES/59/250) recognizes the crucial role of capacity building for achieving the Millennium Development Goals and calls upon the United Nations organizations to increase their support to developing countries' own efforts [1]. Capacity and institution building is a core function of the Food and Agriculture Organization (FAO) of the United Nations. In order to provide structured access to FAO's agricultural learning resources and capacity and institution building services, the "Capacity and Institution Building Portal" (*hereafter referred to as* 'the Portal') project was started in 2006.

Food and Agriculture Organization of the United Nations, Knowledge Exchange & Capacity Building Division (KCE),
Viale delle Terme di Caracalla, 00153 Rome, Italy

hstuempel@gmx.de, {Gauri.Salokhe, Anne.Aubert, Johannes.Keizer, Andrew.Nadeau, Stephen.Katz, Stephen.Rudgard}@fao.org

The Portal will provide direct access to learning resources, such as training materials, guidelines, tool kits, available in any media, which are usable in or pre-pared in support of a learning process by which individuals, groups and organizations can enhance their skills, and develop associated knowledge, attitudes and values, to improve their performance and solve problems in order to achieve their objectives. It will also facilitate access by external users, as well as FAO staff, to the Organization's learning resources and services, thus enhancing member countries' capacities.

To ensure that the Portal can be searched by users and to enable interoperability with other Learning Object Repositories (LOR), one of the core activities of this project was to design an Application Profile (AP) which adheres to standard nomenclature to describe agricultural learning resources. An *Application Profile* is defined as a schema which consists of data elements drawn from one or more namespaces, combined together and optimized for a particular local application.

In the following sections the paper establishes the need for metadata to describe learning resources, analyses existing standards and details the requirements for an AP. Finally, it illustrates the elements of FAO's Agricultural Learning Resources AP.

2   Metadata for Describing Learning Resources

Metadata for learning resources are important to facilitate search, access, use and reuse of learning objects, for instance, by learners or instructors. The learning objects or the relating metadata records are often stored in LORs. Different LORs address different needs and, therefore, have different metadata schemas. To enable interoperability and easy sharing of resources between these repositories (and to facilitate federated search or metadata harvesting), the use of common standards and specifications becomes essential [2]. This section describes some of the common standards used in educational settings.

The Institute of Electrical and Electronics Engineers (IEEE) provides an internationally-recognized open standard for the description of learning resources. The so called IEEE 1484.12.1-2002 Learning Object Metadata Standard (LOM)[2] is based on early specifications contributed by the IMS Project[3] and by ARIADNE[4] [3]. The Standard comprises a hierarchy of elements. At the first level, there are nine categories: general, lifecycle, meta-metadata, technical, educational, rights, relation, annotation and classification. Each of these categories contains several sub-categories and thus, in total, LOM provides 76 data elements. The standard is widely used in educational context and applied in several LORs. It

---

[2] Institute of Electrical and Electronics Engineers: http://www.ieee.org

[3] IMS Global Learning Consortium: http://www.imsglobal.org

[4] ARIADNE Foundation for the European Knowledge Pool: http://www.ariadne-eu.org

forms the basis for many recommendations and metadata APs, such as, ARIADNE, CanCore[5], UK LOM Core[6], SCORM[7] and IMS Learning Design[8]. It is also used for the Agricultural LOR of the Consultative Group on International Agricultural Research (CGIAR).

The International Standards Organization (ISO) sub-committee on "Information Technology for Learning, Education and Training" (ISO/IEC JTC1 SC36) started to develop a metadata standard for learning resources [4]. The group focuses on existing standards and conducted a survey on the use of LOM [5].

Furthermore, the Education Working Group of the Dublin Core Metadata Initiative[9] developed Dublin Core (DC) terms to describe educational resources. They proposed a small number of LOM elements to enhance a DC record[10]. Several learning repositories, such as the Gateway to 21st Century Skills (GEM)[11] and the Education Network Australia (EdNA)[12], follow the recommendations provided by the DC Education Working Group.

3. Considerations for the Application Profile for FAO's Agricultural Learning Resources

An important consideration when developing the AP for FAO's agricultural learning resources was the conformance with existing standards so as to assure that metadata records can be shared with other educational repositories, especially with those providing agricultural learning resources.

A study recently conducted by the Agricultural University of Athens [6] indicates that of the 59 repositories analyzed, 54% use LOM or compatible APs based on IMS and Cancore, and 22% use DC. Although the tendency of most LORs is to use the LOM set, FAO decided to base its standard on Dublin Core, for the reasons listed below.

---

[5] CanCore Learning Resource Metadata Initiative: http://www.cancore.ca/en/

[6] United Kingdom LOM Core: http://www.cetis.ac.uk/profiles/uklomcore

[7] Sharable Content Object Reference Model (SCORM): http://www.adlnet.gov/scorm/

[8] IMS Global Learning Consortium: Learning Resource Meta-data Specification: http://www.imsglobal.org/metadata/index.html Learning Design Specification: http://www.imsglobal.org/learningdesign/

[9] DCMI Education Working Group: http://dublincore.org/groups/education/

[10] DC-Education AP: http://dublincore.org/educationwiki/DC_2dEducation_20Application_20Profile

[11] GEM: Gateway to 21st Century Skills: http://www.thegateway.org/

[12] Education Network Australia: http://www.edna.edu.au/edna/go/resources/metadata

A considerable amount of FAO's resources which have been identified as learning resources already have a metadata record in one of FAO's repositories. These resources are currently described using the AGRIS AP, which is based on DC and the Agricultural Metadata Element Set (AgMES)[13]. This specification is widely used by FAO and its partner organizations. Most of the elements in this standard overlap with metadata necessary to describe learning resources such as title, publisher, date of publication, language, subject etc. To be able to reuse these records would imply immense cost-savings, so an AP based on DC and AgMES was considered the optimal solution.

Additionally, because the AP would be promoted to FAO's member countries, who wish to establish similar LORs, it was important to ensure that it would be easy to use and implement. Thus, it was also important to identify a balanced number of data elements to keep the metadata creation effort manageable and to ensure a high return on investment. An AP which uses the complete set of 76 LOM elements was, therefore, not practical. A survey on the usage of LOM shows, that in practice most communities use only parts of the complete set [5]. Moreover, there is an overlap between the common elements in LOM and Dublin Core.

Given the above circumstances, the most cost effective solution in the case of FAO resources was to set up an exchange profile with Dublin Core, AgMES and LOM elements.

4. Application Profile for FAO's Agricultural Learning Resources

The needs analysis and the evaluation of existing standards resulted in an Agricultural Learning Resource AP (Ag-LR AP) which is created by taking elements from the following namespaces[14]: Dublin Core Metadata Element Set (DCMES)[15], IEEE LOM Metadata Set[16] and AgMES[17].

Twelve elements were taken from the DCMES namespace. Additional, elements from LOM are added to fulfill the task of fully describing a "learning resource". To identify the additional elements from LOM, it was necessary to evaluate the most commonly used LOM elements in other APs. The following elements were chosen from the educational category: "Intended End User Role",

---

[13] Agricultural Metadata Element Set: http://www.fao.org/aims/

[14] XML Namespaces: http://www.w3.org/TR/REC-xml-names/

[15] Dublin Core Metadata Element Set (DCMES):
http://dublincore.org/documents/2006/12/18/dces/

[16] Standard for Information Technology --Education and Training Systems -- Learning Objects and Metadata: http://ltsc.ieee.org/wg12/

[17] Agricultural Metadata Element Set (AgMES): http://www.fao.org/aims/agmes_intro.jsp

"Context", "Interactivity Level", and "Typical Learning Time". These elements, for example, indicate if a resource is intended for a learner or a trainer, if it is supposed to be used in school or training context and the foreseen average learning time.

One of the requirements of describing FAO learning resources was also to use standard terminologies such as FAO's multilingual agricultural thesaurus: the AGROVOC. AGROVOC is used by FAO and its member countries to describe agricultural resources. To allow consistent description of the learning resources in the Portal, it was important to provide the possibility to index resources with AGROVOC thesaurus. Therefore, elements from the AgMES, namely subject refinements and the possibility to explicitly indicate AGROVOC (or any other agricultural thesaurus) were included in the AP. This will allow FAO resources (learning and other types) to be searched simultaneously using the same keywords.

The resulting set of proposed elements as well as an example of a learning resource described and displayed using the AP is provided below.

4.1 Overview of Proposed Elements

An overview of the proposed elements to be included in the AP is provided in Table 1. The table also includes brief information about the controlled vocabularies used, the cardinality, and if it is mandatory or not. The details of each element and guidelines for adding content are available from the Agricultural Information Management Standards (AIMS) Web site[18].

The AP is expressed using an XML Document-Type Definition (DTD). The DTD is used for validating exported XML metadata records. In the future, the same schema may be further expressed and exploited using Web Ontology Language (OWL). Nevertheless, to validate XML metadata records, a DTD is essential.

---

[18] Agricultural Information Management Standards Web site – Learning Resources Metadata: http://www.fao.org/aims/ap_applied.jsp

Table 1. The elements of FAO Ag-LR AP with information about controlled vocabularies used, the cardinality and if it is required.

Proposed Elements	Name-space[19]	Controlled Vocabulary	Requirement[20]	Cardinality[21]
Title	DC	no	M	R
Supplement Title	AGS	no	O	R
Creator	DC	no	O	R
Subject /FAO Categories	AGS	no	M	R
Subject /Keywords	AGS	no	M	R
Abstract	DCTERMS	no	O	R
Notes	AGS	no	O	N-R
Publisher	DC	no	M	N-R
Date	DCTERMS	no	M	N-R
Type	DC	yes: Type Vocabulary[22]	M	R
Format-Type	DC	yes: Format Vocabulary[23]	M	R
Aggregation Level	LOM	yes: Aggregation Level Vocabulary[24]	O	N-R
Size	LOM	no	A	N-R
Identifier	DC	no	M	N-R
Language	DC	yes: Language Codes	M	N-R
Relation	DC	yes: "collections, translations"	O	R
Coverage	DCTERMS	yes: Official Country Names	O	R
Rights	DC	no	O	R
Cost	LOM	yes: "Yes, No"	O	N-R
Intended End User Role	LOM	yes: "Learner, Teacher, Manager"	O	R
Context	LOM	yes: "School, Higher Education, Training, other"	O	R
Interactivity Level	LOM	yes: "very low, low, medium, high, very high"	O	N- R
Typical Learning Time	LOM	-	O	N-R

[19] Namespaces: Dublin Core (DC), Dublin Core Terms (DCTERMS), Agricultural Metadata Element Set (AGS), Learning Object Metadata (LOM)

[20] Mandatory (M) / Optional (O) / Automatic (A)

[21] Repeatable (R) / Not-Repeatable (N-R)

[22] Type vocabulary: Training/Learning Resource, Training/Learning Support Material, Portal, Best Practice, Case Study, Policy Brief, Reference Material

[23] Format vocabulary: Electronic Document, Paper only Document, Slides, Website, CD-Rom / DVD, Audio, Video

[24] Aggregation Level Vocabulary: 1: raw media data or fragments, 2: lesson, 3: course, 4: e.g. a set of courses that lead to a certificate

4.2 Example of a FAO Resource Described Using Ag-LR AP

Figure 1 shows an example of a FAO learning resource described and displayed using FAO Ag-LR AP.

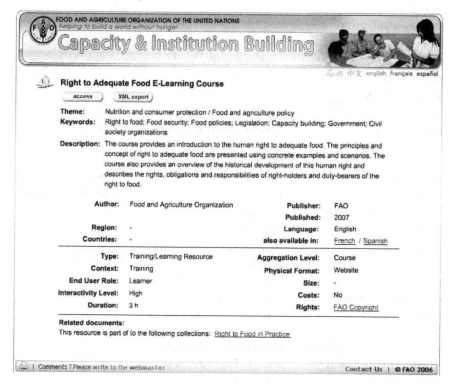

Fig. 1. Example for a record describing an online module on the Right to Food.

4.3 Mapping to LOM

To enable interoperability with other repositories, such as the CGIAR LOR, a mapping of the elements from the Ag-LR AP to their LOM equivalents has to be done. Table 2 provides an overview of the elements and their equivalents as well as possible interoperability issues.

Next to the elements which can be mapped, there are some LOM elements which can be generated automatically for the XML export, e.g. elements from the meta-metadata category.

Table 2. Elements of FAO Ag-LR AP and their LOM equivalents with reference to possible issues for mapping and exchange of records.

Element AP (Namespaces)	LOM equivalent (No)[25]	Possible Issues
Title (DC)	Title (1.2)	
Supplement Title (AGS)	-	
Creator (DC)	Contribute (2.3) / Role: Author	AP does not use vCard
Subject /FAO Categories (AGS)	Classification (9)	
Subject /FAO Keywords (AGS)	Keyword (1.5)	
Abstract (DCTERM)	Description (1.4)	
Notes (AGS)	-	
Publisher (DC)	Contribute (2.3) / Role: Publisher	AP does not use vCard
Date (DCTERMS)	Contribute (2.3) / Role: Publisher / Date (2.3.3)	
Type (DC)	Learning Resources Type (5.2)	customized vocabulary
Format-Type (DC)	Format (4.1)	customized vocabulary
Aggregation Level (LOM)	Aggregation Level (1.8)	
Size (LOM)	Size (4.2)	
Identifier (DC)	Identifier (1.1)	
Language (DC)	Language (1.3)	
Relation (DC)	Relation (7)	
Coverage (DCTERMS)	Coverage (1.6)	
Rights (LOM)	Copyright and Other Restrictions (6.2) /	
Cost (LOM)	Costs (6.1)	
Intended End User Role (LOM)	Intended End User Role (5.5)	
Context (LOM)	Context (5.6)	
Interactivity Level (LOM)	Interactivity Level (5.3)	
Typical Learning Time (LOM)	Typical Learning Time (5.9)	

5. Conclusion

The AP presented above meets the needs of FAO's Capacity and Institution Building Portal which is currently under development. However, more importantly, it is also extendable to the wider agricultural community and its learning resources through the inclusion of AgMES elements (which are used to describe many of the learning resources such as "case studies", "training materials" etc.) and agriculture specific schemes such as AGROVOC. The use of

---

[25] (No): indicates the number of the LOM element.

standard metadata schemas and XML export functionality ensures that information can be shared with other web-based repositories. This interoperability allows for various value-added services.

1. It allows for exchange of information across applications using varying systems that in turn are using different schemas and different encoding guidelines.

2. The generic Ag-LR AP adheres to the unqualified DC metadata set which is used as a common harvesting format by the Open Archives Initiative[26] (OAI) Community. The Ag-LR AP facilitates exposure of the agricultural content to a wider audience by making the metadata harvestable and available.

3. A recent study [7] concluded that more and more resources are being retrospectively added to the Web. Based on this study, availability of good quality metadata allows for retrieval of the original resource, regardless of its actual location on the Web.

References

1. 59/250. Triennial comprehensive policy review of operational activities for development of the United Nations system [59/250]. United Nations General Assembly: Resolution adopted by the General Assembly [on the report of the Second Committee (A/59/488/Add.1)] (2005). http://daccessdds.un.org/doc/UNDOC/GEN/N04/491/26/PDF/N0449126.pdf
2. Friesen, N.: Connecting Collections: An overview of approaches (2006) http://www.cancore.ca/protocols_en.html
3. Friesen, N.: Editorial - A Gentle Introduction to Technical E-learning Standards. In: Canadian Journal of Learning and Technology. Volume 30(3) (2004) http://www.cjlt.ca/content/vol30.3/normeditorial.html
4. ISO/IEC JTC1 SC36: Working Draft for ISO/IEC 19788-2 – Metadata for Learning Resources – Part 2: Data Elements (2005)
5. ISO/IEC JTC1 SC36: Final Report on the "International LOM Survey" (2004) http://jtc1sc36.org/doc/36N0871.pdf
6. Tzikopoulos, N. Manouselis, R. Vuorikari: An Overview of Learning Object Repositories. In: Northrup, P. (ed): Learning Objects for Instruction: Design and Evaluation. Idea Group Publishing, 2007 (accepted)
7. Salokhe, G., Weinheimer, J., Bovo, M.G., Agrimi, M: Structured Metadata for Direct Resource Location: A Case Study (2003). http://www.siderean.com/dc2003/404_Paper84-color.pdf

---

[26] Open Archives Initiative: http://www.openarchives.org/

A Distributed Architecture for Harvesting Metadata Describing Organizations in the Agriculture Sector

Valeria Pesce, Ajit Maru, Gauri Salokhe, Johannes Keizer

Abstract. Providing easy access to updated, accurate and semantically meaningful information about organizations working in the agriculture sector is of primary importance in agricultural information management. Many databases of these organizations already exist but none are comprehensive and all differ in coverage (often overlapping), semantic organization, being up-to-date, quantity and quality of the information they provide. In addition, only very few information systems share and exchange data among themselves. This paper describes a distributed architecture which minimizes duplication in information storage and flow and improves quality of the information provided. In this architecture the data describing an organization are stored in a file as an XML description based on a specific metadata set, and access to these distributed files is facilitated by a central registry file. The proposed metadata set is also discussed, with special focus on those aspects that help to make the architecture coherent.

1 Background

Agricultural sciences, technology and extension boast a large number of organizations, both in the developing and developed countries, mainly because agriculture is the primary industry in many countries. The demand for quality

Valeria Pesce, Ajit Maru

Global Forum on Agricultural Research (GFAR), c/o Food and Agriculture Organization of the United Nations, Viale delle Terme di Caracalla, 00153 Rome, Italy
{Valeria.Pesce, Ajit.Maru}@fao.org

Gauri Salokhe, Johannes Keizer

Knowledge Exchange & Capacity Building Division (KCE), Food and Agriculture Organization of the United Nations (FAO of the UN), Viale delle Terme di Caracalla, 00153 Rome, Italy
{Gauri.Salokhe, Johannes.Keizer}@fao.org

509

information services on "who is doing what" and "who is operating in which areas" is very high.

Information on agricultural organizations is now managed by many different information services[2] with independent databases.

This situation translates into three major difficulties:

1. *on the part of the information services and the data owners*: maintenance is costly (and not cost-effective, since many similar datasets are maintained and updated by different services) and there are no standard exchange formats that allow to tap into external sources;
2. *on the part of the users*: similar information is available from several sources, none of which is comprehensive and all of which differ in: subject coverage, type coverage, semantic organization, quantity and quality of information; selecting only one source is limiting and no cross-searches are possible;
3. *on the part of the single organizations*: visibility in all the existing databases requires submitting the same data about the organization to multiple databases.

Important steps towards improved coherence in agricultural information systems have been taken starting with the Expert Consultation on International Information Systems for Agricultural Science and Technology [1] held in Rome in 2005 and especially with the activities of the Content Management Taskforce (CMTF), set in place by the same Expert Consultation.

In this context the Food and Agriculture Organization of the United Nations (FAO), the Global Forum on Agricultural Research (GFAR) and Wageningen International have developed the Agricultural Organizations Application Profile[3] (or AgOrg AP) and have proposed a special use case for it, with the objective of streamlining the management and flow of information on organizations, thus minimizing the duplication of data, work and costs.

In the proposed use case[4], each organization describes itself using the AP, stores the XML/RDF description on a server and registers the URL of the description with a publicly accessible central registry file so that information services can harvest the descriptions by accessing the Registry.

---

2   Some examples of databases with global coverage are: AROW http://www.isnar.cgiar.org/arow/index, InfoSys+ http://www.infosysplus.org/, WISARD http://www.wisard.org/, the FAO NARS database http://www.fao.org/sd/researchinstitutions

3 Presented at the Content Management Taskforce meeting in Wageningen (March 2007) [2] and now available on the Agricultural Information Management Standards Web site (AIMS) (www.fao.org/aims) at: http://www.purl.org/agmes/organizationap/dtd/

4 The project paper detailing this proposal is available for comments on the EGFAR Web site (www.egfar.org) at: http://www.egfar.org/egfar/website/opensite/collabwebsite?contentId=1599

1.2 Approach

The idea behind this project is that while the adoption of a common metadata set would facilitate information sharing and allow information systems to access each other's data, a distributed architecture where data are only managed by the owners and harvested by the information services would also minimize the problems related to maintenance.

Consequently, beside adopting the above mentioned AgOrg AP as a standard exchange format, it was decided to create an infrastructure for a completely distributed architecture, having learnt from past lessons that data are most easily managed (stored, updated and made accessible) where they were originally created, which is where they can be easily updated and where they are most probably used to deliver desired services that meet local needs.

The whole architecture is designed so that data about an organization should be stored and managed by the organization itself and stored and maintained in one single place.

2 Proposed Architecture and Workflow

The proposed architecture is based on a central Registry which stores the locations of the distributed organization metadata files.

The elements of the proposed architecture are:

Data Providers.   These are the organizations themselves: each organization should describe itself and the description should be in the form of an XML/RDF record (compliant with the AgOrg AP) stored in a file. If the organization has the capacities, it can create the XML/RDF record, validate it against the prescribed Document Type Definition (DTD), store it on a web server and register the URL of the file with the central Registry. Otherwise it can use the services of a gateway provider (see below). The description is always maintained and, if necessary, edited by the organization itself.

Registry.   Through a simple web application, URLs would be appended/updated to a central Registry File. The data in the Registry would be stored in XML/RDF format, so as to allow ease of access and reuse. For each organization, there will only two pieces of information stored: an identifier (see below the paragraph on unique identifiers) and the URL for retrieving the XML/RDF description.

Gateway Providers.   These are the organizations that can provide facilities for other organizations, like: a) a web tool for creating the XML/RDF record; b) web hosting for the XML/RDF file with related tools for updating the record and registering it with the Registry.

Service Providers (harvesters).　　All the organizations/services that want to provide information services based on the descriptions of the organizations. Service providers would access the Registry file, either directly or via web services, and harvest all the URLs. With this information, they can then individually access the metadata records, read the data that they need and create the desired value-added services. Since the XML/RDF descriptions, at each URL, are created and maintained by the owners themselves, they will allow for the implementation of quality information services.

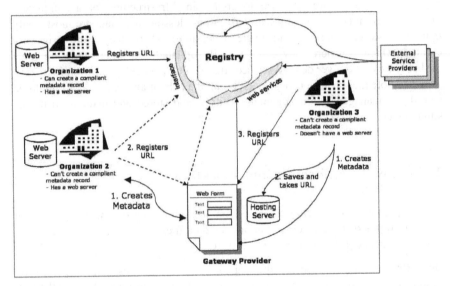

Fig. 1. Architecture and workflow

3　The AgOrg AP

Studies on the available systems that contain organization information, indicate that most of them have been created to meet their individual needs[5]. The AgOrg

---

5 Some of the information systems mentioned earlier in this document use a set of fields for describing organizations, but have not designed a metadata set for general purposes. In a broader field than that of agricultural organizations, the Common European Research Information Format (CERIF) standard was released in 1991 to foster the diffusion of research information across Europe. This standard was created to exchange project information, however the documentation of the updated version (2000) includes other types of information including organizations. The standard is stable but has a complex structure with different information types integrated within. The result is a high number of elements of which most are mandatory. This makes the standard not flexible or easily interoperable with others standards.

AP was designed to define a basic general standard set of metadata elements. The AP does not aim to be an all inclusive and comprehensive standard for describing organizations, their units and their personnel. Rather, it limits itself to describing the type of organization and its location information: a business card for an organization.

As in the case of any AP, the AgOrg AP reuses metadata elements from existing namespaces, namely: Dublin Core[6] (DC), DC Terms[7] (DCTERMS) and Agricultural Metadata Element Set[8] (AGS). The elements that were evaluated as necessary for describing an organization are as follows:

Table 1. Elements of the Organizations Application Profile.

Proposed Elements	Namespace	Controlled Vocabulary	Require-ment [9]	Cardi-nality[10]
organizationName	AGS	no	M	R
> ID attribute				
- fullOrganizationName	AGS	no	M	N-R
- organizationAcronym	AGS	no	O	N-R
address	AGS	no	M	N-R
- streetAddress	AGS	no	M	N-R
- country	AGS	dcterms:ISO3166	M	N-R
telephone / fax / telex / email	AGS	no	O	R
identifier (scheme "dcterms:URI")	DC	no	O	N-R
description	DC	no	O	R
subject	DC	no	M	R
- subjectThesaurus	AGS	yes [11]	O	R
organizationType	AGS	recommended	M	R
relation	DC	no	O	N-R
- isPartOf (scheme "dcterms:URI")	DCTERMS	no	O	R
- replaces (scheme "dcterms:URI")	DCTERMS	no	O	R
date	DC		M	N-R
- created / modified	DCTERMS	dcterms:W3CDTF	M	N-R

6 http://www.dublincore.org/

7 http://www.dublincore.org/

8 http://www.fao.org/aims/

9 Mandatory (M) / Optional (O)

10 Repeatable (R) / Not-Repeatable (N-R)

11 Scheme refinements are provided for the most widely used thesauri in the agricultural field and in related fields: AGS:AGROVOC, AGS:CABT, AGS:ASFAT, AGS:NALT, DCTERMS:MeSH, DCTERMS:LCSH

3.1   The AgOrg AP in a distributed framework

Unique IDs

Theoretically, the Registry could just consist of a list of URLs, with no need for unique identifiers, since the URLs, though not permanent, are unique.

However, assigning a unique identifier to an organization allows to: a) change the URL of the record without creating a second entry in the registry file; b) (to a certain extent) avoid duplication; c) performing faster harvesting; d) most important of all, create and maintain relations between the records (impossible with URLs since they can change).

The unique ID would be stored in the ID attribute in the metadata and it would be generated according to an agreed algorithm. Rather than establishing an assigning authority, it was decided to devise an algorithm so that the ID can be generated also locally and the calculation is repeatable. Every feature of this architecture should enhance the distributed approach.

Semantic coherence

Considering that different organizations might be familiar with different vocabularies or classifications and that different information services harvesting the records might use different taxonomies or Knowledge Organizations Systems (KOS), a certain range of values for the scheme refinement of ags:subjectThesaurus is provided[12], in addition to the possibility of using free-text values in dc:subject.

The envisaged architecture also offers other means of achieving coherence and integration, as the web tool for creating the metadata and/or the information services harvesting the descriptions can map terms between different vocabularies[13] and offer real added value.

References

1 Expert Consultation. International Information Systems for Agricultural Science and Technology - Review of Progress and Prospects. FAO Headquarters Rome 19-21 October 2005 (2005). ftp://ftp.fao.org/gi/gil/consultations/final_report_10-02-06.pdf

2 Meeting Report: Content Management Task Force. International Information Systems for Agricultural Science and Technology. Technical Centre for Agricultural and Rural Cooperation (CTA) Wageningen. The Netherlands 1-2 March, 2007 (2007). ftp://ftp.fao.org/gi/gil/gilws/aims/publications/papers/20070416CMTF-Report.pdf

12 In order to promote coherence, the metadata guidelines will encourage the use of AGROVOC, the multilingual agricultural thesaurus produced by FAO: http://www.fao.org/aims/

13 Of course, mapping between different KOS may be a long and difficult task, but some projects have already started, like the mapping between the United States National Agricultural Library (NAL) Agricultural thesaurus and the AGROVOC Thesaurus.

Semantic Location Based Services for Smart Spaces

Kostas Kolomvatsos, Vassilis Papataxiarhis and Vassileios Tsetsos

Abstract Enhancing the physical environment of users with IT and communication elements is one of the main objectives of the pervasive computing paradigm. The so-called "smart spaces", which are typical pervasive computing environments, combine computing infrastructure with intelligent and context-aware services in order to advance the users' computing experience. In this paper we describe a metadata-based infrastructure that is required for delivering semantics-aware location-based services in smart spaces. This infrastructure involves geometric and ontological spatial representation as well as graph- and knowledge-based navigation algorithms.

1 Introduction

Nowadays, one can observe an integration of the technology with the environment, giving the opportunity to people to utilize it at every time and any place. This is the core idea in pervasive computing [3] and it deals with the distribution of computing devices, such as wearable computers, sensors and other computational elements, in the physical world. Through this highly distributed infrastructure, users are able to gain access to various information sources and services. This way, the physical environment is transformed to a "smart space". Among the core applications for "smart spaces" are the Location Based Services (LBS). LBSs are information services, usually accessible through mobile devices, that correlate spatial and non-spatial data in order to enable location-aware content delivery [1]. However, existing LBS systems have limitations in the management of dynamic location-dependent content as well as in the interoperability between different platforms and application domains [12]. These limitations are mainly due to the poor representation techniques that are adopted for spatial data and application content. For example, most existing systems rely on geometric spatial

Kostas Kolomvatsos, Vassilis Papataxiarhis and Vassileios Tsetsos

Pervasive Computing Research Group, Department of Informatics & Telecommunications, University of Athens, Panepistimiopolis, Ilissia 15784, Greece.

{kostasks, vpap, b.tsetsos}@di.uoa.gr

information, which is incapable of expressing location semantics and does not adhere to some standard, especially for indoor spaces, where GPS is not available.

Navigation services are the most challenging LBS due to their complexity. In a smart space, they should take into account users' physical and perceptual characteristics as well as the dynamic environmental semantics (e.g., temporary obstacles in the path elements). Both the path selection and guidance processes should reason over the current user context, in order to provide optimal user experience.

It is expected that Semantic Web technologies can provide solutions to the aforementioned problems by providing means to resolve interoperability issues as well as to implement intelligent and personalized LBS. Based on the Semantic Web, a semantic navigation service would be based on a spatial ontology and on appropriate knowledge-based inference for path selection. In this work we present such a semantic navigation system that can help users, even with sensory, physical or mental disabilities, to navigate in an indoor environment. The proposed solution is also applicable to outdoor navigation scenarios and to other types of LBS.

The present paper focuses on selected practical issues not covered in the literature (e.g., semi-automatic population of spatial ontologies). More details on the entire LBS platform can be found in [4]. In Section 2 we give a short description of the ontology used to define the spatial elements as well as a GIS-based methodology for the creation of the ontology instances. Section 3 describes the algorithms that can be supported by this approach and that have been implemented in our system. Some related work is surveyed in Section 4. The paper concludes with a brief discussion on some key research issues.

2 Spatial Modeling

2.1 Spatial Ontology

Our approach is based on a semantic description model that exploits concepts from a spatial ontology in order to describe basic elements of navigation paths. The ontology used is an extended version of the Indoor Navigation Ontology (INO) [4], [18], based on the OWL-DL language [19].

As one can see in Fig. 1, INO defines concepts that correspond to every basic spatial element typically found in an indoor environment, and particularly in (or near) a path. Some key concepts are *Space, Path, Path_Element, Path_Point, Corridor, Passage, Obstacle*, etc. (their definition can be found in [4]). Additionally, INO includes several relationships among concepts. Moreover, many concepts are defined through necessary and sufficient conditions based on these relationships. This design decision considerably simplifies the ontology population process (see Section 2.3). Specifically, the class of each passage is deduced from the class of its endpoints. Hence, during INO population we only have to classify the Path_Points. The passages are automatically classified by the reasoning engine.

Furthermore, INO contains relationships that relate its individuals with users, typically defined in a user ontology. The user ontology we have used for demon-

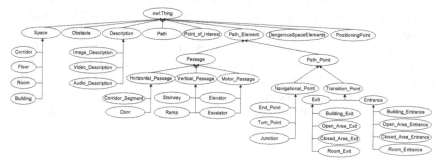

Fig. 1. The main concept hierarchy of INO (arrows represent 'is-a' relationships)

strating our services can be found in [17]. This way, we are able to provide personalized services based on INO. Finally, each spatial concept is associated with actual content, information useful during guidance or for advanced path selection techniques (see also Section 3.4). A specific property is used in order to connect *Path_Element* individuals of INO with the ontology used for content annotation. Through a graphical user interface of the system the user adds content and its metadata (i.e., content ontology instances) on the building floor maps.

All reasoning involved in path searching and user guidance is based on the INO instances extracted from a GIS, axioms holding for the INO relationships (e.g., transitive relationships) and rules (i.e., user profile). In the following sections we describe the phases involved in INO population: a) annotation of GIS data, and b) automatic creation of the ontology instances from GIS data.

2.2 Ontology-driven map annotation with GIS

As described in the previous section, the INO ontology provides a number of concepts for spatial element representation. In order to define the instances of these concepts for an indoor environment, we use a GIS system. In our approach, we categorize points according to the concepts defined in INO. Hence, we decided to use a layered architecture, where each GIS layer corresponds to a concept in INO ontology. For example, there are layers that describe points of building entrances/exits, room entrances/exits, elevators, ramps, etc. (see Fig. 2).

The blueprints of each floor constitute the lower layer and are used as a reference layer. Based on each floor's map, corridors are drawn in order to be used as reference for the markup procedure of the spatial points. Each corridor segment is represented by a straight line. Upon these lines, the various points are defined, as well as their most important semantic features (i.e., floor in which each point is located, its coordinates, its identification number, its label and a short description).

In our approach, 16 layers of points are used for each floor. The most important of them are layers related to navigational or transition points. However, there are also layers devoted to facilitate users' guidance. Hence, we have used an "alert points" layer in order to provide information about very important or dangerous path elements (i.e. stairways, junctions, end points, etc) to users before they reach to the specific location. For orientation purposes (see Section 2.4), auxiliary points are defined close to transition points (i.e., room entrances). Specifically, these points are placed on the side of the corridor that the path element is really located and, thus, they determine the real coordinates of the transition points (all other points are projections of the respective path elements to the corridor lines).

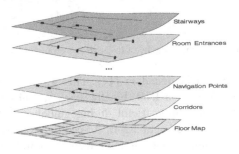

Fig. 2. GIS Layers

2.3 GIS-based Ontology Population

Once the GIS data are in place, one can proceed with the actual ontology population. Each of the GIS layers is exported as a shape file which is further imported in a table of a spatial database. Subsequently, a series of algorithms are used to create the instances of the class corresponding to each layer (see also Listing 1). First of all, we use an algorithm in order to decide for every point in a floor to which line it belongs to. The second step is to discover the endpoints of each line in order to help us in the next step (i.e., discovery of adjacent points). This procedure is repeated for all floors of the building and for all lines and points in a floor. The result is that for every point we store its floor, the lines in which it belongs to and its adjacent points in the floor. The final step is to create the individuals based on INO and the information that we have extracted from the previous steps.

2.4 Orientation Issues

An essential precondition for an indoor navigation service is the ability to determine, at any given time, the orientation of the moving users. Orientation information includes data such as cardinal points and deviation from cardinal directions and, combined with positioning data, it can be translated into directional information, such as "left" or "right". Exploiting orientation information in the context of indoor navigation services has not been widely explored yet, although it can advance the user experience through more intuitive routing instructions (e.g., "the third door at your left", "the door opposite to the coffee machine"). The main obstacle encountered in orienting users in indoor spaces is the lack of efficient ways to directly acquire orientation information, since, unlike the outdoor navigation case, most built structures prohibit the use of GPS devices.

```
CreateIndividuals(INO, spatial DB tables)
Begin
  Create a list of the Floors
  Foreach Floor F
    Foreach line L in F
    Find the points that belong to L
    Find the endpoints of L
    Endfor
  Endfor
  Foreach Floor F
    Foreach line L in F
      Foreach point P in L
        If P is an endpoint then
          Find one adjacent point (based on coordinates)
        Else
          Find two adjacent points (based on coordinates)
        Endif
      Endfor
    Endfor
  Endfor
  Foreach Floor F
    Create INO Floor instances
    Foreach point P in F
      Create an instance in the INO class indicated by its GIS
        layer
    Endfor
    Foreach line L in F
      Create and INO Passage instance
      Perform reasoning (the instance is classified based on its
        endpoints and its definition in INO)
    Endfor
  Endfor
End
```

Listing 1. Algorithm for instance creation

In order to resolve this issue, our approach exploits geometric information as well. Specifically, an angle between the direction of successive corridors belonging to the path is estimated through mathematical computations, in order to identify left and right turns. A similar methodology was adopted in order to estimate whether the entrance of a room resides on the left or the right hand of the user while she traverses a path. For that purposes, an extra layer of points is explicitly represented in the GIS layers, as already mentioned in Section 2.2.

Furthermore, a predetermined, arbitrarily chosen corridor segment, with known deviation from the North is used as reference, in order to decide in real time where a point is located with reference to the user orientation. As a result, the corridors can be classified, depending on their deviation from North, into one of eight cardinal directions (*north, northeast, northwest, east,* etc.). Whether a point is at the left or the right of the user, is decided by taking into account her orientation (e.g., through a digital compass) and the direction of the current corridor.

3 Hybrid Navigation with Graphs and Rules

The INO instances, along with the ontological representation of user profiles and the content semantics, which are described in [4], can be used in a wide range of LBS/navigation algorithms. In order to exploit these metadata, a core part of these algorithms is implemented through rules. In the following sections some key design decisions and algorithmic issues for our system are discussed.

3.1 Why Rule-based Navigation?

A navigation algorithm can be considered as a special case of a path-searching algorithm applied to spatial graphs. Such algorithms typically try to calculate optimal paths with regard to some optimization criteria. For graphs representing spatial environments, the most common, and usually the only, criterion is the Euclidian distance. There are many efficient algorithms for computing shortest paths, such as A* and optimized versions of the Dijkstra algorithm. However, when one introduces more than one criteria to a shortest path searching algorithm (e.g., quickest path, most popular path), its complexity increases dramatically. Specifically, we have a Multi-objective Shortest Path problem [5], which belongs to the broader category of multi-objective combinatorial optimization problems (known to be NP-hard [6]). Moreover, it is usually quite difficult to extend such an algorithm by adding more criteria. For example, let us assume that we have a spatial graph where each edge (i.e., corridor segment) is assigned a weight vector representing its physical edge and width. We also assume that we have designed an algorithm that calculates the shortest routes with edges exceeding a minimum width threshold. If we further want to add the height of each edge to its weight vector, the algorithm needs to be redesigned (maybe a non-trivial task). Moreover, the computational complexity of the new algorithm will increase considerably. Obviously, things become worse as more constraints are added to the algorithm.

Since in personalized human navigation systems we expect to have many different constraints (per user) during route calculation, we decided not to adopt such a "monolithic" approach. In particular, the complexity of the route instructions is a very important factor in human navigation, since people usually do not follow the shortest but the simplest path. The simplest-path algorithm proposed in [14] computes the "easiest-to-describe" path in a graph and has similar computational complexity with a shortest path algorithm. Although the resulting path is, in general, somewhat longer than the shortest one, it is simpler to be followed.

Hence, we have separated the path selection process to two discrete parts: a) identification of k-simplest paths, and b) application of constraints (in the form of simple, Horn-like rules) and preferences to these paths. The path that satisfies all or most of the constraints is guaranteed to be the simplest acceptable path. This modular approach has the following benefits:

- We take into account the route distance, i.e., the main criterion in navigation.
- We can enforce as many constraints as we want and express them in a rather intuitive form of rules.
- The computational complexity does not scale exponentially with the addition of new route selection criteria. In fact, the MOSP problem is decomposed to a k Shortest Paths Problem and to the matching problem involved in rule triggering. The latter problem has been addressed since many years with efficient solutions even for large rule sets (in our case, navigation restrictions) [7]. Nowadays, efficient algorithms have been implemented for both problems. Yen presented a generic solution of k Shortest Paths which can be implemented in $O(kn(m+n\log n))$ [16]. In recent years, RETE algorithms [15] have been proved efficiently in rule execution, facilitating the inference process.

3.2 The Navigation Algorithm

The implemented indoor navigation algorithm constitutes a hybrid rule-based approach of computing the "best traversable" path depending on the user profile, which is comprised of user abilities as well as preferences. In particular, the algorithm computes the optimal path with regard to a number of criteria, such as the total path length and the simplicity of route descriptions.

The first step of the algorithm involves the creation of a "user-compatible" building graph, based on the user profile. This graph is obtained after applying a number of disability rules over the INO instances. These rules eliminate the path elements that cannot be traversed by a particular user. Once this restricted graph is calculated, the execution of the k-simplest paths algorithm follows. We should note that all rules used in the prototype implementation are expressed through the SWRL formalism [13], maintaining maximum compatibility with the OWL language that was used to represent the system ontologies.

```
Navigate(INO, origin, destination, user profile)
Begin
  Create the building graph from INO
  Apply disability rules to INO instances
  Foreach Path Element PE
    If PE is accessible by the user
    Discover and remove the corresponding node and its edges from the
    building graph
    Endif
  Endfor
  Compute the k-Simplest Paths from origin to destination
  Foreach of the k-Simplest Paths
    Foreach Path Element PE
      Assign bonus/penalty value to PE, according to perceptual
      rules and user preferences
    Endfor
    Compute the total path length
    TotalPathRank = f(path length, bonus vector, penalty vector)
  Endfor
  Return the path with the maximum TotalPathRank
End
```

Listing 2. Outline of the navigation algorithm

Afterwards, several other rules assign bonus or penalty values to path elements, based on the user profile. In addition, the total cost of each path is computed as a function of the bonuses and the penalties of the path elements and the total length of the path. Finally, the simplest path is selected based on the total cost of the paths computed in the previous step (see also Listing 2).

3.3 Path Selection Example

A path selection example that demonstrates the execution results of the algorithm presented in the previous section is the following. Fig. 3 depicts the floor plan of a building. Initially, we assume that the user is located in point A and wants to move to point H. There are three possible loopless paths that she may follow. Examining these routes, it is established that the path ACFEH is the shortest path between A and H, but not the simplest one, due to the intersections it contains. On the other hand, the path ACFDGH is neither the shortest nor the simplest one. In fact, it is the longer and the most complicated path between A and H and, as a result, it cannot be selected by the algorithm. Finally, the path ABDGH is the simplest, since it contains only two turns (points B and G). Moreover, it is not much longer than the shortest one and, consequently, it is presented to the user as the "best traversable" path between A and H. For more details on path complexity, one can refer to [14].

3.4 Navigation Alternatives Supported by our Approach

Given that different users and application domains have different requirements for navigation, new navigation algorithms should be devised. This is possible in our approach:

Example 1 - Content-based Navigation. A tourist is interested in ancient weapons and war exhibits. When she visits a large archaeological museum, she uses a tour guide that plans some routes of variable duration/length, all of which mostly containing exhibits of interest.

Example 2 – Presentation-based Navigation. A blind user needs some auditory assistance in order to find his way in a building. The building's spatial elements and points of interest are semantically annotated with descriptive images, texts, and/or sounds, which are used in the instructions provided by the system. In case the system knows that the user is blind, it can calculate paths that will be easier to describe to him (i.e., annotated with sounds and text, since the latter can be transformed to speech through appropriate software).

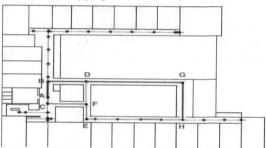

Fig. 3. A sample floor plan

4 Related Work

Several researchers have recognized that semantics can improve the way location services work. For example, in [8] the authors present a Semantic Web framework for context-aware and location services. This framework defines a context ontology used to annotate spaces and deliver advanced services to pedestrian users.

Semantic spatial representation is at the heart of semantic LBS, since the quality of LBS algorithms depends heavily on the spatial modeling of the physical environment. As far as indoor navigation is concerned, only a few researchers have proposed practical, yet expressive, models. In our view, the most important one is presented in [9]. It is a hybrid model, which represents the space as semantic hierarchies of "locations" and "exits" that also carry geometric information (e.g., coordinates). More ontology-oriented approaches are presented in [10], [11]. Although these models are useful for developing LBS, we are not aware of any methodologies for (semi-) automatic instantiation of the respective models.

5 Conclusions and Discussion

Enhancing traditional context-aware services with semantics seems a promising solution for future pervasive computing environments. In this paper we have described some necessary elements and methods for implementing such services, with a special emphasis on personalized pedestrian navigation. We showed that delivering such services is feasible with the aid of Semantic Web technologies. However, there are some issues that require further research. For example, several problems become obvious when trying to represent complex environments and their features, such as open areas without many physical boundaries (e.g., museums or airports), or spatial updates (e.g., a temporary locked door). Regarding technology issues, existing SWRL rule engines are not fully integrated with OWL ontology reasoners, thus complicating the inference process. Furthermore, some features of spatial environments should be expressed through non-symbolic information (e.g., uncertainty), raising also the need for more expressive representation formalisms (e.g., fuzzy extensions to OWL).

References

1. Virrantaus, K., Markkula, J., Garmash, A., Terziyan, Y.V., 'Developing GIS-Supported Location-Based Services', In *Proc. of WGIS'2001 – First International Workshop on Web Geographical Information Systems.*, Kyoto, Japan. , pp 423–432, 2001.
2. Weiser, M. 'The computer for the twenty-first century', Scientific American, 265(3):94–104, Sept. 1991.
3. Satyanarayanan, M. "Pervasive computing: vision and challenges", IEEE Personal Communications, Aug. 2001, Vol. 8, No. 4.
4. Tsetsos V., Anagnostopoulos C., Kikiras P., and Hadjiefthymiades S., "Semantically Enriched Navigation for Indoor Environments", International Journal of Web and Grid Services (IJWGS), Vol.4, No.2, Inderscience Publ, December 2006.
5. Current, J., and Marsh, M. "Multiple transportation network design and routing problems: taxonomy and annotation", European Journal of Operational Research, 65, 4—19, 1993
6. Serafini, P. Some considerations about computational complexity for multi objective combinatorial problems. In J. Jahn and W. Krabs, editors, Recent advances and historical development of vector optimization, volume 294 of Lecture Notes in Economics and Mathematical Systems. Springer Verlag, Berlin, 1986.
7. Forgy, C. "Rete: A Fast Algorithm for the Many Pattern/Many Object Pattern Match Problem", Artificial Intelligence, 19, pp 17-37, 1982
8. Bikakis, A., Patkos, T., Antoniou, G., Papadopouli, M., and Plexousakis, D. "A Semantic-based Framework for Context-aware Pedestrian Guiding Services", 2nd International Workshop on Semantic Web Technology For Ubiquitous and Mobile Applications (SWUMA), Riva del Garda, Trentino, Italy, August 2006
9. Hu, H., and Lee, D.L. (2004) 'Semantic Location Modeling for Location Navigation in Mobile Environment', IEEE Mobile Data Management, pp. 52-61.

10. Coenen, F. and Visser, P., 'A Core Ontology for Spatial Reasoning'. Department of Computer Science, University of Liverpool, 1998.

11. Flury, T., Privat, G., Ramparany, F. 'OWL-based location ontology for content-aware services', Proc. Artificial Intelligence in Mobile Systems, Nottingham, pp52-58, 2004.

12. Kim, J. W., Kim, J. Y., Hwang, H. S., Park, S. S., Kim, C. S., Park, S. G. 'The Semantic Web Approach in Location Based Services', in 'Computational Intelligence and its Applications', ICCSA 2005, Singapore, Springer, pp 127-136.

13. Horrocks, I., Patel-Schneider, P.F., Boley, H., Tabet, S., Grosof, B., & Dean, M. (2004b). SWRL: A Semantic Web Rule Language Combining OWL and RuleML, W3C Member Submission, 21 May 2004.http://www.w3.org/Submission/SWRL/.

14. Duckham, M. and Kulik, L., "Simplest Paths: Automated route selection for navigation," Accepted for COSIT'03, Lecture Notes in Computer Science, Springer-Verlag, 2003.

15. Forgy, C.L. 1982. Rete: A fast algorithm for the many pattern/many object pattern match problem. Artificial Intelligence, 19:17–37.

16. J. Y. Yen, Finding the k shortest loopless paths in a network. Management Science, 17:712-716, 1971

17. User Navigation Ontology, available at http://p-comp.di.uoa.gr/ont/UNO.owl.

18. Indoor Navigation Ontology, available at http://p-comp.di.uoa.gr/ont/INO.owl.

19. OWL Web Ontology Language Guide, Retrieved January 19, 2008 from http://www.w3.org/TR/owl-guide.

How to Overcome Stumbling Blocks of Traditional Personalization Paradigms[*]

Yolanda Blanco-Fernández, José J. Pazos-Arias, Alberto Gil-Solla, Manuel Ramos-Cabrer, Martín López-Nores

Abstract N

owadays, users are exposed to an overwhelming amount of information in several application domains. Recommender systems fight such an overload by selecting the products which are more appealing to each user, according to his personal preferences or needs. Current personalization techniques are based on more or less sophisticated syntactic methods which miss a lot of knowledge during the elaboration of the recommendations. In this paper, we propose an approach that effectively overcomes the drawbacks of the existing personalization techniques by resorting to reasoning mechanisms inspired in Semantic Web technologies. Such a reasoning provides recommender system with extra knowledge about the user's preferences, thus favoring more accurate personalization processes.

1 Introduction

Nowadays, users are exposed to an overload of information in numerous application domains (e.g. WWW, e-commerce, Digital TV). In this scenario, it is necessary to develop recommender systems which select automatically products interesting for each user, according to his/her preferences or needs (modeled in a personal profile).

In order to predict the relevance of a product for a given user, some personalization techniques establish simple comparisons between the main attributes of this product, and those defined in his/her profile. In contrast with these strategies, other approaches dismiss these content descriptions and only consider the levels of interest contained in the user's profile. All the existing personalization techniques have

ETSE de Telecomunicación, University of Vigo, 36310, Spain
e-mail: {yolanda,jose,agil,mramos,mlnores}@det.uvigo.es

[*] Work supported by the Spanish Ministry of Education and Science Project TSI2007-61599, and by the Xunta de Galicia Project PGIDIT05PXI32204PN.

a common drawback, due to the fact that the selection of the recommendations is based on **syntactic** mechanisms which miss huge amounts of knowledge about the user's preferences. Such knowledge is related to the **semantics** of the user's interests and of the products available in the recommender system. This limitation reduces the quality of the offered suggestions, and causes weaknesses in the personalization techniques adopted by existing recommender systems.

In this paper, the aim is to fight these syntactic limitations, by taking advantage the experience gained in the Semantic Web field. As stated in [5], this initiative permits to discover semantic relationships among resources annotated by metadata, which are formally represented in a knowledge ontology. Specifically, we explore the benefits provided by an approach of semantic reasoning to the current recommender systems. As a result of this synergy, we define personalization techniques which, instead of resorting to traditional syntactic approaches, infer semantic relationships between the user's preferences and the products available in the recommender system. These relationships provide the system with additional knowledge about the user's interests, thus favoring more accurate recommendation processes. In this regard, note also that our reasoning mechanism is flexible enough to be employed in multiple personalization applications and systems. In fact, the only element that binds our approach to a specific domain is the knowledge ontology, which formalizes the concepts and relationships typical in the context of each recommender system.

This paper is organized as follows: Sect. 2 describes how the most-used personalization paradigms work, along with their main limitations. Sect. 3 presents the way in which our reasoning approach overcomes such limitations, and finally, Sect. 4 draws some conclusions and outlines possible lines of future research.

2 Current Personalization Paradigms

Two principal paradigms have been proposed in literature, namely *content-based* and *collaborative filtering*. The main difference between both strategies is the kind of information used during the personalization process. This way, while content-based filtering considers the descriptive *features* of items, collaborative proposals use the *ratings* that users assign to these items in their profiles. Consequently, content-based filtering only works when dealing with domain where feature extraction is feasible and attribute information is readily available. As collaborative filtering uses content-less representations, it does not face this limitation, even though suffers from another weaknesses.

2.1 Content-based Filtering: How does it work?

The so-called **content-based filtering** suggests products which are similar to those the user liked in the past. This technique compares the user's preferences with available products, by considering their respective content descriptions (i.e. their main attributes).

Several similarity metrics have been proposed in the content-based recommender systems described in literature, such as TV Advisor™ [11], TV Show Recommender [27], and PPG [1] in TV domain. Some approaches establish simple syntactic comparisons among a set of keywords; more advanced metrics rely on the predictive capabilities of automatic classifiers (e.g. Bayesian networks, decision trees, neural networks) to decide about the relevance of a product for a given user. These approaches have a common weakness related to their syntactic nature, which only permits to detect similarity among products sharing the *same* attributes.

The strength of content-based filtering is related to the fact of offering accurate recommendations to a user without knowing other users' preferences. Its Achilles heel are the employed syntactic metrics, which lead to **overspecialized** suggestions including only products very similar to those the user already knows.

2.2 Collaborative Filtering: How does it work?

Collaborative filtering suggests to a user products which were appealing to others with similar preferences (henceforth his *neighbors*). Firstly, the technique forms the user's neighborhood and, next, it predicts his level of interest in the products defined in his neighbors' profiles.

2.2.1 Neighborhood formation:

Traditional collaborative approaches compare users' preferences by considering only the levels of interest defined in their respective profiles. Specifically, these approaches create a vector for each user containing his ratings in each product available in the recommender system[2]. Next, the correlation between the considered user's rating vector and the vectors of the remaining users is computed. Finally, the N highest correlation measures are selected, since these values correspond to the N nearest neighbors to the user. From this explanation, it follows that traditional collaborative approaches only detect that two users share preferences when there exists overlap between the products contained in their respective profiles, as explained in [25].

---

[2] A rating 0 is assumed in case the user has not yet rated a product.

2.2.2 Prediction of the user's interest:

To predict the interest of the user in the products defined in his neighbors' profiles, the existing collaborative approaches compute a weighed average of their ratings in these products, using as weights the correlation values (between their preferences) previously measured. Therefore, a collaborative system suggests to the user the products which are most appealing to his nearest neighbors.

As collaborative systems do not only consider the user's preferences (but also his neighbors' interests), they offer diverse recommendations and, therefore, overcome the overspecialized suggestions of the content-based approaches. Notwithstanding, the existing collaborative filtering tools, such as Bellcore Video Recommender [14], MovieLens [18], TV Scout™ [3], and Moviefinder™ [19] have revealed some critical weaknesses:

- **Sparsity problem:** As the number of available products increases, it is unlikely that two users rate the same products in their profiles, thus hampering the selection of the user's neighbors.
- **Scalability:** As the number of products available in the recommender system increases, the user's rating vector also increases in size. In this case, the creation of his neighborhood (based on computing correlations between users vectors) becomes too demanding in computational terms.
- **Latency problem:** Since collaborative systems only suggest products defined as preferences of the user's neighbors, new products cannot be included in a recommendation before a significant number of users rate them in their profiles.

2.3 Hybrid Approaches: How do they work?

As Burke described in [9], many current systems resort to a hybrid personalization technique by mixing content-based methods and collaborative filtering (for instance, PTV [20], TiVo™ [26] and Recommender [2]). Most of the hybrid proposals adopt the so-called *"collaboration via content"* paradigm by Pazzani [22], based on computing the similarity between two users's preferences by considering both their content descriptions (just like in content-based approaches), and their respective levels of interest (considered in collaborative filtering). This way, Pazzani fights the *sparsity problem* by detecting that two users have common preferences even when there does not exist overlap between the products contained in their profiles. However, in order to measure similarity in this case, it is necessary that these products have common attributes. For that reason, Pazzani's approach is still limited by the syntactic metrics used in the traditional content-based techniques.

In order to fight these limitations, our approach defines metrics that compares the user's preferences with the available products in a more flexible way. Instead of using syntactic techniques, our metrics reason about the semantics of the compared products. To this aim, we take advantage of the inference approaches developed in the Semantic Web.

3 Reasoning-based Personalization Techniques

In order to reason about the semantics in a specific domain, it is necessary to formalize an ontology by a language expressive enough to represent typical concepts and relationships. The former proposals were RDF [4] and RDFS [8], which added a formal semantics to the purely syntactic specifications provided in XML. Next, DAML [10] and OIL [12] arose, which have been finally fused and standardized by W3C as OWL [17]. Nowadays, OWL is the most expressive language in which three sub-levels have been defined (Lite, DL and Full).

In our approach, such a domain ontology represents the products available in the recommender system, along with their main attributes. As an example, we show in Fig. 1 a brief excerpt from a ontology in television domain. In this figure, it is possible to identify several instances that identify specific TV programs, which belong to a hierarchy of classes referred to different genres (e.g. *Fiction, Sports, Music, Leisure*). The attributes of these TV contents (e.g. cast, intented audience, topics) are also identified by hierarchically organized classes, and are related to each program by means of labeled properties (e.g. *hasActor, hasIntendedAudience, isAbout*).

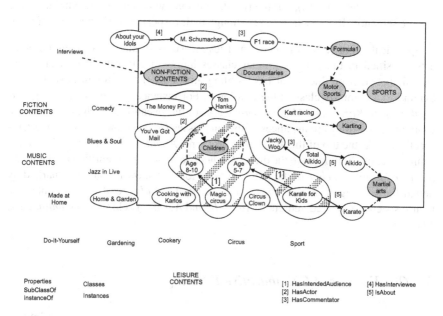

Fig. 1 A brief extract from an ontology about the TV domain

3.1 Our Enhanced Content-based Filtering

Thanks to the reasoning, we overcome the overspecialized nature of the traditional content-based recommendations by resorting to a **semantic similarity metrics**.

- In literature related to semantics research, it is possible to find numerous similarity metrics which measure resemblance by looking at the *hierarchical relationships* established in a taxonomy, such as those described in [24, 15, 23]. According to these proposals, the hierarchical similarity measured between two products depends on the existence and the depth[3] of a class which is ancestor of both of them in a hierarchy. This way, the deepest the *lowest common ancestor* (denoted by LCA) of the two products in the taxonomy, the higher the value of hierarchical semantic similarity between them.

- As Ganesan *et al.* explained in [13], *"taxonomy-based approaches do not accurately capture similarity in certain domains, such as when the data is sparse or when there are known relationships between the compared products"*. For that reason, we extend the existing similarity metrics by mixing the hierarchical relationships included in the domain ontology, with other *associations hidden behind the properties* explicitly defined in it. Thanks to these associations (described in detail in [6]), our metrics detects that two products are similar if they are semantically associated, even though their respective attributes are different.

Specifically, our reasoning-based metrics measures similarity between: (i) products classified in the ontology under classes hierarchically related to each other, and (ii) between products that have sibling attributes (i.e. different attributes belonging to a common class in the ontology). For instance, in Fig. 1, the programs *Cooking with Karlos* and *Made at Home* are similar because they share the *Leisure Contents LCA* (they are instances of the subclasses *Cookery* and *Do-It-Yourself*, respectively). At the top of this figure, the programs *About your Idols* and *F1 race* are similar because both involve the driver *Michael Schumacher* (identified by the *union instance M. Schumacher* in the ontology). Besides, as shown in an area marked by dotted lines in Fig. 1, *Magic Circus* and *Karate for Kids* are also related because their respective intended audience (*Age 8-10* and *Age 5-7*) belong to the *union class Children*.

3.2 Our Enhanced Collaborative Filtering

Our collaborative approach uses semantic reasoning both in the phase of neighborhood formation, and in the prediction of the interest of the user in a generic product (not necessarily rated in profiles available in the recommender system).

---

[3] The depth of a class in a taxonomy is defined as the number of hierarchical links between it and the root node.

In order to form the user's neighborhood, we extend the *"collaboration via content"* paradigm, so that we reason about the semantics of the users' preferences instead of using only their content descriptions. For that purpose, we propose a **taxonomy-based approach** to create the user's rating vector. Instead of including his levels of interest in the available products, our vector contains his ratings in relation to the categories under which these programs are classified in the ontology. The hierarchical organization of these categories permit us to fight the *sparsity problem* and the scalability-related limitations present in the traditional collaborative approaches.

- On the one hand, such an organization allows to detect that the preferences of two users are similar even when their respective profiles do not contain neither products nor attributes identical. In our approach, it is only necessary that the categories of the considered products share a common ancestor in the hierarchy defined in the domain ontology. For instance, according to the hierarchy defined in Fig. 1, our taxonomy-based approach uses *Motor sports* category to detect similarity between the preferences of two users who have viewed a formula 1 race (classified under *Formula1* subcategory) and a karting competition (belonging to *Karting*), respectively.

- With regard to scalability concerns, note that as the number of available products increases in the system, our rating vectors do not necessarily increase in size (just like in the existing collaborative approaches). This is due to the fact that many new products can belong to the same hierarchical categories in the ontology, thus reducing the computational cost of our neighborhood creation process.

Once correlation between users has been computed and the N nearest neighbors have been selected, it is necessary to predict the user's level of interest in the considered product. In contrast with current collaborative approaches —which only consider the contribution of the neighbors who have already rated this product— we explore the full neighborhood of the user. This way, if a neighbor has rated the considered product, the prediction is based on the level of interest defined in his profile; otherwise, we predict this level by measuring the semantic similarity between his preferences and the target product. Thus, our reasoning-based collaborative filtering enables to suggest (without unnecessary delays) products which are completely novel for all the users in the system. Consequently, we eliminate the *latency problem* of the traditional approaches, in which a product must be rated by many users before being suggested.

4 Conclusions and Further Work

Semantic reasoning permits to overcome unresolved limitations of the current personalization techniques. Our reasoning approach is flexible and generic enough to be applied in multiple domains (and, consequently, in numerous recommender systems). To this aim, it is only necessary to provide an ontology where the knowledge of the specific domain must be conveniently formalized.

Our reasoning-based recommendation techniques have been experimentally evaluated in Digital TV domain with a set of 400 undergraduate students from our University. We have included these techniques in two personalization systems: a tool that suggests TV shows according to the viewer's preferences (see [7] for details), and a t-learning system that offers personalized courses by considering the user's interests and the acquired knowledge, as we described in [21]. Our experiments compared the proposed enhanced strategies with several approaches defined in literature which are devoid of reasoning capabilities. The obtained results revealed significant increments of average recall and precision in relation to the existing approaches (up to 35% of recall and 47% of precision with regard to the best strategy).

We plan to continue the experimental evaluation of our strategies by involving the subscribers of the Spanish operator R^4. Specifically, we have incorporated our techniques into a recommender system named R-AVATAR, that has been deployed over the cable networks of this operator, which has 80000 subscribers and broadcasts daily 43 TV channels, yielding about 1000 TV programs to reason about (considering 25 contents per channel on average). Besides, we are also working in the integration of our recommendation strategies into the MiSpot system [16], a technological framework that enables new and more effective forms of publicity in the IDTV field, both for in-home and mobile TV settings. MiSpot combines two basic ideas: non-invasiveness, to ensure that publicity does not interfere with the viewers' enjoyment of the audiovisual contents; and interactivity, to deliver online trading services through the TV. In this context, a personalization engine with the kind of abilities discussed in this paper comes as a crucial element to turn advertising into a source of useful information for each individual viewer and, thereby, maximize the revenues of publicity.

References

1. Ardissono L., Gena C., Torasso P., Bellifemine F., Difino A. and Negro B. User modeling and recommendation techniques for personalized electronic program guides. In *Personalized Digital Television: Targeting Programs to Individual Viewers*, pages 3 – 26. Kluwer Academics Publishers, 2004.
2. Basu C., Hirsh H. and Cohen W. Recommendation as classification: using social and content-based information in recommendation. In *15th National Conference on Artificial Intelligence (AAAI-98)*, pages 714–720, 1998.
3. Baudisch P. and Bruekner L. TV Scout: guiding users from printed TV program guides to personalized TV recommendation. In *1st Workshop on Personalization in Future TV*, pages 151 – 160, 2001.
4. Beckett D. RDF Syntax Specification. Disponible en *http://www.w3.org/TR/rdf-syntax-grammar*. 2004.

---

[4] www.mundo-r.com

5. Berners-Lee T., Hendler J. and Lassila O. The Semantic Web: A new form of Web content that is meaningful to computers will unleash a revolution of new possibilities. *The Scientific American*, 279(5):34–43, 2001.
6. Blanco-Fernández Y., Pazos-Arias J., Gil-Solla A., Ramos-Cabrer M., López-Nores M., García-Duque J., Díaz-Redondo R., Fernández-Vilas A., Bermejo-Muñoz, J. A flexible semantic inference methodology to reason about user preferences in knowledge-based recommender systems. *Knowledge-Based Systems Journal*, http://dx.doi.org/10.1016/j.knosys.2007.07.004. In press.
7. Blanco Fernández Y., Pazos Arias J. J., Gil Solla A., Ramos Cabrer M., López Nores M. and Bermejo Múñoz J. AVATAR: Enhancing the personalized television by semantic inference. *International Journal of Pattern Recognition and Artificial Intelligence*, 21(2):397–422, 2007.
8. Brickley D. and Guha R. RDF vocabulary description language 1.0: RDF Schema. Disponible en *http://www.w3.org/TR/rdf-schema*. 2004.
9. Burke R. Hybrid recommender systems: survey and experiments. *User Modeling and User-Adapted Interaction*, 12(4):331–370, 2002.
10. DAML: The DARPA Agent Markup Language. *Disponible en http://www.daml.org*. 2000.
11. Das D. and ter Horst H. Recommender systems for TV. In *Recommender Systems: Papers from the AAAI Workshop*. *Technical Report WS-98-08*, pages 151 – 160. American Association for Artificial Intelligence, Menlo Park, California, 2001.
12. Fensel D., van Harmelen F., Horrocks I., McGuinness D. and Patel-Schneider P. SOIL: An ontology infrastructure for the Semantic Web. *IEEE Intelligent Systems*, 16(2):38–45, 2001.
13. Ganesan P., Garcia-Molina H. and Widom J. Exploiting hierarchical domain structure to compute similarity. *ACM Transactions on Information Systems*, 21(1):64–93, 2003.
14. Hill W., Stead L., Rosenstein M. and Furnas G. Recommending and evaluating choices in a virtual community of use. In *Proceedings of International Conference on Human Factors in Computing Systems (CHI-95)*, pages 194–201, 1995.
15. Lin D. An information-theoretic definition of similarity. In *15th International Conference on Machine Learning (ICML-98)*, pages 296–304, 1998.
16. López Nores M., Pazos Arias J., Blanco Fernández Y., García Duque J., Tubío Pardavila R., Rey López M. *The MiSPOT System: Personalized Publicity and Marketing over Interactive Digital TV*. E-Business and Telecommunication Networks. Springer-Verlag, 2007.
17. McGuinness D. and van Harmelen F. OWL Web Ontology Language Overview. W3C Recommendation. 2004.
18. Miller B., Albert I., Lam S., Konstan J. and Riedl J. Movielens unplugged: experiences with an occasionally connected recommender system. In *ACM Conference on Intelligent User Interfaces*, pages 263–266, 2003.
19. Moviefinder Recommender System. Available information in *http://www.moviefinder.com*.
20. O'Sullivan D., Smyth B., Wilson D. and McDonald K. Improving the quality of the personalized Electronic Program Guide. *User Modeling and User-Adapted Interaction*, 14(1):5–36, 2004.
21. Pazos-Arias J., López-Nores M., García-Duque J., Díaz-Redondo R., Blanco-Fernández Y., Ramos-Cabrer M., Gil-Solla A., Fernández-Vilas A. Provision of distance learning services over Interactive Digital TV with MHP. *Computers & Education*.
22. Pazzani M. A framework for collaborative, content-based and demographic filtering. *Artificial Intelligence Review*, 13(5):393–408, 1999.
23. Rada R., Mili H., Bicknell E. and Blettner M. Development and application of a metric on semantic nets. *IEEE Transactions on Systems, Man, and Cybernetics*, 19(1):17–30, 1989.
24. Resnik P. Semantic similarity in a taxonomy: an information-based measure and its application to problems of ambiguity in natural language. *Journal of Artificial Intelligence Research*, 11(4):95–130, 1999.
25. Sarwar B., Karypis G., Konstan J. and Riedl J. Item-based collaborative filtering recommendation algorithms. In *10th International WWW Conference (WWW-01)*, pages 285–295, 2001.
26. TiVo, Inc. TiVo: TV your way. Available in *http://www.tivo.com*, 2002.

27. Zimmerman J., Kurapati K., Buczak A., Schafer D., Gutta S. and Martino J. TV personalization system: design of a TV show recommender engine and interface. In *Personalized Digital Television: Targeting Programs to Individual Viewers*, pages 27 – 51. Kluwer Academics Publishers, 2004.

A Semantic Matching Approach for Mediating Heterogeneous Sources

Michel Schneider, Lotfi Bejaoui, Guillaume Bertin

Abstract Approaches to make multiple sources interoperable were essentially investigated when one are able to resolve a priori the heterogeneity problems. This requires that a global schema must be elaborated or that mappings between local schemas must be established before any query can be posed. The object of this paper is to study to what extend a mediation approach can be envisaged when none of these features are a priori available. Our solution consists in matching a query with each of the local schema. We designed a first prototype which showed that the approach could be efficient. We propose in this paper a new more sophisticated prototype. A friendlier query language is available. The detection of matching is more successful. This kind of system can be installed on super-nodes in P2P networks in order to facilitate accesses to data by their semantics. It can thus contribute to the pervasive computing paradigm.

1 Introduction

The interoperability of multiple heterogeneous sources represents an important challenge considering the proliferation of numerous information sources both in private networks (intranet) and in public networks (internet). Heterogeneity is the consequence of the autonomy: sources are designed, implemented and used independently. Heterogeneity can appear for different reasons: different types of data, different representations of data, different management software packages.

One interoperability approach which has been studied for several years is based on mediation [23], [5]. A mediator analyzes the query of a user, breaks it down into sub-queries for the various sources and re-assembles the results of sub-queries to present them in a homogeneous way. The majority of mediation systems operate in a closed world where one knows a priori the sources to make interoperable. There are several advantages to this. First it is possible to build an integrated schema which constitutes a reference frame for the users to formulate their queries. Then it is possible to supply the mediator with various

Michel Schneider
Cemagref, 24 Avenue des Landais, 63172 Aubière Cedex, France
michel.schneider@cemagref.fr

Lotfi Bejaoui
Cemagref, 24 Avenue des Landais, 63172 Aubière Cedex, France
lotfi.bejaoui@cemagref.fr

Guillaume Bertin
LIMOS, Complexe des Cézeaux, 63173 Aubière Cedex, France
bertin.guillaume2@gmail.com

informations which are necessary for the interoperability and particularly to resolve heterogeneity problems. The different kinds of heterogeneity to be resolved are now clearly identified: heterogeneity of concepts or intentional semantic heterogeneity; heterogeneity of data structures or structural semantic heterogeneity; heterogeneity of values or extensional semantic heterogeneity. Different solutions have been studied and experimented on to solve these problems. For example we can cite the work of [7] and [9]. From these initial investigations, very numerous works intervened to propose automatic approaches of integration of schemas. An approach was particularly investigated: the mapping of schemas. It led to the elaboration of several systems such as SEMINT [12], DIKE [18], COMA [3], CUPID [13]. One will find analyses and comparisons of such systems in [19] or [6] or [16]. The practical aspects of the application of such systems are discussed in [1]. The role of ontologies was also investigated. In [2] and [15], the interest of ontologies for the semantic interoperability is underlined. Several approaches of integration of information based on ontologies were suggested. One will find a synthesis of it in [22]. It is necessary also to quote the work of [10] suggesting a logical frame for the integration of data. In all these works, the objective is to build a global schema which integrates all the local schemas.

When one operates in an evolutionary world where sources can evolve all the time, the elaboration of a global schema is a difficult task. It would be necessary to be able to reconstruct the integrated schema each time a new source is considered or each time an actual source makes a number of changes. To overcome these drawbacks an another approach has also been investigated: the query based approach. In this approach no global schema is required. The integration problems are solved during querying. Three main systems can be classified in this category: Information Manifold system, InfoSleuth system and Singapore system. Information Manifold [11] uses sources capabilities to determine how a query can be solved. InfoSleuth [17] is an agent-based system using ontologies for performing information gathering and analysis tasks. Singapore system [4] proposes an object language to formulate exact or fuzzy queries.

Our approach can also be considered as query-oriented. It is based on a semantic matching between the user query and each source schema. The user formulates its query by using its knowledge of the domain. Only the sources whose schemas match with the query are considered. The user query is rewritten for each of these sources according to its information capacity. These sources are then interrogated. Results are formatted and integrated. This approach offers several advantages. The rewriting process is simpler. A new source can be inserted at any time; the only obligation is to provide an adequate representation of this source. We have implemented a first prototype [21] to validate this approach.

The second prototype which we present in this paper possesses various advantages on the first. The query language is more intuitive and so is more convenient for a non specialized user. The matching between a query and a source is more successful. The system is capable of identifying itself the potential sources available on the Web.

We will consider in this paper only XML sources, but our approach can be adapted to deal with any kind of sources.

The paper is organised as follows. In section 2 we explain the principle of our approach. Section 3 describes the architecture and the working of the system. Section 4 is devoted to the OWL representation of sources. In section 5 we explain the main features of our matching algorithm. Section 6 is devoted to some experiments with the second version of our prototype. Section 7 presents some others features and section 8 presents a number of conclusions and perspectives.

2 Principle of the Approach

Our approach does not use a global schema or some predefined mappings. The user thus formulates his query by using his implicit knowledge of the domain or by making an explicit reference to an ontology of the domain.

The syntax of our query language is inspired by that of SQL. The query is cut in three clauses with the reserved words Select, From and Where. The "Select" clause defines the searched elements and the "Where" clause specifies the properties which have to verify these elements. The "From" clause is not indispensable because the user does not know the structures in which elements must be looked for. It is the system which has the task to localize these structures. Nevertheless it is necessary in certain situations for introducing alias of elements. The "Where" clause contains the conditions. We need two types of conditions: "link conditions" allowing to specify the existence of links between elements of the query, and "valuation conditions" allowing to impose values on certain elements of the query. For example suppose that a user looks for the name of the customers living in the same region as a supplier having a name "easymarket". He has to specify in the query that name is linked to customer, that name is linked to supplier, that region is linked to customer, that region is linked to supplier. In our query language this query is specified as:

```
Q1 : Select a()name
from customer a, supplier b
where a()region=b()region and b()name="easymarket"
```

We use the double symbol () to specify a link condition between two elements.

The alias in the "From" clause have a precise signification. For example using the alias a for customer imposes that it is the same instance of a that is connected with name in a()name and with region in a()region. So query Q1 can be paraphrased as follows : search for an instance ain of customer and an instance bin of supplier such that ain is connected to an instance of name and an instance rin1 of region, bin is connected to an instance of name whose value is "easymarket" and an instance rin2 of region, the values of rin1 and rin2 are equal.

Fig. 1 XML trees of two sources

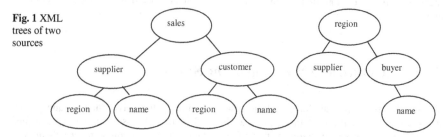

A correspondence (matching) is established with a source if each term of the query has a correspondent in the source and if each link is present in the source. A term has a correspondent if it exists in the source the same term or a synonym or a hyponym. Synonym and hyponym are determined by scanning a domain ontology. A link a()b is present in the source if it exists a semantic connection between the correspondents of a and b. We will explain further how this connection is detected.

We will illustrate how the matching can work with the two XML sources of figure 1. It is straightforward to infer that the query Q1 matches with the first source since the supplier element and the customer element are both connected to an element the name of which is region. A matching for the second source cannot be inferred so immediately. First the matcher must discover that buyer is a hyponym of customer. Then it must found the connection of buyer and supplier with the shared element region. Supplier is not connected to a name element but since supplier is a leaf element it can suppose that its value represents its name. So this second source matches also with the query since it respects the semantics of the query.

The rewritings of the query in the user language for the two sources are respectively:

```
Select a()name
from customer a, supplier b
where a()region=b()region and b()name="easymarket"
```
(same as the initial specification)

```
Select a()name
from buyer a, supplier b
where a()region=b()region and b="easymarket"
```

The system proposes all the rewritings to the user. The user can then ask the execution of some of them. The system has to rewrite each one in the source language.

Two other points must be mentioned about our query language.

- Since the user does not know the structure of the data sources, it is not possible for him to indicate that a term corresponds to an element or to an attribute. So the system will have to look both for elements and for attributes when searching a correspondence.

- No difference is made in the query user between lower case and upper case letters. The system will make sure the exact writing of a term is retrieved for the rewriting of the query.

Presently we do not handle the problem of the semantics of a link condition. For example in a source it can exist a link between employee and department which means that the employee works in the department and in another source a link which means that the employee manages the department. The specification employee()department in our query language does not make distinction between the two situations. We plan to handle this problem by allowing the user to introduce a verb to specify the semantics of the link. So the specification employee(manage)department allows to look for only the links of which meaning is manage. Note that the matching can be solved only if the sources are suitably annotated.

3 Architecture and Working of the System

The matcher is the central element of the system (Figure 2). It receives the user query, and has the task to determine if this query can be applied to a data source. To achieve this processing, it possesses a representation of each data source in a common formalism (we propose OWL to support this formalism, cf. section 4). It must search for a correspondence between the query and each source by taking into account the terms and the structure of the query. A source can answer a query, if the terms of the query correspond to those of the source and if the linksof the query corresponds to that of the source. Correspondences between terms of the query and terms of sources descriptions are established by using a domain ontology.

The working of our system comprises three phases.

In the first phase the system initializes the connection with the ontology and the OWL descriptions of the sources. The system is then ready to handle queries.

In the second phase, when the system receives a query, it first interrogates the ontology to retrieve the synonyms and the hyponyms of the terms of the query. It then initiates the operation of matching for each of the sources. Several rewriting possibilities can be proposed on one or several sources.

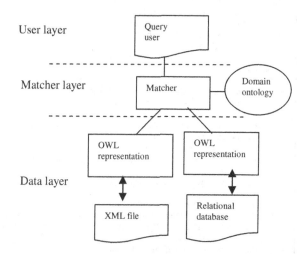

Fig. 2 The architecture of the system

The third phase triggers the execution of one or several of these rewritings on the corresponding sources. Execution can be triggered automatically or by the user. The user can choice a rewriting to be executed on the basis of the terms and the links included in this rewriting. An execution necessitates a new step of rewriting in the language of the source (XML, relational, ...).

4 OWL Representation of the Sources

Presently we are working only with XML sources. To make the matching, the system could directly work on the DTD or on the XML schema of the sources. We preferred to describe every source in OWL for various reasons. At first, as we want to operate with several types of sources, the matching will be implemented with a single kind of description and will be so independent from the types of the sources. Then it is possible to take advantage of OWL features to implement the matching. Finally we foresee improved versions of the matcher, in particular by placing semantic annotations in the description of sources. The management of these annotations will be made more rationally with an OWL representation.

We elaborated an algorithm with which a DTD can be mapped into an OWL representation. This mapping is bijective: from the OWL representation, it is possible to regenerate the DTD. In the following we give the principles of the mapping.

The main idea is to represent every element of the DTD by an OWL class. Every father-son link between two elements is then represented by an OWL property. An attribute is also represented by a property. When a father element has only a single son element, the cardinality of this son is represented by creating a restriction on the property connecting the two elements. When the father element is a complex element, we add an intermediate class to be able to express correctly all the cardinalities.

```
<owl:Class rdf:ID="ORDER">
<rdfs:subClassOf> <owl:Restriction>
<owl:onProperty rdf:resource="#ORDER.&complex1;"/>
<owl:cardinality rdf:datatype="&xsd;nonNegativeInteger"> 1
</owl:cardinality>
</owl:Restriction> </rdfs:subClassOf >
</owl:Class >
<rdf:Property rdf:ID="ORDER.&complex1;">
<rdfs:domain rdf:resource="#ORDER"/>
<rdfs:range rdf:resource="#&complex1;"/>
</rdf:Property>
<owl:Class rdf:ID="&complex1;">
<rdfs:subClassOf> <owl:Restriction>
<owl:OnProperty rdf:resource="#&complex1;.CUSTOMER"/>
<owl:cardinality rdf:datatype="&xsd;nonNegativeInteger"> 1
</owl:cardinality>
</owl:Restriction> </rdfs:subClassOf>
...
<rdfs:subClassOf> <owl:Restriction>
<owl:OnProperty rdf:resource="#&complex1;.PRODUCT"/>
<owl:minCardinality rdf:datatype="&xsd;nonNegativeInteger"> 1
</owl:minCardinality>
</owl:Restriction> </rdfs:subClassOf>
</owl:Class>
<rdf:Property rdf:ID="&complex1;.CUSTOMER">
<rdfs:domain rdf:resource="#&complex1;"/>
<rdfs:range rdf:resource="#CUSTOMER"/>
</rdf:Property>
```

Fig. 3 OWL representation for the ORDER element and its sons

Agreements for the names of classes and properties are as following. The class representing an element will be named with the name of the element. For an intermediate class (associated to a complex element), the name of the class will contain the names of elements with their separator, all in brackets. When this name is long, an entity can be used. A property between two classes will carry the two names separated by a point. For attributes, the symbol '@' is used to separate the name of the class and the name of the attribute.

As an example let us consider the element ORDER defined as follows:

<!ELEMENT ORDER(CUSTOMER, STATUS, PRODUCT+)>

In order to obtain its OWL representation, a class ORDER is created and also an intermediate class the name of which is (CUSTOMER, STATUS, PRODUCT+). For clearer under-standing, the entity &complexe1 is introduced to replace this name in the OWL file. Then a property connecting ORDER with the complex class is created, and the cardinality in the class ORDER is restricted. In the definition of the complex class the limitations of cardinalities are introduced for each of the elements. For CUSTOMER and STATUS, the cardinality is forced to be 1. Then properties are created to connect the complex class with each of the classes CUSTOMER, STATUS, and PRODUCT (figure 3).

Using the same principles, it is possible to design an algorithm which maps a relational schema into an OWL representation. So our approach can be extended to deal also with relational sources.

5 Matching Algorithm

The first step of the matching consists in extracting from the ontology synonyms and hyponyms (by possibly limiting the level of these last ones) for each of the terms of the query. A source is a candidate if it contains for every term of the request a synonym or a hyponym. Sources which are not candidates are definitively discarded. This step does not put particular difficulty.

The second step of the matching consists in determining if every link condition of the query is verified in each of the candidate sources. We then say that such a source matches with the query.

Let a()b be a link condition of the query and let a' and b ' be correspondents (synonyms or hyponyms) for a and b existing in the source S.

First matching rule: If in source S, a' and b ' are directly connected (i.e. they are linked by a property in the OWL file in the direct direction or in the inverse direction), then S satisfies the link condition.

Example: Let us consider again the query Q1 of section 2 which looks for the name of the customers living in the same region as a supplier having a name "easymarket".

```
Q1 : Select a()name
from customer a, supplier b
where a()region=b()region and b()name="easymarket"
```

Each of the link conditions is verified for each of the two sources of figure 2. So, these two sources match with the query.

But this first rule does not cover all the situations where one can find a matching for a link condition. Let us consider for example the query Q2 and the source of figure 4.

```
Q2 : Select a()name from customer a
where a()city="Aubière"
```

The link condition a()city is verified because buyer is a correspondent of customer, urban-center is a correspondent of city and these two correspondents are not directly connected but by an intermediate node which does not change the meaning of the connection (address being a hypernym of urban-center). One can make the same analysis with the link a()name. So this source matches with query Q2.

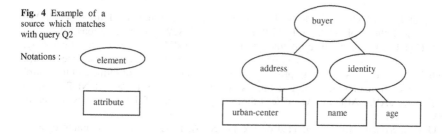

Fig. 4 Example of a source which matches with query Q2

Notations :

This induces us to propose another matching rule for a link condition.

Second matching rule: If in source S, a' and b' are indirectly connected (i.e. they are linked by several sequential properties in the OWL file in the direct direction or in the inverse direction), then S satisfies the link condition of the query if each intermediate class is a synonym or a hypernym or a hyponym of the previous class or the next class.

We give below a description of the matching algorithm.

Algorithm
Resources : OWL descriptions of a set T of sources; an ontology of the domain
Input : a query Q
Ouput : the set of matching queries for Q
1- For each term of Q create the list of correspondents with the term, its synonyms and its hyponyms at level < k; let L be the set of lists so obtained.
2- S:= set of sources of T which have in their OWL description at least one member of each list of L.
3- For each source of S
  3.1 - Generate the different combinations C for associating a correspondent to each term of the source;
  3.2 - For each combination of C
  If it exists a link in the source for each link in Q (test by using the matching rules) Then generate a new matching query by replacing each term in Q by its correspondent and by prefixing each attribute by the symbol @.

The overall complexity of this algorithm is linear with the number of sources. For a given source the complexity is linear with the number of combinations generated in stage 3.1. This number depends of the parameter k (exploration depth in the ontology for hyponyms). For our experiments (section 6), we have chosen k=3.

Note that a matching query for a source must be rewritten in the language of this source. In our case, each matching query is rewritten in XQUERY. We do not detail this rewriting process. To construct the various paths of the FOR WHERE RETURN clauses, one starts from the matching query and one organizes its terms into a hierarchy. The FOR clause contains the definition of the paths which allow to reach from the root of the XML document the highest terms previously defined. The paths of the WHERE clause integrate the link conditions and the valuation conditions. The RETURN clause contains the searched elements, i.e. those associated to the SELECT clause of the matching query.

6 Prototype and Experiments

The prototype which we built implements the architecture presented in figure 2. We incorporated the tool SAXON-B [20] to access the OWL representations. We used WORDNET [14] as the domain ontology. Since WORDNET is in fact a general ontology, we shall use sources for our experiments which do not contain highly specialized terms. WORDNET is thus used only to provide synonyms and hyponyms of terms and to control that a succession of terms along a link is acceptable. Access to WORDNET is made through the JAVA API Java WordNet Library [8]. The body of the matcher is written in JAVA.

Our experiments were conducted on six sources A, B, C, D, E, F containing data on sales of products. Sources contained from 8 to 14 elements. Every element had on average two attributes. They were built manually. OWL files were generated automatically by our transformation algorithm. We submitted ten different queries to the matcher. To save space we give only the results obtained on sources A and B for the first two queries. Extracts of the schemas of sources A and B are given in figures 5 and 6.

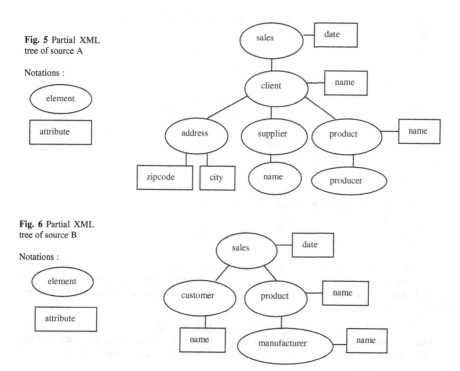

Fig. 5 Partial XML tree of source A

Notations :

element

attribute

Fig. 6 Partial XML tree of source B

Notations :

element

attribute

Query 1 : Names of the customers which live in "Aubière" and which have "Castorama" among their suppliers.

User query:
```
SELECT a()name FROM customer a, supplier b
WHERE a()b AND a()city="Aubière" AND
  b()name="Castorama"
```

Matching query n° 1 for source A provided by the matcher:
```
SELECT a()@name FROM client a, supplier b
WHERE a()b AND a()address()@city="Aubière" AND
  b()name="Castorama"
```

Rewriting n° 1 for source A provided by the matcher:
```
FOR $a IN sales/client
WHERE $a/address/@city="Aubière" AND
  $a/supplier/name="Castorama"
RETURN {$a/@name}
```

For this query the matcher proposes a unique matching for source A. It uses the term customer as synonym of client. We observed that attributes are well detected and are marked with symbol @ in the matching query. No matching is proposed for source B.

Query 2 : Names of the products of the brand "Siemens".
User query:

```
SELECT a()name FROM product a, manufacturer b
WHERE a()b AND b="Siemens"
```

Matching query n°1 for source A provided by the matcher:
```
SELECT a()@name FROM product a, producer b
WHERE a()b AND b="Siemens"
```

Matching query n°2 for source B provided by the matcher:
```
SELECT a()@name FROM product a, manufacturer b
WHERE a()b AND b="Siemens"
```

Rewriting n°1 for source A provided by the matcher:
```
FOR $a IN sales/client/product
WHERE $a/producer="Siemens"
RETURN {$a/@name}
```

Rewriting n°2 for source B provided by the matcher:
```
FOR $a IN sales/product
WHERE $a/manufacturer/@name="Siemens"
RETURN {$a/@name}
```

In source A, the term producer acts as a synonym of manufacturer. It is a leaf element and is used for the valuation condition. In source B, manufacturer has an attribute name which is used to specify the condition. In both cases, the matcher provides the correct rewriting.

For the studied queries the performances of the matcher are good or very good. Lacks in the matching occur when ambiguous words are used in the queries or in the sources. Our matcher does not consider in the immediate the sense of words. Improvements in this direction are so envisaged.

7 Other Features

To increase the efficiency of the system it is interesting to be able to equip it with the possibility of automatically incorporating new data sources. We have implemented a module in our prototype to try this possibility. The administrator of the system can describe a domain of application by keywords and ask the system, by using a search engine, to look for XML sources (and their DTD) compatible with the keywords. These sources after validation by the administrator are then incorporated automatically into the system (by translation of the DTD into OWL and by insertion in the directory of sources to be used for the matching). This feature appears very efficient.

By leading these experiments we noticed that numerous tags, in XML documents coming from the Web, contained abbreviations which were unknowns from the ontology (WORDNET). For example one often sees terms such as "lastdate" or "pubdate". It is possible with WORDNET to declare these abbreviations as synonyms of existing terms and to make them so accessible by the matcher. We tested this possibility and it appears efficient.

8 Conclusion and Perspectives

Through the results obtained, it appears that our system is able to find data from an intuition of the user, intuition expressed through an implicit vision of the domain compatible with the ontology.

The main advantage of our approach is its robustness with regard to the evolution of sources. When a new source is inserted, it is sufficient to elaborate its OWL representation so that it can be exploited by the system. When a source evolves, it is sufficient to reshape its OWL representation.

The main limitations come from the fact that our system does not actually handle sense of terms and sense of link conditions. These two points are strictly connected. To determine the most adequate sense of a term during a matching it is necessary to know the context in which the user takes place and this context could be be determine through the links.

Our system was designed to handle this problem. By allowing the user in his query to supply the semantics of a link condition, the matcher will get back useful information to characterize the user context. To improve the matching, the OWL representation of sources can be fitted out to memorize annotations on the sense of terms (at the level of the corresponding classes) and on the sense of links (at the level of properties). The main problem is that of the installation of these annotations in sources.

These annotations can be installed manually by the administrator of each source. This solution is now recommended by many experts. We investigate another solution which consists to permit the system to provide some of these annotations during its working. It appears possible to seek the opinion of the user when the results of a query are displayed and to infer so some semantic features of the corresponding source.

We think that these improvements could result in an efficient system.

The system can be extended to deal with other types of sources (relational, object).

We are also engaged in another improvement of our prototype in order to allow the join of results coming from different sources. In that case a query is rewritten in several sub-queries, each sub-queries being relative to a different source. Our matching algorithm can be adapted for this more general situation. It is necessary to verify a link condition by using information coming from different sources.

Another important point concerns the performances of our matching algorithm. Without join between sources (as in this version of our prototype), the complexity of the matching is linear with N, the number of sources, and does not induce any problem to scale up. By implementing the join, we will increase the complexity of the matching (it becomes exponential). We investigate different solutions in order to permit the system to scale up. A possible way would be to explore only the most realistic matching cases, by using for example a learning approach, or by introducing constraints.

Such a system can be very useful for different applications. Incorporated into an intranet system, it would allow a user to reach the data sources without knowing their schemas, by being based only on the domain ontology. In a P2P system, it could be installed on some peers or on the super-peers to facilitate access to data by their semantics. The only obligation for a peer would be to publish its data by using the OWL representation.

References

1. Bernstein, P. A., Melnik, S., Petropoulos, M., and Quix C.: Industrial-strength schema matching. SIGMOD Record, Vol. 33, No 4, pp 38-43 (2004).

2.   Cui, Z., Jones, D., O'Brien, P.: Issues in Ontology-based Information Integration. IJCAI, Seattle (2001).
3.   Do, H. H., Rahm, E.: COMA - A System for Flexible Combination of Schema Matching Approaches. VLDB 2002, pp. 610-621 (2002).
4.   Domenig, R., Dittrich, K.R.: A Query based Approach for Integrating Heterogeneous Data Sources. CIKM 2000, pp. 453-460 (200).
5.   Garcia-Molina, H., Papakonstantinou, Y., Quass, D., Rajaraman, A., Sagiv, Y., Ullman, J., Vassalos, V. and Widom, J.: The Tsimmis approach to mediation: Data models and languages. Journal of Intelligent Information Systems , Vol. 8, No. 2, pp. 117-132 (1997).
6.   Hai, Do H., Melnik, S., Rahm, E.: Comparison of Schema Matching Evaluations. Web, Web-Services, and Database Systems. pp 221-237 (2002).
7.   Hull, R.: Managing semantic heterogeneity in databases: A theoretical perspective. Proc. of the Symposium on Principles of Database Systems (PODS), Tucson, Arizona, pp.51-61 (1997).
8.   JWNL. Java WordNet Library. http ://sourceforge.net/projects/jwordnet.
9.   Kedad, Z., Métais, E.: Dealing with Semantic Heterogeneity During Data Integration. Proc of the International Entity Relationship Conference, pp. 325-339 (1999).
10. Lenzerini, M.: Logical Foundations for Data Integration. SOFSEM 2005. pp 38-40 (2005).
11. Levy, A.L., Rajaraman, A., Ordille, J.J.: Querying Heterogeneous Information Sources Using Source Descriptions. VLDB 1996, pp. 251-262 (1996).
12. Li, W.S., Clifton, C.: SemInt-a tool for identifying attribute correspondences in heterogeneous databases using neural network. Data Knowl. Eng. 33(1), pp. 49-84.
13. Madhavan, J., Bernstein, P.A., Rahm, R.: Generic Schema Matching with Cupid. VLDB 2001, pp. 49-58 (2001).
14. Miller, G.:Wordnet: A Lexical Database for English. Communications of the ACM, Vol. 38, pp 39-41 (1995).
15. Missikoff, M., Taglino, F.: An Ontology-based Platform for Semantic Interoperability. Handbook on Ontologies. pp 617-634 (2004).
16. Mohsenzadeh, M., Shams, F., Teshnehlab, M.: Comparison of Schema Matching Systems. WEC (2), pp 141-147 (2005).
17. Nodine, M.H., Fowler, J., Perry, B.: Active Information Gathering in InfoSleuth. CODAS 1999, pp. 15-26 (1999).
18. Palopoli, L., Terracina, G., Ursino, D.: DIKE: a system supporting the semi-automatic construction of cooperative information systems from heterogeneous databases. Softw., Pract. Exper. 33(9), pp. 847-884 (2003).
19. Rahm, E ., Bernstein, P.A.: A survey of approaches to automatic schema matching. VLDB Journal 10(4), pp 334-350 (2001).
20. Saxon. SAXON: The XSLT and XQuery Processor. http://saxon.sourceforge.net/.
21. Schneider, M., Thevenet, D.: Mediation without a global schema: Matching queries and local schemas through an ontology. Second international Conference on Web Information Systems and Technologies (WEBIST 2006), Setubal, Portugal, CD-ROM Proceedings, 10 pages (2006).
22. Wache, H., Vogele, T., Visser, U., Stuckenschmidt, H., Schuster, G., Neumann, H., Hubner, S.: Ontology-based integration of information - a survey of existing approaches. In Stuckenschmidt, H., ed., IJCAI-01 Workshop: Ontologies and Information Sharing, pp 108-117 (2001).
23. Wiederhold, G.: Mediators in the architecture of future information systems. IEEE Computer, Vol. 25, No 3, pp.38-49 (1992).

Index